Courage High!

A history of firefighting in London

Courage High!

A history of firefighting in London

Sally Holloway

LONDON: HMSO

© Crown copyright 1992
Applications for reproduction should be made to HMSO

First published 1992

ISBN 0 11 701689 6

'Courage High!' is published by HMSO.
Sally Holloway was commissioned to write a history of firefighting
in London by the London Fire & Civil Defence Authority.

HMSO publications are available from:

HMSO Publications Centre
(Mail, fax and telephone orders only)
PO Box 276, London, SW8 5DT
Telephone orders 071-873 9090
General enquiries 071-873 0011
(queuing system in operation for both numbers)
Fax orders 071-873 8200

HMSO Bookshops
49 High Holborn, London, WC1V 6HB
(counter service only)
071-873 0011 Fax 071-873 8200
258 Broad Street, Birmingham, B1 2HE
021-643 3740 Fax 021-643 6510
Southey House, 33 Wine Street, Bristol, BS1 2BQ
0272 264306 Fax 0272 294515
9-21 Princess Street, Manchester, M60 8AS
061-834 7201 Fax 061-833 0634
16 Arthur Street, Belfast, BT1 4GD
0232 238451 Fax 0232 235401
71 Lothian Road, Edinburgh, EH3 9AZ
031-228 4181 Fax 031-229 2734

HMSO's Accredited Agents
(see Yellow Pages)

and through good booksellers

FRONTISPIECE
Saved – London's version of the famous painting which
hung on the walls of so many London firemen's homes in
the early 1900s.
   The unconscious maiden was the daughter of an LFB
fireman.

FRONT COVER:
An LFB firefighter of the 1990s.

BACK COVER:
One of many memorials to James Braidwood after his
death in the great Tooley Street fire, 1861.

KENSINGTON PALACE

London's firefighters have waged an unending battle against
the blazes which have beset the City over the years.
Struggling to keep pace with technological change, using
equipment ranging from buckets, hooks and manual pumps
through to today's sophisticated technical equipment,
firemen have fought heroically against the fires which were
such a regular feature of the medieval City, the Great Fire
of 1666, the blazes of the early years of the industrial
revolution, and the Blitz of the Second World War. More
recently, apart from fighting fires in the capital, firemen
have been volunteering to join international rescue teams in
places like Iraq where their professionalism is at a
premium.

My forbears have always taken the closest interest in the
work of the London Fire Brigade. King Charles II and the
then Duke of York joined those trying to quell the Great
Fire, and then played a major part in the restoration work.
King William III brought the "great sucking worms" to London
from Holland, while my great great grandfather, King Edward
VII, when he was Prince of Wales, regularly donned the
uniform and brass helmet of the Metropolitan Fire Brigade
when he rode out with them to the fires.

This book, written by the grand-daughter of a Victorian
fireman, gives the courage and professionalism shown by
London firemen over the centuries the place in history which
they so richly deserve.

This book is dedicated to the courage
of firefighters throughout the world . . .
and to their partners and families

Contents

Illustrations

(Source and copyright holders in brackets.)

Black & white:

Chief  Officers

LONDON FIRE ENGINE ESTABLISHMENT

1833–1861	James Braidwood
1861–1865	Captain Sir Eyre Massey Shaw

METROPOLITAN FIRE BRIGADE

1866–1891	Captain Sir Eyre Massey Shaw
1891–1896	James Sexton Simonds
1896–1903	Captain Sir Lionel de Latour Wells

LONDON FIRE BRIGADE
(London County Council)

1903–1909	Rear Admiral James de Courcy Hamilton
1909–1918	Lieut. Commander Sir Sampson Sladen
1918–1933	Arthur Reginald Dyer
1933–1938	Major Cyril Clark Boville Morris
1938–1939	Commander Sir Aylmer Newton George Firebrace
1939–1941	Major Frank Whitford Jackson
	(Deputy Chief Officer Commanding the LFB)

NATIONAL FIRE SERVICE 1941–1948

1948–1962	Sir Frederick William Delve
1962–1965	Leslie William Thomas Leete

LONDON FIRE BRIGADE
(Greater London Council)

1965–1970	Leslie William Thomas Leete
1970–1976	Joseph Milner
1977–1980	Sir Peter Howard Darby
1981–1986	Ronald Alfred Bullers

LONDON FIRE BRIGADE
(London Fire & Civil Defence Authority)

1986–1987	Ronald Alfred Bullers
1987–1991	Gerald Dawson Clarkson
1991–	Brian Gordon Robinson

Introduction

AS LONDON HAS CHANGED, SO HAVE ITS FIRES AND disasters and so has the challenge to its firefighters, that curious, courageous and cheerful breed of men and women whose vocation demands that they face work each day, knowing that by the end of any shift they may be called on to give their lives to save others. The history of firefighting reflects the whole development of this great metropolis.

First co-ordinated efforts at coping with fire were late arriving, underlining the general attitude of public and government over so many centuries – and even today – that fires were a fact of life and would not happen to them. Not until 1833 did the first insurance fire companies combine to form the London Fire Engine Establishment, the expense of which was borne entirely by their policy holders. Not until 1866, when faced with the threat of total withdrawal of fire cover from London at the peak of Victorian trade and industry, was the government forced into creating the capital's first publicly owned fire force – the Metropolitan Fire Brigade, led by the gallant Captain Eyre Massey Shaw and supported by the Metropolitan Board of Works. Not until 1938 were the 1,666 fire brigades of Britain taken seriously enough by the government for legislation to be passed co-ordinating them sufficiently to attempt to combat the aerial onslaught of World War II on the major cities. It was 1941 before the first National Fire Service was introduced – and had been dissolved by 1948.

Since then, the London Fire Brigade – and the hazards facing its firefighters – have grown beyond all recognition, particularly in the 50 years following the Second World War.

When Philip Jones, then Chairman of the London Fire and Civil Defence Authority and Gerald Clarkson, then the Authority's Chief Executive and Chief Fire Officer, asked me to write about this history, I knew that I was taking on a big subject. I had not reckoned on the vast area which such a book would cover and I realise now that no single volume could include the entire story. Fire appliances alone begin in the 16th century and would fill a sizeable book. The River Fire Service has its own considerable history. The development of fire extinguishers, going back to the days of glass grenades, is a fascinating subject along with 200 years of sprinkler systems. Brian Wright has already produced a most comprehensive work on Fire Marks. Brian Henham and Brian Sharp have described the badges and maces of the insurance companies' Watermen Firemen in 'Badges of Extinction'. Firemen's verses would fill yet another book.

What has become quite clear has been the effect which each individual Chief Officer has had on the Brigade, influenced in every case by his previous experience. Because of this, I have divided the later chapters into the periods covered by each 'Chief' and tried to show how the Service has changed in that time.

Reducing so much to a single volume has meant cutting away much which I would like to have included in the sincere hope that others will, at some time, expand where I have had to contract. I will have left out many events and people, particularly from more recent decades, who were deeply involved in the work of the LFB and who deserved mention. For this, I apologise and hope that they too, or their colleagues, will write down their memories. That great veteran fireman and fire chronicler, Cyril Demarne OBE, has shown the value of personal reminiscences in his book 'The London Blitz – a Fireman's Tale', which brings to life the horror of the Second World War in his own words and those of his contemporaries who fought so bravely to save London from the flames.

My own thanks go to many people who helped me. To HRH Prince Charles who, in his Preface to this book, has paid his own tribute to the courage of London's firefighters – who include some of his ancestors. To the Chief Officers, past and present: Sir Frederick Delve, Joseph Milner, Sir

Peter Darby, Ronald Bullers, Gerald Clarkson and Brian Robinson, all of whom have given up valuable time to recall the events of their period of service and check the chapters concerning them. To Sir Charles Cunningham, for his memories of fire history during the 1930s and the time when he was Permanent Under Secretary of State at the Home Office. To Lady Cuthbert, one of the first women to join the AFS before World War Two, and who led the women's section of the National Fire Service for much of that war. Also to Alan Turney, Deputy Assistant Under Secretary of State in the Fire and Emergency Services Department of the Home Office and Sir Reginald Doyle, HM Chief Inspector of Fire Services. Also, Gordon White, Colin Williamson and the staff of the LFB Public Relations Section. The value of the help I have received from them and from others is impossible to quantify and I feel that their enthusiasm and anxiety to help is, in itself, a tribute to what one Museum described as 'the debt which we owe to our firefighters'.

In alphabetical order therefore, I would like to thank: The Armourers' and Brasiers' Company; Frank Atkinson, Librarian of St Paul's Cathedral; Ernest Allday; Brian Aungiers of Morris Merryweather; Roy Baldwin; Marian Ballott; Ronald Bentley; Tom Bell; Dr E G W Bill and his staff at Lambeth Palace Library; Eric Billingham; Ian Bone; Dr Alan Borg and his staff at the Imperial War Museum; Dr G L Brown; Oliver Budd; Fraser Cantrill and Linda Thompson of the London Toy and Model Museum; The Chartered Insurance Institute; S H Charters; George Clarke, formerly Commandant of the Fire Service College and the Librarians of the College; Mrs Hazel Clisby and D O Clisby; Laurence Cotterell; Pat Cox; the staff of the Courtauld Institute; Cyril Demarne; Dr David Dixon of University College, London; Michael Doherty; Dr Ronald Gray; the staff of the Greater London Council Record Office; at Guildhall, James R Sewell, City Archivist and also John Fisher and Jeremy Smith for their exceptional help in the Department of Manuscripts and Prints at Guildhall Library, to Stefania Vignotto for translating and to the staff of the Corporation of London Record Office; Gavin Morgan of the Museum of London; John Hewish and HM Patent Office; Dave Higgs of the Fire Brigades Union; David Hill of the Sun Alliance Insurance Group; Colin Hinton; Bertram Hoare and Victoria Moger of Hoare's Bank; John Horner; Robin Hamlyn and the Tate Gallery; Peggy Jacobs; John Liffen and the Science Museum; Martin Lloyd-Elliott; Ron Long; Gustav and Christine Milne; A R E North and the Victoria & Albert Museum; Bert Paramor; Malcolm Parker; Lady Paterson; David Pike; Don Pye; John Rodwell and Roy Still at the LFB Museum for constant support, cheerful enthusiasm and a perpetual and welcome supply of tea; Leonard Rosoman RA; Ian Sabiston; Derek Senhenn; Sir Stephen Spender; the Library staff of the Society of Antiquaries; Louisa Steel and the staff of the LFB Library; Sun Alliance; Neil Wallington; Julian Watson, Greenwich Local History Library; Andrew Wells and the Company of Watermen and Lightermen; Dr David Woolley and the staff of the Fire Research Station at Borehamwood; Jack Woodgate, Chaplain of the LFB. Also to staff at the British Museum; the National Gallery, the National Portrait Gallery and the London Transport Museum.

On a personal note, I would like also, to thank David, my encyclopaedic husband and my wonderful family for their constant help and practical support (including forcing me into using a word processor) and to the many friends who have shown so much patience and forbearance over my pre-occupation with fire in recent years.

Sally Holloway
Barnes, 1992

1

London Burning

'Cognosco I Segni Dell' Antica Fiamma'

('I know the symptoms of the ancient flame'...
   Dante's Inferno'.)

London's Burning, London's Burning,
Fetch the Engines, Fetch the Engines,
Fire! Fire! Fire! Fire!
Pour on Water, Pour on Water!

traditional canon.

FIRE AND DISASTER HAVE AFFLICTED LONDON FROM the moment that man – and woman – first built their wooden homes on the edge of the Thames and long before Julius Caesar made his first sortie to Britain in 55 BC. In those days, the settlement was little more than a collection of huts, but it was already a small, thriving port when the main force of Romans took it over and the weapon of fire was used in the efforts of the natives to oust them. Deep below the modern concrete mass of office buildings which line the Thames to the north of London Bridge lie two separate layers of reddened earth, speckled with blackened charcoal and scraps of Samian pottery, a hidden but permanent memory of the London which Boadicea (Boudicca), Queen of the Iceni tribe, put to the torch in AD 61 in an effort to rid the country of the hated invaders, and to the fire which swept the Roman city of Londinium in AD 120–130.

Predictably, it was probably not until after the burning of Roman London by Boadicea that the first steps towards fire protection were attempted. (To this day, firefighters talk of 'stable door' legislation.) The famous Legions who travelled to this unwelcoming and chill outpost of their empire would, perhaps, have marched up from the south coast, accompanied by detachments of *Vigiles*, the Roman firefighters who worked alongside them. The soldiers would have followed the traditional eagle standard; the *Vigiles* carried their own 'mace' aloft, topped by one of their particular gods. Some would have been trained in the sophisticated, organised and disciplined firefighting system through which ancient Rome was ringed with fire stations, each with its satellite outposts – *excubitoria* – for storing equipment and providing shelter for the men who patrolled the streets at night, on the look-out for small fires which could be extinguished before they grew into conflagrations. The *Vigiles*, or *'Sparteoli'* – 'bucket boys' – as they were nicknamed, were famous not only for their courage and efficiency, but for their liveliness and devilry, recorded by an assortment of writers of the period. Their main duties would have involved patrolling the city at night, to spot fires while they were small enough to deal with by bucket chains. Once past that stage there was little that they could do with their primitive equipment.

From excavations in Italy and from contemporary descriptions, we learn that they were highly trained and drilled and the main forces were stationed in barracks which at times contained several hundred men. *Vigiles* wore uniform togas and sandals, carried buckets and had an

1

assortment of equipment, the modern counterparts of which can still be identified on fire and salvage appliances at the end of the 20th century. It included *scalae* – ladders; *dolabrae* and *ascina* – long and short-handled axes; *hamae* or *secchae* – buckets (made of tarred Esparto grass – hence the nickname '*Sparteoli*') *centones* – fire blankets; *serrae* – saws; *mallei* – hammers; *perticae* – scaffolding equipment; *ferramenta* – iron tools and *spongiae* –sponges (probably for mopping up operations when the fire was out.) Occasionally, there were *siphones* – force pumps – not unlike the stirrup-pumps of the 1930s and 40s.

They almost certainly came to Britain. The *Notitia*, the official record of military establishments of the eastern and western Roman Empire records that at the beginning of the 5th century there was a '*Praefectus Numeri Vigilum Concangios*', a cohort of night watchers or firemen, stationed at Greta Bridge in North Yorkshire, not far from the Roman Wall, and another at Chester-le-Street.

Whether they existed in London has not, so far, been established, although it seems likely that there would have been units there with the Roman army of occupation, combining their firefighting skills with work as night watchmen or guards. But when the Romans finally abandoned the cold shores of Britain, the city and the country as a whole, reverted to a general acceptance that fires were an Act of God against which nothing could be done, other than to pray and, in later centuries, to endow, anoint and inscribe special church bells with prayers to protect them from the flames. Although, again, no trace of these survives in London, one which remains in Sherborne, Dorset, exhorts:

> '*Lord, quench this furious flame*
> *Arise, run, help put out the same.*'

Another, in Coventry, bore the message:

> '*I have been called the common bell*
> *To ring when fire breaks out to tell.*'

For generations, it was the custom to ring the bells backwards as a fire alarm and not without cause. In the years 798, 982, 1086 and 1211, London was swept by massive fires, despite the fact that William the Conqueror, within two years of coming to power in 1066, had embarked on a tough regime of '*couvre-feu*' or '*curfew*' as it came to be known. Every night at eight o'clock, all lights and fires had to be extinguished and severe penalties were imposed on anyone found with a fire burning in their home after curfew. Excavations in London have revealed pieces of pottery from this period which were undoubtedly the remains of ceramic curfew covers – large dome-shaped objects with handles on

top which could be put over the fire in the middle of the room to extinguish it completely or at least, to prevent sparks emerging from it. (Later 'couvre-feu' were made of metal and one example, in the Victoria and Albert Museum, is handsomely decorated with St George and a fire-breathing dragon.) Although curfew was intended as a fire precaution, it was also regarded in many English homes as a badge of servitude to the new Norman masters, and a tyrannical custom which brought great misery on cold winter nights, as one poet recorded:

> *The shivering wretches at the curfew sound,*
> *Dejected, sunk into their sordid beds,*
> *And through the mournful gloom of ancient times*
> *Mused sad, or dreamed of better.*

The dream came true, to some extent, when Henry I repealed the Curfew Act in 1100 and once more, fire protection reverted to prayers, bells and buckets of water until Richard I, Richard the Lionheart, for all the religious fervour of his Crusades to the Holy Land, decided that perhaps the rites of the Church were not adequate for fire protection. Within a year of his accession in 1189 the wardmotes, the early parish councils of the City of London, had laid down rules for preventing loss of life and destruction of property by fire. It was one of the earliest edicts of this relatively new gathering of citizens as London took its first steps towards becoming an organised and independent city, governed in its own right.

The wardmotes' rules, which included a curfew again, demanded:

> '*Item:* That all persons who dwell in great houses within their ward have a ladder or two ready and prepared to succour their neighbours in case misadventure should occur by fire.

> *Item:* that all persons who occupy such houses have, in summer time and especially between the Feast of Pentecost and the Feast of St Bartholomew (24th August) before their doors a barrel of water for quenching such fire if it be not a house which has a fountain of its own.

> *Item:* that ten reputable men of the ward with ten aldermen provide a strong crook of iron with a wooden handle, together with two chains and that the beadle have a good horn and loudly sounding. Of persons wandering by night, it is forbidden that any persons shall be so daring as to be found wandering about the streets of the city after the curfew, rung out at St Martin's-le-Grand and St Laurence, upon pain of being arrested.'

At this time too came the first of many fruitless attempts to prevent fire by controlling building methods. Henry Fitz-Ailwyn, the first Lord Mayor, laid down in the London Assize of 1189 that houses in the City were to be built only of stone with party walls of a minimum size and thickness and with roofs made of material other than thatch of reeds or straw – in other words, slate or clay tiles.

Despite this, fire broke out in the Church of Our Lady of Cannons in Southwark, just south of the City across the Thames, on 10th July 1212, destroying the church of St Mary Overy and burning down the houses which had been built across London Bridge. Crowds poured in to try to rescue the victims and put out the flames but at the end of the day, contemporary records report that 2,000 people were drowned and an estimated total of 12,000 perished in what, until 1666, was known as the Great Fire of London. Certainly far more lives were lost here than in the later disaster.

It was this blaze which prompted King John to have a survey of the City carried out and, as a result of its findings, to order that all the wooden houses in Cheapside be demolished or altered to comply with the existing fire laws – some indication of the public's indifference to fire safety measures in previous years. New regulations were introduced controlling the building of ale-houses in London and the populace were firmly reminded of Fitz-Ailwyn's strictures of 1189 concerning the installation of water tubs outside their homes during the summer months.

Already London, like many other European cities, was beginning to develop as a major port and a centre of trade. Young men arrived every day from all over the country, anxious to make their fortunes as money dealers, merchants, craftsmen or tradesmen, lured to the town whose pavements were reputed to be paved with gold. Instead, they found tight-packed houses, streets fouled and stinking with refuse, gutters clogged with rubbish and ordure and cheerful maidservants who would open a gable window and with a merry cry of 'gardyloo' (from the French 'look out for water') hurl the contents of the family chamber pots into the streets below. Behind the scenes of growing municipal awareness and pride, the fashions of the gentry and the splendour of the wealthy was a seething, hard-drinking, hard-wenching, devil-may-care populace who thought little of the danger of fire until it affected their own homes – if they had a home. This it did so frequently that by the end of the 13th century a prominent citizen was writing that the only inconveniences of London were 'the immoderate drinking of the foolish and the number of fires', despite the fact that the dangers of fire were being publicised nightly by an order of the Corporation which had appointed a night watchman to patrol the streets, watch out for possible sources of fire and advise on the state of the weather. 'Fire! Fire!' as well as 'Past three o'clock and a cold, frosty morning' was a regular background of London life.

Still the houses burned down and by 1430, the Minutes of the Court of Aldermen record their agreement that every new Alderman, within a month of his creation and every new Sheriff within a month of his admission to the Court 'shall cause 12 new buckets to be made of leather for the quenching of fire… Merrington to make all buckets of leather.' Another entry records that money was to be paid to 'poor people who labor'd at quenching of fire in the Vintry'. The same volume mentions orders for ladders and hooks for firefighting and the sending of 'certain persons to Minories to see damage caused by fire.' As a result of their report, £40 was paid 'to the Abbess and Nuns for the purchase of cotton-russet for their habits', presumably to replace those damaged in the fire.

Wealthier home owners were already installing chimneys to enclose the smoke from their hearths and waft it away above the rooftops, but unfortunately the new flues were fashioned from hollowed out tree trunks, setting off another wave of fires. By the middle of the 15th century, the Lord Mayor was forced to declare that anyone who lit a fire under a wooden chimney would be fined 6s 8d (38p), a goodly sum in those days

London – the town to which Dick Whittington had come and been Lord Mayor four times – was now one of the most prosperous ports in Europe, developing rapidly within its old walls and building more and larger warehouses along the banks of the Thames to store the goods brought back by the merchant adventurers who were sailing the 'Main' from the ports of northern Europe through the Bay of Biscay and down to the Mediterranean and beyond.

Not all earned good, honest livings. Some more modern problems existed even in those days and an Act of 1429 suggests an early protection racket which must have worried those concerned with the dangers of fire. The Act laid down that 'if any threaten by casting bills to burn a house if money is not laid in a certain place and do after burn the house, such a burning shall be adjudged High Treason.' The Penalty for High Treason was death.

Houses in the City were often dual-purpose, with merchants and shopkeepers living upstairs and storing and selling their wares from the downstairs rooms and cellars. Servicing them, with their stores and workshops packed in between the dwelling houses, were tradesmen whose craft might demand fires of intense heat to be kept burning, sometimes day and night. Blacksmiths, armourers and brasiers, swordmakers, foundrymen, coopers and many more tradesmen and craftsmen were all there, winter and summer. Sparks, swept aloft in the swirling winds would land on the still illegal thatched roofs or drift in through open windows to set off yet another blaze.

The whole city was a hotchpotch of buildings although there was some element of method providing a key to the names which survive to this day in the City itself (as opposed to the area of Greater London which lies outside the line of the old walls). The type of thoroughfare at that time depended on the number of hearths in a building.

Streets were the main roadways, edged with the larger houses of the more wealthy citizens which had between five and nine hearths.

Lanes were narrower, with houses of between four and five hearths, tending to be homes for craftsmen in metal or wood and all using fire to a greater or lesser degree in their work.

A Yard or Court would be a turning off a street or lane, enclosed by buildings with four hearths.

Alleys held the smallest dwellings of three hearths or less and occupied by the poorest craftsmen and artisans.

Houses of the wealthy might have small gardens, perhaps with a well or a fountain which would be a useful source of water for firefighting at a time when it was hard to come by. From the period when it had begun to outgrow its original streams, London had always had water problems and as early as the 13th century the Corporation had begun to intercept the springs which fed the Tyburn watercourse and divert them into reservoirs near what is now Marylebone Lane. From these, it flowed in a six-inch lead pipe down to Charing Cross, along the Strand and Fleet Street, over the Fleet River by a bridge and up to a conduit at the western end of Cheapside. The water, which came from the Marylebone subsoil, was so unpolluted and hard that there was no danger of lead poisoning from the pipes.

The cost of the piping was paid for by certain merchants in Ghent, Bruges and Antwerp in return for exemption from river dues on the goods they brought up the Thames and into London. The King also had a share in the bounty by taking a free supply of water for his stables which were then on land close to where St Martin-in-the-Fields church stands now. The reservoirs were a considerable feat of building and were covered with arches where, once a year, a banquet was held for members of the City Corporation on their annual visit of inspection.

As the City grew, this supply became inadequate and the Corporation looked to other sources. In 1582 a Dutchman, Peter Morrys, was granted permission to build a water wheel under the arches of London Bridge and this supplied power to work a force pump which raised water from the Thames and drove it through lead or wooden pipes laid in the streets. The wooden pipes were made of tree trunks,

hollowed out through the middle and pointed at one end so that they fitted snugly into each other. Smaller pipes known as 'branches' led off the 'trunk' lines. At one time, 16 pumps were worked by the wheels under London Bridge, each 7 inches in diameter and with a 30 inch stroke. They worked 3,025 strokes per tide and there were 708 tides in a year. By 1761, three arches had wheels beneath them and by 1767 there were five with a 10 hp atmospheric engine for use on the neap tide or when the tide was on the turn, to keep the wheels revolving. At this stage it was pumping 2,704 gallons a minute to 10,417 paying customers. By 1820 the number of wheels under the bridge had increased until 26 million hogsheads of water a year were being supplied at the rate of 216 gallons a minute. Some of the pipes had survived for 300 years. The whole system slowed down the flow of the Thames so much that in extremes of cold it froze from bank to bank sufficiently for ox-roasts to be held on the surface in the famous 'Frost Fairs'.

Soon after the London Bridge works began, a Welsh goldsmith, Hugh Myddelton, was granted permission by the City Council to bring the Chadwell and Amwell streams down the 38 miles to London from Ware, in Hertfordshire and after many difficulties, the water reached the village of Islington in 1613, where New River Head remained the headquarters for London's water supply until after the Second World War. It was metered through pipes which were somewhat enigmatically described as 'the size of a goose quill' but more specifically as 'through a pipe half an inch in diameter.' There seems little doubt that there was, as one might say, money flowing like water since Morrys's family eventually sold their London Bridge Company in 1701 to a goldsmith, Richard Soames, for £36,000.

By the time that Henry VIII was in power and disposing of wives in rapid succession, the City was packed even more tightly and so many fires were breaking out that the nightly patrol of bellmen was increased and given the added task of keeping an eye open for fires, ringing their handbells and intoning '*Take care of your fire and candle, be charitable to the poor and pray for the dead.*'

Within three years of the accession of the Virgin Queen Elizabeth I the first St Paul's Cathedral had been struck, in 1561, by another frequent cause of fire, described in this case as '*a marvellous great fiery lightning*' and, at the same time, '*there was a most hideous crash of thunder.*' Flames began to pour from the roof, wreathing the ancient steeple '*like a garland.*' The Lord Mayor, the Bishop of London, the Lord Treasurer and the Keeper of the Great Seal were called to the scene. As they argued as to whether they should shoot the steeple down with cannon or hew a gap in the roof to act as a fire break, Londoners poured through the streets carrying buckets of water which proved totally useless.

At the height of the uproar and chaos, the great golden cross and eagle toppled from the roof and fell in a shower of blazing debris, crashing through the rafters and setting fire to the aisle. Only when the Lord Mayor was warned that the Bishop's Palace, close behind the Cathedral, was in danger did they reach a decision. Ladders and axes were sent for and a hole was cut in the roof. It halted the spread of the fire but 500 men and women continued to fight on until finally, long after dark, the flames were subdued.

The Cathedral was partly saved but the indecisiveness of the authorities in taking steps to halt the fire in its initial stages should have worried the people and the Corporation.

By 1575, the City was charging Londoners for the cost of providing new leather buckets to be stored in all the churches as well as ladders and huge fire hooks and chains for pulling down rafters. Many of these hooks were now 20–30 feet long and took several men or even a horse and cart to transport them to the scene of the fire and put them into action.

So great was the fear of fire that in 1585, as Elizabeth prepared her fleet to face the Armada, the City Fathers of London issued regulations which had about them all the ring of a Tudor version of the Auxiliary Fire Service of 1938:

'For the military government of the City, in view of the threatened invasion of the Spaniard it is laid down that:

Item: for quenching sudden fires it will be necessary to have a thousand trusty persons to carry leather buckets and ladders and that to them of the graver citizens there be appointed leaders to lead them as need may be by the hundreds and fiftys to be ready to relieve any fired place.'

And further:

'That one of the Watch Houses at the water's side be near the engine that serveth the City with water for that, above all others, is most present and abundant to that purpose and most ready for quenching fire and therefore is specially to be guarded.'

It would appear that the Dutchman's water wheel was already proving too valuable a source of water for firefighting to allow it to be damaged by any Spanish force which might manage to sail up the Thames.

The fear of invasion passed and with the burgeoning of Elizabethan England, new inventions for pumping water out of ships and for watering gardens were now being turned to the problem of putting out fires. One of the earliest was a bronze squirt (or 'squrt' as it was occasionally called) like a huge garden syringe, sometimes large enough to need three men to work it, two holding it aloft and one pushing the plunger so that the water emerged through the nozzle on to the flames.

Fire scoops – wooden shovels shod with iron were also used for scooping water from butts or gutters to throw on burning embers.

It was a period of rapid expansion in Europe, of feuds and battles when no city was totally safe from marauding foreigners. It was also a time when men were beginning to think of scientific developments and not only did they travel to trade and to fight but also to exchange ideas. Already, news was reaching London from France, Germany and Holland about machines which might attack fires more efficiently than buckets, 'squrts' and scoops.

Towards the end of the 16th century, a variety of primitive pumps were emerging, and in 1584 a visitor to London from Germany wrote of a *'contrivance for putting out fires'* which he had seen spraying water into the crowds to clear a way for the Lord Mayor's procession. It was almost certainly an early development of the squirt, with a pear shaped cylinder, filled by buckets through a hole in the top and forced out by turning a handle at the lower end which pressed the water up and out through an elevated nozzle at the top end. It was sometimes mounted on wheels and sometimes on a sledge but was almost certainly the first 'fire engine' to reach the streets of London.

Shakespeare might have seen it as he prowled the streets of the City, and would, no doubt, have welcomed it on the evening of 29th June 1613, the first performance of his new play 'Henry VIII' at the Globe Theatre on Bankside in Southwark. An over-enthusiastic effects man had produced the sound of cannon fire with a real gun and ammunition. A cannon ball, recklessly discharged, lodged in the thatch of the Globe's roof and produced a fire which destroyed the entire theatre.

By 1612 a *'force pump'* was being reported from France and from Nuremburg in Germany. The writer, Saloman de Caus, published a document under the title '*Les Raisons des Forces Mouvantes*' in 1615 describing such a pump which appeared in illustrations as a large wooden tub, fixed to a sledge base, with a handle on one side to pump up the water and a long, fixed metal nozzle ejecting water on to a burning building.

Suddenly, a whole wave of inventions for pumping water began to emerge. London had already set up a system of registering patents for inventions to prevent them from being copied without the permission of the originator. One of the earliest (Patent Roll No 2329, 22 pt 6, no 12) dated 26th February 1625, detailed a fire engine *'for the casting of water through a spout made of copper and brass.'* The patentee was a Roger Jones of London, but although the patent was granted in his name, it seems likely that the idea

Men – and women – manned the 'squirts' in Shakespeare's London, c.1590 (LFCDA.)

for such a machine was suggested to him by his brother, John, who had travelled widely on the Continent, particularly in Germany.

The Patent is particularly interesting as this is probably the earliest fire engine, as opposed to a device invented primarily for pumping water from the holds of ships, to have been patented in London.

It reads (somewhat breathlessly):

'John Jones of London merchant in his travailling over the seas hath found out and discovered and he and Roger, his brother, by their great industrie and paines and greate costs and charges have perfected a newe, profitable and commendable invention art or skill and way of making and using an Engine or Instrument artificiallie wrought with scrues and other devices made of Copper or Brass or other metall into any house shippe or other place taken with fire in such a manner with the help of tenne men to labor at the said engine or instrument water may be cast into any house, shippe or other place with fire with more ease and speed than five hundred men with the helpe of Bucketts and laydels can perform without it and that without danger to these that shall labour about it and with that certaintie and assuredness that the fire by God's blessing shall not spreade to the endangering of houses or places adjoining which nowe are preserved onlie by pulling them down to their utter destruction and the danger of manie mens lives, which said engine or instrument.... hath not heretofore been knowen or putt in practise and brought to perfection within anie Realme and Dominions....'

The Patent, ostensibly written by King James I, gave Roger Jones the sole right of making, selling and using the engine 'in England, Ireland, Wales and the town of Berwick-upon-Tweed for fourteen years'.

We hear more of Roger Jones in Fuller's book 'Worthies' (1662) which suggests that he was a merchant, living in Austin Friars, who 'fetched the first form thereof from Nurimberge' and that he had died during a Plague which raged through London in 1625 and 1626, soon after the Patent was granted. Fuller mentions that two engines had been brought to London by Jones but that others had been made later.

Interestingly, an entry in the quill-pen written Minutes of the Court of Aldermen for 11th November 1624 reads:

'Order'd that £50 be paid to Mr John Jones for two Engines by him brought over from beyond the Sea which

Minutes of Court of Aldermen ordering fire engines, 1624. (Corporation of London Records Office.)

are conceived to bee very necessarie and usefull within this Cittie for quenching of fyre.'

In the ensuing pages of Minutes, the fire engine saga continues:

'*18th November 1624.* Order'd that Mr Alderman Hamersley and Mr Alderman Moulson shall send for from beyond the seas two Engines such as is Mr Jones the Marchant, to be used within this cittie upon the occacion of fier.'

'*17th May 1625:* Order'd that Ald Hammersley be paid £50 upon his account of charges disbursed in the matter of obtaining such engines.'

'*16th October 1625:* This Court, being informed that Mr Alderman Hamersley by the direction of the Court, hath caused a further provision of two water engines or spoutes for the Cittie's use, which are now come from Hamburgh, ordered that £100 be paid to his servant to defray the charge of the two water spouts.'

'*13th June 1626:* The Court being informed by Alderman Hamersley that by direction of the Court he had procured 11 Engines or water spouts to be sent over hither from beyond the seas, order'd that they be distributed and remain as follows: the heart of the xj (sic) to be at the Lord Maiors house and so yerely from Maior to Maior; two at the Guildhall; two at Leadenhall; one at

German fire engines of type ordered by the City, 1630. (Society of Antiquaries of London.)

St Hellen's in Bishopsgate Streete; one at Bowchurche in Cheape; one att Christchurch; one at St Albones Church Cripplegate; one at St Andrewes in Holborne and one at the Bridghouse. The Aldermen of the Ward to which any of the Engines shall be sent to take order that the same be kept in some convenient place from wett.'

'3rd July 1638: Chamberlain to pay £44 to Leonard Lambert, the City's Founder, for two Engines or spouts of water by him lately made to the City's use for quenching fire.'

'15th October 1644: City Founder order'd to view the engines at Leadenhall and in the wards and to report.'

20th November 1644: Detailed Report of City Founder giving location of engines and their state of repair and accessibility. (Some described as 'kept in a house made for that purpose'. List includes several engines belonging to some Companies as well as those in the Wards and Parishes.)

From this it would seem clear that for some years before the Great Fire, the Corporation of London was not only aware of the fire risks but was spending money on the latest means of firefighting available to them by importing fire engines from Germany and having them copied in London. There seems little doubt that after the death of the patentee, other 'founders' or foundrymen began making and supplying fire engines not only to the Corporation but to the Livery Companies and others.

Interesting too, is the story of William Harvey, a distinguished physician who spent part of his time tending the sick in St Bartholomew's Hospital in Smithfield and part of it researching into the circulation of blood. Harvey, who would have been regularly walking through the City at about the time when the Corporation had distributed its primitive fire engines, is said to have stopped one day to watch such an appliance playing water on a fire. This was before a balancing mechanism had been developed to produce a single, smooth jet and he noted particularly the way in which it emerged from the pump in spurts. In a letter to a friend he compared it with the way in which blood spurts from a cut artery at every contraction of the heart, pointing out that:

'Just as water by the force and impulsion of a fire engine is driven aloft through pipes of lead, and we may observe and distinguish all the forcings of the engine, even though it be a good way off, in the flux of the water when it passes out, the order, beginning to increase and vehemency of every stroke, even so it is with the blood from the orifice of a cut artery.'

In 1628, after years of study, he published his treatise 'Exercitatio Anatomica de Motu Cordis et Sanguinis' in which he expounded his theories of the circulation of the blood.

Harvey's observations had been opportune. In 1633 came reports of three improved fire engines 'of the type made in Germany by Hautsch', in use at a fire on London Bridge:

'The effect of this Engine is to throw out water to a great distance and to what place you will by the compression of water forced out through a tube.... that which is most peculiar about it... is that the Course of the water issuing out of the Tube that darts it is continued, not being interrupted.'

A method of producing a constant stream had, at last, been discovered.

The fire on London Bridge was described in detail in a diary written by Nehemia Wallington, a deeply religious Londoner who lived on Fish Street Hill near the Bridge. It described the scene as 'a fearfull and dreadful fire, vaunting itself over the tops of houses like a Captain flourishing and displaying his banner' but left a feeling that the engines, fine though they were, might have been more effective if there had been water to supply them. As it was, his friends escaped the flames which enveloped the Bridge

'having nothing on their bodies but their Shurts and Smoke.... The Fire it burnt so fiercely that it could not be quenched till it had burnt downe all the houses on both sides of the way... and although there was water enough very neere to, yet they could not safely come at it, but all the conduites were never open and ye watter swept down with broomes which helped enough... the three Engines which are such excellent things that nothing that ever was designed could do so much good, yeet none of these did prosper for they were all broken and y tide was very low that they could get no watter... some ladders were broke to the hurt of many for some had their legges broke, some their armes and some their ribs were broke and many lost their lives...'

Despite this, there seems to have been no doubt as to the general success of the new fire engines – provided they had 'watter' and were not broken, but clearly there were not enough of them and in 1637 the King Charles I wrote to the Lord Mayor and Court of Aldermen 'Concerning Provisions of Engins in London for Accidents of Fier' complaining that while they had been useful in a fire near Arundel House (close to the Temple) there were not enough of them near at hand and more were needed in the parishes, particularly outside the confines of the City itself.

A year later, he was again urging the Lord Mayor to provide more 'engines for the quenching of fire', intimating that the Lords of Council would be responsible for providing them 'in the liberties' – the areas immediately outside the City. So much pressure was brought to bear that in 1642, the Lord Mayor sent a precept to the chief City livery companies requesting each of them 'to provide an engine for preventing fire.' Records show that the Goldsmiths and the Ironmongers complied immediately while the Carpenters agreed 'to contribute to the parish churchwardens for the purchase of an engine.'

The Lords kept to their word and by 1639 there was an engine, plus buckets and hooks at St Giles and by 1649 the Inner Temple had invested in one. By 1650 the Middle Temple had bought one for £30 and the Board of Greencloth (the financial committee of the English Royal Household which still survives, if only in symbolic form) had installed fire engines at Scotland Yard for the protection of Whitehall Palace nearby. William Burroughs, who owned a foundry in the City, claimed that he had improved the Jones brothers' engine and had produced about thirty between 1625 and 1660, which had been distributed throughout the City.

It was a time of turmoil in the country, of Roundheads against Cavaliers, with King Charles I beheaded in 1649 and a Commonwealth government in control, under Puritan Oliver Cromwell and later Richard Cromwell, until 1660 when King Charles II was restored to the throne. The new King was a highly intelligent and academic man, concerned particularly with the development of the arts and sciences and under his rule, despite the still frequent ravages of fire, London continued to thrive and expand beyond its old walls.

Within 50 years of the death of Queen Elizabeth I, in 1603, its population had doubled in size from 250,000 to half a million people. Houses were packed closer and closer together, the building regulations were blatantly ignored and any form of hygiene was at a minimum. Citizens accepted unquestioningly the suggestion in a remarkable broadsheet printed by one Lord Mayor, that most small fires could be extinguished by 'gentlemen gathering together in a circle and pissing on it.' In 1665 there was a massive outbreak of plague, brought into the port by rats from the ships, which killed thousands of people and changed the cry of the Night Watch to a constant and mournful 'Bring out your dead.'

Charles II, who was so interested in firefighting that he would row along the Thames looking for a good blaze at which he could direct the attack, was so concerned that in 1665 he vehemently reiterated the previous warnings to the Lord Mayor of London to take precautions against the possibility of a major fire. Yet they were virtually ignored, the

City still expanded and by 1666 its suburbs had spread, particularly to the west, beyond the Lud Gate across the Fleet River, through the Temple and on towards Westminster. These were good King Charles's golden days, when Nell Gwynn was charming – or scandalising – the Court, when rich Londoners could take a sedan chair to the Theatre Royal in Drury Lane or, like Samuel Pepys the diarist, might attend church on the Sabbath with the hope of finding a pretty and willing maid to fondle during the sermon. It was an age of intellectual as well as geographical adventure when you could enjoy your leisure by reading Milton's latest poems, listening to the music of Purcell or admiring the architectural delights of Dr Christopher Wren.

Conversation over dinner might dwell on the prophecies of the seers and astrologers. Walter Gostelo, in 1658, had warned 'Oh London! London! Sinful as Sodom and Gomorrah! The decree is gone out, Repent, or burn as Sodom and Gomorrah!' Mother Shipton, the famous witch and prophetess, foresaw that London should be burnt to ashes in 1666. Gossip would have revelled in the naked Quaker who had walked through crowded Bartholomew Fair with a pan of fire and brimstone on his head, warning Londoners of their potential fate.

Little attention was paid to such outbursts, but spurred by the monarch and to be on the safe side, the Lord Mayor again issued a long and detailed warning of the hazards of fire and the precautions to be taken by every householder to prevent it.

Attitudes of mind were beginning to change rapidly. In 1660 the new King and his intellectual friends had founded the Royal Society. Thomas Sprat, later to become Bishop of Rochester, wrote of the 'learned and inquisitive age' in which he lived, praising the new freedom of scientists who were, under Charles II, no longer bound to fit their discoveries into the rigid dogma of religious beliefs. It was a crucial time for theologians and for the men of science including such pioneers as Edmond Halley the astronomer and Sir Isaac Newton the mathematician. While many of them had little personal interest in firefighting it was their work for science which began to change public opinion and to question the widespread belief that fire was, indeed, an Act of God against which there was no remedy.

The trend was being repeated throughout Europe. The Low countries, at a zenith of commercial prosperity, were competing with England for trade in the Far East and the warehouses of Amsterdam were already crammed with goods and ripe for fire. Two young brothers, the Van der Heidens had been concerned for the inherent dangers and when Amsterdam took the inspired decision that it needed a Fire Department, it was the Van der Heidens who were put in charge.

They began their intensive research into firefighting methods, emphasising the need not just to attack fire from the outside but to get in to burning premises to take it at source. For this, the rigid metal nozzles of the existing fire engines were useless. Something longer and more flexible was needed. Their experiments produced at first a longer fixed nozzle and then they discovered that if you riveted strips of leather together you could produce a long, flexible tube – a hosepipe. Their countrymen – and the English when it reached them – dubbed it 'The Great Sucking Worm', but that was later.

Now, in 1666, London was sweltering under a long, hot, dry summer. The Dutch navy had already sailed into the Medway and was threatening the mouth of the Thames. The City, still recovering from the devastating Plague of the previous year, was on tenterhooks. By the 1st September Londoners were looking forward to the cooler days of autumn. This was a Saturday. At the end of a busy day's toil the workers and servants had to be paid, the money counted and the books made up for the week. Late in the evening was the time for a relaxing drink, or two, or more; for long conversations with friends.

By the small hours, most honest – and dishonest – citizens were soundly asleep in their beds.

2

The Great Fire of London – Annus Mirabilis

'In Sixteen Hundred and Sixty Six
London burned like rotten sticks.'

BY TWO O'CLOCK IN THE MORNING OF 2nd September 1666 most Londoners were sleeping heavily. Thomas Farynor, the King's baker, whose home and bakehouse were in Pudding Lane, not far from the Thames, swore that before retiring he had closed all the doors and windows of the building, checked the rooms and raked out all his embers. He was so certain that there was no spark left because later, at about midnight, he had wanted to light a candle and had gone down to his oven to see if there were any red embers, but there were none. Farynor went back to bed. The house was silent until soon after 2 am when his assistant woke to find the room full of smoke. He shouted to Farynor who woke his wife Hanna, his son, Tom, his daughter and their maid. By now the fire was licking up the staircase. The baker just had time to notice that the fire was nowhere near his oven or the pile of wood which had been stacked in the courtyard ready for the next day's baking when he realised that they were trapped. The only escape was through a garret window and across the roof to a neighbour's house. Choking but together the family crawled to safety, but their maid was too frightened to follow. She became the first victim of the Great Fire of London.

Thomas Vincent, 'citizen of London', described it as it happened:

'The fire begins, is quickly taken notice of, though in the midst of the night. "Fire! Fire! Fire!" doth resound the streets; many of the citizens start out of their sleep, look out of their windows, some dress themselves and run to the place.' *(Other contemporary reports suggest that the*

citizens of London were so accustomed to the cry of 'Fire!' *that they probably turned over and went back to sleep.)* 'The Lord Mayor comes with his officers; a confusion there is . . . . . London, so famous for its wisdom and dexterity can now find neither brains nor hands to prevent its ruin . . . .'

There seems little doubt that the Lord Mayor, Sir Thomas Bludworth, was deluded into thinking that this was a small fire when the reports first reached him. His initial response was the remark *'Pish! A woman might piss it out.'* Whereupon he went back to bed. Samuel Pepys, the diarist, who kept valuable notes on the development of the Fire, had little regard for Bludworth, describing him as *'a silly man, I think.'* In fact, Pepys himself had also been deluded into underestimating the seriousness of the outbreak. He wrote in his Diary:

'2nd. Lord's Day. Some of our maids sitting up late last night to get things ready against our feast to-day; Jane called us up about three in the morning, to tell us of a great fire they saw in the City. So I rose and slipped on my night gown and went to her window; and thought it to be on the backside of Markelane at the farthest; but being unused to such fires as fallowed,' (sic) 'I thought it far enough off, and so went to bed again and to sleep.'

While Pepys and many of his fellow citizens were sleeping, the families who had already realised what was happening tried to hurl buckets of water on the blazing buildings while others rushed out with squirts. Some reports mention that *'engines'* were being used, but whether there were insufficient men to man the pumps' handles or whether they were too cumbersome to haul out in the panic, they played a minimal part. Within a few hours the flames, fanned by a stiff easterly wind, were leaping through the tight-packed buildings, homes, businesses, warehouses, already out of control. All that might have saved the City at this stage was to bring in the army, blow up a section of houses and create a fire break, but the more influential citizens whose homes were not yet burning, resisted this course and the flames roared on. Water was short, particularly after the London Bridge water system was put out of action and many of the water 'mains' ran dry – as they would nearly 300 years later when London burned again in the 'Blitz'.

Vincent takes up the saga, his words reflecting the bitter enmity which still existed between Roman Catholics and Protestants:

'The beginning of the Fire at a time when there had been so much hot weather which had dried the houses and made them more fit for fuel; the beginning of it in such a place where there were so many timber houses and the shops filled with so much combustible matter; the beginning of it just when the wind did blow fiercely upon that corner to the west of the City which was then like tinder to sparks; this doth smell of a Popish design, hatched in the same place where the Gunpowder Plot was contrived.' *(This was the plot by Guy Fawkes and his fellow Catholics to blow up Parliament in 1605, remembered in 1666 more venomously, perhaps, than in these modern days.)* 'Now, the trained bands are up in arms, watching at every quarter for Outlandish men' *(foreigners)* 'because of the general fears and jelousies and the rumours that fire balls were thrown into houses by several of them to help provoke the furious flames.'

Pepys, awake now, records:

'About 7 a.m., rose again to dress myself, and there looked out at the window and saw the fire not so much as it was, and further off. So to my closet to set things to rights after yesterday's cleanings. By and by Jane comes and tells me that she hears that above 300 houses have been burned down tonight by the fire we saw, and that it was now burning down all Fish Street Hill by London Bridge.'

After going out into the streets and realising how fast it was spreading, he describes

'poor people staying in their houses as long as till the very fire touched them and then running into boats or clambering from one pair of stairs by the waterside to

another. And among other things, the poor pigeons I perceive were loath to leave their houses but hovered about the windows and balconies till they were some of them burned, their wings, and fell down.' *(It was a sight to be remarked on repeatedly by the firefighters of 1940.)*

He hired a boat himself and travelled to Westminster

'and did tell the King and Duke of York what I saw, and that unless His Majesty did command houses to be pulled down, nothing could stop the fire'.

The King, clearly worried by the report,

'commanded me to go to my Lord Mayor from him and command him to spare no houses but to pull them down before the fire, every way. The Duke of York' *(later King James II)* 'bid me tell him that if he would have any more soldiers, he shall.'

Pepys returned to the burning streets,

'and at last met my Lord Mayor in Canning Streete like a man spent, with a handkercher about his neck. To the King's message he cried like a fainting woman "Lord, what can I do? I am spent! People will not obey me. I have been pulling down houses but the fire overtakes us faster than we can do it." That he needed no more soldiers and that, for himself, he must go and refresh himself having been up all night.'

They parted and Pepys noted seeing people, almost distracted, with houses

'so very thick thereabouts and full of matter for burning, as pitch and tar.... and warehouses of oyle and wines and brandy and other things.'

Later that day, he, with his wife and friends, took a boat to Bankside on the further shore, to watch the blaze from an ale-house.

'So near the fire as we could for smoke; and all over the Thames, with ones face in the wind, you were almost burned with a shower of Firedrops – this is very true.... houses were burned by these drops and flakes of fire....'

They sat watching it until long after sunset when

'It being darkish, we saw the fire as only one entire arch of fire from this to the other side of the bridge and in a bow upon the hill, for an arch of above a mile long. It made me weep to see it. The churches, houses and all one fire and flaming at once, and a horrid noise the flames made and the cracking of the houses at their ruine.'

Next day, the fire had approached so close that, like

thousands of his neighbours, he packed up his home and

> 'my Lady Batten sent me a cart to carry away all my money and plate and best things to… Bednall Green, which I did, riding myself in my nightgown in the cart and Lord, to see how the streets and the highways are crowded with people, running and riding and getting of carts at any rate to fetch away things.'

Anyone with a cart was indeed, charging 'any rate' and being paid by the frantic citizens, watching their wealth literally melt away before their eyes.

The City was, by now, in total chaos, with all hope of firefighting long forgotten. The King and the Duke of York, with their men, rode up and down the streets trying to keep order. The Duke, whose links with the City, like many noblemen, were strong – was not only heir to the throne but Lord High Admiral, (which put the services of the Navy in his hands for firefighting purposes), Governor of the Royal African Company and the Hudson's Bay Company in Canada, as well as being a powerful shareholder in the East India Company. The homes and warehouses which were now burning were those of his close friends. One can imagine his feelings as he watched shops and houses being looted. Many of those who owned carts were charging up to £30, a phenomenal sum, to carry goods away to the fields of 'Bednall Green', to the east and Soho to the west, while the Thames was alive with boats laden to the gunwales with everything from household furnishings and musical instruments including virginals, to 'children and women in labour.'

The King was determined not only to see what had happened but to take part physically in fighting the flames and helping his subjects. His keen personal interest in fires and firefighting was already known by his own circle of friends, but now he was seen working alongside the men and, at one stage, on the roof of a building opposite the Watermens' Hall, assessing the situation. Here, he realised that the only hope of salvation was to blow up surrounding houses and this was done, but in vain. A contemporary letter described

> 'his Majesty and the Duke of York handing the water in bucketts when they stood up to ancles in water, and playing engines for many hours together as they did at the Temple and Cripplegate, which people seeing, fell to worke with effort, haveing so good fellow labourers….'

The whole of London seemed to have succumbed not only to fire panic but to fear of the Dutch and French taking advantage of the disaster to launch an attack. Londoners turned on any foreigner who was foolish enough to show his face on the streets. One terrified Dutchman wrote:

> 'all foreigners alike were held to be guilty…. and many who were known to be of good character and upon whom no suspicion could rest, were cast into prison. Amongst them was Mr Germanus, who looks like a Frenchman and because of that he was grossly mistreated. A Dutch baker in Westminster heated his oven to bake bread and the people, seeing smoke coming from his chimney, cried out that the rogue was setting the town on fire at that end and they dragged him out into the street, severely wounding him and they nearly beat him to death…..It will be a long time before the people of London forget their wild rage against the foreigners.'

Despite this, some order gradually ensued. State papers for that period (Calendar State Papers Domestic, 1666-67) show that London had eight fire fighting posts at which constables of the parishes were ordered to attend, each of them with 100 men. At every point there were to be

> '30 foot soldiers with a good, careful officer, 2 or 3 gentlemen who are to have the power to give a shilling to any who are diligent all night. These men are to be relieved from the country tomorrow. £5 in bread and cheese and beer are to be allowed to every post. Two companies of trained bands are to guard peoples' goods in Lincolns Inn Fields, Grays Inn Fields, Hatton Garden and St Giles Fields' (all close to but outside the actual City of London) 'and a good officer to go round several posts at this end of the town to see these orders executed.'

Meanwhile, Sir William Coventry was noting that the Duke of York

> 'fears for the want of workmen and tools tomorrow morning and wishes the deputy Lieutenant and the Justices of the Peace to summon the workmen with tools to be there by break of day.'

From the Tower of London, John, Lord Berkley ordered all 'water engines' remaining in store at Deptford and Woolwich to be delivered to him

> 'on account of the dreadful fire now raging. Also for all persons capable either by hand or judgement to assist in the preservation of the Tower' (of London).

Tuesday 4th September brought worse news. The wind still blew strongly from the east and the fire had now leapt beyond the City walls and was eating up the western suburbs. The diarist John Evelyn noted

> 'all Fleet Street, Old Bailey, Ludgate Hill, Warwick Lane, Paul's Chain and Watling Street now flaming and most of it reduced to ashes. The stones of St Paul's, like grenades, the lead melting down the streets in a stream

and the very pavements..... glowing with fiery redness so that no horse or man is able to tread on them.'

Added to which, the fire was by now passing the Temple at the further end of Fleet Street and blowing towards Whitehall where the King's Palace stood. That night the Exchequer was evacuated to Nonsuch Palace in Surrey and the King's most valuable possessions taken to Hampton Court.

Wednesday 5th September dawned to find John Pill and Christopher Parker, the King's printers, defying the approaching flames and working at their presses to produce his latest proclamation:

'His Majesty, in his Princely Compassion and very tender care, taking into consideration the distressed condition of many of his good subjects whom the late dreadful fire hath made destitute of habitations and exposed to many exigencies and necessitites; for present remedy and redress whereof His Majesty, intending to give further evidences of his Grace and Favour towards them as occasion shall arise, hath thougt fit to declare and publish his royal pleasure:

That as great proportion of bread and all other provisions that can possibly be furnished shall be daily and constantly brought not only to the markets formerly in use, but also to such Markets as by his Majestie's late Order and Declaration to the Lord Mayor and Sheriffs of London and Middlesex have been appointed. viz: Clerkenwell, Islington, Finsbury Fields, Mile End Green and Ratclif; His Majesty being sensible that this will be for the benefit also of the Towns and Places adjoyning as being the best expedient to prevent the resort of such persons as may pilfer and disturb them.

And whereas also, divers of the said distressed persons have saved and preserved their goods which nevertheless they know not how to dispose of, it is His Majestie's pleasure That all Churches, Chappels, Schools and other like Public places shall be free and open to receive the said goods when they shall be brought to be there laid. And all Justices of the Peace within the said Counties of Middlesex, Essex and Surrey are to see the same to be done accordingly. And likewise that all Citties and Townes whatsoever shall without any contradiction, receive the said distressed persons and permit them the free exercise of their manual trades, His Majesty resolving and promising that when the present exigent will be passed over, he will take such care and order that the said persons shall be no burthen to their towns or parishes. And it is His Majestie's pleasure that this shall be forthwith published not only by the Sheriffs, Mayors and other chief officers in their respective precincts and limits but by the Constables in every parish...'

King Charles spent the whole of the next day handing out money from a pouch of golden guineas which he wore slung round his shoulders, to soldiers and workmen, exhorting them to work harder in the rescue. Much of his time was spent on foot in bucket chains or helping to dig out people trapped in the debris, his fine costume bedraggled with mud and soaked with water like the rest of the firefighters.

It was, in the end, the King and the Duke of York who, defying the wealthy citizens who still wanted their properties preserved, took the bold step of ordering all buildings in the path of the fire to be blown up. Starting outside the City, they had enough houses destroyed in Westminster to create a fire break between there and the City. Next, they turned to the City itself where still, according to contemporary reports, 'the gentry were only minded for their own preservation.' By then, most of the rest of the population were so distressed and devastated that they hardly knew what they were doing, and many of the poorest 'minded nothing but pilfering.' Came the end of September 4th and the King's troops began blowing up houses near the Tower.

On Wednesday morning, September 5th, Thomas Vincent wrote:

'the Lord hath pity on poor London; his bowels begin to relent, his heart is turned within him and he stays his rough wind in the day of the east wind. The wind is now hushed; the commission of the fire is now withdrawing and it burns so gently..... that it is not hard to be quenched.'

Yet still there was no peace. As the exhausted Londoners prepared to find some rest for the first time in four days, the cry went up 'Arms! Arms!' and rumours flew that the French were coming, armed against them to cut their throats and spoil them of what little they had managed to save from the flames. Thankfully, it was yet another rumour.

By Thursday 6th September, Pepys was reporting a small, isolated outbreak at Bishopsgate, on the northern boundary, but this was quickly quenched. It was, he wrote,

'pretty to see how hard the women did work in the drainage channels, sweeping of water', (to fill the buckets, scoops, syringes and pumps) 'but then they would scold for drink and be drunk as devils.'

On the 8th September, the Official London Gazette which had been delayed by the Fire threatening its printing works, was published with a full description of what had happened each day, and disclosing just how close the fire had come to destroying the Tower with its store of arms and explosives, 'so as though it has pleased God to visit us with his own hand, he hath not, by disfurnishing us with the means of carrying on the War, subjected us to our enemies.....'

The soldiers and sailors who had been summoned to help were congratulated by the King and returned to base. An army of 'rakers' moved in to sift the ruins for valuables. Slowly, the citizens began to creep back into their homes. Vincent, still thundering on, wrote:

'Thus fell great London, that ancient City! That Populous City! Which was the Queen city of the land and as famous as most cities in the world..... And yet how is London departed like smoke and her glory laid to dust!'.

In the space of five days fire had destroyed more of the square mile of the City of London than the whole of the German 'blitz', which brought back the flames in 1940. The loss was estimated by some at £10,000,000. Thomas Delaune, a non-conformist writer, detailed the extent of the damage in his book 'The Present State of London.'

Diagram showing damage caused by Great Fire and that deriving from the air raids of World War Two. (Christine and Gustav Milne.)

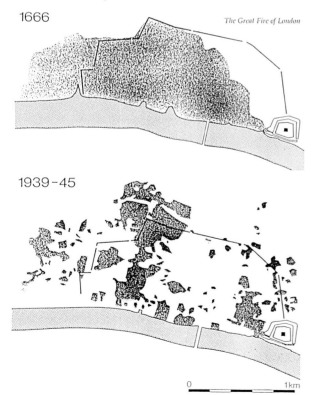

1666

The Great Fire of London

1939–45

0   1km

'Within the City Walls there were 460 acres and the Fire devastated 373; whilst without the Walls it devastated 63 acres and three roods.'

'Out of 15,000 houses, 13,200 were destroyed besides public buildings.'

The detailed list – and the cost in cash – read:

87 parish churches at £8,000

6 consecrated chapels at £2,000

The Royal Exchange at £50,000

The Customs House at £10,000

52 Halls of Companies = £78,000

3, City gates at £3,000 = £9,000

Gaol of Newgate at £15,000

4 stone bridges, £6,000

Sessions House, £7,000

Guildhall (with courts and officers' belongings) at £40,000

Bridewell Gaol, £5,000

St Paul's Church, £2,000,000

Wares, Household Stuff, moveable goods, lost or spoiled, £2,000,000

Printed books in shops or warehouses, £15,000

Wine, Tobacco, Sugar etc of which the Town was at that time very full, £1,500,000

A Pamphlet 'Observations on the Fire of London' by Rege Sencera, published in 1667 in 'Harleian Miscellanies' (iii, 295–350,) quoted:

12,000 houses burnt, £3,600,000

87 churches and other buildings, £1,800,000

Goods and furniture etc, £1,800,000

20 wharves for coal and wood, £20,000

Hire of Porters, boats, etc for removing goods, £150,000

And from another account:

'Out of 26 wards, 15 were destroyed, the remainder scorched ruins and uninhabitable. 400 streets destroyed and 89 churches, schools, hospitals and libraries.

More than bricks and mortar and personal possessions perished in the Great Fire. At this period, under the Licensing Act, only 20 master printers were allowed to publish in the United Kingdom and of these, all but the two University Presses of Oxford and Cambridge were based in London. Because of this, an enormous number of books and documents were destroyed, and it seems likely that among them were copies of the original drafts for Shakespeare's plays and much of his third folio, printed in 1664, which was almost certainly destroyed.

The rest of Europe considered that London was now finished as the greatest centre of trade and commerce. No city could fight back from such destruction and wreckage.

They were, of course, wrong.

Within days, the City Fathers had met and first, declared that the Second of September should be a day of prayer and humiliation for ever (provided that it was not a Sunday). Then they set to work on the task of re-building. The whole City was piled with blackened rubble, so that it was impossible to work out where one house ended and another had begun. Pepys wrote of it '.... *all the town burned, and a miserable sight of Pauls church, with all the roofs fallen – Paul's school also – Ludgate, Fleet Street… and a good part of the Temple the like.*' He gives us some idea of the problems facing him and other Londoners as he writes of '*being all in dirt from top to bottom*' and seeking '*any place to buy a shirt or a pair of gloves but without success.*' He has to walk well beyond the City gates to borrow a shirt from a friend and to wash. Nevertheless, he writes within a few days that '*certainly, never so great a loss as this was borne so well by citizens in the world.*' In his own case, workmen arrived to rebuild and refurbish his home within days of the fire ending and within two weeks he reports, with some satisfaction '*Home to bed and, to my infinite joy, many rooms clean and myself and wife lie in our own chamber again. But much terrified in the nights nowadays, with dreams of fire and falling down of houses.*'

So many people had similar fears that suggestions for fire prevention poured in to the City Council. One of the more imaginative which appeared in Andrew Yarranton's pamphlet '*England's Improvement by Sea and Land*' suggested that fire commissioners should be appointed '*to quench and prevent the spreading of fire*' and that these should have a special staff of engineers, plus two 'sentinels.' The latter's task was laid down in some detail:

'That a sentinel be placed on the highest steeple in the City whereby he may look all over the town and every two hours of the night he plays half an hour upon a flageolet,' *(a small flute)* 'being very delightful in the night; and he looks round the City; if he observes any smoke or fire, he presently sounds a trumpet and hangs out a bloody flag towards that quarter of the City where the fire is.'

Whether or not the Lord Mayor favoured the idea of a little flageolet music in the night is not recorded. Bludworth had gone and his successor moved quickly now. A 'skilful citizen' was appointed to wait on the Lord Mayor at fires and to give advice on which houses should be blown up instantly to prevent flames spreading and another fire sweeping the entire city.

Nor was the King sitting idle after his experiences as an auxiliary fireman. He had a comprehensive set of regulations drawn up

'to be observed within His Majesties Palace at Whitehall in case of Fire happening there and for Prevention of Danger thereby.'

The detailed orders demanded first that anyone living in the Palace must provide a bucket of water for every chimney in the Palace and 'that no person makes use of the said Boquetts for any ordinary or private use' and, among a long list of orders

'That on Thursday in Easter-Week yearly every person respectively upon penalty of five shillings for his Default, do cause to be sent into Scotland-Yard all the Boquetts he is charged withall, full of Water, to be called by the List and viewed by the Officers appointed to search and try whether the same be sound and in sufficient repair, who are thereupon to give notice to the Gentleman-Usher of any defaults, that the same may be reformed…' Also:

'That in case any Chimneys shall happen to be on fire it is Ordered that they do not fire any Guns up the Chimneys but rather clap a wet sheet very close against the Mantle and Jambes, that no Ayre draw in, which will readily extinguish…'

(Noble intentions, but despite this, Charles's Palace at Whitehall burned down in 1698, 13 years after his death, when a maidservant left her wet washing draped round a fire to dry for so long that 'in an instant, as it were, the merciless and devouring flames got such advantage that notwithstanding the great endeavours used by the Water Engines, numerous assistance and blowing up houses to the number of about 20, it still increased with great fury and violence all night, till about 8 of the clock next morning, at which time it was extinguished, after it had burnt down and consumed …. about 150 houses, most of which were the lodgings and habitations of the chief of the nobility.' Poor Charles must have turned in his grave.)

There is little doubt that the King's experiences in the City made him determined that London should never burn again through such carelessness. But first to find the cause. Despite official and unofficial inquiries, investigations and endless speculation, nobody can be quite certain how the Great Fire of London began. Master Farynor, the King's baker and his family maintained their strenuous denial that it was their carelessness in not extinguishing their fire. The 'mobs' blamed the Dutch, the French, in fact, anyone not born and bred a Londoner and were eventually placated when a young Frenchman, Robert Hubert, described as '*a poor, distracted wretch, weary of this life and chose to part with it this way*', confessed to starting the blaze and was promptly tried, found guilty and executed. Three months later, a Parliamentary inquiry decided that the fire had not been started by him, nor as a result of any Papist plot, but '*by the hand of God upon us, a great wind and the season being very dry.*'

Added to that, more recently, have been the findings of a team sent in by the Museum of London to excavate the site of the bakehouse in Pudding Lane. Contemporary reports had described the Pudding Lane area as one in which shipowners bought materials for making their vessels watertight. Archaeologist Gustav Milne describes the modern detective work in his book '*The Great Fire of London*' (Historical Publications, 1986):

Meticulous digging and sifting in the area pinpointed the bakehouse but also discovered, immediately next door to it beneath generations of debris, '*a cellar, full of the remains of barrels, covered with a tar-like substance once contained in the barrels.*' It had formed a hard crust on the upper surface of the blackened brickwork and had percolated between the bricks, staining their sides and discolouring the earlier surfaces beneath.

Scientific analysis of samples taken from this deposit was conducted by the British Carbonisation Research Association. It concluded that '*the carbonaceous material had the open spherical structure associated with the later stages of carbonisation of pitch*.' Further tests indicated that the remains were of a particular type, known as '*Stockholm Tar*' which was often used for waterproofing ships and that they could not have oozed from the barrel staves because these were made of non-resinous oak. Further detailed examination of the surrounding layers of debris produced a fascinating picture.

It seems that Master Farynor's neighbour kept a shop at street level, but in his cellars he stored barrels of Stockholm Tar or Wood Pitch for waterproofing the ships which came into the then busy harbour of Billingsgate, barely 100 metres away, down the hill on the edge of the Thames. Had the fire been confined to the King's Bakery, it might well have been contained. It was the cellar full of pitch barrels, well alight and blown by the strong wind, which set London ablaze with such speed and ferocity.

One might have thought that the population of a City already weakened by Plague and who had faced all the psychological trauma of such a fire would have given up, but not Londoners. By Christmas, 1666, some of the houses had been restored and plans were under way to rebuild the City as a whole.

Architects, including Sir Christopher Wren, drew up great schemes for a city with wide streets, built on a reasoned, grid pattern, but this was not what many citizens wanted. They were already squabbling over boundaries – where exactly their house had stood, whether the walls were one foot to this way or that. Parliament dealt with all this by setting up a Fire Court in February 1667 (18–19 Chas II, 7) which eventually continued its sittings for nine years to deal with all the disputes. A second measure, (18–19 Chas II, 8) represented the most far-reaching and comprehensive set of guidelines for development which the City of London had ever experienced. (This second Act was modified and extended in 1671, [22, Chas II, 11]).

Under this legislation, the new City would be brick or stone built with wider streets and better drain pipes and gutters.

The '*Act for the Rebuilding of the City of London*' laid down not only the regulations for the '*uniformity and gracefulness*' of the new London, but '*to the end that great and outrageous fires may be reasonably prevented. . . .*'

Only four types of houses were to be allowed in the City:

'The least sort to be built in by-lanes two storeys high.

'The second sort in streets and lanes of note to be three storeys high.

'The third fronting high and principal streets – four storeys.

'The fourth type "of the greatest bigness" and not fronting a street must also not exceed four storeys.'

The authorities meant business. Penalties for not obeying the law were severe. The Lord Mayor was commanded that, by 1st April 1667 a decision must be made as to

'how many streets shall hereafter be deemed by-lanes, streets or lanes of note, or high and principal streets. All the said streets intended to be rebuilt shall be marked and staked out so that the breadth, length and extent thereof shall be better known and observed.'

For anyone caught removing the stakes, the penalty was three months imprisonment or a fine of £10. If the offender was 'a person of low and mean condition', unable to pay the fine, he was to be 'openly whipped till his body be bloody.'

That having been settled, all buildings had to be of brick or stone, all with party walls of a specified width of bricks according to the type of building and the level of each storey. (Oak, normally used for house-building, was in short supply as naval actions at the time were demanding more ships, built of oak. More inflammable pine had often to be substituted for roofing timbers.)

For once, the government took serious steps to try to prevent fire, by laying down that 'trades and occupations judged noisome or perilous in respect of fire may be prohibited in the high and principal streets.' This was convenient for the wealthy but did nothing for the poorer citizens living in premises where dangerous processes might still be carried on behind the 'high and principal' streets.

This was also the law which ordered the setting up of a Monument, 'the better to preserve the memory of this dreadful visitation.' The Monument, designed by Wren, was duly built, not on the site of the baker's shop, but close to it, a pillar of Portland Stone, 202 feet high and with a staircase inside leading to the gallery surrounding the top, just below the vase of gilded flames which surmounts it. The pediment bears fiery scenes in bas-relief including one showing King Charles 'affording protection to the desolate City and freedom to its rebuilders and inhabitants.' After the trial of Titus Oates who, in 1678, claimed that the fire had been the combined work of 80 Jesuit priests, a further, somewhat inflammatory inscription was added:

'The burning of this Protestant City was begun and carried on by the treachery and malice of the Popish faction, in order to better the effecting their horrid plot for the extirpating the Protestant religion and English liberties, and to introduce Popery and heresy.'

Anti-Popish feelings were high in London at that time and the site of the bakehouse in Pudding Lane was also marked with a plaque bearing the equally biased message:

'Here by ye permission of heaven, hell broke loose upon this Protestant City from the malicious Hearts of barbarous Papists. by the hand of their agent, Hubert, who confessed and on ye ruins of this place declared the fact for which he was hanged, ... that here began that dreadful fire which is described and perpetuated on and by the neighbouring pillar.'

This too, was eventually removed and presented to the Guildhall Museum in 1876.

Not all agreed with the inscription and the Lord Mayor who had added it, Sir Patience Ward, was scathingly decried in a poem by Thomas Ward, (no relation) who wrote in his 'England's Reformation' in 1710 that Titus Oates:

'... swore, with flaming faggot sticks
In sixteen hundred sixty-six
That they through London took their marches
And burned the City down with torches;
Yet all invisible they were
Clad in their coats of Lapland air.
That sniffing Whig-Mayor Patience Ward

To this damned lie had such regard
That he his godly masons sent
T'engrave around the Monument.
They did so, but let such things pass,
His men were fools and he an ass.'

Thomas Bludworth, the ineffectual Lord Mayor whose faltering confusion in the earliest hours of the fire had led to such criticism, left at the end of his term of office within a month of the fire. Meanwhile, a Relief Fund had been set up and donations poured in from all over Britain and Ireland, but Bludworth's immediate successor as Lord Mayor, Sir William Bolton, was rapidly suspended from office when he was discovered filching the cash for his personal benefit. In 1668 he was convicted of embezzling a major part of the Fund.

In effect, the City was initially slow to be rebuilt and by 1668 Samuel Rolle was writing:

'Is London a village that I see, the houses stand so scatteringly? The major part of the houses built upon the ruins let out to alehouse keepers and victuallers to entertain the workmen employed about the City. Few expect to trade within the walls till the City be rebuilt.'

But rebuilt it was. By 1675, Christopher Wren's design for a new St Paul's had been approved and work on the foundations had already begun on the Cathedral which still dominates the City 300 years later.

Yet despite all the Acts of Parliament and by-laws and dire threats of punishment for anyone responsible for starting a fire, the problem still faced London. In November 1666 Pepys is writing of a 'horrid great fire' burning the Palace and the Horse Guards. Charles II himself, by now, a seasoned firefighter, attended in person another massive fire which swept through Southwark in 1676, along with the Duke of Monmouth and the Earl of Craven and, according to one Thomas Jordan, gent.,

'being pleased to go down to the bridge foot in his barge to give such orders as His Majesty found fit for putting a stop to it, which, through the mercy of God, was effected after about 600 houses had been burned and blown up. The fire was stayed at St Thomas's Hospital and, there is reason to believe, through the instrumentality of a fire engine with leathern pipe, now first used in this country.'

But the skyline of the City itself was resolutely growing, with many of the public buildings paid for by a hefty tax on the one product which everyone needed for light and fuel — coal. All coals (and the Thames was daily packed with coal boats and reputed to be 'full of sin and sea-coal') brought into London, were to be sold by the chaldron or tun and a tax of 12 pence paid to the Mayor for every tun.

By incredible good fortune, very few people had died in the Great Fire although it was not easy to be certain of the number with so much debris. The Bills of Mortality, listing the deaths in each area, mention six people, including Thomas Farynor's maid and an old woman in St Paul's churchyard, but others put the figure higher. Far more, particularly the poorer people, died during the hard winter which followed when they had no shelter and had to camp out in the fields beyond the walls of the City.

On the whole, London's rulers at this time were more concerned with property and finance than with people, but, under pressure from Parliament, the Court of Common Council agreed on and decreed some specific fire precautions. The City was to be divided into four districts, each of which would be provided with 800 leather buckets, 50 ladders of different sizes from 12 to 42 feet long; two brazen hand squirts to each parish, 24 pickaxe sledges and 40 shovels.

Each of the twelve livery companies were to provide themselves with *an engine, thirty buckets, three ladders, six pickaxe sledges and two hand squirts to be ready upon all occasions.* The twelve would have been the premier livery companies, led by the powerful Mercers, but the new Acts also required that the inferior companies should provide *such a number of small engines and buckets as shall be allotted to them by the Lord Mayor* and added to this *that the aldermen past shrievalty do provide their several houses with four and twenty buckets and one hand squirt each, and those who have not served in that office, twelve buckets and one hand pump each.* To make sure that these were supplied with water, pumps were to be fitted to wells and plugs were to be fixed in the main water pipes supplied by the New River and Thames Waterworks.

For Londoners, particularly wealthy businessmen, the talk in the new coffee houses was all of property and of their monetary losses. Conversation, from the taverns to the dining rooms of the better-off was of compensation. How could a man recover from such a fire? For all the business men who had bounced back, there were many more suffering total bankruptcy who had been shown no sympathy but simply thrown in to the debtors' gaol. One of many who had been dealt with in this summary way, had a six-page pamphlet printed and distributed, calling on King and Parliament to show mercy to these *miserably singed citizens.* The writer asked that a tax, or even voluntary contributions, be collected to help them, pleading that

> 'the sufferers are worthy objects of your help and interposition for the stopping of the merciless fury of their creditors whereof the prisons about London are severe testimonies, and this countenanced by the Law

because of debt, without any reflection upon the Hand of God that disabled them.'

The very fact that such a desperate plea was ignored must have worried the businessmen of London, only too aware that despite all the long words and legislation, fires were still breaking out – and on a devastating scale. The new phrase being heard in the coffee houses was Fire Insurance.

General insurance was not new. Over many years shipowners had contributed to schemes of marine insurance against the loss of their great merchant fleets on the high seas. Insurance for goods in transit went back to the days of the Assyrians. But with the hazard so high, nobody had been fool enough to venture into insurance against damage by fire although it had, in the earlier part of the century, begun to be discussed. As long ago as 1609 a scheme of fire insurance had been put forward in London, followed by three more in 1635, 1638 and 1660. The 1635 scheme was actually laid before the Privy Council, suggesting a plan for fire insurance in the City at 1s per annum. It was followed in 1638 by a venture which included the provision of fire-engines in every Ward of the City as well as a nightly watch for fires and the deposit of £5,000 in the Chamber of London as security for those insured through the scheme. Although Charles I had been pleased to grant his petitioners a 'Patent according to the petition and propositions' of the 1638 proposals, nothing further was heard of the scheme – probably because the country was soon in the throes of Civil War. Soon after Cromwell's death and the restoration of the Monarchy, another scheme was put forward 'by several persons of quality and eminent citizens of London' but, again, this foundered. There was some individual underwriting of fire risks by the Lombards in Italy and merchants in some of the cities of Germany, but there was no fire insurance in London on the 2nd September 1666.

Now, however, times had changed. Under the restrictions of the 1667 Building Act only some 9,000 brick or stone houses were to be erected to replace the 13,000 of the pre-Fire days. Already, too, the City was offering its legal powers to compel *constables, bailiffs and private citizens* to turn to and help put out fires. The risks had been considerably lowered.

Smoke in their noses no doubt cleared the heads of the brighter young business men of the time, not least one who was reckoned to be among the most enterprising ever to emerge. He was one of twin sons born to a prominent member of Cromwell's government, Praise-God Barebones. The brothers were given the unfortunate baptismal names of *Christ Came Into The World To Save* Barebones and *If Christ Had Not Died Thou Hast Been Damned* Barebones. The more lively of the two rapidly changed his name to

Nicholas Barbon and set off on a succession of careers, some of which sailed fairly close to the wind. As one of his contemporaries commented later, people were uncertain which of the twins was Nicholas but he was certainly known as 'Damned Barebones.'

In fact, Nicholas Barbon was well-educated and trained as a physician, but recognising that there was quick money to be made after the Fire, he turned his hand to building. He was not concerned with architecture, merely to putting up as many houses as possible on any piece of land he could buy up at the lowest possible rate. He must have been one of the earliest 'jerry builders', of mostly small family houses, which, in his words, were 'economical on the ground.' Some were so economical that one, in Mincing Lane, collapsed when the vaults fell in and he nearly faced financial ruin – not to mention the fury of the new owner.

After this, he turned his attention outside the City walls, buying up fire-damaged properties in the Strand area and turning them into 'houses and tenements for taverns, alehouses, cooks shoppes, vaulting schools' and the gardens adjoining the River into 'wharfes and woodmongers.' By now he was established as an entrepreneur, a 'developer of land of good address' and when he began rebuilding the Temple he was described as 'an excellent mobmaster, he knew the art of leading, winding or driving men as herds.' By 1690 he was a Member of Parliament and by 1692 was 'improving' Chancery Lane and Lincoln's Inn.

Whatever the rights or wrongs of the quality of his building efforts, there was no doubt that he knew the hardship brought about when uninsured buildings burned down. So it was, that in 1667, as soon as the City had recovered from the first shock of the devastation and while the losses were still raw in their minds, Barbon worked out a new scheme for fire insurance, confiding to his friends that he 'reckoned to get vastly by it.'

In that year, he set up and launched 'The Insurance Office at the Backside of the Royal Exchange', offering to insure the citizens of London against loss by fire, in return for premiums set according to the size and quality of their homes or work places. It was brilliantly timed. The scheme not only caught on but was copied, in 1669, by Benjamin Delaune who had written so extensively about the Fire. His proposal would, he hoped, be backed by municipal finance, but the City Corporation refused to co-operate. Instead, in 1682 they drew up their own scheme for fire insurance. By now, Barbon's company was becoming so successful that he publicly challenged the Corporation, comparing their scheme unfavourably with his own in fairly fiery language.

Although they had received nearly 1,700 proposals, they were forced out of business and the Chamberlain was instructed to repay all the money which had been advanced to them.

All seemed to be going well for Barbon until, in 1683 two more enterprising men, William Hale and Henry Spelman, set up in competition, founding their 'Friendly Society for Securing Houses from Loss by Fire.'

Barbon was not pleased. He claimed that his was the only real insurance company, that he now had 4,000 subscribers and that the Friendly Society's proposals were far inferior to those which he offered his own customers. He had, by now extended his original policies with a new 'bait'. His company would, he announced with a flourish,

> 'provide a group of men versed and experienced in extinguishing and preventing fire...Servants in livery with badges who are watermen and other lusty persons who are always ready when any sudden fire happens, which they are very laborious and dextrous at quenching and not sticking in cases of necessity to expose themselves to very great hazards in their attempts.'

The Friendly Society's founders retaliated equally firmly, arguing that they had a right to launch their own scheme to which they too, hastily added a band of lusty firefighters. Barbon promptly applied to King James II for a monopoly of fire insurance 'within the Bills of Mortality' for the next 31 years, but the Friendly Society, now distinctly unfriendly, filed a counter-claim.

King James and his advisers pondered on the problem and came down on the side of the Friendly Society but Barbon, furious and undaunted, challenged the decision. The King, in a Solomon-like judgement finally awarded Barbon a monopoly, but for one year only, after which the underwriting was to alternate quarterly between Barbon's Office and the Friendly Society, each seeking customers and carrying on their work at intervals of three months. Such a scheme was clearly unworkable and both companies eventually continued until gradually more insurance firms came on to the scene.

For the first time in its history, London had teams of organised firemen who, although most of them were only part-time firefighters, were at least receiving some training in fire extinction and the workings of their primitive fire engines. Their objective was to save property from destruction and in so doing, reduce the cost of fires to the insurers. Saving life was not necessarily included.

3
The Watermen Firemen

'The Hand-in-Hand the Race begun
Then came the Phoenix and the Sun,
The Exchange where old insurers run,
The Eagle where the new....'

ALTHOUGH REGULAR SOCIAL HISTORIANS MIGHT not agree, there can be little doubt that from a viewpoint of London fire history, among the more important landmarks of the 18th century were insurance firemen, Queen Anne and the Industrial Revolution.

As the 1600s came to an end, new fire 'engines' were beginning to appear with greater frequency. Sir Samuel Morland, Master of Mechanics to King Charles II, was advertising engines using a 'cyclo-elliptical' pump instead of the previous force-pump. Records for December 1689 show a Patent granted to John Lofting and Nicholas de Wael for their 'engine for the quenching of fire the like never seen before in the country ..... spouting water at 300 or 400 feet high'. John Lofting, a merchant who had come to London with William III, had studied firefighting problems with the Van der Heiden brothers in Amsterdam. In 1690 he was advertising another appliance, 'the new Sucking Worm Engine' introducing, apparently for the first time, a suction pipe on a fire pump. The hose, described as 'canvas or leathern' was strengthened by binding with wire. His advertisement in 1715 features his engine and 'sucking worm', suggesting that it might also be used for pumping out ships and watering gardens – and showing it working from what must have been one of the earliest fire floats.

The whole atmosphere of London was changing now. No longer was the City a place where one concentrated one's entire life, with workplace and home under the same roof – or close by. Many people who considered themselves

Londoners already lived a mile or more beyond the boundaries of the old City with the better-off and those who supplied them with their amusements, centred to the west. The docks, the great warehouses and the working classes were situated to the east. Northward was still an area of villages like Clerkenwell, and beyond these, the hills through which much of London's water supply was piped.

By the turn of the century, much of the business of insurance was being carried out in the many coffee houses which had spread rapidly, replacing the mass of old ale-houses and cutting down, for the time being at least, some of the drunkenness which had marred the London scene for so much of the preceding centuries.

This was a time when 'tay' and coffee were becoming increasingly popular with both men and women. Social life was developing fast, new theatres were being built – pleasure gardens began to develop, crowds of people gathered together for entertainment. Art, great music, the magnificent architecture of Wren, were all gracing the capital, but for the man (woman and child) in the street, there was still little regard for fire. True, there were still the remains of the old engines which had been based outside the livery halls and in the yards of some of the larger churches. King William III had brought with him among his courtiers, men who were influenced, no doubt, by the Van der Heiden brothers who had successfully spread their new methods of firefighting throughout Europe. Fire 'en-gins' with fixed nozzles were useless, they argued. Fighting fire

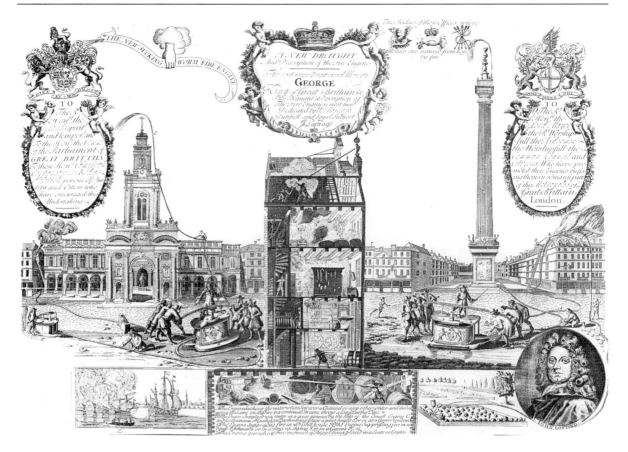

— 13. This Day, between Four and Five of the Clock in the Afternoon, the Boy of one *Walker*, who kept a small Gunpowder Shop near *Bear-Key*, in *Thames-Street*, between the Custom-House and *Billingsgate*, being in an upper Room with a Light, and making Rockets and Squibs, unwarily set Fire to the Gunpowder; upon which the House blew up. The Wind being very high, the Fire soon spread from that House to others towards *Billingsgate*, and backwards towards the Warehouses on the Keys, did great Damage there, cross'd the Way to the North-Side of *Thames-Street*, and burnt up *Water-Lane*, and the back Part of *Harp-Lane* to *Tower-Street*, taking *Baker's-Hall* and *Trinity-House* in its destructive Career, which, about Five of the Clock the next Morning, was stopp'd in *Tower-Street*, over against *Mark-Lane*; above 120 Houses were either burnt or blown up, and great Quantities of Sugar, Oil, Wine, and other rich Goods and Merchandizes, were consum'd and destroy'd. The Loss was computed at above 500,000 *l.* and above 50 Persons perish'd in the Flames, or were bury'd in the Ruins of Houses.

1715

Above: John Lofting's great sucking worm and engines. (Society of Antiquaries of London.)

Left: Early firework disaster. (Guildhall Library, Corporation of London.)

successfully demanded that the water should, if possible, be provided by some attachment to the pumping engine, rather than relying on buckets to fill it. After this, the water should be directed on to the flames from as close a source as possible – and a fixed nozzle on a fire engine meant that not only the appliance but its operators also – were in danger of being burned. The solution lay in their new sucking hose-pipes which could be taken in to the source of the outbreak, and, if necessary, directed through metal 'branches' or nozzles up to six feet in length.

Flexible leather hoses were used throughout the world until woven canvas hoses replaced them in the 1870's. (Jean Rudolf Hegner had invented a loom for weaving flaxen yarn into seamless pipes or tubes *'suitable as a substitute for leather hose'* as early as 1792, but it was not until the discovery that they could be lined with rubber or gutta-percha and made waterproof that the invention caught on.)

Although leather hoses were valuable in their time, they were immensely heavy – four times the weight and bulk of canvas pipes – and careful steps had to be taken always to prevent them from cracking. At least four times a year they had to be thoroughly anointed with special oil. One commonly-used recipe for hose oil read:

'Take two lbs of perfectly clean tallow, free from salt and mix with it when hot, 1 gallon or 9 lbs of cod oil'.

The smell alone must have heralded the arrival of the firefighters.

The two brothers had published a number of papers on their work including one, in 1690 – 'A Description of the newly invented Fire Hose' which was illustrated with steel engravings demonstrating a section of a burning house and showing flexible hoses in use, as well as one of their engines – an oval cistern, 5 feet by 2 feet and 2½ feet high, two barrels and an air vessel with the delivery pipe attached. The air vessel was used to ensure a constant stream of water from the pump instead of the intermittent jets which had been peculiar to most previous engines. (Some reports suggest that one of the earliest engines with a constant stream was produced by fire engineer Nathaniel Hadley, of Cross Street, 'West End' in London. His business was later linked by marriage with others and, eventually, was taken over by the famous Merryweather company, which is still in business 300 years later in the 1990s.)

Although the work of the Van der Heidens was known in England and their machines examined and improved on by the fire engine makers of London, such experience was not enough to prevent yet another 'sudden and most dreadful fire' at Execution Dock in Wapping in 1703 which consumed 50 dwelling houses in four hours, 'most of them the habitation of seamen, seamen's wives, sea-artificers and traders at sea'. So much devastation was caused that Queen Anne, who had only acceded to the throne the previous year, gave permission for house-to-house and church collections to be held throughout the land to help the victims.

The distress, particularly among the women and children, must have left its mark. Four years later, Anne, with her advisers and government, finally produced what was to be the first major legislation dealing with fire.

'An Act of Parliament for the better preventing of the Mischiefs that may happen by Fire' came into force on 1st May 1708 ('or as soon as may be') and its strictures were to apply for more than 200 years. It recalled the serious fires of the recent past and pointed out that much of their intensity and damage might have been prevented had there been

sufficiently strong 'party' walls in buildings (which had, of course, been mandatory but conveniently ignored by architects and builders). Less use of timber in construction and better water supplies were also essential, said the lawgivers. This new Act, brought about solely by the pressure of fire hazard, was aimed at making the whole population more aware of the problems of fire. More than that, it activated the great change in general architecture, pioneered by Wren, which brought in the magnificent Queen Anne style of houses – for the wealthy at least.

The Act laid down that all houses erected after May 1 1708 'within the Bills of Mortality', were to be built with front and rear walls of brick or stone, and between each house was to be a party wall at least two bricks thick in the cellar and 14 inches thick from there through each storey. There was to be no timber under the eaves.

Each parish was to have and maintain in good repair a large engine and a hand engine and a leather pipe for filling the engine with water without having to resort to buckets.

Churchwardens in every parish were to fix stopcocks on the water pipes which ran through the streets and marks showing the position of these stopcocks were to be fixed to nearby houses so that their position could clearly be seen. (They still exist in the modern hydrant signs.)

Turncocks were to be paid one shilling (5p) for opening up 'plugs' in a street to provide water for firefighting.

Servants whose negligence caused fires were to be fined £100 (an impossibly high amount for any servant to pay) or be sentenced to 18 months in the Workhouse.

As soon as a fire broke out in London or Westminster,

'all Constables and Beadles…shall immediately repair to the Place where the said Fire shall happen, with their Staves and other Badges of their Authority, and be aiding and assisting as well in the extinguishing of the said Fires, and causing People to work at the Engines, as also in preventing Goods being stolen; and shall seize and apprehend all ill-disposed Persons that they shall find stealing or pilfering from the Inhabitants; as also the said Constables and Beadles shall give their utmost Assistance to help the Inhabitants to remove their said Goods.'

There were penalties for failure to carry out the letter of the law and rewards for the first, second and third engines to reach a fire, provided that it was in good working order and complete with an effective hose.

Although the practical workings of the Act were not totally clear, it seems, from the various records of parishes within the City of London, that the 'Engine-keepers' of the first, second and third appliances to reach the fire had, when it was all over, to visit a magistrate and be given a specially prepared note certifying their arrival. This was then taken to the parish council who would pay the fee, thirty shillings (£1.50p) for the first engine, twenty shillings (£1) for the second and ten shillings (50p) for the third, although over the years the amount appears to have varied and later, tokens were given in payment for pumping and for buying beer. In those days the parish councils were the heart of their areas, dealing not only with religious matters but helping, advising, and sometimes caring for or providing money to help nurse the sick, the dying or such problems as 'wandering and drunken females' or 'foundlings'. Minutes of the regular meetings of some parishes show how seriously they took Queen Anne's 'Parish Pump' Act, as it came to be known – as well as the problems which it brought them.

Vestry Minutes for St Dionysius Backchurch, in the City for example, show that within months of the Act being passed, the churchwardens had chosen a Mr Fox 'for y Engine-Keeper for extinguishing fire and has appointed such consideracion for his Trouble as y Church Wardens should think fit.'

The law evidently allowed two churches to join together to provide the necessary equipment and in 1709, the vellum-bound accounts for 'the united Parishes of St Marten's Ongar and St Clement's, Eastcheap' had, fixed inside the cover 'The Inventory of the Things in the Engine House'. The list, which survives in the Guildhall Library of the City, reads:

'1 Large Engin and Hand Engin.

2 Brass pipes.

3 Iron Turn Cocks.

1 Large Brass Fire Cock.

1 Chest, lined with lead.' *(The water tank.)*

'20 yards of leather pipe for St Marten's Ongar.

10 yards of leather pipe for St Clement's Eastcheap.

The Inscription on the En-gines and Brass Fire Cock followeth:

"This Engin belongeth unto the United Parrishes of St Marten's Ongar and St Clement's Eastcheap." The Same on the large Brasse Fire Cock.'

Further entries track the history of the *'en-gine'* and include 10/- paid in May 1714 *'for playing ye engine 4 times'* and, on a sadder note, *'April 21 1714: Paid for 2/3rds of wheels for the Engine, broke att y fire – 12/-* (60p). In 1717 they were paying out yet again, *'to Mr Faithfull for Plumbing work done to y Firecock, 3/6d (17¹/₂p) for digging up y pavement and mending firecock.'*

Many of the records which have survived mention their parish 'pumps' and from St Margaret's, Westminster, close to the Abbey, comes an elaborately hand-written contract, signed in November 1742, laying out the Articles of Agreement between two churchwardens, Richard Bridge, a cofferman and John Stagg, bookseller, on behalf of the parish and John Gray, an engine maker, *'for a New Engine and keeping the old ones in repair for the Term of seven years.'* This evidently involved carrying out repairs to their *'large engine and small squrt'* and suggested what would appear to be a 'trade-in' deal to exchange an old pump for a new one, with meticulous details of how it was to be built. Included in the 'deal' was the clause that John Gray

'shall and will', four times in every year '...play the same Engines either in their Church Yard or in New Palace Yard...to the intent that the Church Wardens...who shall be assembled together may View and see that the said Engines are in good Order and Repair.'

It is possible that this John Gray (or Grey) was the partner of another fire engine maker named Maundell, both part of the growing band of engineers who were setting up business in London – often in Long Acre – and not only providing engines for this country but already exporting them abroad, and particularly to 'the Americas'. The growing towns of New York and Boston were built almost entirely of wood, and fire was a constant hazard. Among the exporters of these early 'enjins' from London were Maundell and Grey, and Fowke, who produced a range of small engines which could be mounted on a wheelbarrow-type chassis as well as 'constant-flow' machines, some of which could play two streams at once. Records from the 'New World' show that in 1707, two pumps were imported from London to Boston and again, in 1711, three more were received.

London was increasingly famous for its fire engine inventors including John Blanch, whose pump could, he claimed, pump fifty yards (45.7 m) high; Charles Simpkins; Joseph Bramah of Piccadilly who patented *'a hydrostatical machine upon a new construction in which the pistons had their motion round a centre in a rotary direction rather than reciprocating in a straight barrel'* which was normal at that time, and Roundtree, of Great Surrey Street in south east London who was also making semi-rotary engines.

Supreme among engine makers of the 18th century though, was Richard Newsham, the son of a button-maker, who patented his first fire engine in 1721 and became known as the 'Father of Fire Engines.' One of the major changes which he brought about was to alter the pumping mechanism from the front or rear to the sides of the engine. Newsham's appliances had two long 'stretcher' handles, one on each side, so that two teams of four or five men, pumping in parallel, could increase the power of the jets. By the middle of the century he was hailed as a national hero by a contemporary writer, *'having given a nobler present to his country than if he had added provinces to Great Britain.'*

His first patent was for a water engine

'for the quenching and extinguishing of fires, contrived to work with more winches or cranks on the outside than any water engine heretofore made (none having more than two cranks to work with) a new contrived winch or crank in imitacion of a crane called a crane crank, acts as a double mocon' (motion) 'and hath a new invented clack with four half-wheels, also a new fashioned worm which works without racks or ladders, so fixed that one forcer begins before the other hath left forceing, and causes a continued stream without intermission, and with such force that it throws out or emptys one hundred and ten gallons of water in one minute's time or a little more, and at a greater distance than any other water engine can, and as it excells all other water engines in the performance, so it likewise differs in the invencon and contrivance and the patentee conceives it may be properly called a perpetual engine for quenching and extinguishing fires.'

(He added a 'supplemental improvement' to this in June 1725.)

His workshops in Cloth Fair (close to St Bartholomew's Hospital, off West Smithfield) were kept busy making and adapting engines and eventually he devised a pump which was not only worked with long handles on either side but with men who, according to a contemporary report, were taught to 'tread or dance in rhythm' on a lever on the top of the appliance, to add to the force of the jets.

Other improvements included a bent axle so that the body of the machine was lower and therefore easier for the men who were pumping to work the levers. Because of the rails on top which the 'dancers' used to steady themselves, this early style was known as a 'bed-poster' and some were still being used in the mid-1800s.

Newsham described each pump in detail in his advertisements, usually headed with an illustration which showed them at work on a particularly fierce fire. One, he said, had

'an oak plank cistern, joints lined with sheet copper. Easily moved by pole and cross-bar in front of the engine, the cross-bar built to slide back under cover of the cistern. Mounted on solid wheels, the hind axle fastened under the bottom of the cistern, the fore-axle tree on a strong bolt/pin horizontally fastened in the middle of the front of the cistern base'.

The engine could

'stand firmly on rough or sloping ground as if it were level'

and had a leather pipe which could be screwed on and off a brass cock at the lower end of the cistern. The other end could be immersed in a cistern or pond or water from a fire-plug – there was no need for buckets to pour water into the tank, but if this proved necessary, it was strained through an inbuilt copper sieve. The force of water from the pumps was so strong, he maintained, that it could break windows with its pressure.

Before long, Newsham was by far the biggest maker of fire engines in London and on May 6th 1731, the inhabitants of New York were drawing attention to his pamphlets in a petition to their City Council for improved fire protection for their mostly wooden town. On May 6th 1731, the Council agreed:

'With all convenient speed to procure two complete fire engines, with suctions and materials thereto belonging, for the public service; that the sizes thereof be of the 4th and 6th sizes of Mr Newsham's fire engines; and that Mr Mayor, Alderman Cruger, Alderman Rutgers and Alderman Roosevelt, or any of them, be a committee to agree with some proper merchant or merchants to send to London for the same by the first conveniency and report upon what terms the said fire engines, etc, will be delivered to this corporation.'

(Size 6 was Newsham's largest, with a cistern holding 170 gallons of water which could be discharged at the rate of 170 gpm for a distance of 40 yards. It cost £70. The smaller, Size 4 engine held 90 gallons, discharged at 90 gpm for a distance of 36 yards and cost £40).

The Committee set to work and on December 3rd 1731, the machines were unloaded from the ship 'Beaver' and ceremoniously hauled to the City Hall. Four days later, the Boston Weekly Newsletter, in its 'News from New York', was reporting:

'Last night, about twelve o'clock, fire broke out in a joiner's house in this city. It began in the garret where the people were all asleep and burnt violently; but by the aid of the two fire engines which came from London in the ship "Beaver", the fire was extinguished after having burned down the house and damaged the next.'

Newsham died in 1743, leaving his business to his son who died in the following year so that it was passed on to his widow and a cousin, George Wragg. It was a time when fire engines were in steady demand and would continue so to be. Not only were the parishes trying to keep their appliances in working order but more and more insurance companies were developing and even individuals were buying engines. Archbishop Thomas Secker noted in his diary for 1761, as he prepared for the Coronation of George III:

'This year I bought for the use of my Successors as well as Myself, a Coronation Cope which cost me £52 & a Fire Engine which cost me £54.'

This was a century in which the coffee houses which had quickly caught on with Londoners, rapidly began to identify with their own type of clientele. Politicians gathered in 'The Cocoa Tree' or 'St James's', poets and writers at 'Will's' in Covent Garden. In the City itself, Edward Lloyd's Coffee House had become a centre for merchants and business men where they could not only sup their coffee and smoke a pipe of tobacco, but exchange news of shipping movements, of commodity supplies, of politics and prices – there was no 'media' to provide all these. Lloyd's was the great centre and it was here that many of the new insurance companies had developed.

Many distinguished men of the period were among the Directors of these new companies, not least Sir Christopher Wren, who, with customary perception and depth of vision, had included a site for a major building, labelled 'Insurance Office' in his new plan for London in 1667 (and had later joined the board of one of the new fire insurance companies, the 'Friendly Society'). Barbon's Fire Office had already been taken over and become the 'Phenix', which itself eventually sank back into the ashes after a series of disasters culminating in the 'South Sea Bubble' incident of the 1720s.

(The later 'Phoenix' was a totally different organisation, founded in 1782 and absorbed now into the 'Sun Alliance' Insurance PLC.)

In November 1696, Tom's Coffee House in St Martin's Lane, Westminster, had seen the rise of 'The Contributors for Insuring Houses, Chambers and Rooms from loss by fire by Amicable Contribution' – which became the 'Hand-in-Hand'. 'The Exchange House' amalgamated in 1710 with the 'Sun' (which joined with the Alliance in 1959 to become the 'Sun Alliance') followed in 1714 by the 'Union' which became the 'Alliance' after 1906 when it had fallen on hard times after the San Francisco earthquake and its subsequent fires. The 'Westminster' emerged in 1717 and, interestingly, took for its badge and fire mark the portcullis of Westminster, surmounted with the Prince of Wales's feathers in recognition of the 'invaluable assistance at the fire in the French Chapel and library at Spring Gardens in 1716' rendered by the Prince who later became George II. The year 1720 saw the arrival of the 'London Assurance' and the 'Royal Exchange' and so it continued. The 'Westminster' paid 4½d for casting its marks, 10d for gilding – a total of 1s 2½d – and charged policy holders 1/8d.

Most of the companies now offered their own firefighting service, often equipped by Mr Newsham, and to distinguish between them – not least for publicity as the increasingly large fire engines roared through the town, drawn first by men and later by horses – they decked them out in brightly coloured uniforms similar to those which are worn to this day on State occasions by the Queen's watermen and the winners of the annual Doggett's Coat and Badge race on the River Thames. By the middle of the century, the cry of 'Fire' could bring a hasty response not only from the parish pumps but from half a dozen different insurance brigades. Sallying forth from the 'stations' where the engines were stored, London's watermen firemen were a colourful sight. The top coats were of double-breasted 'Brummagen' type, which the watermen usually wore on the River to keep out the cold winds. They soon found the long skirts too cumbersome for clambering up and down ladders so trimmed them short and produced a tunic in a style which was to remain with the fire brigades of London for nearly 250 years.

The tunic and breeches were the outstanding part of the rig though and the 'Sun' company was soon advertising that it had

'Thirty lusty and able-body'd firemen who are clothed in blue Liveries and having Silver Badges with the 'Sun' Mark upon their arms, and twenty able Porters likewise, who are always ready to assist in quenching fires and removing goods, having given Bonds for their Fidelity.'

The 'Hand-in-Hand' wore 'Caps, coates and breeches' in 'Blew lined with red, a red edging being put upon ye same'. The 'Royal Exchange' men, by contrast, wore 'yellow lined with pink' and were also equipped with '35 steel caps, covered with leather, 35 pole-axes, 35 girdles, 2 iron crows, 2 pick-axes, and 35 preventers in the nature of boat-hooks'. The 'Phoenix' dressed its men in 'a coat of Crimson Livery Cloth lined with light Saxon Green, turned up with light Saxon Green Shag' (shag was a cloth with a long, coarse nap). Conscious, perhaps, of the Royal presence, the 'Westminster' took on a more restrained and regal look, wearing blue jackets with elaborate gold cuffs, and gold braiding, repeated on the waistcoat, over black knee breeches, white stockings and gold garters.

One can only surmise what these looked like after hours spent fighting fires, soaked with water, stained with smoke and the mess of post-fire chaos. This, and perhaps, a certain acidity of Cockney humour, may have been the reason why, the 'Royal Exchange' men quietly slipped out of their pink and yellow and were later seen in a distinctly more sober pea-green plush.

Free watermen plying on the Thames always wore a metal badge on their sleeves to show that they were qualified and registered. Those employed by specific companies, perhaps in the docks or warehouses, wore the badges of their employers. The badge itself was usually a large oval plate, elaborately engraved with a suitable symbol and made of silver or some other metal. Minutes of the earliest proceedings of the 'Hand-in-Hand' show some confusion over the actual metal used. An entry for August 29 1699 reads that 'Coates and Cappes of Leather and also Copper Badges.....to be put on and wore when they are Imployed in Extinguishing of Fires'...but a similar record of the following week's meeting reads '...Also Badges of Silver,...with the Marks of the Office, And also Strong Leather Capps that may come down to their Shoulders, for each man to wear, haveing a Badge of Brass also upon the same...'. Uniform buttons were often die-stamped with the badge of their company.

As well as firemen, most companies employed porters – the predecessors of the Salvage Corps – equally strong and reliable men who 'understand taking down and removing all manner of Household Furniture, Wares and Merchandizes with speed and the least Dammage.' Almost all of them would have been working watermen, whose daily job would be ferrying customers up, down and across the Thames.

The river was still the main thoroughfare while the narrow roads remained muddy in bad weather, rutted in the dry heat of summer and, in the quieter areas of the 'suburbs' sometimes dangerous. For speed and ease of travel, Londoners took to the Thames and the watermen (carefully trained, examined and registered at the Hall of the Watermen's Company) stood ready at their 'stairs' all along the river bank, rather as taxis sometimes wait at ranks now, and were hired in much the same way. When fire broke out, they were called to their nearest engine house by a messenger. Some watermen firemen advertised their employers' insurance companies by means of elaborately painted backboards on their boats and later in the 18th century, several companies bought special barges, mounted fire pumps on their decks and used them with as many as twenty pumpers a side.

Daniel Defoe, author, among other books, of 'Robinson Crusoe', was born shortly before the Great Fire, and in later years devoted a chapter of his 'Tour through Great Britain' to the City of London, waxing enthusiastic with a colourful and comprehensive description of the fire scene:

'No city in the world is so well furnished for the extinction of fire.

1 By the great convenience of water which, being everywhere laid in the streets in large timber pipes as well as from the Thames as the New River, those pipes are furnished with a fire plug which the parish officers have the key of and, when opened, let out not a pipe but a river of water into the streets so that making but a dam in the kennel (a 'canal' or watercourse in main streets) the whole street is immediately under water to supply the engines.

2 By the great number of admirable engines of which almost every parish has one and some halls also and some private citizens have them of their own, so that no sooner does a fire break out but the house is surrounded by engines and a flood of water poured upon it 'till the fire is, as it were, not extinguished only, but drowned.

3 The several ensurance offices…have each of them a certain sett of men who they keep in constant pay and who they furnish with tools proper for the work and to whom they give jack-caps of leather, able to keep them from hurt if brick or lumber of anything of not too great a bulk should fall upon them; these men make it their business to be ready at call, all hours and day or night, to assist in case of fire; and it must be acknowledged, they are very dextrous, bold, diligent and successful. These they call "firemen", but with an odd kind of contradiction for they are really, most of them, watermen.'

Competition for the appointment as a waterman-fireman was fierce, not just for the uniform. The men were paid a 'retainer' by the insurance companies who employed them,

plus a set amount for regular training drills and extra for any fires they attended. Firemen and porters were usually nominated by one of the insurance company's managers, and as far as the 'Sun' company was concerned, records show that the men had to have completed their apprenticeship at Waterman's Hall and had to be at least 5ft 7 inches tall. (By the early 1800's, they had also to be literate and under 29 years old.) Because of the work they were engaged in – and the appalling record of looting from fires which went back for centuries and also involved, at times, arson, the Insurance fireman had to deposit £100 as security in token of his good character and behaviour – a very large sum of money for those days.

A number of these security warranties survive in the Guildhall Library, naming the waterman fireman concerned, his warrantors and the terms of his employment:

'that the said……. shall and do at all times hereafter, as often as he shall be informed, know or have notion of or from any person whatsoever, of any Fire happening or which shall be within the Cities of London or Westminster or Suburbs thereof or any neighbouring village or place, and doth attend such Fire, doth not purloin or embezzle any money, wares merchandizes, household goods or other goods or things, of or belonging to any person or persons inhabiting at or near the place or places of such fire, but in the best manner the case will at that time allow, take down, remove, carry away and safely preserve the same in some neighbouring place and give notice thereof immediately to the owner or owners thereof. And also the said……… shall indemnify the said society and every member thereof from all damage, complaints or troubles arising from any neglect, omission or commission of the said……. And also that the said……. shall and do, at all times hereafter civilly and quietly demean and carry himself towards each of the members of the said society and obey, execute and perform and conform himself to all orders, directions and instructions which from time to time shall be sent to him.'

Failing this, his blue coat and silver badge and all other things belonging to the Society would be removed from him.

The insurance brigades were usually small – 30 men was an average number, although sometimes this was considerably higher. In the early days of some companies, the firefighters had to pay for their uniforms, but this idea was soon abandoned (no doubt after vociferous protests by the men). Problems over uniforms arose from time to time – men went off to sea, taking their smart outfits with them, and for many years a tribal chief in the Pitcairn Islands was reported to be wearing the uniform of a London insurance fireman as his ceremonial dress, 'won' in some way, from a seaman who had mutinied on the 'Bounty'. The records of the London Assurance Company also show that on 29 August 1739, Francis Bludwick was discharged after he had pawned his badge and chain of office.

London Assurance had divided London into four districts and each fireman had a particular area in which he normally worked – usually close to his home. Clients of the company were given a complete list of the men and divisions on the reverse of their fire insurance policies so that a speedy messenger could be sent to the nearest '*station*' if fire broke out. The men were chosen from long waiting lists by ballot and occasionally, there were problems. In 1750 a young man, Richard Birth junior applied to become a London Assurance Fireman, but was brusquely turned down with the explanation that the Company '*would not give two coats in the same family*' and he must wait until his father was dead before applying again. His father lived and served for a further 33 years and nothing further was heard from Birth junior.

The 'Sun' reported problems in 1717 when the firemen's foreman, a man called Vaughan, was dismissed and six of his loyal firemen friends who threatened to leave if he went, found themselves also without a job.

London Assurance records show that both firemen and porters received the same pay, 1s for the first hour at a fire and 6d for each additional hour provided that they appeared at the fire within *an hour* after the outbreak. Their general instructions insisted that 'Cloathes and Badges must be worn constantly', Engines had to be tested on the first Monday of every month.

New uniforms were usually issued in June or July and this was followed by a '*Day of Marching*' when the entire Brigade paraded before marching through the City in full fig. Not only did this show off their new outfits, but was a massive advertising campaign as they handed out leaflets along the five-mile route, inviting the admiring public to take out fire insurance policies with their employers. London Assurance records that bands were paid to provide 'Musick' for these occasions, varying from a regular £2.18.6d during most of the 18th century to an inflationary five guineas in the early part of the 19th century. The day's celebrations were followed by a dinner in the evening at a cost of 11/3d per head for the four foremen and 9s per head for the firemen and porters. (On the Day of Marching in July 1789, fire porter Joseph Cartwright is reported to have taken advantage too freely of the lavish refreshment provided and consequently to have been dismissed the service.)

Although the uniforms were obviously splendid and costly, the generosity of the companies did not always extend as far down as the feet of their men, and on 1st February 1754, the London Assurance Fire Committee was solemnly presented with a petition by four representatives of their firemen, asking for boots to be supplied for walking through the water and mud at fires, as these had not been renewed for four years. The Committee accordingly granted them one guinea each for new boots.

Footwear was clearly a sore point, as the company later records another piteous appeal:

'To the Governors and Directors of the London Assurance:

The humble Petition of the Porters and Watermen belonging to that Corporation SHEWETH that amongst all the Dangers and hardships to which Your poor Petitioners are exposed in the discharge of the Duties of their Office, there is none more sensibly felt than those which they experience from the want of Boots as their Leggs are frequently torn with Nails, Barrs of Iron and such kind of Rubbish as Fire occasions. That the late dreadful Fire at Shadwell particularly evinced the great Necessity of Boots, as several of Your poor Petitioners were up to their Knees in Water, hot from the Water-Works and Instantly after plunged into Cold Water, by which Deplorable case great Numbers of Your Petitioners Lives were endanger'd by Coughs and Colds which they caught, which Calamity Your Petitioners presume to suppose, might be in future happily prevented were their Leggs defended by Boots. That as the health, and Indeed the Lives of many of Your poor Petitioners might be in a great measure preserved by the use of Boots; Your Petitioners humbly Submit this Matter to Your Consideration, And humbly hope, that as Your poor Petitioners may be Justly deem'd usefull Members of Society, the Preservation of their Lives and health will be thought Worthy of Your Attention and Engage Your favouring this Petition by Ordering Your Petitioners Boots for the Use and Purposes aforesaid. And Your poor Petitioners as in Duty bound shall Ever Pray.

Robert Huxley.   Willm. Medcalf.   Luke Dickenson. Joseph Archer.   John Mayrick.   Henry Hill.   Willm. Little.   Thomas Parker.   John Moring and others.'

Sadly we have no news of whether the petition succeeded. It was simply marked '*Not read in Court*'.

Boots or not, there was one extra and important 'perk' for any man with no wish to be kidnapped by the 'Press Gangs' who wandered the streets looking for likely young men to be 'impressed' into the Navy or the Army. Watermen-firemen who were on the books of the insurance companies were registered at the Admiralty and were given certificates of exemption from service because of their importance to the City as firemen. The exemption had been granted as part of Queen Anne's Act:

> 'Whereas the insurance offices retain in their service and give coats and badges unto watermen for service in extinguishing fires, who are always ready at call and provided with hooks, hatchets and other instruments at the charge of the insurance offices; which watermen by custom and skill venture much further and give greater help than any other persons not used to come into danger, not exceeding thirty of them for each office to be exempted from being impressed or liable to go to sea, their names being registered and entered with the secretary of the Admiralty.'

These certificates had to be carried by the men at all times and there are peevish reports of the trouble which companies were put to when some men forgot, fell foul of the Press Gangs and had to be 'bailed out' through the Admiralty and restored to their families – and jobs. One certificate which survived, reads:

> 'These are to certify to all Press Masters, Constables and all others concerned that the Bearer thereof, Benjamin Braithwaite Cummings, Five feet six Inches high, wearing his own dark brown hair, Man of the age of Twenty-five Years, is one of the thirty persons entertained by us for the service of this Office and registered in the Admiralty Offices pursuant to the said Act of Parliament....'

It was dated 23rd October 1821.

An even earlier certificate which had obviously been folded and carried for some time by its owner, has been preserved by the Company of Watermen and Lightermen. Dated 29th September 1807, it certifies that:

> 'Henry Christopher Pullum, Waterman, being Number 26, living at Temple Stairs, aged twenty, is one of the Watermen employed by the said Company of Insurers' *(the 'Hope' Fire Office of Ludgate Hill, London)*, 'for extinguishing Fires, and his Name and Place of Abode registered at the Admiralty-Office, as applies under the Hand of William Marsden Esq, Secretary to the Rt. Hon. the Lord High Admiral of Great Britain....'

The certificate, a printed document with spaces left to fill in the individual names, made clear to the Pressmen that the

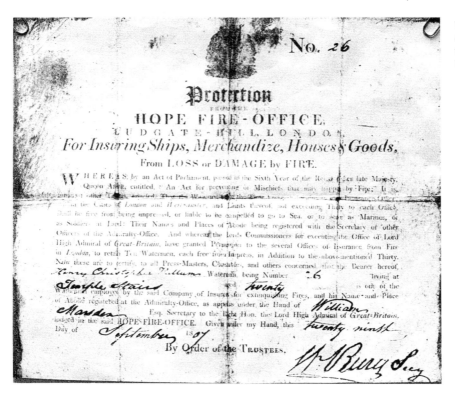

Waterman fireman's certificate of exemption from the press gangs. (Company of Watermen and Lightermen.)

holders of such certificates: 'shall be free from being impressed, or liable to go to Sea or to serve as Marines, or Soldiers at Land; Their Names and Places of Abode being registered with the Secretary or other Officers of the Admiralty'.

Although the insurance companies only provided brigades of watermen firemen in London, they encouraged self-help outside the capital, sometimes by contributing towards the cost of providing an engine and advising on the provision of a firefighting service if there were a sufficient number of people there who were insured against fire with that office. In 1756, the Sun was providing an engine and 'a proportionate length of pipe' to Wapping and Shadwell at the request of the insured in the area, and a similar engine to 'Mr Smith's wharf at Horsleydown' (by the river in Southwark). The 'Sun' also made a contribution of 50 guineas (£52.50) towards building a reservoir containing 18,000 gallons of water outside St Peter's church in Cornhill, in the City.

Steadily the number of 'stations' at which engines were kept and to which people could run for help when fire broke out increased and by 1789 the Sun was reporting these available at Ratcliffe Highway, Holborn, Swallow Street, Lincoln's Inn Fields and Horsley Down, all of them maintained and repaired by independent contractors. The 'Sun' also had by now invested in two special fire engines, mounted on barges, for use at riverside fires. These were available either to pump water directly on to wharf or warehouse fires, or to pump up water from which land engines could draw to fight the fires.

Throughout this time, the developing insurance brigades existed primarily for the benefit of patrons of their companies. Homes insured with the companies were identified, at a time when numbered houses in streets were hardly heard of, by means of a 'mark' or plate bearing the same badge as that worn by the firemen. The earliest were mostly made of lead, but later – and well into the 19th century – of other metals, many of them brightly painted. Most of them bore not only the company's mark but the number of the policy holder. Their manufacture was a cottage industry for many years, going back as far as the 1680's when the Friendly Society had a lead badge of five arrows intertwined with a snake and the policy number panel at the base. Among the most numerous to have survived (often in recent years, forged or copied) were the 'Sun' Company's marks, which varied over the years and were originally devised in the early 1700s by Charles Povey, 'father' of the company, who had a deep interest in astronomy. Many of the badges were produced by women in their home kitchens and the boiling lead must have been a considerable health hazard with small children running

about. The Sun Fire Office's Minute book records:

'December 12th 1745.

Order'd That Ann Bagley be paid Fifteen pounds 10/8d for casting 1,000 Sun marks.

July 28th 1748. Order'd that Mary Maynard be paid Thirteen pounds Eleven shill. for Gilding 500 Sun marks.'

One woman who had begun as one of these 'out-workers' was Hester Bateman, wife of a gold chain maker, who took over her husband's business in 1760 after his death. Although she could neither read nor write and she was then 51 years old, she registered her own silver mark a year later and by 1774 had registered with the Goldsmith's Company and was accepting commissions in her own right. By 1776 she was taken on to make badges for the 'Hand-in-Hand' and later for the 'Sun'. Hester's son and her grandson, were trained silversmiths and both made badges for the 'Sun', but although she kept the right to her own hallmark until she was 81, it seems unlikely that she actually made the badges herself.

(Details and excellent illustrations of fire marks and maces and arm badges of the watermen firemen are given in three books, 'The British Fire Mark' by Brian Wright, 'Badges of Extinction' by Brian Henham and Brian Sharp and 'Fire Insurance Company Buttons', by Fergus Bain and Brian Wright.)

Although many fire marks have survived, the badges of the watermen firemen are much rarer. It seems unlikely that any supplied to the earliest brigades of the Fire Office, the Friendly Society and the Hand-in-Hand still exist. One might have thought that because of their size and value, they would only have been worn on special occasions like the 'Days of Marching' but they seem to have been carried regularly – possibly as advertisements and possibly to warn off the Press Gangs. Old ones which had worn out were returned to the manufacturers – usually London silver-smiths – in part exchange for new badges. All the firemen's arm badges bore their number and porters' numbers were also marked on the bags which they carried when they were rescuing property from fires. The numbers were useful for identifying the men at a particular fire – for praise, complaint or simply as a means of checking who had turned up. These identity numbers were also added to the Press Gang exemption certificate registration information at the Admiralty.

Normal wear and tear of these elegant pieces of silverware was increased by the need for them to be regularly cleaned and this was evidently carried out by boiling them at least once a year to remove the accumulated grime. The hazard of appearing without the badge during the annual cleaning process was made clear in the minutes of the 'Hand-in-Hand' for 20th April 1718, a time when men were urgently needed for the Navy in countering the Spanish in the Mediterranean and the Press Gangs were particularly lively. The note read:

> 'Ordered that the Badges be not Boyled this year lest some of Ye men should suffer for want of ym during ye present pressing.'

Among other works of art involved with firefighting at that time were the maces, topped with the magnificent silver badges of their companies and carried aloft by the foremen at the head of their columns on the Days of Marching, rather as the Roman Vigiles had carried their symbols aloft in earlier days.

As the years passed, competition emerged between the parish beadles and the insurance brigades to reach a fire first and there were tales of fights and the slashing of hoses in some of the worst cases. Not all the watermen-firemen were as noble and angelic as they looked in the illustrations which survive. In 1723 a foreman was suspended for his insolent behaviour to his employer; in 1757 came an allegation that at a fire in Old Jewry the engine was withdrawn before the

fire was out; in 1763 a magistrate committed four Sun firemen to the Round House of St Martin's Church while they were fighting a fire (although it was said that he later had to apologise for this) and in 1770 a fireman was discharged for being drunk and abusive.

Despite all precautions and provisions resulting from the aftermath of the Great Fire, London still suffered from the hand of the Fire King at all too frequent intervals. One outbreak in Change Alley in the Cornhill Ward of the City in 1676 had burned 200 houses. In 1794 an enormous fire at Wapping burned 630 houses and another in an East India Company warehouse which contained 35,000 bags of saltpetre resulted in a reported loss of £1,000,000. In 1799, 50 houses were destroyed in the King's Bench area of the Temple. Several times the water works alongside London Bridge which produced a supply not only for general use but for firefighting, caught fire itself, including one outbreak, in 1779, which destroyed the high tower. In its place, an elegantly designed receiver and distributor was erected in 1780 with an elaborate system of pipes. Details of this advanced and intricate piece of machinery were delineated in plans 'most humbly inscribed' by their chief millwright and surveyor John Foulds 'to the Trustees & Managers of the

18th century water receiver and distributor. (Guildhall Library, Corporation of London.)

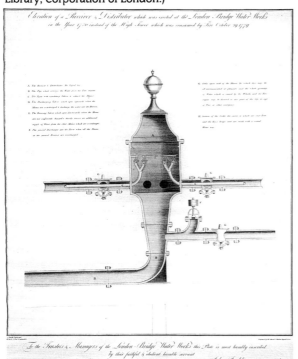

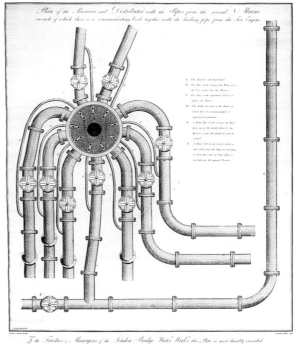

London Bridge Water Works.' They show 'the Receiver and Distributor with the Pipes from the several Mains on each of which there is a communicating Cock together with the leading pipe from the Fire Engine', suggesting that as early as this, there were, in some places, more than the wooden plug knocked into the main as the only means of obtaining water for firefighting.

There is no doubt that the insurance brigades were efficient – as far as was possible with the equipment of the period and the uncertain water supplies, but the same could not always be said of the parish pumps. As time passed, some churchwardens kept their books and fire-fighting equipment in good order, but not all were so careful. Just as many builders, particularly of the increasing number of slum houses for workers, were conveniently forgetting the Queen Anne Act, so quite a few parishes had quietly let slide the efficiency of their fire fighting equipment.

Charles Dickens, in his 'Sketches by Boz' offers a picture of a typical fire scene, albeit of a slightly later period:

'We never saw a parish engine at a regular fire but once. It came up in gallant style – three miles and a half an hour at least; there was a plentiful supply of water and it was first upon the spot. Bang went the pumps, the people cheered, the beadle perspired profusely, but it was unfortunately discovered, just as they were going to put the fire out, that nobody understood the process by which the engine was filled with water, and that eighteen boys and a man had exhausted themselves in pumping twenty minutes without producing the slightest effect!'

Pumping was carried out by hand – the men would line up on either side of the engine, gripping the long horizontal bars then raising and lowering them in unison. On some engines, in Newsome style, men stood on top, working the pumping mechanism with their feet. It was an exhausting job – the manual workers could usually only pump for five minutes before they had to be rested while others took their place. Passers-by were often recruited to help out and a regular shout of 'Beer-oh, Beer-oh' accompanied the rhythmic movement. If sufficient strong liquor was not forthcoming to slake their enormous thirsts, the pumping stopped. (Merryweathers have a set of jugs, produced specifically for carrying beer to pumpers, the largest of which holds four gallons – 20 litres.)

London was still expanding fast and was an acclaimed centre of fashion and art. Talented playwrights produced a wave of exciting theatrical productions – John Gay's 'Beggars' Opera'; Sheridan's 'The Rivals' and 'The Critic'; Goldsmith's 'She Stoops to Conquer' – and with the darlings of the audiences, such great stars as David Garrick, Peg Woffington, Mrs Siddons and John Philip Kemble to whip up

enthusiasm, bigger and better theatres and leisure places were being built with no particular attention to anything so frightfully boring and tedious as fire prevention.

Theatres with their canvas scenery, lavish costumes and candle lighting, burned down all too frequently, but it was in 1809 that the great Theatre Royal in Drury Lane succumbed to the flames and was burned to the ground. It was a spectacular but sad event for the firemen. The newspaper 'The Courier' described it:

'The men of the "Phoenix" Office were the principal sufferers. On their arrival with their engine at the great door under the Piazza, they were met by Mr Kemble.... They were humanely apprized by him .... of the great danger of entering at that door. He told them that the rooms of the "Shakespeare", immediately adjoining, were used as a warehouse to the Theatre and were filled with powder, oil and other very inflammable matter, and entreated not to run any risk. These brave and bold fellows answered – "Where danger is, there is our duty" and rushed forward.'

In the ensuing inferno several 'Phoenix' firemen were killed and others suffered horrific injuries.

The theatre was rebuilt, and to celebrate its re-opening on 14th August 1812, the committee invited the public to send in 'compositions', the best of which would be read at the opening ceremony. They must have been staggered when 112 such 'addresses' arrived. Although a number of notable writers submitted entries, two brothers, James and Horace Smith, took it upon themselves to write a whole series of 'compositions' in the style of famous authors of the day. They failed to win the prize, but although the manuscript of their book 'Rejected Addresses' was originally turned down by John Murray – already an established publisher, it was printed elsewhere and rapidly became a best-seller. So much so that seven years later, in 1819, John Murray bought the copyright after the book had already run through 16 editions. The brothers wrote in the style of Byron, Samuel Taylor Coleridge and many more, but one – in imitation of Sir Walter Scott – offers a rare and fascinating, if tongue-in-cheek picture of a London fire at the peak of the insurance brigades' power.

After setting the scene at wordy length, it continues:

'The summon'd firemen woke at call,
And hied them to their stations all:
Starting from short and broken snooze,
Each sought his pond'rous hobnail'd shoes,
But first his worsted hosen plied,
Plush breeches next, in crimson dyed,
His nether bulk embraced;
Then jacket thick, of red or blue,

Whose massy shoulder gave to view
The badge of each respective crew,
In tin or copper traced.
The engines thunder'd through the street,
Fire-hook, pipe, bucket, all complete,
And torches glared, and clattering feet
Along the pavement paced.
And one, the leader of the band
From Charing Cross along the Strand
Like stag by beagles hunted hard,
Ran till he stopp'd at Vin'gar Yard.
The burning badge his shoulder bore,
The belt and oil-skin hat he wore,
The cane he had, his men to bang,
Show'd foreman of the British gang, –
His name was Higginbottom. Now
'Tis meet that I should tell you how
The others came in view:

The Hand-in-Hand the race begun
Then came the Phoenix and the Sun,
Th'Exchange, where old insurers run,
The Eagle where the new;
With these came Rumford, Bumford, Cole,
Robins from Hockley-in-the-Hole,
Lawson and Dawson, cheek by jowl,
Crump from St Giles's Pound:
Whitford and Mitford join'd the train,
Huggins and Muggins from Chick Lane,
And Clutterbuck, who got a sprain
Before the plug was found.
Hobson and Jobson did not sleep,
But ah! no trophy could they reap,
For both were in the Donjon Keep
Of Bridewell's gloomy mound!

E'en Higginbottom now was posed,
For sadder scene was ne'er disclosed;
Without, within, in hideous show,
Devouring flames resistless glow,
And blazing rafters downward go,
And never halloo "Heads below!"
Nor notice give at all.
The firemen terrified are slow
To bid the pumping torrent flow,
For fear the roof should fall.
Back Robins, back! Crump, stand aloof!
Whitford, keep near the walls!
Huggins, regard your own behoof,
For, lo! the blazing, rocking roof
Down, down in thunder falls!
An awful pause succeeds the stroke,

And o'er the ruins volumed smoke,
Rolling around its pitchy shroud,
Conceal'd them from th'astonished crowd.
At length, the mist awhile was clear'd,
When lo! amid the wreck uprear'd,
Gradual a moving head appear'd
And Eagle firemen knew
'Twas Joseph Muggins, name revered,
The foreman of their crew.
Loud shouted all, in signs of woe
"A Muggins! to the rescue, ho!"
And pour'd the hissing tide.
Meanwhile, the Muggins fought amain,
And strove and struggled, all in vain,
For rallying but to fall again,
He totter'd, sunk and died!
Did none attempt, before he fell,
To succour one they loved so well?
Yes, Higginbottom did aspire
(His fireman's soul was all on fire)
His brother chief to save;
But ah! his reckless generous ire
Served but to share his grave!
'Mid blazing beams and scalding streams,
Through fire and smoke he dauntless broke,
Where Muggins broke before;
But sulphry stench and boiling drench
Destroying sight o'erwhelmed him quite
He sunk to rise no more.
Still o'er his head, while fate he braved,
His whizzing water-pipe he waved;
"Whitford and Mitford, ply your pumps,
You, Clutterbuck, come stir your stumps,
Why are you in such doleful dumps?
A fireman, and afraid of bumps!
What are they fear'd on? Fools! 'od rot 'em"

Were the last words of Higginbottom!....'

By the second half of the 18th century the London scene was already changing fast. The pattern set by the Royal Society had been taken up and, a century on, inventions were beginning to pour into the books of the Patent Office – and to affect everyone's life. Steam power had been discovered and was already being put to use for industry. The small workshops of the past were being overtaken by factories, most of them in the City and east end where gradually sail was to give way to steam in the ships which arrived at the growing Port of London.

In the 1740's gin-drinking had brought back to the City the squalor and drunkenness which ale had produced in the past. Sales of corn, needed to distil gin, had rocketed – to the benefit of the wealthy producers, and Hogarth was illustrating the horrors of 'Gin Lane' in his pictures while John Gay was underlining it in his 'Beggar's Opera'. Between 1740 and 1742 burials in London were double the number of baptisms and although an Act was passed in 1751 to try to halt the scourge of gin drinking, life in the capital was under the shadow of overcrowding and drunkenness for many years, culminating in the Gordon Riots of 1780 when 70 houses and four gaols were burned by mobs. It was a period of unrest throughout Europe and the watermen firemen found themselves working not just to extinguish fires but to cope with rebellious mobs. On 11th November 1795 the Lord Mayor wrote to the London Assurance Company, thanking them for allowing their firemen 'to assist on Lord Mayor's day in preserving the peace in the City'. On 3rd January 1798 he was again thanking them for their attendance 'on His Majesty's procession to St Paul's on the 19th December' and again, on 21st June 1799 'for the assistance so readily offered by the Corporation in allowing its firemen to act with the Constables... during the time His Majesty inspected the Volunteers.'

Whether the men eventually grew tired of being used in this way and made their feelings known is not recorded. Certainly, by 29th October 1800, the London Assurance Directors were resolving

'that as the business of Firemen is particularly to be in constant readiness to attend fires immediately upon their breaking out, in and near the metropolis, and it being in the power of the Lord Mayor to nominate and appoint as many other persons as he may judge necessary to act on the above' (Lord Mayor's Show) 'day, it appears that the employment of their men as constables is not necessary to the preservation of the peace of the City: and having found it to be attended with many inconveniences and evils to the Corporation' (of the London Assurance) 'they must request his Lordship will dispense with their attendance.'

Despite this, the Lord Mayor still requested the services of the insurance firemen for his protection in the following year's Show, only to receive a cold rebuff in the form of a copy of the Minute of the meeting on the subject plus a further note that it was 'the earnest wish of the Governors and Directors that his Lordship would dispense with the attendance of their men on the present occasion.'

All the men possible were needed for firefighting now, as London launched itself into the Industrial Revolution. Steam power threatened the whole traditional way of life not only in the capital but the entire country. One of its earliest industrial uses was in London at the Albion Mills, close to Blackfriars. Until now, corn had been milled entirely by wind or water power which meant that at times of calm weather or drought, when the mills slowed down or even stopped completely, the price of bread could rise so high that it was beyond reach of the poor. Steam power meant that the price of bread could remain steady, but many of the more powerful traditional millers could see their livelihoods being threatened and there was considerable opposition to the new methods. Many fire insurance companies showed some hesitation in accepting the Albion on their books, and the Westminster Company had refused altogether. Nevertheless, the Mill opened, using one of the first Newcomen steam engines. Disaster struck only a short time later.

On 2nd March 1791, the Albion Mill went up in spectacular flames and fire engines from all the surrounding areas galloped – or were dragged – to try to save it. At one time it was surrounded by appliances, including barges with pumps mounted on them which attacked the fire from the river itself. Several lighters alongside the wharf were burned and at least 300 people who had worked in the Mill were thrown out of work. An official inquiry was held but it discounted incendiarism as the cause of the outbreak, ascribing it possibly to flames from the flue igniting corn in a kiln.

Ordinary Londoners, who saw the bread literally being taken out of their mouths, viewed the verdict with some scepticism and almost immediately, a crudely printed handbill was on the streets suggesting that here was no accident:

'This noble building burnt so fast
Blackfriars Bridge could not be past,
Nor could they get the engines nigh
These mills did burn so furiously.
And now the folks begin to chat
How the owners they did this and that,
But very few did sorrow show
That the Albion Mills were burnt so low.

Says one "they had it in their power
For to reduce the price of flour
Instead of letting the bread raise!",
But now the Mills are all ablaze.
Now pray God bless us, one and all
And send the price of bread may fall
That the poor with plenty may be found
Though the Albion Mills burnt to the ground.'

Hazards of industrial expansion were not alone among the fast-increasing causes of fire. At the Siege of Acre in 1799, Turkish soldiers had, according to reports of the time, had the 'hookahs' through which they smoked, destroyed by gunfire. In desperation, they used the paper supplied for touching off their guns for a different purpose – they rolled tobacco in it, set light to the end and produced the first cigarettes. It was eventually to become one of the biggest fire lighters of all time.

Firefighting had, by now, become increasingly chaotic. The Queen Anne Act of 1707 had been extended to allow the reward for early attendance at a fire to be paid to anyone with a fire engine, not necessarily the insurance companies or the parish pumpers. By the end of the century, any rag, tag and bobtail who could reach a fire with a vehicle which might pass as a 'fire engine' was careering in, getting in the way of the trained firemen, upsetting the beadles with their pumping volunteers and starting fights which frequently ended with public brawling and hoses being slashed while properties burned to the ground.

Among the more flamboyant of the 'pirates' were '*The Bridewell Boys*'. All were lively young men-about-town who had been committed to the Bridewell Prison at Blackfriars for various youthful misdemeanours, but were allowed out for firefighting forays. A report from the period described them:

'Clustered like bees to the tow-ropes they started off with a hallooing and shouting which was sufficient warning to clear a way before them, while the cheering of the populace encouraged them upon their errand of mercy. Arrived at the scene of danger, they went to work with a will and energy found only in volunteers and contrasting strikingly with the not less zealous but more methodical proceedings of their rivals.'

Firefighting clearly needed some form of organisation and in 1791, three of the major fire insurance companies, the 'Phoenix', the 'Royal Exchange' and the 'Sun' combined to form a small, joint, private fire service called 'The Fire Watch'. With the approval of the Lord Mayor, this was centred on the 'Sun's' engine houses in Southwark, Lincoln's Inn Fields and Great Swallow Street; the 'Royal Exchange's' at Guildhall and the 'Phoenix's' in Well Close Square.

The 'Sun' provided 12 men for duty each night and the other two Offices, nine men each. The Watch continued with diminishing success until 1805, when the 'Phoenix' complained at the cost of the patrol being borne by the three great companies alone. Other plans for combining forces were proposed but no agreement was reached, the fighting and chaos grew and along with it, so did London.

As the 18th century gave way to the 19th, the metropolis was facing another population explosion. People were still pouring in from the impoverished rural areas, hoping to find work in the new factories. Endless slum streets of small, terraced, back-to-back houses were being built, alarmingly quickly, particularly in the eastern and some northern suburbs. Between them and beyond, were the factories and the mounting number of warehouses and wharves where more and more ships arrived to load and unload their cargoes. The lessons of the past were still being ignored. Restrictions on the intensity of building and the areas in which goods were to be stored, contained in the 1774 Fires Prevention (Metropolis) Act, were almost universally flouted and little heed was paid to the potential fire hazards of the goods stored in them.

'*Red sky in the morning, shepherds' warning*' quoth the new arrivals from the country as they looked up through their grimy windows, for a sign of the weather to come, but the dawn of the new century was all too often red with the flames of yet another major fire.

4

Insurance Brigades and Parish Pumpers

SHEPHERDS' WARNING MIGHT WELL HAVE BEEN firemens' warning. In 1800 yet another big fire hit London when a brewery and a whole area of sugar warehouses in Lower Thames Street burned so fiercely that it caused £300,000 of damage – and set light to the rigging of several ships off Bear Quay. Others were soon to follow – mills and granaries in Limehouse Cut cost the insurers another £50,000 and again, Todd's Warehouse at Red Lion Wharf – £50,000, which could have been far worse had the firemen and their helpers not managed to grab and move to safety a whole consignment of gunpowder. Although the explosive was supposed to be banned from the City it figured again in a fire at the old Custom House when a store intended for the Volunteers blew up and flattened the area between Bear Lane and Water Lane. Yet still the warehouses and wharves filled without restraint or supervision and by 1814 the revenue of the Port of London was increasing phenomenally.

Fire was no selector of victims. The Drury Lane Theatre fire in February 1809, had struck only 14 years after the theatre had re-opened after an earlier inferno. Sheridan (who was said to have been seen dejectedly watching the original blaze and, when interrupted, complained 'cannot a man warm his hands at his own fireside!') had poured money into the new building, including in the plans a huge water tank in the roof for fire protection and for aquatic theatrical effects. The theatre re-opened in 1794, complete with a newly invented cast-iron safety curtain which was lowered during the interval and beaten with a stick to prove to the audience its strength and resistance to fire. The leading actress even mentioned it in a special address:

'The very ravages of fire we scout

For we have wherewithal to put it out

In ample reservoir our firm reliance

When streams set conflagration at defiance.'

After which the iron curtain was raised on a scene with water pouring down the back set into a small lake on the stage with an actor rowing a boat round it. 'The audience' we are told 'could hardly constrain themselves with excitement and approbation.' Alas, after 14 years of safety, Drury Lane had burned again.

By now, the voices of the insurance companies were being joined by the general public, in growing alarm at the danger of fires and the clear inability of the existing brigades – parish pump with volunteers or insurance company with professionals – to deal with them or to make any attempts at saving life.

In 1817, a letter appeared in 'The Times'. Signed 'Palatinus', it drew attention to 'the truly alarming list of Fires that have happened in the Metropolis in 1816: – 41 – (although more have been omitted.)' The fire loss in financial terms had been £80,000 'and yet no building of consequence burnt, nor have fires extended to many adjoining houses.' Several people had, however, been burned to death and others injured. 'How long' asked Palatinus, 'is the Metropolis to suffer for the want of a public establishment by which light carts, laden with fire escapes, might be had always in readiness and the inhabitants of houses on fire rescued from imminent danger and the most dreadful deaths. I should hope this enormous evil will attract the notice of the House of Commons…'

But the House of Commons, having just survived a series of wars with Napoleon, struggling with the Irish problem and sorting out its growing Empire, apart from a variety of home problems, had neither time for, nor interest in, dealing with fires. And so they continued, some small and domestic, others, like the fire at Pickfords wharves and warehouses in the City Road Basin in 1824, enormous and frightening, although crowds, who had little other forms of entertainment in their lives, packed the streets all round to enjoy the thrill of the flames. So much so that a bridge over the nearby canal was solid with sightseers, several of whom fell off the parapet, and James Fogo, fireman of the Royal Exchange, either fell or was pushed into the canal too. Reports spoke, yet again, of valuable packages being cut open and much looting, with an insurance loss of £30,000 (the value of which can only be judged when one considers that a wage of £1 was considered adequate.)

Now, with each new fire and the growing list of casualties, social consciences were being stirred and in 1826, a group of philanthropists met, laid firm plans and proposed the establishment of the Society for Preventing the Loss of Life from Fire.

Writing from 85, Cheapside on October 28 1828, their Secretary, John Hudson, explained in a printed letter:

'It has ever been a source of great anxiety to every feeling mind when reflecting on the dreadful situation in which all are liable to be placed in this extensive Metropolis in case of Fire. The great height of many of the houses, and the almost impossibility of escape from so devouring an element, has led to many ingenious contrivances, but, as yet, no plan has been adopted for carrying these praiseworthy efforts into effect.

A society is just formed, and is now proceeding upon the same excellent principles as the Royal Humane Society, the prominent features of which are as follows:

1st A Committee of Management, chosen from the Governors.

2nd A Depot or Station in the centre of every district, (being one square mile) throughout the Metropolis, containing Apparatus under the care of persons properly instructed and in constant attendance.

3rd A selection of two or more able men will be made in every Ward or Parish, to act as Assistants, and who will be remunerated at the discretion of this Committee.

4th Active characters (who are willing to assist in cases of Fire and who shall conform to such regulations as are approved by the Committee) will be accepted as Honorary Members.

That such an establishment is most desirable for the safety and protection of the inhabitants of this extensive Metropolis, has been proved by numberless instances of the destruction of human life, including all ages and descriptions of persons. The same philanthropic feeling, therefore, which prompted the establishment of a Humane Society for rescuing life from drowning, may naturally be expected to operate successfully in the support of a Society for preventing loss of life by Fire.

Although much ingenuity has been displayed … by the invention of fire-escapes, it has been proved that these alone are very inefficient. The blind, the cripple, the infant, the aged, the infirm, the bedridden, and indeed, all absorbed in sleep, require the assistance of men trained in such manner as will enable them to render immediate and effectual aid in the moment of danger.'

The scale of subscriptions ranged from £5 5s (£5.25p) for a Life Governor down to 5s (25p) for a Member and the letter added a note that 'the co-operation of two or three respectable inhabitants in every Parish would insure the speedy establishment of Stations throughout the Metropolis.'

Surprisingly, the appeal was not well supported at that time and although the Society survived briefly, it finally collapsed. Nevertheless, the germ of the idea stayed in the minds of many people and was taken up later when, in 1836, the Royal Society for the Protection of Life from Fire was established. It began with £800 pa and six 'escape' ladders, but by the middle of the century it had become such a popular cause that its income had risen to £10,000 a year – entirely from voluntary contributions – and it was providing a force of 100 men (5 inspectors, 89 conductors and 6 supernumeraries) manning 85 fire escapes. Part of the income was devoted to rewards for saving life from fire all over the world and in its first twenty years, the men of the Society attended 7,828 fires and saved 972 lives.

The RSPLF escapes were stationed at strategic points around Central London, often close to the bigger churches and squares. In winter they were manned by a conductor from 8 pm until 7 am and in summer from 9 pm until 8 am and the 'escape man' sitting by his ladder, often with a dog for company, became one of the regular sights of London. When the alarm was raised, the fire brigade was called from the nearest station by one runner while another ran to the escape post which could be some distance in the opposite direction. The conductor would whirl his wooden rattle to summon help and as soon as he had a minimum of two volunteers to help trundle the heavy escape they would set off, frequently led by the dog with a lantern in its mouth.

The escape was unusual by modern standards – a massive, wooden ladder, between 32–35 feet long, mounted on a spring carriage with large travelling wheels, it had a canvas trough fastened the entire length of its underside, strengthened with copper wire mesh and forming a chute large enough for the rescued person to descend without having to be carried down the ladder. A folding ladder, some 20 feet long, was jointed to the main ladder about ten feet from the top and if more length was

Right: **Royal Society for the Protection of Life from Fire, escape in use. (Guildhall Library, Corporation of London.)**

needed it could be swung up and over by means of ropes attached to iron levers. When greater height was needed, a further short length of ladder could be fitted to the top making a total of some 60 ft. The folding ladder could also be detached and joined to a 16 ft ladder to rescue victims from windows which opened into narrow courts and alleys where the big escape was not able to penetrate. The whole escape weighed 9 cwt and a larger size was available for work in 'high-class' districts where houses tended to be taller.

To those who *rescued life from fire* the Society presented a silver medal showing a man in a toga rescuing a woman from the flames and with the somewhat enigmatic inscription: '*Actions are ours; results are God's.*' Those who rescued life from the *danger* of fire (a fine difference) received a cash award or a testimonial on vellum.

Decisions over which award was to be made sometimes seem incongruous. Conductor Wood of Whitechapel – famous for his many rescues – ran his escape to a fire in Colchester Street and, according to a description of the occasion in the Reports of the Society:

'On his arrival, the fire was raging throughout the back of the house and smoke was issuing from every window; upon entering the first-floor room, part of which was on fire, he discovered five persons almost insensible from the excessive heat. He immediately descended the ladder with a woman on his shoulders and holding a child by its night clothes in his mouth; again ascended, re-entered the room and having enabled the father to escape had scarcely descended with a child under each arm when the whole building became enveloped in flames, rendering it impossible to attempt a rescue of the remainder of the unfortunate victims....'

For this, Wood was evidently reckoned only to have saved life from the *danger* of fire and accordingly received only a testimonial on vellum for his courage.

There is no doubt, however, that this was a period of boom in the production of 'ingenious contrivances' for fire safety and protection. From the time of Queen Anne, the Patent Office had been logging inventions of all kinds for saving life from fire in one way or another – some sensible and practical, others less so.

As far back as 1735, Obadiah Wyld had worked out a way of 'treating linen and cotton so that they will neither flame nor retain fire ....' It consisted mainly of 'allom, borax, vitreol of copper dissolved and mixed with pulpy substance.'

In 1763 came an idea 'that will infallibly alarm the sleeping persons before a fire can have arisen to any dangerous height in even the most remote parts of the house,' and which consisted of an elaborate arrangement of strings which would burn through and release weights to drop and set off an alarm bell.

Others included 'a square box or frame containing a large pulley and chain to fix to the front of the house, the said chain to be momentarily let down by means of a moveable bolt and hinges which operate by pulls from the bedside in case of fire.' The victim would, after operating the 'pulls' from his bed, be lowered to the ground in a wicker basket.

1772 brought an alarm which not only gave notice when fire broke out but, in the words of Henry Solomon, its inventor, 'sets off an alarm and releases springs which grab any burglar and hold him fast in such a manner that he can neither retreat or proceed.' Mr Solomon gave no details of what to do if the 'intruder' chanced to be a hapless fireman, coming in to rescue the householder.

More to the point was an escape ladder, patented by John Page, in 1786. This was mounted on a four-wheeled carriage for easy movement.

Not all the inventions came from men. In 1803, Elizabeth Bell, worried, no doubt, at the injuries caused to the small boys who were sent to climb up inside chimneys to sweep them, patented 'an invention for sweeping chimneys and extinguishing fires – a rope or chain with brushes fixed to a pulley in the roof and pulled up and down to brush the chimney' or, 'in the event of the chimney being foul and actually on fire, arrangements are made for the sending up of a vessel containing water and made of such material as is not liable to fracture, the vessel is provided with a valve which is opened by pulling a string or wire, when the vessel arrives at the place where the fire is burning – or that locality.'

By 1807, Joachim Smith had patented a complicated fire escape which, he claimed 'affords more ample means of relief to all in so perilous a situation than is to be found in any other contrivance for the purpose...' Made of strong sail canvas, it was a form of chute, with a lattice framework across the top, which could be folded up and hidden in 'an elegant piece of furniture' in one's bedroom, and, when hurled from the window in the event of fire, was firmly fixed to the heavy piece of furniture at one end while the other end could be hooked to a railing or post in the street. Anyone trapped by fire could escape by sliding down this, but in addition, firemen or rescuers could also haul themselves up inside the chute, and below the lattice work, hand over hand to rescue others from the burning building.

A variety of pieces of heavy furniture were coming on to the market at this time – dressing tables, desks and even bedsteads which contained rope ladders or chutes for escaping from fire – all beautifully made and carefully hiding their purpose.

Joachim Smith's fire escape. 1807. (Guildhall Library, Corporation of London.)

Thomas Collins, in 1810, patented a ladder 'jointed together in numerous short lengths and proportionately varying in strength and weight from the strongest at the lower end to the lightest at the top.'

1812 brought Sir William Congreve's invention of what must have been one of the earliest practical sprinkler systems. Congreve, a scientist, was comptroller of the Woolwich Laboratory and had already invented the Congreve rocket which was used during the Napoleonic Wars. His sprinkler system consisted of perforated pipes running along the ceilings of premises containing hazardous goods. One turn of the tap outside the building and the whole interior could be drenched with water.

Soon after this, a retired Army Officer, Captain Manby, produced a portable fire extinguisher, similar to the modern soda-acid type, but charged with compressed air and a mixture of water and pearl ash – long accepted as a fire extinguishing medium – which he described as 'Antiphlogistic fluid.' Later, he asked the government to have the streets patrolled at night with teams of 'fire police' drawing small hand-carts, each equipped with four of his cylinders.

By 1819 the first practical street fire-escape, with sliding ladder sections which could be extended and which was mounted on a two-wheeled carriage, was invented by one J. Gregory. This was to be the prototype for the fire escapes which became a familiar sight on the streets of London for the rest of the century.

Public concern for fire protection continued to grow – increased by the printing of cheap leaflets describing, usually in excruciating verse, the horrors of the latest fire, particularly if children were involved.

Several attempts at combining the insurance brigades had been made after the collapse of the Fire Watch. In 1808 Sir Frederick Morton Eden, the founder of the 'Globe' Insurance Office had proposed that all the London Fire insurance companies should join together to set up a Fire Committee to run a brigade comprising 20 men from each company, with each office paying an equal contribution towards the cost of such a service. There was no suggestion of a municipally maintained service – public opinion at this time would not even contemplate a police force to encroach on their liberty, let alone a publicly maintained fire service, yet the streets of London were rife with crime and daily threatened with destruction by fire. Eden's scheme too, fell by the wayside.

It was not until 1828, and in the teeth of fierce opposition, that Sir Robert Peel, the Home Secretary, succeeded in forcing a Bill through Parliament, 'An Act for

Improving the Police in and near the Metropolis', (10.George IV, c 44) which began to bring some order to the chaos of London's streets. Although it was described by its opponents as 'an invidious attempt to enslave the people by arbitrary and tyrannical methods', it meant, in fact, that a uniformed, trained, disciplined and properly organised force took over from the parish beadles, the often corrupt 'constables' and frequently the troops who, until now, had been responsible for keeping order. The new 'Bobbies' or 'Peelers', nicknamed after their founder, were quickly brought into action in controlling the huge crowds who frequently ran riot at fires, obstructing the firefighters, looting and generally creating havoc. Not all, however, was sweetness and light. Among those who were initially critical of the new Metropolitan Police Force were the directors of the insurance companies who felt that the police were cutting across the duties of their fire fighters.

In 1830, the Secretary of the London Assurance complained to Sir Robert Peel:

'I am directed by the Court of Directors of the Corporation of the London Assurance, to represent to you that their Firemen and Porters have made various complaints of obstruction from the new Police in the execution of their arduous duties, and from the investigation which they have made the Court feels satisfied that the servants of the different Fire Offices do not meet with that assistance and co-operation from the Police force which the object and nature of their employment appears to entitle them to.

'I beg leave to enclose a copy of the instructions which are issued to the Firemen and Porters of this Office and to state that the Court insists on a rigid compliance with them and also that all their men are dressed in the regular uniform of the office and that each man wears a number on his badge, which number is also worked on the sleeve of his waistcoat and may consequently be easily known and recognised by the Police.

'The Court of Directors feel assured that it would be your wish to afford the firemen every protection and that they need only request your attention to this important subject to procure the issue of such instructions to the police as will ensure their giving to the firemen the most efficient aid towards the extinction of fires and the preservation of that property in which most cases the Fire Offices are so deeply interested and where in all cases the exertions of their servants are of so much importance to the public.'

Peel replied personally, saying that he would investigate the complaints himself, and from that time, relations with the new police force improved considerably.

After an assortment of legislation in the 18th century which had done little to alter the course of firefighting, 1830 brought a somewhat obscure Act 'to Make Provision for the Lighting and Watching of Parishes in England and Wales,' more commonly known as the 'Lighting and Watching Act.'

This was important because, although it laid no obligation on any authority in England and Wales to provide a municipal fire brigade, it at least allowed them to levy a general rate on their community

'to keep up fire engines with pipes and other utensils proper for the same .....and to place such engines under the care of some proper person or persons, and to make him or them such allowances for his or their trouble as may be thought reasonable, and the expences attending the providing and keeping of such engines shall be paid out of the money authorised to be received by the inspectors under the provisions of this Act.'

(The Act was repealed in 1833 (3 & 4 Wm IV, c 90) but re-enacted in extended form, so that there was no alteration in the provisions relating to fire protection.)

By now, the situation in London had become impossible. Fires were increasing, set off, in some cases, by thirsty layabouts who knew that once the brigade arrived, volunteer pumpers would be needed and the beer would flow to 'lubricate' them. Discipline in the insurance brigades was failing and there were reports of increased fighting between them. The number of engines had dropped from 50 to 38, and not all of them in good condition. The time had come for determined action.

It was Charles Bell Ford, Company Secretary of the Sun Fire Office who proposed that ten of the largest insurance companies should get together to form a combined force. Inevitably, there were arguments, the pros and cons were discussed at length, but London was still burning and the situation was becoming desperate. Eventually the Alliance, Atlas, Globe, Imperial, London Assurance, Protector, Royal Exchange, Sun, Union and Westminster joined forces. They agreed to spend £8,000 a year on setting up a fire service with 19 engine houses or stations, 80 men and two fire floats, one to be moored at Southwark Bridge and the other at King's Stairs, Rotherhithe in the heart of the docks. It would be called the London Fire Engine Establishment.

Right: **Proposals for London Fire Engine Establishment. 1832. (LFCDA.)**

The following Companies present by their Representatives —
Sun — Protector — Royal Exchange — Imperial — Glo...
Alliance — Westminster — London Union — Atlas, and ...
London Assu...

REGULATIONS

FOR THE

PROPOSED

General Fire-Engine Establishment of London.

20th JULY, 1832.

Adopted —— A Committee of Management, to consist of a Director or Secretary from each of the Fire Offices in London concurring in the Measure of forming a GENERAL FIRE-ENGINE ESTABLISHMENT :—Three to be a Quorum.

The Establishment to consist of

Adopted ———— A Superintendent,
Consid⁻ Postponed ———— An Assistant Superintendent,
Adopted ———— 14 20 Engines, 20 Engineers, and 100 Firemen. *5 Spare Engines*
Adopted ———— 1 Floating-Engine.
Adopted ———— Salary of Superintendent, £250 per Annum.
Consid⁻ Postponed —Do. Assistant do. £120 do.

adopted { 5 Foremen (1 in each District) to be paid each at the rate of £80 per Annum.. } To be permanent and regular Weekly
9 Engineers to be paid each at the rate of £75 per Annum .... } Servants *their wages to be regulated hereafter the Comm⁻ⁱᵉ but in all not to exceed ...*

adopted { 100 Firemen to have each at the rate of £55 per Annum, and to find their own Lodgings —— (which are to be within a short distance of the Engine Stations,) to be permanent —— and regular Weekly Servants. *their wages in all not to exceed £3850* *suggested that 20 should receive 24/6 per Week 38 of the Men 21/ea* }

adopted —One Suit of Clothes to be provided for each of the Engineers and Firemen every Year *at a cost of*
adopted —The Superintendent to pay the Men's Wages weekly by Cash issued by the Committee.
adopted the detail with the Comm⁻ⁱᵉ —The Men to be fined for non-attendance at Fires. Roll to be called twice a day *by the Superintendent or some one appointed by him*
Consid⁻ Postponed —The Superintendent to reside in or about Gracechurch-Street in the City : the Assistant to reside in or about King-Street, Holborn.
adopted { The whole Force to be under the directions of the Superintendent, and at Fires to be directed by him, or his Assistant if the Superintendent be not in attendance.

The Town to be divided into Two Districts, viz. *as follows.*

Consid⁻ Postponed { No. 1.—From Eastward to St. John's Street, Far- } Within which District the Superin-
ringdon-Street, and Blackfriars-Road. } tendent is to attend all Fires.

No. 2.—From St. John's Street, Farringdon-Street, } Within which District the Assistant-
and Blackfriars-Road, — Westward, } Superintendent is to attend all Fires.

5

The London Fire Engine Establishment

ON 1ST JANUARY 1833 THE LONDON FIRE ENGINE Establishment was set up with its headquarters at Watling Street in the centre of the old City and still the business heart of London. There had, for the first time, to be a man in charge of this, London's first united company of firefighters. Competition for the post was fierce, but the man they chose was already seasoned in the art of firefighting. James Braidwood had been Firemaster of Edinburgh for nearly ten years. His salary as Superintendent of London's first organised and combined fire service was £400 a year.

Pictures of Braidwood – and there were many, since Londoners were deeply interested in this new organiser – show him as a tall, dark-haired, handsome man. One report described him as 'a qualified surveyor and civil engineer, the first fire chief to weld together small units into one; quiet, unassuming, technically competent, strict but kind and of fine physique.'

He was composed, quick to weigh up a situation. Clear, concise orders were given in a quiet voice. A man of deep Christian feelings, religion was in his blood, his grandfather had been a member of a strict Scottish religious order the 'Bowhead Saints'. He settled 'above the shop' at the new headquarters in Watling Street and was soon involved not only with the men of the service and their families, but in helping out wherever possible among the poverty-stricken people of the surrounding area and involving himself with the establishment of the 'ragged' schools which were being founded at that time.

London's first fire chief had been born in Edinburgh in 1800 and educated at the Royal High School, but he had always been interested in fires and firefighting and became Superintendent of Fire Engines there when he was only 23 years old. Within three weeks he was to face the Great Fire of Edinburgh which destroyed the old centre of the city, killing ten people and making hundreds homeless. Luckily the shrewd townsfolk took Braidwood's advice, despite his youth, and pioneered the establishment of a regular fire-fighting organisation in the city, with men, often from the building trades, whom he had personally chosen for the job of firefighters. Although they carried on with their own work until a fire call came, they were expected to parade at 4 am on one day a week – not just 'bloody-mindedness' by their

Left: James Braidwood, first Superintendent of the LFEE. 1832. (LFCDA.)

Right: First headquarters of the LFEE, Watling Street, (LFCDA.)

chief but because, he explained, it gave them the opportunity of carrying out procedures, running out the engines and coupling up hoses in the total darkness which real fires often demanded. They were soon able to run out the engine complete with three lengths of coupled hoses in ninety seconds. He rejected the old method of pouring as much water as possible on to a fire, haphazardly, emphasising instead the need for getting in to a fire and attacking it as close to the source as possible. His men went in with a will, pouring sweat, even collapsing in the heat as they dealt with over 100 fires a year. For the first time in history, firemen were put through a course of gymnastics to reach and maintain peak fitness. Braidwood was no theorist. He trained his men and he worked alongside them – in one fire he saved nine people himself, dragging and carrying them from the flames.

By 1829, his work had attracted so much attention that the Society of Arts in London awarded him a silver medal for his description of a chain-ladder fire escape which he was using for rescue work at a time when London still had no such equipment in general use.

In 1830 he published the first serious book on firefighting ever to appear in Britain, 'On the Construction of Fire Engines and Apparatus: the Training of Firemen and the Method of Proceeding in Cases of Fire.' It was written, he emphasised, 'in the hope of inducing others to give further information on the subject......my aim will be obtained if I shall have succeeded in imparting it or directing the public's attention to the advantage which may be derived from the systematic training of firemen.'

Edinburgh was understandably loath to lose him. They presented him with a gold watch and, from his loyal men, a silver cup engraved 'Presented to James Braidwood by the City of Edinburgh firemen as a token of their admiration for him as their leader and of deep respect for him as a gentleman.'

Small wonder that after all this, firemen throughout the country were beginning to be known as 'Jim Braidy's.' As London's new chief he already had a firm programme in mind. His Establishment comprised 19 fire stations and 80 full-time professional firemen, drawn almost entirely from the cream of old insurance company teams. (Among them was Robert Tozer of the Hand-in-Hand, who was speedily promoted to Engineer in charge of Baker Street LFEE station. His son was to be at Braidwood's side when he died, and since then at least six generations of Tozers – all 'born under a hose cart' – have taken their places in the history of British firefighting, not only in London but as Chief Officers in Birmingham and Manchester.)

Gone, now, were the bright – and impractical – colours of the old companies. Braidwood's men wore long jackets of sombre grey with matching trousers, leather top boots and black leather helmets, crested to break the impact of falling debris. All the men wore a black silk scarf under their collar to prevent red-hot embers from slipping down inside their tunics. (London firemen are still issued with black scarves, no longer silk, but fire-retardant NOMEX.)

London was divided into four districts, each with a foreman in charge who had three engineers and three sub-engineers in his area. The men were charged with knowing every inch of the area which they covered:

'Any buildings supposed to be particularly dangerous should be carefully examined and all the different places where supplies of water can be obtained for them noticed. A knowledge of the locality thus obtained will be found of great advantage in case of a fire breaking out. Indeed, all firemen, especially those having the charge of engines, should be instructed carefully to examine and make themselves acquainted with the localities of their neighbourhood or district. Such knowledge will often prove valuable in emergencies, the proprietors or tenants of the property on fire being sometimes in such a state of alarm that no distinct intelligence can be got from them.'

Braidwood too, set up the London tradition which was to last for more than a century, of preferring to employ ex-sailors as firefighters. (Although it was officially abandoned in the 1890's, ex-seamen were undoubtedly preferred until the late 1930's). In earlier days, he had selected carpenters, masons and slaters as firemen. Now, he decided that 'seamen are to be preferred as they are taught to obey orders and the night and day watches and the uncertainty of the occupation are more similar to their former habits than to those of other men of the same rank in life.'

For him, as for his men, working hours were 24 hours a day, 365 days a year (yes, 366 in Leap Years). If he was not training the men or working on his plans and statistics, or out fighting fires or taking his family to church or on good works, he occasionally allowed himself time to sleep, but he had a speaking tube fitted in his bedroom to keep him in constant touch with the watch room below.

The few proper engine houses which he had taken over were adapted to 'modern' use and a programme of rebuilding began, paid for by the insurance companies. Soon after arriving in London, Braidwood had met the enterprising Mr Moses Merryweather, whose family had, one way or another, already been concerned with fire-engine manufacture for more than a century and a Mr Tilley who also made fire engines. Although a steam fire engine had already been invented several years earlier, they decided that manual pumping was to be preferred (provided the supply of beer could be maintained). Very soon, they introduced the London Brigade Manual Engine. It was a remarkably poor decision for anyone as 'canny' as Braidwood, for although the new appliance's pumps, seven inches in diameter with an eight inch stroke, were too wide for efficiency, one would have felt that, in that period, almost any form of standardisation of equipment was welcome after the hotch-potch of the old insurance brigades engines which could rarely share nozzles or hoses – even if their operators stopped fighting long enough to consider it.

Most of the men still lived in their own homes, but close enough to the stations to be available instantly when they were needed. At first, they were drilled daily, but once they had been licked into shape, drills were reduced to two or three a week. Conditions were tough, discipline strict and heavy fines were imposed for misconduct. One of Braid-wood's earliest pronouncements made clear to the public that LFEE men could be recognised by their grey uniforms with a number in red on their left breast and he added the polite request: *'In the event of any of them acting improperly, it is requested that his number be taken and a complaint made forthwith to the Superintendent at the Chief Station, no. 68, Watling Street.....or to the Board's secretary.'*

Despite all this, competition for the job of a London fireman was still intense, there was always a waiting list and vacancies were rare. Applicants had to be between the ages of 18 and 25 years and those selected had to find a 'gentleman' willing to act as security for their 'good behaviour' to the tune of £25, (following the tradition of the old watermen firemen.) As soon as there was a vacancy, several men were chosen from the waiting list and sent to the Surgeons to the Establishment, Mr Brown of Walworth Road and Mr Smith of Finsbury Square, who chose the candidates they considered to be the fittest. The final decision was then left with the Board, who, in turn, made Braidwood responsible for choosing his man.

Once appointed, the recruits started drill immediately with a salary of 21s (£1.05p) per week with 2/6d (12½p) deducted for rent for married men and 1s (5p) for bachelors if they were living on the premises. A man was given a high number (worn in red on the left breast) when he joined and as he moved up in seniority, the number was lowered. When it reached No. 55, he was automatically given a pay increase of 3/6d (17½p) a week and promoted to Senior Fireman. Sub-Engineers were chosen from these senior men and on qualifying, received a further increase of 1/6d (7½p) per week. Before long the Establishment was so much part of the London scene that many people assumed that it was run by the State rather than the insurance companies.

'Jim Braidys' were as efficient as their Chief could make

them and as effective as the equipment with which they were provided, but this was not always necessarily the latest or the best. Braidwood could be stubborn, sometimes with good reason, although the trait was bolstered by the enthusiasm and praise of fashionable London. He read papers on fire-fighting to such auspicious bodies as the Royal Society of Arts; he was consulted on fire prevention and protection by industry and big business, he became an Associate of the Institution of Civil Engineers and a well-known figure throughout the City. Cabmen liked him because he was always 'a good fare'. Policemen approved of him because although firemen carrying messages to and from fires were expected to run all the way, policemen were allowed to call a cab 'on expenses.' Cockney urchins worshipped him – they could earn up to 15s a week as runners, calling out the men to a fire or fetching the turncock to open up the water mains.

He could, undoubtedly, be tough and had a lifelong feud with one of Merryweather's directors. Their archives record that 'the energies he put into his inspections is remembered' – particularly when it came to testing hosepipes. 'He took with him an iron ball of the exact diameter the hose was supposed to be, would have the lengths suspended from the upper windows into the street and the ball would be put in at the upper end of the hose. Only if it passed through and fell into the street would it be accepted.'

Above all, he appeared to dislike change for the sake of change. He kept his men on, sometimes until they were well over 60, which slowed down promotion and led to dissatisfaction in the ranks. Younger men, with no hope of advancement for years, would drift off to join other forces in private companies or factories, in or beyond London. He refused ever to allow the telegraph to be introduced into his stations, but most puzzling was his objection to steam-powered pumps, which seemed to rest primarily on his argument that there would not be enough water available for them.

It was during the latter part of the 18th century that an engineer named Bramah had begun experimenting with steam for powering fire-pumps, but it was not until 1828 that two men, Ericsson, a Swede and an English engineer, James Braithwaite, perfected their elegant and efficient steam fire engine which was powered by a steam boiler instead of requiring teams of perspiring volunteers, plied with endless streams of beer. There was no doubt as to its efficiency, but critics suggested that something of less power but more portable would be better.

Already Braithwaite had spent £1,700 on developing the appliance but, as he wrote later, 'nothing daunted, I adopted the suggestion and constructed another to be drawn by two horses and which, by appointment, was taken to the Regent's Canal Basin.' It was still a mighty engine, weighing 45 cwt with two horizontal cylinders and pumps, each steam piston and that of the pump being attached to one rod. Water steam from the cylinders was conveyed through the tank containing the feed water by means of two coiled pipes, giving the feed water a good temperature before it was pumped into the boiler. Within 13 minutes from the first fire being lit, the steam was up at 50lbs pressure and a column of water was being thrown to a height of 80 feet and a distance of 130 – 140 feet at the rate of 45 tons per hour.' Although everyone seemed to be impressed and well satisfied with this, the LFEE refused to consider it, preferring, instead, Mr Merryweather and his manual pumps.

Braithwaite and Ericsson staunchly hauled their appliance to a fire at the Argyll Rooms, a theatre, where the weather was so cold that all the manual pumps were frozen solid and totally useless, but the new steam engine pumped without pause for five hours, and considerably restricted the area destroyed by the fire. Soon after this, it went to work at fires in Wells Street, Charles Street, Soho and the English Opera House as well as Barclay and Perkins' Brewery – a particularly bad fire. In a letter to the Mechanics' Magazine soon after this, Braithwaite wrote, not without some understandable sarcasm:

'The superior merits of the steam fire-engine over every other, all admit; but to myself, beyond the thanks of owners of property on the spot, and the liberal treatment, I am happy thus publicly to acknowledge, I and all my people received from the hands of Messrs Barclay, Perkins and Co., and one sovereign (£1) given to my men ... by Mr Braidwood, ... I have neither received reward nor encouragement – nay – until the New Police was introduced, nothing but obstructions and annoyances.'

(Steam-engine and men were indeed, attacked again and again by other firefighters and the beer-swilling pumpers who saw their source of beer disappearing. The engines were damaged and the hoses slashed.)

Braithwaite turned his efforts next to a fire float with steam-powered pumps. For more than a century fire floats had been a common sight on the Thames – there were usually two available at any period and paintings of big riverside fires often show them clearly, with the pump mounted on their deck and teams of pumpers working away at the long handles on each side. Each float needed 40 men, relieved every 10 minutes, to work the pumps effectually. Now, and evidently with some encouragement from directors of the insurance companies, he drew up plans for a new style fireboat and submitted them. They were immedi-

ately passed to Braidwood who, having examined them, sent his reply:

68, Watling Street, 14th Sept., 1835

Sir, – I am directed by the Committee for managing the London Fire-Engine Establishment to return you their best thanks for the sight of the plans you have been kind enough to favour them with; and to inform you that they do not deem it advisable to execute them at present; but, should they do so at any future time, they will be most happy to have your valuable assistance.

I have the honour to be, Sir, Your most obedient servant, James Braidwood, Superintendent.'

It was to be nearly 20 years before Braidwood brought steam power to the fire service – initially on a fire boat in 1852 – but not until July 1860 was a land steam engine to be bought for the LFEE.

Time was to prove that London certainly needed something other than Mr Braidwood and his brave manual pumpers to cope with the damage that was to come. Socially, the capital was reaching one of its worst eras. Building developers, still ignoring with impunity the laws for party walls and fireproof exteriors, were throwing up street after street of potential slum housing, back-to-back with little more than the occasional alley between the outdoor earth closets and as many dwellings as they could possibly squeeze into a minimal space. Between them – still – were the factories where the inhabitants, men, women and small children, were employed, with both homes and workplaces squalid and hazardous. Matches – lucifers they were called – had been invented and gas lighting was beginning to be developed on a growing scale. The two combined were proving an infernal source of trouble to Braidwood and his men as fire followed fire across the capital.

Never too far from the endless small fires came the enormous conflagrations – and within two years of the LFEE's establishment, the government was feeling the heat of the flames. On October 16th 1834, a clerk in the Parliament building at Westminster decided to dispose of a load of unwanted wooden 'tally' sticks, which had been used in the exchequer, pouring them with enthusiasm into a suitable stove and disappearing home without a backward glance. The ensuing fire burned so fiercely that it set light to the chimney and before the night was out, had achieved more than Guy Fawkes could manage. The Mother of Parliaments was virtually destroyed.

By the time the fire was discovered, at 6.20 pm on a wintry evening, the whole of the upper part of the House of Lords was on fire and the mass of the building, including the end of the ancient Westminster Hall, was burning. A westerly wind, blowing hard, fanned the flames and by 11

Firemen's dog 'Chance' at Houses of Parliament fire, 1834. (LFCDA.)

pm there was little hope of saving Westminster Hall itself. At 11.30 pm a floor fell in and a fireman named Hamilton was killed, another fireman had his leg broken, yet another his skull fractured and several more were severely injured. Soon after this, the gable wall of Westminster Hall collapsed and the Painted Chamber and Library of the House of Lords were reduced to ashes. *'On the Hall taking fire, a noble struggle was made by the firemen to save that venerable building and their bold and daring hearts accomplished that desirable object'* said a hastily printed news report, sent through the streets on a handbill. *'At one o'clock the flames continued to ascend from the interior of the buildings, in a manner that no hopes were left of saving the mass, the Speaker's House now being reduced to ashes.'*

As in the present day, the danger and stress of the disaster brought out the worst in the way of humour. The same handbill reported approvingly that Mr Hume, Mr Gordon and Lord Palmerston rendered very great service in rescuing the journals, papers and volumes of the House of Commons which they conveyed to St Margaret's Church, but commented *'it was distressing to witness the great levity which was manifested on the spot, expressions such as "it's a pity the bishops and lords are not there"* and *"Mr Hume's motion is carried by fire."*

Braidwood sent 12 engines and 64 men – a considerable part of his force – but with no hope of extinguishing a fire

with such a hold. The old Houses of Parliament were left to burn themselves out while the men concentrated on saving what they could of Westminster Hall, which they achieved successfully, dragging their pumps into the building, battling all night with pumpers provided by a detachment of Guards, and cutting away part of the roof where it was joined to the blazing house of the Speaker, which was eventually destroyed. Westminster Hall was saved, but two of Braidwood's men were so badly injured that they had to be invalided out of the service.

Contrary to the handbill's report, *The Times* next day applauded the behaviour of the onlookers:

'The conduct of the immense multitudes which, in the course of the evening, flocked together to view this spectacle of terrible beauty was such as to inspire respect… the general feeling seemed to be that of sorrow, manifested either by thoughtful silence or by occasional exclamations of regret. The admiration of the sublimity of the scene, which seemed to impress every mind, was subdued by the pain of losing these noble memorials of the wisdom and greatness of bygone ages. On common occasions of general concourse, the English are sufficiently noisy in the demonstration of their feelings; but on this occasion all was grave, decorous and becoming a thinking and manly population.'

There was no comment on the feelings or the thinking of the manly population on the valour of the firefighters or the death of one and injury to others. Nor was there mention of the chaos caused by 'gentlemen in authority'. During the inquiry into the fire, Sir Richard Mayne, Chief of the Metropolitan Police, protested that 'Lord Hill and myself ... endeavoured to get the engines to play at the only point which appeared to be of importance, but the fire engine men refused to do what we asked them to do.' He maintained that the saving of Westminster Hall was mainly due to their exertions – a claim which was vehemently denied by another witness who insisted that 'the preservation of Westminster Hall was entirely owing to Mr Braidwood and his men, two of whom were disabled for life by it.'

Braidwood himself put blame for the rapid spread of the blaze on a number of causes:

1   The total want of party walls throughout the building.

2   The passages which intersected the building in every direction and acted as funnels to convey the fire.

3   The repeated alterations in the buildings which had been made with more regard to expediency than to security.

4   The immense quantity of timber used in the exterior.

5   The great depth and extent of the building.

6   A smart breeze of wind. (Not the 'hurricane' of the Press.)

7   An indifferent supply of water which, though ample for any ordinary occasion, was inadequate for such an immense conflagration.

8   My own and the firemen's total ignorance of the localities of the place. In fires in private dwellings, warehouses or manufactories, some idea may generally be formed of the division of the premises from observing the appearance of the outside, but in the present case, that rule was useless.'

The fire clearly caused a furore, not just because the whole process of government had been disrupted but because it was suddenly and abundantly clear that had the insurance companies' brigades – who had no legal obligation to attend – not been kind enough to do so, the whole building and the surrounding area could have been devastated. The only firefighters obliged to attend would have been the parish pump of St Margaret's Church, across the road and any others which happened to be in the neighbourhood. The buildings were not even insured with any fire office, since the Government carried its own risks and had never allowed Braidwood to enter the building to inspect it for fire hazards.

After Braidwood had submitted his report to his employers a remarkably acrimonious battle of words developed between the Board of the LFEE and the Duke of Wellington, who was acting Prime Minister at the time. Within two years of the inception of their brigade, the companies were clearly questioning their wisdom in relieving the government, locally or nationally, of their duty to provide some form of official fire service, as they had with the police force.

Their letter to the Duke firmly spelled out the situation:

'The engines and men employed by the fire insurance companies, although always ready and anxious to afford all the assistance in their power upon every occasion of fire, are nevertheless private establishments, maintained for the immediate purpose of protecting the interest of their employers. They still form the main security of the public against the spread of fires; but where their service might require to be absorbed in the protection of the peculiar interest of the insurance companies, the uninsured portion of the public and the Government works must necessarily be left to the care of other engines.

Thus, if during the late conflagration at Westminster, any insured property in danger, or any simultaneous fire or fires in other parts of the town, had imperatively called upon the Superintendent to devote the services of the engines elsewhere, Westminster Hall and the public property adjoining must have shared the fate of the two Houses of Parliament.

The only provision made by law for the suppression of fires will be found in the 14 Geo III c.78, sec 74. By this Act, parishes are directed to maintain engines in an efficient state; but the experience of this Committee justifies them in stating that neither the power of the engines, nor the means of prompt attendance, nor the independent and unsystematic plan upon which they are worked, will ever enable them to render any very effective service, unless they should be placed under some general superintendence and, more especially, be restrained on some occasions from placing themselves in the way of the more effective engines of the offices and exhausting their supply of water.

Though it is scarcely within our province to intrude on his Majesty's Government any suggestions for remedying these defects, we nevertheless (having judged it highly important to request your Grace's attention to them at a time when recent events have strikingly exemplified their existence) venture to state generally our views on the subject. With great deference, therefore, we give our opinion, that many of these evils would be corrected merely by placing the parochial engines under the inspection of the Commissioners of Police, as to their repair and efficiency for service (the fine of £10 imposed by the Act above referred to on the churchwardens for neglect in this particular, appearing sufficient if rigidly inforced), and by placing the public and parochial engines at fires under the orders of one directing officer.'

It was six weeks before the Duke bothered to reply. The Committee could only have been amazed at his letter of 28th February, 1835;

'I beg to assure you in reply, that I am not disposed to deny that there are cases of fire in which what you recommend might be productive of beneficial consequences; but nevertheless it appears to me that in the majority of instances, the interference of Government would be productive of little benefit, while it might and probably would relax those private and parochial exertions which have hitherto been made with so much effect and so much satisfaction to the public.'

So, among the few benefits which emerged from the fire were the new building, which still stands, and a magnificent painting of the fire by Turner, who was returning from the country when he saw it and managed to make sufficient sketches at the scene to produce his memorable record.

While the Board was still swallowing Wellington's statement, which evidently had the support of many of his contemporary politicians, Braidwood and his men fought on. In the same year the laundry at Millbank Penitentiary, a women's prison, close to the present Tate Gallery site, caught fire and again the insurance companies' brigade attended. More was to come.

Meantime, the London Fire Engine Establishment had settled down sufficiently for *The Times*, in 1836, to write a feature article on the improvements in firefighting which had been introduced by Braidwood and on life in the service generally.

It noted the great number of additional sets of stronger scaling ladders – the men could now join together seven lengths to make a 40-foot (10–15m) ladder and raise it in as little as 21 seconds. Canvas sheets with lead weights to steady them had been introduced after a fire in Burlington Arcade, to be used for covering gratings over drains and preventing the waste of water. Short axes with a cutting and a ripping end, worn in leather sheaths from waist belts had been provided for some men and the force had also been provided with candle-powered lanterns fitted with powerful reflectors carried on the engines and by some firemen. Others carried portable canvas fire buckets. By now too, coupling and tripling joints had been added so that the

water of two or more engines could be discharged in a concentrated stream and new, improved engines were being built (all manual – Braidwood would still have nothing to do with steam.)

'*The Times*' noted strong camaraderie in the stations:

'Whenever an engine is called to a fire the man left in charge of the office puts a large coffee boiler on the fire, so the instant the men return a full supply of good, strong coffee is ready to be served out to them.'

It also noted that

'while at work at a fire a moderate allowance of beer or spirits is served to the men at the expense of the Office, the foreman of the district regulating the quantity according to the length and nature of the service…To guard against all danger of excess, the men are strictly prohibited from taking any refreshment offered to them by strangers when they are on duty. As a means of encouraging the men, they are assured that their incomes are secured to them for life with no other condition than good behaviour. If disabled by natural disease or by accident, their pay is continued all the same. Good conduct is the only qualification required to ensure promotion – the mere claim of seniority is disallowed.'

It was very much a family service at that time, with Braidwood carrying on the good Scottish tradition of a Hogmanay party every year when the men would gather together for yarning and to sing the popular songs of the period, which included their 'anthem' – a ballad called '*The Waterman Fireman*.' The tune has long been lost but the words began:

In Hungerford Market a maid
Dwelt who never had thought o' man
Till by Cupid her heart was betray'd
And she fell in love with a waterman.
His person had every charm
And grace that could be had by man
He wore a gold badge on his arm
For he was a waterman fireman……'

The not altogether moral story continued for a further seven long verses, and was undoubtedly a high spot of the cosy evenings in the engine house which enlivened an otherwise hard existence. A description by Charles Dickens brings its details to life:

'The cry of "Fire" suddenly resounds from a distant street. The heavy boots of a policeman clatter along beneath our window. The cry is repeated by several voices and more feet are heard hurrying along. The fire is in a squalid court, leading into a mews which runs close to the backs of the houses on one side of a great square. We hastily struggle into an overcoat, snatch up a hat and issue forth to follow the alarming cry....... Somebody arrives at the gates of the chief office of the fire brigade in Watling Street and seizing the handle of the night bell, pulls away at it with the vigour which such events always call forth.

'The fireman on duty for the night immediately opens the gate and receives the intelligence, cutting short all loquacity as much as possible and eliciting the spot where the fire has broken out and the extent to which it was raging when the person left. The fireman then runs to the pipe, hears a voice ask "What is it?" The fireman hears his own voice sound, as if at a great distance, while the voice, actually remote, sounds close in the mouthpiece with a strange, preternatural effect. The bell-wire reaches up to the Superintendent's bedside and the bell being rung. Mr Braidwood raises himself on one elbow and applying his mouth to the end of the tube, answers and gives orders.

'A few words of dialogue conducted in this way suffice. Up jumps Mr Braidwood, crosses the passage to his dressing room (armoury we ought rather to call it) and in three minutes is attired in thick cloth frock-coat, boots and helmet of the fire brigade, fixing buttons and straps as he descends the stairs.

'Meanwhile, all the men have been equally active below. No sooner has the fireman aroused Mr Braidwood than he rings the bell of the foreman, the engineer and the "single men's bell" – which means the bell of the division where the four unmarried men sleep. He then runs out to the stables calling the "charioteer" by the way and two other firemen lodging close by, after which he returns to assist harnessing the horses.

'Owing to the simultaneous action, each according to his special and general duties, by the time Mr Braidwood reaches the bottom of the stairs, the engine has been got out and put in working order. All its furniture, implements and tools are placed within or packed about it. *Short scaling ladders* made to fit into each other are attached to the sides, *six lengths of hose*, *branch pipes*, *director pipes*, *spare nozzles*, *suction pipes*, *goose necks*, *dog's tails* (the first to deliver water into the engine, the second are iron wrenches), *canvas sheet with rope handles round the edge* (to catch people who will boldly jump out of windows), *dam board* (to prevent water from plug flowing madly away,) *portable cistern*, *strips of sheep-skin* (to mend bursting hose), *balls of cord*, *flat rose*, *escape chair*, *escape ropes*, *mattock, saw, shovel, pole-axe, boat-hook or crow-bar* (such a fellow!) to burst through doors or walls or break up the pavements, *instruments for opening fire plugs and keys for turning stopcocks* of water mains and etc.

'All being ready, the Superintendent mounts the engine to the right of the driver and the engineer and foreman and firemen mount also and range themselves on each side of the long red chest at the top, which contains the multifarious articles just enumerated.

Off they start, brisk trot, canter – gallop! A bright red gleam overspreads the sky to the westward. The superintendent knows that the fire in the court has reached the mews and the stables are in flames. Full gallop!'

6

'Jim Braidys' in action

QUEEN VICTORIA HAD SCARCELY BEEN ON THE throne for a year when late on the freezing cold night of 10th January 1838, as firemen were still 'yarning' about the excitements of recent years, flames burst out of the Royal Exchange, barely a stone's throw from their headquarters in Watling Street. This was the second Royal Exchange to be built in the City, the first, erected by Sir Thomas Gresham between 1565 and 1570, was destroyed in the Great Fire. It was rebuilt and opened in 1669. Walter Thornbury in 'Old and New London' recalls the scene on the night of the fire:

> 'The flames, which broke out probably from an over-heated stove in Lloyd's Coffee-House, were first seen by two of the Bank watchmen about half-past ten. The gates had to be forced before an entrance could be effected and then the hose of the fire-engine was found to be frozen and unworkable.'

He might have added that the plugs in the water mains, stuffed round as always, with damp straw, usually taken from stable floors, had also frozen solid so that they had to be chipped free before stand-pipes could be wedged in their place. By the time any effective fire-fighting could begin the flames had taken a complete hold of the old building with its handsome gate tower and cupola and its fine clock which Londoners were so accustomed to hearing as it chimed daily at three, six, nine and twelve o'clock. On Sundays it played the 104th Psalm ('*Who maketh His angels spirits, his ministers, a flaming fire*'); on Mondays: '*God Save the Queen*'; on Tuesdays: '*The Waterloo March*'; on Wednesdays: '*There's nae luck aboot the Hoose*'; on Thursdays; '*See the Conquering Hero Comes*'; on Fridays: '*Life let us Cherish*' and on Saturdays '*The Foot Guards' March.*'

In the bitter darkness of this January night as the pumps creaked, the pumpers roared, the porters heaved out as much as they could of the furniture and records, the water hissed and the crowds cheered, flames licked over the roof and leapt up to engulf the recently finished tower. The hands of the clock pointed to one o'clock of a cold winter's morning, and the crowd was suddenly silent. In a last frenzy the bells were ringing again – '*Life let us Cherish*', '*God Save the Queen*', and as the tower shuddered and began to give way, '*There's Nae Luck aboot the Hoose*'. Then all eight bells crashed down, shattering the roof of the entrance hall in a last, terrible chord.

The east side of nearby Sweeting's Alley and all the royal statues except one – of that great firefighter Charles II – were destroyed. As news came in from outside, it emerged that the glow of the fire had been clearly seen from Windsor, more than twenty miles to the west and at Roydon Mount, near Epping, to the north-east.

Braidwood drew breath and London went on with its old, complacent ways until, on the 30th October 1841, the fire fiend struck again – and this time its target was the Tower of London.

The Tower, an impregnable castle which had stood for 700 years without assault, fell victim now to an enemy within. By luck the damage was confined to one main building. Unfortunately, it was the Armoury, where the collection of magnificent armour was kept. It had been formed by James II and added to ever since his time. In all, 2,800 pieces of arms and armour were destroyed or damaged beyond hope of repair. The keepers of this, of all places in London, might have been assumed to have obeyed the law and been protected from fires. Now it was clear that only a handful of ancient pumps and small engines had been provided by the authorities, many years previously, and these were derelict and useless. An official inquiry was held, but to no purpose. The Press was vitriolic in its criticism and the new satirical magazine '*Punch*' emphasised some of the sillier events including the fact that the sentries under orders to keep out all comers, had firmly refused entry to the firemen.

Much of the criticism was justified. The financial loss –

£250,000 – was bad enough but the destruction of the priceless armour was a historical disaster.

The inept handling of the Tower fire, was in no way the fault of Braidwood. Like the Houses of Parliament, the Tower was not insured by any City company – and his men were clearly hampered in all they had tried to do – as they had been at Westminster. Sadly, another of the Establishment's men died in the blaze, but as ever, the humour of the evident chaos was not lost on the local inhabitants and within hours of the ashes being sifted, yet another handbill was circulating, the verse, it was recommended, to be sung to the air: 'The Good Old Days of Adam and Eve.' It began:

'Fire at the Tower of London'

'Oh dear, oh dear, this conflagration,
Caused alarm without exaggeration,
The flames so awful, shone so bright sir,
All over London on Saturday night, sir;
The girls did shout, the boys did holloa,
The men did run, & women follow,
The dustmen cried 'the world is undone
There's a dreadful fire at the Tower of London.'

CHORUS

They holload, squalled and thousands did run,
To see the fire at the Tower of London.......'

Not only was London's history now being steadily eroded by fire, but fires in industrial premises continued to grow in size and frequency. Letters of complaint about the insufficient strength of the firefighting forces increased, and more big commercial organisations set up their own private fire brigades to complement the LFEE, which was – inevitably – underfunded, undermanned and under-equipped to deal with the still growing Metropolis. In 1848 there were letters in the Press pointing out that no fire cover whatsoever had been provided for the newly built up areas of St John's Wood, Belgrave Square or Kensington, but the insurance companies argued that it was not their responsibility to provide a municipal fire service.

Among the assortment of private brigades set up by owners of factories and other premises to protect their own property, one stood out above all as an example of philanthropic fire protection. Its founder was Frederick Hodges, a fashionable young man who had inherited the gin distillery in Pratt Walk, Lambeth, in a house adjoining which, he had been born in 1830. By coincidence, the site, close to Lambeth Palace, was just behind the present LFB headquarters. Hodges, educated at Munich University, was no fool and had seen the damage wrought by fire in neighbouring

factories. His premises adjoined candle works, firework manufacturers, tallow factories and bone boilers and he was taking no chances. In 1851 – on the day the Great Exhibition opened, he established his own Fire Brigade.

It must have been a remarkable sight in Victorian London, with its fire station and a spectacular observation tower. He described them both in a letter he wrote to 'The Fireman' in later life:

'The keystones of the window were formed by the life-size figure of a fireman on the look-out. The spandrels of the same of some implements as a fire bucket, a hose and branch-pipe, cross ladders, helmets, etc. The fire alarm forming the crowning point of the house was a neat, gothic belfry with a powerful steel bell, worked by a ratchet wheel and weight, always kept wound up ready to go off when the call came. The door and windows were all plate glass and the house was in the middle of the distillery premises.

'The engines were embellished also with various emblems of fire extinguishing apparatus and with American steam engines...'

The crews came from distillery workers, trained in the skill of firefighting and dressed in smart, dark blue uniforms with brass buttons, black helmets and high, shining boots. Beneath this splendour and warming their manly chests, were white flannel shirts, described by a contemporary admirer as having

'printed on them in colours, alternate illustrations of a steamer going to a fire and a hand engine doing likewise, with horses and men attached.'

With such heroes available at the call of 'Fire!' it was small wonder that the Company suffered a spate of false alarms until Hodges built his observation tower, from which a look-out man could scan the horizon for the tell-tale smoke of a genuine fire. Hodges, again, described the landmark:

'It was a fire observatory, a mast of wrought iron with an ornamental gothic gallery of cast iron work. The mast was 120 ft high and the bottom 21 ins in diameter, tapering gradually to 12 ins at the top. The body of the mast was ¾ inch plate at the bottom, gradually reduced to ¼ inch at the top. The mode of ascent was from the outside by means of a short cage, open at the top and hauled up by means of one of Weston's Differential Pulley Blocks. This I afterwards altered, not having speed enough..... This cost me the sum of £456 and became at once an ornament for miles around and on high days and holidays waved a Union Jack, 30 feet in the hoist and 60 feet in the fly. The whole construction reflected the highest credit upon the engineer, Mr Charles Beeden King.'

Small wonder that in no time, local urchins were chanting:

'If fire you want to put in
Try Hodges' Cordial Gin;
But if fire you want to put out
Try Hodges' Engine and spout.'

The distillery became a centre for a growing band of firefighting enthusiasts in London. Inventions were tried out, usually with an appreciative audience which often included the Prince of Wales (later to become Edward VII), and his close friends, the Duke of Sutherland and the Earl of Caithness, both of whom shared his enthusiasm and had their own private fire brigades on their country estates. It was a fashion which spread rapidly, with footmen and stable staff of stately homes trained in firefighting and dressed in special uniforms – often in the racing colours of their employers. Like Hodges' Brigade, they would not only cope with outbreaks of fire on their own premises but would go out to fight fires in their neighbourhood. Not all kept records of these sorties, but Hodges was able to announce that between 1851 and 1862 his Brigade had attended a total of 521 fires in south London.

In token of this, the grateful citizens of Lambeth offered to buy him a silver tea service, but he modestly declined, adding that he would prefer a fire engine. The opulent vehicle which must have bankrupted the entire area, is on display in the Museum of London. Fully operational, it was capable of discharging 140 gallons of water a minute when manually pumped by a full crew of 30 men.

The designer was an Italian, Sr GM Casentini and on each side of the upper portion of the engine were six panels of different sizes, the centre one having a pedimented top in which were placed bronzes in bas-relief of firemens' helmets and axes. The main shaft at the back passed through the mouth of a golden dolphin and the driver's seat, richly ornamented, had at the back the motto *'Publicae Utilitate'* while the footboard was supported by a bronze dragon. In the centre of one side was an inscription:

'Presented to Frederick Hodges Esq., by the inhabitants of Lambeth and the Metropolis as a memento of their appreciation of his services rendered for many years by his Fire Brigade and in recognition of his heroic and unparalleled exertions to protect life and property from fire.'

The intense interest of this group of fire enthusiasts must have encouraged many of the engineers who were working to improve firefighting methods. Hodges himself welcomed young James Merryweather, who, with his brother Richard, had introduced some of the earliest steam land-engines and two engines, the *'Torrent'* and the *'Deluge'* were the pride of the Hodges Brigade (although not always appreciated by other London firemen. These were said to have refused, on one occasion, to allow them access to a water plug until one of Hodges' firemen dismounted and imperiously settled the matter. It was the Duke of Sutherland).

Another source of encouragement was a succession of trials of fire engines and equipment, sometimes held on the shore of the Thames and on other occasions at Hyde Park or Crystal Palace, with competitions for the most efficient crews.

While all this was happening, Braidwood soldiered on, life in the Establishment settled down into disciplined routine and he was clearly satisfied with the behaviour of his men who, according to his Annual Report to the Board for 1853 had dealt with 900 fires, 261 involving severe damage. It was during this year that the LFEE was called to one of its strangest duties – at Windsor. Far beyond the limit of their normal 'beat' they had been summoned by Prince Albert, husband of Queen Victoria.

The square Prince of Wales tower of the Castle, close to the East Terrace and the State Dining Room, housed mostly servants and it was a young cook who raised the alarm after finding his room filled with smoke when he went to bed. Prince Albert himself, in his meticulous way, had later tried to discover the cause of the fire, but could only ascribe it to a smouldering beam, charred when a furnace fire had overheated and eventually burst into flames. The result was spectacular. The pregnant Queen Victoria (whose eighth child was born only three weeks later), watched the firefighters from a nearby room as the Castle's own fire brigade was joined by local volunteers from Windsor and Eton. There seems little doubt that Albert took charge of the proceedings and before long messengers were sent racing down into the town to summon the Guards from their barracks to help the pumpers.

By 10.30 pm 700 soldiers had arrived and by 11 pm more than nine engines were at work. The Castle, under the shrewd eye of the Prince, had already installed a large water tank which prevented any shortage for the pumps, but as midnight approached, Braidwood was called. One can imagine the nightmare. The message had to be transmitted by telegraph to Paddington, then to the Strand and on to Watling Street. Braidwood turned out his men and set off for Waterloo, only to be told that there was no service to Windsor and he would have to go to Nine Elms station. Once there, trucks were lined up to transport the engines – and the horses – and the whole troop were finally packed on board to arrive at Windsor by 1.30 am 'By half past two o'clock the fire had perceptibly succumbed; before four o'clock it was entirely extinguished' reported the 'Illustrated London News'.

A comparatively small incident, but it was to have a profound effect on the young Prince of Wales who, throughout his adult life, was fascinated by fire and, encouraged by Hodges and his society friends, considered firefighting as one of his more colourful hobbies.

Not all the disasters dealt with by the LFEE were caused by fire alone. On 4th September 1847 the 'halfpenny steamer' 'Cricket', a steam-powered paddle-boat which plied between the City and the West End, had made two journeys between the Adelphi Pier and London Bridge when, at 9.30 am, loaded with 150 passengers and ready to cast off, its low pressure condensing engines blew up, hurling most of the passengers into the river. Miraculously, only four died and 15 were injured, but Braidwood's men were once more called to damp down the remains and clear up the wreckage.

London in the 1840s, particularly the eastern side, was at one of its lowest ebbs. The slums were rife with disease and death, factories were often dangerous and squalid, the Thames was so polluted by sewage and the effluent of factories that there had been a terrifying epidemic of cholera. This was not helped by the fact that with the ever increasing population and the wave of deaths from disease the churchyards were literally overflowing, and rotting corpses protruded from many graves after bodies had been piled, one on another, again and again. Slum houses were often built over cess pits which overfilled and seeped through the floorboards. When the use of cess pits was forbidden, to try to stem the disease caused by this, sewage was simply diverted into the Thames – in one case a few yards from a point where drinking water was being fed into the mains. Within a short time, London was rife with cholera.

There had been more and more fires in the warehouses of the Pool and the ever growing dock areas below London Bridge and in 1858, Braidwood was instructed by the Board of the LFEE to go over the whole of the East and West India Dock warehouses, to report on their hazards and inspect their fire engines, hose, water supply, hydraulic engines and anything else that he felt was relevant.

His reply, in June 1858, was horrifying. He detailed warehouses of more than 2,000,000 cubic feet with no attempt at divisions between the storage areas and the docks and with timber stacked against the walls of warehouses packed with inflammable cargoes. At this time, when the railways were rapidly extending all over the country, wooden sleepers were being imported by the shipload, and steeped in creosote before joining the piles already stacked between the warehouses. In one seven-storey warehouse, he noted molasses, spirits, shell, horns and cork in the basement; jute and coir on the ground floor and on the upper floors, 'tea, coffee, etc.' In another 'sugar, rice, jute, saltpetre, coffee, etc and 300 tons of palm oil lying in front of the warehouse.' And in another, 'passengers' baggage stored in the warehouse with hemp, jute, castor oil, gutta-percha, palm oil and wool.' Massive fire risks were created when mahogany and other timber, popular among the growing number of furniture makers in London's East End, were stored above rum and other spirit vaults. Cargoes were packed away, he said, 'as they come'. No docks had any special supplies of water laid on, so there was none available for firefighting.

After his first report, calling for safer storage methods, more fire doors to break up the huge open spaces, proper water supplies to all warehouses and water tanks on every floor, plus more fire engines and more firefighters in the docks specially trained for this work, he went on to inspect other areas in the Port of London. These must have caused him even greater nightmares, yet although some minor action was taken, his reports and the exhortations of the insurance companies, appear to have fallen, for the most part, on deaf ears.

In 1858 he was sufficiently worried to write to a friend RW Warrington, FCS, Chemical Operator to the Society of Apothecaries, asking for technical advice on the possible progress of fire if it broke out in a cask of rum in the centre of one of the enormous stacks which he had seen outside a warehouse. The reply came back from Warrington:

'I consider that if any of these casks should take fire, the flames would rise with intense heat to a great height and as the liquid rum flowed, it would spread in all directions under and around the neighbouring casks, causing them to be burnt in succession, thus rapidly increasing the evil.

'No doubt some of the fluid would be absorbed in the earth, but when the ground became heated the greater part of the spirit would be vapourised and inflamed. Any that might flow .... over the quay side would, from the gentle descent and low specific gravity of the spirit, tend to rest on the water and thus spread the conflagration among the shipping.'

The Report was confirmed all too often – even in the bombing of the docks during the Second World War.

Braidwood continued his reports on the docks – St Katharine's passed muster, with only some replacements of firefighting equipment needed. Of the Victoria Docks he wrote 'not anywhere seems less attention to be paid to the risks of fire either in construction, mode of stowage or means of extinguishing fire. There is no such thing as a party wall. Spirit vaults are in direction communication with warehouses above 2,000 to 3,000 tons of sleepers, injected with creosote, lying on the ground.'

And cynically, of storage in the London Docks:

'The effort seems latterly to have been to cover the greatest possible quantity of goods at the smallest possible cost, independent of the risk of fire.'

So it continued. To-day we shudder at the dramatically sordid scenes of Dickensian London in modern films. One can only imagine Braidwood's fear when he walked through the original sites. Worst of them all was the Steel Yard, a plot of ground between Upper Thames Street and the river, with a frontage to the Thames of some 400 feet. Much of the ground was entirely covered by

'three ranges of the most ruinous old brick and timber warehouses that I recollect ever to have seen used for the stowage of merchandise. Except at one point, the whole three ranges are in direct communication by doorways, running bridges between buildings are covered in timber, there are numerous holes in the worn out floors.'

The warehouses, with a content of some 1½ million cubic feet, ranged between two and three storeys high and were, when he inspected, filled with brandy, drugs, castor oil, rags, cotton, jute, hemp, tow, sugar rice and 200 bags of saltpetre. Half had vaults full of palm, coconut, fish and earth oils. Immediately to the west on the same site was a complex of rotting sheds filled with timber. The only provision for stopping fire consisted of two firecocks outside the premises in Thames Street and eight feet of hose which had been borrowed to wash down the yard.

One can almost feel the weariness in his heart as he gave up advising or suggesting and simply made his recommendation: '*Take down the lot and re-build in accordance with the Building Acts.*'

His final warning must have chilled him as much as it should have frightened everyone in authority who read it.

'My belief' *he wrote*, 'is that if a serious fire were to take place on the lower floors of any of the large warehouses, either in very dry weather or very hard frost with a fresh breeze or wind or when the Dock is very full of timber in front and stacked up along the back of the warehouses, the losses might be very great indeed.'

How great that was, he would discover to his own cost.

Braidwood's reports were brought to the attention of all the dock owners concerned, as well as the companies involved in insuring them, but the only effect seems to have been an increase in the survey of warehouses by insurers. Very little money was spent on fire prevention and protection.

Nevertheless, he and his men carried on and did their best. Prince Albert, who had inspired scientific and industrial development as wholeheartedly as Charles II before him, had been the inspiration for the Great Exhibition of 1851 where a variety of new fire engines had been displayed, some of them steam-powered. Braidwood, whatever his obstinacies, was always interested in any new development and soon after his arrival in London had welcomed a gift of an all-enveloping fireproof suit containing breathing apparatus from the commander of the Paris Fire Brigade, M. Paulin. Interestingly, the gift came with the request that it should be kept for Mr Braidwood's personal use and was not to be copied. In 1840, Braidwood had a similar suit made, with some adaptations and this, after careful testing, was used by his men in conditions when breathing was difficult.

Despite his early objections to steam power, he relaxed his prejudices after the Exhibition and in 1855 paid £7,000 for a large self-propelling floating steam fire-engine, built with locomotive boilers and a double steam engine, and with a top speed of 9 mph. The same engines provided four streams of water through the 1½ inch branches. But it was not until 1861 that he ordered the first land steam fire engine for his brigade.

Braidwood was now over 60 years old and must have been growing weary of the struggles of everyday life, although he showed no sign of it and still reckoned to be on

Braidwood's early breathing apparatus. (Guildhall Library, Corporation of London.)

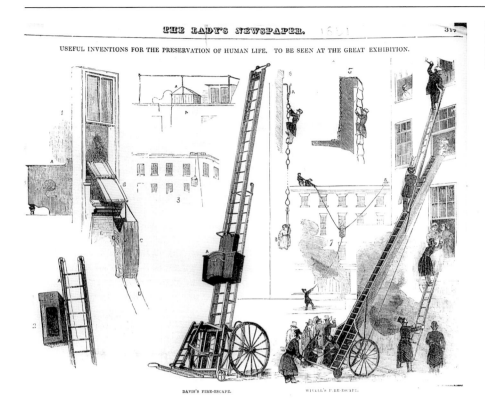

THE LADY'S NEWSPAPER.

USEFUL INVENTIONS FOR THE PRESERVATION OF HUMAN LIFE. TO BE SEEN AT THE GREAT EXHIBITION.

DAVIS'S FIRE-ESCAPE.   WIVELL'S FIRE-ESCAPE.

Fire escape inventions at Great Exhibition of 1851. (Guildhall Library, Corporation of London.)

duty all day, every day. The Victorians talked of 'The Demon Fire' and of 'The Fire King' almost as if they believed that there was, indeed, a demon waiting to set off yet another great blaze in London.

As long ago as 1839, a poem had appeared in a magazine called 'The Town' which must have lodged in the mind of London's Fire Superintendent. It was entitled 'The Fire King':

> "I'll do for that Braidwood then, said he,
> And the whole of the Brigadier brood.
> I'll make them respect my dignity
> As every fireman should.
> I'll set the Thames on fire and see
> If he bilks me of my food.
>
> Then away he tooled to Tooley Street
> And selected a warehouse of oil.
> 'Tis true he didn't admire the treat
> For he very much suffered from bile.
> But a glass of turpentine taken neat
> Soon settled his inward turmoil.

> The Thames all over was in flame
> As with lighted oil 'twas running.
> To save the craft was each one's aim
> But his craft exceeded his cunning
> And the Fire King laughed when he found he could tame
> The Fire Brigade with his funning.
>
> When they threw the tide on the burning mass
> Quite fruitless was their desire,
> And the bravest heart cried out 'Alas'
> And shrank from the Fire King's ire.
> Things were come indeed to a pretty pass
> When water wouldn't put out a fire."

Perhaps the memory of this doggerel crossed Braidwood's mind when he wrote in 1854 to the first commissioner of Public Works, Sir William Molesworth, commenting on plans for a proposed warehouse in Tooley Street, just downstream from London Bridge on the Southwark bank:

> 'The whole building, if once fairly on fire in one floor, will become such a mass of fire that there is now no power in

London capable of extinguishing it, or even retaining its ravages on every side, and on three sides it will be surrounded by properties of immense value'.

Surely, too, it must have been there on the evening of 22nd June 1861. It had been an ideal day by the Fire King's standards – a hot afternoon with the sun pouring down on the cobbles and roofs of the narrow streets and brick-built warehouses that he knew and dreaded. Scovell's warehouse in Tooley Street was one of the better equipped – thanks to Braidwood's constant nagging at the authorities. Inside, great iron, fireproof doors divided the different bays which were tight packed from door to ceiling with every kind of cargo – bales of hemp and cotton, sacks of sugar, casks of tallow, jute, tea, spices, oil. In theory, the day's work had ended and the fire doors should have been tightly shut. In practice the odd one, here and there had been left open just a crack. It was enough for the stray breeze to find its way in at the moment when the bales of damp cotton, warmed by the sun, were heating up. One last breath of wind and, with

spontaneous combustion, a bale began to burn. Soon the rest of the stack ignited and by the time the smoke rolled into the open, the fire had taken hold. A runner flew to the fire station along the street – the engines turned out instantly and a message was rushed over to Watling Street.

Braidwood's force had increased since its inception. He now had 117 firemen and officers, scattered through his original four divisions, 15 drivers, 37 horses, 27 large, horse-drawn manual engines, two floating engines worked by steam (one 40 hp the other 80 hp) one land steam fire engine and 28 hand pumps. Nearly the entire force poured over the Thames and down Tooley Street as the flames belched from the upper floors of the warehouse, but with little hope of doing more than preventing the blaze from spreading. Within minutes of their arrival the fire had leapt across to the adjoining Cotton's wharf, then to Hay's and Chamberlain's wharves. Braidwood's dire warnings were coming into appalling effect as the fire fed on a glorious banquet of oil, paint, sulphur, cheese, flour chicory, rum, brandy. No time to ponder now on the effect of heat on

The great fire of Tooley Street, 1861. (Guildhall Library, Corporation of London.)

spirits. Within an hour the whole river bank was ablaze and with it the river itself as the burning rum joined with molten tallow literally to set the Thames on fire. Ships cast off and fled from the flames which seemed to chase them as they sailed or rowed desperately away. Sightseers had packed London Bridge, delaying the relief engines. Some had jumped into small boats for a closer view and as they sat and watched in horror, the flames engulfed them and they drowned.

Pumps from the smaller private industrial brigades ran in and fell over the parish pumps which had rumbled over the cobbles, interfering with the efforts of the few still-remaining insurance firemen and infuriating the men of the LFEE. Wave after wave of pumpers strained at the levers until the cry of 'Beer-oh' became a croak that no amount of alcohol could slake.

It was seven o'clock in the evening when one of the LFEE men ran up to Braidwood, typically in the heart of the action. There was a problem: the fire floats fighting the fire from the river were themselves being scorched by the heat. What should be done? Braidwood turned into one of the narrow alleys that ran from Tooley Street itself, down to the water's edge, pausing only for a moment to unwind the red silk Paisley kerchief from his neck to wrap it round the hand of one of his men who had been cut and was bleeding from the gash. With a word of comfort, he moved on again, with a senior officer keeping pace alongside him.

Years later, one of the young firemen, JE Palmer, who had been with Braidwood at this point described what happened as they heard a wall begin to groan.

'Braidwood turned and called "Palmer – mind the wall! I said "Hi Hi Sir" and saw the walls begin to crack. I called to my men "run for your lives".....there was a groan, the high warehouse wall beside them bulged, cracked and with a great roar, collapsed on Braidwood and his officer. They were buried under the mass of bricks and killed instantly.'

It was a disaster in every sense. News of the death of the man who had led them for 28 years ran through the ranks of his firefighters, already weary and daunted by the impossibility of the task which faced them. He had no deputy. The Committee of the LFEE had never appointed one. Braidwood had always been there. The officers did their best but the manuals' jets could scarcely reach halfway up the buildings and it was not until the new steamer and several privately owned steam engines went into action, including those belonging to Fred Hodges, that the water came anywhere near the roofs of the warehouses.

Hodges sent a messenger to the long-established fire manufacturing works of Shand Mason in Blackfriars Road and a steamer which was under test was rushed out to help, but to no avail. The fire burned, totally out of control for two days from London Bridge to the point at which Tower Bridge stands to-day. It took a whole month before it was completely extinguished.

The bodies of Braidwood and his officer lay below the debris for three days before they could be recovered, then the buttons were cut off his uniform and distributed among his men.

James Braidwood's funeral was almost as spectacular as the fire which had killed him. London, which had loved him, came to a standstill. Crowds packed the streets from Watling Street to Abney Park cemetery where he was buried, alongside his stepson, also a fireman. Over a thousand policemen were in the cortège, as well as 700 men of the London Rifle Brigade (including three of his sons), the band of the Royal Society for the Protection of Life from Fire, 400 men from the City Police, superintendents and men from all the water companies; representatives from private and local fire brigades as well as the Board of the LFEE. The bells of all the parish churches in the city tolled and the mourners were led by his widow, his children, the Duke of Sutherland and the Earl of Caithness, both of whom had a strong interest in firefighting and had been his close friends.

Queen Victoria sent her condolences to the family and similar messages came from fire departments all over the world. The Superintendent of the Sydney Fire Brigade in Australia wrote 'on receipt of the sad news, our large fire bell was tolled, the British Ensign hoisted half-mast high and crape attached to the firemens' uniforms as token of respect for one of the noblest, most self-denying men that ever lived, who spent and lost his life in the service of his fellow creatures.' A fund had been set up for his widow but the insurance companies stepped in and offered to pay 'the full value' of his life. The fund was diverted towards helping the two elderly sisters he had supported throughout his life.

Tributes and poems to the 62-year-old Chief Officer appeared in newspapers, magazines, 'memorials' and on cheap printed handbills, sold to the public on the streets and all commemorating his courage. Staffordshire china figures were produced in his memory. There were calls for a monument and one was placed on a wall as close as possible to the spot where he fell. It remains to this day, in Tooley Street, not far from London Bridge. One of the more ingenious tributes came in the form of a card, sold in the streets on the day of his funeral:

IN MEMORIAM

ACROSTIC

Being

AN EPITAPH

On the Late

Mr JAMES BRAIDWOOD,

Superintendent of the London Fire Brigade,

Who lost his life at the

Great Fire of Tooley Street, on

June 22nd, 1861

J—oined with a feeling wisdom, the swift skill

A—nd grasp of energy – an iron will.

M—ost resolute when danger threatened most.

E—ngland laments for these, in Braidwood lost!

S—till ready to dare Fate at duty's call,

B-ridling the flames, breasting the red-hot wall.

R—edeeming wealth (amassed by years of toil.)

A—nd life (more precious) from the fiery coil.

I—n those bright haloes, ranked with chief and sage

D—escends thy glorious name from age to age!

W—here shall we seek so firm, so brave a mind?

O—r where, his men reply, a heart so kind?

O—h not in vain didst thou resign thy breath;

D—evoted hero conqueror in death!

★

Indeed, his death was not in vain. It marked one of the
great turning points in the history of firefighting in London.

7

Interregnum – Enter Captain Shaw

TOOLEY STREET BROUGHT THE FIRE INSURANCE companies to their knees. Although they all honoured the claims made for compensation, the total amount, estimated at some £2,000,000 brought gloom and despair to their board rooms and the decision that this must, indeed, be the end of their provision of a firefighting service for the whole of London. No other large city in Europe, let alone a capital city, relied on private funding for their firefighting. Edinburgh, Glasgow, Manchester and Liverpool already had municipally-maintained fire companies. London must take action.

Until 1855, this would have been difficult. Apart from the Corporation of the City of London – still restricted to the square mile in the centre – metropolitan London had no overall governing body. In that year, more than 300 different groups of people who, since Tudor times, had been responsible to a greater or lesser extent for the public services of its people, had been brought together under one authority, the Metropolitan Board of Works. Now, at least, there was a single overall body which might take over responsibility for a municipal fire service, if it were not to be wholly State run.

Meanwhile, in a near-panic reaction to their loss and an effort to restore their funds, the insurance companies raised their premiums and laid down conditions of storage which were considered impossible to sustain. London's merchants howled with fury as the rates went up from 4s 6d per cent to 15s per cent (22p to 75p).

Grouping together in opposition, they petitioned the Lord Mayor, asking him to convene a public meeting to discuss the problems which had arisen as a result of the fire and emphasising that the companies had, for many years, received premiums for the insurance of merchandise and property which had given them a good profit even after compensation for fire losses had been paid. It went on:

'The recent fire in Southwark was of an extent never equalled in the metropolis since the foundation of the Insurance Offices and consequently of an exceptional character. The offices nevertheless have, in their panic occasioned by so serious a loss, endeavoured to establish a tariff of premiums which, if submitted to, would render to them far more than an equivalent to their risk – in fact, would convert an extraordinary calamity into the basis of a permanent source of excessive profit. To exact the high rates now proposed by the offices who, by combination, exercise a practical monopoly against which at present the mercantile community is powerless, would be to encourage non-insurance, and thus to stimulate an improvident habit of trading, the evils attending which could hardly be exaggerated and which we earnestly deprecate.'

In short, they claimed that the new premiums, once they had made up the Tooley Street losses, would provide the insurers with an excessive profit at the expense of the merchants, many of whom might, as a consequence, fail to take out any insurance.

The meeting was duly called and the insurance companies defended their actions on the grounds that, for ten years before this, mercantile insurance in London had been unprofitable and this justified the new rates. Once changes had been made in the safety of storage of goods coming into the port, the premiums could be lowered.

The merchants were still dissatisfied. In defiance, they decided to set up an insurance company of their own to challenge the new rates. In fact, they proposed eight new fire offices – the Braidwood, Britannia, City of London, City and Provincial, Empire, Public, Mercantile and Commercial Union, but only two – the Mercantile and the Commercial Union were floated and a year after this the Mercantile merged with the North British, but the Commercial Union survived. The established insurance companies drew back from the ferocity of the attack by the merchants and reduced their premiums from 15s (75p) to 12s 6d (62p) per cent. However, they stood firm on the question of improved warehousing and refused to reduce their safety requirements for storage of goods.

The matter did not end here. Relations between merchants and insurers were anything but friendly. More immediately important, London was without a fire chief. The Board of the LFEE met in August 1861 and appointed, in his place, a young Irishman, virtually unknown in London, who had been Chief Constable and Chief Officer of the Fire Brigade of Belfast, Captain Eyre Massey Shaw. Under him, the Establishment carried on, struggling still with too few stations, too few men and too little equipment to cope with the never-ending demands made on it as London blossomed with yet another Great Exhibition and, stemming from it, more people, more industry, more ships pouring supplies into even bigger warehouses.

But, even as they made the appointment, the insurers were determined that this would only be an interregnum. No longer were they prepared to burden their customers with the enormous cost of providing London with a public fire service.

In February 1862 they wrote to the Home Secretary, Sir George Grey. Calmly they pointed out that they considered it was no more part of their duty to protect the lives and property of the people of London from fire than it was to police the capital. For thirty years they had put out any fires which occurred, regardless of whether the owners were insured or not. Costs had soared as London grew and the more efficient the insurance cover, the less the parishes bothered to keep up their own provision for fighting fires. It was now up to the government to make suitable arrangements for a municipally-financed fire service. This time they made it quite clear that they would no longer be responsible for the duty and accordingly, they were going to disband the LFEE and transfer its stations and engines to such Authority as the Government might see fit to appoint.

There was no doubting the seriousness of their intent. Put into the words of the man in the street, they were fed up with carrying the fire bucket and were about to kick it. Meantime, and on a temporary basis, they would carry on under Captain Shaw.

Unlike the Duke of Wellington, Sir George at least took action. In the manner of all good politicians, he played for time by setting up a Select Committee 'to enquire into the existing state of Legislation and of any existing Arrangements for the Protection of Life and Property against Fires in the Metropolis.' Its Chairman was Thomas Hankey, MP, and its 15 members included the Lord Mayor of London, The Rt

Hon William Cubitt; The Commissioner of Police for the City of London, Mr DW Harvey; The Commissioner of the Metropolitan Police, Sir Richard Mayne; The Chief Constable of Liverpool, the Chief Fire Officers of Glasgow and Manchester; Mr Samson Lowe, secretary of the Royal Society for the Protection of Life from Fire; Captain Shaw and in addition, representatives of the Metropolitan Board of Works, parishes, vestries, insurance companies, water companies, ratepayers and the commercial interests. (As Shaw was to comment acidly, on a later occasion, 'the Committee took the advice of all who were in a position to offer any and many who were not.')

If the intention were to delay action, the Committee must have disappointed the Home Secretary. Their first session was held on 25th February 1862. Their Report was published on 8th May 1862, six weeks after they had examined the last of their 42 witnesses.

The picture which emerged was alarming in the evidence of fire cover for London and confusing as far as the advice on ways to solve the problem was concerned. The Committee were told that compulsion to provide any firefighting service depended entirely on the Act passed during the reign of King George III, in 1772 (12. Geo III, c.73) which called on parishes in London to be responsible for fire extinction, under pain of punishment if they failed to comply. This had in most areas (as Dickens had made so clear) become a farce. Sir Richard Mayne, of the Metropolitan Police, said that he had never heard of a conviction against a parish for non-compliance with the Act and (somewhat surprisingly) it was no duty of the police to enforce it. To his knowledge, 106 parishes kept fire engines of one sort or another but 104 did not. Most of them were kept either in the churchyards or at the workhouses, usually in the charge of a parish beadle who was paid a small amount for the responsibility.

At great fires, most parish engines were useless and at small fires they were not needed. They were clearly raced to fires solely ('vexatiously' he called it) to demand the reward for first, second or third attendance when, in effect, it was an advantage if they did not attend. Any law founded on the old parochial system was useless for London now. Their area was too limited, their boundaries too irregular, there was no executive power in the parishes for the purpose.

Pursuing his theme, Sir Richard pointed out that an undue risk was now being incurred by the public from the want of a general system under some official authority. He thought it 'most serious in an extraordinary degree' that there was 'an utter neglect of arrangement by any public authority for the safety of buildings of the highest importance.' The public felt strongly the want of provision for saving life at fires. He most certainly did not think that protection against fire should be entrusted to bodies without responsibility. There should, he maintained, be a public establishment with adequate means supplied by law and with adequate powers.

John Bowing, Clerk to the London Union, filled in the picture of the parish pumps. There were 98 parishes in the City itself which were still paying engine keepers' salaries, (as they had since the days of Queen Anne,) to what might be termed 'engine men, engine women or engine children' as the case might be. In many cases they were parish old women or schoolboys. One parish engine was bricked up behind a blacksmith's shop wall. The only reason why most parishes kept a pump was to claim the reward for attendance. They did more harm than good and were not the slightest use at a fire.

Added to which, he assured the Inquiry, the 1772 Act was as useless as the engines. The City of London was entirely dependent upon the LFEE.

Job Hyam, a vestry clerk of Christ Church, Spitalfields, supported this. It cost them £50 a year to pay their 'engineer' to look after their pump, he said, but although it was efficient it was never called out as the police and local people preferred the LFEE. 'They actually pass our door to go to an Establishment station – from which, perhaps, they receive a little more beer.' Other witnesses referred to the parish pumps as 'futile', 'perfectly worthless', 'so insignificant as to be valueless', 'a farce', 'a delusion' and all agreed that the money spent on them was totally wasted. Indeed, as one aptly commented 'it is money thrown in the fire.'

Remarkably, considering his position as chief of the LFEE, it was Capt. Shaw who, whilst he accepted that many parish engines were useless, argued that some of the bigger parishes were running efficient units, listing 16 of these which included the two he considered the best, Hackney and St Marylebone.

Problems varied in different parts of London. The City itself, for instance, covering less than 700 acres, was still divided into 98 parishes. Hackney, with 3,200 acres had five engines with a full-time engineer and deputy engineer, both of whom had served in the LFEE. The parish spent over £400 a year on their 'brigade'; their part-time firemen were well trained and well drilled.

Marylebone, with 1,509 acres and a population of more than 160,000, kept two large engines in Marylebone Lane and a full time engineer receiving 25/- (£1.25p) a week 'and all the rewards'. Already, residents in nearby St John's Wood were petitioning for an engine to be sited near them and this was being considered.

Experts described the London Building Acts as 'faulty and inadequate' and 'far inferior to Bristol and Liverpool'. They were still, in any case 'extensively evaded.' Remarkably, it transpired, the docks with their huge, undivided buildings, were exempted from the Acts.

There was no doubting that London, the capital of the country, lagged far behind other major industrial cities in firefighting terms. The LFEE had increased by only 47 men and one station since it was formed. To have a pro-rata force with Manchester, for instance, it would need to take on 500 men.

Most of the existing fire stations were close to the heart of London – within a radius of three miles of the Royal Exchange – where the biggest fire hazards lay in insured warehouses and factories. With the increasing size of all these industrial buildings, the Committee of the Establishment had recently had to order six new steam fire engines – and already the cost of fire protection for London had reached £25,000.

It was generally agreed that the LFEE was efficient but it was too small, it lacked 'the power of the law', it needed to be an independent body commanded, in the words of the Lord Mayor '*by a person who in time of need should have power as despotic as that of the captain of a line-of-battle ship, being only responsible and amenable to public opinion and the Secretary of State.*'

Nobody seemed to want to alter the situation of the Royal Society for the Protection of Life from Fire, whose secretary said that they now had 77 men and four inspectors on full pay, and had saved 71 lives a year for the past five years and a total of 748 lives since 1844. In its first 20 years of existence, the Society had attended 7,823 fires and saved 972 lives.

The individual insurance companies seemed uncertain as to whether they wanted the fire fighting service to be run entirely municipally or whether they would continue themselves, but with considerable support from public funds. The death of Braidwood had clearly left them in a dilemma. As John Drummond, Secretary of the Sun and Chairman of the Committee of the LFEE explained, 'we were then like a ship at sea without anybody to lay hold of the rudder; he had performed these duties so long and so well that we really thought it impossible to replace him.'

However, the Metropolitan Police Commissioner, Sir Richard Mayne, had no doubt that any future fire brigade should be part of his police force. Preservation of life and property from fire ought to be as much a part of the duty of the police as preservation from thieves and murderers and he was confident that he could run such a force for an addition of one penny on the police rate – which would raise £56,000. It would also mean that it would be worthwhile installing an electric telegraph for both police and fire duties – a service which he clearly felt unnecessary, uneconomic, or both – for the police alone. Explaining this, he pointed out that by a system of established routes and using message 'runners', as the fire brigade did, a communication could be sent and an answer received from every station throughout the police district within two hours.

He was supported by the Chief Constable of Liverpool, where the fire brigade had been under police control since 1837. With a population of 475,000, Liverpool had 15 manual engines, one 'steamer' on order and the cost of the service was only £2,871 (£350 of which was paid by the insurance companies.) 155 Liverpool policemen, 'selected for their health, strength and intelligence', were paid an extra 2/- (10p) per week in addition to their policemens' pay of £1 to act as firemen.

Arguments continued as to whether a new London fire service should be part of the police force, whether it should be independent and funded from the rates; whether the cost should be paid by the government from the tax which they levied on insurance policies (which was eventually abolished in 1869) and how much the insurance companies should contribute towards the cost.

Only one witness, William Hall, a wharfinger of Tower Hill, looked into the future far enough to assert, a century before its time, that *the protection of life and property against fire should be under one commission upon a large and comprehensive scale, embracing the whole of the United Kingdom.*

The Committee's Report was a model of concise brevity. On five pages and in 40 numbered paragraphs, it offered its comments and produced its recommendations.

There was little support for the 'useless', even 'injurious' parish pumps. Money wasted annually on these within the capital was reckoned to total some £10,000. The LFEE was praised for its efficiency and was suggested as the basis for any future service.

Then came the recommendations:

'1   That a fire brigade be formed, under the superintendence of the Commissioners of Police on a scheme to be approved by the Secretary of State for the Home Department, to form part of the general establishment of the Metropolitan Police, and that the Acts requiring parishes to maintain engines be repealed.

2   That an account of the expenditure of the new police fire brigade be annually laid before Parliament, together with the general police accounts; in such a manner that the special cost of the brigade may be ascertained.

3   That the area of the new fire brigade arrangements be confined within the limits of the jurisdiction of the Metropolitan Board of Works, with the option to other parishes to be included, if within the area of the Metropolitan Police.'

In concluding, the Committee added a footnote that in their opinion no amount of legislation would alter the fact that everybody should treat fire with respect, should take care not to start fires and should one begin, that it should be tackled immediately to stop it growing into a conflagration.

The government responded to the recommendations by asking Captain Shaw to draw up a working plan for a new fire service to cover the entire Metropolitan Board of Works area. This, in itself, was a colossal task for a man who had come to London comparatively recently and was now faced not only with organising and running his own Establishment with virtually no administrative help, but with producing a scheme which would cover the 117 square miles of the MBW area instead of the ten square miles of Central London which were the limits of his existing force.

Shaw, undaunted, drew up his plans with new fire stations, more men and more equipment at an overall cost of £70,000 a year. The Home Secretary was aghast. 'Out of the question' was his comment. There was no way in which the Government could consider such an extravagant proposal. Shaw returned to his home 'over the shop' in the City and his oil lamps burned deep into the night as he cut down his estimates to £52,000. Once more the scheme was turned down, with Sir George Grey, the Home Secretary, indicating that if the cost were cut to £50,000 – a completely arbitrary figure which bore no relation to the necessary costs of such a service – the government was prepared to consider any Private Member's Bill proposing the transfer of the present service from the insurance companies to whatever authority might be agreed. Instead of the penny rate, suggested for a police/fire service by the Metropolitan Police Commissioner, this amount was based on a halfpenny rate.

Once again, Shaw went home and set to work, producing eventually, proposals for a force which would increase the number of fire stations in London from 19 to 43 and the number of firemen from 129 to 232. The boundaries of the new force would extend to Hammersmith, Hampstead, Stoke Newington, Bow, Woolwich, Lewisham, Tooting and Wandsworth and the cost would be kept down, with difficulty, to £50,000.

The concept of a police brigade was immediately the subject of arguments between the City of London police and the Metropolitan force and it was finally agreed that the overall authority should be the Metropolitan Board of Works. After three years of to-ing and fro-ing, *'An Act for the Establishment of a Fire Brigade in the Metropolis' (28 & 29 Vic., c 90)* became law in July 1865, declaring that the new Metropolitan Fire Brigade should be born on January 1st 1866. It would cover the City of London and 'all other parishes and places' within the jurisdiction of the Metropolitan Board of Works. The Board was to take responsibility for providing an efficient force of firemen, and to provide them with all such fire engines, horses, accoutrements, tools and instruments as might be necessary. The stations, fire engines, plant and other property of the LFEE were to be transferred to the Board who would also take over their pension responsibilities.

Added to the contributions from the parishes of the MBW would be an annual payment not exceeding £10,000 from the government towards the cost of protecting government buildings. Any insurance company operating a fire insurance scheme in the area was also to pay the Board a sum in the rate of £35 per million gross insured by it. In addition the Board of Works might borrow a sum not exceeding £40,000 to cover any extra costs under the Act – a ludicrously niggardly amount if the essential expenses of establishing the new service had been seriously considered.

The new Brigade would not take over salvage duties, but if the insurance companies decided to form a salvage corps, the two would be expected to co-operate fully with each other, with the fire brigade sending daily reports of all fires in their area to the participating insurance companies. Any part of the fire brigade could, if necessary, be employed on special duties.

The insurance companies seemed happy enough with this solution to their problems. £35 in a million was not excessive – they reckoned that it would probably cost them some £12,000 a year which was less than half the amount which the London Fire Engine Establishment had cost – and they would be relieved of all responsibility for its maintenance and control. In fact, the first year of the new Brigade cost them only £10,200. They also donated more than £18,000 which was the balance between the value of the plant delivered up from the LFEE and its liabilities.

In handing over the London Fire Engine Establishment to its new owners, the Metropolitan Board of Works, Shaw was meticulous in his actions, drawing up a detailed record and summary of all the information collected during the 33 years of the Establishment's existence, including a series of tables which were, he explained 'the largest amount of trustworthy Fire Statistics hitherto collected in a methodical form.'

The total number of calls received by the Establishment during its existence had been 35,145. Of these 2,769 were false alarms; 3,307 were chimney fires and 29,069 were for fires, of which 9,635 resulted in serious damage and 19,434 in slight damage. Twelve men had been killed on duty, but the number maimed or wounded had, he commented, been very large and in addition there were 'men who from over-fatigue and other causes incidental to the profession, have either died or been disabled in the service'. Not all the men had stayed – the Establishment had employed in its service over the years some 600 men, of whom 129 now remained.

He also provided a complete inventory of every implement and item of gear with their original cost and their current value – including those mentioned by Dickens – the Goose Necks and Dog Tails (30 Goose Necks at £22.10s had retained their value – as had the 107 Dog Tails at £8.0.6d the lot).

The original ten insurance companies who founded the LFEE had changed over the years, – two more had joined them in its first year and the number supporting the Establishment had risen to 30 in 1864. As the change-over approached, it had reduced to 28.

Under the Act the newly founded Metropolitan Fire Brigade had to have a leader. There could, by now, be no doubt as to whom it should be. The Chief Officer of London's first municipally-funded fire brigade was Captain Eyre Massey Shaw.

8

Facing the Challenge

N O VICTORIAN MELODRAMA COULD HAVE MATCHED
the action which faced the Metropolitan Fire Brigade
on the day of its birth, 1st January 1866. One could
almost see the Fire King emerging in a cloud of red smoke to
hurl down the gauntlet as Braidwood's successor took over
at Watling Street, not as leader of a Fire Company or
Establishment but with the full ringing title of Chief Officer of
the Metropolitan Fire Brigade.

Within minutes of reaching his desk, Shaw was interrupted by a breathless messenger reporting a fire at St
Katharine's dock in Lower East Smithfield, a stone's throw
from the Tower of London. With Tooley Street in the
forefront of his mind, he leapt into action. Already the flames
which had begun in a jute store were spreading along the
wharf and he brought in all the appliances within range –
municipal or private. More 'steamers' than had ever before
been used at any fire in Europe were rushed in, along with
two fire floats, three steam engines due for delivery to
customers abroad which were sent in pro. tem. by their
manufacturers, one steamer belonging to Hodges's volunteer brigade and an assortment of manuals.

The whole atmosphere was one of frenetic enthusiasm.
In the course of the action, according to a contemporary
report 'one engine of the brigade had its boiler deranged and
had to be sent away; two had their boilers so damaged that
several hours' work was required to get them right; another
was set leaking and a fifth had its crank shaft broken.'
Criticisms that his men had been 'less than thorough' were
vehemently denied by their new Chief, although the
insurance loss was £200,000.

His task now was to consolidate his £50,000 scheme
within the tight parameters laid down by the government
and to assess the problems ahead – which were manifold.

In one area, if in no other, the government and the Board
of Works had shown wisdom in their choice of a leader for
the new Brigade and there was no doubt that London, after

nearly a lifetime of Braidwood, was looking at Shaw with an
intensely critical eye. Who was this increasingly powerful
and popular Irishman?

Eyre Massey Shaw was certainly something of an
enigma. Here was a man clearly devoted to the whole

**Captain Sir Eyre Massey Shaw, first Chief Officer of the
Metropolitan Fire Brigade. 1866. (LFCDA.)**

business of firefighting yet he was not an engineer, although, in 1865 he had sought a patent for an adaptation to improve a steam fire engine. (It was granted, but only on a temporary basis owing to lack of detail!) In the brief period during which he had led the LFEE, he had already made many friends in London, particularly among the upper classes, yet could be brusque to the point of rudeness with other experts and particularly, as years passed, with his employers, the members of the Board of Works. He was, like Braidwood, loved by the ordinary people as a hero and defender; admired and criticised by his men – and his peers. He had the bearing to attract all eyes at a fashionable society function, was on friendly terms with Queen Victoria – and with Edward, the heir to the throne, yet could be seen, again and again, his uniform dirty and soaked through with water, fighting the fires of London alongside his fire crews and returning home weary and sometimes injured, only to change into dry 'gear' before setting off again. As time passed, it was also noted, with a raised, fashionable eyebrow, that he could do his rounds of inspection of fire stations with a different society lady at his side every day of the week. He was to be mentioned in one particularly sticky divorce scandal yet he remained happily married and evidently devoted to his wife and children (a tribute, surely, to the patience and forbearance of Anna-Maria Shaw.)

His age, when he stepped into Braidwood's shoes at Watling Street in 1862, is uncertain – he was either 30 or 32 years old. His place of birth was just outside Cobh in southern Ireland, almost within sight of the sea and close to Cork, where his father was a merchant. His family were of Scottish descent and he was closely related to General Eyre Massey, who was raised to the peerage of Ireland in 1800 as the first Baron Clarina. (One of Shaw's sons was named Clarina after his distinguished ancestor.) His grandfather's name was Bernard and he was distantly related to George Bernard Shaw.

When he was barely in his teens he was already experienced at sailing his father's yacht round the tricky waters of the local coast. He always loved the sea and had, since a very young boy, had his own small sailing boat. He had a reputation as no 'dandy' spare-time amateur but as a competent sailor who could 'bear a hand' in any part of a ship. Even in his earliest youth he often visited the great sailing ships which put into Cobh and occasionally went with them on voyages.

Originally he was meant to be a clergyman and indeed, he entered the Divinity School of Trinity College, Dublin, when he was 15½ yrs old and by 1847 had a Bachelor of Arts degree. Even then, he must have realised that the Church was not for him, and later in life, he wrote that he was on the point of being ordained but 'after the ordination sermon had been preached, I returned furtively in my college robes and leaving these and my other small belongings in my College rooms... took ship and after many long weeks, found myself at the Western side of America......' Whether he was, indeed, at point of being ordained is doubtful, but there is no doubt that he not only went to the United States but spent some time there – possibly as much as four or five years, covering the period of the great Gold Rush which attracted so many young Irishmen, anxious to make their fortunes. Shaw may, or may not have been a part of this, but there is no doubt that he travelled around America. Certainly, in his evidence to the Select Committee of 1862 when he was questioned about his life there, he claimed to have seen fires in New York, Philadelphia, Washington, Boston 'and a great many other places.' It was a period when the New World was expanding rapidly, with a vast natural supply of readily available timber used in the building development. Fires broke out with alarming frequency – sometimes on a small scale, but all too often spreading in the fierce winds to involve great areas of the major cities.

What Shaw did in America, other than look at fires, is difficult to discover but it seems likely that family pressure – and the offer of a commission in the North Cork Rifles – brought him back to Ireland and he stayed in the regiment for six years, reaching the rank of Captain and marrying, in 1855, a local beauty – and heiress – with Portuguese connections, Anna-Maria Dove. The North Cork riflemen seem to have been a lively crowd and Shaw must have learned much about organisation and discipline as he led his contingent, but Army life failed to satisfy him. Married now with three (later to be four) children, (including his beloved daughter Anna who was to stay single and devote herself to caring for him in his old age) his restless nature drove him on. After a particularly serious fire, the City of Belfast was looking for a new chief officer to take over their now combined police and fire brigade (and to oversee the Sanitary and Lighting Departments). From 50 applicants, Shaw was successful. June 1st 1860 found him in Belfast on a salary of £300 a year with no apparent experience but immense confidence in his own ability. Looking back in later years he wrote 'I took a good house, furnished it in a sumptuous manner, far beyond my means, and thought I should never move again.'

One of his greatest shocks came when he discovered that there was 'no published information and ... nowhere the theoretical knowledge without which ... no profession can keep pace with ... growing requirements.' There was, of course, Braidwood's book on dealing with fires, but that had been thirty years previously and Shaw might not even have known of its existence. It was a tribute to his enormous organising ability – and his unshakeable self-confidence – that he went ahead with the job with considerable success and even enjoyed the excitement, not least as Chief of Police, recalling: 'where politics run high as between Orangemen and Papists ... and in some difficult cases when both sides fought with unusual ferocity and blood ran freely I had to act with vigour and was accused of "undue violence"; which means that I had used the strong arm at my disposal without waiting for a magistrate to read the Riot Act.'

It was typical of Shaw to enjoy the fray, to take the law into his own hands if necessary, to impose strong discipline and, at the same time, to be able to say 'notwithstanding my position, I was on very good terms with both sides, particularly the Papists, although I did not belong to their creed...' These were certainly high among the characteristics which came through during his time in London.

There is no doubt that he made mistakes and even, in his energy and enthusiasm, put his own life and that of his men at risk, but he was certainly cutting his firefighting teeth in Belfast and, as he wrote later 'I may now frankly acknowledge that some of the most painful humiliations of my life were undergone at that period.'

Perhaps too, he had some gambling instincts, for in taking over the London Fire Engine Establishment, he had no guarantee that the post would continue beyond the time it would take for the insurance companies to offload the responsibility on to some other organisation. Now, however, his future was assured for as long as anyone could foresee. His salary had been the subject of some argument with the Board of Works – one of his earliest crossing of swords with his new masters – but he seems finally to have accepted their offer of £750 per annum, plus a house and the other allowances (including £50 from the British Museum which he had been paid under the LFEE and other 'perks' which were only hinted at.) It was a high figure for that period, particularly as he had relatively little experience of firefighting, but, as he was quick to point out, he had never spared time, money or toil in acquiring knowledge of the profession and had studied the working of fire brigades 'in every city of importance not only in England but all other countries.' He certainly loved travel.

According to Jack While, the fire correspondent of *The Times*, there was no more popular figure with all ranks of the population in London than the six-foot Shaw,

'all lithe, active, without an unnecessary ounce of flesh on his body, with a commanding presence, the eye of an eagle that sees and knows from afar. Intensely intellectual and alert and his appearance generally so out of the common that he would take the eye in a group of a thousand men. He had a marvellous knowledge of men and a great capacity for reading character, almost at a glance. When he had once engaged a fireman, you could be certain that he knew that man from head to foot, inside and out. His men knew him, loved him and feared him. He instantly became known as "The Skipper" and the name remained to the day he left the force, still as beloved and esteemed as he had been throughout his service. He was a stern disciplinarian, but a thoroughly just man and I never heard a fireman say that he had not had a straight deal by "The Skipper", even if he had given him his dismissal. He was fearless, calm and cold as ice at the biggest fire that ever happened during his period of command and with an eye for the most remote possibilities of disaster. He never told his men to take up a position to which he would not unhesitatingly go himself and his attitude in emergencies which looked most grave was one which instinctively inspired confidence in all.'

His superiors and contemporaries soon discovered that this was no Braidwood, quietly religious and devoted to good causes. Anna-Maria and Shaw's two daughters – Anna and Zarita – worked ceaselessly to help the firemens' families, but for Shaw himself, life was dedicated to firefighting and the good life of Victorian high society.

In his earliest days, however, his brigade had to be organised. As in the LFEE, the fire force was divided into four districts, now labelled A,B,C and D. 'A' covered the West End; 'B' Central London; 'C' was the East End and 'D' was the whole of the area south of the River, with headquarters in Kennington. Every station had a Superintendent and Engineer-in-Charge.

New firemen had to be enrolled. A number of firemen from the old LFEE, no doubt missing the family atmosphere of the Braidwood era and being apprehensive of Shaw's tightening discipline, had left before the new Brigade had begun. Some, no doubt, were not altogether happy about the pay and conditions under which they would be expected to work – a strict 24 hours a day, seven days a week all the year routine, with a minimal amount of time off, dependent on the goodwill of the station Superintendent. Some found new jobs as theatre firemen, or enrolled in private or industrial fire brigades.

Faced with starting virtually from scratch Shaw made it clear that he was looking for ex-seamen (which again, upset the critics who still maintained that men with experience of the building trade were preferable.) He thrust aside the allegations that seamen were the scum of the earth, arguing, from his own experience, that these were what he needed now – skilled men who could be quickly trained – and sailors could be trained more quickly to the Brigade's needs than any landlubber. Sailors would work the long watches that his meagre budget and shortage of manpower demanded. Sailors accustomed to running up rigging in a storm, trimming sails or heaving at the capstan were the men who could drag the hoses, hold them as they kicked under the pressure of water, swing the escapes up into position and then stand, cool-headed on a narrow wall or the top of a ladder, high above the crowds, with the wind and rain beating against them while the smoke and flames licked round their feet. They could live in cramped quarters, accept discipline, react quickly to an emergency.

But his advertisement for recruits demanded more than just a successful career at sea. It spelled out his exact needs:

'Candidates for appointment must be seamen; they should be under the age of 25, must measure not less than 37 inches round the chest and are generally preferred at least 5 feet 5 inches in height. They must be men of general intelligence and able to read and write; and they have to produce certificates of birth and testimonials as to character, service, etc.

'Each man has to prove his strength by raising a fire escape, single-handed with the tackle reversed' *(the equivalent of lifting a straight, 244lb – over 2 cwt – or approx 150 kilo).*

'After they have been measured, had their strength tested and been approved by the chief officer as stout, strong, healthy-looking, intelligent and in all other respects apparently eligible, they are sent for medical examination before the surgeon who, according to his judgement, either rejects or passes them, in either case giving a certificate.' *(The certificate guaranteed that the man was* 'free from disease and well suited for the situation of a firemen in the Metropolitan Fire Brigade.')

Following this, and a three-month probationary period, the man was examined again and, if satisfactory, was taken into the service.

He was also trained. Shaw reckoned that an experienced seaman could be ready for duty inside two months while a man without the advantage of a seaman's training would take from six to eight months to be reasonably prepared. Men lived at their stations but attended classes dealing with the management of engines and engine gear, and also with escapes after the MFB took over the escapes of the RSPLF in 1867. During this period of training they were only allowed out with the experienced crews in cases of extreme emergency because, in Shaw's words

'no amount of numerical strength, even when combined with discipline, can compensate for the absence of skill and knowledge, and on this account I consider a proper system of training before attending fires, the only true method for making men real firemen.'

His emphasis on skill was to be questioned a century later when the grading of firemen as unskilled, semi-skilled or skilled was to become a major bone of contention between the authorities and the trade unions after World War Two.

Shaw changed the uniform too. Irritated by the welter of assorted volunteer or private brigades which still seemed to turn up at all major fires, he rejected Braidwood's dark grey outfits with black leather helmets. Instead, he opted for a seamanlike navy blue – a tunic with brass buttons, cloth trousers, boots, belt, pouch and axe, plus a top-coat for cold weather, as the 'Number One' outfit. Working uniform was a duck jacket, ('duck' was a form of coarse cotton, often used on small sails), duck trousers, round cap, similar, again, to the Royal Navy caps and, for the steam men, a similar suit of woollen serge. The tunic was made of stout blue 'kersey' – a thick woollen cloth, double-breasted with a 1½ inch high

Raising escape as recruitment test of strength. (LFCDA.)

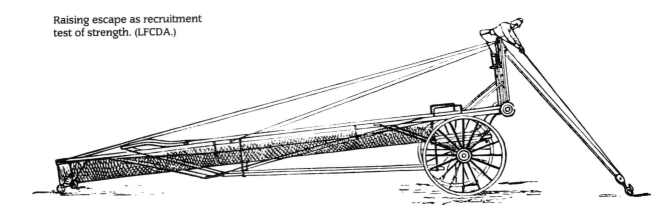

stand-up collar which was rounded off at the front and faced with scarlet cloth. There were two rows of flat brass buttons, marked 'MFB' in old English lettering and the top part of the tunic was lined with woollen plaid. (In the 1930's, John Horner, who later led the Fire Brigade Union and became an MP, worked as a London fireman and commented on the high quality of the uniform, particularly the lining of the upper part of the tunic with what he described as close woven tweed, intended to keep out as much water as possible and to protect the shoulders from burning embers.) The trousers were also made of blue kersey, lined with grey cotton and, like sailors, with a whole 'fall' or flap, instead of flies in the front, fastened with bone buttons. Boots were best grained leather and double-fronted with the top made high enough to reach above the calf but below the knee. The kersey tunics were 37 inches long compared with the shorter 'duck' tunics.

Superintendents' uniforms were similar to the men's but of finer cloth and single breasted while the Chief Officer's was distinguished by its rounded silver buttons.

The outstanding feature of the new brigade was the brass helmet. Shaw, in his visits abroad and particularly to Paris, reckoned to have studied 'all the helmets in existence' before deciding on the type which made his men so famous. The design he settled for was inspired by the French 'pompiers', and, he explained that it combined the strength necessary to give protection with lightness and the absence of any projections which might stop men getting through narrow apertures. 'In America' he said, 'I have always been astonished at the shape of the helmets which appeared to me to be so encumbered by the enormous back-flap, and so defective in point of protection, particularly about the eyes, that I should suppose it to be absolutely impossible for the men to go through such openings as for instance, the panels of doors, etc. which we are in the habit of doing.'

The new helmet which Shaw had designed for his men's protection – and appearance – had a front peak which shaded the eyes without interfering with the vision, a back peak which protected the neck and ears from molten lead from roofs, but was slightly cut away at the ears so that he could still hear without difficulty; a 'comb' on top, strong enough to resist the force of a blow from falling masonry or timber and the pattern intended to make sure that if a man did drop unconscious, his helmet would protect his face or the back of his head whether he fell forward or backward. (The dragon embellishing the sides of the crest was said to have been designed by Shaw's daughter, Anna.) The material – brass – was not important, other than to distinguish MFB men from the rest.

Shaw reckoned that leather helmets probably gave as much protection and both were liable to be penetrated by sharp objects such as falling slates. One practical advantage of the brass design was that any section which had been damaged could be easily unscrewed and a new piece screwed back in its place. (In later years, helmets which were so damaged as to be useless were sometimes taken to pieces in the Brigade workshops and made up into miniature helmet-shaped money boxes to collect cash for the Widows and Orphans Fund.) The Chief Officer himself could be quickly recognised in any group – his helmet was silver.

Shaw's intensive recruiting drive had to be backed up by a major building programme. Many new fire stations were needed and he set a target of increasing the old LFEE quota to 43.

Immediately, under the halfpenny rate squeeze, he ran into financial problems, but never one to be daunted by apparent lack of funds, he pressed on and new stations were steadily built while the old ones were improved wherever this was possible – and economical. Between 1867 and 1871, 26 'modern' fire stations were opened and because Shaw felt that the service would be more efficient if he had his men where he could keep an eye on them, he made sure that as soon as the budget would allow, these included not only space for appliances and the watch room but quarters for married men and their families and for single men. Married men usually had two rooms per family; single men shared a dormitory. In addition, there was a basic mess room, a watch room, a room where wives could do their washing and hang it up to dry and some communal provision for washing and bathing. (Some stations had the luxury of drying cupboards for laundry and wet uniforms.) Gradually too, provision was made for a watch tower, where a man would be on constant alert for smoke rising from a possible fire (if he saw it, he put the engine on stand-by, ready with steam up for when the call came through) and where hoses could be hauled up by ropes and dried out after use.

For the first four years until 1870, all the new stations were designed by Edward Cresy, who had been private secretary to the Chairman of the Board of Works, was the son of a London architect and seemed to act independently of the Board's Superintending Architect, George Vulliamy. His buildings were typically Victorian, solid malm bricks (made from a mixture of clay and chalk) relieved by red bands and Minton tiles.

Cresy died suddenly in 1870 and although he was succeeded by his assistant, Alfred Mott, most of the stations after this were attributed to Vulliamy. Mott, however, was mainly responsible for them, producing a solid Victorian Gothic style until 1879 when a new assistant, Robert Pearsall, took charge of the elevations of the new stations and changed to a more distinctive design with an angular outline, paired windows, careful detailing and crenellated look-out towers. By this time, look-out towers combined with hose-drying facilities had become a 'standard fitting'. Quarters were slightly more generous but still cramped and outrageously restricted for most families, not only in size but by the rule that all accommodation could, at the Station Officer's will, be open to inspection to make sure that each fireman's wife was keeping her rooms clean and tidy.

Outside contractors were used for the building and maintenance work and it was not until the LCC took over in 1888 that an Architect's Department was set up with a special Fire Brigade Section.

Shaw 'played the field' in his search for the best equipment, often setting one manufacturer against another in his attempts to arrange a sharp financial deal. Allegations that he favoured one firm rather than another were proved false by the variety of suppliers noted in his record books. His two main engine and equipment manufacturers, however, were Shand Mason of Upper Ground, Blackfriars, who had supplied Braidwood as well as many private fire brigades, and their fierce rivals, Merryweathers of Greenwich. (Their company, founded in 1692 by Nathaniel Hadley, had passed to his son who, equally successful, took on a partner, called Simpkin and carried on the business with him, changing their range until they decided that they needed new blood.

They took on a third man in 1791, the smart son of a country squire who had joined them in Long Acre as an apprentice and was taken on now as a partner in the firm of Hadley, Simpkin and Lott. Later, another apprentice joined them from his home in Yorkshire, became a partner and married Lott's niece. His name was Moses Merryweather and within his lifetime, he took over the company and gave it the name which was to be famous in the world of fire engines from then until the present day.)

Braidwood had dragged his feet over using steam-powered appliances, not altogether surprisingly as they were still in their early days and their weight was enormous – one of the early Shand Mason steamers took three strong horses to move it. Even with the lighter engines, rails were sometimes fitted into the sloping floors of the new fire stations to allow them to be got 'on the run' or under way quickly and pushed back 'off the run' when they returned. Both phrases stayed in London's fire brigade vocabulary until the present day. (Similar rails were found in the excavations at the ancient Ostia fire station outside Rome, suggesting that even in the Roman Empire the firemen had some form of weighty transport for their equipment.) Shaw, well aware of the steamers' increased power and their economy of running (a few buckets of coal were infinitely

cheaper than teams of pumpers who had to be paid in cash and beer or beer tokens,) pressed the manufacturers to produce improved, lighter patterns and this, gradually, they did. Like Braidwood, however, he was concerned that water mains, still in the hands of a variety of private companies, would not be able to cope with the increased pumping power of steam.

With the arrival of the new Service, the RSPLF was gradually disbanded, so from his meagre grant, Shaw was faced with adding the saving of life to the saving of property. The chief fire escape makers to the MFB in the early days appear to have been Messrs EH Bayley & Co of Newington Causeway, near the Elephant and Castle, although there was some competition from Bray's – a smaller firm in Deptford. Apart from the cost of the equipment, this was a further drain on his manpower.

Fire engines were drawn by horses, hired at a fixed annual rate from horse-masters. Again, Shaw surveyed the field before settling on a major contract with Tillings of Peckham, which was the equivalent of a modern, nation-wide car hire company. Tillings provided horses for everything from buses to doctors' carriages. They supplied fodder, instantly replaced any animal which was injured, sick or died and kept a constant eye to make sure they were in tip-top condition at all times. Sick horses were taken to their special 'hospital' at Peckham where they had 60 loose boxes, each horse having its bill of health and treatment pinned to its door. The Brigade needed horses which were strong and powerful but, at the same time, calm under chaotic conditions and sensitive to control and, after some discussion with Tillings, Shaw persuaded them to breed animals specifically for the MFB's needs. Usually these were greys, partly so that they might be seen more easily at night (as if the noise of the engine wheels and the racket of the firemen's shouts were not enough to warn the unwary of their approach). They stood between 15 to 16 hands, sturdy but not so heavy that they could not gallop for some distance pulling a load of up to five tons of engine, equipment and men. The Brigade contract was quite specific about their characters – all London fire horses had to be 'quiet to drive and ride.'

The horses were remarkably intelligent too. While the Parisian and New York fire horses were trained in special schools for up to 12 months, London's horses made do with three months' intensive work-out before going out 'on the run.' Tillings accustomed them to the noise of traffic by using them as leaders of a four-horse coach which ran between Peckham Rye and Oxford Circus, but they would normally work in pairs hauling the engines, with an occasional three-in-hand. Their leather harness was decorated with small brass bells and only the letters 'TT' advertised that Tillings had provided them. (A fact often commented on by wags in the crowd who reckoned they knew why the same letters were not engraved on the men's helmets – few firemen were 'TT' – teetotal – in those days.) Mares or geldings, they came to the Brigade when they were between five and seven years old and were kept in the service for about five years, although a particularly good pair might stay on for as long as twelve years. Some horses were imported from America; some from Ireland, a few from Holland, but they were always selected in pairs by size so that they could run easily and efficiently, side by side.

This led to some remarkable friendships between the animals, with tales of horses pining if their team-mate was ill and off the run. In the old Chatham Road fire station at Battersea, it was some time before their coachman noticed that one of a pair of greys was almost completely blind. The weakness must have developed over a considerable period of time, during which its partner had led it so well that the men were completely deceived. The blind horse was immediately retired, but its partner pined to such an extent

that its 'mate' was brought back and they continued to run as a pair until both were eventually retired together.

Horses were very much a part of station life and, throughout the Victorian period, there was competition which reached not only national but international proportions, with tales of their prowess being exchanged up and down the country and across the Atlantic, usually in letters to the firemen's magazines.

As soon as they were delivered to a station they came under the care of their driver, or coachman and were immediately 'spoiled' by the men and their families, stabled in clean stalls, thickly spread with dry straw, well-fed and with a special bonus of treacle with their hot bran mash once a week. One writer described them as being treated as well as the firemen treated their own children, but the children must have come out second best – cuffed, chivvied, made to do the chores (which often included using a mutton bone to rub dubbin into their fathers' fire boots – a long and arduous job when done properly, and woe betide them if they did not include the instep between the sole and heel,

Brigade horses were carefully matched in pairs. (LFCDA and author.)

where the leather was liable to split when it dried out if it was not kept supple with the grease.)

The horses' stalls were usually set in a yard behind the engines so that all they had to do when the bells went down was to trot forward into the shafts and wait for the harness to be fastened. On one of Shaw's visits to America he saw their clip-on style harness and introduced this to London. From then, the horses had a period of two hours 'on watch', standing between the shafts with the harness above their heads, ready to drop down and be quickly fastened with clips instead of the more intricate buckles. (Again, there are stories of horses knowing to the minute when their two-hour stint was up and stamping their hooves or neighing to be replaced by the next equine 'watch'.)

Undoubtedly, one of the great sights of Victorian London came just after the alarm was raised at a fire station. Firemen would shoot down the stairs (or later in the century, down the new brass poles, inspired by American fire houses) leap to the engines, the doors would swing open and the horses rear on their hind legs – eyes rolling, manes flying as they lunged forward, taking the weight of the engine on to the road before galloping off, hell-for-leather along the street.

Some horses were said to be so intelligent that they would glance at the board which indicated where a fire alarm had been pulled and then turn left or right out of the station, according to the site of the alarm and with no guidance from their 'coach', who always controlled them through the streets. Beside him stood the fireman with the largest lungs, hand cupped to his mouth, bellowing 'Hi! Hi!' in a voice which cleared the busiest street as the horse-drawn cabs and buses scattered into the kerbs and the crowds cheered – and often followed them to the fire.

Once they reached the fire, the horses would be unharnessed and taken to a quiet corner where they enjoyed the attention of the crowds, sedately accepting offerings of carrots, sugar lumps, apples or buns. Occasionally, if an urgent message needed to be taken back to the station, a firemen would ride one of the horses bareback at full gallop through the streets.

At least one responsibility was lifted from the new Brigade. In the old insurance company days, the fire companies always included porters for salvage work as well as the firemen. In 1867, the London Salvage Corps was established by the combined insurance companies to go out with the MFB on fires of any size and to be responsible for protecting the property of the owners from excessive water damage, smoke and from looting. The Salvage Corps vehicles became almost as well known on the London fire scene as the fire engines themselves and the Corps remained in existence until after the Second World War.

Now, though, added to the task of organising the new Brigade, Shaw with his statistical mind was anxious to discover and list the causes of fire to see what could be done by way of prevention – if this were possible. He already had some idea, from the files of the LFEE, and from the Insurance Record of 12 January 1866 which had published an analysis of over 25,000 fires in England and the United States indicating at the top of the list, 'accidents and carelessness' as the major causes.

After these came:

Chimneys, flues, stoves, pipes, furnaces or other heating apparatus, defective or overheated, along with arson and incendiarism including 'malicious mischief' and 'mischief of boys', then:

Curtains and bedding igniting.

Candles and lamps.

Gaslights, leakage, explosions etc.

Clothing on the person*, airing or drying.

Sparks from chimneys, forges, locomotives etc.

Fire heat in manufacturing or in ovens.

Shavings.

Children playing with matches or lucifers, fire or gunpowder.

Matches

Pipes and cigars.

Spontaneous combustion.

Camphine fluid and coal oil.

Fireworks and gunpowder.

Intoxication.

Ashes and cinders.

Lightning.

Friction of machinery.

Steam boilers.

'Mysterious'

Cats and rats (excluding matches*).

Causes not reported or unknown.

*Clothing on the person included, for a short period of high fashion, womens' crinoline dresses. Apart from the most expensive models, the enormous skirts were draped over a bell shaped metal frame. These were so wide that all too often and particularly in the cramped rooms of some of the less opulent houses, the fabric would brush against the open fire and catch light. The space beneath the dress formed an air pocket and the frame prevented the victim from being rolled in a rug or blanket which might have extinguished the flames. In some cases, the skirts were ten yards in circumference at the hem and, in the more expensive models, contained hundreds of yards of highly inflammable tulle. 'Punch' was one of the magazines which thundered against the fashion, claiming that 3,000 women a year lost their lives because of it, but to no avail. Women continued to die until the fashion itself faded away.

Another strange cause of accidents at that time came about when gas lighting began to grow in popularity. Gas and water were brought into houses through lead pipes and for some reason, rats discovered that they could get a drink by gnawing through the water pipes. Unfortunately they were not clever enough to distinguish between water and gas pipes and if they made a mistake, gas leaked out and on several occasions caused sizeable explosions. Equally odd was 'rats gnawing lucifers' as a cause of fire. Evidently they found the wax used on the matchsticks was very palatable and would carry away any they found lying around the house to sample in their holes under the wainscoting. If their teeth ground on the phosphorous heads, the match would catch fire and ignite any dust or rubbish in the rat's nest and this too, began a number of fires in London.

Added to all this was the continuing growth of slum housing, of factories, of theatres using highly inflammable and increasingly complicated scenery and props, not to mention amazingly ambitious productions which sometimes involved lighting fires on the stage itself. Small wonder that Shaw had his work cut out keeping fires at bay in London.

9

The Hose of Common Sense

HOW SHAW MANAGED TO GET SO MUCH DONE SO quickly is hard to understand. Despite the confusion caused to the LFEE with no-one to take over after Braidwood's death, the Metropolitan Board of Works still saw no need to provide its new Chief Officer with a Deputy. He carried the main burden alone and, apparently with no administrative staff other than his senior officers, who were based at stations and constantly being called out to fires, plus such help as his wife and daughters could offer.

Nor was he at ease with his employers and the government – there were constant questions, arguments, even Select Committees throughout the period in which he led the MFB. Nevertheless he found time not only to examine in detail the fire hazards of Victorian London,

particularly in theatres, to meet and negotiate with manufacturers of fire equipment, and to deal with a never-ending stream of inventors. These offered every kind of helpful device, from coiled springs under firemens' boots to allow them to leap unaided to upstairs windows, to helmets with built-in water sprays to protect their faces from the heat of the flames. One of the strangest was a pair of leather trousers with a strong belt to which an umbrella could be attached in the event of fire. The trapped victim needed only to climb out of the nearest window, open the umbrella and jump. At times it must have seemed as if everyone in the country was offering an invention – even the murderer Charles Peace was said to have spent his last days in the condemned cell, working on an aid to firefighting.

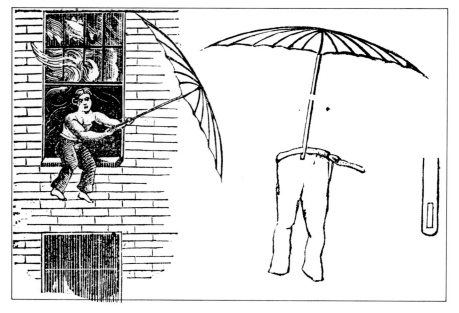

Inspired invention for escaping from fires. LFCDA.

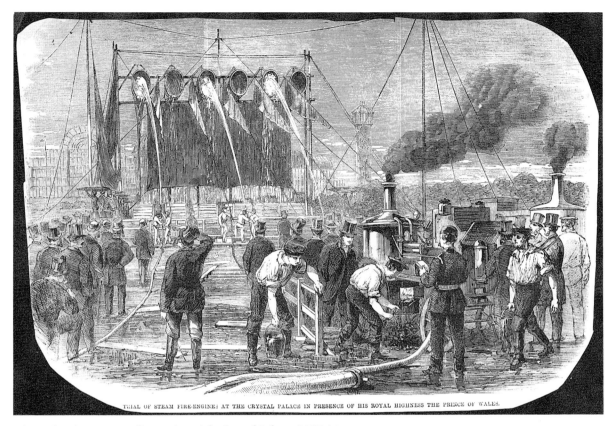

TRIAL OF STEAM FIRE-ENGINES AT THE CRYSTAL PALACE IN PRESENCE OF HIS ROYAL HIGHNESS THE PRINCE OF WALES.

Prince of Wales at steam fire engine trials, Crystal Palace. (LFCDA.)

In his leisure moments, Shaw made more and more friends in high places, not just the Prince of Wales, but the 'Hodges' Set', men like the Duke of Sutherland, by now the largest landowner in the country and one of its richest men, and the Earl of Caithness, who had become a Fellow of the Royal Society with a great interest in engineering. Shaw was also on the Committee which had organised the first fire engine trials, held at the Crystal Palace in 1863 – in the presence, inevitably, of the Prince of Wales.

Queen Victoria herself received him on a number of occasions, and it was to him that she turned for advice on the fire protection of Osborne House, her home on the Isle of Wight, and of Sandringham House. In return for his help, she presented him with an inscribed clock – now in the Museum at Southwark. But it was her son and heir, Edward, Prince of Wales, eventually to become King Edward VII, who developed a passion for fighting fires and became one of Shaw's closest friends – and an invaluable ally in his battles with the government and the Board of Works, both of whom were clearly influenced by his noble associates.

Whether the Prince of Wales had been lured into firefighting by his experience of the Windsor Castle fire has never been proved. Certainly it was in 1865, not long after Shaw had taken charge of firefighting in London, that we hear of him with his friend Sutherland and Lord Richard Grosvenor, another 'pyrophile', turning up at a fire in Saville House, Leicester Square, *partly in the dress of a fireman.*

Soon after, the Prince was off fire-spotting again, this time in Oxford Street, not far north of his home in The Mall. According to a newspaper report on 24th February 1866, fire broke out at the premises of Messrs Laune and Marner, coach builders and:

'Within a few minutes, engines had arrived from Wells Street, King Street and Baker Street, as well as the parish engines of St Anne's, Soho and of Marylebone. Turncocks arrived, plugs were drawn in Hanover Square and Oxford Street and the water flowed up almost as high as the first floor of the houses. At this moment, HRH the Prince of Wales, the Duke of Sutherland and the Hon Captain Howard arrived. His Royal Highness looked on with much admiration

Prince of Wales, later Edward VII, in uniform of the Metropolitan Fire Brigade, on a fire ground. (Gernsheim Collection, Harry Ransom Humanities Research Center, University of Texas at Austin.)

at the alacrity displayed by the firemen who were assisted by the Duke of Sutherland in getting the hose from the engines properly connected so as to get the water to bear upon the burning pile.......'

Clearly this fuelled his interest and later he was to appear at fires in the full uniform of the Metropolitan Fire Brigade, complete with helmet, belt, axe and boots. Shaw would send a messenger to Marlborough House to alert him if a 'good' fire had broken out and the Prince, if he were free, would hasten to the nearest station, at Chandos Street by Charing Cross, slip into his uniform and gallop off on a fire engine. (On one of these 'jaunts' when he was riding an unusual appliance, drawn by three horses instead of two, the route led off the main thoroughfare and into a street where the road was being dug up. The first horses, the 'wheelers', slid into the hole, the engine lurched, flinging off the firemen but, by a miracle, it didn't overturn and they all, including their Royal colleague, managed to scramble clear,

continuing at a more sedate pace to the fire.

The friendship between the two men undoubtedly caused some jealousy and Shaw was often criticised – not only for this but because of his cavalier treatment of anyone who disagreed with him – rightly or wrongly. However, he held his ground and defended his men in the face of all attacks. Throughout his time as Chief Officer, he was beset by inquiries of one sort or another, from his employers, from the government, from manufacturers, from other fire brigades – all over the world – and from the public, but he coped with absolute confidence and carried on with his work of building up a Brigade which was rapidly becoming respected as the finest in the world.

In 1867, within a year of the establishment of the MFB, he was called to give evidence at the Select Committee set up by the government to look into firefighting generally in the United Kingdom (a follow-on from the Committee which recommended the establishment of the MFB). Apart from major cities like Manchester, Birmingham and Liverpool, firefighting was almost non-existent and arson, particularly insurance fraud, was rife, despite the penalty of 10 years transportation.

Shaw, in his evidence to the Committee, gave a glimpse of the problems which he himself was facing. Questioned about the storage of paraffin, a comparatively recent arrival on the household scene and one which was already a regular cause of fires, he replied: 'in London, by law, almost any goods can be stored in any way......' Fires in warehouses still bedevilled his force – as well as many other industrial premises in the capital and despite the *Waterworks Act of 1847 ('An Act for Consolidating Certain Provisions usually contained in Acts authorizing the making of Waterworks for Supplying Towns with Water,' 10. Vic. c.17)*, failure of water pressure in the mains was another major difficulty. (The Act had called for better supplies of water, fire plugs in all mains at not more than 100 yards

apart for extinguishing fires, keys to be deposited at the fire stations and the plugs to be kept in good order, plus a notice in the street indicating the position of the plugs, and no charge to be made by the companies for supplying water to fight fires). It was not helped by the fact that the supply of water was divided between eight private water companies in the Capital.

It was in this Committee that Shaw was attacked by CTF Young, an ardent amateur fireman and author of '*Fires, Fire Engines and Fire Brigades*', who accused him of failing to allow volunteer fire brigades to help at fires. Shaw denied this, saying that he was prepared to accept their help (he often needed the men, his own force was so undermanned and overworked) but that he was not prepared to have them wandering round the fire ground getting in the way and failing to obey his orders, or those of his officers. He complained that volunteers often 'came when they liked, amused themselves as they liked, and went when they

Shaw and the Fire Fiend.
(Punch & LFCDA.)

liked'. They copied the MFB uniform and when he brought in the brass helmet, they had copied that too. Young had maintained that the Sapeurs Pompier in Paris were far better than the MFB, and held London's Brigade in low regard. Shaw, who had visited Paris on a number of occasions and knew their fire officers well, replied 'those gentlemen in Paris are intimate friends of mine and have assured me that Mr Young's statement is incorrect.' He couldn't avoid a dig at his employers and the government in adding that the Paris force had an annual income of £100,000 – considerably more than his own Brigade – so they could afford to be better equipped.

Shaw had recently introduced the electric telegraph machine to improve communications between his stations and Young accused him of using the Wheatstone system, which was 'an apology for a telegraphic system.' Shaw flattened him with his reply – expressing himself amazed at Mr Young's ignorance of the fact that the MFB was using the highly efficient Sieman and Halskes' system.

The Select Committee reported back with a series of recommendations. They included the need for a new Building Act to include more stringent regulations for warehouses and shops; no petroleum, paraffin or other mineral oil with an ignition point of less than 110 degs Fahrenheit to be sold for lighting purposes, and penalties for breach of such a law, plus the setting up of machinery for inquests to be held into major fires throughout the country.

Following the customary pattern, the Inquiry was a waste of time as very little action was taken by the government on the recommendations of its Committee. However, the idea of the inquest into suspicious fires must have been remembered by at least one authority, and in 1888 the City of London, which had suffered from a spate of arson attacks for some years, had a local Act of Parliament passed - 'The City Fire Inquests Act' – which gave their Coroner the unique power to have all fires reported to him and to hold an inquest into such fires. (These inquests are no longer held.)

For Shaw, finance was still a nightmare. The product of the halfpenny rate had, admittedly, risen from £30,913 in 1866 to £33,869 in 1869 and the insurance companies' contribution had gone up from £11,050 to £14,391, but the government's offering for the protection of their buildings had stayed at the original £10,000 and London was still growing fast.

In 1869, the Metropolitan Board of Works Loan Act authorised the interest on borrowed money to be paid and the principal redeemed out of the proceeds of the Metropolitan Consolidated Rate, apart from the halfpenny set aside for firefighting purposes. It also laid down that the amount to be raised for the working expenditure of the

Brigade each year should be equal to what would be produced by a halfpenny in the £ on the gross annual value of property rather than, as had happened previously, on the rateable value. This, however, was insufficient as far as the MFB was concerned.

The over-riding fact remained that Shaw was desperately short of men and those already in the Brigade were appallingly overworked. While provincial city brigades enjoyed a whole day off every two weeks, London's firemen were lucky to get four hours off a week. Two men were on watch at night in every station and while they could try to doze on the hard wooden benches alongside the telegraph machine in the watch room if there was no fire call, they were not allowed to remove their boots, their belts or their axes. These were reckoned to be 'on duty', while the rest of their colleagues, whose daily 'on duty' period spanned 16 hours, were allowed to sleep in their beds provided that they did not leave the station. For the remaining eight of the 24 hours they were still considered to be 'for duty' and could be called out at a moment's notice.

When in 1866, the Brigade took over the work of the Royal Society for the Protection of Life from Fire and with it, their escape stations, it meant that every night 100 heavy fire escapes had to be pushed out from their daytime resting places in churchyards or on street corners, to their night, stations by 100 firemen who then had to spend the night in tiny wooden 'sentry' boxes alongside the escapes, ready to push the ladders on their great wheels to any fire which broke out in the locality – helped by such kindly passers-by who had the strength to lend them a hand. The boxes were hot in summer, freezing cold in winter and the one blanket with which they were issued was not enough to keep them sufficiently warm to allow them to sleep. Instead, they often wrapped it round their shoulders and stamped up and down trying to keep warm.

In the morning, the escapes had to be pushed back to their daytime base, after which the men returned to their fire stations to help clean, polish and check over the equipment, sweep out the yard and make sure that the rest of the station was in first-class condition. If there were no fire call, they could, after their mid-day meal, rest during the afternoon, but if there happened to be a major fire, they carried on. It was not unusual for men to work for 60 hours without any sleep, and at times it was 120 hours. The strain was intolerable – their wives and families barely saw them, although they lived above or close by the stations – and conditions grew worse as the number of fires continued to increase until even drills had to be abandoned.

Shaw lost men by the dozen. Many of them felt that even the hardships of unemployment were preferable to the misery of these long hours of duty and although the pay

Various methods of using fire escapes, mid 19th century. (LFCDA.)

was good compared with many working men, it was not remarkable.

By the 1870's the London firemens' income was:

Superintendent: £200 pa

Engineer 1st class: £128 pa

Engineer 2nd class: £109 pa

1st Class Fireman: £1.15.0d (£1.75p) per week

2nd Class Fireman: £1.11.6d (£1.53) pw

3rd Class Fireman: £1.8.0d (£1.40p) pw

4th Class Fireman: £1.4.6d (£1.22p) pw

The Chief Officer, Superintendents and Engineers had free quarters, coal and light, but the men had to pay rent and for these services. There was no automatic promotion after a set length of service as there had been in the old insurance brigades. Promotion was slow and the men had many complaints, not least the strictness of Shaw's discipline which, he defended as *'a form of freedom since it releases men from any necessity to make decisions themselves.'*

Above all, the men were concerned about their pensions – and what was to happen to their wives and families if they were to be sufficiently badly injured, or developed any serious illness due to their work and had to leave the Brigade, or if they were killed on duty. In the days of the

insurance brigades and the LFEE, the companies were always generous in their allowances and care of firemen and their families if they fell on hard times. The Metropolitan Board of Works had no such scruples. If a fireman fell sick, or died, his widow was probably young enough to go out to work herself to support her family. They were not prepared to mollycoddle her with municipal support.

Eventually the Brigade was losing men at such a rate that Shaw, in desperation, turned again to his old antagonists, the volunteers, for help to ease the pressure on his exhausted crews. In 1875, after consulting some of his Society firefighting friends, he set up the *London Auxiliary Fire Brigade*, to work alongside the professionals. It was organised on the lines of a gentlemen's club with an entry fee and an annual subscription. Candidates had to be recommended by an MFB Engineer and two other members, after which a ballot was held with one blackball in five being enough to exclude them from membership. The volunteers bought their own uniforms, which were the same as professionals but with black buttons instead of brass, black-painted brass helmets and with a black band instead of red round the 'undress' sailor hat. Like the Auxiliary firemen of World War II, they trained and drilled alongside the professionals and had, at all times, to obey the orders of the MFB officers.

By 1871, Shaw was being criticised by the insurance companies. With their most valuable clients centred within the City of London, they wanted the MFB to concentrate on this area – if necessary at the expense of the rest of London which was already crying out for better fire cover. Eventually, with his reluctant advice, but against his wishes, the Board of Works closed two stations as an economy measure, one at Farringdon Street on the edge of the City and the other in Sloane Street, Chelsea. It was a bad decision. Within a matter of weeks, in February 1871, fire broke out at the Pantechnicon – a large warehouse covering two acres of ground in Motcombe Street, Belgravia. It had been solidly built some 40 years earlier, advertised as being completely fireproof and was used by the wealthy to store their valuables – antique furniture, paintings, jewellery, even armour – while they were abroad or during the fashion-dominated 'seasons' when they were staying at their country estates. Without the recently closed Sloane Street fire station, which would have been within a few minutes of the site, the call was taken by a volunteer brigade who failed to alert the MFB and in whose inadequate hands the fire took massive hold. It was half an hour before the Brigade received any message and by the time they arrived, the whole building was in flames. A financially and historically priceless assortment of antiques was totally destroyed and although the insurance companies paid out £1,850,000 in compensation, many of the depositors had relied on the fireproof reputation of the building and had not gone to the expense of taking out insurance.

Fire after fire continued but by now there were other problems. The Victorian period was seeing the expansion of science as well as industry, and this involved more and more dangerous substances. For some time the Brigade and the Press had warned of the dangers of transporting hazardous goods across the metropolis.

It was 2 am in the morning of 2nd October 1874. The steam tug 'Ready', hauling a small fleet of barges – the 'Jane', 'Dee', 'Tilbury', 'Limehouse' and 'Hawkesbury' – quietly chugged its way along the Grand Union Canal at the start of a journey to Nottingham. Its cargo, neatly divided between the narrow-boats, included sugar, nuts, coffee, strawboard, '2 or 3 barrels of petroleum' and five tons of gunpowder, much of it stored in barrels but some 'boxed' in canisters and flasks. It was still dark as they slid through Pentonville and Camden Town, past the cages of the London Zoo and on through Regents Park. Just before 5 am as the leading boat was approaching the Macclesfield Bridge which linked Avenue Road with the Outer Circle road round the Park, there was what was described as 'a rapid burst of blue light' on the 'Tilbury'. The steamer and barges stopped, presumably to discover what had happened, but evidently satisfied that there was no serious problem, the skipper of the 'Ready' re-started his engines and the convoy moved on.

Within seconds there was a deafening roar and the 'Tilbury', now passing under the bridge, blew up. Almost instantly the 'Limehouse' sank, the 'Dee' was damaged and the Macclesfield Bridge was totally destroyed. By a miracle, only three people were killed, and although there was some damage in nearby houses, there would have been devastation in most of the surrounding area had the barges not been passing through steep-sided banks at that moment, which deflected the worst of the blast upwards instead of sideways.

Londoners were physically and mentally shaken by the incident, which was followed by a wave of protest against the transport of dangerous goods through the capital. The influential 'Illustrated London News' carried pictures of the scene and stormed:

'Explosive substances are carried through the heart of London every day. The inhabitants of the Metropolis are constantly in proximity to a danger so appalling that were it fairly appreciated, efficient means would certainly be taken to avert it. Gunpowder, nitro-glycerine and other materials of its kind are passed to and fro as articles of commerce under restrictions (if restrictions they can be called) so loose that the wonder is not that accidents should sometimes happen but that they should happen so rarely. Parliament must see to this.'

Ironically, a century later similar protests were still being made in London against the transportation of equally, if not more hazardous, nuclear materials through the capital.

Meanwhile, for the firefighters, a small ray of hope penetrated the fire scene in 1875 when the Public Health Act (An Act for Consolidating and Amending the Acts relating to Public Health in England, 38, 39, Vic. c. 55) came into force, Section 66 of which demanded that every authority must install fire plugs – with a notice above them to make their position clear for the firemen. Unfortunately, no details of what they meant by 'plugs' were given. Nor was any uniformity mentioned, so that round threads, 'V' threads, gas threads of many different pitches, 'bayonet' outlets – one a type which had never before been heard of, were all used and were to cause chaos, even as late as the Blitz in 1940, when brigades came together to co-operate in fighting major fires. Shaw settled for round threads. They were eventually changed during the Second World War, but the LFB Veterans Club still called themselves 'The Round Threads'.

In the midst of all this, Shaw kept up his pressure for better conditions and for pensions as of right for his men and eventually, in 1877, another Select Committee was set up by Parliament, under the Chairmanship of Sir Henry

Selwyn Ibbotson, to enquire into 'The Constitution, Efficiency, Emoluments and Finances of the Metropolitan Fire Brigade.' It had been precipitated not by the representations of Shaw and others concerned with fire in London so much as the reports coming in from other countries of a spate of major fires in Vienna, Berlin, Boston, Chicago and New York which had been fanned by strong winds and caused immense devastation.

Shaw was one of many witnesses who gave evidence, and, not one to mince words, he told this Committee bluntly that in the ten years of the Brigade's existence, 640 men had resigned through sickness, bad pay, long working hours, lack of superannuation and the miserly attitude of the Board of Works towards pensions for the widows and children of men killed on duty. When the Brigade had started there had been a long waiting list of applicants wanting to join. Now there was none and recruiting was a nightmare. It was not unusual for men to be on duty for 120 hours without a break. There was no statutory time off. His men were, to all intents and purposes, on duty or on call for 24 hours of every day of every year. If they had any time off at all it was regulated by the goodwill of their Station Officer and the number of fires now occurring.

Bitterly he pointed out that it cost £100 to train a London fireman, and in the past ten years, £60,000 had been wasted on men lost to the Brigade. Since he had sent the Home Secretary his plans for the new fire service in 1865, the population of London had increased by 17%, yet he had 84 fewer men than he had suggested then as an absolute working minimum. What he now needed for an efficient firefighting force for London was 931 men manning 330 engines and 200 escapes. He had nowhere near that number (and to be honest, had no hope whatsoever of achieving it).

Among the men who supported him at the Inquiry were his two faithful senior officers, First Class Engineers William Port and George Duck. Both men emphasised the misery of the firemens' lives, the endless hours of being confined to the station with a half crown fine if they set foot outside. For a young man, it was virtually impossible to get acquainted with a girl without breaking the rules – or meeting her at the back door of the fire station, not the most romantic setting with horses snuffling in the background and the bells liable to go down at any moment. The only women allowed in any station were the wives and daughters – and they had to keep out of the way in their own quarters. Shaw, with his insistence on discipline, kept a book showing the various offences his men committed against the rules and it's small wonder that one of the most frequent at this time was 'encouraging a female in his watch box,' – with considerably more 'sinning' when the small 'boxes' were replaced with

somewhat larger huts containing a bed.

The Board of Works retorted that there would be enough men if Shaw were not so meticulous in expecting them to polish their engines and equipment every day and that it was his strict discipline which had driven many of them away. They blustered over pensions, but several cases which underlined the Board's meanness had occurred at that time and they were in a poor position to argue.

One of these which had brought a particular outcry concerned Fireman Joseph Ford, who had been on watch with a street fire escape on the night of October 7th 1871 when he was called to a fire over a chemist's shop in Grays Inn Road. Despite the intensity of the smoke and flames, he ran his ladder up to the top window and one by one, carried five people down to safety. He was almost exhausted when he heard the screams of another woman, climbed back to rescue her but half way down she slipped from his grasp. He made sure that she fell safely into the arms of the rescuers below, but his belt became entangled in the mesh of the chute attached to the back of the ladder and, trapped against the flaming building, he was roasted alive in full view of the crowds until, in agony, he managed to break away and fall to the ground. He died soon afterwards and Shaw, in his daily Record Book, describes in detail the accident and the ceremonial attached to his funeral including the order of his procession with detachments of firemen and police.

Almost certainly under the influence of the publicity surrounding his heroism, the Board of Works awarded his widow a pension of £1 a week. However, the press and ballad mongers gave the event massive (and justified) publicity, while the 'Graphic' went further and published a heart-rending poem which ended:

'He falls! He falls! Is there none to save?
Ah! Cruel to think that one so brave
Who snatched six souls from a fiery grave,
Should perish by the same.

Not really cruel. If Providence
In place of our dull earthly sense,
More godlike eyes had given;

Like Jacob's Ladder years ago,
Perchance the fire escape would glow
With angels passing to and fro
To point the way to Heaven.'

The ensuing public subscription raised £1,000 for his widow, whereupon the Board of Works decided that she was sufficiently provided for and cancelled her pension.

In another instance, an Engineer named Radford, a

married man with a family, had contracted consumption –
tuberculosis – which was made worse by his working
conditions. When he became too ill to continue his duties his
pay was cut to 15 shillings (75p) a week and when he died
his widow was given an outright payment of £20 and told
that she was lucky because in some cases widows were only
allowed £2.

The men repeatedly asked for some kind of superannuation scheme, but to no avail and in 1874 a group of them got
together to send the Board a '*Memorial*' which read (still in
the cringing tones of their predecessors in the insurance
brigade, begging for boots):

'We...view with consternation and alarm the position
we hold with regard to the future of ourselves and our
families, in the event of our becoming incapacitated,
either through accident, ill health or old age, from further
service.

We therefore beg leave to remind your honourable
Board that last year we humbly petitioned you to
consider an appeal made by us to lay down a scale of
pensions and received an answer to the effect that the
Board were not then prepared to do so; and also that
since that time several of our men have broken down,
and have been dismissed from the service without any
provision whatever for their future; and therefore it is
that we desire most respectfully and seriously once more
to draw your attention to the great necessity which
exists of adopting a scale of pensions, whereby any one
of us, through any of the above causes, or, in case of
death, our wives and families may be entitled to receive
a pension according to the position held by us at the
date of our incapacity....'

Their requests were modest – a contributory pension
scheme; a pension of five-eighths of his pay for any man who
was so disabled on duty as to be unable to earn his living;
retirement payment for each year of service and a widow's
pension, as of right, for the wives of men killed on duty.

Again, they were totally ignored by the Board.

There was no doubt that the Select Committee was
impressed with the pension problem, just as the long hours
of duty had worried them. In the latter case, though, it was
not the effect of the long hours of work on the mens' health
or family life which bothered them, but the possibility that it
might prevent them from attending church on Sundays.
Several witnesses were closely questioned as to whether
their hours of duty affected this.

After a year of evidence, during which time the Board of
Works had suddenly and miraculously come up with a
pensions scheme for the MFB, the Committee produced its
recommendations. They thought that the hastily cobbled

together pension plan for the firemen was a good idea and
should be put into force. They agreed that Shaw was right
and he had far too few men, but suggested no action to be
taken. Then, for no apparent reason whatsoever, they
wanted the Brigade to be transferred from the control of the
Board of Works and taken over by the Metropolitan Police,
with a special Assistant Commissioner in charge.

They also recommended:

That the halfpenny rate should be increased to one
penny to include the new combined Police Force and Fire
Brigade.

That a single authority should be set up to control water
supplies.

That hydrants should be fitted throughout London
immediately.

That existing theatres should be made safer from fire
hazards and that newly built theatres should incorporate
specific fire prevention and safety devices; that theatres
should be inspected regularly and that anyone breaking
fire regulations should be prosecuted.

The Report caused uproar. Shaw was furious. The Board
of Works instantly issued a statement insisting that there
was no evidence that change of control of the Fire Brigade to
the Police was wanted by the Board or the Police. The 1862
Committee had recommended a Police-controlled fire brigade but the Government had turned it down then, with no
disastrous results which might justify such a change now.
'To declare what was done then was a mistake should be
supported by strong evidence of failure and by the most
cogent reasons' it argued.

It was no more than a storm in a fire bucket. Yet again,
the whole exercise had been a waste of time as none of the
recommendations were put into effect, other than to speed
up the installation of fire hydrants in the streets.

Despite all this, Shaw carried on 'leading from the front'.
He said that when he first came to London he had, (like
Braidwood) risen at 3 am and walked from Watling Street to
stations as far off as Kensington or Rotherhithe to train the
men or instruct them in the management of the engines and
equipment. Later, his walks began at 7 am and others
helped with the instruction courses.

By 1878, the Watling Street Headquarters which had
been adequate for the small LFEE were becoming far too
small. The piece of waste ground at the rear of the building,
used as a drill yard, was no longer available and some new
central station had to be found. Shaw, determined to raise
his own status and that of his Brigade, demanded adequate
quarters for the Service and, for himself, a house with a

minimum of sixteen bedrooms. In the event, he was provided with a fine house, but had to make do with slightly less in the way of sleeping accommodation.

The site chosen was 1¾ acres of ground on the site of the old Winchester House in Southwark Bridge Road comprising the original buildings which exist to this day (1992) and a new fire station adjoining them. At one time it had formed part of Southwark Park, the property of the Bishop of Winchester and during the period of the Great Plague, in 1665, it was used as a burial ground for victims of the disease – the explanation for the grisly relics which still come to light every time the forecourt is dug up. It seems that the area became popular when a man called Thomas Finch discovered a spring there in 1770. He snapped up the land cheaply, claimed that the spring had medicinal qualities, laid out the land round it as a pleasure garden, built an octagonal house, installed an organ, provided

orchestral music and invited the public in. It became known as 'Finch's Grotto' until it was eventually sold to a man named Williams who added spectacular firework displays to the other attractions, but on such a scale that he eventually went bankrupt. For a short period it was a public house, which bore on its front a board with the verses:

'Here herbs did grow and flowers sweet;
But now 'tis called St George's Street.'

The nearby St Saviour's church acquired the site then for a workhouse and much of this building still stands. In the early 1800's it was bought for a hat factory by a Mr Rawlinson Harris, MP for Southwark, who erected two houses on the site, one of which, the present Winchester House, he used as his own residence. The whole area was well known to Charles Dickens. Lant Street, opposite, was where Bob Sawyer's party took place, Marshalsea Debtors'

Southwark headquarters of Captain Shaw's MFB. (LFCDA.)

Prison, Mint Gate and the Rules of the Mint ran where Marshalsea Road now stands while Quilp Street was named after another of Dickens' characters.

The magazine '*The Builder*' described the new development in its issue of 15th June 1878:

'Winchester House, as it originally stood, set back from the road, formed three sides of a quadrangle. What has been done principally in the way of new building is that a block has been added to each of the wings. This new addition, on the front line, represents the engine station, writing room and watch room on the ground floor, which is capable of containing the largest engines and the three storeys above are intended as quarters for some of the men and officers. There is a watch tower, 78 feet high springing out of the block, with communication from the top to the watch-room by a speaking tube. Up aloft on this tower and commanding a good view in every direction, a watch will be kept so that a fire illumination anywhere will itself be an alarm that will put everything in order for turning out when the exact intelligence comes.

The front part of Winchester House is devoted to the use of Captain Shaw, the frontage to the road where the garden was, being used as a fire escape yard and the other two sides of the edifice looking into the quadrangle, are for more quarters for the men and the basements for education, bath and washing rooms and hose-shops. This quadrangle courtyard, a broad open space, will be used for the purpose of exercising the men, especially in fire-escape practice.

There is a dummy front of a house on one side, with window-like apertures at the top, opening on to the roof. The roofs are so arranged with a level platform that the men can practise running about at a considerable height. The other block added contains stabling accommodation for the horses so that the stables are immediately opposite the engine stations and no time will be lost in getting the horses 'put to'.

At the rear of these are a large smithy, workshops and store room while there are several outbuildings including a long fire-escape shed. The buildings are of brick, dressed with stone. The alterations and additions have all been completed within 12 months, the contractors being Messrs Hook & Oldrey of Kensal New Town, and the architect is Mr G Vulliamy, assisted by Mr Mott.

The ground with the buildings upon it cost the MBW £35,000 which was increased to about £38,000 by the

Bearded look-out on Southwark HQ tower. (Guildhall Library, Corporation of London.)

purchase of certain leaseholds and trade interests. The cost of the buildings is £32,000, making the total about £70,000.

There is accommodation for 52 firemen, (28 married, 24 single) 14 horses, 16 engines and 20 fire escapes.'

Although it provided the latest in contemporary luxury, it had no telephones, (they had only been patented two years earlier), no fire alarms nor any electric light. Communications between the new Headquarters and the other fire stations was by telegraph – a large and cumbersome piece of equipment like a clock with the letters of the alphabet instead of numbers and a brass pointer in the middle. The sender of the message turned the pointer to each letter of the message he wished to send until it registered in a notch, checking the accuracy of the message on a smaller clock face nearby. If this showed the letter '*R*', for '*Repeat*' they had to start again. If it was correctly received the letters '*OK*' appeared. It was not the fastest of communication methods.

The Brigade – and the Shaw family – moved in and Shaw now had a fine carriage with two horses – fire brigade greys – to draw it and a top-hatted coachman 'on the box'.

10
Crest of The Wave

THE MOVE TO SOUTHWARK PUT SHAW ON THE CREST of the wave. One feels that he almost relished his battles with the authorities, for whom he had scant regard or respect. His home was beautifully furnished and kept by Mrs Shaw and her daughters with a modest staff of servants (and, thanks to the help of Shaw's grandson, Sir Bernard Shaw, some of it, at least, has now been restored to its original state). Shaw had his own bedroom – presumably to avoid disturbing his wife when he dashed off on one of his nocturnal fire calls, from which she was rumoured to be totally excluded. Here, he kept a row of uniforms, hanging in a neat line, ready to change into after each soaking, and a row of jackboots 'standing erect, shoulder to shoulder, like a well-drilled regiment.' He worked at a desk 'surrounded by innumerable speaking tubes' which kept him in touch with the rest of the building and when anyone wanted to contact him they blew up the tube which sounded a whistle to alert him. Like Braidwood, he had a '*blower*' as these primitive telephones were nicknamed, over his bed to rouse him in the night if a fire call came through.

His days were often spent inspecting buildings, and particularly theatres, for the vulnerability of these 'palaces of entertainment', their audiences and actors, worried him. He knew of some appalling theatre fires abroad in the 19th century. One, in St Petersburg, with 800 casualties; one in Karlsruhe in 1847 with 631 casualties and another, in China, with 1,670 people dead and injured.

London's theatre fires had, fortuitously, been less severe, but they were certainly numerous. Drury Lane had been one of the greatest victims; Astley's Amphitheatre had been destroyed by fire in 1794, 1803, 1830 and 1841. During the 19th century alone, fire had broken out in (and usually caused extensive damage to) the Surrey Theatre; Covent Garden (twice); the Royalty; the English Opera House (later to become the Lyceum); the Argyle Rooms (a particularly bad fire); the Garrick; the Islington Fields; The Pavilion,

Whitechapel; The Standard, Her Majesty's in the Haymarket and many smaller venues.

Voluminous stage curtains were seldom fire retardant, (although an assortment of methods for fireproofing fabric had been known and used for at least 200 years). Footlights were simple gas jets or candles; carpenters heated their pots of glue over naked flames; paint shops, stores and wardrobe rooms were all packed together behind the scenes as the managers prepared their extravagant productions, some of the most dangerous of which were intended as a token of praise for the fire brigade.

Typical of these in 1884 (the year in which 1,200 people were killed when 41 theatres burned down across the world), was a production at the Pavilion in London. Under the glowing headline '*Fire Fighting reaches the theatre*', the magazine '*The Metropolitan*' reported:

'Mr Fred Abrahams has produced at the Pavilion "The Streets of London", a performance which has not been excelled in any of the West-end theatres. Viewed from the auditorium, the whole stage appears to be in flames from top to bottom and the destruction of the theatre itself seems to be imminent..... The modus operandi is as follows:

'The house to be destroyed is placed towards the front of the stage and perforated gas pipes are attached to the framework to increase the flames. At a convenient distance behind the scene, an iron frame is set up and covered with loosely bound tow, saturated with a light spirit such as naphthalide; a gallery, upon which are pans containing coloured fire, runs across the upper part of the doomed house. A "sycopodium pot" is used to kindle the fire. The pot is made in the shape of a large pepper box and contains a sponge, saturated with spirit, attached to a wire. This fire pot is jerked about at different points of the stage and a very good representation of an outbreak of fire is produced. The tow on the iron screen is now ignited and in a few minutes the stage presents the appearance of a building which has succumbed to the fiery elements!....... It is at this juncture that one of Messrs Merryweather and Sons "London Brigade" Steam Engines with a full complement of firemen, dashes upon the scene, drawn by a couple of horses with steam at full pressure and whistle blowing. Two lines of hose are run out, the firemen attack the flames which are rapidly extinguished and the curtain drops.... In order to obviate all chances of danger, firemen are stationed in the wings throughout the performance with hoses attached to the high pressure fire-main in the theatre.'

Small wonder that Shaw, deeply concerned, toured the London theatre scene imploring and exhorting the owners to look out for the high risks which they were taking, and in 1878, after reports had swept the country of a disastrous fire which had killed 283 people in a Brooklyn Theatre, he published his book 'Fires in Theatres', which at least stirred the government into adding theatre safety to the 'brief' of its 1877 Select Committee (whose findings were, for the most part and yet again, conveniently set aside). True, an Amending Act the following year gave the Board of Works power to 'require' alterations where necessary in existing theatres, but these applied only to theatres above a certain size and no more than 'moderate expenditure' could be insisted on. Even this small piece of legislation brought bitter complaints from theatre owners and other interested parties. Nor did they affect the scores of Music Halls where the poorer Londoners packed together for their entertainment in buildings which were often more dangerous than theatres.

In 1880, a fire in which more than 500 people died at the Ring Theatre in Vienna spurred the Government to ask the Board of Works to report on what was needed to be done to all London theatres to make them safe – regardless of the expense. They, in turn, passed the task to Shaw.

Immediately, he set to work, demanding detailed drawings of 41 theatres in the London area plus information on all the relevant facts he needed for protection of the actors and audiences from fire, and for their safe exit should one break out. It was a heavy task – even for Shaw with his acknowledged superhuman energy. (He seldom needed more than three hours sleep a night.) When the MFB was ordered to take over the work of the RSPLF with only 48 hours notice in 1867, he and his men had worked for 100 hours without a break, but the theatre investigation was worse than this and in April 1882 he was reporting to his employers:

'....the labour and responsibility are so great and have been so continuous that I own to being almost overwhelmed by them.'

He sought help from the Civil Service, suggesting that the Lord Chamberlain's Department and the Home Office might lend a hand, since they were being paid to control the theatres. As he might have expected, help was not forthcoming and rather than leave London theatre-goers at further risk, he and his staff of working firemen carried on, completing the inspection and producing a detailed report in seven months.

It ran to 370 pages and shows why, for once, he had been reduced to admitting that he was almost totally exhausted and in need of help. The findings were, in some cases, quite shocking. The theatres in which the greatest stars of the Victorian stage performed were often death traps, including some in which it took more than ten minutes to evacuate the audience. In the Strand Theatre, Shaw found false wooden ceilings, defective gas and water supplies and fittings and he reported 'the theatre, under its present conditions, would, if once lighted, burn as quickly as a match box or a prepared bonfire and is absolutely unsafe for the reception of an audience.' It was immediately rebuilt. The Prince of Wales Theatre, known as 'the Dust Hole', had a wall in imminent danger of collapse, unsafe lath and plaster walls between the stage and auditorium, dangerous wooden floors plus defective firefighting apparatus and water supply. Again, immediate action had to be taken.

As a result of Shaw's report, some of the worst buildings were closed down immediately and active measures put in hand to make the rest safer. The success of his immense task was indicated by the fact that in the 17 previous years there had been 14 major theatre fires in London and in the 17 years following the Report there were seven. Sadly, one of these came within six months of the Report's publication.

Meantime, and despite his criticisms of theatre safety, Shaw himself was an enthusiastic theatre-goer and on 25th November 1882, soon after returning from a trip to New York, he attended the first night of the new Gilbert and Sullivan comic-opera 'Iolanthe' at the Savoy Theatre. WS Gilbert, the librettist, apparently, noticed Shaw sitting in the stalls before the curtain went up, and took immediate action to amend the libretto. So it happened that as the Fire Chief relaxed in his front seat, the Fairy Queen stepped down from the stage and, to his surprise and embarrassment addressed the song which was supposed to be aimed at the sentry, Private Willis, to Shaw himself, trilling:

'On fire that glows with heat intense
I turn the hose of common sense
And out it goes at small expense.

We must maintain our fairy law
That is the main on which to draw –
In that we gain a Captain Shaw!'

Then, in an aside, and an allusion to his reputation with the ladies, she added:

'Oh, Captain Shaw!
Type of true love kept under!
Could they Brigade with cold cascade
Quench my great love I wonder?'

According to his grandson, Bernard, the subject of the solo was furious. In fact, the theme was not unique. Many years before, an old pantomime song was popular in the music halls, with the words:

'My heart's on fire, not all the Fire Brigade could
Subdue the flames, though led by Mr Braidwood...'

Whatever Shaw's feelings, he had little time to brood on them. Only twelve days later, the Alhambra Theatre in Leicester Square went up in flames. Ironically, it had been designed by one of the more responsible theatre architects, CJ Phipps, but nevertheless Shaw, in his report on the theatre, had warned the Board of Works of a number of defects, including the fact that since it was not divided up by party walls, any fire which was not extinguished within five or six minutes would be disastrous, although he felt that the external walls were of sound material and construction and appeared to be capable of resisting any fire or shock which might occur.

This was the fire at which the Prince of Wales missed death by minutes when the walls did collapse. The fire had broken out several hours after the end of the performance of a *'gorgeous, unrivalled spectacle, The Silver City of Atalanta, with the silver-clad Amazons from Babil and Bijou... Last 3 nights of Marian, the Amazon Queen......'* At 1 am the theatre fireman, on his regular tour of inspection, discovered that fire had taken hold in the balcony stalls. The call reached Chandos Street fire station at 1.05 am and by the time its engines had arrived the Alhambra was blazing 'like a Christmas tree.' The telegraph clicked at breakneck speed as steamers galloped in from the entire length and breadth of the Brigade's area, bringing with them not only the flower of London's noble fire brigade but the Prince of Wales himself, no doubt riding one of the engines from Chandos Street. He was reported to have been seen balanced on the roof of the theatre attacking the fire with a hose and branch in the thick of the smoke and flames. He had safely reached the ground when the cry of 'run for your lives' went up and with a rumble and roar, the roof on which he had been working

collapsed, killing two of Shaw's firemen. Remarkably, no newspaper included the activities of the Prince in their reports of the fire next day, but Jack While, the famous Fire Correspondent of *The Times*, included it in his memoirs many years later and it became a legend among the men of the Brigade, not least because of the cigars which the Prince's aide always distributed after a 'good' fire.

Theatres were not alone among the problems facing the Brigade. Warehouses were still a regular source of fires including some which produced unusual – and irritating – consequences. A burning pepper store devastated the crews when it exploded, scattering pepper dust across the area and reducing the men to helpless sneezing. The weight of water playing on a burning flour mill brought down the roof, covered the men in white flour and buried the whole fire ground in a quagmire of flour and water paste. Fire in a perfume factory sent them home with their uniforms reeking suspiciously of the latest expensive scent while the sparkling brass on the engines, helmets and equipment reacted with fumes from a burning spice warehouse and turned green. It took hours of 'elbow grease' to restore them to their customary scintillating state.

Meanwhile, Shaw and the Prince of Wales were setting a

Chandos Street fire station. (LFCDA.)

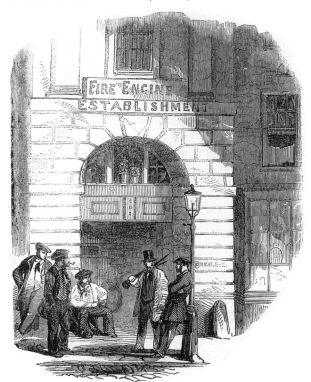

fashion for firefighting among their Society friends. The sight of the gallant men of the MFB, galloping through London with, as Hilaire Belloc put it '*Courage high and hearts aglow*' warmed the hearts of the Victorian populace who respected them as heroes. There were calls for paintings of firemen to be hung in the Royal Academy, and famous artists of the period including Sir John Millais were among those who produced heroic scenes, often showing a gallant fireman emerging from a blazing building with an unconscious young woman, clad in a white nightgown, draped across his arms.

Millais is said to have been irritated by the 'drumbeating' for the armed services and to have written to a friend: 'soldiers and sailors have been praised a thousand times. My next picture shall be of a fireman.' He travelled round London watching firemen at work and finally burned planks in his studio to obtain the most lifelike effects for his painting '*The Rescue*', now in the National Gallery of Victoria in Melbourne.

The *Times* launched an appeal for books for firemen to improve their educational standard and Queen Victoria was among many who responded, sending in a number of volumes including her own '*Leaves from my Life in the Highlands*' and even '*More Leaves from my Life in the Highlands*'.

In this heyday of the patriotic ballad, the billiard rooms of many a fire station rang to such renderings as '*The Song of the Fire Brigade*':

'*Our soldiers and sailors are gallant and brave*
And they well serve their Queen on the land and the wave.
With nerves that are strong and with hearts that are true,
And we gladly give honour where honour is due.

But tonight I would ask you to think upon those
Who go forth to fight the most deadly of foes;
Who boldly, with danger and death undismay'd
And our blessings are breathed for the Fire Brigade.

When the terrible flames are extending around
And no other succour or help can be found,
Our men and our children are saved by their aid
And our blessings are breathed for the Fire Brigade.

With their lives in their hands they advance to the spot,
Though the rafters are creaking and walls are red-hot
And the march of the cruel destroyer is stayed
By the daring and skill of the Fire Brigade.

Their hardships are many, but few are their rants,
And well by their conduct they merit our thanks,
Their deeds are heroic and never shall fade –
Three cheers and one more for the Fire Brigade!'

Fireman as hero in advertisement. (LFCDA.)

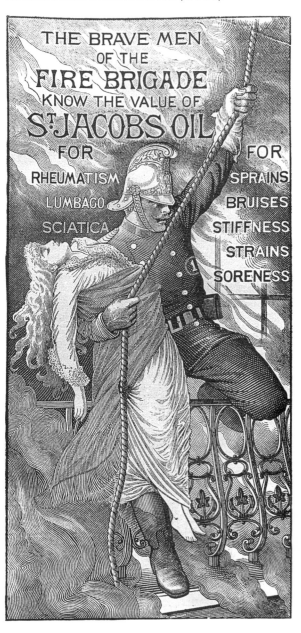

Their hardships were, indeed, many, but although they ranted among themselves, there is no doubt that they were aware of the high regard in which the public held them, and that they respected and admired their '*Skipper*' or, as he came to be known, '*the Long'un*'. His reliance on discipline was emphasised by the pattern he had laid down for their duties, so that there was never any confusion no matter how large and terrifying the fire facing them from the day they entered the Brigade. All too familiar with the horrors that a great fire might present, with smoke and flames and the screams of trapped victims ringing in a fireman's ears, he wrote:

'Occasions may arise when the maddening influence, which the scene of a fire seems to have on persons unaccustomed to it, may place serious obstacles in the way of a fireman carrying out his duty in the mode here indicated' *(the mode, laid down by regulation, was children first, then women, with their skirts, if time allowed, fastened round their ankles to prevent any immodesty, or getting them caught up on the escapes, then men).*

'At such times, a fireman must be resolute and determined in having his commands obeyed, and nothing must induce him to allow the men, of their own accord, to take precedence as they will almost always try to do.

'If he be perfectly cool and collected, as he ought to be, his mere command will generally be sufficient, as there is a sort of instinct in most persons which, even in the agony and madness of a panic, teaches them to follow and obey a man who speaks and acts with the resolution and power and confidence of knowledge.

'At such a moment, there is an important duty to be performed, that of saving the greatest possible number of lives; and very little time in which to carry out that duty, probably not more than one or two minutes at the utmost; and there is also a principle at stake, that of giving the first help to those who need it most; and if the fireman should hesitate or vacillate in the smallest degree, he throws away the very power on which alone his success in saving life depends, and that at the critical moment for coping with the exigencies of which he has been specially appointed, trained and trusted....

To do this work properly, a fireman must be strong, active, quick, fearless and intelligent; but above all, he must be resolute.....'

Recruits spent three months in classes and daily drill at the Southwark headquarters, learning about engines and escapes and practising how to use them, wrestling with the specific knots which firemen used, discovering how to hold a jumping sheet for rescue work, how to scramble safely about roofs and above all, the special skills of entering a house, using the axe with minimum damage and restricting the use of water to a minimum. Again, Shaw had made his instructions clear.

They also learned some basic first aid for the injured. Commands were given in naval fashion, brief and easy to understand in the heat of the moment. Engines were numbered according to their station, so that orders like '*Down with number 60*'. '*Avast number 44*', '*Knock-off nearside delivery of number 5*' brought an instant reaction. Only when they were completely competent were the new firemen given a number and posted to a station and only then could they begin firefighting as professionals. Even the brass numbers worn on the breast of their tunics were significant, with the lowest indicating to an officer at a fire that he was dealing with a man who was new to the brigade, and changing according to time served so that the higher the number, the more experienced the man.

By the mid-1880's life on the stations was settled – if still hard. Most LFB fire stations had five pairs of horses, with two always '*on watch*', their collars hitched to the roof with a rope to ease the weight on their necks and other ropes attached to their blankets so that when the alarm sounded they could be released instantly to run to the shafts. The famous '*London*' manual appliance had been joined by a growing number of 'steamers', each of which had its crew of one officer, one coachman and four firemen. *No 1* was the officer who stood on the nearside of the engine, by the brake. *No 2* stood by the brake on the off-side. *No 3* stood behind the officer and *No 4* behind *No 2*. *No 5* dealt with the boiler fire and kept up steam, standing on a step at the back. The coachman handled the reins, sitting at the front.

As soon as they reached a fire, 1 and 2 made sure that the brakes were on, then went to the fire; the coachman removed the horses out of danger and if necessary rode back with messages to the nearest station (although eventually portable telephones were carried on the engines and plugged in to the nearest fire post in the street.) No 3 opened the tool box and passed out the hydrant shaft, hoses, etc, while No 4 received the hose and connected it to the water main, either in a dam or tank of canvas or directly into the main. No 3 took the delivery hose and while No 5 connected the suction pipe, fixed the branch or nozzle to the hose with the help of No 4. Between them, they then took the completed hose and nozzle to the fire itself, connecting new lengths of hose as they were required and, if necessary, keeping up the pressure with a succession of pumps.

Meantime, the engineer was raising a head of steam ready for the water to open up as soon as the signal was given. At the biggest fires, coal carts would be sent along to keep the boiler fires going.

London 'steamers' were small and nippy, able to twist and turn in the narrow streets of the City, but while they were normally able to throw 300 gallons a minute using a 1 inch nozzle, it was known that some other big cities, like Liverpool, with similar problems of big dock and factory fires like London, had bigger engines capable of throwing considerably more water through a 2¼ inch nozzle. American brigades also worked on the principle of using bigger engines which could deliver more water through bigger nozzles, but London, with its powerful links with the insurance companies, was always reluctant to use more water than was absolutely necessary, feeling that this could, in many cases, cause more damage than the fire itself.

On the whole, firemens' families lived in reasonable conditions, the children playing in the yard until the fire call came, when they knew that they had to make themselves scarce immediately. There was, however, one pattern of fire service life which affected the children considerably. Every two years, the men moved to another station in a new area so that they might gain experience of different types of fire. So it was, that a man might go from Manchester Square, with its big houses and shops, to Rotherhithe with its docks and warehouses or to Whitefriars or Cannon Street for City offices and the intensive workshops of these areas. Few children spent more than two years in a school before being uprooted and having to start again with new teachers and above all, new schoolmates, many of whom had already formed into their own small 'gangs' which were loath to welcome the newcomers. 'Father's moves meant that fire station families were a tight unit, keeping themselves to themselves and not making many friends in the neighbourhood where they lived' recalled Mrs Edith Want, who had been born and bred in the fire stations of Victorian and Edwardian London. 'Single men were eventually allowed to see their young ladies within the station itself if they were seriously "walking out" together, and two wooden chairs were placed under the station staircase for them to sit on and talk.' The main source of entertainment was the 'dance' held in the billiard room on Friday nights. Her father, Peter Gray, had four children, and space was always short in their LFB flats. But when her brother, Douglas, developed appendicitis it was the Fireman King's surgeon who carried out one of the earliest operations on the boy, without fee. Their lives were hard, toys were often home-made from scraps of wood, and there were no clothes for relaxing in. 'The boys wore sailor suits, made by mother, for much of

Firemen and families had no money for leisure clothes. Peter Gray and family, c. 1906. (LFCDA & author.)

their lives and father wore his uniform whether he was on duty or off.'

Food was basic, heavily dependent on the skill of the wives for variety and enlivened occasionally by bags of bones, often scrounged from sausage factories or hotel kitchens, and made into soups and, if a station were in a wealthy area, by basins of 'dripping' (fat from roasted meat) passed on by obliging cooks. Fresh fruit was too expensive to buy, but the children sometimes scavenged it from the markets. Tea was the staple family drink, usually with condensed milk. The average fireman's family diet would have reduced a modern dietician to a state of distraction. Nevertheless, many of the children grew up to live long and healthy lives.

For Shaw himself, relief from the stifling pressures of London life lay in his frequent visits abroad. Paris was a favourite jaunt, with visits to his friends the *Pompiers*. In 1871, during the time of the Commune, he wrote to the Foreign Office in Whitehall offering to organise a firefighting force to travel to the French capital to support the authorities there. Typically, the letter was sent without any prior consultation with the Board of Works, who were not amused. However, they soon received an official request for help from the French Government (prompted, perhaps, by the hand of Shaw) and they did, then, agree to send as many men and engines as were needed. (The upheaval had ended before the London fire force could be sent and Shaw, meanwhile, had swanned off privately, to be cheered by a guard of honour of Sapeurs Pompiers shouting '*Vive le Capitaine Shaw*' as he set off on his journey home.)

This was the year in which the Foreign Office asked him to visit Egypt to advise on fire prevention in Cairo, soon after the opening of the Suez Canal. He evidently carried out his duties with customary enthusiasm, not only advising but drilling a fire force and reporting on fire protection in Alexandria, Ismailia and Port Said too.

It was during the 1880's that he made most of his visits overseas, visiting France, Austria and Spain and crossing the Atlantic several times to visit his colleagues – trips which he obviously enjoyed, but which his American friends might not always have welcomed wholeheartedly.

About this time, Shaw was on immensely friendly terms with the Prince of Wales and had, indeed, been invited to Buckingham Palace to present a display before the Prince and his Princess, the Duke and Duchess of Edinburgh and an assortment of politicians. He arrived with nearly a fifth of his force – three fire escapes, thirteen steam fire engines and five manuals, plus 150 men 'in fire repressing order' who immediately displayed their skills by climbing all over the back of the Palace (breaking one or two balustrades in the process), rescuing each other from a mock blaze and demonstrating their chair knot system. '*The Princess of Wales*' (the beautiful Alexandra) '*spoke frequently to Captain Shaw – happy man!*' – commented a contemporary report, while others noted that he had '*discussed technicalities with the Prince and Mr Merryweather who supplied the London Brigade with much of its equipment.*'

In the following year the Prince visited the United States to attend one of the great parades of firemen in New York (where it was not unusual for 1000 companies of volunteer firemen to parade at one time). Edward undoubtedly reported back to his chum, Shaw, not failing to mention that at midnight the whole city was illuminated by a torchlight procession of firemen, all in full uniform. In 1882, Shaw set sail for New York and started the strong link of co-operation – and sometimes rivalry – which has existed between that city and London ever since.

London's Chief Officer must have noticed somewhat wryly that New York, still a small city compared with his own, had, according to its Chief Engineer's report: '14 engineers, 52 engine companies containing 2,196 members, 55 hose companies containing 1,184 members and 18 hook and ladder companies containing 568 members, giving a total of 3,960 men engaged in controlling and extinguishing fires in New York alone.' In addition, they had 27 steam fire engines in good condition when London had, at that time only a dozen; 19 hand engines, 55 horse carriages, 18 hook and ladder trucks plus 76 assorted hose, coal and wood tenders.

Firefighting in America was part of the old Colonial tradition, and had, for many years, been the work of volunteers who considered it not just a necessary service but a social grace. Many of America's greatest sons including George Washington, Thomas Jefferson, Paul Revere and Benjamin Franklin had all served their time in the Fire Volunteers. Pennants and decorative panels at the time of the American Revolution often carried the motto: '*In war, militiamen; in peace, firemen.*'

It was the National Convention of Fire Engineers in Cincinatti which had tempted Shaw to cross the Atlantic again, during the course of which he was made a life member of the National Association of Fire Engineers of America, and there is no doubt that his presence caused a stir. For once, we hear of his voice, when the Fireman's Journal of America commented 'he is apparently over six feet in height and his blonde hair, moustache and Imperial have now a strong sprinkling of silver... Born in Ireland, he has been in England long enough to acquire a very decided London accent...' They also felt that he was critical of American firemen – which Shaw hotly denied. However, he had, when the fire chiefs of New York put on a special show for him to prove how quickly their 'steamers' could turn out, shrewdly realised that it was a 'fix', pulled the wrong lever and had the personal satisfaction of seeing the men, primed to follow the original plan, go to the wrong destination. It was not, perhaps, wholly accidental that later in the visit, a display by water towers – which were virtually unknown in London at the time – went wrong and somehow Shaw was drenched to the skin.

His speech to the Cincinatti Convention seemed harmless enough, if remarkably prophetic. He described his Brigade in London, the problems of the water supply and his concern over the increasing height of buildings, in both countries.

'There is nothing I should like so much as to see buildings erected not over 60 feet high' *he explained, adding with immense foresight:* 'But this is not likely. There is no chance for it. I believe that before 20 and 30 years are over our heads, we shall still see higher buildings. I am prepared in London, if I live long enough, to see buildings 130, 140 and 150 feet high. I look upon it as an absolute certainty.' *(By the 1990's London's highest building, at Canary Wharf in the Isle of Dogs, was 800 feet high.)* 'It is

becoming perfectly gigantic . . . . . . You have the means for the enlarging of your areas here which don't exist in the old countries and until you have exhausted these areas you may, perhaps, keep down the height of your buildings, but the moment the area is exhausted, you will have to go up higher as we have done, as Hamburg has done and Berlin and even Paris. All firemen, and particularly the younger ones, should look to what will happen in the next 20 years and make their arrangements accordingly.'

Although it provoked little reaction at the time, there were some acid comments as Shaw returned to England. He was accused, among other things, of being a dandy and a snob and his Brigade was declared 'a product of way back' which to some extent, was true. On the whole, though, the visit set up some good links between the firemen of the two countries, which included a lively correspondence in 'The Fireman' concerning the relative intelligence of American and London fire horses and dogs during which the Americans vowed that they had a ghost fire engine in San Francisco which would gallop through the mists wreaking

Firemen with station pets. 1909. (LFCDA.)

havoc in the streets, and a fire horse which refused to eat oats on Friday in deference to its driver's Irish-Catholic feelings.

London in turn, swore that it had a dog which could not only down a pint of mild and bitter in one gulp but knew when it was the night before the Queen's birthday and could trot to a special cupboard and drag out the Union Jack, ready to be run up the flagpole next morning.

Many fire stations in both countries had pets – the Americans specialised in dalmatians which ran to the fires alongside the engines, while in London the range over the years included dogs, cats, monkeys, parrots and a goat, while, during the Second World War, pigs and rabbits were added, but mainly to alleviate the boredom and the paucity of the meat ration.

Among the most famous London fire dogs was 'Chance', who belonged to the insurance firemen. He was believed to have been thrown over Blackfriars Bridge as a puppy and rescued by the firemen who treated his mange with tobacco water and cossetted him to such an extent that he devoted his life to running with them to fires and helping them detect victims or, if necessary, dig out the fire plugs. An illustration of the fire at the Houses of Parliament shows him as a solid retriever-size mongrel, pawing at a plug and wearing the brass collar, bought for him by his firemen friends to keep him safe as he moved from one fire station to another on his regular rounds. It was inscribed:

'Stop me not but onward let me jog

For I am Chance, the London firemen's dog.'

At one time it was suggested that the firemen preferred spaniels because they had a cavity above their nose which made them particularly expert at sniffing out unconscious or dead victims at fires. Many of the dogs, like *'Baron'* the Great Dane at Whitefriars, became pets of the families, giving the children rides round the yard when they were not 'on duty'. Usually they ran alongside the engines, and all too many, including *'Baron'*, were killed under the wheels when the appliances had to swerve.

Pets apart, there was always a language difference between London and America and *'The Fireman'* felt obliged to offer a brief translation of terms for the benefit of both sides:

ENGLISH	AMERICAN
Branch pipe	Play pipe
Breeching pipes	Siamese connection
Breeching water valve	Hydrant gates
Fireman's helmet	Fire hat
Buckets	Tin pails
Preventers	Pull-down hooks
Hose clamp	Hose jacket
Ladder hook	Hose suspender
Hose reel	Jumper
Jumping sheet	Life net

Great interest developed between the firemen of the two countries, but on their pay, and with popular air transport nearly a century from fruition, there was no hope, at that time, of them crossing the great 'Pond' which divided them, although Shaw went back to America several times and also entertained their fire chiefs at Southwark.

Back home in London, fires continued. Not all shops were as small as they had been in the past, and one of the biggest, Whiteley's of Bayswater, was particularly unlucky. Five times fire broke out in the store during the 1880's. All the incidents were caused by arson, which was another problem facing the MFB, since almost any business man who fell on hard times seemed to be tempted to recoup his losses by setting fire to his premises and claiming on his insurance.

Whiteley's fires were different, however, and seemed to result from spite or vindictiveness. The last outbreak, in 1887, was the worst when two firemen were killed and twelve firemen and a number of policemen were seriously injured. This was by far the biggest fire to have faced the MFB in its entire existence. At one point a gas main ruptured and exploded, destroying a fire engine as the men tried to cope, struggling through the huge building with its network of gas pipes feeding the lights in every department.

The shortage of men became all too obvious at a conflagration of this immensity. One fireman nearly collapsed after working 108 hours without a break and others were on duty for 24 hours without relief. Altogether, the whole store and 15 adjoining buildings were destroyed, causing a total loss of £525,000 – but the insurance cover was only £16,000 since no company would take on more after Whiteley's previous history of arson. Despite this, it was re-built and re-opened nine months later, such was the resilience of traders in those days.

Among other shopkeepers who suffered heavy loss by fire at that time was Mr Charles Harrod. His staff had been busy dealing with Christmas orders and snow was falling heavily when fire broke out at his premises in Brompton Road on December 8th, 1883. Before the fire brigade could do anything, the building had become a seething mass of flames. Lesser men might have given up, but Charles Harrod was made of sterner stuff. Even as nine steamers were pumping water into the ruins, he salvaged as many orders as he could, retired to a nearby pub, sorted them out and wrote letters to all his esteemed customers which read:

'I greatly regret to inform you that in consequence of the above premises being burnt down, your order will be delayed in the execution a day or two. I hope, in the course of Tuesday or Wednesday next to be able to forward it. In the meantime, may I ask you for your kind indulgence.'

Indulgence he received, all the orders were 'executed' by Christmas, the Harrods reputation for service was started and in record time, he had opened an even larger store, eventually to become the great emporium which was still thriving in the 1990's and where the grandsons of the Victorian firemen helped to save the store at another fire and an IRA attack, many years later.

It was not until the end of this decade that the London firemen's conditions began to improve slightly. Shaw's constant battering at the Board of Works was paying off; they were granted twenty-four hours' leave every two weeks plus seven days holiday a year – unheard of luxury! Pay was still poor and conditions tough, but at least there was a chance to sleep occasionally and to be with their families.

Chandos Street fire station, haunt of the Prince of Wales, had been replaced by the new and handsome Great Scotland Yard station, with its Portland stone facings, still standing a century later, although long since abandoned for firefighting purposes.

Under its dashing and fashionable Chief Officer, the Metropolitan Fire Brigade had been raised from a handful of rough ex-sailors to a force which was loved and respected throughout London, with a strong back-up of steam-powered pumps, noble horses, a small fleet of fire-floats with steam-powered pumps, riverside fire stations and for rescue work, fire escapes throughout their area.

To some extent the Brigade had been brought together not only by Shaw's discipline but by the magazine, 'The Fireman', produced by Merryweather, and another, 'Fire & Water', both of which kept firefighters throughout the world, and especially the British Empire, in touch with what their colleagues were doing, as well as providing details of all the latest developments. It was not through the pages of these magazines, however, that the country learned of the scandal in which Shaw was heavily involved and which could have cost him his career. The writer Anita Leslie describes in detail in her book 'Edwardians in Love', the divorce case of Lord and Lady Colin Campbell in which Shaw, along with several other prominent Victorians, was cited as a co-respondent. Campbell, a barrister and son of the Duke of Argyll, had married a somewhat unusual young lady, referred to during the divorce hearing as 'very popular, attractive and accomplished.' She was heavily involved in the fashionable occupation of Good Works for the Poor, but also fenced,

swam, rode, painted, played a good game of lawn tennis, smoked cigars and cigarettes, posed in the nude for the artist Whistler and had been described as 'a glamorous nymphomaniac.'

During the case, which lasted 18 days in December, 1886, Lord Colin Campbell sued on the grounds of his wife's adultery with four men including the Duke of Marlborough, her doctor, an army General and Captain Shaw. His wife countered by charging him with adultery with their housemaid. It was an odd story, since one of Shaw's daughters had been a bridesmaid at the Campbells' wedding and both families had been close friends.

The jury, faced with a mass of conflicting evidence, including an argument over how much could have been seen by the butler through a keyhole, had no doubts in their minds. They cleared Shaw, who was granted costs. The magazine 'Society' summed up the event:

'Captain Shaw....left the court without a shadow on his fair name and blameless, honourable life'.

(Captain Shaw was fortunate. It was a well-known secret that the Prince of Wales, when he had nothing better to do, would sometimes visit Shaw at Southwark in the evening. The daughter of a subsequent Chief Officer recalled her father describing how Edward – or 'Bertie' as he was known – would arrive at MFB headquarters and leave his coach there while the two hired a hansom cab and in her words: 'both naughty old boys used to go "foraging" together... One day, as they were leaving the gate, a fireman saluted. The Prince turned angrily to Shaw and said "I told you I wanted to come incognito" whereupon Shaw replied "it's all right Sir – he was saluting me!"'.)

After the Campbell case, the Chief Officer must have returned to work heaving a sigh of relief. He was instantly turning his attention to such continuing problems as advising on the fire protection for many of London's major buildings, including St Paul's Cathedral. At his suggestion, two new water mains were reported to have been run from New River Head to the north side of the Cathedral for use in firefighting and, in addition to this, several other precautions were taken by the Cathedral authorities, in co-operation with Merryweathers, who still have the original plans for the work.

In 1860, during Braidwood's time, static water tanks had been installed in the Stone Gallery and the South aisle roof of the Quire.

Later Cathedral records show:

'1867... "Fire Annihilator" installed.' (An early form of fire extinguisher.)

1873... Additional tanks on Stone Gallery and additional

'Extincteurs' and public segment of the dome lined with 'Branum's Patent fire-proof coating'.

1876... Extensive fire precautions installed.

1884... Hydrants installed around base of the Dome.

1888... Fire precautions... Better communication between upper systems and protection of Crypt doors with brick walls and iron plated doors.

By the 1890's, London's firemen were spreading their wings. They had formed a sports club for athletics, a cricket club, a minstrel troupe for concerts and a brass band – the latter two aimed at raising money for the recently formed Widows' and Orphans' Fund. (In 1880 one of the Brigade's admirers, Miss C Morris, had provided 600 guineas (£630) to found the *Morris Fireman's Charity*. Soon after, the title was changed to '*The Captain's Club*' – presumably named after Captain Shaw – and later became the *London Fire Brigade Widows and Orphans Fund*. Members paid 6d (2½p) per week towards it and on the death of a fireman, his widow would receive £50 from the Fund plus £2 a month pension. The fund also paid for the Firemens' Corner in Highgate Cemetery.)

Now, however, a major change had taken place. Under the Local Government Act of 1888, the old Metropolitan Board of Works had breathed its last. In its place, on March 21st 1889, came the new *London County Council*, bringing together elected representatives from all over the capital with a strong political mixture. To this new authority, the Board of Works handed the Metropolitan Fire Brigade lock, stock and barrel, admitting in writing, with a final burst of honesty, that it had been '*left in a condition of insufficiency when the necessities of London are taken into consideration.*'

Shaw had led London's firefighters for nearly 30 turbulent years. He had been injured several times at fires, had fallen off a fire engine more times than he could have counted (anyone who has ridden at speed on a horse-drawn fire engine with its iron-rimmed wheels, will understand why). Gallantly, he faced his new employers who decided that an Annual Parade would be held and medals presented to the Metropolitan firemen by the Princess of Wales.

With his genius for organisation, Shaw would have taken this on, but the new Council decided that it was their duty. The Presentation, scheduled to begin in the early afternoon of Saturday, 25th May 1889 on Horse Guards Parade, was widely advertised and although tickets of admission had been issued in advance to various dignitaries, no barriers had been erected to keep back the crowds who, without such diversions as the cinema, radio or television, poured in by the thousand to see their firemen perform.

Shaw personally mustered his 100 picked men, including the medal winners, but was dumbfounded when the whole event degenerated into a near-riot. The Royal Party, which included Lady Shaw and her family, was bogged down in the crowd and had to fight their way through from Marlborough House. Shaw's daughter was cut off as she tried to present the Princess with a bouquet and had to be rescued by firemen and brought out of the fray on a 'steamer'. The police were powerless, as were the small contingent of troops brought in to help them. All hope of a display by the Brigade was wiped out. Even the Royal guard of honour was knocked sideways by the throng. Eventually, sufficient space was cleared for a handful of fire engines to gallop past before the firemen were hastily handed their medals and the ceremony abandoned.

Never in his life had Shaw or his men been involved in such a fiasco, and one over which he had been completely powerless. He was livid. His men were furious. The crowd were disappointed and one can hardly feel that the Royal Family were best pleased. Questions were asked in Parliament. Eventually the fury subsided and an unbelievably inadequate official statement was issued. There had been, it said, '*some misunderstanding between the LCC and the police.*'

It was about this time that rumblings began to emerge from the City. Whispers of equipment which might not always be as efficient as it should be; of reluctance to snap up new ideas from abroad; slowness in 'turn-outs'. Shaw, as always, stood by his men, but he was shrewd enough to have seen an amber, if not a red light ahead. Before his new bosses could begin to criticise, he struck first, handing in a report containing his extensive – and expensive – plans for the improved fire protection of London. Defiantly, he issued it simultaneously to all the newspapers.

As London grew, he said, he had always been concerned that while some places were within easy reach of several fire stations, others were at a considerable distance from any of the existing points for appliances or escapes. To carry out his plan, he now needed 32 new fire stations involving, apart from the capital sum for sites and buildings, an annual outlay of £32,000 a year. They would also need 15 more 'steamers', 25 manuals, 50,000 feet of hose and other equipment totalling £20,000. There were still 127 escapes, manned only at night but no funds were available for a day service. Shaw felt that escapes should not be more than half a mile apart (more than enough, one feels, considering that they still had to be run to a fire by the man on duty and two volunteers). To allow for this, their numbers should be increased to 472. Allowing three men for every two escapes, the renewal of 26 escapes a year and other expenses, the present cost of £20,320 would have to rise to £75,000 a year for 472 stations manned at night only and to £150,000 if they were to be manned day and night, (a sum considerably more than his entire service was now costing.) If the whole of this scheme were adopted, the cost would be £275,000 p.a. but, as he hastily pointed out, this was infinitely less than the cost of firefighting services in other major cities, including New York. It would, he explained, mean that each citizen of London was paying 1/2d (about 7p) for fire protection while those of New York were paying 5/7d (about 27p) per head.

Under the new Act founding the LCC, restrictions on the use of rates for fire protection had been eased, so that Shaw was somewhat astonished when the Council accepted at least some of his suggestions by levying a higher rate for fire protection. This allowed for new fire stations, particularly on the outskirts of the London area, and 113 more men. Supplies were increased and the installation of hydrants in the streets was stepped up until by the early 1890's there were 2,428 of them. Pressure in the water mains still varied between the seven supplying companies, from 40lbs in some to 75–80 lbs per square inch in others, but by now a new gadget had been devised so that the pressure in all the companies' mains was recorded on a continuous roll of paper at the Southwark headquarters.

The statement had come as a shock to the LFB and a delight to the Press, but other new forces were at work now. Throughout the country workers, tired of being downtrodden, were beginning to organise themselves. 1880 saw the Great London Dock strike, the 'Tanner' strike for 6d (2½p) known as 'a tanner', an hour instead of 5d, which was the first successful attempt to organise unskilled labour. It saw too, an American, Eastman, producing amateur Kodak cameras for use with celluloid film and the birth of Charlie Chaplin. Times were changing.

Now, for the first time in the history of any fire service, London's men threatened to go on strike. Not for shorter hours, not for better conditions, not for higher pay, but for that old fire service bugbear, boots.

The subject matter recalled the insurance men's prayer for boots a century previously, but this was no forelock-pulling plea. The London men should, they claimed, have been issued with new boots for Christmas but no replacements had been forthcoming. They wanted their boots. They were determined to have them, so London could burn and be damned. Suddenly this was a new breed of firemen who, one suspects, might have taken some of their lead from their Chief Officer.

Their threat was effective. The Council sent an urgent letter to the contractors and explained to the men (something which the Board of Works would never have dreamed of doing) that 1,800 pairs of boots had been ordered at 18/- (90p) per pair, made of best leather with soft leather linings and thick leather soles, but the contractor in Northampton had gone bankrupt so that the order had to be placed with a firm in the West End of London. So far, only 130 pairs had arrived. The shock of being treated as human beings had its effect. The strike threat was withdrawn and an uneasy peace ensued.

However, the Brigade which, for years, had for the most part run itself, was now being subjected to interference from above. The new Council wanted to know how its money was being spent and was offering suggestions as to how improvements might be effected. By the beginning of 1891, six senior officers had handed in their resignations. Rumours whisked round London that even Captain Shaw was being asked searching questions about his month-long trips abroad, which he had always justified by pointing out, quite truthfully, that he used them not only as a change from London life but in order to discover more about the latest methods of firefighting abroad. (Nobody who saw his lamp burning throughout the night as he worked at his desk in Southwark, could have suspected that London was not getting value for money. Shaw was no clock-watcher.)

Gradually relations worsened. Nobody has, to this day, discovered what sparked off the final explosion – whether it was spontaneous combustion as opposed to simple friction. The fact remains that on 26th June 1891, Shaw wrote a brief letter to his employers. It read:

M.F.B., Southwark.

'Gentlemen,

Having completed 30 years' service in the brigade, I desire to obtain my pension in accordance with the regulations. I shall, however, be glad to remain in charge for any reasonable time to be agreed on, if your honourable Council consider that such a course will be of advantage to the department, pending the appointment of my successor.

I am, etc.,

Eyre M. Shaw. Chief Officer. MFB.''

After a brief, shocked silence when the letter was read out to them, one member asked if any information could be given as to the reason for Capt Shaw's action. The answer came back that all the information available was contained in the letter.

Another member, Mr Boulnois MP, suggested that there might, at least, have been some expression of regret from the Fire Brigade Committee, at the retirement of Capt. Shaw after 31 years of faithful and meritorious service. The people of London would view with profound regret the retirement of an officer whose place would be difficult to fill. On the other hand, Mr Benn leapt in to say he 'could quite understand Mr Boulnois's desire to advertise his friend, Captain Shaw (cries of "Oh! Oh!") at the expense of those who had done their duty properly ....'

The arguments continued until eventually it was decided that Captain Shaw should be asked to reconsider his decision.

Shaw's response was prompt – and final:

'Gentlemen,

I have received your letter of July 22nd, informing me that you have passed a resolution expressing regret at my retirement and asking me to reconsider my letter of June 26th with a view to withdrawing it. I am much obliged for this compliment, and I do not hesitate to say that I would gladly do anything in my power which would enable me to remain where I am; but I am compelled to look at all the circumstances from a point of view which may not have presented itself to your notice, and I regret to have to express my conviction that, under the existing conditions and terms, I could not continue to hold my position with advantage either to your honourable Council or to myself.

I have the honour to be, Gentleman,

Your obedient Servant,

Eyre M. Shaw. Chief Officer. MFB'

Those who knew Shaw had often remarked on the striking effect of his steely blue eyes. One wonders what sparkle must have been in them as he penned the words 'your obedient servant.' Whatever he had done for his masters over the previous 30 years, he had never, for one moment, been an obedient servant.

The news quickly leaked out to Londoners, many of whom had never, throughout their lives, known another fire leader. The effect was quite remarkable. They were shattered, appalled and wanted to know, above all, why? The answer was never forthcoming, officially. The minority suggested that he was autocratic, dictatorial, that he could see retirement looming and was already feathering his nest by finding himself a good position in the private sector. The vast majority saw it as the commander of a gallant force whose efficiency had been restricted only by the notorious 'Board of Perks' in the past, and now by the equally irritating political in-fighting of the London County Council. Shaw offered no explanation but remained firm in his purpose.

'Punch' printed a fine cartoon, captioned 'The Fire King's Abdication' and alongside it, a long poem which became known all over the world. (For its source, see again 'Rejected Addresses' by J & H Smith. The last line of the second stanza refers to the satirical poem 'The Cloud King' by Monk Lewis.)

'My palate is parched with Pierian thirst,
Away to Parnassus I'm beckoned;
I sing of the glories of Fire King the First!
(Whose fit to be Fire King the Second?)

Captain Eyre Massey Shaw is a Fire King indeed!
Abdicating? Alas that too true is,
For he's a Fire King of a different breed
From the Monarch described by Monk Lewis.

Not mere King of Flames, fiery faced à la Skelt,
Inhabiting regions most torrid,
With a breath that is warranted copper to melt
And eyes indescribably horrid.

He hath not a blazing Bardolphian nose,
He is not flamboyant or furious;
His Crown's a brass helmet, his Sceptre a hose;
True Fire King – all others are spurious.

For he rules the flames; he has done so for long
And now that he talks of retiring
Men mourn for the fire-queller, cautious and strong
Whose reign they've so long been admiring.

Clear-headed, cool Captain, great chief MFB,
All London is sorry to lose you;
As kindly as kingly, from prejudice free;
No danger could daunt or confuse you.

As doffing your helmet and dropping your hose
You bid us farewell, we all own you
As one of Fiend Fire's most redoubtable foes –
As that, thirty years we have known you.

Our Big Boards might jib and our Bigwigs might jaw,
But spite of their tricks and their cackle,
Our Chief we could trust, we were sure that our Shaw
His duty would manfully tackle.

So farewell great Fire King!
Your crown you lay by;
E'en you cannot lay by your credit.
Ignipotent Knight? Well you ought to stand high
In the next Honours List –
Punch has said it!'

Typically, Shaw left as he started, in a blaze of publicity. This time, one feels, he was determined to show the LCC the difference between his organisational powers and theirs. For several years he had been President of the National Fire Brigades' Union, formed in 1887 by a number of mostly provincial brigades 'to promote the efficiency of Fire Brigades throughout the United Kingdom by the holding of periodical meetings in the winter at which subjects of interest to firemen would be discussed and to establish meetings for friendly drills during the summer.' One of its main aims was to induce Parliament to amend the Public Health Act of 1875 and to make compulsory the establishment of Fire Brigades by local authorities.

This was the first time that fire officers had come together in an efficient organisation to discuss their problems and to seek joint action. Shaw, while not prepared to involve the MFB, at least showed his sympathy with their aims by accepting their offer to become President.

By July 1891 the Union had produced a standard drill book so that when brigades were called on to join together, they at least knew what the others were talking about or doing. Annual summer camps with drill competitions for firemen were started, although their efforts to introduce a standard national fire uniform were less successful.

Nevertheless, they were, in a short time, remarkably successful and the timing of their first great national review and demonstration at Crystal Palace was fortuitous. It was a magnificent occasion for Shaw's last public appearance as the Chief Officer of the Metropolitan Fire Brigade. The Prince of Wales, still waiting to succeed his mother to the throne, still fascinated by fire, attended in full regimentals with his wife, Princess Alexandra. His cousin, the Emperor of Germany, was in London at the time and the Prince asked him, as another devotee of firefighting, to officiate.

On a glorious day then, Kaiser Wilhelm II, wearing a white uniform with the blue Garter ribbon across the front, and a golden helmet surmounted by an eagle, accompanied by his Empress and by the Duke of Clarence, the Duke of Edinburgh and other royal personages, drove into the ground and up to the dais. 1,413 firemen with 56 fire engines from 131 brigades were drawn up in front of him and after a display, a march past and a gallop past, Shaw made his Presidential Address, affirming 'we are proud to appear before one who understands and appreciates organisation, and whose well-known public utterances shew an unfailing confidence in the power of skilful combination to ensure safety.'

This time everything went smoothly and strictly according to plan, the day ending with the finest display of fireworks ever seen at Crystal Palace.

Back at Winchester House, he finished his last report to

the LCC, sending it with a final letter in which he wrote:

'I have completed every reference made to me from committees and answered every letter which I have received and there are no arrears of work in my department.

On taking my leave, I respectfully commend the existing force to the favourable consideration of your honourable Council.'

Punch's prediction had been correct. On the morning of his retirement, 30th October 1891, London's Fire King was knighted by his Queen and it was Sir Eyre Massey Shaw who walked into the recreation room at Southwark that night to find as many men as could be spared from duty – 300 in all – gathered to wish him Godspeed. With them was Lady Shaw, daughter Anna and their son Clarina (pronounced as in 'Rhine'). Shaw's deputy, Captain J Sexton Simonds offered the congratulations of all the men on the knighthood, then read an illuminated address and presented the 'Skipper' with a silver plate which had been bought with subscriptions from all the men, a ring for Lady Shaw and a brooch for Miss Anna.

For once, their Chief Officer, now 61 yrs old and perhaps more sensitive to the emotion of the moment than he might have been in the past, read his speech in a voice which was surprisingly faltering for so determined a character. Speaking almost softly, he sent the crews who had been under his command a final message, which recalled his past love of ships:

'Shadows may come across your route, mists and fogs may obscure the vision of those in charge, the darkness of night may come down and obscure her on every side, yet there is a compass on board and those in charge can continue their course onward, confidently and patiently, until the mists disperse and the day dawns. We all have our trials and in your case the compass of duty has indeed aided you to keep your course clear.......

'You know your duty. Your position is this: The inhabitants of this vast metropolis, numbering some five million persons, desire to be protected from the ravages of fire and have employed you for the purpose....

'It is your duty always to be loyal...'

At five minutes to midnight a message went out to all stations:

'Captain Shaw, on leaving, wishes to say goodbye and good luck to all members of the Brigade.'

11

Sexton Simonds: Success – and Failure

James Sexton Simonds, Chief Officer, 1891–1896. (LFCDA.)

THE SCRAP OF DOGGEREL FROM 'PUNCH' EXEMPLIFIED the situation at London County Council Headquarters. Shaw's resignation had caught them by surprise. Faced with finding a successor, arguments disrupted the General Purposes Committee as they sifted through 41 applications for the post. Should it be Shaw's deputy, Capt J Sexton Simonds who had been in the MFB for many years. or should they opt for an officer and a gentleman with no experience of firefighting? They decided on the officer, a Capt WP Campbell, but this caused such uproar in the Council that they rapidly changed their minds and appointed Simonds.

It was to prove an unfortunate choice.

The magic which Shaw was able to weave and which had kept his men disciplined by their affection for him as much as their acceptance of his command, had vanished. Simonds was a totally different character with his black hair greased close to his head and his moustache waxed neatly over his upper lip.

At first things went smoothly. The men now had their annual week of leave and their one day off a week was generally honoured. The annuity to widows of First or Second Class firemen was increased from £15 to £20 year and a compassionate allowance of 1/6d (7p) a week was allowed for each child (not a lot, but in the days when a child's haircut could cost as little as a halfpenny – old money

Fire stations varied. *Above:* Portland Road; *Right:* Bishopsgate. (LFCDA.)

– with a toy monkey on a stick thrown in – it was, at least, a move in the right direction).

By 1892, and without the strong influence of the Prince of Wales, now a middle aged-man and increasingly involved with affairs of State which left him little time for jaunts on a fire engine, and the Duke of Sutherland, who had died, much of the sparkle had gone from the 'backing group' of Shaw's great company of friends. Only Fred Hodges remained from the lively team of Society firebrands, still writing letters to newspapers and magazines.

The Council, free at last from Shaw's autocratic hand, launched out on a wave of building. New fire stations were to be erected at Wandsworth, East Dulwich, New Cross, Brompton and Hackney. Extra living quarters were to be added to Cherry Garden Pier for the men of the fire floats.

Several existing land stations were to be enlarged and more were in the planning stage.

Pay was again reviewed and a 'generous' increase made in wages as well as a reduction in working hours (although wages were still meagre and working hours excessively long.) The Brigade now numbered 825 men and the cost of maintaining it had risen to £128,783.

Fire alarm points, which had been set up throughout London and beset by false alarms, were increased by 129 so that there were 520 places where the public could pull the brass handle and call the fire brigade – even if – as so often happened among the massive immigrant population of the East End – they could not speak English.

The new Council called on the Water Companies immediately to implement the Water Act of 1871 so that by

1893 there were more than a thousand hydrants, indicated by a letter 'H' nearby.

Simonds had taken over quietly and gone about his business quietly. Only one major problem emerged. His business appeared to be not only that of the Metropolitan Fire Brigade but a certain amount on his own account. Rumours began to ripple, at first through the Brigade and then further. On 10th December 1895, the bombshell was dropped. A report to the LCC from its Fire Brigade Committee dealt with the allegation that the Chief Officer of the Metropolitan Fire Brigade had been associated with a certain Mr G Bray in obtaining a patent for improving fire appliances and that because of this association, six hose tenders at a cost of £900 had been bought by the Council.

Soon after this, questions were raised concerning fire escapes manufactured by Messrs Rose and Co and Messrs Bayley and Co. An investigation was set up and Simonds was questioned. He strongly denied that he had used his influence as Chief Officer of the Brigade to buy items in which he had a personal interest, but it seemed clear enough that this was a fact.

Simonds was undoubtedly a skilled engineer and had used his expertise to perfect several small items of equipment which he had recommended for use by the Brigade, but in these cases he had always declared his interest. There was, unfortunately, one £9,000 order which he explained, had not been declared because it had 'slipped my memory.'

The Council were not interested in excuses. After a four-hour debate, they called for his resignation. He refused, complaining that he had been condemned unheard and had been given no chance to vindicate his actions. Added to that, he would now lose all compensation for his 15 years service in the Brigade. John Burns, himself a fiery left wing politician, had alleged that a sum of £17,400 had been involved. Challenged by his fellow councillors on the accuracy of these figures, he rose, apologised and admitted that they were wrong. The sum, he said, was nearer £28,000.

The debate continued but to no avail. Simonds was struck off the strength of the Brigade and given a gratuity of £1,650.

Once more, the heads of the LCC came together to choose a new Chief Officer for their Fire Brigade. A working fireman, with experience of London's problems, or an officer and gentleman? Once more there was a shower of applications. This time they turned away from fire experience in favour of the officer and gentleman.

12

All Change with Wells

COMMANDER LIONEL DE LATOUR WELLS WAS certainly an officer and a gentleman. His lineage could be traced back to the year 1100 in Alsace, and one of his ancestors, Henri de Latour, had been Marshal of France in the 16th century, while another, André de Latour was executed during the French Revolution. Lionel was variously described by his contemporaries as 'flamboyant', 'exuberant', 'good humoured' and 'the handsomest man in the

Captain Sir Lionel de Latour Wells, Chief Officer, 1896–1903. (LFCDA.)

Navy' and is said to have danced a pirouette round his bedroom when the news of his appointment was brought to him, but even he, experienced sailor and good-natured as he was, would hardly have described himself as a fire expert. True, as a naval officer he had some slight experience of fire-fighting. He had hardly had time to develop his sea legs when the cargo of his ship caught fire. The *Times* reported the incident:

> 'Midshipman Lionel Wells … a naval officer who has not quite reached the age of sixteen years, constituted himself with universal consent, the director of operations there. With a mixture of good-humoured badinage and encouragement, he kept his men to their work. Although a few of the amateur pumpers working under his directions were so fortunate as to merit the approval of his ripe and critical judgement, there were still fewer of them, seeing the youngster's coolness and courage, who were not impressed with the thought that young Wells had in him the stuff of which good sailors are made.'

His early life had been less than happy, according to the biography written by his wife, Ida Caroline Wells (privately published in 1934 by AJ Davis). He was born in India in 1859 when his father had been serving there in the period of the Raj, but had returned to England and was still only 11 and at school when his mother died. Lionel had adored his mother and was now bereft. Nevertheless, he seems to have found some compensation later, when, after leaving school in Cheltenham, he joined his uncle in the Navy, was nicknamed 'Dicky' after him and described his period of sailing round the world as 'very happy days … spent in learning many things, every spare moment going off to fish or shoot in some of the lovely Canadian rivers or Newfoundland bays and merrymaking in the South or the West Indies.' With a reputation for 'a touch of the blarney', he evidently had a perpetual string of young ladies in attendance. He was known to be a good leader 'always kind to junior midshipmen'. If a man needed disciplining, Wells would take him aside and talk to him, rather than dress him down in front of his fellow seamen.

His love of animals led to him frequently defying Naval regulations and keeping pets in his cabin including, at one period, a pair of silver jackals. When his ship was in Portsmouth after one voyage, he took a bevy of girl friends aboard to show them his cabin and his pet parrot. As they were leaving, the bird, which had until then, maintained a discreet silence, suddenly hopped up and down on its perch and screeched admonishingly 'Dicky Wells kisses the girls!' Apart from all this, he had written two brief books, one called 'Jack Afloat' which illustrated the various phases of life of a RN seaman and the other a shilling souvenir of Nelson's flagship, the 'Victory'.

During his years in the Royal Navy he had served in the Egyptian War of 1882, as a sub-lieutenant on the Royal Yacht and had been promoted to Commander before his appointment as Chief Officer of the Metropolitan Fire Brigade.

So after the Christian goodness of Braidwood, the aristocratic autocracy of Shaw and the ineptitude of Simonds, a totally different character entered the London fire scene, chosen from a field of 83 candidates – all serving officers from the armed forces. Nobody could doubt his enthusiasm and his honest determination to do a rattling good job for London. The men, on the whole, liked him, but their longstanding dissatisfaction with their tough conditions was beginning to come to a head. Education for 'the masses' had started. Political parties concerned for the welfare of the downtrodden 'working classes' were at last beginning to make headway. The successful strike for the 'dockers' tanner' had made its mark. In the year that Wells took over, firemen had taken their first joint industrial action. Led by a serving sub-officer, James Diaper, they asked for some form of representation at County Hall, some way of having their conditions improved. When this was refused, they asked for delegates from all London fire stations to be allowed to meet at the Southwark headquarters. The Acting Chief Officer at the time, Sidney Gompertz Gamble, had refused to allow the meeting to take place, whereupon the men formed up two deep 'in a disciplined and orderly fashion' and marched to Cleopatra's Needle on the Embankment where Diaper addressed them. He called for a petition to County Hall and asked John Burns, a radical MP and member of the LCC who had been successfully involved in leading the dockers' strike, to help.

No action was taken on their petition although Diaper, a 39-year-old, conscientious fireman with nearly 20 years service in the Brigade, found himself reduced in status by nearly 100 places to a point where he had no hope of further promotion. Writing about the incident later, he pointed out that 'it was not until the whole Brigade was seething with rage' that any action was taken by the Council.

Life in the fire stations was still much as it had been in Shaw's time although, as he had predicted, the number of false alarms had increased until in 1895, an Act had to be put through Parliament prohibiting the giving of false alarms (58 & 59 Vic. c28) which laid down a maximum penalty of £25 and/or three months imprisonment. Despite this, the false alarms continued and were to continue, particularly in the period following the 'going home' times for schools and pubs.

Wells began work in November 1896, and immediately altered two rules which had been a source of irritation among the men for years. In the past, any infringement of the rules affected a man's chances of promotion. Under the new scheme, he was punished and the incident was finished, so that when his time came for promotion he lost no places – as Diaper had done. The other change affected the wives and families too, since it allowed married men who lived in or close to their stations to go home for meals if they were not out at a fire. He also arranged that fines paid for misdemeanours should not go into London's general rate fund as they had in the past, but into a specific fund for improving the mens' recreation facilities. Soon after this, he managed to change the old system of 'grace and favour' fortnightly leave days, so that they could be taken as of right and were not dependent on whether the Station Officer decided it was convenient.

There seems to be no doubt that without Shaw's eagle eye for more than four years, the Brigade was in need of a Spring Clean and, in the Spring of 1886, Wells set to work with gusto, bringing everything up to date from the fire stations, workshops and appliances to the Widows and Orphans Fund. Somehow he managed to influence the members of the Fire Brigade Committee, which, as ever, was short of cash. Skilfully using determination and tact he managed to extract enough money to set a number of schemes in action, including the use of oil instead of coal for the engines, interchangeable fire escapes and some of the earliest portable telephones.

Just before taking over, he had met one of his earlier girl friends, Ida Caroline Busk. By February 1897 they were engaged and in April of that year they were married at the Church of Annunciation, Bryanston Square, with a wedding present of silver candelabra from the officers and men of the Fire Brigade and a silver salver from the LCC.

Back in harness, he continued rapidly to improve the service, changing the old system of men dragging the escapes from street points to the fires, by providing horse-drawn escapes which were quicker in attendance and a distinct improvement for the firemen. The new sliding carriage escapes were telescoped into a shorter length which made them easier to manipulate through narrow streets. From then, all the notorious street escape stations within a three quarters of a mile radius of any fire station were closed and the men and equipment transferred to the fire station. As time passed, he re-organised the Brigade, making it possible for 100 men and their equipment to be concentrated in any high risk area within a total of 15 minutes and setting a time for first attendance at 5 minutes. Pursuing his philosophy of encouraging the men, he presented a silver cup annually now, for '*the smartest job of the year*' – a jolly if somewhat indefinite description which he later changed to a competition for the best fire escape drill.

At about this time he noticed during his inspections of crews, that many of the men looked 'remarkably lean', so ordered canteen vans for the Service, to be taken to all major fires. If the men were to be on duty for long hours, he maintained, they must at least have something to eat and a hot drink provided for them. (For some years, Station Officers had been instructed to ensure, if possible, that hot water for baths or 'wash-downs' should be available for men returning cold and wet from fires, and to take particular care for the hazard of fumes from acid which could affect their lungs and sometimes took a while to produce symptoms.)

London was, by now, divided into five districts for fire fighting purposes, still identified by letters. 'A' District was the West End, with the District Superintendent's Station at Manchester Square. 'B' was Central with the Superintendent at Clerkenwell; 'C' was East and North-East, with Superintendent at Whitechapel; 'D' to the South-East with Superintendent at New Cross and 'E' was South-West with the Superintendent at Kennington. Headquarters was known as 'No 1' – Southwark.

All the stations were in 'electric' communication and every day, lists and details of fires attended from 6 am one day to 6 am the next were sent from every station to headquarters. By 1898, the average of calls worked out at ten a day, many caused by the overturning of paraffin lamps, overheating of flues, drying and airing of linen too close to the fire and, as ever, children playing with matches.

In addition to the standard fire engine equipment, small hand-pumps had been in use for some years. Filled with water from a bucket and pumped by foot from a narrow gauge hose and nozzle, they were often sufficient to put out a small fire with minimum damage.

The 'steamers' were always cleaned after every fire, and the fire was usually re-laid in the boiler to be kept ready for the next incident. Lighting the fire was a work of art – and the reverse of the normal, domestic procedure. Coal went in first, at the bottom of the grate, then wood, with shavings on top. A 'fusee' or 'steam-match' would then be lit and dropped down the funnel. The steam-matches were made specially for the Brigade and once struck, would continue to flame even if they were dropped into water. The fire would, in any case, have a head start. Years earlier, Shaw had arranged that a gas jet was kept burning under the boiler to maintain the water at a high temperature. This was disconnected before the engine left the station and the fire then took over to keep up steam. Only the firemen themselves knew that on occasion, when they had a shrewd suspicion that they were being called to a false alarm, would they drop a lighted oily rag down the funnel so that smoke would pour from the top, giving the impression that the fire was alight and saving them the trouble of constantly re-laying it.

Every steamer carried 500 feet of hose, made in lengths of 100 feet (costing about £7 a length without connections) which could take a supply of water at 300 lbs per square inch. By now, the old leather hose, with its smelly 'anointing' oil, had been abandoned and all hose was made of best flax canvas lined with rubber, much lighter and easier to move around. As soon as the men returned from a fire, the hose was unrolled, scrubbed and hauled up into the hose tower to dry.

By this time, London's transport was beginning to include trams, running on rails set into the centre of the main roads with a narrow gap between them. The gap, essential to take the 'plough' which ran from the base of the tram to pick up electric current from an underground rail, was a nightmare for horse-drawn vehicles, whose narrow, iron shod wheels were often caught in it. To counter this hazard, London's fire engines were fitted with special broad, wavy-shaped iron 'tyres' which extended over the side of the wooden wheels and prevented them from slipping on the tram lines. Even the horses' harness was specially adapted so that an animal which slipped and fell could be released instantly by a quick turn of the swivel-bar at the end of the harness-pole, and helped to its feet.

Drills were still part of daily life and the training period remained at three months before a man was allowed to attend a fire. Before being accepted, recruits had still to have been in the Navy, to be between the ages of 21 and 30 and to be able to raise a fire-escape ladder from the ground by the levers. Only after all this were they allowed to start training.

Their education as firemen usually began with Indian club drill followed by practice with the engines, the escapes, the jumping sheet and the chair knot, with the skill of carrying and rescuing people high on the syllabus. Shaw's words, quoted from his book '*Fires and Fire Brigades*' were constantly in their ears – '*watch and study, labour and learn, flinch from no risk in the line of duty and be liberal and just to fellow workers of every grade.*' This solemn sermon was not enough to prevent some high jinks, particularly when two or three unfortunates were ordered away to dress up in long skirts for practice in carrying females to safety. At other times, the recruits were divided into groups of 14 men to hold the jumping sheets – standing in a circle, gripping the edges of the tough canvas as their mates leapt from the top windows of Winchester House. The art of controlling the sheet lay in leaning well back so that the force of impact as the victim hit the target area did not result in the canvas sagging to the ground – with fatal consequences. Victims were warned not, in fact, to jump but rather to fall as a dead weight. Too much spring in the step brought about much the same result as a trampoline.

Rescue by rope was another lesson to be learned. All engines carried lengths of tanned manilla rope and a fireman was taught to fasten one end of this to two firm objects, possibly chimney stacks, then two loops were made using what was known as a 'Tomfool's knot' with one loop slung under the victim's arms and the other under the legs. A guiding rope was attached and with these, they were lowered to the ground.

Ladder and escape drill involved a knowledge of all the types used by the Brigade, including in 1897, the new 40-foot ladders with one extension and others with a succession of extending ladders rising to a height of up to 70 feet. (By this time an Act of Parliament had provided that all new buildings above a certain height must have iron staircases attached for escaping from fires.) Men were taught to run safely to the top of a ladder and then fasten themselves by a rope to the top rung before breaking a window and entering a burning building. In the dense smoke a fireman was likely to find inside, the rope ensured that he could find his way back to the window – and the escape.

Some escapes still had chutes of canvas or wire netting attached to the back and in the case of multiple rescues, the fireman would carry the rescued person to the top of the ladder and send them down the chute, feet first. He himself would take the last victim, somersaulting from the top and descending head first, holding the victim by the arms and regulating the speed of descent by pressing his elbows and knees against the side of the chute. Chutes, which had been used throughout the Victorian period, were being phased out, so that training concentrated mostly on carrying victims down the ladder in the traditional 'fireman's lift.'

In America, water towers were already in general use, with the hose attached to the side of the ladder, but in London, the men carried the hose themselves – a 100 ft length weighed up to 65 lbs, and that without the water inside. At the shout of '*Water on!*', the '*steam-man*' on the engine would pull the warning whistle and the firemen holding the branch and nozzle would brace themselves to take the strain as the water surged through at considerable pressure. Branch pipes – the guiding pipe from hose to nozzle – were shorter now and easier to handle, while nozzles could usually be adapted to vary the stream of water which emerged from a direct jet to a spray.

Although equipment had been constantly updated throughout Shaw's days, the Brigade Report for 1897 shows that no fewer than 808 fires were still extinguished by buckets, 460 by hand pumps, 98 by engines and 466 by hydrants and stand-pipes. Drill was specified even for the Brigade buckets, which were made of white canvas and carried 2½ gallons of water. The top and bottom were made rigid by cane rings for ease of filling, but the bucket could be collapsed flat for stowing away.

Chimney fires – common at a time when central heating was almost unheard of and coal was the universal fuel for all forms of heating – were usually dealt with by hand-pump. A small amount of water was poured on to the fire in the grate and the steam from this belched up the chimney and usually put out the fire. To make sure of success, the men would climb on to the roof and finish the job with a bucket of water poured in from the top. Other methods included blocking both ends of the chimney with wet mats or sacks to cut out oxygen from the fire or throwing salt on the fire (a method which had been described in the days of Charles II!) The heat would decompose the salt, release a gas and choke the fire.

First-Aid was included in the training, with the anatomy classes helped by a human skeleton. Among all the equipment, the mattocks and shovels, saws and spanners, turncocks, keys and the general paraphernalia carried on fire engines was always a box of medical and surgical supplies. These would include 'Carron' oil, believed at that time to be the correct treatment for burns and so-named from the Carron Iron Works, in Scotland, where it had been used for generations. This wonder-treatment comprised equal parts of linseed oil or olive oil with limewater, and along with it on the engines were triangular and roller bandages, surgeon's lint and cotton wool. (A century later, under the Health and Safety, [First Aid] Regulations, all appliances carried sterile First Aid equipment including bandages, eye pads, adhesive plaster, antiseptic solution [Savlon], specialist burns dressings, a Brook airway, bleached burns/body sheet [both stored in sealed plastic bags], a safety knife, sterile water/emergency eye wash, a reflective foil survival blanket and a foil strip of 'cooling draught' tablets – salt and glucose for cases of dehydration. The Carron Oil had been long discontinued!)

Under the new regime, it was arranged that at least 30 recruits would be in training at one time and they were never called away to do other work which might interrupt this, as trainees had in the acute manpower shortages of the recent past. At the end of three months, if they had passed all the tests, they were drafted into the ranks as firemen 4th class.

Wells was not beyond realising his own human limitations, and before long had asked for the appointment of a third officer to spread the work load which was divided between himself and Sidney Gompertz Gamble. The Council's Fire Brigade Committee pondered and finally appointed yet another young naval officer, Lieut Sampson Sladen.

For the Chief Officer, the first disaster struck on November 19th 1897. The Cripplegate area of the City with its nickname 'The Fire Island,' was notorious for its old, close-packed buildings and narrow streets. This was the centre of the fancy-goods trades which specialised in trimmings, paper decorations, candles, a whole range of inflammable bits and pieces which were made up and packed, mostly by women, in poor conditions and considerable fire hazard. Now it was lunch time and as the City workers began pouring into the streets to stretch their cramped legs and find something to eat, the cry of 'fire' went up and once more the major part of London's fire brigade converged on the centre. One of the City's businessmen, James Blomfield, a wool broker, happened to be in the area. His description of the event, in a letter to a friend, epitomises the fire scene in London at the time:

'The hoarse shout – you know it. It always frightens me. Unnatural. Unearthly. What is it? A fire engine. The heavy rumbling, the tinkling bells' *(at this time there were no fire bells on the engine – only the small bells on the horses' harness and the shout of the 'Hi! Hi!' man).* 'Every horse is at once reined in to make room for it. People stand alert, ready to lend a hand, to make the way clear so that the engine may go fastest to save life and property ...'

He reached the St Martin-le Grand end of Aldersgate: 'but see here, a fireman riding bareback on a horse, galloping his hardest, not for fun or pleasure but in dead earnest.......I went a few yards out of my way, drawn irresistibly....'

The fire had started in the Wells Street premises of a firm specialising in ostrich feathers. Many of the six-storey factories and warehouses were undivided so that yet again, despite all the centuries of building regulations, the flames swept through, unhampered by any fire-resistant party-walls or doors. Fifty-one steaming fire engines manned by 228 officers and firemen, among them their new Chief, battled valiantly. Wells himself had a narrow escape when a plate-glass floor light fell on his helmet and nearly cut through the metal. Despite all their efforts, by the end of the day all that remained in this heart of the City was a bare and blackened patch of ruins where more than one hundred buildings and warehouses had stood. Total losses were estimated at well over a million pounds but added to that, 4,000 workers – men, women and girls – found themselves destitute, unemployed and out on the streets. Newspapers published whole supplements describing the blaze and its after-effects. Small wonder that the relief fund, opened for them by the Lord Mayor, was well subscribed.

One of the comparatively new fire inquests was held at Guildhall and the jury, for some reason which was not altogether clear, decided that the fire had been *'wilfully caused by some person or persons unknown.'* More to the point, they added that while the officers and men of the Fire Brigade were equal or superior to any similar body of men, they were not satisfied that their appliances and equipment were what they should be. What was needed, they said, were more fire alarms, better indication and improvement of fire hydrants, that City fire stations should all have two steamers, one of which should always be *'under steam'* and ready for instant action and that members of the Brigade should be better acquainted with the geography of warehouses.

The last recommendation was particularly interesting. For at least two centuries, maps had been available to the insurance companies showing the layout and hazards of many of the bigger buildings in London as an aid to assessing the premiums. They were drawn on a large scale and showed the boundaries of individual buildings, the material from which they were constructed, the number of storeys, the position of skylights and the use to which they were put. Their whole purpose was to identify fire risk and yet one wonders whether London's firefighters, including Braidwood and Shaw, had ever been made aware of their existence.

Most prolific among these map makers was Charles E Goad, who set up his own specialist company which, from 1886 to 1970, provided plans for all the rival insurance companies. Because of their large scale and their detail, they would have proved a rich source of information for fire officers, but they seem only to have been known to the 'closed-shop' of underwriters.

Inevitably, the Cripplegate fire resulted in an immediate, steep rise in fire premiums in the City. It also resulted in the LCC deciding that the Board of Works had been wrong in cutting down on the City's fire cover. Within a short time they bought the site of the old Lady Holles school in

Redcross Street for £31,000 and built Redcross Street Fire Station.

Wells, with his interest in mechanical things, had already heard of experiments with new engines driven by petroleum power and began looking further into this with the long view that it might eventually be used for powering fire engines. For more than fifty years, efforts had been made to discover some means of propelling fire engines other than by man or horse-power. Steam had been successful to a degree, but steam powered engines were, of necessity, large, heavy and hard to manoeuvre. Petrol power might be the answer and Wells was keeping his eye on the possibilities. At the same time, his love of ships had turned his attention to the river fire service and already he was busy drawing up plans for a new, faster and more efficient fire boat.

1897 had been a busy year of social gatherings and preparations for Queen Victoria's Diamond Jubilee. The Wellses took part in many of the jollifications including the Royal Garden Party, and the Duke and Duchess of York, in return, attended a Fire Brigade Review on Clapham Common. Young Mrs Ida Wells clearly enjoyed her position in her 'charming house' at headquarters

> 'with spacious rooms, adjacent to the look-out tower and hose drying tower, as well as accommodation for the men under instruction and married quarters for the Second Officer, Chief Superintendent and some of the men.' *She kept in close touch with the other wives and wrote* 'we seemed like one big family.'

> *Unlike Shaw, Wells seems to have been a conscientious husband as well as Chief Officer. His wife continued:* 'L. made our home lovely by constant visits to Covent Garden. He used to say that as we could not have a garden we must be well supplied with flowers. A wonderful copper-headed young woman who went by the name of "Copper-Top" was often to be seen coming into the quadrangle with a huge basket on her head, filled with the most exquisite, freshly unpacked bunches of flowers from Covent Garden.' *It was here too, in 1898, that their daughter, Iris, was born.*

There is little doubt that the Cripplegate fire helped Wells's efforts to persuade the LCC to grant more money for fire protection and by July 1898 when the average number of fires in London every day was reported as 'thirteen – of good size', he was already holding trials for the experimental fire-boat which he had invented.

Things were going well and more than 50,000 people attended the now regular annual Fire Brigade Review in Victoria Park in 1898 when the new horse-drawn fire escapes were displayed to the public. By January 1899, he

had added a collapsible hand pump to the equipment of his Brigade and had patented and installed a new system of telephone fire alarm posts. But not all his work was practical and energetic. In the same year he appeared before yet another Select Committee, set up by the government. This was

> 'to inquire and report as to the existing arrangements for the provision of Fire Brigades …in England and Wales, excepting the Metropolitan Fire Brigade, the adequacy of such arrangements for the due protection of life and property from destruction or injury from fire; and the Amendments, if any, which are necessary in the Law on the subject.'

Although it was not intended to deal with the MFB, the Committee took evidence not only from Wells but from Shaw, who had been in retirement for eight years.

Wells, who had been out of the Navy and into firefighting for all of three years, nevertheless gave his evidence with quiet confidence, listing points which had struck him including irregularity of system, no training to qualify for fireman, uneven scales of pay and haphazard selection of appliances. Brigades, he said, were often raised or augmented in time of panic; there was insufficient interest by many local authorities to make the best use of their officers and men, or indeed, to establish a brigade at all; lack of the proper enforcement of the three authorising Acts which now existed, and absence of unbiased independent professional advice, without which local authorities were, in many cases, entirely dependent upon the makers of fire apparatus and their agents. He felt that it was illegal for local authorities to help pay for volunteer brigades in their areas 'which often left much to be desired in discipline and efficiency and performed careless and ignorant work though done with the best intentions.' He assured the Committee that further legislation was necessary.

Shaw, called from retirement to give evidence, made it clear that while he thought some local brigades were 'quite good', others were exceedingly bad when the local authority had not taken the trouble to use its powers. There had been a great deal of apathy, the number of fires was excessive and the waste of public money had come to a point where it was desirable to prevent it going further. In a far-seeing statement, Shaw made it quite clear that he thought it was the duty of the State to look after fire protection.

Both men, questioned on the need for some form of overall inspection of brigades, were in favour of such a scheme. 'I would not force it on large towns but most of them would be very proud to be inspected' said Shaw. 'It would be of the utmost value' agreed his successor. 'Any ship or regiment takes inspection as a compliment except

Early electric street fire alarm. (Guildhall Library, City of London.)

where it is likely to reveal inefficiency or slovenliness.'

Among other suggestions made during the Inquiry were the drawing up of standard specifications for all types of fire appliances, the granting of legal rights to Chief Fire Officers to visit any premises to assess fire risk and the establishing of a government-run central training school for fire officers. The latter caused such interest that Commander Wells was asked to research the matter, draw up proposals and submit them. He did so, with alacrity and efficiency, suggesting a staff of fifteen under a Commandant with a salary of £1,500 per annum.

The Committee's report, with recommendations to the government, was issued the following year. There was no mention of wider powers for Chief Officers, of any form of inspection, nor of any overall authority for fire brigades, let alone a training school for officers.

It was all of no consequence for, yet again, the recommendations were ignored. However, the subject was to become immensely important forty years later, when the government, faced with the prospect of a second world war, found that times had hardly changed since the 1899

Commission and they were dealing with more than 1,600 assorted fire brigades throughout the country, using a wide variety of equipment, much of which was incompatible with neighbouring brigades and certainly with London. Even the beginnings of government action at this stage might have prevented the problems facing the country when the 'Gotha' air raids of World War One and certainly the Blitz of World War Two started.

One cannot help feeling that Wells must have returned to his normal duties with some relief and, as the twentieth century dawned, the London Brigade was already working on the idea of a petrol-powered fire engine and welcoming the new fire boat which had been designed by their Chief Officer. This addition to London's small fleet of river boats was stationed at Blackfriars Bridge. Wells had drawn on his naval experience, particularly his work as Commodore of a torpedo boat flotilla, in designing the boat which was based on the 'Heron' type of shallow-draught gunboats of the Royal Navy, intended for use on tropical rivers. It had a pump capable of throwing 1,250 gallons of water a minute, drew far less water than the old boats and could get close to a fire no matter what the state of the tide.

Wells's original design had proved too expensive for the LCC but the new boat had been built on similar lines. At the same time, he altered the arrangement of the river service stations. Until now, there had been five, but this meant that as a general rule, it was more than 15 to 20 minutes after an alarm call was received before a tug was under way with its fire float. (The delay was caused partly because of the time it took for the tug to raise steam and partly because the crews had to be called from home). Wells reduced the number to four stations: Battersea, Blackfriars, Rotherhithe and Deptford, with crews always on 'stand-by' and appliances ready to steam away at once. The staff from Blackfriars were lodged at the newly built Whitefriars Station, in Whitefriars Street, close to the Embankment and Blackfriars Bridge, which had been opened on 21st July 1897.

Until Shaw's time firefighting from the river had been carried out mostly with pumps mounted on barges or 'floats' (although Braidwood had introduced an early steam-powered fire boat shortly before he died.) The earliest boats had been rowed by Thames watermen, who manned the pumps when they reached the fire, but the later floats or barges were attached to steam tugs and hauled into position. This not only meant that twice the number of craft were needed but it was not always easy to get close enough to the shore for efficiency. Wells had decided to combine pumping and propulsion in the same vessel and this was the first he produced.

Merryweather's had by now invented a new oil driven fire engine, the cumbersome 'Fire King', but this clearly had its drawbacks, and Wells spent many hours with his sleeves rolled up, working alongside his men in the Brigade

Early self-propelled fire engine. (LFCDA.)

workshops until, by 1901, they had adapted the chassis of a steamer to accommodate a petrol driven engine. It was not a success, and was eventually withdrawn from service and converted back to steam and horse power, but by now, the eyes of the senior officers were firmly fixed on a future brigade with petrol-driven appliances although there were still many old hands who growled that 'it would never happen.' Happen it did, and the twentieth century brought a succession of rapid changes to the organisation which, in 1904, altered its name, by Act of Parliament, from the *Metropolitan* to the *London Fire Brigade*.

An assortment of replacements for horse-drawn appliances was tried out during the first decade of the new century, among them an electric-driven escape, with batteries stored under an elongated bonnet, which weighed two tons and, again, had no great turn of speed. In 1903 a petrol-powered motor tender with chain transmission was introduced. This carried a small tank from which water was expelled by pressure of carbon monoxide gas. Within a few years, motor pumps were appearing with tanks of 60 gallons capacity from which water was forced by compressed air.

Laurels for the first self-propelled, petrol-motor fire engine in the whole London area have to go to Finchley, which at that time was outside the jurisdiction of the London Brigade. Finchley's Chief Fire Officer, a Mr Sly, had a great interest in the new petrol-driven car industry and had joined with Merryweather's to produce an appliance with a 30 hp engine capable of reaching a speed of 20 mph and carrying a pump with a capacity of 250 gpm. It had a soda-chemical powered 60-gallon water tank and carried 180 feet of hose. More were to follow.

Meanwhile, in 1901, Queen Victoria had died and the Prince of Wales had become King Edward VII. His Coronation procession through London had, by chance, been 'improved' by the appearance of a fire engine galloping past on its way to a fire, which must have brought back nostalgic memories to the new monarch.

All seemed to be going smoothly with the LFB. Legislation had even been passed in 1902 combining all the London water companies into one body – the Metropolitan Water Board. But then Wells's luck suddenly failed. On 9th June 1902, around 5 pm, fire broke out in a City workshop. The five storey building belonged to the General Electric Company. On the top three floors were their offices and below them, the rest of the building was used for the manufacture of decorative lamp holders, using celluloid, rubber tape and rubber adhesive solution. Almost all the workers were young women and it was in the lower section, reeking with fumes from the adhesive liquid and packed with supplies of celluloid, that the fire began in a waste paper basket. Although the building had its own fire hydrant and its own fire force, orders had been given not to call the London Fire Brigade if fire broke out but to leave it to the staff firemen. Because of this, no call was made to the Brigade for at least ten minutes, when a member of the public saw smoke and ran to give the alarm.

The Queen Victoria Street tragedy was to become a landmark of firefighting history. It made headlines throughout the world and was described by one London newspaper:

> 'The smoke rapidly increased in volume. Someone ran to the fire station in Watling Street, not a minute's run. The firemen promptly arrived with fire escapes and reared them against the building. But by now.... great volumes of smoke were issuing from the fourth floor windows and flames began to shoot forth.
>
> 'Men and women cried for the escape to save them and the frenzied girls above waved their arms to the crowd below. But the Watling Street fire escape stood idle. The brave firemen's weapons so to speak, broke in their hands. While the victims were yet shrieking ... while they were wildly waving to the crowd in their agony, while thousands of persons stood appalled at the spectacle, a fire escape, six or ten feet too short was reared helplessly against the building and the firemen had to look on – impotent – while nine people were sacrificed.'

There were no turntable ladders and no hook ladders in the Brigade at this time, but there were ropes and jumping sheets, so that there was speculation as to why these were not used. A special 70ft escape ladder was galloped in from Southwark and several girls were rescued by it, but at the end of the day, eight young women and one young man who had run over the rooftops to try to rescue them from above, were all dead.

The fire brought a bitter reaction from the Press and public, who as so often happens to this day, laid the blame not on the owners of the business who had allowed such dangerous working conditions, but on the Fire Brigade and the London County Council. Wells took the brunt of the responsibility although the jury at the City Fire Inquest were remarkably kind to the firemen. After agreeing that the call to the Brigade had been late in coming and that considering the appliances at their disposal, there was no legal negligence, they added a series of riders which read:

> 'We consider that the Watling Street Station is totally inadequate to meet the demands of the district in which it is situated and that it should be immediately reconstructed as a first-class fire station. We consider that the London Building Act of 1894 should be made retrospective as regards life-saving. We consider that the

General Electric Company by evading the Factory Act and misleading the district surveyor, render themselves responsible for the loss of life and we give unqualified praise to the Metropolitan Fire Brigade and the Salvage Corps.'

In the aftermath of the fire – and inquest – the General Electric Company managed to prove that the premises were not a workshop as specified in the Factories and Workshops Act of 1901, and that the building was exempt from the legislation of the 1894 Amendments to the London Building Act (which laid down safety codes including fire escapes, for buildings of more than 60 ft in height) because it had been built before the Act applied and the legislation was not retrospective.

The remains of the ruined building were demolished and Cannon Street Fire Station was built on the site by the LCC, but still the backlash was concentrated on Wells, not just from the press and public but in a small and venomous book which was written soon afterwards under the pseudonym 'Phoenix' and published with the title 'The Decay of London's Fire Brigade.' The book castigated Wells, accusing him of being hostile to such innovations as hook ladders which were used in many continental countries; refusing to fit bells on appliances (long avoided because of the fear of frightening the horses) and relying instead on the old fashioned shout of 'Hi! Hi!'. It suggested that his policies had sent the death rate – and the insurance premiums – soaring and, more than this, that he was self-satisfied, inefficient and responsible for a decline in both the morale and efficiency of the London Fire Brigade.

In many ways, the criticism was unfair. Wells had made many efforts to improve efficiency. Fire stations were now equipped with brass poles so that the men could slide down at speed instead of having to run down stairs and brass bells were fitted to fire engines. Fire horses were kept harnessed to escapes on two-hour shifts at key fire stations and – more long-lasting – hook ladders were quickly introduced as part of standard Brigade equipment. The hook ladder which was also known as the 'Pompier' ladder, because it was invented in Paris and had been used there since 1826, was 13 feet long and weighed some 28 lbs. It had a large, barbed hook at one end, making it possible for a fireman to scale the outside of a building to almost any height provided there were enough window-sills for the ladder to be hooked over – and provided he had sufficient balance, strength, agility, head for heights and courage. Before long the entire Brigade

was equipped with and trained in the use of hook ladders, which were to stay with them for the next 50 years.

Wells stood the heat of the controversy for another year, but the attacks continued. His wife described the problems, revealing for the first time the temptations and hazards facing the Chief Fire Officer of a city the size of London. In her biography, she wrote:

'Owing to his firm stand in never truckling under to any appliance makers, L. had no doubt made enemies. On one occasion, many thousands of pounds was (sic) offered him if he would recommend some special appliance. It seemed now as if all his enemies combined to behave in the most hurtful way, added to which the 'Daily Mail' made the most virulent attack upon him. It was a terribly trying time and it always seemed to me that the LCC might have given him greater support as they really had an immense respect and admiration for all he did.'

Shortly before Christmas, 1902, Wells was taken ill with scarlet fever – a serious event in pre-antibiotic days. After recovering, he went abroad to visit fire brigades in Berlin, Hamburg, Dresden and Bremen, some of which had been given fulsome praise in the 'Phoenix' book, but found them no better than London. In May 1903, their second daughter was born, but died almost immediately and his wife was seriously ill after the birth. It was at this time that the Conservatives offered him the post of Chief Agent to their Party. To the regret of his wife and evidently, his men, he accepted.

'It was a great wrench to leave the headquarters of the MFB where we had spent such happy years except for the trying time in 1902' wrote Mrs Wells. 'The men assembled in the recreation room to bid their Chief good-bye and it was said that amongst all those brave fellows there was not one with dry eyes. A beautiful centre-piece was their parting gift.'

Wells never settled down with the Conservative Party, leaving them within a few years and living restlessly until returning to the Navy during the First World War. He was knighted in 1923 for his public services and in 1928 was elected as Vice-Chairman of the Playing Fields Association. He died in 1929 after a short illness.

Once more, however, London, in 1902 was without a Chief Officer for its Fire Brigade.

13

Sparks from The Phoenix

THE IDENTITY OF 'PHOENIX', AUTHOR OF THE BOOK which had contributed so much to the downfall of Wells, was no secret. While London's Chief Officer was occupied with his new engines and boats, Edwin O Sachs had been making his mark on the fire scene. Sachs was born in 1870 and started his working life as an architect specialising in theatre design, but even as a student he had been fascinated by fire. He knew of Shaw's obsession with theatre fires and was concerned that those which he designed should be as safe as possible. He was also genuinely upset by the number of deaths caused by the use of two highly inflammable fabrics – flannelette and celluloid. Hundreds of babies – as well as adults – died every year when their flannelette nightgowns went up in flames. Hundreds more were maimed or died when their celluloid hair ornaments, combs, brushes, brooches or labour-saving collars caught fire.

Sachs was never a member of the London Fire Brigade, but his passion for fire safety led him to take time off from his professional work (at the age of 28 he had installed the first electrically operated stage – at Drury Lane Theatre) to gain experience in the problems of fire. At one period he signed on as a scene shifter in a London theatre, earning 2s 6d a night to discover, by personal experience, what went on behind the scenes. As a result of this, he led a campaign which brought about more stringent fire regulations in theatres including the statutory provision of fireproof safety curtains. Following this, he extended his expert knowledge by travelling widely on the continent, serving as an ordinary fireman in the municipal brigades of Paris, Berlin and Munich and, apparently, being commissioned in all of them.

On returning to London, he gathered together a group of influential men including Robert Mond, (a founder of Brunner Mond, later to become ICI), Sidney Gompertz Gamble, a senior officer in the London Fire Brigade, Sir Arthur Sullivan (of Gilbert and Sullivan – and 'Iolanthe'

fame), who was immensely influential in the theatre world, and several other interested people. With their support and the backing of an increasing number of high-powered businessmen he established the British Fire Prevention Committee in 1897. For the first time, the hazards of fire and of the materials which were now being produced by scientists and industrialists, were to be examined scientifically with a view to discovering what effect they would have on the customers. From this, half a century later, developed the government's Building Research Establishment, although the Joint Fire Research Organisation had been formed in 1946, in partnership with the Department of Scientific and Industrial Research.

Until the beginning of the 1990s there had been very little in the way of scientific fire testing, although the appalling losses from big fires, particularly during the first half of the 19th century, had produced considerable interest in fire proof buildings.

As early as 1723 a Mr Ambrose Godfrey had invented what is believed to have been the first fire extinguisher, filled with gunpowder and a secret mixture 'which never corrupts nor alters when.. pure water would soon putrefy and stink.' Godfrey's fire extinguishing 'bomb' was tried out at a public experiment in Belsize Park in front of an audience which included the Lord Chancellor and Members of the Royal Society. Unfortunately the explosion which followed when the glass 'bomb' was thrown into the burning building not only failed to extinguish the flames by its force, as was planned, but scattered them throughout the building and as a bonus, blew Mr Godfrey off his ladder.

Not to be deterred, more inventors followed using such known fire-extinguishing substances as alum, soda, borax, hyposulphite of soda, silicate of soda (water glass), chloride of lime, tungstate of soda, sodium chloride (common salt), potash, bicarbonate of soda and ammonia. Thousands of glass bottles – plain and coloured – were filled with an assortment of liquids with the claim that they would extinguish fire, but none was proved to be effective on any but a small outbreak which might have been equally efficiently put out with plain water. It was only when extinguishers such as the '*L'Extincteur*' and its successors appeared on the scene in the mid 1800's that a reasonably effective first aid for fires proved itself. In 1776 an inventor, David Hartley, had lined his house in Putney with a system of patented metal plates designed to provide a complete barrier to fire, and managed to stay unharmed on the first floor while fire burned beneath him. The experiment appears to have been successful to some extent, if expensive and cumbersome and for many years an engraved stone commemorating the event stood on Putney Heath.

So many people were concerned about fire in the late 18th century that in 1791, the Associated Architects Club of London was formed to consider the causes of frequent fires within the limits of the Act of George III, entitled "*An Act for the Further and Better Regulation of Buildings and Party Walls . . . . .*' The Club later became the Royal Institute of British Architects and survives to this day.

Now, however, Sach's Committee set up the first fire testing station in Europe, close to Lord's cricket ground between Lodge Road and North Bank. The main building had four testing chambers, the largest 22ft 3ins by 15ft and with gas-fuelled furnaces.

Tests were carried out into building materials and other items, including fire alarms and fire extinguishing equipment, with fees ranging from £105 – £185 for furnace tests to £75 for smaller items. By 1904 they had carried out 79 fire-resistance tests, issued 57 publications of test results plus 22 other fire prevention publications and lost over £6,000, fortunately made up by subscription and other funds.

Their work was generally welcomed by conscientious organisations in Britain and throughout Europe and the USA and gradually similar testing centres were set up in Berlin, New York and Chicago, although not on the scale of London. Applications for tests came from the US, France, Germany, Denmark and Switzerland and in 1904, the Committee organised the first World Conference on Fire Safety at Caxton Hall in London which welcomed over 800 delegates from all over the world and included an exhibition of fire equipment at Earls Court. (None, however, from the Metropolitan Fire Brigade. Their memories of the '*Phoenix*' affair were still too bitter to allow them to participate.) Some idea of the increasing hazards already facing firefighters can be gathered from the programme.

Among the subjects discussed at the conference were building construction and equipment, electrical safeguards and fire alarms, the storage of oil, spontaneous combustion, fire surveys, fire patrols, fire losses and insurance, fire tests and standardisation. Papers were read in a number of different languages and talks included the storage of petrol, explosives and chemicals, particularly in densely inhabited areas, as well as the need for international standards for fire resistance. Among the resolutions passed was one which called for the phrase '*fire-resistant*' to be used instead of the misleading '*fire-proof*' which confused the public.

In the teeth of opposition from many architects, Sachs campaigned for the greater use of reinforced concrete in big buildings particularly (it was first used in London in 1899) and it was Sachs who played a part in founding the Concrete Institute which later became the Institution of Structural Engineers.

Sachs was, by now, well-known in Europe and, as the backing of wealthy and successful business men was increasingly lost to the LFB, he was to become more influential on the fire scene in London, as Wells discovered to his cost. There was little doubt that Sachs was the author who, under the pseudonym '*Phoenix*', had written the attack on the Chief Officer after the Queen Victoria Street disaster. For the next two decades he was to snap at the heels of London's firefighters with remarkable success.

14

Motorisation – James De Courcy Hamilton

WHAT POSSESSED THE LCC TO APPOINT REAR Admiral James de Courcy Hamilton as the new Chief Officer will never be known. It was said more than once that he knew little about the fire brigade when he arrived in July 1903 and about the same when he left in 1909. Jack While of *The Times*, reckoned that 'he never really seemed in love with the fire brigade' and so it

appeared. Nevertheless, his time at Southwark was a period of many developments which, one suspects, were prompted and executed through the devotion and enthusiasm of his deputies, who included the redoubtable Sidney Gompertz Gamble, Lieut Sampson Sladen and a young engineer called Arthur Dyer.

Times had changed from the old days when Shaw's word was law and men needed any available, steady work to keep a roof over the heads of their families and were not going to jeopardise it by taking their complaints too far. Now the whole Labour movement was gathering force. Workers all over the country, miners, steelmen, iron foundrymen, the postal workers and, as ever, the dockers, were in a growing state of discontent and the firemen were increasingly determined to replace their 24-hours-a-day duty system with a more acceptable shift procedure.

Sachs and his followers were, meanwhile, not slow to point out the growing and changing challenge of fires in London. For some time the public had stopped to stare in wonder at the phenomenon of the motor car as it rolled and coughed its way through the streets, preceded by a man with a red flag. Motor cars needed petrol and the storage of this was proving a new fire hazard. Along with it came the storage of celluloid, still being used on a large scale and often kept in blocks which were anything but safe. The notoriously inflammable fabric, flannelete, was continuing to kill at the rate of around 1,000 people a year and Sachs was skilled in publicising such deaths.

The Brigade was, by now, committed to changing from horse-drawn steamers to petrol-powered and driven pumps. Astonishingly, the last of the manuals had not been pensioned off until 1899, but a new age was beginning. Courses in driving the new vehicles had to be set up, training laid down and examinations established. Even when a driver was considered competent, there were more problems when owners of the traditional horse-drawn buses and cabs

Rear-Admiral James de Courcy Hamilton, Chief Officer of the London Fire Brigade. 1903–1909. (LFCDA.)

complained, in colourful Cockney, that the new fire engines were frightening their horses.

Brigade workshops had to change from maintenance of steamers and escapes to the new internal combustion engine. Steam-propelled engines had been known for more than 50 years, the first almost certainly invented by Paul Hodge, although the first in London was built by William Roberts of Millwall in 1862. This raced along at 12 mph (19.3 km) and on one ambitious day took on an incline of one in sixteen. It soon became a 'white elephant' and it was not until the end of the 19th century that Wells and his engineers had begun to take the new petrol engine seriously as a possible means of propulsion and of pumping. The standard horse-drawn steamer which they had managed to convert to steam power was not a success and was soon abandoned and in 1903 the Brigade 'lashed out' on a four-cylinder petrol tractor of 24–30 hp which appears to have comprised a four-wheeled front section with seats for a driver and companion. This was attached by a perch-bolt to the back end of a normally horse-drawn steamer so that the resulting vehicle had a total of six wheels of three assorted sizes, all with solid tyres. Unfortunately, the weight of the steam boiler at the rear resulted not only in the front section being almost lifted off the ground at times, but in a tendency to skid and, most distressing of all, to jack-knife. This leviathan cost £750, ran 3,180 miles in all and attended six fires (although it only worked at one.) It was sold in 1909 for £8.10s (£8.50) after costing £156 in repairs.

In the same year, a 10–12 hp two-cylinder motor chassis fitted, unusually, with pneumatic tyres, was bought for £463 and converted, again in Brigade workshops, at a cost of £93, into an appliance carrying three men, a small pump and a box containing 500 ft of hose and other essentials. By the time the mechanics had finished with it, the petrol motor could drive the pump as well as the vehicle. It achieved 8½ miles to the gallon but, again, was not used for long. Experiments were made with electrically-powered fire engines but these too proved unsuccessful, not least because of the enormous weight and bulk of the primitive batteries.

Finally, the Brigade settled for petrol powered 'appliances' and gradually increased their number, so that 'first-aid' vehicles – pumps and escapes – were all fuelled by petrol. By 1907, three new fire stations had been designed and built specifically for motorised appliances – Wapping first, then Lee Green in 1906, followed by Tooley Street. The problem of skidding remained. Experiments with chains wrapped round the tyres, metal studs and traverse bands of balata belting were all tried out and at one stage, gyroscopic action was tested, but abandoned. The most successful grip seems to have been effected by enclosing one front and one back wheel with extra heavy, steel-studded leather covers.

These were only some of the new problems facing the Brigade. Public entertainment now included the growing attraction of the bioscope or cinematograph and from the mid-1890s, the celluloid film it used had added a further fire hazard to the existing headache of celluloid goods. Without stringent precautions the film was liable to catch fire and there were a number of tragic accidents, including a fire at Newmarket in 1907 when 500 people, crammed into a hall for a 'Bioscope Entertainment', knocked over the projector and a pile of film spools alongside it which had been sited close to the only exits. In the panic which ensued, three women died and 50 people were injured.

The problem of unaccompanied children in cinemas was dealt with as part of the Children's Act of 1908. This not only introduced a penalty of £10 on parents if a child under the age of seven was killed or seriously injured by being left in a room with an unguarded, open fire, but demanded an adequate number of attendants at any cinema performance where the majority of the audience were children.

But it was 1909 before the passing of the first Cinematograph Act (9 Edward VII, c.30) with its regulations for licensing cinemas for the showing of films. These demanded the provision of adequate exits as well as suitable firefighting equipment and the enclosure of the projector and film reels in a separate, fire-resistant compartment. At about this time too, the LCC began to consider bringing in its own local legislation. (In 1922, the government passed the Celluloid and Cinematograph Act to control the use and storage of the substance.)

In 1909 too, a Frenchman named Bleriot made headlines when he stepped into a flimsy aeroplane and managed to fly across the English Channel. It was a memorable 'first' and it not only produced a closer 'entente' with neighbouring France, but a totally new and worrying prospect. England, protected in the past by its island status, was now within easy range of possible enemy action. For London's firemen it had ominous portents. For its Chief Fire Officer, however, it held no headaches. He had been offered a directorship of the Army and Navy stores and had accepted it.

15

Sir Sampson Sladen – The Committee Man

THE APPOINTMENT OF LIEUTENANT COMMANDER Sampson Sladen in 1909 was not welcomed with wild applause by the officers and men of the Brigade, who considered him more a 'committee man' than a full-blooded firefighter. Many of them had hoped that Gompertz Gamble would, at last, take command and those who were pressing for improved conditions reckoned, not without some justifi-

Lieut. Commander Sir Sampson Sladen. Chief Officer, 1909–1918. (LFCDA.)

cation, that Sladen was 'in the pocket' of his employers, the London County Council, and as such was inevitably at a distance from his work force. They, increasingly, were determined that their 24 hours a day duty, – barring sickness or leave – must come to an end.

Sladen, however, set to work conscientiously and meticulously, dealing with all aspects of his administration but making no particular personal impact. In 1911 the Brigade took delivery of a new, motor powered fire boat 'Gamma II' from Thornycroft's yard. Like Wells's boats, it had a shallow draught (3½ ft), was 66½ ft long by 11 ft 6 ins beam with interior headroom of 6 ft 6 ins. It had accommodation for three men in quarters aft, furnished with sofa beds and equipped with a table, cooking 'range' and a lavatory. Forward were the store and hose room. (All London's fire boats, 'Alpha', 'Beta', 'Gamma' and 'Delta', named from the Greek alphabet, had 'II' after them, not because they were the second in their class, but probably because other boats with the same name had already been registered.)

By this time, the suffragette movement was beginning to make an impact as women began increasingly to emerge from their homebound lives in considerable numbers and demand wider opportunities. Above all, they wanted the vote. Peaceful approaches had proved totally unsucessful in producing universal suffrage and now came a much tougher campaign which featured disruption of public occasions and often involved the Fire Brigade.

It was only one of the hazards facing the organisers of the Coronation of King George V in 1911. Edward VII had died after only a comparatively short period on the throne and one of his last official engagements was on 19 July 1909 when he inspected the London Fire Brigade's Annual Parade in Hyde Park. In his speech, he thanked the firemen for all that they were doing, recalling that, as a young man – and an amateur fireman – there was nothing that he had liked more than helping to extinguish fires, and even now, he still took a great interest in the work. He had, he told the Brigade, never seen a finer body of men, and exhorted them to continue 'always zealous and active' in their duties.

At about this time, he instituted the King's Police and Fire Services Medal, with a clause that it was to be awarded to

'those of our faithful subjects who, being members of ... a properly organised Fire Brigade within our Dominions, have performed acts of exceptional courage and skill or have exhibited conspicuous devotion to duty.'

(The awards were changed later to become the King's Police and Fire Services Medal for Gallantry and the King's Police and Fire Medal for Distinguished Service. In 1952, the gallantry award was replaced by the George Medal, except in posthumous cases, and the Distinguished Service Medal was divided into separate groups, with a Queen's Fire Service Medal and a Queen's Police Medal. Both of these had special classes for posthumous awards.)

After Edward's death, official plans for the Coronation of his son, as King George V, must have been discussed with Sladen, but it was Sachs who stepped in and stole the publicity with the fire precautions which his Committee considered should be borne in mind in preparing for the processional day. Until then, he claimed, nobody had been concerned – the Home Office, the Police or the London Fire Brigade. There were no plans for public guidance. Sachs produced them.

Edwardian ladies were walking fire hazards, he asserted. Their long, trailing dresses of voile, muslin, flannelette, with celluloid ornamentation, were all an open invitation to fire. Even the huge and elaborate hats with their ostrich plumes and celluloid trimmings were a fire risk. Cigarette smoking had been increasingly popular since the turn of the century and now, as open top buses drove past, passengers often tossed their still-smouldering cigarette ends over the sides to land on the hat of some unsuspecting woman, passing by below, and set it alight.

Decorations too. The streets of London were to be draped with swathes and banners from end to end – all of them inflammable.

Sachs drew up a list of warnings and guidelines against the fire hazards of Coronation Day, had them printed as leaflets and posters and distributed by volunteers on a stupendous scale. Posters and handbills warning, particularly, of the dangers of lighted cigarette ends, were put up all along the processional route, with the support and help of practically everyone from the Dean of St Paul's, the railway, bus and tram companies, the Board of Trade and even Dr Barnardo's Homes. Kodak, the photographic company, distributed 5,000 warning 'slips' and the public was bombarded with 14,000 posters, 13,000 handbills, 4,000 letters (to household and shopkeepers along the processional route) as well as announcements in 400 newspapers and periodicals throughout the country.

Not to be outdone, the Brigade offered advice to the authorities on fire protection, particularly in the stands outside St Paul's and Guildhall, where smoking was absolutely forbidden and firemen were posted at strategic points to make sure that nobody broke the rules. The LCC and the Metropolitan Boroughs Joint Standing Committee also issued strict instructions on conditions for safety in signs and decorations – on the route and elsewhere. This was probably the first major exercise in fire protection on a great public occasion in the capital and it proved remarkably successful.

The Coronation aside, a somewhat casual attitude to fire hazards seems to have been widespread in the corridors of power at that time, and, despite the obvious dangers of celluloid, urgent action was not considered necessary since there were so few big fires caused by it. This totally ignored the fact that small fires often caused horrendous injuries to individuals and bigger ones were disastrous. Arding & Hobbs department store, close by Clapham Junction railway station, set out an elaborate window display of celluloid dolls, toys and decoration for Christmas 1909. Through some mild overheating, it burst into flames and started a fire which was so intense that the heat was reputed to have cooked all the turkeys hanging outside the poulterers' shop across the road. More important, it resulted in the deaths of nine shoppers and assistants but despite a further public outcry, no government legislation was brought in for another 13 years. (Flannelette had been dealt with in the *Fabrics (Misdescription) Act of 1913*).

Changes were undoubtedly taking place within the Brigade however. Already the motor fire engines were reaching speeds of up to 50 mph and an intensive building programme which had started in Hamilton's time as Chief Officer, was being intensified. Lee Green at Lewisham had a watch room equipped with electrical indicators from the various fire alarm call points, telephones and '*an ingenious device so that as soon as the fire bell is rung, the electric lights are automatically switched on in the station – and the mens' bedrooms.*' A fine contribution, no doubt, to marital bliss, particularly as not only did lights go on in the bedrooms but bells rang out above the bedroom doors. There was a gymnasium, 'with dumb-bells, Indian clubs, etc' and a full-size billiard table. Electric light, hot water for baths and heating and a complete laundry were provided in the basement along with drying closets. There was a separate oil store and 'a little iron cupboard' in the station yard, stacked with cans of petrol.

Pre-1914 petrol driven appliances. (LFCDA.)

Accommodation was provided for the men and their families over the station and in cottages close by, behind which was '*a novel hose-drying tower consisting of an iron tripod frame about 60 ft high, so constructed that it can be used for drills with fire escapes and hook ladders.*' When the bells went down, the appliances were reckoned to be on the road within 30 seconds. This was the pattern for the ensuing stations. Knightsbridge had followed rapidly. With a 500 year lease at £790 a year ground rent and costing £11,250 to build, it was still being used at the end of the century.

In 1911, an unusual and provocative challenge faced the Brigade. On 24th January, a group of anarchists who, on the previous day, had shot and killed three policemen, were holed up in a house in Sidney Street, deep in the slum area of London's East End. Police and the Scots Guards, who were called to the scene, closed in with rifles and shot guns and sealed off the whole surrounding area. After a long, uneasy calm, smoke was seen coming from the house in which the anarchists were trapped. An onlooker called the Fire Brigade and the Home Secretary, Winston Churchill, who, because of the unusual importance of the occasion was among the officials in attendance, later described the ensuing events:

'…Suddenly, with a stir and a clatter, up came the Fire Brigade, scattering the crowds gathered on the approach to the scene and thrusting through them until they reached the police cordon at the beginning of the danger zone. The Inspector of Police forbade further progress and the Fire Brigade officer declared it was his duty to advance. A fire was raging and he was bound to extinguish it. Anarchists, automatic pistol danger zones – nothing of this sort was mentioned in the Regulations of the London Fire Brigade. When the police officer pointed out that his men would be shot down, he replied simply that orders were orders and that he had no alternative.

'I now intervened to settle the dispute, at one moment quite heated. I told the Fire Brigade officer, in my authority as Home Secretary, that the house was to be allowed to burn down and that he was to stand by in readiness to prevent the conflagration from spreading.' *The fire burned on with troops and police at the ready.* 'At last,' *wrote Churchill*, 'it became certain that these human fiends had perished… a detective inspector walked quickly to the door and kicked it open. There was nothing but smoke and flame inside the building. The firemen rushed forward with their hoses......'

The Sidney Street Siege was over. Winston Churchill, had survived his first brush with the London Fire Brigade but was to meet them on more than one occasion thirty years later when he led Britain as Prime Minister throughout the Second World War.

Although there were still big fires in London, the use of sprinklers in major buildings was developing and reducing the risk of the old 'conflagrations' in which fires had spread rapidly from one building to another.

The idea of an automatic fire sprinkler went back to the late 18th century when the earliest types had simply been pipes with holes bored at intervals which could be primed by turning on a water tap. In 1806, a Londoner, John Carey, took out a patent for a rose sprinkler in which pipes were fitted in various parts of a building and operated by pulling ropes. Water was supplied by tanks on the roof, dependent on a good supply of rain and when this disappeared the sprinklers stopped work. In 1807 a French patent for an automatic sprinkler was registered and shortly after this, Sir William Congreve patented a system of perforated pipes which worked on a combined automatic / manual method. Valves attached to the water pipes were connected by cords secured in a cement which was fusible at 110°F – or less if the machinery went wrong. An assortment of similar devices followed until in 1864, a Captain Stewart Harrison of the 1st London Engineers devised a sprinkler which consisted of a rose with perforations through which water was forced, with an internal valve controlling the water and secured with solder which melted in heat. This was the first sprinkler to work with any degree of efficiency and it was followed in 1874 by another, even more successful, called, after its inventor, 'The Parmelee'.

One of the best systems in the Victorian period was the Draper Hetherington. By the beginning of the new Georgian age many of the bigger London buildings were equipped with even more sophisticated and efficient systems for dousing fires as soon as they started, among them the bigger hotels and stores. The chief risk with these was accidental triggering, which could cause more damage than a fire.

Despite this, 1912 brought another devastating blaze in the City, when a Christmas card factory in Moor Lane burned down and nine people were killed. Yet again, celluloid was the culprit. A consignment of 1,500 lbs of German celluloid was stored on the premises when an unsuspecting youth, parcelling it up, dropped hot sealing wax on to a small block of the material which burned so fiercely that within minutes the fire was out of control. The only extinguishers on the premises were buckets of water and despite the widespread publicity of previous years, the manager of the works said that he had thought there was no danger. There had been no fire drills on the premises, nobody had known what to do and the whole affair was described as 'a comic opera.' Not, however, for the victims and their families.

The jury at the inquest into the Moor Lane fire urged the Home Office to introduce more stringent controls generally on the use and storage of celluloid and primarily as a result of this, a Government Committee was established which set to work diligently. It held 29 meetings, took evidence from 40 witnesses, visited France and Germany and finally, in a report issued in December 1913, called for regulations restricting the amounts and demanding safer means of storing raw celluloid.

One is tempted to assume that the result of such recommendations might have gone the same way as its predecessors, but at least, the LCC, under pressure from Sladen and his officers, promoted the *London County Council Celluloid & etc Act* in 1915 which demanded essential, if basic, precautions to be taken in places of entertainment against the risks involved with the use of celluloid and other inflammable materials. It was not until 1922 that the general legislation was brought in by the government's *Celluloid and Cinematograph Film Act*.

Before this, events had overtaken the whole country which evidently pushed the problems of fire into the background. In August 1914, the Great War – World War 1 – broke out and the minds of government and people were concentrated on a very different danger.

With these professional challenges and a growing atmosphere of industrial unrest, 1914 was a particularly unhappy period in LFB history. Gone was the gallant image of the Massey Shaw fireman, all galloping horses and glistening brass. Many of the men were increasingly discontented. The officers were struggling to maintain discipline and, at the same time, to cope with the external dangers facing them. When the LCC had taken over from the Board of Works in 1889, they had cancelled the order that all firemen should have previously been seamen, but nevertheless, many of them had served in the Royal Navy. As the war broke out 1,251 men were on the books of the LFB. Almost immediately, 280 of the reservists, were called up for duty with the Navy or the Army. No move was made to prevent this, but the LCC did agree to allow their families to continue occupying Fire Brigade quarters and their service pay was made up to the level of their civilian wages. Patriotic fervour was high and another 140 men volunteered for service 'at the Front', so that by October 1914 the Brigade was already more than 400 men under strength.

If industrial unrest had been in anyone's mind, it was sharply dealt with by the LCC announcement that in view of the shortage of firemen, the whole question of increasing days off from one day a fortnight to one day a week would, of necessity be deferred, although they agreed to reconsider this after a period of 6 months. Nevertheless, they urgently needed more men and offered a reward of ten shillings to any fireman who introduced a suitable recruit to the Service.

The attitude of the Government, which had always been lukewarm to the needs of firefighting, was less sensitive. The war was being fought on the battlefields of France and Flanders. They could see no reason to fear that it might strike closer to home. Admittedly, when the first Zeppelin raids occurred, mostly in East Anglia in the Spring of 1915 and Field Marshal Lord Kitchener, as Secretary of State for War, was asked whether he felt that firemen should be expected to join the services he had replied that they '*would be doing their duty for King and Country equally well at home as those who had joined the Army for service on the traditional battlefield*'.

It did, however, make the London County Council realise that London might yet be the target for German bombers and in May, 1915, arrangements were made with the General Officer commanding the London districts for one officer and a number of sappers to help the Brigade, along with members of the Salvage Corps, the Metropolitan Water Board and the Kodak private brigades, but this help would only be available during air-raids. Indeed, London's professional firemen were not exempted from call-up for the armed services when conscription was introduced in 1916 and as the trained and skilled firemen left for the trenches of Flanders, their places were taken by men, mostly over military age, serving with the London Rifle Volunteers, recruited to the LFB after a brief and inadequate training period.

Apart from one or two minor incidents, plus a Zeppelin raid when 29 fires were caused in the most vulnerable part of the City around Wood Street, during which 22 motor pumps were in action and one fireman was killed, fire damage from enemy air attacks was slight during the earliest part of the war.

Despite this, the indefatigable Sachs was deeply concerned at the potential fire risk from enemy air attack. Perhaps because he moved in such influential circles, he was able to browbeat sufficient members of the government to allow him to form a volunteer force of auxiliary firemen and this he did, on a remarkably large scale. In the earliest days he had contacted the authorities to ask what steps they were taking to protect the population from aerial poison bomb attacks, only to be told (somewhat complacently,

considering the gas attacks which took place during the battles in France) that the only bombs which might be expected were high explosives and incendiaries.

An official report, published later by his Fire Prevention Committee showed that the permanent Civil Department of the government had 'cordially welcomed' the offer of help from the Committee. '*Some government departments*', it said, '*did not realise the necessity for fire prevention with the result that the destruction by fire of munitions, food, forage etc, was somewhat large and the loss to the community considerable.*' Not surprisingly, it added that many complaints had been received by the Committee over the lack of fire and safety precautions, the absence of precautions for munitions factories, the danger of accumulation of hazardous stores, the difficulties of water supplies to sensitive areas, of poor communications, of dangerous processes and some degree of carelessness in such inspection as there was into hazardous risks.

Equally important, surprising and significant was the report's assertion that '*similarly, the military authorities were inclined to ignore the question of fire prevention from the scientific point of view, resulting in much fire loss in camps, hutments etc.*' As a result of this indifference and ineptitude, it was Sachs and his supporters who provided a 24-hour telephone advisory service on fire prevention and the effect of bombs on building material, particularly concrete, as well as on ways of minimising the effect of possible incendiary bomb raids.

His faithful volunteers, often using their own transport and unpaid, apart from some travelling expenses subsidised by the War Office for the inspection of hutment camps, visited and produced surveys on 35 army camps and 2,500 hospitals up and down the country, on the basis of which they issued comprehensive fire warning posters in English, translated into Urdu and Punjabi for Indian troops; Arabic for Egypt and Palestine; French and Flemish plus Braille for the blind. Their warnings and advice covered hospitals, Red Cross work-rooms, munition works, churches, schools, theatres, Christmas entertainments, farms and petrol stores.

From their West End offices, they set up a technical advisory service, answering questions from the armed services and government departments which ranged from the incendiary effect of thermite on different building materials, suitable protective clothing for munition workers, protection of naval gunners against back-flash, the chemicals from which fumes might be dangerous to firemen, the possibility of safeguarding aircraft from outbreaks of fire, the classes of structure which it would be a waste of effort to bomb during aerial attacks on Germany, through to the precautions which the public should take in the event of air raids. Added to this, Sachs, with his wide experience of

THE BRITISH FIRE PREVENTION COMMITTEE
(FOUNDED 1897—INCORPORATED 1899)

FREE ISSUE
FOR THE
PUBLIC USE
No. 17a

SPECIAL
FIRE SURVEY
FORCE
WAR CAUTION

WARNING!

FIRES DUE TO AIR RAIDS

NATURE OF BOMBS USED AND HOW TO DEAL WITH FIRES ARISING THEREFROM

- Buckets of water (supplemented where feasible by ordinary hand pumps) are recommended as the most suitable and economical fire appliances, and, where oil or spirit is used, buckets of sand.
- Don't wait until a fire occurs to find the best way out in the dark. Think of a couple of ways out beforehand.
- If there is dense smoke from a fire remember that the air is clearer near the ground, so crawl on the floor, with a handkerchief, wet rag, or respirator in front of your mouth.
- Ascertain the quickest means of obtaining assistance from the Fire Brigade and Police. Post up the necessary particulars, nearest fire-alarm, &c., on the ground floor.
- Don't run off shout. Keep calm as an example to others.

1. THE ORDINARY EXPLOSIVE BOMBS employed by the enemy rarely cause a fire per se, but where a building is injured or collapses, fires are frequently caused by open lights or fires, etc., and their spread is assisted by escaping gas from broken mains or arcs from broken electric cables.

   Fires thus caused indirectly by Explosive Bombs can as a rule be dealt with as ordinary fires in their incipient stage. Any gas or electrical supply not cut off prior to the outbreak should, if possible, however, be cut off at the earliest possible moment.

2. THE INCENDIARY BOMBS employed by the enemy readily fire buildings and their contents owing to the fierce nature of the flames and the molten metal generated by the chemicals used.

   Fires caused by Incendiary Bombs may be prevented from spreading, regardless of the high temperature generated at the actual seat of the outbreak, if water be promptly applied in fair bulk, force and continuity, say from a series of buckets energetically thrown, or hand pumps vigorously worked. Sand or loose soil similarly thrown might be useful in the absence of water, but would not have the necessary cooling effect. The application of single buckets of water, single shovels of sand, etc., would be comparatively valueless, a concentration of the available liquid first-aid appliances being required to obtain the necessary result.

   Note: In order to deal with fires from Incendiary Bombs, their make should be understood and the following describes one of the types frequently used:

   (a) The bomb as a rule, is conical, of 10 inches diameter at the base, corded round, and has a metal handle at the apex (see A).

   (b) The base is a flat cup, on to which a pierced metal funnel is fitted, having the ignition device and handle fitted at the top.

   (c) The funnel is generally filled with Thermit, which upon ignition generates intense heat and by the time of the concession has taken the form of molten metal of the extraordinary high temperature of over 5000° Fahr.

   The molten metal is spread by the concussion.

   (d) Outside the funnel is a padding of a highly inflammable or resinous material bound on with an inflammable form of rope. The resinous material creates a pungent smoke.

   (e) There is generally some melted white phosphorus in the bottom of the cup which develops noxeous fumes.

   (f) In some cases celluloid chippings are added and occasionally a small quantity of petrol.

Sketch A. Appearance of an Incendiary Bomb.

Ignition Device

Thermit

Resinous matter

Melted white phosphorus

Rope

Cup

SECTION OF INCENDIARY BOMB.

3. FUMES: The fumes of the Bombs are generally very pungent, and a simple form of respirator (that can be readily damped) should be kept handy and used where necessary.

   Firemen and others whose duty it is to attend incendiary fires would do well to carry simple respirators in their uniform.

PRECAUTIONS:

SHOULD DEFINITE INFORMATION BE RECEIVED OF THE APPROACH OF HOSTILE AIRCRAFT OR ACTUAL BOMBARDMENT COMMENCE IN THE VICINITY, REFUGE SHOULD BE PROMPTLY TAKEN IN THE CELLAR, BASEMENT OR LOWER FLOOR:

- ALL GAS LIGHTS or stoves should be turned out, and the gas supply turned off at the meter.
- ALL ELECTRIC LIGHTS should be switched off, and the supply turned off at the main switch near the meter.

FURTHER, IF TIME PERMITS:

- ALL OIL LAMPS should be extinguished and taken into the cellar or basement.
- ALL OPEN FIRES above basement level should be extinguished.
- ALL DOORS should be closed.
- ALL WINDOWS should be closed, also shutters where such exist.

BUCKETS OF WATER SHOULD ALWAYS BE AVAILABLE AND WHERE SPIRIT IS USED ALSO BUCKETS OF SAND.

Offices of the Committee:
8 Waterloo Place, Pall Mall,
London, S.W. 1916

Issued by THE BRITISH FIRE PREVENTION COMMITTEE
(By Order of the Executive).

Any Technical Inquiry regarding special precautionary measures during the War will be dealt with by the British Fire Prevention Committee upon written application.

[Approved Copyright Form]

European firefighting, was able to offer invaluable detailed and accurate information on the firefighting arrangements of 'certain enemy cities.'

At Sach's suggestion, a fire committee was set up in the Ministry of Munitions, with the major aims of safeguarding British arms dumps in France and improving safety in munition factories and stores at home – all matters which one might have thought would have already been the responsibility of the government.

Some idea of the contemporary official view of the importance of firemen and firefighting can be assessed by the outcome of an appeal made to a special Tribunal, set up in London in 1916 when the government had refused to withdraw exemption from military service from all firemen below the age of 25. Sladen supported the Chairman of the LCC in pleading for 119 trained and experienced London firemen below that age to be allowed to stay but in vain. The answer came back that 2,000 young postmen had already been granted exemption and these totally untrained 'conscripts' could be used for fighting fires – which was evidently regarded as an unskilled task needing no more than a couple of hours' training.

They were soon to be proved wrong. In the summer of 1917, a group of German Gotha bombers flew over the Capital. Watched in horror by Londoners, scarcely able to believe their eyes, the planes circled St Paul's before dropping their bombs in the heart of the City, completely unchallenged. In three daylight raids a total of more than 200 people were killed. HE and incendiary bombs set light to the General Post Office a stone's throw from the Cathedral and started a trail of other fires as well as destroying a number of buildings.

In the ensuing panic, the government ordered all members of the London Fire Brigade serving in the armed forces to be recalled (or those of them who had survived the carnage of battle). The Home Secretary was asked to co-ordinate all the 90 local fire brigades which existed in the 750 square miles of the London area and this he did, on 25th September 1917, under the Defence of the Realm Act, setting up a Greater London Fire Brigade Co-ordination Committee to implement suitable plans.

The procedure involved two or more 'moves' in the event of a raid. The first called for the attendance in London of at least nine motor fire engines from outside brigades while others closed up on stand-by. The second provided for a greater concentration of motor fire pumps in London and for a considerably larger number of motor and horsed appliances to close in and stand by. The first scheme was activated 19 times and the second, larger, scheme only

Warnings to the public of fire hazards in First World War. (Guildhall Library, Corporation of London.)

once. The order, initially intended for use only during air raids, was later extended to include any fire at a Naval, military or air force establishment or ammunition factory within the whole Metropolitan area.

All the fire stations in the new area were now linked by special emergency telephone lines so that they might be notified by the Commissioner of Police as soon as enemy bombers were spotted. It was then their responsibility to set off maroons warning the public of a potential air raid – a situation which led on the Sunday morning of 19th July 1917, to 79 fire stations simultaneously detonating a series of ear-splitting maroons, which brought practically every citizen of the metropolitan area out of their beds and diving for shelter. In the event, enemy planes had only been seen crossing the Essex coast and the threat never reached the London area. Additional telephone lines kept the fire brigade headquarters in touch with the GHQ of the Home Forces, the Metropolitan Police, the assorted gas, light and electric companies and the Metropolitan Water Board. These were duplicated with lines to Euston fire station which was designated as a substitute Brigade HQ under the Divisional Commander, North, should Southwark have been put out of action.

It was a bold and proper move, but caused endless problems, not only of appropriate financial compensation for the outer London brigades but through incompatibility of equipment. The LFB 'round thread' screws seldom fitted on to the variety of joints being used by other brigades and special adaptors had to be hastily fashioned to fasten together the different lengths of hose.

For the most part though, despite the teething problems, the scheme worked well. In the next serious air raid, in December 1917, six German planes dropped 276 incendiary bombs and started a record 52 fires. It was the first time that London had experienced a fire raid and, unfortunately, not the last. Two people were killed and six injured in the attack which was followed a few weeks later by another raid in which two firemen were hurt. The fires were successfully dealt with by brigades from as far out as Twickenham and Wembley which roared in to help out the beleaguered inner London crews although this was, at times, reversed as the bomb attacks were not concentrated solely on the inner city but scattered throughout the suburbs.

The biggest challenge came in the last serious raid on the capital, on 28th January 1918, when 33 high explosive bombs and one incendiary fell, killing 41 people. The bomb which caused the most casualties landed on Odhams printing works in Long Acre, close to Covent Garden Market and, by chance, the home of many of London's earliest fire engine manufacturers. It penetrated a basement which was being used as an air raid shelter, and firemen, drawing on their training and experience, were able to tunnel into the debris, extricating the bodies and rescuing more than 100 injured civilians.

It was not only bombing which caused casualties. As Sachs had repeatedly emphasised, many of the manufacturing processes of war produced their own hazards, principally those in munitions factories. His teams of experts had toured these, pointing out the risks and urging precautions and care. Nevertheless, there were numerous incidents in a variety of factories concerned with armaments. Reports of such accidents were officially censored, but nobody could hide the results of the worst which took place in January 1917.

A small fire had broken out in a vast munitions plant at Silvertown near the Thames estuary in east London and a detachment from the West Ham fire brigade was dealing with it when, shortly before 7 pm, a devastating explosion demolished the entire factory. West Ham's pump was wrecked, a sub-officer and fireman were killed instantly, the fire station a few hundred yards away was shattered and two of the resident firemen's children killed. Windows of houses in Blackheath, on the far side of the river, were smashed by the force of the blast and 69 people, including 26 women and children, were killed in the houses nearest to the factory, with a further 400 injured.

The casualties would have been greater had there been workers inside at the time, but the fire spread rapidly. Within minutes a gas holder containing nine million cubic feet of coal gas went up in flames and the sparks from this blew across the Thames and set light to a tar manufacturer's yard in Greenwich. Added to which, terrified local people increased the chaos by setting off practically every street fire alarm in the East End.

West Ham called in the London Fire Brigade who were already attending the fires which had broken out in Greenwich and Blackwall as a result of the initial explosion but they sent 29 motor pumps and two fire boats to help their West Ham colleagues and the combined fire force was in attendance at Silvertown for ten days.

Peace came at last to the country with the signing of the Armistice document between Germany and the victorious Allies on 11th November 1918. For the London Fire Brigade though, the rumblings of discontent were reaching a climax which brought the very real threat of the first firemen's strike in the history of the capital.

Life in the Brigade had undoubtedly changed for the better during Sampson Sladen's period in office, at least in the pre-war days. Stations were bigger, better built and provided far more facilities for the men and their families than there had been in the past. There was a Brigade Athletics Association which included branches for angling, boxing, cycling, cricket, football, swimming and running. The Annual Sports Day in one of London's parks was already a regular event, often enhanced by the music of the London Fire Brigade Band under the baton of its Bandmaster, Peter Anderson. The Band was also commissioned for concerts at other events throughout London.

Within the Brigade promotion no longer relied on years of service alone. An examination system had been set up in the 1880s dealing with general and technical knowledge and by now an ambitious young man could, within reasonable time, rise to Sub-Officer, Station Officer, District Officer, Superintendent and Senior Superintendent, although the senior posts tended still to be reserved for 'officers and gentlemen.'

The uniform had changed slightly since Shaw's days. Now, a Sub-Officer wore an epaulette without sidepieces on his right shoulder, a Station Officer a full epaulette, a Superintendent had one row of buttons on his tunic but a District Officer had two. The undress uniform of a Superintendent and all ranks above was a blue serge suit with a cloth peak cap having an oak leaf pattern round the peak while the cap of a Sub-Officer had only a glazed peak. All ranks below Sub-Officer wore an undress 'sailor' style cap without a peak. Helmets, epaulettes and buttons of the principal officers were silver-plated while a Superintendent and ranks below him were brass.

Re-organisation on this scale, plus the problems of the War had brought heavy pressures to bear on Sladen, who had been faced with bringing together a service which had lost many of its best young men and taken in a rag, tag and bobtail of auxiliaries and conscripts with little idea of what to do at a fire, let alone working out ways of dealing efficiently with the destruction wreaked by successive air raids. Records show that the Brigade had worked at three raids in 1915, three in 1916, thirteen in 1917 and five in 1918, seven of them carried out by Zeppelins, eighteen by aircraft. Of these, 22 were at night and three by day, with the last on the night of the 19th/20th May, 1918. 922 bombs were dropped including 355 incendiary and 567 HE in the London area, killing 524 people and injuring 1,264.

Jack While of *The Times* wrote:

'The catastrophe which beset the entire civilized world from August 1914 until close on Christmas 1918 swept away many traditions, wiped out all records and created many new ones; but it did one unmistakable thing: it made us abandon for ever the comforting thought that we Britishers previously hugged to our bosoms – that our insular position made us perfectly safe from the approach of foreign foe.'

It was While too, who remarked 'it is a pity that officialism did not rise to the occasion .....to meet the emergency. The powers-that-be scorned the idea that terrified women and children wanted shelters or even warnings to get to the shelters....but when they found that the Zeppelin raids were followed by the Gotha raids, that great areas of London in the very central and most important districts were attacked not only by night but in broad daylight, they began to bestir themselves ... and so, out of the scenes of confusion and devastation and terror arose some sort of system which undoubtedly saved many lives in succeeding raids.'

In glowing words of the day's journalese he bore witness to 'the splendid work of the London firemen..... and their gallantry in all the circles of raids, which has been too little noticed by the authorities.' *He deplored the fact that* 'when unknown civil servants who had spent the war sitting in their offices had received honours, the work of the firemen had practically escaped the attention of the authorities'

Some had been maimed and gassed (presumably from broken gas mains) while dragging victims from the wreckage of ruined buildings. In other cases, the enemy planes had returned to the scene of an attack and dropped bombs on the firemen as they fought the flames. Jack While suggested publicly that a special Air Raid Medal should be struck and awarded to all the people who did systematic service during air raids, but no action was taken on this, although 47 officers and men of the Brigade were decorated by King George V for their gallantry. For the rest, as While wrote later:

'they did many gallant deeds which have never been recorded and which, as a result of the modesty of all brave men, will remain unrecorded.'

Now the battle of peace began.

The war had taken an enormous toll of the nation's physical and mental resources. Almost every family had lost someone in the four years of horrific trench warfare and bombardment. The leisurely, luxurious days of the pre-war wealthy Victorian and Edwardian upper classes contrasted starkly with the lives of the working population who had, as the war dragged on, become increasingly hit by food shortages and the rising cost of living. As far back as 1909, a conference of fire chiefs acknowledged that *conditions to-day call for firemen with a knowledge of electricity, chemistry and other subjects*' yet this had never been reflected in the men's pay and conditions of service. Gradually, 'extra' duties had crept into their unwritten terms of reference. In 1912 a team of reluctant firemen were called in to use their hoses in breaking up a workers' demonstration during a strike in the London Docks. Other, less tendentious, work included helping the police to chase miscreants over roofs, rescuing cats from trees, opening doors for those who had forgotten their keys, checking on dangerous chimneys, inspecting places of entertainment, inspecting private fire appliances, plus checking 1,500 street fire alarms and 20,000 hydrants every two months. Their quarters were still subject to inspection and had to be kept spotless by their wives while the men spent hours every day cleaning the station and checking and polishing every item of equipment – including their own boots, buttons and brass helmets.

Wages in London, when the First World War started, ranged from £1.6.6d (£1.32p) to £1.15s (£1.75p) plus some 'gratuities' and a non-contributory pension scheme. Added attractions in the LCC's official advertisement for firemen included free uniforms and free medical treatment. Nevertheless, the starting wage for a fireman at that time was already reckoned to be 20% less than the national average wage and the peak of £1.15s per week was only reached after ten years' service. The pension was only paid after 28 years' service. As late as 1912, a man who had been ill for any length of time could be evicted, with his family, from Brigade quarters and would have to find some temporary lodgings until he was fit enough to return to duty, the explanation for this being that it was *to provide an inducement to a man to resume duty as quickly as possible.*'

Hours of duty meant that a London fireman had to be in his station day and night for 13 days of continuous duty before being allowed a day off and his annual holiday was one week's leave away from the station. Days off could still be cancelled at a moment's notice in the event of a big fire, an inspection or even a drill. (One seasoned fireman, a well-disciplined ex-seaman, was so incensed when his particularly vindictive Station Officer called a drill at the precise moment that the man was chatting up his fiancée at the Station entrance, that he carried out the drill impeccably before chasing his superior round the watch room with an axe. It did his cv no good, but released a great deal of personal tension.) At times when large fires had drained the nearest stations, men were transferred over to 'hold the fort' at neighbouring areas, which often meant hours away from home and a long walk back at the end of it, as there were no 'expenses' for any transport on these occasions.

In 1911, the LCC had granted their employees a six-day week, but specifically excluded firemen from this, arguing that it would require more men, £11,000 extra a week in wages, £15,000 capital expenditure for new quarters to accommodate the extra firemen and £3,500 for training them. An added excuse was that the men had not positively demanded one day off and also that they were allowed to read and smoke on duty!

Although it was true that many firemen still preferred to work the long hours rather than risk their homes by causing trouble, the atmosphere was already changing in the service. Although several efforts had been made by the Labour movement, one as early as 1902, to start up a trade union for firemen, a majority of London men had rejected the idea. In 1913, despite murmurings of mutiny and breach of discipline, a fireman's branch of the National Union of Corporation Workers (later to become the National Union of Public Employees) was established claiming 864 members from firemen in the capital (although not all from the LFB – many came from private industrial brigades.) Its first meeting was held in the Bell Hotel, Old Bailey, and following this, the men's demands were presented to the Press and the LCC. There were five points:

1   One day's leave in eight.

2   Removals from station to station to be paid for by the County Council. (Particularly important, considering that they moved home every two years.)

3   The granting of subsistence allowances when men were temporarily sent to other stations to stand-by.

4   The withdrawal of a regulation which required sons of firemen to leave their homes on the station when they reached the age of 18.

5   The reduction of the period of service to qualify for a pension to be reduced from 28 years to 25.

The result was a suggestion by the Fire Brigade Committee of the Council that a representative or staff committee of 12 elected Brigade members might be set up with the title of 'The London Fire Brigade Staff Committee' to present the views of the men on changes in their welfare to the Chief Officer. He could then, if necessary, arrange for a deputation from the Staff Committee to attend on the Fire Brigade Committee. Their reasonable expenses would be paid by the Council.

The men pondered on the offer but rejected it, saying that they would prefer trade union membership. Meanwhile, their Union continued its work. It now tackled the problems of the young firemen. Those taken on as single firemen who later married, were only allowed married quarters when they had served a minimum of three years in the service. Should they marry before this, they had to find their own accommodation outside, but continue taking their meals in the single mess quarters, paying a compulsory 1/- (5p) a week for the use of its lighting and heating. The branch pressed for all married firemen to be provided with suitable quarters, on site.

Soon after this, a petition was handed to the Chief Officer

again outlining changes in pay and conditions which a majority of the men were seeking. And so the arguments had continued until the beginning of the war had put paid to any further consideration of the men's demands. The bitterness of the established firemen was deepened when they discovered that the authorities who had denied them their extra shilling a week were now paying a wage of two guineas (£2.10p) a week to the recruits taken into the Special Fire Service Force which had been organised by Sachs and his British Fire Prevention Committee.

Patriotism and extra work brought on by the departure of so many men to the war, kept the London men quiet for two years but by 1916 they had put up another petition for a wage increase. In 1913, they had been told that they could not petition the Council and must work through the Chief Officer. Now they were assured that they could not petition the Chief Officer. Small wonder that there was a rift between them and Sampson Sladen.

Despite the war effort, 1917 became a year of industrial ferment. Shipyard workers, miners, dockers, factory workers were again up in arms, frequently on strike, and there were even threats of mutiny in the armed services. In August 1918, shortly before the war ended, a climax was reached when the Metropolitan Police came out on strike.

The dispute was settled quickly, with an assurance that there would be a substantial pay increase and no victimisation on condition that no policeman joined a trade union. Instead, they and the prison staff were allowed to form an elected organisation, the Police Federation, to put forward formal representations and complaints. This concession formed the basis of the Police Act of 1919.

It was a significant move. Until this stage, there had been parity between the pay of the firemen and police. Now, it was the firemen's turn to increase pressure on the authorities to provide some means by which they too, might submit requests concerning their pay and conditions.

A 'round table' discussion was set up between the men's union representatives and the LCC Fire Brigade Committee, but the result proved unsatisfactory. Both sides agreed to submit the main problem of union representation to arbitration. The Government was approached and in September 1918 Sir George (later Lord) Askwith, was appointed to act as arbitrator. Until this time, action had been centred on the lower ranks, but now, despite warnings from the Chief Officer that he would 'deplore' such action, the sub-officers withdrew from the Staff Association and joined forces with the men. Askwith, who had been chief of the labour, commercial and statistical department of the Board of Trade before the war, was an experienced Chief Industrial Commissioner. It was he who listened to the mens' case (although neither he, nor the Council knew at the time that the men had already taken a vote and agreed on strike action should their demands be turned down out of hand).

The firemen were represented by their Union Secretary, Jim Bradley, a former London park-keeper and avid trade union man. He maintained that firemen's unions were recognised throughout the world and by many authorities in England. Only the LCC had quibbled over accepting union representation. On the other hand, the LCC argued that the County Council was responsible for the safety of London and they, as well as everybody else, including the Government, believed that in a disciplined force it would be fatal to introduce an outside body between the Chief Officer and the Council.

Askwith went away, pondered and produced a verdict, establishing the right of every London fireman to belong to a Trade Union if he so wished. It was a memorable result, although it was not all that the unions had hoped for, since it offered the alternative of a Collective or Representative Body and the men now opted for this.

It also divided the unity of the Brigade, since it made clear that the award only applied to the ranks below that of Station Officer – those who had united to present the case. The Representative Body was soon established, with 12 members including three sub-officers and Jim Bradley. Soon after this, they achieved a five shilling (25p) pay increase on the 'war wages' and ten shilling a week widow's pension, plus one day's leave in ten days. The Representative Body and the Trade Union were to work side by side for the next twenty years.

Meanwhile, the strain had become too much for Lieut-Commander Sladen. His 19 years of service, with ten years of command, had drained him. He had been criticised frequently for having lost the confidence of his men and the Council Minute noting his resignation included no expression of thanks or word of recognition for the undoubted burden which he had carried conscientiously throughout his period of office. They did, however, award him the pension which he would have been entitled to after the normal 25 years of service 'to mark its sense of the unparalleled conditions which had obtained during the last few years when the work of the Brigade has been carried out under special difficulties owing to war conditions.'

Once more, London was faced with finding a new Chief Officer. This time they opted for 39-year-old Arthur Dyer, a skilled engineer who had joined the service in 1904 as a Principal Officer by direct entry. The post of Principal Officer which became vacant on his promotion was filled – again through direct entry – by an ambitious young naval officer, Commander Aylmer Firebrace, of whom more was to be heard later.

LEFT Young waterman-fireman in the 'Sun' Office uniform with Newsham pump and 'dancers' in background.

BELOW Late 19th century advertisement for the Sun Fire Office shows 18th/19th century insurance fireman and salvage porter.

OVERLEAF The Great Fire of London, this painting by an unknown Dutch artist shows the Tower of London, which escaped the flames as the end of London Bridge, the City and St Paul's Cathedral burned in September 1666.

SUN FIRE OFFICE
LONDON
ESTABLISHED 1710.

ABOVE A rare bargeboard from one of the Phoenix Company's fire boats, showing two Phoenix watermen-firemen, the Thames and the City of London in the background.

BELOW The first steam fire engine to be built in England by Braithwaite and Ericsson, 1830. This was initially boycotted by London's firefighters.

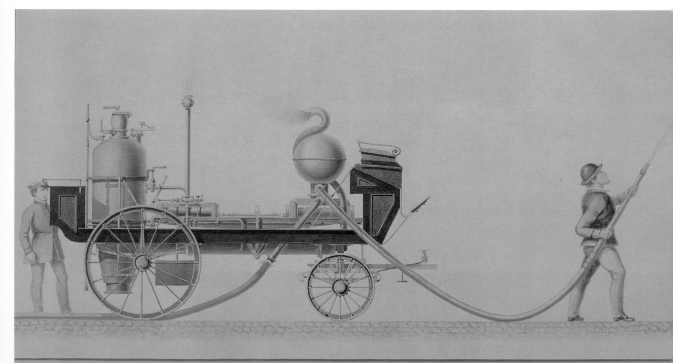

FIRST STEAM FIRE ENGINE CONSTRUCTED IN ENGLAND. A.D. 1830.
BRAITHWAITE AND ERICSSON, INVENTORS AND CONSTRUCTORS, LONDON.
WEIGHT OF ENGINE.2 TONS,1 QR.
QUANTITY OF WATER THROWN OUT OF A 1¼ INS NOZZLE
14933 LBS PER MINUTE,OR 40 TONS PER HOUR TO A HEIGHT OF 90 FEET.

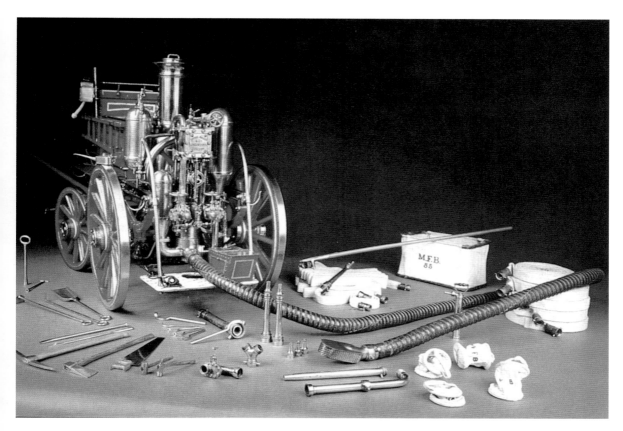

The range of equipment carried on the Brigade's steamers – and the appliance itself – are shown in this fine Shand Mason salesman's demonstration model, built by Thomas Coates in 1888 and now in the London Toy and Model Museum.

Frederick Hodges, gin distiller, doyen of Victorian London's private fire brigades and friend of King Edward VII, was presented with this ornate manual pump by the citizens of Lambeth and London in gratitude for his dedication to firefighting. It is on display in the Museum of London.

One of the earliest conflagrations of the Industrial Revolution – land engines and fire barges rush to the suspect outbreak at the Albion Mills in 1791.

OPPOSITE ABOVE The Moorgate Underground disaster – one of the worst problems to face London's emergency services in their entire history. Here, firefighters struggle to penetrate the tangled wreckage.

OPPOSITE BELOW Out of hell's gates – weary fire crews climb from the fire-scarred entrance to King's Cross Underground station where Colin Townsley, Station Officer of Soho, lost his life along with 30 travellers, after the escalator fire on 18th November, 1987.

By the 1980s, transport accidents were bringing big problems to the Brigade. Clapham Junction was one of several major rail accidents which London's firefighters – men and women by now – struggled with.

Sir Peter Darby CBE, CStJ, Chief Officer, 1977–1980.

Ronald Bullers, Chief Officer, 1981–1987.

Gerald Clarkson, BA, Chief Officer, 1987–1991.

Brian Robinson, Chief Officer, 1991–

Speed and improved service came from the new,
computerised Control Room at Lambeth headquarters.
The LFB receives 200,000 calls a year.

LEFT Television – and particularly the dramatic London Weekend Television series 'London's Burning' – increased public interest in firefighting. Members of the cast helped the Brigade with fire safety campaigns.

BELOW Continuing the royal tradition, Prince Harry eagerly takes the wheel of a vintage Leyland Metz fire escape after he, his mother, the Princess of Wales and his brother, Prince William, attended the service at St Paul's Cathedral on 25th October, 1990, to commemorate the 50th anniversary of the Blitz on London.

OPPOSITE Close to St Paul's Cathedral on 4th May, 1991, HM Queen Elizabeth, the 90 year old Queen Mother talks to Chief Officer Gerry Clarkson after unveiling the memorial to the firefighters of Britain who lost their lives in the air raids of World War Two.

OPPOSITE ABOVE LEFT
Waterman fireman, 1792.

OPPOSITE ABOVE RIGHT The
firefighter of the 1990s –
with a totally new style of
helmet and visor, trying out
the experimental BA Control
Telemetry System which
includes a heat sensor,
monitoring unit, earpiece,
speech interface, press to
talk switch and radio. In a
burning building, the eye
level heat sensor's red light
gives a temperature warning
– the green light indicates
'you should be on your way
out . . .'

OPPOSITE BELOW Heavy
rescue unit, used for serious
accidents, 1992.

RIGHT Versatile Bronto
Skylift can rescue several
people at a time and has
radio communication
between base and top.

LEFT Saxon pump/ladder.

BELOW Saxon pump/ladder, showing some of its standard equipment, including Hol-Metro hydraulic rescue gear.

16

Arthur Dyer – The Invaluable Engineer

ARTHUR REGINALD DYER WAS A QUIET MAN, TALL, fair haired, handsome. He had been born at Alton in Hampshire in 1870 and educated at St John's College, Hurstpierpoint. Firefighting was in his blood. His father was one of the most respected volunteer firemen of his generation, a founder and, for many years vice-president of the late-Victorian organisation for volunteer firemen, the

Arthur Dyer, Chief Officer, 1918–1933. (LFCDA.)

National Fire Brigades Union. After leaving school the young Arthur served four years apprenticeship to a mechanical and hydraulic engineer and passed his technical examinations as an Associate Member of the Institution of Civil Engineers. The new century found him in America between 1900–1902, working for the Westinghouse Electric Company in Pittsburgh, Pennsylvania, where he passed through all the mechanical and electrical sections, staying on with them when he returned to England until he joined the LFB as a principal officer in 1904. His career in the Fire Service was decribed as 'conspicuously successful'. It was a time when the Brigade needed, above all, the excellent technical qualifications which he was offering, and with his quiet, equable temperament, he clearly got on well with his colleagues. When Sladen resigned in December 1918, Dyer was a Senior Divisional Officer and second in command. While the Council advertised the post, he took over as Acting Chief Officer before being appointed to full command from a short list of four selected candidates.

His electrical and engineering expertise had already proved invaluable to the Brigade throughout the period which had seen such a massive change in appliances and equipment, so much so that the Council had stubbornly refused to release him for war service. As a result, he had been on duty during every air raid on London, proving by his work in the dangers of wartime fire grounds that he was no 'fair weather' fireman. Although he was to prove efficient and successful as a Chief Officer, he was dogged by ill-health throughout his term of office, mostly as a result of injuries received at fires. On one occasion he was so critically hurt that he was on sick leave for nine months after nearly dying in hospital. During the Sidney Street Siege, as Winston Churchil had mentioned in his report, five firemen had been seriously injured as a wall collapsed. One of them was Arthur Dyer, who was buried beneath the debris. Later, at a fire in Whitechapel he fractured his skull, collar bone and four ribs,

Kens. Fire Station. "A" Watch. Sept. 1. 1921.

The last horsed escape at Kensington fire station, 1921. (LFCDA & Kensington fire station.)

although he managed to escape unscathed after taking command in the earliest and most dangerous stages of the fire which followed the great Silvertown explosion. He was quietly to see the Brigade through the next 14 years, a non-controversial man, well-liked by his officers, men and employers.

It was to be, above all, a period of industrial unrest, during which the whole country suffered from the world-wide recession. Despite this, he applied his mind not only to all aspects of firefighting but to fire prevention and he was in command when one of the biggest breaks in tradition was commemorated. Shortages during the war had led to many horses being 'conscripted' and taken to France to haul guns, waggons and other assorted forms of essential transport, requisitioned from every possible source, including the fire service. This had speeded up the transition to full petrol-driven appliances and the last horse-drawn London fire engine was finally pensioned off in a ceremony in Kensington on 24th November 1921. The *'Daily Telegraph'* reported the occasion:

'Punctually at two o'clock in the afternoon a gentleman undistinguished from the well dressed passers-by in Kensington High Street approached the fire station and rang the bell. A daring thing to do, but the police looked on and never interfered. The double doors were thrown open and with that alacrity which the London Fire Brigade never fails to display, there tumbled out in succession, all fully manned, a fire-escape on a motor carriage, two motor pumps and – finest sight of all – the horsed escape, drawn by two perfectly-conditioned and groomed bay horses. Lucy and Nora knew the meaning of the alarm quite as well as the firemen and had ears as acute.

'"Hi-Hi! Hi-Hi!" How good it was to hear the cry again as the horsed vehicle dashed into the traffic of Kensington's busiest street. Four brass-helmeted comrades rode with Coachman G H Cox and they gave the great fireman's cry with lusty vigour. Those who heard the cry distantly fade away realised that something had gone out of London's life. The London Fire Brigade had had its last horsed turn-out.'

It was Major Percy Simmons, Chairman of the LCC, who had pulled the alarm bell, sending the appliances off on a quick sortie to Queen's Gate and back. On returning to the station, Lucy and Nora took a 'photo call' in the street with their escape before Major Simmons made amends for calling them out on a false alarm by emerging from the station bearing a silver salver on which was an array of carrots and sugar lumps. Both horses enjoyed munching them, to the whirr of an early news-reel camera, before setting off on their final mission to haul the escape back to Southwark headquarters. They had already been bought from the Brigade by a sympathetic friend and were now to be transported to the country to enjoy their retirement.

Life was less sentimental in the Brigade generally. During the previous years the industrial unrest had continued, not only in London but among firemen throughout Britain. Over the latter half of the 19th century, firemen's organisations, mostly for volunteer or provincial brigades or for fire officers, had been established, but in the years immediately following the Great War, there was a movement to update these and sort out the membership. The National Fire Brigades Union (nothing to do with the later Fire Brigades Union) became the National Fire Brigades Association. The Association of Professional Fire Brigade Officers became the Professional Fire Brigades Association, since most of its members were rank and file firemen. London's firemen left the Corporation Workers on 1st April 1919 and amalgamated with the Firemens' Trade Union, Three years later it was to break away from the private brigades and form a separate organisation under the secretaryship of George Gamble, with James Bradley as his assistant and later as the Secretary of the Fire Brigades Union. (The name was changed as it had been confused with the men who shovelled coal on railway locomotives.)

Sachs's Committee had already suggested the establishment of one united organisation to represent all firefighters throughout the country, professional or volunteer, but this was ignored – as were so many of the forward-looking ideas which he and his Committee proposed.

All the assorted groups formed meeting points for a variety of firefighters from all types of brigades, but so far, there was no organisation solely concerned with technical competence – and education. Immediately after the war, at the end of 1918, various chief officers from outside London had formed a committee to launch such a body – the *Institution of Fire Engineers* – which would run on similar lines to the Institutions of Civil, Mechanical and Electrical Engineers. (Although Sladen had promised his support for

this, London, traditionally isolated, had in fact, maintained that the Committee's examinations were less difficult than the LFB's own promotion examinations – probably with justification – and ignored the new organisation, apart from saying that if any LFB man wanted to take the examinations of the IFE they would not hold it against him!)

The new body planned to hold annual examinations in technical subjects which related to firefighting, including mechanics, hydraulics, chemistry, electricity and building construction and its aims were to provide some form of diploma which would guarantee technical competence and, by so doing, 'to place the fire service generally on a higher level than has hitherto been accorded it and... compel the recognition it deserves from local and national authorities.'

At this time there were virtually no textbooks for young fireman. Sachs (who had died in 1919) and his Committee had published a series of 'Red Books' dealing with some aspects of firefighting; the LFB had a succession of drill books; there were the books written by Braidwood, Shaw, Young and Gamble, but none of these dealt with the contemporary situation. Despite this, the Home Office refused to support the application for a new Institution of Fire Engineers to be registered with the Board of Trade – as it had to be under the Companies Act.

The reason, they said, was that the Government had decided to take the problem of firefighting in Britain seriously. It was to set up a Committee, under the Chairmanship of Sir William Middlebrook (the Liberal MP for South Leeds and a former Lord Mayor of Leeds) 'to Inquire and Report upon the Hours, Pay and Conditions of Service of Firemen in Professional Fire Brigades in Great Britain.' It had four members, one of whom, Major Vivian Henderson MC MP, was later, as Sir Vivian Henderson, to be heavily involved in fire service preparations for the Second World War.

Although at this time the government had no specific statutory powers over local authority fire brigades they issued a White Paper in 1920, outlining the recommendations of the Committee which, they felt, embodied many of the problems in the forefront of the programme for a possible re-organisation of the fire service. These suggestions had included standard rates of pay, commencing at £3.10s (£3.50p) a week plus a variety of increments for firemen rising commensurately for officers up to £750 – £1,000 for Chief Officers; free quarters for all ranks or a non-pensionable allowance in lieu; a standard uniform for the whole fire service; the opportunity for firemen to transfer from one brigade to another without loss of pension rights; special (non-pensionable) allowances for skilled men; one day's leave a week and half a day on alternate Sundays; short leave for special purposes and annual leave for firemen of 14 days, rising to 21 days for Divisional Officers and with

Chief Officers' leave by mutual arrangement. Plus a compulsory retirement age of 60 years for all ranks below Station Officer and 65 for higher ranks.

Nobody was particularly surprised when, after a singularly chilly reception from many local councils, a letter from the Home Secretary was read to the Annual Meeting of the Professional Fire Brigades Association saying that it was not proposed to introduce any legislation to enforce the recommendations. History, once more, was being repeated, although the Conference passed an angry resolution to be sent to the Home Secretary, demanding immediate action on the recommendations.

Even before this, the organised pressure from London's firemen through their Representative Committee, had forced the LCC to agree to a two-shift system of working and although the Council, knowing that a Government Inquiry was likely to be set up, had asked the men to await the result of this, the men (having experienced the non-results of so many previous Select Committees and official inquiries, no doubt), refused to wait, demanding parity with the Metropolitan Police immediately. This was finally granted in December 1919, and with the recruitment of new men into the Brigade, the two-shift system began at selected stations throughout London in the summer of 1920 on the understanding that the men, through their Representative Body, would not apply for a three-shift system and a 48-hour week before July 1922.

It was a triumph for the men, since the terms included an agreement that no fireman below the rank of Station Officer need live in a fire station and that they would receive a grant of 8/6d (42½p) towards the cost of renting accommodation outside. The LCC refused to allow senior officers to live outside stations on the grounds that it would be impracticable. Such officers, anyway, were not involved in the Representative Committee. The new scheme demanded that numbers in the LFB should be almost doubled and an additional officer was appointed to deal with this. The candidate chosen by the Council was Major F W Jackson, who had been a senior assistant in their Education Office after leaving the army, where he had served on the Western Front for four years. He had been awarded the DSO and mentioned three times in despatches. Many years later he was to lead the Brigade into the carnage of the Blitz in the Second World War.

With the new shift system in force and the 144-hour week reduced to 72 hours, 600 men had to be recruited as rapidly as possible. Sir Aylmer Firebrace, at that time a young senior officer, only recently recruited himself, recalled the anxious men, many returned from the battlefields and desperate for a good, regular job, standing in queues four or five deep down Southwark Bridge Road, waiting their turn to

be measured for height and chest expansion, to have their strength tested and to be given an elementary educational test before being interviewed. Even then, only one in every hundred was offered a place in what, by now was becoming, indeed, an élite corps. One young man who had been job-hunting for a year or more, was so delighted when he was taken on that he ran the four miles to his East End home in tears of relief to tell his widowed mother that, at last, they would have a regular pay packet coming in at the end of the week.

Meanwhile, the fury of the assorted fire brigade organisations over the rejection of the Middlebrook Committee's Report resulted in further pressure on the government for a Royal Commission. Accordingly, on the 19th January 1921, *The Royal Commission on Fire Brigades and Fire Prevention* was set up under the Chairmanship of Sir Percival Maitland, a retired judge from the South African Supreme Court. It was, perhaps, one of the worst examples of such an inquiry. It sat on 48 days between February 1921 and March 1923, asked 14,501 questions, and produced its final report in a volume of 265 closely printed pages of more than 100,000 words, culminating in 142 conclusions and recommendations which were so appallingly pompous and badly written that they became something of a Civil Service joke. Among its considered conclusions were such world-shattering discoveries as: *'Buckets of water are not only simple and cheap but effective appliances, though their utility is limited by the impracticability of throwing the water above the head line.'*

The Report cost the public eight shillings to buy – a week's rent for many working class families, and had cost the nation £3,081.9s (£3,081.45p) to produce. Apart from minor suggestions about training, standardisation of equipment, safety in factories, and the problems of transporting and storing celluloid, its chief recommendations concentrated on the more realistic proposition that boroughs and country districts should be the units for fire service administration with the possibility that this might be extended to county administration. They also felt that *'an expert official'* who might be designated the *'Fire Adviser'*, who had a thorough knowledge of the problems of fire prevention and fire defence, should be appointed to the Home Office, although even this was opposed by some of the members.

There seems little doubt that the ludicrous length and verbosity of the document played some part in the fact that the majority of its recommendations were, once more, ignored. A few minor amendments were made to the Building Acts and an honorary 'Fire Adviser', Lieut-Col Guy Simonds, was appointed to the Home Office. One major development, however, came soon after this when the

Institution of Fire Engineers received its registration and was established.

For Arthur Dyer, settled now as Chief Officer, life had been anything but quiet. There were continuing social events and in 1920 a Royal visit to Southwark when the Prince of Wales, (later, and briefly, King Edward VIII) presented fire service medals and certificates to the men. Soon after this came the annual Brigade Sports Day at Herne Hill. More to his interest, there was a constant stream of new developments on the firefighting scene, including foam and 'suds' for oil and petrol fires, motor cycle and even bicycle 'fire engines' to test (and reject) and the great talking point of the 1920's – wireless for entertainment and, even more important from the Brigade's viewpoint, for communication. On May 14th 1920 the Marconi Company gave a demonstration of the possible applications of the latest 'wireless' for fire brigade purposes.

A standard Marconi aircraft transmitter and receiver were placed on a table at headquarters, with the aerial wire suspended between the towers used for drying the hoses. A similar apparatus was fitted to a fire tender which then drove seven miles to Putney Common, almost on the boundary of the Brigade area, with 85 lbs of wireless equipment stashed in a cupboard on the back. Within a minute of stopping, the men had raised a ladder and hooked an aerial wire to a tree. Two copper gauze nets were laid on the grass to establish the earth connection and the scene was set. Three calls were made through the transmitter to LFB HQ at Southwark and to everyone's delight and amazement, communication was established. The wavelengths, roughly 500–700 metres were liable to interference by other stations which was a drawback, and conversations were said to be *'liable to be interfered with by ships' wireless'* but, as the report on the experiment pointed out: *'this can be easily remedied by working on different wavelengths and there is no reason why, if fire brigade wireless develops, it should not have wavelengths of its own.'* They considered that it would probably be more convenient to introduce the 'duplex' system to do away with the delays caused by the change-over system but they were so enthusiastic that the tender gave a further demonstration on the way back, stopping in a street at Clapham, looping the aerial over a couple of lamp posts and laying the netting on the roadway.

Petrol engines were developing fast and now came a period of discussion over the merits of self-starters and the feeling that they might lower the standard of engine efficiency, although it was reckoned that if they were kept in tip-top condition they could maintain an eight second getaway time using a battery and coil switch. This was high theory compared with the practical problems of the day. Sir Aylmer Firebrace recalled the early 1920's when he was allotted an old-fashioned fire tender, painted fire engine red but so primitive that

> 'climbing steep hills … we did not ring the fire bell as so many vehicles were passing us that it would have looked ridiculous. We endeavoured to give the impression that we were returning from a fire when, of course, bell ringing is not allowed!' *He admitted that on the level, the vehicle was reasonably fast, but remarkable at skidding……* 'Once, in the middle of Oxford Street, we described a full circle and then proceeded on our way trying to look as if nothing out of the ordinary had happened.' *Life at the top on a fire engine was raw in those days.* 'This machine' *he continued* 'had not even the suggestion of a windscreen. Perched high up, driving through every kind of weather, we sometimes arrived half-frozen at the fire and often, after getting wet through, were completely frozen by the time we returned to our station.'

Small wonder that, until the first appliances with enclosed accommodation for the men were introduced in the mid-1930s, the motorised fire engine was know in the LFB as *'the pneumonia waggon'*.

Petrol itself was still a problem. Fires were frequently caused by its storage and its careless use, particularly in homes where many people had found it useful as a 'dry'cleaning liquid but failed to realise the danger of its vapour. Its transportation was yet another headache for the Brigade as more big tankers began to sail into the Thames, sometimes offloading petrol and oil to shore installations and sometimes into barges. The implications of this horrified the Brigade, particularly after one nightmare event.

It happened on the night of 20th August 1920. The unattended barge 'Dorcas', laden with petrol, was moored off North Woolwich on the Thames in south-east London when she caught fire. The mooring ropes burned through within minutes and with no crew on board she drifted away, pulled by the tide, swirled by the current and flaming from end to end. Lurching in mid-river she bumped into two tugs, setting them alight before colliding with Woolwich pier, igniting that and several other barges before careering off again, glowing golden with the heat, until she hit land at Laboratory Wharf by Woolwich Arsenal.

Here, ten motor fire pumps were waiting for her, but before they could take action she exploded, setting light to the whole surrounding area of land and water. Three of the fire engines were enveloped immediately and had to be abandoned. Flames, 300 feet high set light to two large warehouses 100 feet away and released more burning oil on to the river.

By the time the 'Dorcas' finished her night out on the

Thames she had destroyed two tugs, nine barges, a ferry boat and three fire engines and seriously damaged a pier and two warehouses along with an assortment of railway trucks and sheds.

For the Brigade and its Chief Officer it was an experience to remember, and remember it they did, when, in 1925, the Port of London Authority approached the LCC for permission to amend their 1912 by-laws governing the transportation of petroleum on the Thames so that large petrol-carrying vessels might be allowed to dock higher up the river. Under the present by-laws, petroleum spirit and low-test petroleum had not been allowed above Thames Haven, seven miles below Tilbury where the river was nearly 1½ miles wide. The proposals put forward by the PLA would allow the vessels to proceed as far as Crayford Ness, west of Purfleet and 14 miles nearer London, where the River was some 600–700 yards wide. There, they planned to offload petrol tankers, virtually on the borders of London. Under pressure from the Chief Officer, the London County Council refused to relax the existing regulations.

Again, in 1927, the Port of London Authority at the request of the Standard Oil Company of America (later to become 'SO' – 'Esso'), sought permission for ocean-going tankers 'to sail and discharge petrol above the Mucking Light at Thames Haven'. This time, an official inquiry was set up which lasted for 28 days and although many witnesses were heard, only one was allowed to represent the fire service. During a whole day of giving evidence, Chief Officer Arthur Dyer recalled the incident of the 'Dorcas', emphasising the risks involved if the great new tankers were to be allowed upriver to within five miles of the county boundary. Those who supported a ban on tankers offloading close to the edge of any big city included the Conference of the Institution of Fire Engineers who passed a motion 'considering with alarm the proposal of the Port of London Authority to permit ocean-going tankers to proceed to within 14 miles of London Bridge'. Not only was their message passed to the PLA but to the Prime Minister, the Home Secretary and relevant government ministers as well as the other riparian authorities in Essex and Kent.

By fortuitous chance, the Inquiry coincided with an incident in which the American tanker 'Seminole' carrying thousands of tons of naphtha, petrol and other spirits, broke her back in the Mersey, close to her landing stage in Liverpool. Disaster was averted only because the tide was ebbing and the massive leak of petroleum spirit which flowed from her split side, either evaporated or was swept out to sea.

This underlined all that Dyer had said. The LCC's refusal to allow the change of its by-laws was officially endorsed and the major petroleum companies were forced to change

plans and to build their refineries nearer to the Thames Estuary at Shellhaven, Thames Haven and on the Isle of Grain.

More legislation concerning petrol arrived in 1929 under the *Petroleum (Consolidation) Act, (18 & 19, George V, c 42)*. Under this, it became illegal to store more than three gallons of petrol without a licence and there were strict provisions for licensing, for methods of storage and transportation, for inspection and for the notifying of accidents, all concerning petrol.

It was not only petrol which caused trouble on the river. The ghost of the Victorian dock fires still walked, and in 1926, Chief Officer Dyer, with his deputies, Firebrace and Jackson were all 'eating smoke' as they led their men into the inferno when a warehouse full of resin and other highly inflammable material burned at Wharf Road, Cubitt Town. Flames reached a phenomenal height and the new fire float 'Beta III' set up a record by working non-stop for 14½ hours. Using one monitor and four deliveries, she threw 1,710,000 gallons of Thames water into the burning building.

Brigade news during the first post-war years certainly contained variety. It included 12 men trained in the use of new, self-contained breathing apparatus; LCC amendments to their Theatres and Music Halls legislation which demanded that only electricity might be used for lighting on-stage (an end to the old candle or gas-lit footlights); the 'take-over' by Merryweathers of their old rival, Shand Mason and the beginning of public agitation over the development of 'skyscrapers' when in 1923, the LCC raised the height restriction for buildings from 60 ft to 80 ft (although requests had been made by developers for 120 ft.) In 1923, new regulations were issued by the Home Office to minimise the danger of fire and panic in 'cinema theatres'. Operators were required to rewind and repair film in a room separate from the public enclosure.

Arson had been a problem for more than a century with many unsuccessful shopkeepers and business men trying to raise money on fire insurance by setting fire to their premises using a variety of means – among them, tying a kipper to a paraffin oil lamp and leaving a cat alone in a shop with it. The cat grabbed the kipper, the kipper upset the lamp and another unsuccessful arson attempt was eventually discovered. It was only one of hundreds of ingenious efforts.

More successful were three arsonists who had left a trail of fires in London's East End. The full story of their activities emerged in 1923, when Joseph Engelstein, Bernard Stolerman and Julius Brust were sentenced at the Old Bailey to six, five and four years penal servitude, respectively. Engelstein, know as 'Dandy Joe – a maker of the most lovely fires at moderate prices' had posed as a prosperous City merchant,

Early emergency tender, 1920s. (LFCDA.)

with a large house in Hackney, complete with several servants. His tariff ranged from £100 for arranging a small fire to £1,000 for a 'conflagration,' and over a period of two years, he and his confederates swindled the insurance companies with a succession of 200 fires throughout the East End. The 201st was his downfall. Two young East End traders reported his activities to the police who closed in, catching the 'team' in the act of setting light to the premises. It was not, however, to be the end of arson in London.

During the early 1930s, there was a spate of warehouse fires throughout the capital and in Manchester. The Brigade, as well as the police, suspected that they had fire-raisers on their hands once more, and not without reason. In 1933, one of the most notorious gangs of arsonists was brought to trial at the Central Criminal Court – the 'Old Bailey'. Their leader, Leopold Harris, had been a respected member of an old-established City firm of insurance assessors and his activities were believed to have started ten years previously, when he began bribing assessors and building up a complicated organisation of spurious companies, supplied with false stock by his brother-in-law. It was only the suspicions, followed by years of tireless tracking down by a solicitor specialising in insurance work, William (later Sir William) Crocker, that finally led to their prosecution.

The charges involved 16 members of the gang and the

trial lasted 33 days – at that time the second longest criminal trial ever held. Among the documents produced was one, known as 'Willesden Junction' because of its compexity. It showed a diagram of 29 serious fires, marked round the edge of the document and linked by lines to the names of members of the gang, marked in the centre of the page, who had started them. It was this damning piece of evidence which brought a revised plea of 'guilty'. The men were sentenced to varying lengths of imprisonment. For Harris, it was 14 years penal servitude; for the rest, sentences ranging from four months to five years.

The public and the Fire Service settled back with the comforting thought that arson could be pushed into the background for the time being, but three months later, electrifying headlines announced the arrest of the Chief Officer of the London Salvage Corps. Capt B E Miles MC, had been a member of the London Fire Brigade, which he had joined by direct entry as an officer after the war. Five years later, he had joined the London Salvage Corps as Deputy Chief Officer to the famous Colonel Fox, who had six months to serve before retirement.

Miles succeeded him, as planned, with a comfortable four-figure salary plus free quarters and other 'perks' of the position. It was, once more, the indefatigable investigations of William Crocker, during the Harris period, which had led him to realise that the gang must have had some form of inside information. Crocker had, understandably, discussed the arson problem frequently with Miles. Now, he realised that the information had been passed back to the gang – at a price. Miles was convicted, sentenced to four years penal servitude and dismissed instantly from his post with the Salvage Corps.

Facing the music in a completely different way was the new Fire Brigade Band, funded initially, by Lloyds of London in gratitude for the war-time courage of the LFB. All were firemen, some of whom had never tackled an instrument before joining the Brigade. Now, under a special arrangement with the Guildhall School of Music, they were taught music under Sir Landon Ronald with the Professor of trumpet and cornet, Peter Anderson, instructing them in his subjects. Before long, there were weekly concerts at headquarters and an annual 'date' at the famous Queen's Hall (bombed to the ground during World War Two).

By 1924, the new, enlarged Brigade was proving as impressive as Shaw's company of firemen, and with no shortage of tough and healthy candidates, the Chief Officer laid down that the standard height for recruits was to be raised from 5ft 5 ins to 5 ft 7 ins. It was a period of both

seriousness and triviality. 'Froth' extinguishers came on the market to join with the newly invented 'Fire Suds' in dealing with petrol and chemical fires. At the same time, advice was offered by the Brigade on model fire appliances for the Queen's Doll's House at Windsor Castle. Outside the capital, the 1920's were bringing a spate of devastating fires in stately homes, but within its boundaries, chemicals and gases were extending the technical ingenuity and expertise of the London Brigade.

Acid was a staple component of batteries for cars and in accumulators which were increasingly used domestically for powering 'wireless' sets, selling fast as the new British Broadcasting Company set up its studios on Savoy Hill. Spilt acid could, in some cases start fires. Wireless receivers, despite their name, demanded wires leading to an aerial on the roof and these were occasionally struck by lightning. In 1924, the Brigade issued a note for the public on the fire hazards of radio sets, reassuring them that 'trouble should not be caused by the source if the antennae are properly protected. Aerials may be safeguarded by a lightning arrestor, installed in the lead-in wire as near as practicable to the point where it enters a building…'

By now, as electricity increasingly replaced gas lighting,

London Fire Brigade band. (LFCDA.)

heating and cooking in many homes and offices, came the first reports of electric cables falling from the ceilings of burning buildings. Some had already dropped across the firemen's helmets, injuring them when the brass had acted as a conductor. In 1925 a London sub-officer died when he was electrocuted at a fire in Finsbury Street. The jury at the inquest added a rider to their verdict, asking that the LCC should take steps to prevent a recurrence of the accident by insulating firemens' helmets. Shaw's magnificent headpiece was rapidly becoming a potential killer and the first rumblings began, which were eventually to end in its replacement. Not, however, before the Fire Brigade Committee had discussed the matter of possibly replacing the brass with fibre or leather and remarked sagely that *'firemen could still be electrocuted through wet clothing'* or *'we are convinced that there are no means whereby the possibility of accidents of this kind can be avoided'*. They discussed too, the feasibility of current passing along the jet to the branch pipe and causing accidents but decided that these risks were all part of the inseparable duties of a fireman and as they had not happened very often, *'the risk can be regarded as exceedingly small'*.

Old wounds had caught up with the Chief Officer and he was seriously ill for much of 1924 although by November he was reported to be 'making good progress'. He was well enough, by 1927, to lead his daughter, Joan, to the altar of Southwark Cathedral for her marriage, after being drawn in a coach hauled on ropes by cheerful firemen and walking in through a brass-helmeted, spick-and-span guard of honour from the Brigade.

Throughout this period industrial unrest had continued, to some extent within the Brigade but, more devastatingly, outside it, as many working class areas, particularly in the North of England and in the Welsh mining valleys, came near to starvation as the economic situation worsened. In 1926, after months of industrial strife over mercilessly low wages and appalling conditions, a group of miners were locked out by their employers for refusing to accept a 13% pay reduction. Immediately, a General Strike was called and workers all over the country withdrew their labour in a mass protest. Although it was rumoured that London firemen had been used against their striking fellow workers, this was not true. The Askwith Award had made it quite clear that no fireman was allowed to take part in any industrial dispute. Nor did the firemen withdraw their labour, although they too had suffered from the stringencies of the economic situation when the LCC asked them to accept an *'economy cut'* of 5% in their wages. The Representative Body protested with such force that the Fire Brigade Committee suggested a compromise of 2½% for one year only. As this would keep them at parity with the police, the firemen accepted the cut which

averaged some eight shillings a week off an already lean wage.

It was not the end. With workers' pay throughout the country being slashed (a left-wing newspaper described it as *'a frontal attack on the whole working class by the capitalists and their Government'*) more cuts were to come and in 1923, as unemployment began to reach unprecedented proportions, the LCC presented their firemen with a demand for a 20% reduction in pay. The case was put to the arbitration of an industrial court that it was illogical to destroy the accepted situation of parity with the police, after employers and men had accepted it only a year previously, The court found in favour of the firemen, agreeing that it was too soon to depart from police/fire brigade parity.

One bright spot in the welfare scene came in 1925 when a Private Member's Bill in Parliament was passed with Government support. The Fire Brigades Pension Act conferred pension rights on all professional firemen, with a pension of half-pay after 25 years service and two-thirds pay after 30 years. It also provided for pensions due to any injury received on duty, or through ill-health.

Apart from the ever-present, major problems of petrol and celluloid, the fire scene was, on the whole, no worse than usual and, at times, remarkably peaceful. On New Year's Eve in 1924, (as had been the case in 1918,) no fire calls were received throughout the London Region and only eight calls were received on November 5th – Guy Fawkes Night – in 1925, a period when few London families other than the wealthy, had money to burn. (The figure increased dramatically in succeeding decades until, by the 1980s, massive safety campaigns were launched by the Brigade in an effort to cut down the injuries caused by fireworks. One of the worst years was 1982 when over one thousand people were injured and the Brigade responded to more than 3,000 calls involving fireworks.)

It seems remarkable that for more than a quarter of a century, celluloid had been causing fire after fire with very little legislative control over its storage or sale. After a spate of fires in cinemas, demands were made in the House of Commons for celluloid factories to be brought under the same stringent restrictions as those where explosives were produced. In addition there were calls for legislation to be introduced to control not only the manufacture of film for cinema use but also that used in cameras, which were becoming increasingly popular. As if to underline the problem, the Brigade was called out to a particularly bad fire at St Pancras which involved a store of film waste. As a result of this and the Parliamentary pressure, new regulations came into force on 1st April 1928, governing the manufacture of cine-film and also cine-film stripping, and revoking the 1921 regulations which were by now inadequate.

Unemployment was worsening and competition to join the London Fire Brigade was still intense. With hundreds of applicants ready to step into a fireman's job at a moment's notice, this was no time for making demands on one's employers, although the cuts in wages of the earlier years had bitten hard.

A major discussion topic among brigades nationally now, was centred on ways of producing better educated firemen, trained and prepared to cope with the increasingly sophisticated problems which the rapid advance of science was posing almost daily. Firemen were expected to drive engines, about which many of them knew very little, and face fires in factories and workshops which might present them with hazards of which they had no knowledge. There was talk of the pressing need for a college or centre where senior firemen could be educated in the modern needs of the service – for one large building as a training and social centre for the fire services of the nation. Already, visits to overseas brigades and conferences were on the increase and it was pointed out regularly that when representatives of British fire services went abroad they were excellently entertained, but when the foreign representatives came to London there was no centre to which they could be taken that could be regarded as a national building belonging to the fire services of Great Britian.

London, it was agreed, should be the centre for such a building, and in December 1929 the magazine 'The Fireman' was stressing in an editorial that 'the London Fire Brigade has long been recognised as the world's best training ground for firemen,' plus the fact that 'a large proportion of the officers who hold responsible commands in British territory at home and abroad received their early training in London'. But times were increasingly hard, and a government which had turned down the recommendations of an expensive two-year Royal Commission was in no mood to spend money on a 'fancy' school for firemen.

By the end of 1930, the national economic situation was so acute that with the unemployment figure touching 3.000.000 the political parties combined to form a National Government which enforced pay reductions for all public employees, including teachers and the police. In line with police parity, London's firemen were faced with a further pay cut of their lean wage, this time by 10%. Under the leadership of Percy Kingdom, the Fire Brigades Union took the matter to an Industrial Court and as a result, the cut was deferred until 1933, but it was imposed then. Within months, the LCC had proposed yet another wage cut. Once more, the matter went to the Industrial Court and Sir Richard Redmayne, the arbitrator, maintained that since the police had recived no further cut, Fire Brigade wages should not be reduced either.

Whether the country could afford it or not, fire losses were increasing annually and reaching dangerous proportions. The year 1929 had brought a death toll of 800 people in fires which had cost some £15,000,000 and, in January 1930, the Home Secretary, the Rt Hon John Clynes, received a deputation from the Institution of Fire Engineers urging him to introduce 'at an early date' legislation to give effect to the recommendations of the 1923 Royal Commission.

They emphasised that the main reasons for the increased losses were lack of any national effort to deal with what was a national peril; the increasing use of highly inflammable materials; the financial inability of some local authorities, and the neglect of others, to maintain fire brigades in a proper state of efficiency (there were, by now, more than 1,500 assorted fire 'brigades' in the country); and the creation of new industrial areas which, owing to their low rateable value, had to rely upon an inadequately equipped fire brigade service with volunteer personnel.

The deputation urged **that the fire service should be recognised as an essential service to the State; should be accorded statutory powers and that some central supervision should be established without, however, stifling local interest in the maintenance and work of the brigades.**

All in all, it was a considered and vitally important message which, had it been accepted and acted upon, would have made a great difference to the fire defences of Britain when the Nazi Blitzkrieg struck its cities ten years later.

Instead, it was met with a diplomatic 'thank you' from the Home Secretary and the quibble that the Royal Commission had not, in fact, recommended in so many words that the fire brigade service should be put on the same footing as the police with central supervision, central inspection and a Government grant. Their main recommendations had, he maintained, been that local authorities should be put under a statutory obligation to maintain, or combine in maintaining, an efficient fire service and that county councils should act as the initiating and co-ordinating authorities with power to act in the default of any other local authorities.

Mr Clynes expressed his sympathy with the objects which the deputation had in view and promised that he 'would keep the matter constantly before him with a view to legislation as soon as the opportunity can be found'. In the meantime, he felt that much more might – and indeed should – be done by local authorities and the fire brigade officers in the way of co-operation between and co-ordination of the available services.

A vital opportunity was laid aside but the matter had clearly disturbed many members of the government and, in

May 1932, at the annual congress of the Professional Fire Brigades Association, the Home Secretary, Sir Herbert Samuel, said that much as legislation was needed *'to remove the imperfections of the present parochial methods of firefighting'*, the national exchequer could not find the necessary money. *'We recognise to the full that the organisation in this country for firefighting is inadequate, and that it is imperfect in many particulars, and we welcome suggestions for the improvement of the present organisation'* he said. There were plenty of suggestions but with a bare exchequer they were sterile — and this within seven years of another great war.

1933 brought a report that the Home Secretary, by now Sir John Gilmour, was being represented by Mr A L Dixon and Lieut-Col Symonds at a conference in Holt, Norfolk, to discuss a co-ordinating scheme for local fire brigades. The dreaded word *'nationalisation'*, which had been whispered for several years, began to be brought into the open.

London would barely have been affected had the proposals been put into force, as it already had a highly efficient fire brigade, but later, it was to reckon with the problems of co-operating with a heterogeneous assortment of brigades, equipment and even verbal fire commands when the Second World War started.

Not only was the technical 'language' of the LFB different from that used in other parts of Britain but the columns of *'The Fireman'* had showed the marked differences between London and the American fire service phrases.

While the nuances between the brigades in Britain may have been less marked, they certainly existed, as did the use of different connections. London stood doggedly by its 'round threads' and these, along with the different command phrases, were to cause many problems in the days of the 'Blitz'. It was not until 1989 that the ISO — the International Standards Organisation brought together a team which included DCO Michael Doherty from London and fire chiefs from Canada, France, Japan, and Germany to produce an internationally-agreed glossary of firefighting terminology.

Discussion in London turned now to the increasing height of buildings. The LCC building regulations had been altered in 1932 to allow, in certain cases, slightly higher buildings, but only subject to fire precautions. Shell-Mex House, close to the Savoy Hotel on the Victoria Embankment was, as a result, one of the first to be built with a statutory provision of special hydrants and dry rising mains. At about the same time, in 1933 Merryweather produced a new, 100-foot turntable ladder to help cope with the increasing height of office buildings, particularly in London.

In many ways, the romance was disappearing from the fire scene, although the Press reported in June 1933 that crowds in the City Streets stopped in wonder at the sight of firemen 'who might have come out of a fairy tale' returning to their station after subduing a fire in the store-room of a metallic powder manufactureres in Aldersgate Street. Water from their hoses had mixed with the gold metal dust and the spray had covered them from head to foot in glistening gold which shone brilliantly — and embarrassingly — as the 'fairies' drove hastily back to base.

What effect the dust had on the firemen's lungs is not recorded but already there was growing concern for the danger to firemen posed by the substances they were forced to face in the course of their duties. Liquid bromine was one such chemical. This was being carried round London in glass vessels which, as the manufacturers mildly observed, *'did occasionally fall from vehicles and fracture from time to time'*, despite warnings from the importers to carters of the risks involved should there be breakages. The gas released could cause pneumonia and death. The public had to be kept away from the area of the breakage and firemen dealing with such an incident had to wear respirators which would, it was hoped, be sufficient to cope with the gas. But what if it were a gas which the respirator could not filter? It was to be more than 20 years before the London Fire Brigade itself launched a scheme for providing firemen with essential information concerning chemicals, particularly in transit, and the 'HAZCHEM' system was accepted internationally.

As for the old 'conflagrations', just as the Brigade might have felt that these were part of their past, fire broke out at Butler's Wharf, in that old jinx area of Tooley Street on 7th March 1932. It was a bitterly cold day as the 'Brigade Call' went out, alerting every station to prepare to move in as hundreds of men and dozens of appliances headed for the river by Tower Bridge. Two fire boats *'Alpha'* and *'Beta'* hove to and joined in the pumping but the spray froze as it flew, stiffening the mens' clothing and sealing their hands to the brass branches as they swung the nozzles to attack the flames. Gigantic icicles formed on the ladders and one crane, top-heavy with ice, toppled and fell, missing the firemen by inches. Despite intense heat from the fire, one man, doggedly playing a hose from high up on a girder, was frozen solid and had to be chipped off his perch and carried down, rigid, by his mates. The seven-storey warehouse crammed with rubber, tea and an assortment of other goods, was almost totally destroyed but at least the fire was contained and no other buildings were badly damaged. It was a cruelly harsh job, excellently carried out, and a message from Chief Officer Dyer, who had attended the fire himself, congratulated his men and thanked them for all they had done.

It was to be his last major fire. On March 31st, 1933,

Icicles at Butler's wharf fire, 1932. (LFCDA.)

Arthur Dyer retired. A report presented to the London County Council listed some of the important changes which had occurred in the Brigade during his period of command: full mechanisation, the introduction of high, turntable ladders and the use of mechanical methods for fire fighting. His supervision of all these and his entire administrative work, had kept the service at a very high level of efficiency. The smooth working and successful results of the two-shift system for sub-officers and firemen was also a tribute to his organisation. The Council placed on record their

'high appreciation of the services rendered by Mr Arthur

Reginald Dyer, AMICE, as Chief Officer of the London Fire Brigade during the period from 1919 to 1933.' *The Fireman* was more fulsome in its tribute:

'A man of outstanding courage, resource and tact, he is an ideal leader, who early gained and has always retained the respect and affection of his men. No British fireman has ever more worthily upheld the great traditions of the service and none has carried with him into retirement a greater measure of esteem and good-will'.

17

A Troubled Horizon for Major Morris

I T CAME AS NO SURPRISE WHEN THE LCC APPOINTED Major Cyril Clark Boville Morris as the seventh Chief Officer. He had been educated at Haileybury, a distinguished public school, followed by four years training as a pupil at the Great Eastern Railway Locomotive Works at Stratford and three years during which he was Engineer-in-Charge of the Great Eastern Motor Department. He was also a member of the Institution of Mechanical Engineers.

In July 1908, the year in which Eyre Massey Shaw died, he had been appointed Assistant Divisonal Officer in the LFB, one of the experts who were taking it out of the horse era and into the age of mechanisation. He continued in this capacity until he left in 1914 to fight in the Great War as an officer in the Army Service Corps (Mechanical Transport Division.) No doubt his experience in the Brigade was partly responsible for his rapid promotion and by February, 1917, he was appointed Deputy Assistant Director of Transport, staying in France and fighting at the desperate and memorable battles of Ypres and the Somme, where he commanded one of the largest Mechanical Transport Units. He was awarded the Military Cross, mentioned twice in despatches for bravery and held the Royal Humane Society's Bronze Medal for a rescue from the St Omer canal in the small hours of a cold autumn morning in 1914. London missed him badly and he was one of the first to be recalled when the bombing raids intensified in 1917 and the government allowed the Brigade to bring back its key men. By the time of his appointment as Chief Officer he had served as Principal Officer in the Brigade for 24 years and from 1919 had been second in command to Arthur Dyer. This had included frequent periods of full command when his Chief had been on sick leave.

The Fireman commented on his appointment in an editorial:

> 'he is not merely a firefighter but an expert engineer who takes the keenest possible interest in questions of fire prevention, and it is safe to predict that during his term of office, fire risks in London will be at the irreducible minimum as far as reasonable and intelligent exercise of the powers vested in the Chief Officer of the London Fire Brigade can effect such a result.'

Morris was an experienced organiser and one of his

Major Cyril Morris, Chief Officer, 1933–38. (LFCDA.)

earliest schemes was a new development, 'Section X', by which a group of senior Brigade officers set up a complete 'office' in empty premises or in a van close to any big fire, installed an emergency telephone, prepared plans of the fire and the proposals for fighting it, arranged for reliefs and kept in constant telephone touch with HQ. It was the start of the 'mobile' fire control system to be developed over subsequent years until it became a permanent and sophisticated part of London's fire defences.

Headquarters were still at Southwark, where the training school and fire station were all on the same site and had become increasingly cramped as the Brigade numbers – and responsibilities – grew. For some time there had been talk of the need to expand, but the site was restricted and the LCC decided to look further afield for a new base.

Ironically, the two-and-a-half acre site costing £85,000, which they chose at Lambeth, alongside the old Royal Doulton pottery, had been the wharf where, in dense fog on 30th January 1918, two sub-officers and five firemen had lost their lives when a wall collapsed as they were fighting a blaze.

The incident was immortalised in a poem by another fireman, F Barber Wells:

'Honour the Fire Brigade!
Honour the men who fell
Seven heroes brave – a gallant band –
Mid fire and flame, see how they stand,
Begrimed, bespattered, hose in hand,
Their duty done so well.
Honour the name they made!

Honour the Fire Brigade!
Peace to the noble seven,
Fighting the foe at duty's call
Not theirs the lance or rifle ball –
The crashing wall their funeral pall
Seven souls, swift-winged to Heaven.
Honour the name they made.

Immortal dead! The price they paid
Unstamped on scroll of fame.
Proudly the Soul her paean sings
Proudly enshrined their memory clings,
There, homage yields her offerings,
Eternal lives their name!
Braves of the Fire Brigade.'

The old wharf, drained and reinforced, was to become the basement of the new building and later, after further reinforcement, the Operations Centre of the London Fire Service throughout the war – which was still only on the horizon. The headquarters, designed by the LCC Architect's department, was opened by King George VI in July 1937. It cost £389,000 and was divided into several sections. The front of the main building, a ten-storey block, 100 feet high, faced the Albert Embankment, close to the new Lambeth Bridge. Seven 'run-outs' for appliances were spaced along its 210ft and above the appliance bays were the rest of the fire station, the administrative offices, quarters for the Chief Officer and his family, his deputy and ten other officers as well as a recreation room and a canteen.

Behind this was a drill yard, 250 ft by 112 ft, with a brick-faced, fireproof tower, 100 ft high, for training exercises at one end. At the other stood a bandstand for the Brigade's musicians who played at all the regular Wednesday displays put on for special visitors and for the public.

Across Lambeth High Street was a five storey block with garages on the ground floor, plus the Brigade training school and more accommodation above. New Brigade workshops were located behind this building and, at the rear of these, the arches of the old Southern Railway viaduct were used for storage.

Dominating the entrance hall, leading in from the Albert Embankment, was a bronze and marble memorial, donated to the Brigade by Lloyds underwriters and inscribed: 'To the memory of the officers and men of the London Fire Brigade who throughout the years laid down their lives whilst doing their duty.' Carved into its central panel was a contemporary firefighting scene and above it, a similar group showing an escape and steam fire engine drawn by galloping horses. On either side were bronze panels inscribed with the names of men who had died on duty – at that time, 62. Since then, the names of all the men and women killed on duty in London have been added, including the 327 who died in action during World War II.

At that time, the Brigade Museum was based on the ground floor of the new building but this eventually, was re-sited in Shaw's quarters at Winchester House, and on 31st October 1967, the Massey Shaw suite was opened there by Sir Arthur Hutchinson, Chairman of the Fire Service Research and Training Trust, which had met the cost of furnishing the suite.

The ceremony was attended by Sir Bernard Shaw, grandson of Sir Eyre, who presented the Museum with a gold watch which had been given to Shaw by a volunteer brigade. Later, the Shaw family presented many more items, including furniture and a valuable scrap book of newspaper cuttings and letters which had been preserved by the devoted Anna. Unfortunately, her elder brother, Massey

Tribute to firemen, killed at Albert Embankment, 1918. (LFCDA.)

The new HQ at Lambeth, 1936. (LFCDA.)

Early enclosed pump escape. 1935. (LFCDA.)

who, for much of his adult life seems to have been at loggerheads with his father, burned most of Shaw's private papers when they finally came into his possession.

The move to the new Headquarters ran smoothly and work continued with increasing efficiency under Morris's quietly competent leadership. His engineering training was always dominant and he designed the first fully enclosed motor-pump, filled with 60 gallons of water and complete with 40-ft extension ladder and oxygen apparatus, which was taken into the Brigade in 1935. He also designed a vehicle to speed up the process of laying long lengths of hose. Since then, the 'pump' has been a major part of the Brigade's fleet, its interior fitted with baffles to prevent the water from 'slopping' inside and affecting the safe steering of the vehicle. (Firefighter Eric Billingham, an expert on the Brigade's vehicles, recalls that the capacity of these pumps was later increased to 100 gallons of water and until 1965 they were always dual purpose, carrying ladders as well as men and water. Until the capacity was increased to the present 300–400 gallons, firemen always made a point of refilling the tank from the nearest hydrant before leaving a fireground in case they had another call to a fire on the way back to the station.)

Morris's entire period of office was a particularly busy and varied one, starting with a full re-organisation. This was followed by what, from the public point of view, was a major event in Brigade history – the adoption of a new helmet. The famous old brass helmet was too dangerous to be worn in modern incidents and in December 1934, Merryweathers produced a revolutionary, black 'super safety helmet'. It was, they claimed, 'shockproof, waterproof, flameproof, unbreakable and lighter than leather or brass …. four ply virgin cork treated to ensure insulation, adhered and insulated with pure rubber solution covered with cotton drill steeped in non-alkaline, flame-proof solution and covered in heat-resisting enamel to withstand a temperature of 350 degrees Fahrenheit without change'. The comb was built up with solid cork – treated in the same way as the helmet and inside was a corrugated sponge rubber headband. No metallic substance was used and it had been tested to withstand excessive impact, water resistance and electrical resistance up to 11,000 volts. The old brass helmet had weighed 36 ozs – the new one weighed 22 ozs. The helmets were tested by Shoreditch firemen for 12 months before being introduced in London early in 1936.

Until then, most of the work of the Brigade had been, as

its title suggested, firefighting, but as motor traffic increased on the roads, rescue began to play a greater part in the daily call-outs. In 1934 the Brigade and what was then the authority responsible for all the public transport – buses, trams and the underground rail system in London, the London Passenger Transport Board, – met and agreed to co-operate on providing specialist equipment for lifting heavy vehicles involved in accidents to release anyone who might be trapped underneath. Much of this was stored at bus garages.

The LCC decided, at this time, to permit warehouses to increase in height to 100 ft, – if they were provided with suitable fire-prevention and firefighting equipment. Already, though, the 1930s were increasingly becoming the age of aviation and with this in mind, in September, 1934, a

strange new plan for a Central London Airport was put to the City of London Corporation for consideration. This was to take the form of an enormous reinforced concrete platform over the Thames in the neighbourhood of Tower Bridge. The height was to be not less than 200 feet, 'in order that there may be no danger of aircraft colliding with St Paul's Cathedral and other tall buildings' and it was to stay within the jurisdiction of the City Corporation in order that they should have control of this 'port of aerial commerce which, in time, is likely to be as important to trade as the Port of London'.

After recovering from their initial shock the Brigade, with admirable restraint, suggested that it might pose a considerable new problem of fire protection. The plan, which was described as 'not only in the air but likely to remain so'

New helmets and cumbersome breathing apparatus. 1936. (LFCDA.)

seems, to the relief of the LFB, to have died a natural death. Fifty years later, however, a City airport was, in fact, built, but on derelict land in the disused London docks area – and with the full co-operation of the LFB.

While large fires still bedevilled London, other problems were increasing, and by the beginning of 1935, reports came back from a meeting of firemen in Atlantic City of new dangers from the increasing commercial use of hazardous substances, including asbestos, 'Heavy Water', iodised air, radium paint and radioactive matter. At precisely the same time, firemen in Britain were meeting to urge the government, yet again, to consider whether the inadequacy of the fire service as a whole in Britain did not merit their urgent attention, whether a re-organised fire service should be the first stage of national defence and the fact that police control of the fire service (as applied in a number of large cities) could not be accepted.

National defence had at last come into the open and was being taken seriously by both government and the fire service.

For London, however, another fire hit the headlines – world wide. The Crystal Palace with its two enormous towers, 284 feet high, had been designed by the great Victorian master of glass and iron, Joseph Paxton, and had stood on Sydenham Hill in South London ever since it was moved out of Hyde Park after the Great Exhibition of 1851. It was one of the biggest landmarks in the country, a centre for exhibitions, choirs, concerts; a museum of wonders from all over the world. Its huge park with a unique collection of stone prehistoric monsters was a meeting ground and strolling place for thousands of Londoners and an attraction for visitors to Britain. Its firework displays were memorably spectacular and within weeks of being erected at Sydenham, its own railway was being run from London Bridge to carry the crowds who packed its glass walls and leafy gardens on Saturdays, Sundays, high days and holidays.

Although there had been times when it had fallen into slight decay, it was always restored and in 1920 the Great War Exhibition had been held there (later to be moved back to London as the Imperial War Museum). John Logie Baird had started his experiments into the infant medium of television within its glass walls and some of the earliest pictures were transmitted from the site.

On 30th November 1936, within months of its complete renovation, a group of musicians were rehearsing in the orchestral area of the central transept when they smelt smoke and left the building. A small spark, probably from a faulty piece of electrical wiring under the ladies' lavatory nearby, had been fanned into a flame by the powerful

Left: **Devastation after the Crystal Palace fire. (LFCDA.)**

draught under the floor and within minutes, had set light to the wooden floorboards, tinder dry after 80 years of underfloor heating. Because the Palace had been constructed of iron and glass, those of the public who had considered it at all had assumed that it would not burn. In fact, the whole shape of the building, long and narrow with no fire breaks or fireproof doors, was a perfect natural air tunnel. Near the area where the fire started was a paint store and a massive stack of 2,000 wooden chairs as well as a stock of inflammable black pitch. Beyond were wooden fitments, a huge screen and a giant organ. If the Demon Fire King had wanted a bonfire to dance round, this was it.

For nearly half an hour the flames spread until, at 7.59 pm, Penge Fire Station received the initial call for help. Although the Palace was set on top of a steep hill, the first firemen were in attendance by 8.03 pm. They were aghast. Penge was outside the LCC area and therefore had only a small, local brigade with three appliances. Its Chief Officer had been ill for some time and the handful of firemen realised that this was far beyond their competence. A desperate call for help went out to London headquarters and to neighbouring brigades, including Croydon, nearby.

Never before, nor since, even in the wartime blazes, could Londoners have seen anything quite like the great Crystal Palace fire. Thousands packed the streets to watch from as far off as Hampstead Heath, where children were hoisted on to their fathers' shoulders and told to look and remember the flames and the vicious orange glow in the sky for the rest of their lives. No doubt they did. Police, drafted in, battled to clear the way as crowds blocked the path of scores of fire engines struggling to reach the fire. A '*Daily Mirror*' photographer who flew over the site described it:

> 'through blinding, whirling black smoke, I saw gaping below what looked like the blazing crater of a volcano. Red-hot metal was piled up in huge, shapeles heaps. The whole of London was visible in the intense glare..... you could see Croydon Airport to the south and Osterley Station on the Great West Road. I flew at about 1,000 ft and the highest flames were barely 200ft below. Roads radiating around were thronged with the congested traffic, and the crowds of people who gathered in the glare made it a scene like hell...'

The fire brigades fought valiantly and their efforts were shown in cinemas throughout the world on the different 'newsreel' features. Because of the risk of falling debris, the Press and newsreel camera men were kept at a safe distance, but one wily cine-photographer handed his camera to a London fireman, showed him quickly how to use it and sent him to the forefront to give the world a close-up view. The result was a spectacular newsreel 'scoop' and when the delighted cameraman commented on the steadiness of the shots, the fireman explained: 'holding a cine-camera steady is a ..... sight easier than holding a branch and nozzle'.

Frederick Delve, then Chief Officer of Croydon Fire Brigade and later to control the London Region of the NFS and become Chief Officer of the LFB, arrived early with six appliances. More than 50 years later, he still vividly remembered it all, particularly the heat and the problem of getting water to the area:

'For the first time in 15 years of fighting fires, I saw men wearing their helmets back to front so that the longer rear peak helped to protect their faces from the intense heat. We all worked together, the London Brigade, our Croydon men alongside the others from Penge and Brigades from the south eastern side. As the night wore on, members of the Royal Family arrived; I remember particularly the Duke of Kent being shown round by Commander Firebrace as we struggled to get more water from the foot of the hill. When I arrived, I had reported to Major F W Jackson who was in charge of the London contingent and directing all the fire fighting operations there. He asked me to stay with him to assist and it provided me with invaluable experience, especially in maintaining communications over a large area between the forces fighting the fire and in relaying water over large distances. There was no radio in those days. I realised that few brigades had experience in relaying water, from pump to pump, across big areas and both lessons were foremost in my mind later when the NFS was formed, and when the relaying of water over long distances, the spacing of pumps and the pressures to be observed were given priority training.'

Section by section, with groans and crashes as the iron bent and the glass exploded, the Palace sank to the ground. One great moan, like a dying giant, frightened the crowd and puzzled the firemen, but it was the heat from the flames forcing air through the pipes of the great organ before that, too, succumbed. The transept collapsed with an explosion like thunder which echoed across London.

By next morning, the fire was out and all that remained was a great black, broken skeleton in a pile of smouldering ashes. 100,000 panes of smashed glass littered the ground. 15,000 tons of puddled cast and wrought iron was hardening in the earth. Only the towers had withstood the inferno and these were demolished in 1940 as they would have been too obvious a landmark for the Nazi bomber pilots heading for London. (When the bombers did come, in the autumn of 1940, one of their first targets was Croydon Airport. Ground staff there told the local firefighters who came to their rescue that the bombers were so low that they could recognise the pilots as the German aviators who had flown in with the civilian 'Lufthansa' air liners of the pre-war period. They would undoubtedly have homed in on the Palace towers had they still been there.)

Fire appliances returned to their stations. Equipment was cleaned. The normal life of the fire brigade began again, but now a greater threat was looming.

18
Pathway to War

PUBLIC OPINION ALMOST UNIVERSALLY AGREED THAT the First World War of 1914–1918 had to be the war to end all wars. Men – and women – who had suffered the mud, misery and anguish of the trenches were determined that their children would never become 'cannon fodder' and face the same terrors. From now, there must be peace. The feeling was so strong that for more than fifteen years, no political party dared to appear even to be thinking of the possibility of another war. Yet in the earliest days, there were still those in and around Whitehall who were convinced that such a danger could exist.

Although Sachs had died in 1919, his Committee continued and in 1923 they issued one of their 'Red Books' dealing with air raid damage in London. In it, the authors, Major E C P Monson and Mr Ellis Marsland voiced their fears:

'Take it for granted' they wrote, *'that in the next war, cities will be bombed without warning; what has been done in the past will be altogether eclipsed by the horrors of future aerial bombardments'*. Reasonable precautions to be taken should include regulations to ensure that all large new buildings should have heavy concrete floors to provide shelters which would offer *'almost complete immunity'* against explosive bombs. The two-storey houses of suburbia and, indeed, most of working and lower middle-class London could, they felt, offer no such protection, while nothing had so far been discovered which would offer immunity from all forms of poison gas. The document concluded with the ominously far-seeing words *'it would be unwise in the extreme to allow building construction to proceed without due regard to risks of future enemy attack'*.

Nobody wanted to know. Britain, along with much of the rest of the world, was struggling with economic problems. Only a few people were conscious of the growing threat to peace as Germany emerged from its post-war despair to find the country in the power of the extreme right-wing National Socialist Party – the Nazis. Their leader, Austrian-born Adolf

Hitler, had been a corporal in the German Army during the recent war and now had high aspirations for his country, in alliance with Benito Mussolini, leader of the equally right-wing Fascist party of Italy. Before long, they were both extending their territories, Hitler in Europe and Mussolini in Abyssinia. Disturbing reports began emerging from Germany of Hitler's determination to produce a pure, Aryan race by destroying the Jews. They were confirmed by a stream of Jewish refugees who began to arrive in Britain from Germany, seeking asylum from the Nazis.

By 1935, the mass rallies of jack-booted, goose-stepping German storm troopers, stiff arms raised in the Nazi salute and chanting in raucous, blood-chilling unison the hypnotically repetitive 'Zieg Heil! Zieg Heil!' ('Hail victory!') were becoming a regular sight on the screens of British cinemas as the 'Movietone' and 'Pathé' news cameras monitored Hitler's growing power. Even so, most ordinary people including the young, still turned their faces away from the horrifying prospect of another war. Behind the scenes, however, the Government was all too aware of the danger ahead.

As early as 1923, the Royal Commission on Fire Brigades and Fire Prevention had actually mentioned (p.220, para. 108) the possibility of schemes for fire defence 'to meet special emergencies', suggesting (para 109) that provision should be made for keeping the emergency schemes up to date through a Standing Committee of representatives of local authorities working in conjunction with the Home Office.

At that time, the possibility of another 'emergency' seemed so remote that, like the bulk of the Commission's Report, little was done to act on the suggestion, but one man, Wing Commander E J Hodsoll, a former serving officer in the Royal Flying Corps, had been appointed as a special Assistant to the Home Secretary, charged with the duty of considering what precautions should be taken in the event of air attacks in an unthinkable, possible, future war. It was a delicate subject, mentioned only when essential and even when, eventually, it became clear that there was, indeed, a threat of war, many politicians preferred to use the euphemism an 'emergency'. Hodsoll was faithful and conscientious and by the early 1930's there were, it was said, whole cupboards in the Home Office, full of his reports and warnings – few of which had been read by anyone.

By 1935, however, things had changed and the word 'war' was at last, beginning to circulate in the cubbyholes of Whitehall. Hitler was terrifying his neighbours with threats of invasion. Mussolini, to the horror of the civilised world, was using poison gas to overcome the peaceful and cultured people of Abyssinia. Ministers had, at last, begun to talk of war as a real possibility and to consider, as a major line of defence on the Home Front, what could be done about the problem of the heterogeneous assortment of brigades which still passed as a fire service in Britain.

In August 1935, the Home Secretary, Sir John Simon, set up yet another Committee to review the whole situation concerning fire services in England and Wales. It was chaired by Lord Riverdale, a banker and insurance director, and its members included Sir Percival Bower, a former Lord Mayor of Birmingham, Lt-Col Sir Vivien Henderson MC MP who had served on the 1921 Royal Commission on the fire service, and Sir Frederick Marquis, head of Lewis's department store in Liverpool and later to become Lord Woolton, (famous as a war-time Minister of Food who gave his name to the bane of all housewives, Woolton Pie).

Their brief was simple and straightforward: 'to review the fire brigade services in England and Wales and to advise whether any steps are needed to improve organisation and co-operation for the purpose of meeting danger from fire'. They reported back after nine months during which they had held 17 meetings and taken evidence from 40 witnesses, among them Major Morris of the London Fire Brigade; Mr A L Dixon (later Sir Arthur Dixon), Assistant Under Secretary of State at the Home Office, Wing Commander Hodsoll from the Air Raid precautions Department of the Home Office and the Rt Hon Herbert Morrison, a Labour member of Parliament and also of the London County Council, as well as a number of professional firefighters or people involved with the fire service.

Not to put too fine a point on it, the Committee 'let the cat out of the bag' in the opening sentence of their report. They had, they said, interpreted their terms of reference

> 'as including not only the organisation of fire brigades in normal times but also the question of whether any improvements can be made in the fire brigade organisation of England and Wales for the purposes of dealing

with conflagrations on the scale which might be anticipated in the event of air raids in the time of war.'

What essentially they needed to know was the difference between the fire risks in peace compared with those in time of a war which could involve aerial attacks with high explosive and incendiary bombs. The two situations could be remarkably different. It was clear that such attacks, particularly on a city like London, were going to be very different from those of the previous war. Equally, they wanted to discover how effective a fire service existed to deal with these risks. Very quickly they described the situation which the senior fire officers had been trying to thrust home for the past fifteen years. Their findings included:

1   That the fire brigade system in England and Wales in 1935 was essentially a local authority service which had grown up without any general co-ordinating agency. Existing powers of the local authorities depended on century old statutes which bore no relation to the new, motor-powered fire service.

2   That there was no statutory obligation on any local authority, except the London County Council and the City of London Corporation, to make any fire brigade provision either by maintaining a brigade of its own or co-operating in the maintenance of a brigade.

3   That no government department was charged with direct statutory functions or responsibility in connection with the control and organisation of fire brigades, nor was there any central supervision or recognised standard of efficiency in respect of the strength, training or equipment of brigades.

4   No direct Exchequer grant to fire brigades in England or Wales was in existence, apart from that of £10,000 a year to the LFB for the protection of government buildings (although local authorities did receive some grants from the State under the terms of the General Exchequer contribution of 1929 which gave block grants towards the relief of local rates including, where they existed, fire brigades).

5   In some places the work of firefighting was delegated to the police by local 'Watch Committees' so that local policemen also acted as part-time firemen.

As a result, it became clear that assuming future air attacks would be considerably more intensive than they had been in the past, they felt that with present resources, a town could be totally overwhelmed if bombing caused ten or twenty fires simultaneously.

Then, almost as if they had said too much, the compilers of the Report added

'it is not our desire to appear to be alarmists, our main consideration..... is the better protection and defence of the civilian population of this country. The enormous increase in the offensive power and range of the aeroplane and the suddenness of aerial attack on which its success so largely depends, now make it essential, on the grounds of humanity alone, that plans and preparations for defence should be concentrated before hand. If this preparation is adequate, then we have much less to apprehend both from the material point of view and that of national morale.'

The Riverdale Report, as it became know, backed the recommendations of the 1923 Committee that

'all the provisions relating to equipment, maintenance and operation of fire brigades should be consolidated in one comprehensive measure.'

Replies to a questionnaire from local authorities had shown that even now, only 770 of the 1,526 brigades had motor pumping appliances. In the Greater London area (including the inner area, controlled by the London County Council) there were 64 separate brigades with a total of 264 pumping appliances in commission. Of these, eight local brigades owned more than eight such pumps and these included the LFB with 112 and, at that time, 1,977 uniformed staff. (West Ham, Tottenham, Walthamstow, Hendon, Willesden, Enfield and Croydon had also scored well on provision of modern pumps.)

It seemed clear that because of the largely haphazard growth and the many small units, some areas were inadequately covered while others had more equipment – at a high cost to the ratepayers – than would have been the case if the matter had been dealt with on a broader basis. 'Better service could have been provided at less cost if brigades in some large centres of industry and population were provided jointly with those of adjoining authorities' said the Report. Localities which they felt might benefit from this included parts of Greater London. It was to be more than 20 years before this suggestion bore fruit under the Greater London Council.

Clearly the Committee felt that many local authorities were looking to the government for advice and guidance. Witnesses at the Inquiry had been inclined to accept:

1 The principle of a measure of intervention by a department of central government in firefighting, especially in the event of war. Some, but by no means all, also welcomed the idea of State Inspectors of the fire service.

2 There was still a strong feeling that local fire brigades should remain under the control of their own local authority, however small that might be, although many welcomed the idea of increased co-operation between neighbouring areas, with the Home Office exercising a more general supervision over the fire service. Many fire officers however, seemed to prefer control through Regional Boards consisting wholly or mostly of Chief Officers, either with or without a Central Fire Board.

All agreed that in the event of war, responsibility for the cost of the extra equipment and personnel which would be needed, must be assumed by the State. Also, that a scheme similar to that of World War One, by which men and appliances could be freely moved from one area to another under Defence Regulations, would be essential.

London's defence in the event of war arose when the Home Office representatives put forward their suggestions. Any satisfactory solution must, they maintained, involve a series of ad hoc fire brigade areas, either generally or for large centres of population and particularly the Greater London area, each with a single brigade under unified control and administration. Such a plan would require a special administrative body, possibly a Fire Brigade Board, comprising representatives of local authorities in the area concerned, who would have general control of the administration and financing of the Brigade in their area, plus the power to raise the necessary rate and to appoint a Chief Officer with executive charge of that Brigade.

At this stage, one of the witnesses, Herbert Morrison, Member of Parliament and of the London County Council, had put the case which many local authorities felt. Blind in one eye, with heavy horn-rimmed spectacles and a recalcitrant quiff which tended to fall across his forehead, he was universally know to Cockney Londoners as 'Herbie' or 'Our Erb'. His argument was, fundamentally, that while he agreed that a case might be made for the contention that the fire protection of the whole London area might be more efficient if it were under one control – a Greater London Fire Brigade in fact – an equally good case might be made out concerning the other services of the Council and, in the present economic situation, such a move would have grave repercussions on the structure, stability and comprehensiveness of normal local government machinery. (Ironically, Morrison was the Home Secretary who, at the height of the war in 1941, was responsible for combining the fire forces of the whole country into the National Fire Service.)

It was generally accepted by the Committee that minimum standards for the fire service should be laid down and these were to include *a turn-out time of one minute* for a brigade in a heavy industrial area (four minutes for a smaller area and six for rural areas); *for at least one mobile pumping appliance to reach a fire in not more than five minutes for an area with heavy risks* (10–12) minutes in a residential township and 15 – 20 minutes in a rural area).

Development of an improved fire service should, they maintained, be considered under four headings:

1 Delimitation of fire brigade areas.

2 Area fire brigade schemes.

3 The constitution of Area Joint Committees.

4 Financial arrangements in the areas of Joint Committees.

And the government department upon which the new duties would devolve should be the Home Office, which was already dealing with Air Raid Precautions.

The whole of Greater London would need special consideration because of its size and importance and this could be most conveniently based on what was then known as the Metropolitan Police District.

The Committee recommended that fire brigade schemes should be drawn up for submission to the Home Office by conferences of all local government fire brigade authorities in each area, including Chief Officers of the brigades. Then came the veiled warning:

'We do not desire that local authorities should form the opinion that we are advocationg coercive action or the expenditure of money from the rates without provision for due consideration. Unless the nation is to remain without adequate fire protection to meet both normal and emergency requirements, some time limit must be placed upon the institution of these new schemes and the time limit, to be effective, must carry with it adequate powers in case of default.'

At last, there might be some financial contribution from the government towards the cost of fire fighting, not just in London but nationwide.

A direct contribution from the State, said the Report, should cover 25% of the gross expenditure on public fire brigades in England and Wales (£2,250,000) which would amount to a £700,000 grant plus £300,000 to cover 50% of the administrative costs, making in all the total grant of £1,000,000.

Grants of this magnitude would demand some form of inspection to make sure that the money was spent wisely and correctly and the Committee suggested six or seven full-time Inspectors with regional jurisdiction – 'all of them persons with considerable first-hand knowledge of fire brigade working or some exceptional qualifications or experience which would fit them for the post'.

By this time, the Engineering Standards Association had already prepared British Standards for three types of hose couplings – 'V' thread, round thread and instantaneous – and a revision of this would provide for standard suction hose couplings and branch pipe nozzles. The round-thread screw coupling had been found most satisfactory for fire hydrant outlets and this would be maintained. Specifications were being prepared for portable chemical fire extinguishers. It was agreed that any equipment bought with government grants should be in co-operation with the Department of Scientific and Industrial Research.

One of the most memorable results of this was a call for the provision of light fire-fighting appliances to complement the normal full-size 'engines'. Merryweathers in particular, had been selling a small pump of this kind for some years, but with other companies coming into the market the famous mobile, trailer pumps including the 'Coventry Climax', were mass-produced from 1937 and became, at the outset of the war, a familiar sight in London, attached to the back of taxis and private cars. (The drawbacks were that such pumps, apart from remaining immobile unless some other vehicle was available to tow them, had a tendency not to start up in cold weather and were slung so low that their back axles would hit any steeply sloping kerb. Advantages included their manoeuvrability and ease of crossing rough ground.)

By the beginning of 1938 it was reckoned that to protect Britain's cities adequately, 20,000 emergency pumping vehicles would be needed and would be ready by the middle of 1941. Too late!

Extra officers would need to be trained, and these might be seconded to brigades such as the LFB for advanced technical and professional schooling. *Auxiliaries* including fire brigade pensioners might be taken on in a similar way to the special constabulary although they would need more training, particularly in the use of respirators and protective clothing. There might also be a more localised system of '*Fire Wardens*' who would come under the Home Office ARP department. This time, however, there should be no indiscriminate call-up of professional firemen. At last, the government was beginning to recognise their full value and, with 346 reservists in the London Fire Brigade alone, it was agreed that the LCC should have the right to keep them in the Service.

With hindsight, and recalling the desperate shortage of water in London and many other cities during the fire raids which were to come, it is easy to wonder whether any thought had been given to this. In fact, the Committee concerned itself with the question of water supplies in the event of just such an attack as that which was to ring the City with fire in December 1940 (although they could be

Blessing the trailer pumps, Putney, 1939. (LFCDA.)

forgiven for underestimating the scale of such an onslaught, deliberately timed to strike when the Thames was at its lowest tide).

'...There is no object' *they pointed out* 'in developing an efficient fire brigade if that service is going to find itself put out of action by the failure of water supplies owing to aerial attack. We might as well send our troops into action without ammunition.....We suggest that the government should have further inquiry made into this question, treating it as one of urgency. The matter is of prime importance in London and the larger towns and in the meantime we would direct the attention of all local authorities to the importance of making plans in advance for alternative sources of supply and interconnection between the various pumping stations as well as for the improvement of static supplies of water.'

This was a matter not just for local inquiry but for urgent government action.

In brief, Riverdale, among its 67 conclusions and recommendations suggested that:

1 Fire service laws (some of which went back to Queen Anne) should be combined in one comprehensive measure.

2 Designated authorities should have a statutory obliga-tion to maintain an efficient and adequate service for both peace time incidents or any 'emergency'.

3 The government should make a contribution to help improve and maintain the fire service not just for peace but as an essential part of national defence.

4 Suitably experienced Inspectors should be appointed to ensure that grants were efficiently used and to maintain a national standard.

5 As far as possible, equipment should be standardised.

6 An approved firefighting training school should be established.

7 All the various units of research into fire should be co-ordinated under a properly constituted Research Board.

All in all, the Committee made it clear that they considered that, for the most part, Britain's fire services, other than those in some cities like London, were quite inadequate to cope with the threat of fire in peacetime, let alone in the event of war and they called for steps similar those taken under the World War One Regulation 55B (Defence of the Realm Act) to be instituted, allowing for co-operation between brigades. Stocks of equipment should be prepared and auxiliaries enlisted.

These, then, were the recommendations. At last, they were to be taken seriously.

The Home Secretary moved fast. The report was presented in July 1936. Almost immediately he set up a new 'K' Division in the Home Office to deal with fire at national level. Responsibility for 'K' was handed to Mr Arthur Dixon (later Sir Arthur), who had served on the 1921 Commission and who, although he had for some time been dealing with police affairs, had also kept in touch with the fire brigades' organisations and was well aware of the problems they faced.

Three months later Sir John Simon also set up a Committee on Fire Brigade Reserves, headed by Sir Vivien Henderson. He too had served on the 1921 Commission (both he and Dixon had been perturbed by some of the findings and the verbosity of that report but had been unable to rein in their Chairman). Like Dixon, he had maintained a constant interest in the fire service, so much so that he was the only non-professional fireman to have been President of the Professional Firemen's Association.

The rest of the Committee included Mr E E Armstrong of the Scottish Office; Mr C Birch, (C O Brighton F B); Mr T Breaks (Superintendent, Sheffield F B); Mr F Corby (C O Bedford F B); Mr F W Delve (C O Croydon F B); Cdr A N G Firebrace, (D C O London Fire Brigade); Mr P Methven, (Firemaster of Edinburgh) and Mr A R Tozer (C O Birmingham F B) plus a Home Office official, Mr J C McIver.

Their brief was to advise on recruitment, training, conditions of service and employment of the fire brigade reserves and on auxiliary firemen.

This was a time when knowledge of the latest in firefighting experience was snatched from any quarter which might prove likely to provide it. Aylmer Firebrace, London's Deputy Chief Officer, who clearly enjoyed travelling, had already made a close study of firefighting in the Soviet Union and had visited the Paris Fire Brigade to look at their headquarters before the Lambeth plans were finalised. In the summer of 1936 he crossed the Atlantic on the Cunard's famous flagship 'Queen Mary' spending several weeks meeting firemen and inspecting their buildings and equipment on a semi-private visit to Washington, Montreal and Toronto, finishing in New York where he spent all too brief a period of four and a half days.

He seems to have had no difficulty in filling his time, visiting the New York Fire College with its workshops and clothing department, studying the fire arrangements for the Empire State Building, watching a Rescue Company, an Engine and a Double Engine Company and a high pressure pumping station and being shown a Hook and Ladder Company, and a water tower. The New York Brigade complained that since the economic Depression, they had been short of men they considered suitable for firefighting and had been forced to enrol well-educated professional men, desperate for work of some sort. These were not well regarded – as one smoke-eating fire officer growled 'it's huskies we want'. A sentiment which was to be repeated frequently in London by the old hands of the LFB when the 'soft' white collar volunteers of the AFS came on the scene. He was also deeply interested in the dry and wet rising mains in the growing number of skyscrapers (and was told by his hosts how much they envied London with its 100 ft restriction on the height of buildings. By 1991 London's skyline was to be dominated by the Canary Wharf Building, 800 feet high).

London's Deputy Chief Officer reported back that all New York firemen travelled free on public transport but had to pay for their own uniforms, insurance, a woman for bedmaking (!) and medical attendance for anything not attributable to their work. They were paid no overtime unless a fire was of very long duration and no alcoholic liquor was allowed in any fire house. Radio was already under experiment and it was reckoned that all fireboats would be fitted with this within a year. (London had none at that time.)

Firebrace was clearly fascinated by the 'syrens' on American appliances, writing that 'one aerial truck that I saw had two syrens, one electric and one driven by friction off the fan driving belt. The noise of both, which they worked together for my benefit, was severe.' Uniforms interested him when he discovered that the men bought them from about 25 New York tailors who specialised in fire brigade work. 'The very best material was used – better than that used for officers in the US Navy. The helmets, made of baked leather, cost 11½ dollars (£2.30p).'

Of all the new things which he saw, including smoke extractors, thawing trucks and searchlight units, one which clearly intrigued him to the point of describing it in detail was Dr Archer's Ambulance:

'Dr Archer is a wealthy man, much liked in the fire service. He always rides in his ambulance if he is available, even at 4am in a snow storm. If he is not available, a Department doctor is "special called." A fire enthusiast, he donated the ambulance to the New York Brigade and it was garaged in the fire house nearest to his residence. He has a system of bells in his house and gets all 'third alarm' or greater calls, The ambulance is driven by a fireman who assists Dr Archer at the fire. It is a most elaborate and complete affair, beautifully fitted in all respects and more like a travelling hospital than an ambulance, with a desk for writing reports, two adjustable beds, 18 army beds, a generator under the bonnet to provide for warming pads for the patient's body, snake-bite bottles for use at fires in banana ships and apparatus for pulling persons off electric wires.'

If all this failed, there was a small box containing emblems and holy relics for administering the last rites for the Roman Catholic, Jewish and 'a variety of other religious faiths.'

It was a visit to remember and Firebrace made many good friends in America and Canada who were not to forget their London counterparts in the dark years to come. When the blitz finally struck, the firemen of America and Canada, with their families, raised thousands of dollars to help the firemen in London and other big cities, and many of the canteens which brought welcome hot drinks and food to the parched and exhausted city firefighters bore plaques of good wishes from the kind-hearted citizens of many a small town on the other side of the Atlantic. London firewomen too, restricted by clothes rationing to the prospect of being married in uniform or 'civvies' were able to enjoy walking down the aisle in white, when consignments of high-fashion wedding dresses were sent over by firemens' wives from the U.S and Canada.

With Firebrace back and almost overshadowing Morris with his extrovert personality and his wide knowledge and experience, London faced the prospect of 'an emergency' with added vigour. Civil war had broken out in Spain at the end of 1936 and the fierce fighting between right and left wing forces culminated, on 27th April 1937, in one of the first major aerial bombardments in history. A totally indiscriminate and horrifying air attack devastated the Basque town of Guernica, killing men and women, the old and the children.

Press coverage and cinema newsreels again brought the scenes of violence to the eyes and ears of the people of Britain. The government, having sent a fact-finding team of experts to Guernica to discover what exactly had happened, redoubled its efforts to prepare for the possibility of such an attack on home ground. The raid had been carried out by German and Italian allies of the Spanish Nationalists, using high explosive bombs and one-kilo incendiaries. Spain was clearly being used by Germany and Italy as a training exercise for possible future attacks elsewhere in Europe.

Two months previously, Dixon's new Home Office Fire Brigades Division had sent out a detailed memorandum on Emergency Fire Brigade Organisation to more than 1,000 local authorities, asking them to consider the prospect of possible wartime fire risks in their area, to draw up adequate plans to deal with these and return them to the Home Office. They were warned that a vast expansion in trained firefighters and equipment would be needed and that the Government would provide pumps and equipment on free loan. The authorities were also asked to provide details of auxiliary fire stations, augmentation of water supplies, communications and the training of auxiliary fire personnel.

Towns and cities were to be divided into 'weighted street mileage', of high, medium and low fire risk and had accordingly, to work out how many pumps would be needed. Fire patrols might, it was suggested, tour the streets in the event of an air raid, ready to cope with fires as soon as they broke out.

(The latter suggestion was criticised by fire officers who discovered, as soon as war started, that such patrolling appliances were unable to be contacted by control and directed to any area where fire had broken out in those days when such radio contact equipment as existed had been confiscated on orders of the Home Office. Instead, there were, once the war had started, small emergency fire stations in the care and control of established fire stations in each area at which men and equipment were on stand-by to be called as soon as they were needed in their locality, not unlike the 'satellite' stations of the Vigiles in Ancient Rome).

Having said all this, the memorandum soothingly reassured its readers that the need for such measures 'was not related to any belief in the imminence of war' and that the provision of pumps and gear would be available only to the larger authorities with existing fully-organised fire brigades. (A subtle move to prevent the councils who had hung back on firefighting equipment to stock up at the Government's expense).

London was among a number of local authorities which quibbled over the funding of the new brigades under which pumps and ancillary gear were to be supplied on free loan, but the training and equipping of the auxiliary firefighters as well as various other items, were to be on an undefined grant basis. Despite the grim warning of Guernica, they still maintained that they would order nothing involving the spending of local funds until the financial issues were settled.

Discussions continued, during which time the *Air Raids Precautions Act of 1937 (1 & 2, Geo VI, c.6)* came into force on 1st January 1938. This authorised a government grant of up to 75% on ARP expenditure which could be increased to 90% in areas where the cost was not covered by the levying of a penny rate. Already, in Germany, the 'Luftschutzbund' – 'Air Raid League' – had been formed with 13,000,000 'volunteers' controlled and compelled to attend training under the powers of their Air Ministry.

Throughout this time it was increasingly clear that another war was more than likely and when, in 1937, Japan joined forces with Germany and Italy to form an 'axis' of power, the chances of lasting peace dwindled rapidly. Intensive dicussion had continued between Dixon and his Home Office 'K' Division, fire officers, local authorities and manufacturers of fire brigade equipment throughout the whole of Great Britain and by 1938 a Fire Brigades Bill was ready. Scotland was included in its provisions which called on every borough, urban district and rural district in England and Wales and every burgh and county in Scotland to provide efficient means of fire extinction, either alone or in co-operation with neighbouring authorities. The Home Secretary was given the power to appoint Fire Inspectors to lay down standards of efficiency for the various localities, to establish a training centre, to demand uniformity of appliances and equipment and to appoint a fire service board to take over an area and precept on its rates if, after two years, an efficient fire service had not been provided. There was to be a Fire Service Commission, to review such services which would have the power to enforce co-ordination or area schemes, and to settle any disputes over payment between authorities.

London, however, was excluded from this, other than by the provision of five minor clauses giving powers which had not been included in the Metropolitan Fire Brigade Act of 1865. However, in one major respect, the new Act caused a massive problem. It ignored the Riverdale Committee's recommendation and made no mention of a Government grant to pay for the new fire provision as opposed to ARP provision.

When it was presented to Parliament by Sir Samuel Hoare, the Home Secretary, on May 10th 1938, many MPs were astonished to hear that until now there had been no statutory obligation on local authorities to provide fire protection. One Labour MP was among many who criticised the Government for its dilatoriness in delaying so long. *'It has taken a Government department nearly 280 years to recognise the vital and supreme importance of the fire-fighting services of this country'* he declared.

There were other criticisms, not least the description that it was *'a fly-blown Act, years behind peace-time needs, not to mention the needs of impending war, throwing all the responsibility on local authorities in the most cynical way'*, but, nevertheless, the Bill received the Royal Assent to become the *Fire Brigades Act, 1938 (1 & 2 George VI, c.72)*.

Inadequate it may have been, but for the first time it laid down that, by law, every district fire authority throughout Britain must provide fire protection and that every citizen was entitled to receive the services of a fire brigade without charge. Under its surveillance was a total now of 1,668 fire brigades (1,440 in England and Wales, 228 in Scotland) ranging from the famous and powerful London, Edinburgh, Manchester and Birmingham Brigades at one end of the scale to the 'one man and a pump' in the smallest village. To prevent argument, it laid down that the senior officer present for the district in which the fire originated should have sole charge and control for its extinction.

The new Act repealed 43 assorted previous enactments including parts of the *Lighting and Watching Act* which related to fire. It also relieved the insurance companies of contributions towards provincial firefighting, as a result of which, they generously contributed £600,000 to found a Fire Brigade Training Trust.

One of its major disappointments was the failure to make provisions for standard conditions of service, so that each local authority remained free to establish its own pattern of pay, accommodation and hours of duty which still, in places, ranged from continuous duty to a 48-hour week. After years of struggling, London firemen had hoped that when the Labour Party took power in the London County Council in 1934 they would at last achieve their demand for a 48-hour week but yet again it had been turned down and a long and bitter battle developed between the new Leader of the Council, Herbert Morrison, and Percy Kingdom, Secretary of the Fire Brigades' Union, which ended after five years and only when the Council promised a 60-hour week to come into force on 1st January 1940.

Arrangements were now being made by the Home Office for the establishment of a Fire Service College. A suitable building had been found at Watford and the post of Commandant was offered to Major Morris of the London Fire Brigade. Morris retired as Chief Officer in 1938 after 30 years' service in the Brigade. His five years in command had seen the establishment and official opening of the new Lambeth headquarters, the complete re-organisation of the Brigade, the improvement of equipment and appliances and a considerable contribution toward the preparations for a possible future war.

His successor had been waiting in the wings, somewhat impatiently one might suspect, for a considerable time.

19

Braced for Action – Sir Aylmer Firebrace

AYLMER NEWTON GEORGE FIREBRACE HAD, LIKE HIS predecessor, Lionel de Latour Wells, begun his firefighting career as a midshipman in the Royal Navy. At the age of 16 he was serving in the flagship of the Mediterranean fleet when a call came for help to put out a fire which was threatening to burn down part of the nearby town of Corfu. Given six sailors to command in removing

Commander Sir Aylmer Firebrace, Chief Officer, 1938–39. (LFCDA.)

furniture from a threatened building he raced them to the top floor where, evidently to his surprise, they set to work instantly, flung open the windows and with a cry of 'From under! Below!' began hurling furniture down to the pavement. Other equally enthusiastic sailors leapt into action with the local manual pumps and only the torpedo lieutenant failed to enjoy the exercise, complaining that the fires had all been extinguished before he had time to use the quantities of gun-cotton explosives which he had brought ashore to create fire breaks.

After this brief baptism of fire, Firebrace saw action in the Navy throughout the First World War, finally taking command of the Gunnery School at Chatham, but with the war over, the prospect of any further excitement faded and, in any case, the Navy was clearly going to lay off its excess men. It was in 1919 that he happened to notice an advertisement in *The Times* for a Chief Officer in the London Fire Brigade. Although he had no experience it was, perhaps typical of the general attitude towards firefighting at that period that he assumed that he might stand a chance of getting the job.

In his book '*Fire Service Memories*' he describes his interview with the General Purposes Committee of the London County Council:

'I was asked what I was doing during the war and I replied that I had served in the Grand Fleet in HMS 'Centurion".

"Were you ever in action?" asked a woman member of the Committee.

I told her that I was at Jutland.

"What was your duty during the battle?" she inquired.

"I was in charge of fire control" I replied, intending to convey that my duty was to control the fire of the ship's ten 13.5 inch guns.'

The Committee, with its mind on a new Fire Chief, was evidently so impressed that it came close to appointing him when he realised their misunderstanding and confessed to being a gunfire officer rather than a ready-made fireman. The joke put them all in a good humour however, and he was taken into the Brigade, albeit to the more modest post of Principal Officer. *'Possibly I was appointed solely on my name'* he wrote later. *'Perhaps it was more than any committee could resist than to appoint 'Firebrace' to the Fire Brigade'*.

Even as a Principal Officer, he was at first trained along with all the other recruits, drilling at Southwark and working from antiquated text books because even as late as the 1920s, practically all the sparse education available was handed down by word of mouth, generation to generation.

Hook and ladder work – climbing to 85 feet up the drill tower at Southwark – was a vital part of this training – *'safe to work on, provided a fireman is very carefully trained and is on the look-out for certain well-know dangers…'* Jumping drill involved climbing the tower, bellowing *'Taut sheet!'* and dropping 25 feet into the sheet stretched below. (Jumping sheets were abandoned during the wartime period of the NFS, because of the fear of the public injuring themselves by landing awkwardly or missing the sheet altogether. By then, too, it was felt that it was possible to effect a rescue by safer means.) The new Principal Officer's first attempt at rescue by carrying a man of his own weight down a 50 ft ladder produced a strain in the calf muscles lasting for three days, but he preferred that to being carried down by another trainee. One recruit, he wrote, nearly met with a serious accident when, standing at the head of the turntable ladder he hooked himself on to the wrong rail and was nearly pulled in half as the ladder began to extend. With his wartime gunnery experience he was able instantly to bellow *'Still!'* and save his own life. The man's name was Firebrace – and he was later to warn, from experience: *'if drill instructors do not watch their recruits like cats, somehow or other they will find a way to kill or injure themselves…….'*

Once trained and established, he was entrusted with the massive recruiting campaign which followed the introduction of the 72-hour week, the work period which was to last until the begining of the Second World War. Although he clearly enjoyed a joke and was a great recounter of anecdotes, Firebrace was a serious and conscientious fire officer who, like so many before and since, dedicated his life to the work of the Brigade to such an extent that his family rarely saw him. All aspects of firefighting interested him from appliances, water, fire prevention and ventilation to the pets kept in fire stations.

After some years, a Fireman A P L Sullivan – holder of the Military Medal and bar for courage in the War, (and later the CBE for his wartime work in the fire service) was appointed as a deputy to Firebrace, who recalled the man's action as a fireman, at a blaze in a house in Mayfair, close to Claridges.

Sullivan and another fireman had taken the first line of hose up to the second-floor landing and were standing poised against the back pressure of their jet, in the doorway of a large room. Heads bent down, facing severe heat and smoke, they could see very little when *"Get on in with that branch"* bellowed a voice from below.' Fireman Sullivan took a single step forward and immediately disappeared, leaving his horrified companion alone on the branch and only just able to control it. In the confusion of the dense smoke, neither the men nor their officers had realised that the house was under repair and most of the floors had been removed. Terror-stricken, Sullivan dropped down, hit the skeletal remains of the first floor, rolled over between two joists then crashed down again, to land head first in a heap of sand lying in the stone-tiled front hall.' Mercifully, his brass helmet stayed in place and saved his life, although the inner lining broke and the force of the impact drove the nuts which secured the 'comb' or 'crest' on top, into his scalp, leaving two neat rows of punctured wounds. He emerged slowly from the blazing building, his face white with dust and red with blood, suffering from a strained back, a dislocated finger and, not surprisingly, severe shock. His mate, still balanced precariously with his kicking hose on the second floor, could only revert to the language of his naval past and bellow *'Man overboard!'*

Firebrace was always conscious of the importance of helmets – he had been at a fire in the City on one occasion when a fireman, soaked to the skin and moving along wet ground, brushed his brass helmet against a torn and hanging electric cable and was instantly electrocuted. He was also concerned that firemen during the war had to wear the round-topped steel helmets which afforded very little protection against falling debris.

Sir Aylmer's autobiography contains a succession of anecdotes about London's firefighters in the 1920's and 30's, which makes it clear (as any modern firefighter will confirm) that practical joking has been a perpetual fact of life in the fire stations of the capital, along with the inevitable *'cuppa'* of strong, sweet, tea which encouraged long sessions of *'yarning'* – the re-living of old fires – and did much to ease the tension and the horrific aspects of some sides of their work in the days before professional stress counsellors came on the scene.

Like Wells, too, he was interested in animals, (although not, apparently, to the extent of keeping them in his quarters.) He recalled a dog who lived at Brompton fire station and was adept at stamping out fire with his paws. Another, a Great Dane at Manchester Square, would walk the fire hydrant inspection route with a fireman friend and when a new fireman arrived, would lead him round the route too, making sure that no hydrant was missed. Later in life, the dog suffered from sore pads and if he were out walking alone and found the pavements too hot, would lie in the shade and wait for someone to telephone the fire station, where the officer on watch always happened to have a vehicle passing by at the appropriate moment to give him a lift home. His only weakness seems to have been that, as one fireman remarked, he was *'rather heavy on cats'*.

Cats did not pass unnoticed and Firebrace spotted one strolling across the drill yard at Lambeth. He questioned the Senior Superintendent as to who owned it, and, without a moment's hesitation, was told *'it's a spare sir!'* Another cat which he came across at Euston fire station was Bill, who, on fine warm days, would climb to the top of the 60-foot ladder and sun himself on the top step while he watched the drill in progress in the yard below.

Travelling had always played an important part in the life of the new Chief Officer elect and his journeys to Russia and to the United States and Canada were all to provide experience for the tough task which would be facing him shortly when he took command, briefly of the LFB and later of firefighting throughout the country during the war. Now, there was to be no time to set off on month-long trips abroad – nor to observe the social life of the Fire Brigade pets.

On 6th June 1938 Major Morris left and Commander Aylmer Firebrace achieved the position he had aspired to in 1919. 'It was fortunate that the Brigade was in such good trim when I took over command, for now, except for normal fire-fighting operations and the routine administration of a force 2,000 strong, every minute of the working day and most of what should have been the sleeping night could be given to the many pressing problems involved in preparing for the fire defence of London' he wrote later. (And quoting his long-serving and long-suffering cleaning lady, he added: 'she paused one day from her dusting long enough to point a minatory finger at me and to say *"All this ARP (Air Raid Precautions) – You'll be RIP if you don't look out!"').*

In Brigade tradition, he and his family lived 'over the shop', at Lambeth in a flat with a magnificent view across the Thames. An addition to his normal work was involvement with the LCC's ARP programme and he got on well with Herbert Morrison, who was leading the Council at the time. Because of the heavy work load, however, his Deputy, DCO Frank Jackson, took a considerable share of the firefighting duties.

In 1938, the Auxiliary Fire Service was launched and with it, for the first time in Brigade history, women were invited to join. From the point of view of many of the regulars, this was almost more daunting than the prospect of war. The problems facing Helen Ward, who took charge of the new womens' section were anything but enviable. Long-serving officers went weak at the knees at the thought of women on their fire stations (the very phrase brought back memories of the heinous crime of firemen being caught with women in their fire boxes.) As for women in the watch-room, it was a holy of holies where even the wives who lived in quarters above the fire station were not allowed to cross the threshold. Life would not be easy for either side.

Faced with the request from the Home Office in February 1937 for a fire protection scheme for London to be submitted as soon as possible, the LCC could not be said to have acted with lightning speed, but seven months later it had at least, established a Fire Brigade Committee. The economic situation still meant that the municipal purse strings could only be loosened with the utmost care and there was still no certainty that a war was inevitable – although as time wore on the signs were not good. Even so, no Council was going to spend money which was urgently needed for other essentials on laying in an excess of fire appliances and equipment that were to lie unused and rotting in the stores.

By early 1938 the war clouds were clearly gathering. Calls had gone out for volunteer auxiliary firemen and Chief Officer Firebrace had shared a 20 minute BBC broadcast, appealing for men and women to join the AFS, but the response was lukewarm. In the summer, Hitler marched on Austria and soon after this came reports that a small group of Germans in the Sudetanland were asking him to 'release' them from the control of Czechoslovakia. Suddenly, the ordinary people of Britain woke up to the very real threat of war. In September, the Prime Minister, Neville Chamberlain, flew to Munich for peace talks with Hitler and, in a time of heightened tension, many mothers with children left London for the country, the fear of war and mass bombing vivid in their minds, to return thankfully a few days later when the immediate crisis was averted.

At last, the urgency of the danger had struck home. Action to consolidate the whole of the country's firefighting defences was now needed as a matter of imminent and desperate need. For efficiency in any possible *'emergency'* the country was divided into twelve regions, each under the control of a Commissioner who would take over in the event of any invasion which left Britain without guidance from Westminster.

For the Auxiliary Fire Service, recruitment intensified, particularly in the capital. Posters were distributed throughout London; 60 AFS towing vehicles carried placards round the streets appealing for help; LFB speed-boats flew huge '*JOIN THE AFS*' pennants emphasising the need for crews in the river service and two advertising companies sent up planes to trail streamers above the skies of the capital underlining the need for help. This was particularly effective as people always looked up at the sound of an aeroplane – a rare event in pre-war London.

Fire officers addressed huge recruiting meetings organised by the staff of some of London's biggest stores – Harrods and John Lewis among them, as well as the employees of the Stock Exchange, the LCC and many more.

Meanwhile, back at headquarters, it was not only the Chief Officer who was working day and night to organise the new service. Officers – men and women – had to be appointed. Conferences, training programmes and exercises needed to be laid on; new uniforms, equipment, and quarters had to be found. At the same time, 35 officers were detailed to advise businesses how to protect their premises against incendiary bombs and how to train their employees to fight fires. Added to this was the need to make sure, somehow, that there would be adequate water supplies for firefighting.

'What lingers in my mind' *wrote Firebrace later*, 'is the extraordinary amount of work, all unpaid, done by the auxiliary officers, both men and women, at that time. They worked unceasingly and unselfishly to get things going… One officer paid out of his own pocket the wages of a personal clerk to help speed the work. A woman university graduate wrestled night after night with recruiting and training problems.'

With the high number of professional people now coming in, it was not surprising to find that a senior woman staff officer came on duty one day to discover that another smartly dressed woman was sitting at her desk. Only when she crossed the room did she discover it was a lifelike dummy – finely carved and painted by a volunteer fireman who was also a well-known sculptor and a member of the Royal Academy.

'It was only by such foolery that we preserved our sanity and kept on good terms with each other, despite difficulties which were, for the moment, insoluble and delays which were always distracting,' Firebrace recalled.

This was made worse by the fact that almost every problem had to be solved first for the men, then the women and quite often between the professional firemen of the LFB and the auxiliaries with whom they were not always on the best of terms (although in many stations the initial wariness and antagonism began to disappear as they all combined to get the job of training and absorbing the newcomers into the Service under way, and evaporated more swiftly once the Blitz started).

When one looks back on the task facing them, it is amazing that anything ever emerged from the chaos that had accrued from years of pushing the needs of firefighting to the back of the queue for government action. London was not the only local authority to be dragging its feet until the Government jumped off the fence and came up with some real money in the way of grants towards the heavy expenses which would be incurred in providing all the necessary organisation and equipment.

In his book '*The London Blitz*', Cyril Demarne OBE, a fire officer with West Ham Brigade and later with the NFS throughout the war, describes a typical situation in 1939: 'Plans were laid for the recruitment of an Auxiliary Fire Service but the County Borough of West Ham was at odds with the central Government over the amount of local authority contributions to the cost of the new service. West Ham refused to carry out its obligations under the Act until better terms for depressed areas were conceded. There was also a row over who was to be the Air Raid Precautions Controller for the County Borough. The council wanted to appoint the Mayor Elect but the Regional Commissioner preferred the greater experience of Town Clerk. The situation worsened and the Commissioner threatened to take the matter out of the council's hands altogether. Reluctantly, the council gave way and in March 1939, recruitment for the AFS and Civil Defence began…'

True, Chamberlain had returned from Munich, memorably photographed on the steps of his aircraft, carrying his inevitable umbrella (food for every cartoonist in the land), beaming confidently and announcing that he had negotiated an honourable '*peace in our time*'. All the indications were that this was a frail and uncomfortable agreement, an apprehension increased when, in the following Spring, Hitler marched into Czechoslovakia and began setting his sights on Poland.

Even so, the twelve months' respite granted by the Munich episode gave the Brigade desperately needed time for the defence of the Capital to be organised on a sounder basis. By March 1939, the Home Office questionnaires had been returned, indicating that Britain needed a total of 175,000 auxiliaries. This was a conservative estimate and the Home office experts reckoned that 350.000 would be more realistic. Of these, only some 140,000 had so far been recruited, 65,000 of whom would be available for full-time service if war broke out. The rest would come in at the end of their normal working day and at week-ends.

Now too, the basic pay rates had been announced – £3 a week for men and £2 for women (based on the pay and allowances of a married soldier with one child and slightly higher than the average pay of a semi-skilled worker).

Equipment was arriving more quickly – by June 1939 trailer pumps were being delivered at the rate of 600 a week, to the bewilderment of some local authorities who had no idea where to put them or what to do with them. Croydon's Chief Officer, 'Freddie' Delve had put his to good use when typhoid broke out in the borough and was traced to the local underground reservoirs. The health authorities ordered that all the reservoirs should be washed down to destroy the source of the infection and the local firemen lowered the small, lightweight pumps into the depths and carried out the job at maximum speed and efficiency.

Problems arose, however, with some of the ancillary equipment. Extra hose was but one example. Miles of hosepipe would be needed if bombing destroyed those in normal use. Although the Home Office offered enormous bulk orders, British hose manufacturers had already formed a solid group and refused to quote competitve prices. Nor had they the flax, the machinery or the skilled men to meet the contracts which were being offered. Much of the hose used when the Blitz began had been shipped in from the United States in the form of heavy, cotton-jacketed rubber, difficult to handle, awkward to stow and taking up far more room than the British unlined flax hose.

Although the 1921 Committee had called for standardi-sation there was still no general pattern for equipment. Approaching war found London with 95,000 fire hydrants with six different types of outlet. Stocks of standpipes for all these had to be bought by the different local authorities.

The Home Office now laid down a standard for hose couplings – the 2½ inch instantaneous – for all the emergency hose being issued. It was certainly quick and efficient but London used the round thread couplings, slow to fix and needing a spanner (carried by every London fireman, regular or auxiliary, in a pouch on his belt) to tighten it. With its customary isolation and aloofness, London had despised the instantaneous method – 'competi-tion coupling' they called it – arguing that it was easily damaged and could come apart if hose was being hauled up a building. At first, special emergency hose with round thread couplings was provided for London, but later it became clear that the essentially accurate threads took too long to mass-produce and London finally accepted the Home Office instantaneous coupling.

Water was clearly going to be a problem. If the mains were hit (and when the time came, many of the powerful High Explosive bombs landed in roads producing deep, broad craters smelling nauseously and exposing a fascinat-ing network of shattered gas and water pipes as well as

Brigade workshops prepare for World War Two. (LFCDA.)

electric cable) there would be a shortage of water for fire fighting. Bulk storage in closely built-up areas like the centre of London would be difficult to site, but work went ahead to provide small 'static' tanks, built with steel sheets and holding 5,000 gallons of water, close to any building which seemed to pose any kind of special risk. Even this would be merely a drop in the ocean of flame, since it would only supply a large pump for five minutes.

Portable canvas tanks were bought in quantity and many families donated this type of water container which they had set up in their back gardens during the late thirties and used as family swimming pools. In addition, a fleet of lorries laden with 500-gallon tanks, each towing a trailer pump, was established as a mobile supply for immediate use. British waterways had a few fire boats on the canals but to these were added a small number of emergency craft with a standard heavy unit pump and engine fitted, which could be moved close to any fire on the canal or river bank to supplement the normal service.

In July 1938, London spent £500,000 on increasing its water supplies, with 90% of the cost being provided by the Government and the rest by the London County Council. Half of this was spent on providing a vast underground network of emergency 24-inch water mains, with hydrants attached and special diesel pumps stationed at intervals to force water from the Thames through the areas of highest risk. Although the government had made a similar offer to a number of other cities including Liverpool, Manchester, Newcastle, Nottingham, Bradford, Sheffield and Coventry, not all took up the chance and were to regret it later when sudden air attacks or saturation bombing destroyed their normal supplies.

London spent the rest of its grant on providing pumping stations on the Thames at Blackfriars (where, as a recent addition to the river patrol, the fireboat 'Massey Shaw' was based) and at Charing Cross, as well as installing equipment which would allow the Brigade to draw water from the Metropolitan Water Board's trunk mains. Arrangements were made with local councils for swimming baths and lidos to be used, if necessary, by the Brigade, and many London parks which had yearned in hot weather for paddling pools for local children now found themselves provided with just such a luxury – to be shared with the firefighters.

April 1939 brought the Spring and even greater apprehension. Hitler was demanding Danzig and threatening Poland. Britain and France had guaranteed to support Poland in the event of an invasion. The speed of preparation for war became frenetic. Some fire stations had 1,000 AFS men and women attached to them, who were coming in after work on almost every evening to fit in their statutory 60 hours of training, to drill and to practise with the

equipment. (Many married women fitted in training after giving their husbands their mid-day meal and before the children came home from school.) All firemen and women had been provided initially with overalls, rubber boots, a cap and steel helmet – plus, for the men, a tunic, trousers and waterproof leggings added later as an afterthought. All had gas masks. All needed somewhere to store them ready to change when they arrived at the station. Space was at a premium, so much so that every available inch was taken for service use, including the former family accommodation over many fire stations. In some cases, firemen's families had to find other homes; in others the space above the stations had been let for commercial use as offices, but all in all, 300 flats were taken back for use in a war which still might not happen.

For many years the LCC's Brigade had been divided into five districts, each under the command of a superintendent. The scheme worked out by Firebrace and his men divided the rest of London into another five districts adjoining the outer rim of the LCC area. West Ham, Beckenham, Croydon, Ealing and Tottenham were selected as 'superintendent stations'. All were known to have highly efficient full-time fire brigades and their Chief Officers were to become Assistant Regional Fire Officers (known as 'ARFOs'), under Firebrace. They would act as Assistant Mobilising Officers implementing orders from a Regional Mobilising Officer asking them to send reinforcements to other areas or arranging for help to be sent in to them if it was needed. London remained as a separate entity at this time, under the control of Major Frank Jackson, Firebrace's deputy.

In December 1938, the LCC took over a new block of flats, Whitgift House, close to the Lambeth HQ as accommodation for the auxiliaries but the fire service still needed premises for the six auxiliary fire stations which would be attached to every main fire station throughout London and Station Officers were set the task of searching their area to find possible premises. Not all would prove to be suitable – as their occupants were soon to discover.

Training was now in full swing, with full-time professional firemen – men who had often left school at 14 – finding themselves commanding and instructing men and women from a whole range of backgrounds and professions – solicitors, lawyers, bank managers, artists, and, among the women, top fashion models, journalists, clerks and housewives from all the various social levels of British society at that time. King George VI discovered just how varied the range was when he inspected the Control Room in 1940 and asked one of the women control staff what her peacetime work had been. Springing to attention, she replied 'bookmaker's clerk, sir!' Aux Fmn H S Ingham described it in a preface to the NFS anthology 'Fire & Water', whose AFS contributors were among the cream of young British writers:

'From these new mixtures of auxiliary firemen, individuals would soon emerge. A mess manager would be required, and Smith, who had been a cook in the Merchant Navy, would volunteer. Jones, who was a member of the local Borough Concil, would hear about the Fire Brigades Union, form a branch and become secretary. Williams, a musician, would get together a small orchestra and organize a dance and, when difficulties were experienced in settling accounts and preparing balance sheets, Brown would modestly confess to being a member of the Institute of Chartered Accountants . . . . .'

In the same book, Maurice Richardson describes how he joined the London AFS, and within two months had been trained, sent into the front line, fought dozens of hectic fires and fallen fifty feet from a blazing building.

Mrs Betty Cuthbert, who later became Chief Officer of the Women's Section of the National Fire Service and, eventually, Lady Cuthbert, was the eleventh woman to volunteer. Her husband was a Commander in the Royal Navy:

'I went to Lambeth and was signed on as a firewoman' *she said, recalling the event fifty years later.* 'There was a great deal of confusion and at that stage the Fire Brigade really didn't know what to do with the women who were being suddenly introduced into the Service. There were no women officers. I was trained as a fire man – in everything – and I was given a trailer pump to put on the back of my Wolseley car so that I would be available for any emergency. I particularly hated having to back the car when the trailer was attached – it was a very difficult manoeuvre if you were not used to it.'

Later, she became an officer – 'I remember my husband helping me over the drill, marching the few firewomen we had, along the Embankment and teaching me exactly how to give orders to them. He would walk along beside me with his rolled umbrella and prompt me with the orders in a whisper.'

Slowly and steadily, more equipment began to arrive in London and by hook or by crook (and usually both) space was found for it to be stored. It included nearly two thousand vehicles, from full size engines to trailer pumps; mile upon mile of hose and mountains of bedding. New Ford towing trucks were bought by the LCC for the auxiliaries to train with and smaller Ford vans for the women drivers, many of whom had to be taught to drive from scratch. By the beginning of the war, the LCC had hired 2,381 taxis to haul the trailer pumps – a short-lived exercise owing to the cost of their meters ticking over for 24 hours of every day.

Soon after Firebrace left for the Home Office, the LFB was asked to take over responsibility for fire protection of the entire River Thames, down to its estuary at Holehaven and ten more fireboats were added to its existing complement.

Londoners had been warned of the dangers facing them if war came although they still prayed that somehow the nightmare would end. Gas masks of different types according to need were issued to service personnel, civil defence workers including firefighters, civilians, children and babies in the summer of 1939.

Throughout August the government struggled to keep the fragile peace but by now trenches were being dug and corrugated metal sheets issued to all Londoners for use as air raid shelters (named after the Home Secretary who authorised their issue 'Anderson' shelters.) Week-ends and summer evenings were spent digging holes sufficiently deep almost to bury them in back gardens, shovelling layers of earth on top for extra protection, and 'furnishing' them with old pieces of carpet, blankets, first aid materials, cans of food oil lamps or candles, games, packs of cards and even primus stoves to boil a kettle for all-important cup of tea. Even then, there was still the hope that this was some kind of gruesome game. War could never happen.

A British mission was still in Russia trying to negotiate a somewhat incongruous alliance on September 1st 1939, but Hitler was wasting no more time on words. The dawn found his tanks rolling into Poland at the head of huge armoured columns of highly disciplined Panzer troops.

In all its history, London had never known such a day. All railways stations were taken over and filled with lines of children, labelled with their school number and clutching rucksacs or attaché cases containing a change of clothing and a favourite toy. Their parents, many in tears, waved them off on the great evacuation to safety in the country. The whole machinery of Air Raid Precautions went into action and the Auxiliary Fire Service, 89,000 men and 6,000 women throughout the country, was mobilised for full-time service with a peace-time volunteer and retained service of some 50,000 men under 1,600 different fire authorities. 14,000 emergency pumps had been added to the resources – 12,000 more than existed at the time of Munich.

It is easy to look back and criticise, in retrospect, the lack of preparation which undoubtedly existed. The general poverty of the 1920's and 1930's, had meant that most local authorities of all political colours had very little money to spare on expensive preparations for an event which might not take place, when so much was needed for absolute essentials (or, it has to be admitted, in some cases needed for items which might be more popular with the voters). Because of this, the barest minimum had been spent on the provision of auxiliary fire stations let alone their equipment.

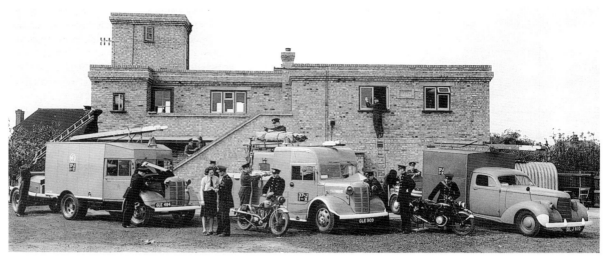

AFS personnel built their own station at Bromley, 1940. (LFCDA.)

The new firemen and women were warned by radio broadcasts to come immediately, bringing two days' rations with them, but not all were able to do even that. They came and were often horrified at what they discovered.

Betty Cuthbert was now in command of a small sub-station at Vauxhall. '*I found it was completely bug infested – there were bed bugs everywhere.*' Another firewoman, all of 19 years old and an early volunteer, was directed to her AFS station – '*a furrier's store until then, with one table and a few collapsible chairs – no beds but a few girls had brought blankets so we scrounged some sandbags and made them into one long bed and shared the blankets. Later we discovered that the place was infested with bugs and were transferred a few yards up the road to a City billiards and lunch club which had been abandoned as the war began. Dirty crockery and empty beer bottles were scattered all over the place but we scrubbed it out and got it shipshape. Unhappily we were rid of the bugs but had much more unsavoury bedfellows – the City ratcatchers caught 80 rats there in one week – and we were sleeping on the floor.*'

And from another of the new firewomen, posted to a sub-station in Chiswell Street, part of Whitbread's City brewery, where they found no beds but a plentiful supply of mattress filling: '*We stuffed sacks with the hops to make palliasses and after a couple of days sleeping and working in one tiny, airless room we were all more or less permanently drugged from the hops and had to have a couple of days' sick leave to rest and recover.*'

Horror stories of emergency fire stations flew round the city, but one, possibly the strangest, affected the AFS crew who were sent to the Royal College of Surgeons, which had been evacuated from Lincoln's Inn Fields. Their dormitory walls were lined with shelves holding rows of glass jars filled with human organs. Prime exhibit was a fully-grown stuffed gorilla which was no contributor to sweet dreams. But there was another side to the situation. A particularly happy young AFS woman reported '*our quarters were in luxury flats – it was the first time I had ever seen a coloured toilet pan!*'

Bromley took matters into its own hands. There, the auxiliaries who included architects, surveyors and builders, acquired a piece of land and built their own sub-station.

The first two days of September 1939 were spent in a fury of clearing up, cleaning, scrounging furniture and beds, blankets and often some means of cooking, for no arrangements had been made for supplying food to the auxiliaries, no matter how long they were to be on duty. Even railway arches had been taken over and pressed into use as fire stations and in some there were not even any lavatories, let alone separate arrangements for men and women.

There was little time for complaint (although the gloomy atmosphere was always eased by a good and constant moan). On Sunday, 3rd September 1939 the whole nation gathered round the wireless – and those who hadn't this luxury went to neighbours who had. At 11 am the Prime Minister, Neville Chamberlain addressed the nation. In a solemn voice he broke the news that Britain had declared war on Nazi Germany.

Within minutes the air raid sirens, which had been installed throughout the country, moaned up the scale and the ghoulish, undulating whine sent shivers up the backs of everyone who heard it. Families rushed for the safety of the sandbagged shelters. In London, firemen and auxiliaries stood side by side, 'tin' hats and uniforms on, gas masks at the ready, appliance engines running. Half an hour later the angelic single note of the 'All Clear' pierced the air. It had been a false alarm when a light aircraft, returning to France, forgot to report its presence to the authorities and was very nearly shot down.

This was the beginning of a period when little was happening on the Home Front. The AFS men drilled with the professionals and worked side by side with them, although there were undoubtedly many problems, not least the difference in pay between the volunteers and the 'pros'. For some years the Fire Brigades Union had been working on behalf of the men and had managed to secure better conditions than had ever existed in the days before firemen were organised to fight together rather than individually for improvements. It had been a tough battle and there is no doubt that the authorities had, for far too long, taken advantage of the unemployment situation which had led to the men's submissive acceptance of appalling pay and conditions.

Playing a major part in the Union now was a young fireman, John Horner, who had joined the Brigade with no great enthusiasm in 1934. He had been a dedicated seaman until, like so many in the early 1930s, he found himself without a job. He was strong and healthy and joined the LFB knowing that, although it was no longer a condition of entry, they still favoured former seamen for the work. He was never happy with the conditions (although he admitted that the uniform was made of first-class material, lined across the shoulders and down part of the sleeves with close woven tweed which helped to prevent sparks from burning through. He always remembered, with wry humour that because the authorities believed that working class men were too common to wear underpants, they were issued with lengths of cotton cloth and their wives were expected to use these to make trouser linings which could be removed at intervals and washed. But despite his bitterness, he kept his London-issue black silk scarf for the rest of his life.)

John Horner became famous as the firemen's champion, doing all he could to improve their conditions through the Union but working from within the Brigade. In June 1939 he was voted in as its General Secretary.

The Union had been in turmoil over the question of the AFS volunteers. Many felt that they were a direct threat, diluting the power of the professional men. On recruitment they had all signed on to serve for an unspecified number of hours. There were no conditions of service, no sick leave, no annual holidays. Recovery from any injuries on duty was restricted to two weeks after which their pay was stopped and they had to resort to the Unemployment Assistance Board (and this applied also for those who, in many cases, had given up good professional salaries to volunteer).

Uniform for the AFS was basic, made of poor quality thin cloth and, for many in London, there was no change of trousers or tunics available, (women were allowed to wear trousers only for certain duties, including motor cycle despatch-riders and lorry drivers). This was bad enough at this stage when fires were much on a peace-time pattern allowing time to change into 'civvies' while they were drying. It was to become a major problem during the blitz, when 'shout' followed 'shout' at such a pace that the men had no time to dry out their clothes and spent much of their time in uniforms soaked from spray. Firebrace expressed his concern at seeing AFS men, returned from hours of hardship fighting the fires of the Blitz, cleaning equipment in their underpants while their uniforms dried out.

When the LFB and the whole London Region were mobilised, there were fewer than six mobile canteens in commission and the Union alleged that, at times, the men were reduced to drinking Thames water to allay the intense thirst which comes in the course of fighting big fires.

Ultimately, the FBU found a temporary solution and, in the month in which the war began, they formed a separate AFS section. John Horner wrote:

'The situation was acute. It brooked no delay. Imagination and decision were needed. The AFS section of the Union was thereupon set up. Speed, direction and organisation were necessary. We could not afford to allow the AFS to remain unorganised… More important, we could not allow some other body, union or otherwise, to organise the AFS…as we later discovered that others had intended to do.'

AFS men paid one penny a week less than 'regulars' in Union dues.

In one brief statement, Horner predicted 'We are living in a time of rapid and radical change. It may be as difficult for you, as it was for me, to adjust your outlook to these changing conditions…' By July 1941, the Executive of the Union comprised nine professional and nine auxiliary firemen, with the understanding that in future, the president or the vice-president might .be an AFS person. It was becoming a force which would, from then on, gain in strength until eventually it would exert a major power over the affairs of the London Fire Brigade.

Apart from the shortages of uniform and the appalling condition of many of the sub-stations, the pre-war insurance schemes had been scrapped and for many men, injuries on duty meant not only that within a couple of weeks, no wages would be coming in but if the injury was severe enough to lead to their dismissal from the service, the decision was often delayed for weeks, during which time they could claim no unemployment pay.

The Union pointed out the problems this raised for both men and women and by November 1939 were meeting officials from the Home Office to demand full pay for London firemen – professional or auxiliary – when they were sick or injured in the course of their work. This was backed up by a Parliamentary debate, fostered by the Union, to press these claims. By December, the government had made provisions for the men to receive two weeks' injury pay and three weeks' sick pay, with injured firemen coming under the terms of the Civilian Personal Injuries Scheme.

This failed to satisfy the FBU. John Horner published a pamphlet 'Your Rights to Compensation' aimed at firemen and firewomen (whom they regarded as having equal status with the men) and a month later, in January 1940, a mass meeting of personnel in London demanded the withdrawal of the scheme. A fierce battle was waged now between various government departments and the Union, with the FBU claiming for full pay during sickness and injury and the Home Office rejecting the demand on the grounds that 'Civil Defence workers are very generously treated'.

By now, nearly a year had passed and the war was going badly on the Continent. For years, the German forces had been preparing for battle and were fully armed, trained and disciplined. The French and the British troops, put into action at a moment's notice, were being pushed further and further back towards the French Channel ports. By comparison, the Fire Brigade was having an easy time and before long they were the target for a wave of abuse from the Press and from their fellow countrymen. This was the period of the 'phoney war' or as some firemen dubbed it 'the Sitzkrieg' as they waited for the attack on London which must surely come. Some of the volunteers were pacifists, unwilling to take life. Pacifists or not, all were accused of being draft dodgers, 'The Darts Brigade' was a favourite name. Cartoons denoted them as living in peaceful luxury while the armed forces were being mown down in battle. Added to this, many of the men themselves felt humiliated and wanted to play a more active part in the war. Resignations from the fire service began to pour in at an alarming rate and one enterprising group took the law into their own hands.

Finland was at war with Russia and needed help. AFS man Anthony Gilkison decided to organise a Fire Brigade Unit to go to their aid – a basic group of eight men which could be increased if all went well. He needed men accustomed to living or working abroad, who could speak foreign languages and settle quickly into a new environ-ment. From his fellow AFS men he chose a former film director, author, lawyer, rubber planter and army PT instructor. Dressed in an AFS-type uniform but with plastic buttons to avoid the danger of burns from the extreme cold, they left Shoreham airfield on 12th March 1940, bound for Finland. Their equipment, which included a heavy-unit type appliance, a Coventry-Climax trailer-pump, a hose lorry and 3,000 feet of American hose, went by sea. By the time they reached Finland, the war there was over, but, with the Russians in occupation, the men from London were trapped. There was nothing to do but join the Helsinki fire brigade and the British crew became famous for defiantly driving round the city in their red appliance with the name 'London Fire Volunteers' on the side and a Union Jack flying from the bonnet. After the invasion of Russia, the Germans took control and it was suggested that some quieter form of employment should be found for the Londoners. They worked in schools or the University until eventually, and with difficulty, they were able to escape and return by devious routes to London.

From the outset of war, the country had been divided into twelve Regions, each under a Regional Commissioner who had, among his senior staff, a Regional Fire Officer as well as a number of Fire Brigade Inspectors, (usually ex-fire officers). Their job was to inspect and report back to the Home Office on the arrangements which had been made for the storage and maintenance of fire equipment, the state of the supplies and to keep in touch generally with the fire service in their area and maintain contact between it and the Home Office.

In London, Aylmer Firebrace had been taken from his job as Chief Officer of the LFB at the outbreak of war and moved to the Home Office to serve under the Regional Commis-sioner, (at first Capt the Rt Hon Euan Wallace MC MP; later and for longer, Sir Ernest Gowers KCB). He had been loath to leave his post and had, indeed, appealed to Herbert Morrison and the Leader of the LCC before reluctantly accepting Command of the whole London Region which, he had assumed, would have been in charge of the combined London Brigades.

Now his place but not his title, was taken by his deputy, Major Frank Whitford Jackson, who became Deputy Chief Officer Commanding the London Region. Jackson had joined the LFB in 1920 with a distinguished war record and became its Second Officer in 1938. When Firebrace was transferred to the Home Office in January 1939, he took over as Officer Commanding the London Fire Service – both the LFB men and the AFS volunteers. For some years before this he had been Station Officer at Euston and not only knew all the ways of the Brigade but was a good administrator. John Horner of the FBU had also served at Euston and knew him

Deputy Chief Officer Commanding London Region throughout the Blitz, Major Frank ('Gentleman') Jackson. (LFCDA.)

well enough to visit him frequently at headquarters and discuss the men's problems with him, on a friendly basis. 'He was a great officer, admired and respected by his men who had a great affection for him. He understood the problems which faced many of them, particularly under wartime conditions and I remember, during the Blitz, going to him to plead that the men must have a change of uniform. Nobody else seemed to want to know that they were fighting fires, going out again and again in soaking wet clothes. With the concentration on the sheer organisation of the AFS and the shortage of supplies it seemed almost impossible to get them a spare uniform but in the end, we discovered that the Post Office had a store of navy blue trousers. Admittedly they had a red line down the legs, and they weren't particularly good quality, but they provided a change and in the end we bought up the whole store – 25,000 pairs'.

Many London firemen fought the fires of the Blitz wearing postmens' trousers. Others discovered that the uniforms issued to them when they joined the AFS were, in fact, second hand and had been handed back by men who had resigned to volunteer for the armed services, which

upset men and women alike in the days when there was no fashion kudos in wearing other people's cast-offs.

Added to the whole problem of the inadequacy of the uniforms was the fact that neither the men nor women auxiliaries had overcoats – other than the drivers – and Lady Cuthbert recalled the chill day in 1940 when the Brigade was visited at Lambeth by the King and Queen and the women marched smartly – and crackling – on to the drill area. Beneath their thin uniforms they had wrapped themselves in layers of newspaper to keep out the cold.

There was no doubt about the Union's increasing power at this time. Its pre-war membership had hovered around the 3,000 mark. By 1942 it had reached 69,000 and was still growing, with increasing Communist domination – acceptable at a time when the Communist Soviet Union was, against all pre-war indications and those of the early 1940's, soon to become an ally of the West. A continuous duty system had been imposed in the fire service on the day the war started but as no air raids developed, it was swiftly changed to a 48-hours on and 24-hours off system of duties (although the other ARP services worked a 24-hours on, 24-hours off system). The regular firemen in the LFB had been promised a 60-hour week by 1940, but they were assured by the authorities that in the circumstances a 110-hour week was inevitable and accepted it without complaint – officially at least.

The period of the 'phoney' war was not easy and the winter of 1939/1940 was bitterly cold. Emergency water tanks had frozen over. Emergency pumps had to be started up every 15 minutes day and night to prevent the engines from freezing. After tidying their stations, polishing the equipment, re-filling and even whitewashing the sandbags, crews read, talked, played cards, listened to the wireless and the more ambitious organised concerts and plays to raise money for the various war-time charities. There were enough professional people in the AFS to make sure that they were first-class productions – often with scenery by professional artist firefighters.

Life for the auxiliaries had been tough, particularly when, without enough peace-time officers to go round, some of them came under control of LFB men who would never have been given command under normal circumstances. The fact that many of the AFS officers had been professional men on good salaries before the war made it all the harder to take. Eventually a special LCC committee was set up to look into the problem and with Home Office approval, decided that every AFS fire officer holding rank was to be given a London Fire Brigade rank along with their conditions, pay and uniform and was to take his place in the LFB hierarchy, with the power to command men who were his junior in either the LFB or the AFS. The scheme applied only to men who could pass the LFB fitness test and came into force in October 1940. Although it had a variety of teething troubles, it was a step towards unifying the volunteers and the 'old-stagers'.

By now, too, the original order granting deferment from call-up for the armed services for serving members of the London Fire Brigade was rescinded and as the numbers fell, they were made up by the 'cream' of the AFS, taken from their grey-painted emergency pumps and allowed the privilege of working from the fire-engine red machines of the regular Brigade. Once more, the FBU protested against the 'Red Riders' as they were known and the issue was only solved when these men too, were made temporary LFB firemen and given the same pay, uniform and conditions of service.

It was not altogether a happy time and it seemed that the whole country was ganging up against the firefighters. In London, two AFS men, with the approval of their Station Officer, removed some scrap building material from an abandoned dump close to their station in an effort to improve conditions. Not only were they arrested and charged with theft but found guilty by a magistrate who upbraided them as 'scroungers' – and all their fellow firemen with them. Both men of unblemished character, they were sentenced to a month's imprisonment, wiped out on appeal, but nevertheless adding to the general depression.

20

Cry Havoc!

'A taste of warlike action..."Massey Shaw"...the little fire float, manned by a mixed crew of AFS and LFB, was instrumental in saving the lives of over 600 soldiers from the beaches of Dunkirk. The Fire Service was greatly honoured to have a part in this brilliant naval achievement...'

Harold Ingham, editor, 'Fire & Water'. 1942.

IF LITTLE WAS HAPPENING ON THE WAR FRONT IN Britain, there was plenty happening on the mainland of Europe. Hitler had invaded Norway and Denmark. By May, Holland and Belgium had surrendered to the Germans. On the 10th May 1940, the first German bomb of the war fell on Canterbury and, more significantly, Winston Churchill took over to become the memorable 'bulldog' Prime Minister for 'the duration'. He was sufficiently far-sighted to see what lay ahead, offering the people of Britain an immediate future of *'blood, tears, toil and sweat'*.

By now, the Germans were streaming through France, forcing the French and British armies to retreat to the Channel coast. With their backs to the sea, more than 300,000 Allied troops were trapped in the small port of Dunkirk. There seemed to be no way out other than surrender or death as they took cover in the town or tried to hide on the surrounding beaches and sand dunes as the enemy fighters swooped low, day and night, to machine gun the exhausted men in the light of the burning oil installations.

Only a miracle could save them. It was called *'Operation Dynamo'*.

Britain had raised many a fleet for battle in the past, but on 30th May 1940, such a naval force as had never been seen before began to gather. Tugs, paddle steamers, pleasure boats cabin cruisers, even rowing skiffs, cast off from their moorings, some from far up the rivers of southern England, and set off for the coast of France.

The crew of the *'Massey Shaw'*, based at Blackfriars, had watched some of them bobbing down the Thames in ragged line astern during the morning. Now a meeting of men of the River Service had been called at Whitefriars fire station, nearby. More than 80 firemen, full-time professionals and AFS, crammed into the station to discover that the Admiralty had asked the London Fire Brigade to allow their fire float, the *'Massey Shaw'*, to go to Dunkirk to help put out fires started by the enemy. Would anyone volunteer?
For a moment there was silence as the astonishing request sank in, then every man in the room raised his hand.

From them, a crew was selected – larger than the *'Massey's'* normal complement, but it was reckoned that it might take several days to cope with the fires and no other reserves would be available. There was the Skipper, Station Officer Youngman, a former Lowestoft fisherman who had joined the LFB some years before and was stationed now at Cherry Garden Pier, two sub-officers, six AFS men and four regular LFB men, including Dick Helyer, a 25 year old fireman who had joined the Brigade after service in the Royal Navy, and of whom much more was to be heard. The AFS men were, typically, a mixed bag, ranging from a manual worker to a City business executive. All gathered now on the *'Massey'* with only two hours to prepare her for a 4 pm departure.

There was plenty to do. The ship had been built at Cowes on the Isle of Wight in 1935, specifically for work as a River Thames fire float. Her only experience at sea had been the journey round to Lambeth for her commissioning. She was 78 feet long, had a beam of 13ft 6ins and a registered tonnage of 50. The twin screws were each driven by a 160 hp Glenifer diesel engine and at fires, these were disengaged to power the pumps, delivering 3,000 gallons of water a minute through her monitors with their nozzles of up to 3½ inches. Her outstanding features were her draught of 3ft 9 inches, which was remarkably shallow for her tonnage, and her low freeboard. The shallow draught enabled her to get close inshore to fight riverside fires or fires on ships in the Thames and this, with her low freeboard, was to prove useful for the task ahead. She had a maximum speed of some 12 knots.

Although her crew were fond of her, she was not without her problems. Dick Helyer described them, with the affection of a proud owner for a favourite race horse:

'she was built for the River and was good in that respect, right for the job, but not intended to go out of the River. She was fine running on both engines, but if one broke down she could turn nasty ... if she was running against the tide she'd turn into it and try to take control and go off where she wanted. She was OK with two screws though'.

How she would react to a Channel crossing was questionable. In the event, the sea, fortuitously, was calm and apart from a tendency to roll badly and some difficulty in steering her, she behaved well.

Because her 'beat' was restricted to the Thames, she carried no compass, and a messenger was rushed out to buy one. There was no time to 'swing the ship' to record its deviation – the errors produced by her own magnetism – consequently it could only provide a rough guide to the courses being steered. At the same time, barrels of foam-making powder were being stowed and food supplies tucked into the galley. On the dot of four, they slipped moorings and set off downstream for the estuary. On the way, they prepared for action, painting the dazzling brass and white fittings a uniform grey for camouflage and boarding up the cabin windows for greater protection. At 9 pm they moored at Holehaven, had supper ashore and spent a night sleeping fitfully. The Commanding Officer travelled down from London to join them for breakfast and bid them farewell as they set off again, this time to Southend Pier, to make sure that they were, in fact, still needed and then on to Ramsgate with a new pilot and typically English summer weather – the sky overcast and a chilly east wind.

Approaching Ramsgate harbour, they signalled in true naval – and LFB – phraseology: 'Fire float "Massey Shaw" from London in attendance.' A young naval sub-lieutenant, carrying only a simple chart and steel helmet, came aboard to take command. Within two hours and flying the white ensign, they were setting course for the North Goodwin Lightship and from there, in a straight line to Dunkirk. In less than an hour their target was pinpointed by columns of black smoke from the burning oil stores, (smoke so dense in a cloud so vast that it could, later, be seen from London).

On board throughout the operation was an AFS man who wrote a full description of the events as soon as he returned to Lambeth. It was published the following year under the pseudonym of 'Proto', in the remarkable anthology of events at that time with the title 'Fire and Water'. He set the scene at their approach:

'there was a good deal of noise, the first of its kind that many of us had heard, and we could see the bursts of anti-aircraft shells over the town. From three or four miles out the roar of the fire was audible and the pall of smoke from it seemed nearly a thousand feet high, jet black and turbulent. Its blackness was accentuated by a foreground of sunlight on bright green meadows and the red buildings of a farm, close to the shore.'

The beaches were packed with soldiers and littered with smashed lorries and army cars, while the sea was awash with the flotsam of shattered, improvised timber piers and small craft. It had also been laid with magnetic mines.

Oblivious of these, the 'Massey' picked her way through until she could put down a kedging anchor within reach of the shore at her allotted beach, Bray Dunes and, because of her shallow draught, nearer than most other boats. Then began the problem of getting the stranded troops aboard. At first they tried using a light skiff 'picked up' in Ramsgate Harbour, but so many men tried to get aboard that 'she failed to rise to a wave, filled and sank in four feet of water, which was happily warm'.

It was now that German bombers closed in above them, only to be furiously attacked by RAF fighters. As the air battle raged overhead, the crew of the 'Massey' struggled to persuade the eight soldiers who had sunk the skiff to wade out and, despite the fact that each wave broke over their heads, they all got through and were taken on board. From then with the help of the Navy and an RAF launch, they made further fruitless attempts including, at one stage, trying to shoot a rocket line ashore, but that too, failed. In the end, Dick Helyer tied a line round his waist, dived over the side and swam ashore, where he eventually managed to fix it securely. Now, under the command of the young naval lieutenant, six men at a time were taken in an orderly fashion into a dinghy and hauled out to the 'Massey', where they could scramble up ropes hung over the side, and reach the low deck.

It was dark by the time the last of the rescued men were taken aboard and finding room for them was the next nightmare. The barrels of foam powder had long since been offloaded – there was to be no question of firefighting in these circumstances – but the 'Massey' had not been built for hospitality and the decks were already swimming in blood. Every inch of the vessel was crammed with servicemen, some wounded and needing treatment, but all soaked to the skin and shivering from cold, shock and sheer exhaustion. Over 30, including the weakest, were crammed into the cabin which had seemed crowed the night before with six crew in it. Many were seasick. Others were in the hose room and the engine room. The rest were on deck, covered in tarpaulins.

It was 3 am before they 'shoved off' and headed for England. 'Proto' recorded: 'the voyage home was uneventful except that shortly after we got under way an enemy aeroplane, attracted by the glow of our wake in the phosphorescent water, aimed a bomb at us which came unpleasantly near.'

By 7am they were offloading 65 soldiers at Ramsgate, ('the forepeak was packed so tight that there was some difficulty in extracting the men when the hatch cover was removed again in Ramsgate Harbour'). The crew scrubbed down the decks and the accommodation below and refilled with fuel and oil. Dinner and a desperately needed rest were interrupted by the naval authorities. They were requisitioning the boat to return to Dunkirk that night. The LFB sub-officer who had been at the wheel throughout the previous trip, guiding her through the wrecks and shallows, volunteered to sail with her again, along with two auxiliary firemen. The rest of the new crew was made up of naval ratings, including two stokers to handle the engines and a gunner for the new Lewis gun which had been fixed to the deck to discourage air attacks.

Completing the complement was a beach party of a dozen men under a RN sub-lieutenant, to cope with the difficulties of getting men from the beaches on to the fire-float and out, this time, to a waiting troopship, moored in deeper water. Once more, the operation was carried out under attack from the air and from land batteries, with shells exploding at intervals, sometimes no more than a couple of hundred yards away. Some came so close that the smell convinced the men that it was a gas attack and for a brief period, they worked in gas masks. 'This was the nearest we came to suffering any casualties on board' said 'Proto'. Now, they were not only embarking men who could scramble up the ropes along her hull, but had to lift stretcher cases on to the deck – and transfer them to the troopship. 'Proto' reported: 'The two naval officers set an example by their bearing throughout the operation, behaving as though at a formal dinner party except when it was absolutely necessary to shout, and never even referring to the shelling.'

There was a constant worry as lines snapped, the tide changed, the waters muddied and, at one stage, the port main engine stopped. The naval stokers, unused to the whims of the 'Massey' used up all the compressed air in trying to re-start and it took half an hour to recharge the air bottles by means of the auxiliary air compressor, during which time, the RNVR lieutenant at the wheel had to manoevre the ship on one engine. It was at this time that, understandably, most of the scars which she brought back, were sustained.

Still the tide ebbed and at one time the troopship, a paddle steamer, was compelled by the falling tide to move into deeper water at a moment when the fire float was fast alongside her paddle-box and in the midst of transferring a stretcher case across to her deck.

'The last two or three hours of the operation seemed, even the next morning, like a dream, and the sequence of events is hard to remember' wrote 'Proto'. 'One had a confused impression of the water crowded with boats in the flickering light of the fires, the gradually increasing irritation of bursting shells, anxiety over the rapidly shoaling water and the calm and polite voice of the officer against a background of gunfire and the shouts of the boats' crews trying to find their own ships. We made about five journeys out from the beach to the troopship and it was calculated that we put approximately 500 men aboard of her. Finally the captain of the troopship told us that he could take no more men, and raised his anchor and steamed for home. The sky had begun to lighten.'

The 'Massey' returned to its beach head and once more, the crew set about rescuing more men. Soon after 3 am, they too, decided to leave, but their anchor was stuck in the sand and nothing would shift it. Eventually, and in desperation, they slipped it and at exactly 3.30 am, headed for England, the last craft to leave that part of the beach. On the way, the compass was so faulty that they began to doubt their position, but a drifter, towing a clutch of small boats, appeared on the skyline and they closed in to follow her past the North Goodwin lightship again, arriving at Ramsgate at 8 am on Sunday, 2nd of June. This time they offloaded between 30 and 40 soldiers.

That evening, the 'Massey Shaw' returned to Dunkirk for the third time, with a Fire Service crew of two auxiliaries and the sub-officer who had been over on the first night, as well as a relief LFB crew, sent down from London. Once more she picked her way through the debris and the minefields and made fast, this time at the jetty. Now though, it was in darkness and the drop to her decks was declared to be too dangerous. Just before leaving to sail back, they were halted by a naval officer and checked to see whether she had been 'de-gaussed' – a safety method to alter the polarity of the magnetic mines which had been laid across the Channel to prevent ships from being blown up. Too late, they discovered that they had been sailing without this protection, and still had to navigate through the minefields ahead without its safety cover – and still with a faulty compass.

They were within sight of Margate when they were overhauled by a French ship, within 200 yards of them, when there was a massive explosion. It had hit a mine and sank within minutes. Immediately, the fire-float put about and went to help the survivors.

With spine-shivering calmness, Dick Helyer has described the scene on a recording, held now in the archives of the Imperial War Museum at Lambeth.

'We picked 40 of them from the water, all French, and struggled to haul them aboard, but they were covered in thick oil from the ship and kept slipping from our grasp. Some had lost limbs – legs or arms. We had to lay them down wherever we could find space and do our best to keep them alive. They were everywhere, in the galley, the toilet, even the engine room.'

Rapid signals to surrounding naval vessels produced one with a doctor on board and in manoeuvring to get alongside with the wounded, the *'Massey'* fouled her propeller on a piece of rope, but still managed to limp back to Ramsgate.

Early on the Wednesday morning, she sailed back up the Thames to London and as she came, the crews of the previous days were sent down to meet her in a speed boat. Each river station she passed turned out to cheer her and at Lambeth, the crew were received by the Commanding Officer and by the wives and mothers of all on board, brought in by the Brigade for the occasion.

Without the gallantry of the men in the little ships, the Germans might have won the war at that moment. Instead, the rescued army had time to lick its wounds and re-form, ready for the next stage. Meanwhile, it was to be the people of London who were on the receiving end of the attack.

The *'Massey Shaw'* returns from Dunkirk. (LFCDA.)

21
The London Blitz

'Apocalyptic fury,
Blaze, blaze, flower of these black skies!
Burst open with vermilion the black night
Of money in the silent city!
With tongues of glory
Of blood, wring eyesight
From the puked lids of long unseeing eyes!
Grind the hearts that ground no bread of pity

Into pity's opposite
Where stones melt, steel smokes, mind
Vomits entrails, love sees hate
Dancing a star of triumph. Let virtue paint a devil
Riding over the ruins in a rite:
That life, by man-made power denied, may find
Song, released by the rejoicing fate
Of world-devouring evil.......'

(From 'Destruction & Resurrection...England Burning' by NFS fireman Stephen Spender.)

IN JUNE 1940 THE FRENCH GOVERNMENT HAD capitulated, against the wishes of many French people, and negotiated an Armistice with the Nazis, who moved their Luftwaffe – a massive air force, far outnumbering the RAF, to a line of airfields along the Channel coast. The scene was set for the final attack which would, they believed, conquer Britain.

First came the attempt to penetrate the air defences, particularly in the southern counties, Kent, Surrey and Sussex where many of the Fighter Command airfields had been set up. The Battle of Britain, fought by young airmen streaking through the skies in Spitfire and Hurricane fighters not only made the Luftwaffe think again but it saved the country, still recovering from Dunkirk. What it could not prevent was the next stage of Hitler's plan – the massive aerial bombardment which began with a series of attacks on 'sensitive' targets in the provinces including the Admiralty's oil storage depot at Pembroke Dock and, on the night of 24th August, on oil installations beside the Thames in London.

On September 5th 1940, the full attack moved to London with a fanfare of bombing which heralded the start of the Blitz.

Mercifully, thanks to the persistence of Arthur Dyer and the London Fire Brigade, the nearest major oil installations to London had been based at the mouth of the Thames estuary, at Shellhaven, Thames Haven and Purfleet. Now, for the first time, the London air raid warning sirens wailed in anger. Late in the afternoon Londoners rushed for their shelters. This time it was no false alarm. All three areas were under attack and their huge, defenceless oil tanks were being bombed and machine-gunned.

London fire officers, called on to help the small, local brigades, were warned by the Home Office not to breach the 1938 Act which put them under the control of the most senior local officer. Knowing the hazards of the area, they took a contingent of firemen – AFS and LFB – with 50 pumps and reported to the local officer in charge. He made it clear that he felt the Brigade had over-reacted and that the situation could be controlled with only five extra pumps. Had it not been so serious, it would have been farcical. Five 2,000 gallon oil tanks were blazing within a 'bund', a large wall, containing seven more large tanks of petrol and oil. The fire was not contained, nor was the temper of the London officer improved when, an hour later, the local officer in charge said he was going home now because he was only a volunteer and had his business to attend to in the morning.

A frantic 'phone call brought Major Jackson into the argument and he sent a fiery Principal Officer from the LFB, red-haired Lieut Commander Fordham, who immediately ordered fifty pumps and three fire boats to the scene, but was told that this was not possible as they were outside the London area and only the local officer in charge – a Cambridge 'don' – could make such a decision. Nor could he be disturbed. The hour was late and he would be in bed and asleep. Fordham threatened to telephone the Home Secretary and eventually a very young man in civilian clothes drove in to take charge. He had never been to a fire before, although he had taken a five-day course in fire-fighting at an ARP school. Fordham had suffered enough. The young man was promptly told to order 50 pumps and three fire boats – and then to keep out of the way.

It was a pitiful mess – not only administratively but for the men, full-timers and AFS, with line upon line of oil tanks either burning, exploding or red-hot. Many of them struggled with their hoses, up to their waists in oil and water and covered in cold – or hot spray. In the darkness, several men stumbled into a bomb crater full of oil and water and had to be hauled out. When women auxiliaries drove in with a canteen van to provide them with the welcome 'cuppas', that too was machine-gunned and the women dived for cover beneath it, before emerging as soon as the coast was clear to brew up again. All night they fought the flames and by morning, miraculously and thanks to the support of the London crews, the fire was out and five tanks were still intact. Next day the German planes returned and the whole procedure started again.

That was the beginning. Far worse was to come.

On the 7th September 1940, many East Enders, off-duty firemen among them, were making their way home after watching their favourite football teams play when, at 5 pm, wave upon wave of German bombers droned up the Thames and circled over the docks. Throughout the evening and all night they came – 600 altogether – dropping great cascades of incendiary and high explosive bombs across the whole of East London. Beckton gas works and West Ham power station were early targets, followed by Woolwich Arsenal, Millwall Docks, Limehouse Basin and the great complex of wharves and warehouses at Rotherhithe. Until now there had been one or two desultory air attacks on the city and the East End, but for 90% of the auxiliary firemen, it was their first real 'blooding'. If this was a baptism of fire it was by total immersion.

The carefully planned Regional reinforcement scheme by which one area could seek help from its neighbours, went into action as West Ham called for 500 pumps. It had seemed a good idea to the pre-war planners, realising that, if

the bombing became intense, houses would be damaged and scaffolding urgently needed, to stockpile a supply of wooden scaffolding poles in one place. It had seemed equally sensible to site these close to Quebec Yard in the Surrey Commercial Docks which had specialised in ships carrying supplies for the timber trade. It was not difficult for the German Intelligence agents to discover this. The ready-laid giant bonfire only needed igniting and the Luftwaffe obliged. Soon the sky above London was glowing with the orange light of the flames, which acted as a beacon to guide the successive waves of bombers in to their clearly visible targets.

Cyril Demarne, then a young fireman with the 'crack' West Ham brigade watched with his mates, horrified as bombs crashed into the huge Ford works at Dagenham and, even as they exploded, more high explosives and incendiaries showered down until it seemed as if half London was burning. The small, slim magnesium incendiaries, sliding into inaccessible corners of the timber stacks, were fed by a succession of oil bombs which quickly produced enormous conflagrations.

Station Officer Gerry Knight of Pageant's Wharf, was a cool, experienced officer who had the fullest confidence of his firefighting crews. Years of service in the West Ham Brigade had left him fully aware of all the official phrases to be used when sending messages but this was more than even he could cope with. As the smoke and flames roared up and surrounded them, he called back to his watchroom. Firewoman Betty Barrett was on duty but even she could hardly believe her ears. Few men, whatever the circumstances, would use 'language' in front of a lady, but there was no doubting Station Officer Knight's message to Control: *Send every bloody pump you've got. The whole bloody world's on fire!*

And so it seemed. Pageant's Wharf was next door to an oil depot which was as vulnerable as all the other targets and during the night, Betty Barrett, with her two colleagues, Myra Barry and 'Brockie' Brockman were manning the watch room and struggling to keep the log book up to date. When they were ordered by District Control to evacuate the fire station, Betty's refusal was not insubordination but purely because the entire building was surrounded by the Thames on three sides and a wall of fire on the fourth.

In his book *'The London Blitz – A Fireman's Tale'*, Cyril Demarne describes the scene:

> 'Lengths of suction hose were coupled up in record time and lowered into the dock water. Hose lines were run out and positioned to stop the spread of fire from stacks hopelessly ablaze, to those already smoking and ready to erupt. But as fast as they knocked down fire in one

stack and switched to another, the first stack began to steam, dried out in the radiated heat from its neighbour and again burst into flame. Telegraph poles began to smoke, then ignite from base to crown, although the nearest fire was many yards away. Then the wooden block road surface ignited in the searing heat. Firemen working in the maze of stacks were driven back, steam rising from their sodden tunics, their faces and hands scorched and eyes smarting from the effects of the acrid smoke and flying sparks. In great danger of being cut off by fire, they were forced to abandon their equipment and run for their lives, passing the fire stations containing their bikes and personal belongings, now blazing as fiercely as the surrounding timber.'

Any hope of Regional reinforcements had long since disappeared as almost every fire appliance in London headed for the dock areas. By now, the water had got under some of the burning road blocks and, as Auxiliary Fireman Bill Ward recalled, *'it was weird – nothing but fire and smoke to be seen everywhere; telegraph poles bursting into flame for no apparent reason and now the bloody road starts heaving'*.

At the peak of the night, a thousand pumps were throbbing in noisy action at the Surrey docks and 300 pumps with more than a thousand men were fighting one big fire alone. 200 pumps were battling at Woolwich Arsenal and at five other targets in the docks there were 100-pump fires, all technically *'out of hand'* – in other words, uncontrolled and spreading. Water mains, gas mains, power cables and the telephone were all out of action. The firefighters were cut off from their control other than by motor cycle couriers – many of them women and teenagers plus a bevy of boy messengers on bicycles. (There was no radio communication in those days although 'Freddy' Delve, an expert in communications had installed it in the Croydon Brigade – against the wishes of the Home Office – and had all the radio sets officially confiscated on the outbreak of war on the excuse that their messages might be overheard by the enemy and used to their advantage. As Delve said, and was to be proved right, if the enemy were dropping bombs, they could see where they were falling and would know that fire appliances were going there anyway. Banning them was only obstructing the efficiency of the fire brigade).

Because the preceding months had been so quiet, many children had returned from evacuation in the country, and now driven from their homes, families were rushing from one shelter to another trying to escape from the walls of flame. Some headed for the Thames hoping to find safety on the floating barges. One group took cover in the shelter at a municipal swimming pool, only to be killed when it took a direct hit.

The writer and Member of Parliament A P Herbert was the Petty Officer in Charge of a patrol vessel, the *'Water Gipsy'*, ordered to sail down to pick up wire from the Lower Pool and take it North Woolwich. He described the trip later in his book *'The Independent Member'*:

'...There was a wall of smoke and sparks across the river. Half a mile of the Surrey shore was ablaze ... warehouses, wharves, piers, dolphins' (mooring buoys), 'barges ... burning barges were drifting everywhere ... we put wet towels round our faces and steamed at half speed into the torrid cloud. Inside, the scene was like a lake in Hell. We could hear the hiss and roar of the conflagration ashore but could not see it; only the burning barges and the crimson water that reflected them ... the main whirl of sparks and smoke went over our head .... it was something to be the only boat in Hell ...'

As the night went on, pumps and crews poured in from as far afield as Birmingham, Nottingham, Brighton and Swindon. In the months to come, the compliment would be reversed as the raids switched to their towns.

During that first night of the London Blitz 436 men, women and children were killed and 1,600 critically injured.

For the next 57 nights, London was to face a similar bombardment.

Families grew accustomed to organising their lives to fit the raids. Although that first onslaught had taken place in daylight, the RAF defence had taken such a toll of the Nazi bombers that from then, the Blitz was restricted to night attacks – particularly intense on nights of a full moon – which came to be known as the *'Bombers' moon'*. At around seven in the autumn and winter evenings, high tea, supper or dinner would be cleared away, food for a late night snack put into a basket and as 'Moaning Minnie' wailed the warning, Londoners would take to the shelters. For some it was a trek to the nearest deep underground station (but several of these took direct hits and in one, many people were killed). For others it was the Anderson shelter in the back garden or the indoor 'Morrison', a solid steel table with meshed sides which was reckoned to be strong enough to hold off the crushing debris of a falling house.

For the firefighters it seemed as if they were on a never-ending treadmill of duty, snatching sleep when they could on a mattress or in a corner or, rarely, in their own homes and then it would often be in the discomfort of a shelter. Some took the chance, stayed in their own beds and got away with it. Others did the same and were cut to ribbons by window glass, shattered in the blast of bombs, or buried in the rubble. There were endless bombing anecdotes, told and re-told. The widespread fatalistic belief that you would only be in danger *'if a bomb has your number on it'*, was reinforced during a raid on a south west London suburb when an incendiary crashed into the pavement outside number 33 in a road and rolled down, leaving scorch marks on the stones until it reached number 45 where it promptly burst into flames. Local firewatchers who went into the attack with stirrup pumps retrieved the casing when it had cooled off. Printed on the side was '45'. Unfortunately most victims had no time to see what the bomb's number was, as more and more Londoners emerged in the dawn to discover huge gaps in the rows of houses where their neighbours had lived until the night before.

AFS personnel, men and women, who had no families at home – wives and children evacuated or husbands in the armed forces – took to sleeping in the fire stations where they could, if necessary, lend a hand whether they were on duty or not, *'if Hitler turned really nasty'*, and while this helped with the firefighting and the administration, it meant that many stations were crammed to the gunwales with staff on duty or trying to snatch a 'kip'.

Health in the service during the intensive bombing, apart from injuries, was remarkably good and the spirit of comradeship meant that nobody who could stand on their own two feet would let down their friends by not turning up for duty. Admirable though this was, it sometimes meant that a bad cold swept through stations and, for some time, anyone who developed a serious cold or similar infectious ailment would be sent to hospital for a few days' isolation and recovery – not always welcomed by the patients. As the raids continued, offers came in from sympathetic owners of big houses in country areas inviting London firefighters suffering from exhaustion or medical shock to recuperate with them, and many of these were taken up.

No longer were firefighters the 'skivers'. The public saw them now, literally, as 'angels with dirty faces', often stopping on the pavement's edge to cheer the battered crews as they drove back at the end of another night of horror.

While the East End and the City took much of the attack initially, the range of bombing gradually spread until the whole of the capital was braced for the nightly 'performance' as the curtain of hundreds of silver-grey barrage balloons rose as a protection against dive-bombers and the perpetual bark of the anti-aircraft guns, stationed on almost every park and common, joined with the 'whoosh' and crump of the bombs. Londoners became adept at identifying the sounds – the deep roar of the heavy 'ack -ack', the comforting clatter of the smaller guns which was so close to the sound of the enemy's 'Molotov breadbaskets'.

In September 1940 alone, some 200 enemy planes a night were offloading their bombs on London, crippling the railways, closing the termini, cutting off telephone communication and blocking roads. In less than 30 days, 5,730 people died and nearly 10,000 were badly injured – and the hospitals were bombed as they tried to treat the wounded. The onslaught continued into October and as the full moon shone down on the 15th of that month it seemed as if the end of the world had come. More than 400 bombers reached the capital, more than 1,000 bombs were dropped; 430 civilians were killed and more than 900 seriously injured in the one night.

For the firemen, the normal hazards of burns, cuts and blows from falling debris were increased by other perils. Bombs exploding in warehouses would suddenly release clouds of devastating spices. Pepper fires saturated the air, stung the eyes and, as the men gasped for breath, filled their lungs with burning dust. The government's official report at the time *('Front Line – 1940–1941*, HMSO) recorded:

'there were rum fires with torrents of blazing liquid pouring from the warehouse doors (nor any drop to drink) and barrels exploding like bombs themselves. There was a paint fire, another cascade of white-hot flame, coating the pumps with varnish that could not be cleaned for weeks. A rubber fire gave forth black clouds of smoke, so asphyxiating that it could only be fought from a distance ......sugar, it seems, burns well in liquid form as it floats on the water in dockland basins. Tea makes a blaze that is sweet, sickly and very intense... A grain warehouse on fire brings forth unexpected offspring – banks of black flies that the firemen's jets wash off the walls; rats in hundreds and the residue of burnt wheat – a sticky mess that pulls your boots off'.

Rice sacks burst, scattering their white grains which swelled up and blocked the drains with watery rice pudding.

One of the firemen described his stint in the heart of the blaze:

'The fire was so huge that we could do little more than make a feeble attempt to put it out. The whole of the warehouse was a raging inferno, against which were silhouetted groups of pigmy firemen directing their futile jets on walls of flame... While we were working on our branch – we had to keep in the same position for hours on end, unable to let go of the branch to take cover when bombs fell – a large cargo ship took fire for'ard... We put this out in half an hour and then went back to the warehouse.

In spite of the numbness you have time to think a little while you crouch over the branch ... occasionally we would glance up and then we would see a strange sight.

For a flock of pigeons kept circling round overhead almost all night. They seemed lost, as if they couldn't understand the unnatural dawn. It looked like sunrise all round us. The pigeons seemed white in the glare, birds of peace making a strange contrast with the scene below. When the real dawn came about five, the Germans eased off their blitz. The All Clear raised a weary cheer....'

In the first 22 nights of the London air raids, firefighters from the Region, with reinforcements from the provinces, fought nearly 10,000 fires, any of which would, in peace time, have made front page headlines for a week in the national press.

November brought 7,500 bombs and then, mercifully a brief lull. In December, as people began to think of decorating their battered homes for Christmas, some 400 bombers joined in with a shower of high explosive and incendiary bombs all over London and on one night, the cloisters of the House of Commons were hit. Churchill called Lambeth headquarters to seek an assurance that Westminster Abbey would be guarded at all costs. Control could only

tell him that every appliance was out and they would do their best to get one to protect the Abbey as soon as possible. In a later raid the Abbey was, in fact, hit – as was St Paul's – but the Brigade was on hand for both events and although the damage in both cases was considerable, it was not irreparable.

Then came one of the most memorable raids of the whole war. Immediately after Christmas, on the night of 29th December 1940, the attack was concentrated entirely on the City of London and after three hours it seemed that no building could survive. Throughout the raids until now, St Paul's Cathedral had stood proudly aloof, to become a symbol of triumph to everyone in London. Many of its regular congregation, concerned as war approached for the safety of the building, had formed themselves into the St Paul's Watch – a curious assortment of volunteers at a time when social barriers segregated the community. The Watch consisted simply of men who worked or lived in the City or who lived outside but worshipped in the Cathedral. Among its members were the Chairman of a major shipping line, an assortment of stockbrokers and business men, the poet

St Paul's dome rising above the smoke of the blitz bombardment. 1940/41. (Popperfoto.)

John Betjeman, a group of postmen from the General Post Office Headquarters nearby, architects, surveyors and many more, coming together on equal terms of matey friendship. Throughout the 'phoney' war they had been taught the basic principles of firefighting by the LFB and had made themselves experts on the ins and outs of the Cathedral's crypts and galleries, narrow corridors and winding staircases.

On this night they watched aghast as high explosives and incendiaries showered on the City. At the height of the raid the Cathedral stood in a great ring of fire, but by then they had no time for fear. Few people who saw the famous Press photograph of the blood-red smoke and flames framing the great dome and flickering on the golden cross realised that inside, this small team of volunteers was racing through the building, seeking out fire in all its stone corners and keeping in touch with LFB control to ask for expert advice or help only when it was essential. Their work eased a little of the responsibility from the full-time firefighters. Mercifully, and for no apparent reason, this only lasted for three hours that night, (although the Cathedral was damaged in another attack.) Later, when the tables were turned and the RAF was raiding German cities, one of the members of the Watch wrote that he and his friends were praying for the victims there, knowing all too well how much they were suffering. The enemy had chosen their onslaught on London with considerable expertise. The tide on the Thames was particularly low when they struck. Shattered water mains forced the firefighters to seek supplies from the river, but reaching it involved struggling knee-deep in mud to the narrow, shallow stream which flowed only through its centre when the tide was this low.

Next morning, as the City workers clambered over the massive debris to their offices, they were to find pile after pile of smoking rubble with scattered groups of wet and weary firemen 'damping down'. Not all was lost. In the words of an observer from Lambeth: '*At last the news came through that water supplies were being restored – and that the miracle had happened – St Paul's was safe. The City, devastated, was still the City.*'

Firefighting humour survived the attacks –
(from '*Heroes with grimy faces*' by Ben Betts.)

22
Inter-Mission

AT THIS TIME, THE UNITED STATES OF AMERICA HAD not joined the battle which was being fought with such devastation in Europe, although it maintained friendly relations with Britain. Clearly, however, the air-raid bombardment of London was creating considerable worries on the other side of the Atlantic and in October 1940, a top secret 'cloak and dagger' mission set out from New York. It was described in detail in a book *'Wartime Defense in London'*, distributed in the Spring of 1941 to the Mayors and Fire Departments of all cities in the United States.

The introduction: *'To my colleagues, the Chief Executives of American Cities'* was written by Fiorello (known world-wide, with considerable affection, as 'Little Flower') La Guardia, the tough Mayor of New York City and President of the US Conference of Mayors. He continued:

'World events have made it mandatory for American cities to be prepared for any possible emergency. The disastrous results experienced in Europe from poorly planned and inadequate defense, both active and passive, are too vivid in our minds to make us feel secure and complacent..... New York City, since Munich, has been studying the experiences of the English cities in meeting their new responsibilities and relating these

American firemen on secret mission meet AFS women. 1940/41. (LFCDA.)

179

experiences to the preparation of an actual civil defense program for New York City. The survey period has passed and we are now ready with detailed fire defense plans, which have been worked out under the supervision of Fire Commissioner John J McElligott, for the protection of the people of this City.'

The ensuing report was the result of a courageous journey to London at the height of the German bombing raids in the autumn of 1940, by three New York firemen – Battalion Chiefs Daniel A Deasy and Frederic J G Wedemeyer with Fireman 1st Grade George G T Scott. It read like the opening of a Humphrey Bogart war film:

'We left New York at 3 pm, October 22 1940, on the "Atlantic Clipper" of the Pan American Airways from La Guardia Field and arrived in Bermuda at 11 pm that night. We departed from Bermuda on the same Clipper at 12.05 am, October 23 1940 and we arrived in Lisbon, Portugal at 11.50 pm that night. Leaving Lisbon on a British Imperial Airways plane on October 24 1940, at 8 am we arrived in England at 4.30 pm' (8½ hours from Lisbon!) 'and promptly reported to the American Embassy in London.

'On October 25th 1940, we proceeded on our mission, to obtain data and information in accordance with tentative instructions received from you; this required visits to the cities of Coventry, Birmingham, Liverpool and other nearby communities.'

Arriving at the height of the London Blitz, the major part of the report was based on their experiences in the capital. Working in co-operation with the London County Council and the London Fire Brigade, the men set about finding out how London and the provincial cities had prepared for the possibility and the fact of intensive bombing. It was a detailed document, running to 70 pages, which not only provided invaluable information for planning the protection of American cities but gave a succinct picture of the organisation and work which had been carried out by Arthur Dixon and his Home Office Fire and ARP departments, and by Firebrace and his staff.

Control of firefighting in Britain operated under the supervision of the Fire Protective Department of the Home Office, with a general plan dividing the country into 13 districts for mutual aid in a plan 'which eliminates friction when one district is without fire protection and another district refuses help, claiming that they require all their personnel and appliances for their own protection,' said the Report.

'In the Regional Control Room in Region Control Headquarters in London, there is a mobilization chart showing all the different districts, their numbers and boundaries. This chart shows the number of pumping units and their capacities, ladder-units, hose laying lorries, rescue companies etc, and anything relevant to personnel in each district.

'When a district is 70% stripped of fire protection, the Regional Control starts operations.' The personnel and equipment sent to that area reported to the Chief in charge who ordered the forces to operating positions or into service in vacant quarters. 'In this manner men and equipment, or men only, are dispatched from one district to another. If only men are required, they respond on buses or trains. If apparatus is also required, it is driven to the scene. These moves take place more frequently at night as at this time the heaviest raids occur....'

There were details of the organisation and response of the London fire force, the gas, water, electricity and sewage supplies, the Underground system, the causes of fire, regional control, telephone services, food supplies, types of bombs used and their destructive force, pumps used in the London Fire Brigade, decontamination for gas attacks, the balloon barrage, the work of observation posts and the general education of the public on what to do in the event of air attack. Every section was dealt with meticulously, numbering each observation and matching it with a recommendation of action to be taken either in New York or in American cities generally.

It was a rich source of factual information. The 700 square miles of London needed 375,000,000 gallons of water a day and during the war, the Water Board had doubled its personnel and assigned ten of its staff to the Fire Brigade as advisers.

The London Fire Brigade area had 1,400 steel tanks, each holding 5,000 gallons of water, placed in the streets with the water changed once a month. (The authors forbore to add that by then, the tanks had usually been polluted with bomb debris, greasy fish-and-chip wrappings, tin cans, bottles, a varied assortment of drowned cats and, if the weather was suitable, become covered with green slime.) In winter, they noted, ice on the surfaces was regularly broken up.

Some private owners of breweries, laundries or big stores had artesian wells – which cut down on the expense of water rates. Since the start of the war, and, if the supply exceeded 200 gallons of water a minute, it had to be made available for firefighting purposes – a rule which applied also to owners of roof tanks holding more than 5,000 gallons of water.

When mains were broken by bombing and the supply could not be shut off, it was easier to relay water to the scene of a fire rather than to try to jump the break with hoses from hydrant to hydrant.

All swimming pools, ponds and lakes had a Fire Brigade attachment. When no water was available through bombing, the army brought in supplies in 5,000-gallon water wagons for domestic use and the Ministry of Health supplied 1,000-gallon water wagons for sanitation and fire extinguishing. Three dirty water mains, each 12 inches wide, ran sub-surface throughout the high hazard areas of London to supply water for fire extinguishing and fed from lakes, ponds and rivers by pumping engines or by connections to the river fire boats which could help to pump water into the system. Every day, mostly as a result of bombing, there were at least 70 breaks in the 6,000 miles of London water mains – a figure which rose dramatically at the time of the full moon when raids intensified. The 33,000 hydrants (of Greater London – increased by more than 1,000 for the war and all, by now, standardised) were inspected every month. Although there was one company which supplied water at very high pressure (750 lbs per square inch) for raising lifts, etc, in the capital, it had not been used for fire-fighting. Most of the water mains in London were from three to ten feet underground. It was reckoned that to be safe from bombing they would need to be at least 60 feet below the surface.

The London Underground system, varying from 20 ft to 200 feet in depth, was used for sheltering from air raids but not before 4 pm, and, if shelterers were planning to sleep underground, they could not bring their bundles of blankets down before 7.30 pm – and had to be away again by 6.30 am. Bunks were being planned (and were eventually installed against the platform walls.) Anyone sheltering in the system needed to buy a ticket – not to ride but to sleep there. The Underground – or 'subway' system, particularly the conditions under which people existed who took shelter there, clearly interested them. They commented on such health problems as 'Shelter Stuffy Throat', caused by the close, dry atmosphere and the unique ailment 'Shelter Legs' caused, particularly among 'the elderly obese', by sitting, or sleeping for too long in a deck chair with the wooden cross-bar pressed against their thighs.

The Thames, which runs for 16½ miles through the centre of London at a width of some 500 feet, had nine fire-boat stations compared with three before the war, each with two or three sub-stations, all independently equipped with telephones to the River or Lambeth headquarters. Three pre-war fire-boats were in service, backed up by 24 emergency fire-boats and three barges mounted with two to four heavy pumping units capable of delivering 1,000–1,400 gallons of water per minute. The emergency self-propelled fire-boats were fitted on average with two heavy pumping units and the three barges, which were not self-propelled, carried four pumping units. The barges were towed either by the fire-boats or by river tugs, pressed into service as needed. In

some cases, when the need was desperate and barges were on canals, they were hauled by hand. All the fire boats had a draught of some 3ft 6 ins to allow them to operate in the shallower reaches of the river. The total pumping capacity of the River service was 54,000 gpm. All fireboats carried foam-making apparatus, three of which were of the type which used 40 lb tins of foam powder while the rest carried liquid foam in five-gallon drums.

Before the war there had been 68 officers and men in the River Service. Now there were 386 and the Marine Repair Shop, which had a staff of 6 now needed 12 men. At present there was no radio equipment on any of the fire boats but, said the Report, 'it is contemplated that radio will be used in the near future and it will be paid for by the Home Defense.' (The River Service was the first part of the LFB to be equipped with radio communication facilities.) During the black-out periods, all the boats ran without lights which they were evidently not happy about but they had to comply with the orders of 'The Military'.

Some idea of the pressure under which the firefighters – on land or river – worked during the attacks on the dock areas particularly, is underlined by the quaintly-worded disclosure in the American report that 'during several operations it became necessary to communicate with the air force and ask them to send planes to disperse enemy bombers which were impairing the efficiency and operation of the Fire Brigade with bombs and machine-gun fire. This was done promptly. An alternative method is to provide a heavy barrage from mobile anti-aircraft guns for the protection of the operating forces.' (One is hard put to imagine a fire commander, in the hell of these enormous fires, politely requesting the RAF to 'disperse the enemy bombers which are impairing our efficiency,' – but such was the language of official reports.)

On Organisation and Response, London was divided into two Divisions, north and south of the Thames, each of which was divided into three Districts, lettered A,B,C,D,E and F. These were further sub-divided into two Sub-Districts. In each District there was an average of ten regular fire stations controlling five Auxiliary Stations, housed independently in temporary buildings which had been specially requisitioned. (These were the oddly assorted mixture of garages, stables, schools etc, which had proved such a problem in the early days of the AFS). Each of the 'Auxiliary Companies' as the Americans called them, had at least five pumping units, giving a total in any of the lettered Districts of 260 pumping units, adding up to 2,000 PU's for the entire Metropolitan area. The pumping units had been bought in bulk by the Home Office which charged the LCC 30% of the cost.

Each Company had up to 50 personnel, receiving (at this time) £3.50 per week. Each member was supplied with a 'cot', two blankets and a pillow. (An optimistic generalisation... some areas could supply more than two blankets – others less than one per man or woman at the time of peak demand – although as the Blitz eased, supplies were better co-ordinated.)

Apart from the pumping units in regular service, the Home Office kept 1,250 PUs in reserve at decentralised locations which could be called on by the Brigade when others had been destroyed. The aim was to keep 2,000 pumps of all sizes in service at all times.

When a fire call came through, the unit nearest to the fire would respond to the location with a Regular officer in charge and a motor cycle dispatch rider (man or woman). If the fire was too large for the unit to manage, a call would go out by telephone or dispatch rider for 20 pumps. Any pumps left at the original station would go to the incident and the number would be made up to 20 by auxiliary stations in the area. The fire would be reported up the line to headquarters and recorded there on a chart and to the Control and Mobilising Officers. As a war time measure, fire escapes were not sent to a fire as a matter of course, but kept back and only sent if a special request was made for them.

In all long-drawn-out fire operations, the local Commanding Officer would ask headquarters to send a Mobile Canteen Unit, operated entirely by AFS women. Food for these was supplied by the Government and included tea, coffee, cocoa, Bovril or Oxo as well as cans of stew, steak puddings and meat pies, heated up in the canteen vans between the explosions and machine-gunning.

The report carried the 'restricted' details which few Londoners were allowed to know – that in less than two months between September 1st and October 27th 1940, assorted bombs in London caused 16,276 'small' fires plus 1,314 which needed between 2 and 10 pumps; 364 'serious' fires needing from 11–30 pumps; 110 major fires needing more than 30 pumps and 14 massive 'conflagrations' demanding an unspecified number of pumps but which, in fact, sometimes had up to 1,000 on site. The New York firemen had also noticed that among the showers of incendiary bombs they saw falling were some with an explosive charge which threw phosphorus for a radius of 30 yards. (Many of these smaller bombs, which lodged in the gutters and penetrated the roofs of thousands of ordinary homes in suburban streets, were dealt with by 'Street Fire Parties', modestly trained groups of local householders who had been issued with hand-operated stirrup pumps which drew water from buckets. These small, lightweight units were cheap to provide, easy to work and kept down the damage done by a great proportion of the small incendiary bombs, although those which had been fitted with explosive charges had to be treated with considerable respect. The

American firemen noted that 150,000 stirrup pumps had been provided for householders by the Home Office plus a further 50,000 supplied to the Fire Brigade.)

Added to the incendiaries were oil bombs: 5–6 feet long metal drums containing up to 50 gallons of old crank-case oil, weighing up to 400 lbs, which exploded on contact throwing their burning contents over an area of 1,500 square feet; land mines carrying up to 2,000 pounds of explosive and two kinds of 'Molotov Breadbaskets' – hollow metal shells, 4 ft high by 18 ins diameter, carrying up to 50 small 2.2lb incendiary bombs and with a timing device to detonate them 100 feet above the ground, when the sides would open and discharge the magnesium-filled bombs over a 200 ft area. (Londoners were well acquainted with all these and could recognise the sound as they fell – particularly the 'screamers' which had a unit in the fins aimed – unsuccessfully – at terrorising the population with a blood-curdling, wind-powered shriek. All were described in detail for the American mayors.)

The equipment for tackling them was outlined too. Before the war, they said, there were 77 six-cylinder 100 horse-power centrifugal pumps in London which could deliver up to 900 gallons a minute at 60lbs engine pressure, with 2¾-inch outlets and 7-inch suctions. The new pump, used mostly by the AFS varied according to the hazards of their areas. The smallest delivered 120–220 gpm, fed by one 3-inch suction with one 2¾-inch outlet and powered by a four cylinder petrol engine. No auxiliary engine was needed for the suction and the whole unit was mounted on a two-wheel, rubber-tyred vehicle and could be demounted from the trailer and pushed on its 'trundle' wheels to the scene of operation 'like a baby carriage'. Originally, they reported, there were 451 pumps of this size in London but they were inadequate to control a fire of any proportions and were being concentrated on the outer London areas where less power was expected to be needed.

The next size up, the Trailer Pumps, delivered 250–300 gpm, 100 gallons at 150 lbs and 350 gallons at 60 lbs and were powered by a 4-cylinder, 10 hp motor which could develop 26 bhp at 3,100 rpm. They too, could be lifted from their trailers and pushed round obstacles such as bomb craters blocking streets, to the scene of a fire. London now had 500 of these.

Third came the 350–500 gallon trailer, a 4-cylinder, 24 hp motor developing 72 bhp at 3,100 rpm supplied by a 4-inch suction with three outlets for 2½-inch hose and delivering 350 gallons at 160 lbs pump pressure or 500 gallons at 80 lbs pump pressure. These weighing 1,755 lbs each, could not be demounted. The Brigade had 500.

Among the largest pumps were the 'heavy units', self-propelled motors delivering 700–900 gallons at 100 lbs pressure from Ford V8 motors. Some, slightly larger, had 6-cylinder motors of around 40 hp developing 90 bhp at 1,000 rpm. These could also be put on the rear of self-propelled units, as the pumping motor was separate from the propelling unit and could, if necessary, be loaded on to four-wheel trailers.

The largest of all the pumps they saw in London were self-propelled, four-wheeled extra-heavy units, delivering 1,100–1,400 gallons per minute at 60 lbs pump pressure, with 6–12 cylinder-type pumping motors generating 100 hp. These pumps had two 7 inch suctions with six outlets of 2½ inches each, placed on the rear of self-propelled vehicles with the pumping motor independent of the propelling motor. Again, the pumping unit could be dismounted and placed on another vehicle. Each of these engines carried 2,500 ft of hose of which 500 ft was 3½ inch and the rest 2¾ inch.

LONDON COUNTY COUNCIL

THE OFFICER COMMANDING THE LONDON FIRE SERVICE

The National Board of Fire Underwriters of the United States, composed of two hundred leading capital stock fire insurance companies, is privileged through the courtesy of His Excellency The Right Honourable,

THE VISCOUNT HALIFAX, P.C., K.G., G.C.S.I., G.C.I.E., His Britannic Majesty's Ambassador to the United States, to present to the London Fire Service this scroll in recognition of the heroism of the fire fighters of Great Britain. Against almost overwhelming odds, and with no thought for their own safety, theirs is the onerous task of extinguishing the fires and conflagrations started by enemy bombs.

The National Board of Fire Underwriters throughout its many years of activities has consistently attempted to instil in the American people a recognition of the need for fire prevention and fire control. Today in celebrating its seventy-fifth anniversary it is stressing the vital importance of National Defense through Fire Defense through a nation-wide fire prevention program.

It is a constant inspiration to the American people to see how the British people are fighting with determined courage an enemy whose ruthlessness is without parallel, an enemy bent on the destruction of that civilization which typifies freedom of thought, word and action, and who would lay waste all the British people hold dear. The American people recognise that true courage is the virtue which champions the cause of right and that wherever there is true courage there is also to be found loyalty of purpose. The American people also pay tribute to those who take so chivalrously the heavy blows of life, who are not only brave but unbroken in spirit.

Therefore it is with deep appreciation and pleasure that the National Board of Fire Underwriters, on behalf of its two hundred constituent members, presents this scroll to the Officer Commanding the London Fire Service as representing the fire fighting forces of Great Britain.

THE NATIONAL BOARD OF FIRE UNDERWRITERS

President
Secretary

General Manager

Vice President
Treasurer

APRIL · 1941

RECEIVED ON BEHALF OF THE FIRE FIGHTING FORCES OF GREAT BRITAIN

Officer Commanding The London Fire Service

Illuminated tribute from US Underwriters. 1941. (LFCDA.)

The New York firemen were evidently surprised to discover that London had no 'front engine pumpers', but noted that although 'water towers' had not, so far, been used, sixteen were now on order. (Experiments with water towers had been carried out in London since Firebrace's visit to America in 1936.)

They reported six hose-laying lorries carrying 6,000 feet of 3½-inch hose which could, if needed, also be laid two at a time for a distance of 3,000 feet at a 'flying' speed of 30 mph. London, and some brigades outside the area, could take suction by using the engine exhaust gases, passing over a jet which was connected with the suction hose, syphoning air from the suction and causing the atmospheric pressure to push water into the pump. This system was activated by throwing a switch which rerouted the exhaust gases from the engine. Once the suction line was filled with water, the handle was thrown back and the pump was then primed.

The Report included other details including the risk of fire from barrage balloons which had broken loose and were trailing their cables, and the system of 'spotting' incidents from the fourteen fire observation posts which had been set up throughout central London.

John McElligott, the New York Fire Commissioner who had been ordered to send his men to London, reported back to La Guardia after their return in January 1941:

'In accordance with our emergency plans, a complete and thorough study has been made of this report. We have based many of the plans on the experience in London, and we are now nearing the completion of fire fighting plans to be available in the event of a war emergency. As you know, we have not acquired, nor are we able to acquire at this time, the enormous amount of additional equipment required.'

It was not the end. Soon after returning, Dan Deasy described to the Greater New York Safety Council a ride on a London fire engine through blacked out, shell-torn streets as *'a jolting journey through a deep, dark tunnel. Bad enough while going but worse when one got there.'* His summary of the general situation in Britain: *'The British will see the crisis through because they have got the guts.'*

Six weeks later, in a ceremony at White Plains, New York, a mobile canteen was handed over for delivery to the London Fire Brigade. On it was the inscription:

'To The Firemen of London:

'There is a tie of brotherhood between firemen the world over which is like unto no other bond of human understanding. It is that rare relationship which has brought to the Firemen of the US the full appreciation of the unsung heroism of their British Brothers in all branches of the Fire Service in the face of the most frightful warfare the world has ever known. In recognition of this courage and of our sympathy, we of the American Fire Service and friends whose names are inscribed on here – together with countless unnamed others – present to the Firemen of London a Mobile Canteen. May this evidence of Brotherhood sustain and strengthen you in your hours of trial and help to bring you safely through until the final 'all clear' is sounded and an honourable peace won.'

How many American cities took advantage of the Report and made the recommended preparations is not known. Eight months later, on 7th December 1941, a large Japanese force which included 300 aircraft attacked the American fleet at Pearl Harbour off Honolulu in the Pacific, killing 3,303 US service personnel and injuring a further 1,272.

From this moment, America was at war with the Axis powers of Germany, Italy and Japan. Thankfully, no full-scale bombing attack was made on any American mainland city during World War Two.

23

A National Fire Service

THE AIR ATTACKS CONTINUED, NOT JUST IN LONDON. From the end of 1940 until the middle of 1941, Coventry, Birmingham, Bristol, Sheffield, Manchester, Portsmouth, Southampton, Plymouth, Cardiff, Swansea, Liverpool, Merseyside, Hull, Belfast and Clydeside were attacked and in some cases – Liverpool for example – suffered, in turn, from short periods of saturation bombing, night after night in a comparatively small area. London had at least escaped this because of its immense size, which meant that bombs did not fall repeatedly on the same streets and there was time to deal with most of the fires before the next night when they would become beacons for another wave of bombers.

Nevertheless, the capital still took the lion's share of the onslaught, with 115 bombers on 16th March 1941 and three nights later, on the 19th, the heaviest raid since the autumn when 500 bombers started, 1,880 fires and killed 750 people. April 16th was another bad night, with 1,108 people killed and 2,250 fires started, followed two nights later by a night when 1,200 Londoners were killed.

On the occasions when the enemy thrust turned from the capital, the firemen and firewomen of London set off to help the cities which had so willingly helped them. Convoys of pumps, escapes and mobile canteen vans set out, often in the middle of the black-out and escorted by men and women despatch riders, to drive on masked and dimmed headlights along unknown roads from which all signposts had been removed (lest they help any potential enemy invaders). Arriving in the smoking ruins of the strange towns they found, all too often, that no arrangements had been made to receive them, there was no food and nowhere to sleep at nights. Tired and hungry, they went straight into action. The women stood by, in equal danger, and one WAFS canteen drove back to London bringing home the bodies of several London firemen who had been killed in the raid, laid out in the back of the van.

Sir Frederick Delve described the scene when, as an assistant officer to Sir Aylmer Firebrace, they dashed to Liverpool, the worst hit of all the cities outside London, with 4,100 people killed in four major raids.

'In early May 1941, concentrated raids were made on Liverpool for eight consecutive nights. The damage and casualties were considerable. On the first night, telephone exchanges were hit and the resulting damage was such that normal communications… were almost impossible. High explosive bombs made craters in roadways destroying water mains and other services, gas, electricity, sewers etc. Reinforcements were called for from surrounding brigades under the Regional Scheme but these were inadequately officered and in view of the extent of the damage and lack of water, little could be done. Saturation bombing continued until, on the second day, the Regional Commissioner applied to the Home Office for assistance.'

The events of the previous six months had made it clear that the existing situation concerning fire services in Britain, with the mixture of professional and volunteer firemen and a wild assortment of efficiency, still, between one area and another which had led to chaotic situations, could not continue. Delve, one of the leading young fire chiefs had been spotted by Firebrace in Croydon and in his work as a government adviser. Now, he called him to serve on his Home Office team to organise what had, for nearly 20 years, been rejected – a national fire service.

So it was Firebrace and Delve, with LFB officer 'Sid' Charteris, who set off for Liverpool by car to see the situation for themselves. A reinforcing contingent of London firemen, under the direction of another senior officer, A P L Sullivan (the fireman who had fallen through the floor in the Mayfair fire some years before) was already on the way.

Firebrace and his group arrived in the outskirts of Liverpool in the afternoon and saw hordes of people from the town on the roads with all kinds of vehicles, even

23, Queen Victoria Street falls into the road. May, 1941. (City of London Police/Museum of London.)

barrows containing their possessions, escaping into the country. In the city itself, fires were raging and not being dealt with. Fire appliances, hose and other equipment were in the streets – abandoned. The London officers booked into an hotel and set off for Fire Brigade HQ as the air raid warning sounded. Immediately the street in which they were travelling was showered with incendiary bombs and they had to take cover. Tall buildings near the fire HQ were well alight and not being dealt with and when they reached the main fire station they were astonished to find men lying on the floor asleep. 'We tried to rouse them and then realised that they were completely exhausted and indifferent to the fact that fires were raging so close to the fire station' Delve recalled. 'In fact, they were barely able to stand. We went to the control where we found the Chief Fire Officer. We told him what we had seen. He pointed to the Mobilising Board and said that showed the position. We asked if he had been out and seen what was happening, with appliances abandoned and fires burning unattended all round. In reply he

referred to a Home Office Memorandum with which he had been issued which said that the Chief Fire Officer was to be in the Control Centre and not leave it. After a hurried consultation the Home Office team decided to take action themselves. They called for:

Properly officered reinforcements to be sent in immediately from the surrounding areas.

The Ministry of Defence to send in military personnel to help with specific duties.

The Liver Building to be the mobilising centre with the roof used as an observation post and teams of firemen directed from here to incidents, guided by motor cyclists who knew the district.

The Home Office to be asked to send special trains with lengths of six-inch steel piping to carry water from the docks to main areas of the town.

The response was immediate. Troops stood by to meet

the special trains bringing in the steel piping. As they unloaded it, they were shown how to make the simple, instantaneous joints before loading the lengths on to their lorries and setting off to lay it in the gutters from the docks. By late afternoon there was some water available, fed into the piping by AFS pumps on the dock side. Other military units patrolled the streets, collecting firefighting appliances and equipment that had been abandoned and taking it all to a park where it was sorted out and re-stowed on appliances. By evening water was available and the crews were refreshed and ready to fight again. Fortunately at the end of eight days, the raids ended.

Although London's firemen had been quick to help and had fought valiantly alongside their provincial 'mates', there is no doubt that in some cases their presence was resented, particularly if their officers, who were often better trained and more experienced, tried to take over command of an area.

Cdr Firebrace was quick to point out to the Home Office the effect of the raids on Liverpool and that they proved beyond doubt the necessity for a national service. Meantime, on the night of November 14/15 1940 Delve and a contingent of 250 London firefighters, were sent to another city under fire. This time Coventry was the victim.

'Again, the City Fire Brigade resources had been overwhelmed and reinforcing crews which had arrived in good time could do little to help as the H.E. bombs had destroyed water mains and deprived the city of water for firefighting. Again, I saw fires burning and the fire crews powerless to deal with them' *Delve reported.*

'An emergency meeting of the City's ARP Committee was being held, which I attended, expecting to hear discussions on the emergency measures to be taken without delay, such as the restoration of water supplies, the clearance of roads and other vital matters. Instead, I listened to criticisms of the Chief Fire Officer and the ineffectiveness of the fire brigade. I pointed out rather forcefully that an army, however successful it might be in possessing adequate, well-trained personnel, would be ineffective without ammunition. The same is the case with the fire brigade – without water fire cannot be extinguished. I told them that their city had declined to provide any emergency water supply, as advised by the Home Office memoranda, until the question of who was to pay for it had been settled. I reported this incident to the Home Office in the hope that it would strengthen the case for a National Fire Service.'

The Coventry affair sparked off another *'first'* in Fire Brigade history. Realising how vulnerable chief fire officers

throughout the country were to this kind of criticism, Delve wrote to them all, explaining the situation and suggesting that to protect themselves from unfair and unjustified criticism the Fire Service should form a Chief Fire Officers' Association, similar to the Chief Constable's Association and based on the rules which governed this. He asked for those interested to send £5 – a generous sum in those days – and had an enthusiastic response. The new Association was set up soon afterwards with an inaugural meeting and luncheon at the Grosvenor House hotel in Park Lane.

Although the move was, to some extent, wasted when the National Fire Service was subsequently founded and the post of Chief Officer disappeared, the Association expanded its membership to include all officers in the NFS and changed the title to 'The NFS Officers' Association'. After the war, when Chief Officers returned, they re-formed their own Association, but included in it Assistant Chief Officers also. All other officer ranks became represented by the National Association of Fire Officers.

There was no doubt by now that the whole organisation of fire services throughout the country was unsatisfactory. The AFS had been formed in haste and although those who produced it did all they humanly could – particularly the fire officers who had been calling for so many years previously for more attention to be paid to firefighting on a national basis, time, resources and the peace-time financial stringencies of many local authorities had simply not allowed for a proper system to be established.

The Home Office had sent out a number of memoranda advising local authorities on steps which might be taken to improve the efficiency of their fire services, but many of these had been ignored. Jackson, who was still in charge of the London Fire Brigade and AFS and had been to Portsmouth with the crews sent from London to help during the attack on that naval centre, reported on the unnecessarily heavy damage resulting from the lack of proper organisation of the fire services. In March 1941, senior fire officers from London spelled out yet again, the need to bring together all the scattered units throughout the country under one chain of command with standardised uniforms, conditions of service, rank badges and ranks and to ensure that an officer of one town had absolute powers when necessary, to give orders to firemen of another town. This, they underlined, could only be done by nationalisation. The response from Sir Arthur Dixon was *'Nationalisation is impossible. The whole of history is against it.'* He was right, history had been against it, but was it impossible?

Time was still short. The viciousness of the enemy attacks on so many cities made it essential for some drastic action to be taken. A letter from Bertram Hoare of Hoare's Bank in Fleet Street (which had been established in London in 1672, soon after the Great Fire), addressed to Herbert Morrison, voiced the feelings of many London business men in criticising the weakness of the combined AFS/LFB organisation. Nobody had anything but the highest praise for the firemen and women. It was the overall organisation which had let them down.

Hoare, who had used his Bank's artesian well to provide water for firefighting and had trained the staff for regular duty as firewatchers, had managed to save their fine historic building when much of the area behind them, including the Temple and the famous Crusaders' Round Church, was badly damaged.

He explained, in his letter, his feelings that the mistakes of the early Blitz could have been avoided *'if someone with a real knowledge of his locality had power to direct a fire brigade to work on the most urgent outbreak in the immediate vicinity, and not necessarily on the one for which it had been ordered. In most districts this might be a senior warden or the Controller at a Report Centre.'* He suggested too, among other things, that the losses in the City due to shortage of water were out of all proportion to the number of fires started by enemy action and called for better provision of emergency water supplies.

While some of his remarks must have raised blood pressures in the Home Office, his was the kind of carefully-argued criticism which added to the pressure being put on the government by the fire service itself for the formation of a proper national organisation.

Events had been moving behind the scenes in the fire administration departments throughout the raids. All the firemen and women now had a second uniform so that they could change into dry clothing after being soaked to the skin. The Civil (Personal) Injuries Act had also been amended to allow injured personnel 13 weeks in which to recover and return to work before having to go 'on the dole'. Even this turned sour when Auxiliary Fireman Harry Errington, the only member of the London Fire service to win the George Cross for gallantry at that time, and who was severely injured in the course of a rescue, was compulsorily discharged after the statutory 13 weeks.

Such insensitivity caused so much outrage that many London firemen started a 'whip round' for the injured men and their families which gradually grew into a fund to which not only fire personnel but the general public contributed generously.

In 1942 the assorted collections were amalgamated into the *National Fire Service Benevolent Fund* for firefighters nationwide and out of this, in the post-war years, grew the *Fire Services National Benevolent Fund*. London, while supporting this with enthusiasm, also kept up its own fund for sick members and their families.

Equipment was constantly being updated, improved and increased and now, every bridge in London had a pumping unit to raise water from the river at any state of the tide. Despite all this, the mish-mash of the professional firemen and AFS was not satisfactory. A succession of leading articles in the more serious newspapers, along with letters from politicians and other leading figures, regardless of their political views, called for action to be taken. Many MPs had seen the results of the muddle in the raids on their constituencies. Eventually, Sir John Anderson, President of the Council, sent a report on firefighting in the bombed towns to Herbert Morrison, now in charge at the Home Office. It coincided with a similar memorandum from Sir Arthur Dixon, head of the 'K' Fire Division of the Home Office.

Morrison acted instantly. At 10 o'clock that night – 18th April 1941 – he called together his senior advisers including Dixon and Firebrace. Four hours later, at 2 am the decision was made to found a National Fire Service. Their proposal was submitted to the War Cabinet on 8th May and on 10th May, the local authorities were told that the Government would take over the whole cost of the emergency fire service and 25% of the cost of their regular fire brigade in a normal year.

Significantly – and to ease the way for the new Bill – Herbert Morrison promised that after the war ended, the Service would be denationalised and returned to local authority control.

There were still some areas where firefighting had been totally neglected – even during the war. One Council had the cheek to complain that an avaricious Government was filching from them 'the brightest jewel in the municipal regalia', but few had time to listen to them.

Only one real stumbling block lay in the path of the new Bill as it approached Parliament – the rank markings of the NFS officers. Firefighters were, despite the work they had carried out under fire, still technically civilians. Winston Churchill was known to oppose anything which suggested that a fire officer might be equal to a military service officer. A Scottish MP had disapproved of any shoulder 'pips' or stars which might smack too much of a fighting organisation. The top fire experts at the Home Office were faced with finding a new symbol in the 24 hours which remained before the Bill was placed before Parliament. Frederick Delve left the meeting racking his brains for a solution. On the blacked-out road back to Croydon, he explained the difficulty to his driver and a few miles further on the man spoke. *'Sir – what about a pump impeller?'* Next day, the idea of the round, flanged, silver impeller – an integral part of a fire pump – was accepted and has been used as the epaulette rank mark in the fire service ever since.

The Fire Services (Emergency Provisions) Act 1941 (4 & 5 Geo VI, c.22) was presented to Parliament on 13th May. Despite criticism from some MP's who felt that it was too little and too late, and others who used the occasion to praise the work of the firemen and women during the raids and (with some justice) to demand better conditions for them, the Bill went through Parliament in all its stages and received the Royal Assent on 22nd May. *By the 5th August the first Regulations were issued and on the 18th August 1941 the National Fire Service took over from the local authorities.*

Sir Arthur Dixon, who was generally respected as having done a fine job at the Home Office, now relinquished his post as Head of the Police Division to concentrate, as Principal Assistant Under-Secretary of State, on the new fire service. Commander Firebrace was appointed Chief of Fire Staff and Inspector-in-Chief of the Fire Services. Sullivan became Deputy Chief of Staff with Frederick Delve as Deputy Inspector-in-Chief of Fire Services.

The part which women had played in the AFS was recognised by the establishment of five grades of women officers, from Leading Firewoman to Senior Area Officer – the senior woman at Regional HQ. Chief Woman Fire Officer at the Home Office was Betty Cuthbert, who had served at LFB HQ throughout the blitz. She now took overall charge of the women's side of the service and spent much of the remainder of the war travelling the country and advising the Home Office.

Under the NFS, England was to be divided into 33 fire areas and Scotland into six areas, each under the control of a Fire Force Commander with an Assistant as deputy. Each division would consist of 100 pumps and their crews and these would be divided into two columns of 50 pumps under Column Officers. The columns were to be split into five companies of ten pumps and crews commanded by a Company Officer with an additional rank of Senior Company Officer for mostly Staff duties.

Although statutory powers were given to the Fire Force Commanders, they were still under the overall control of the Regional Commissioners, each of whom was allocated a Chief Regional Fire Officer who had overall control within the Region.

Officers wore a dark blue uniform and ranks below Company Officer, a fire tunic, with the AFS uniform accepted as the standard. (More than 100,000 had already been issued – to change them would have been phenomenally expensive.) With it stayed the AFS peaked cap. At last the round, 'sailor' undress cap which had been so much a mark of the London Fire Brigade since Shaw's time, finally disappeared.

Uproars were not unusual as the new NFS began to take shape and many of the 1,600-plus Chief and senior officers from the old services began to find themselves demoted. Geoffrey Blackstone recalls in his *'History of the British Fire Service'*, the tough, senior officer of thirty years' service who, at this time, sent a messenger boy to HQ with a letter, adding the admonition: *'And as you leave, see that you salute me smartly lad, because by the time you come back I shall probably have to salute you!'*

Nevertheless, the new Service settled down with its headquarters in Westminster. London, which was again, dealt with somewhat differently from the rest of the country, kept Frank Jackson as its Chief Commander, directly responsible to the Home Office, rather than Chief Regional Officer. The capital now became No 5 Region divided between five Fire Force Commanders under Jackson's direction.

Training on a national basis was essential and the Fire Service College which had been mentioned in the 1938 Act but not actively implemented when the war started, now had to be set up.

Firebrace, as Chief of the Fire Staff and Inspector in Chief of the National Fire Service, decided to go ahead. He sent to the Ministry of Works for a list of ten suitable premises and decided that he and his deputy would visit them on a Sunday morning. Delve looked through the list and remarked casually that one of the possibilities, the Ocean Hotel at Saltdean, near Brighton, would be ideal – adding, from his knowledge of the area – that it had quite a reputation for ringing a bell in the morning so that its guests could return to their own beds. Firebrace ignored the list of practical facilities which the hotel might provide for a College and insisted on looking at every other site on the list, dismissing them all until finally, late in the afternoon, they reached Saltdean. There, he had to admit that the Ocean Hotel had everything they needed – apart from the early bell. There was no doubt of the 'Chief's' views on immorality.

The Ocean Hotel was duly requisitioned and Brigadier C C Hewitt DSO MC, who had considerable experience of technical training in the Army, was appointed Commandant with Mr A W ('Bert') Paramor, an established senior LFB officer as his Director of Studies.

The immediate aims of the College were to raise the standards and 'ésprit de corps' of the fire service by producing good officers and to raise the technical ability of officers and instructors. It was followed later by the setting up of 72 fire training schools in the regions for new recruits, instructors and junior officers. Added to this, for the first time, a National Fire Service Drill Book was produced, laying down standard drills for the handling of every item of equipment in the Service so that wherever a man came from, he could join in with his colleagues without needing to be instructed in their ways and their equipment.

Home Office Control functioned through 458 different volumes of printed NFS instructions, not unlike the King's (now Queen's) Regulations of the armed services, which were backed up by the teams of inspectors who could visit a Fire Force at a moment's notice to check thoroughly and make sure that their work was up to the now national standard.

Firebrace had shied away from any suggestion of immorality in relation to the new College building. Although 'immoral behaviour' was less common (or less publicised) in those days, there is no doubt that when men and women fire personnel were brought into close social contact as they were in the course of their wartime service, some, at least, would fall by the wayside and more than one Station Officer – or even Chief Officer – received letters from worried servicemen, posted away from home, who were convinced that their WAFS wives were 'having it off' with a fireman. The course of action when such problems surfaced in London was quietly to send a senior woman fire officer to inspect the books or check the facilities at the erring wife's station, during which time the officer discreetly kept her ear to the grapevine. If the firewoman in question was not misbehaving, a letter to her husband put his mind at rest. If the station 'buzz' suggested that his fears were well-founded, either she or the 'boy-friend' – and in some cases both – would happen to be posted to new stations as far apart as possible from each other. (Firemen's wives either trusted their husbands or accepted that they would philander with firewomen and seldom complained – officially at least.)

It would be foolish to suggest that there were no lesbian relationships but, again, in the atmosphere of an era in which most women would not even have known the meaning of homosexuality let alone lesbianism before they joined one of the services, the few that may have existed would have been kept carefully 'in the closet'.

With raids continuing, there was very little time to ponder on any of these social peccadilloes.

Not everyone was satisfied. With the lull in the fighting, the NFU launched its *'Firemen's Charter'* campaign in September 1941 'to improve the national status of all firemen'. It called for five main points:

1 The full rate for the job.

2 Full pay whilst sick or injured.

3 A just discipline code.

4 Shorter hours.

5 Promotion on merit only.

There was no doubt that the men had justice on their side. With all that firemen had to put up with, they felt that £4 a week would be a fair rate for the job as a national standard, calling for the 20 rates of pay operating between regulars and auxiliaries to be abolished. They wanted an end to the system of having to apply for Public Assistance after the eight or thirteen weeks of sick pay ended. The regular fireman got full pay. The auxiliary, injured at the same air raid and lying alongside him in hospital was destitute. *'End this anomaly'* they demanded, along with the ending of fines being deducted from pay for misdemeanours and extra hours of duty imposed as punishment.

If there were no enemy action, they wanted a maximum working week of 72 hours, with a two-shift system. Finally, they wanted no preferential treatment or favouritism in the choice of leaders.

The launch was followed by 400 mass meetings and nationwide publicity and for anyone who doubted the part which the firemen had played in the war so far, Horner underlined the facts: *'Imagine armies on the front losing one tenth of their effectives in killed, wounded or sick within four months... No army could endure such losses, yet that is what happened to the Fire Service.'*

Six months later, the Home Office announced that Civil Defence workers were to be treated on the same basis as other Service men during sickness or injury, with full injury pay up to 26 weeks. Not all the points of the Charter had been won, but the campaign, at the height of the war, had been remarkably successful. More was yet to come from the FBU.

Meanwhile, the new NFS had brought a whole wave of other problems and although it was hailed by politicians as one of the finest pieces of large-scale organisation ever to have been carried out in the country at such speed, the six months or so in which it was sorting itself out could have been disastrous if Germany had continued its bombing campaign over Britain. Fortuitously, after a particularly bad raid on London on 10th May 1941, the Luftwaffe had turned its attentions away towards the Soviet Union and soon, cities like Leningrad (St Petersburg) and Stalingrad (Volgograd) were being besieged.

Nevertheless, British Intelligence had given clear warnings that Britain – and London in particular – should not become complacent. Britain was beginning to hit back at Germany, sending fleets of bombers – some of 1,000 aircraft – to cripple the great German cities and ports. It was after the British raid on the ancient port of Lubeck that Hitler declared that he would destroy every British town in Baedeker, (a popular pre-war guide-book) and while such attacks caused damage it was generally agreed that it could have been far worse had it not been for the National Fire Service with its vastly improved organisation.

In London the men of the new NFS had little firefighting to do. They cleaned up their neglected stations and developed bomb sites into gardens and allotments where they grew vegetables and fruit to supplement their now quite stringent food rationing and shortages. Firemen at Hatton Garden and in the Land Registry at Lincoln's Inn were among the groups who kept thriving piggeries – (firemen at Redcross Street fire station, near Guildhall, produced three tons of bacon in two years – the equivalent of one week's bacon ration for 26,000 people). Kingston Hill used their emergency water tank to supply their families with fish, cress and ducks which provided eggs (and – occasionally – meat). One station cut open its sandbags and grew carrots in them; at Walworth the men brought in paper bags full of soil from their gardens – and local parks – to fill boxes where they grew crops. Hayes, on the edge of London, used their nearby fields for growing mushrooms and in the heart of the City, the men at Cannon Street kept rabbits. These, however, proved to be tough and it was decided that they needed more greenery – not easy to find in the heart of the City. The problem was solved when the firemen made an arrangement to cut the grass around St Paul's Cathedral in return for the clippings for their rabbits. One unnamed station somehow produced several turkeys for a Christmas 'blow-out' and arranged for a local baker to cook them. The only vehicle available to collect them was a fire tender which arrived with an escort of thirty dispatch riders and so impressed the local police who, evidently assuming this was a major incident, let them through all the red traffic lights with their piping-hot Christmas dinner.

Fund-raising, for the families of the firemen who had been killed or injured, boomed and appeals were made not only within the Brigade but to the public at large. 'The heroes of the Fire Service must feel that in taking part in a dangerous, selfless work they need not shoulder other worries and responsibilities...' read one such appeal. 'A contribution of £10 will provide an allowance for an orphan for one year. Will you help an orphan?'

The London Fire Force Military Band held concerts to raise money for the Benevolent Fund, including one in the Albert Hall in August 1942 where the many 'stars' who supported them included Vera Lynn, Mantovani, comedians Elsie and Doris Waters and tenor Count John McCormack as well as the London Fire Force Broadcasting Dance Band under its Director, Eddie Franklin. Anne Shelton, a popular singer did so much to help raise money that she was christened the 'Firemen's Sweetheart'.

Not all the work was voluntary fund-raising. During 1943, after consultations with the relevant Ministries and Trade Unions, a scheme was started for firemen and women to take on light industrial work for the war effort and a Brigade publication, 'Extra Hands' (pub 1944) showed that during 1942, 4,500 man hours were being worked and by 1943 output was steadily rising. NFS officers called on local factories to advertise the project and as a result the firemen produced a variety of items ranging from tank fire extinguishers, flare path boxes, bomb pre-selectors and parachute containers to light bench work which involved filing, de-burring, drilling, riveting, making assault craft paddles and wiring mine fuses. The men did the heavier jobs, the women the lighter work during their stand-down and rest periods.

Half of the pay received for this went to the workers, half to the Central Stations Amenity Fund to buy recreational equipment.

Some produced books. 'Heroes with Grimy Faces' by Ben Betts (pub Pearson, price one shilling – 5p) was said to be 'authentic cartoons of life in the Fire Service and the lighter side of the Blitz.'

Many wrote poems, some good, some less so. Some saw the bombing from the view of an ordinary fireman; some through the eyes of the professional writer. Auxiliary Fireman Stephen Spender, already an established poet, later to be knighted and even more renowned, signed on with the NFS at Cricklewood after the blitz and wrote about the bombing of London (although he spent most of his time working as a discussion leader). He describes his training and his later period serving at a station in Hampstead with other distinguished writers including William Sansom, in his book 'World Within World'.

Sansom, Spender and another writer, James Gordon, combined to produce 'Jim Braidy – The Story of Britain's Firemen' – a group of three word sketches describing life in the wartime fire service, and one of Spender's poems is included in another anthology by the wartime AFS members: 'Fire and Water'. Another AFS memory in this was written by author Henry Green.

Throughout the run-up to war and the Blitz, an assortment of professional artists had served valiantly in the London AFS. Now, a number of them joined together to form the Firemen Artists Group. They included: *Enid Abrahams* (Royal Academy Schools); *Leslie Carr*, a commercial artist; *Frederick Cook*, who had designed posters for the LCC before the war; *Paul Dessau* from St Martin's School who had exhibited in London, Canada and the USA; *Stanley Froude* of Goldsmith's College (River Service); *Brian M Gilks*, a furniture designer; *Bernard Hailstone*, an official war artist; *W S Haines*, international artist (River Service); *Norman Hepple*, (Royal Academy Schools) portrait and landscape artist; *Ronald Horley*, commercial artist; *Norman Manwaring*, commercial artist; *Francis Needham*, violin maker; *Francis Nichols*, book illustrator; *Leonard Rosoman*, Royal Academician (who narrowly escaped death when buildings collapsed in front of him in one of the City blitz fires); *E G Turner*, interior decorator and *E Boye Uden*, illustrator and topographical draughtsman. The group was organised by *Rudolf Haybrook*, a theatrical designer with long experience in Britain and abroad.

The Firemen Artists held their first exhibition at the Central School of Arts and Crafts in 1941. It was followed by three more exhibitions at the Royal Academy, attended by thousands of people and at the height of the war, a consignment of the pictures showing 'a kaleidoscope of a fireman's life' was taken across the Atlantic and shown in New York. Among those which stayed in London was a collection which now hangs in the LFB Museum, including an 'action' portrait of *Firewoman Gillian Kluane Tanner*, the only firewoman to be awarded the George Medal, portrayed driving her lorry load of petrol through streets of flame at the height of a bombing attack.

Meanwhile, the new service was being fine-tuned to greater efficiency by the group working at the Home Office.

24
Second Round

AFTER A RESPITE, MARKED BY FOOD AND CLOTHING shortages and permanent anxiety on the Home Front while battles raged in Russia, North Africa and the Far East, London again came under bombardment between January and March 1944. This time it was a series of short raids with incendiary and phosphorus bombs, but by now the Nazis knew that such attacks would bring ferocious retribution from the Allied Air Forces.

Meanwhile, in January 1943, Frederick Delve left his post as Deputy-Inspector-in-Chief on his appointment as Chief Regional Fire Officer for No 5 Region – the whole of the London area. At the same time, what Geoffrey Blackstone referred to as 'the unhappy appointment of Mr Julian Simpson MC' was made, not as Deputy Regional Commissioner for Fire, but 'to undertake the duties of Lieut-General Barker who had previously held the appointment.' Simpson took on the title of 'Regional Commissioner's Representative for the National Fire Service' and soon became extremely unpopular. One of the early results of his term of office was the ousting of Major Jackson, who was diplomatically said to have 'retired to take up an appointment with the Department of Scientific and Industrial Research'.

Jackson, known universally as 'Gentleman Jackson', had been a first-class fireman, quiet, caring, greatly respected by the men and women of his Service whom he had led courageously and conscientiously and modestly throughout the blitz. There is little doubt that his 'retirement' was enforced and his men resented and regretted it – a sentiment which was made clear not only at his 'retirement' party but by their memories, which were still bitter, fifty years later. Their retirement gift was a silver salver, engraved: 'To F W Jackson CBE DSO, Chief Fire Commander, London Area. Their Old Comrade and their Leader in the Battle of London… The deeds of the leader shall live, And the hard won glory of his exploits…'

Frederick Delve and his fellow Commanders already had

wind of hush-hush new enemy weapons. Knowing that Hitler would certainly be seeking retribution for the Allied air onslaught on Germany, they took immediate action to protect London and other major cities. Together they drew up a plan dividing the resources into two – Home Cover and Task Forces. Both were to prove outstandingly successful.

The Home Cover units were to be the equivalent of the peace-time fire stations and would deal with fires not resulting from enemy action. The Task Forces would comprise 100 appliances in the care of an Assistant Fire Force Commander and divided up into columns, companies and sections, with special appliances such as hose-laying lorries and control units attached to them. Above all, each Force would be wholly mobile, so that it could be despatched to deal with any number of fires in one area rather than a building or group of buildings. It was, in effect, a miniature and independent fire brigade, needing only one message to deploy it. At first the Fire Staff at the Home Office had reservations, but later, after top-level discussions, it was accepted.

Never one to miss a chance, particularly for better communications, Freddie Delve took advantage of this meeting to stress the urgent need for radio links – on which he was still an expert. The NFS River Thames Formation (some 70 craft including requisitioned boats as well as the peace-time fleet) covered the Thames from Teddington to the Estuary but could not be contacted in darkness. As the result of Delve's pressure, this now became the first NFS unit to be provided with radio communication. It was an asset which proved particularly useful in the preparations for the D-Day invasion of France when ships of all kinds were being assembled in the lower reaches of the Thames carrying deck cargoes of highly inflammable and explosive materials. Remarkably, no enemy attack was made on this massive concentration.

Some idea of the acceptance of the rapidly growing

King George VI inspects LFB dispatch riders. (LFCDA.)

Trades Union power can be gauged by the fact that before being put into action, the whole Task Force Plan was discussed with the Fire Brigades Union by Delve and received their wholehearted co-operation, although it meant moving many men from their existing fire stations to other areas. By the time the '*hit and run*' raids of early 1944 took place, 700 fires were the most to be started and these were quickly dealt with by the new Task Forces. There was, however, one marked difference between the raids of the early war years and those in this 'second round.' The earlier attacks, which could start up to 2,000 fires, lasted for periods of eight hours or more. The later raids were lightning strikes lasting at most for 14–15 minutes and although they set off a lot of small fires, they were dealt with far more efficiently by the well-trained and better equipped Task Forces, helped by the huge 'army' of trained fire-watchers – the staff of buildings throughout London who were now keeping guard every night in their places of work.

One such raid on Fleet Street in March 1944, prompted a second letter to the Home Secretary by Bertram Hoare of Hoare's Bank, this time to praise the 'fine performance' of the NFS. At the time of the first raid on their area, he explained, there had been no water, other than from his Bank's own well. This time there had been plenty; in the first raid there had been no AFS assistance; this time the fire

service had attended within five minutes. Formerly, the Fire Guards had no co-ordinated scheme of operation. This time, following previous co-operation and instruction from Whitefriars Fire Station, every bomb was tackled at once, so that no building was lost and there was only minor damage to a few roofs. The NFS had established a fire zone in the entire section covering the Temple Bar area of Fleet Street and the Temple. Sufficient appliances and teams were immediately available to fight all the fires and the NFS worked side by side with the volunteers whom they already knew. While the firefighters worked, the Salvage Corps was covering furniture with rubber sheets, reducing damage to a minimum. '*Nothing could have worked better from start to finish and the co-operation was the main reason for the success*' wrote Hoare. '*The occasion has cemented a warm friendship between us and Whitefriars fire station, based on mutual respect… In the eyes of the local inhabitants, the firefighting services have won their spurs.*'

Spurs were needed. It was at this period of the war that the '*Second Front*' – the attack on the European mainland – was being planned, and fearing German attacks on the enormous stocks of equipment being concentrated in Southern England in preparation for this, NFS leaders planned '*Operation Colour Scheme*'. The NFS north of a line drawn from the Severn to the Wash would be reduced by half as units were directed south to help protect the supply lines. The utmost secrecy had to be maintained as more than 9,000 firemen and 2,000 firewomen with 1,240 pumps and other equipment were moved, at a week's notice, into areas which were graded by colours – *red* for reinforced areas; *brown* for reinforcing areas and *green* for those who stayed as they were. The brown areas from which the detachments had been sent were reduced virtually to peace-time levels of personnel and equipment. The *'Colour Scheme'* detachments were to stay for several months, working alongside the troops, tackling ammunition dump fires and patrolling the huge stores of trucks and petrol, laying special pipe-lines and manning fire boats dotted among the armada of small ships waiting for D-Day when they would surge across the Channel.

At one stage, it was decided that firemen would accompany the troops to France and a force of 2,000 men with ten fire boats was prepared for this. They wore normal uniform, identified by red shoulder flashes marked *'Overseas Contingent'*, a blue beret instead of a cap, plus khaki boots and anklets. Eventually, the problems of taking what was still essentially a civilian organisation overseas with the Army became too difficult and the job of firefighting was turned over to the Army Fire Service, in which a large number of former firemen from London and other parts of the country were serving. Only later, after the invasion had proved successful, was a detachment of firefighters including many men from London, sent to France to help protect the British and American installations from fire.

Meantime, in the lower reaches of the Thames, NFS men worked day and night, hosing out the mud to keep a way clear for the great concrete 'caissons' which were to form the Mulberry Harbours, so that they could be floated out into the estuary and dragged across to the French coast. Theirs was an essential but thankless job which often meant long hours spent at the end of a branch, hosing round the concrete and covered from head to foot in mud. At about the same time, detachments of NFS men stood by at the London Docks to provide fire cover for the American Liberty Ships as they waited in line to deliver hazardous military stores to the Royal Docks – comforted only a little by the thought that the vessels were limited to carrying not more than 2,000 tons of explosives each!

The Allies were within days of the long awaited Second Front – the invasion of France. The enormous fire force was poised to back them up. As the seconds ticked away it came as a considerable shock for the Home Secretary, Herbert Morrison when, out of the blue, his Civil Servants discovered that the National Fire Service was an illegal organisation. Through an oversight, due probably to pressure of work at the time, the main Regulations of 5th August 1941, under which the NFS had been constituted, were never laid before Parliament for formal approval. Although MPs would have had the right to have any part of it annulled within 28 days of the laying date, nobody had noticed it inside three years. An Indemnity Bill had to be brought in to validate the error after Morrison had made an embarrassed apology to his fellow MPs.

D-Day finally came. On 6th June 1944, France was invaded by the Allies, but by now, news had come from Intelligence sources that the Germans were ready to use a new and deadly secret weapon, not on the fighting services but on civilians – primarily in London.

On 12th June 1944, within days of the Allied invasion, Londoners were puzzled at first as a self-propelled, torpedo-shaped bomb with short, squared off wings, buzzed through the sky above the capital sounding like a clapped-out motor cycle. Only when the engine stopped and the device nose-dived to earth did they discover that this was a flying bomb – a *'V1'* – packed with high explosive and each one enough to blast down half a street of houses. There was little time to acclimatise to these horrors. Three days later, 73 *'buzz-bombs'*, as they had rapidly been christened, exploded in the London area, causing such devastation that many firemen took on the work of full-time rescue workers, struggling to haul people out of the wreckage of their devastated homes.

At least Londoners could hear the *V1*'s coming and take cover. Everyone grew adept at ducking, head in arms, and diving for the nearest shelter, whether or not the siren had sounded, when they heard the *'putt-putt'* of the bomb's engine. Even on public transport, the driver would pull in to the kerb as the familiar buzz rattled in the distance and his load of passengers would disappear under the seats until the noise had passed over, when they would emerge, dust themselves down and carry on reading their papers or picking up the dropped stitches of their knitting. Sadly, not all passed over and the silent seconds between the cut-out of the engine and the explosion as the warhead hit the ground were the worst suspense of all.

Less predictable was the next range of Hitler's deadly secret weapons. The *V2* rockets, fired into the sky from their coastal hide-outs in France and Belgium were aimed at London again, but this time there was no warning noise. Many of their victims were carrying on with their normal lives and never heard the explosion which blew them to bits. The warhead of these fearsome weapons was even greater than the *V1*s, so that whole areas of streets were flattened as they landed. Although the NFS had spotters on watch to try to track them, the *V2*s fell at such speed that all the firemen could do was pinpoint the area in which they had landed and direct a mobile fire force to it immediately.

In many ways it was almost worse than the Blitz. The silent rocket bombs landed all over London, regardless of military targets. Although *V1*s were sometimes shot down in mid-air by fighter aircraft, to do so was dangerous because they could explode, damaging the attacking plane, or fall away from their target but still causing carnage when they landed. There was no way of stopping the *V2*s in mid-flight. Only when their launching pads were all wiped out was London safe again, and by then the war in Europe was almost over.

From the first day of the flying bombs in June 1944 until the last one fell on 28th March 1945, a total of 2,380 landed in London, most of them during the summer of 1944 including the worst day, 3rd August, when 97 crashed and exploded. The first *V2* landed in Chiswick on 29th September 1944 increasing to a maximum of 116 in February 1945 and 115 in the following month. Altogether, 511 lethal rockets fell in the London area.

The capital never gave in, and by now the Allied onslaught in Europe had finally defeated the Germans. On 8th May 1945, the lights went up in London again. The war in Europe was over, (although the battle against the Japanese continued in the Far East until 14th August 1945).

Londoners went mad with joy as the lights went on again, gathering in Piccadilly to celebrate with long-hoarded bottles of champagne. In the East End, where timber from the debris was piled into great bonfires in the streets, the firemen's gallant wartime work was temporarily forgotten as, to the fury of the celebrators, they tried to put out these fires which were threatening to cause more damage.

The process of totting up began.

The original 25,000 AFS personnel of September 1939 had expanded to 42,159 full-timers in the London Region by March 1942. At the peak of its power, the London Region Fire Service controlled 10,000 vehicles including its peace-time appliances, the war-time additions, trailer pumps, cars and fireboats. The single Brigade workshop at Lambeth (descendant of the previous workshops at Southwark and at

Below: **Firewomen's Day, Queen Elizabeth and Princess Elizabeth inspect NFS women at Lambeth. (LFCDA.)**

Right: **Wandsworth Fire Station destroyed by bomb, 1940. (ADO Paul Purvey, LFB.)**

Braidwood's headquarters in Watling Street), had been joined by three large and eight small workshops to service and maintain the enormously expanded fleet.

The division between AFS and full-timers had long since passed, particularly as the casualty figures emerged. Death was no selector of victims. More than 327 firemen and women serving in the London force were killed in action. A further 3,087 were injured, some severely, as they fought the flames. More than 662 assorted fire stations and stores were damaged.

All London's firefighters were given the Defence Medal, although specific awards were fewer than their courage merited, and those who received recognition were quick to point out that there were many others who deserved them equally. Nevertheless, London's fire heroes notched up one George Cross, 38 George Medals, 3 OBEs, 13 MBEs, 118 British Empire Medals and 11 King's Police and Fire Service Medals.

In a letter to Herbert Morrison on January 8th 1945, Winston Churchill wrote: 'They are a grand lot and their work must never be forgotten.'

Wandsworth Fire Station appliance bay, 1940. (ADO Paul Purvey, LFB.)

25

Peace and Problems

ALTHOUGH THE END OF THE WAR BROUGHT PEACE and new hope to Londoners, it was a time of chaos for the firefighting system nationally. Herbert Morrison had promised the local authorities that the National Fire Service would be only a war-time expedient; they would have their own fire brigades back when it was all over. Nevertheless, the national service had been proved to have many advantages over the old system with its widely scattered groups, its variety of equipment and its wildly different standards of efficiency. Now, too, the Home Office had its own established and powerful Section dealing with firefighting and its needs. Was all this to disappear? On the other hand, there were still many opponents who believed, in the words of one who wrote to the *Sunday Times*, that 'the NFS, quite apart from the mass of bureaucratic red tape with which it is bound up, has become an almost perfect microcosm of the totalitarian state.'

Strangely, perhaps, the Left-Wing FBU came down on the side of those who wanted the service de-nationalised, although hours and conditions had been standardised and considerably improved under the NFS.

For nearly two years the arguing continued, during which a variety of other difficulties arose. Many of the men who had joined London's service as AFS men were not of the standard which would have been demanded in the old, proud, London Fire Brigade days. Clearly there would have to be some 'weeding out'. At the same time, those who were up to standard had no long-term contracts guaranteeing pensions at the end of their service, as the professional firemen had. The Fire Brigades Union fought to have them included if they were to stay in the Brigade.

Significantly, too, the Union was now a powerful force to be reckoned with at a time when thousands of men were returning from the Forces with a determination that the old, class-ridden Britain in which the workers could be kept on the lowest possible wages, must end. Winston Churchill in war-time had become almost a god – the old British bulldog, growling out defiance to Hitler. Now he found his Conservative government defeated as Labour swept to power, to introduce a whole new scene for education and a revolutionary Social Security system which included a National Health Service entitling everyone to free health care. For those who remembered the struggles of pre-war days it was, indeed, a brave new world which brought massive power to the workers.

Regardless of what final decision might be made about the Fire Service, it was clear that many more men would be needed in peace time to bring it up to scratch. Already it was beginning to run down and the Home Office, concerned lest, whatever the outcome of the NFS argument, they finished up with too few men for a viable force, sent recruiting teams overseas to vie with industry in trying to tempt men to sign on for the fire service when they were 'demobbed'. In 1944, hours of duty had been reduced throughout the NFS to 84 hours a week (24 hrs on, 24 off) which would mean a far larger force than was needed for the long working hours of pre-war days. The project was not altogether successful. Few men who had spent the war in uniform and under discipline wanted to return home to the same conditions – particularly when fire service pay was, for the most part, lower than that being offered by industry.

By now, Morrison was no longer Home Secretary. His place had been taken by the Rt Hon James Chuter Ede and under his aegis, the *1947 Fire Services Act (10 & 11, George VI, c. 23)* began to take shape. One thing was made quite clear. The days of the old 1,600 or more brigades were over. The new Fire Service would be controlled by the councils of county boroughs and counties in England and Wales and, in London, by the London County Council. The idea was given a widely mixed reception, since many of the district councils resented the county councils' 'interference' and not all county councils wanted the responsibility, which would push up their rates bill. On them all, however, would rest the duty of providing an efficient Fire Service along with powers to join with neighbouring authorities if necessary, to improve efficiency.

Now too, the Home Office would have the power to make regulations concerning pay, hours of duty and discipline, to control the establishment figures of staff and machinery for brigades and also the standards of training and of the design and performance of equipment.

The long-called-for College for training firemen, which had proved so successful in Saltdean during the war would need a new home. The Ocean Hotel was to be returned to its owners, but a new College was to be established with a Governing Board representing equally the local authorities and the Home Office.

To keep an eye on all this, a team of Government Inspectors would be appointed and to help with the initial cost, there would be a 25% Government grant. Among the 39 Sections of the Bill was a detailed table of pensions and the arrangements to be made for Brigades in adjoining authorities to co-operate in providing reinforcements for major incidents.

Particularly important, a Central Fire Brigades Advisory Council would be established to advise the Home Secretary on any matters resulting from the Act, other than on pay, hours, ranks and discipline, which would be dealt with by an Industrial Council – another major breakthrough.

The new Act would repeal an assortment of past legislation including the *Fire Brigades Act of 1938*, *the Fire Brigade Pensions Acts of 1925 and 1929* and (as Shaw, no doubt, turned in his grave) the *Metropolitan Fire Brigade Act of 1865*, (apart from one or two sections which dealt with the contributions from insurance companies and co-operation with the London Salvage Corps – contributions which were to end when the Salvage Corps was absorbed into the LFB in 1985).

During its first reading on 27th March 1947, there was a concerted attack from some members who wanted a 50% grant to local authorities, (one, indeed, indignantly sought 75%, on the grounds that the Home Secretary was calling the tune and the local authorities were paying the piper). Another member maintained that the Fire Services were part of our national defence and as the armed forces were not paid for from the local rates – nor should the Fire Service be.

Some minor amendments were made during the passage of the Bill through Parliament, but it received the Royal Assent on 31st July 1947. From then, Britain's fire protection was taken over by 151 new fire authorities (later reduced to 141) as the National Fire Service came to an end.

The problem of appointing new Chief Officers brought great grief to many who had been demoted in 1940 when the NFS took over and had looked forward to the end of the war for restoration of their powers. For some senior officers it was a normal retirement time and these included Sir Aylmer Firebrace and Sir Arthur Dixon, both of whom left the Home Office with considerable nostalgia, to rest on their glowing laurels.

All the posts had to be advertised and the London County Council duly complied, although by October 1947 they had no doubt in their minds as to who should lead the re-formed London Fire Brigade on 1st April 1948. They had, indeed, already charged him with planning the 'take-over.'

26

A First Class Life – Sir Frederick Delve

FREDERICK WILLIAM DELVE WAS A SUSSEX MAN WITH a brilliant career in firefighting behind him when he took over as Chief Officer of the newly reconstituted London Fire Brigade on April 1st 1948. His entry into the profession had been a strange one and is worth recalling since its influence stayed with him for the rest of what a doctor had once discerningly declared on a fire service

Sir Frederick Delve, NFS Regional Commander for London, and Chief Officer, LFB, 1948–1962. (LFCDA.)

medical form to be a 'first class life.' He was born in Brighton in 1902, an 'afterthought' in the family of a respected local master tailor who already had four daughters and had given up all hope of a much longed-for son.

Young Frederick was all the family could have wished for – tall, athletic, blonde, straightforward. It was hardly surprising that towards the end of the First World War his favourite Sunday afternoon occupation was walking along the promenade with his friends, keeping an eye open for the pretty young 'flappers' who were pursuing the same recreational course. On one such Sunday in the summer of 1918 a young woman, separate from the rest, approached the tall 15-year-old and pinned to his lapel a white feather to indicate his cowardice at not being away fighting in the war.

Almost certainly, she was unaware of his age, but the action embarrassed the schoolboy so deeply that he decided to volunteer for the Royal Navy and, despite the sadness of his parents, he enlisted on his 16th birthday – October 28th 1918. At the time it seemed an appalling mistake. He was taken immediately to an east coast recruiting centre, stripped of his civilian clothes, put through a disinfectant bath and had his head shaved to the skin. By the end of his first long day, bawled out, having to respond to every command 'at the double', he lay in his bunk and wept with exhaustion and despair. The course which followed was equally tough on the sensitive youngster – days of rowing round Harwich harbour in the bitter winter cold, having his frozen knuckles rapped by a sadistic bo'sun if he made the slightest mistake. To add to the irony, when he had served for only two miserable weeks, the war had ended with an Armistice on November 11th 1918.

Once the worst of the initial training was over, he accepted the situation, settled into the life of the Service, did well in his exams and was allowed to choose radio communications as his expertise in the Navy. One of his father's arguments against enlisting had been that he needed to spend longer on his education. The words came back to him as he realised how little he knew, of mathematics particularly, but his senior officers, spotting his potential, readily helped him and by the end of 1919 he was sailing across the Mediterranean in a battleship to help with the evacuation of British nationals from the Black Sea ports, besieged by the Red Army at the height of the Russian Revolution. His job was transmitting messages back to London by way of a succession of land stations based across Europe.

His skill and interest in communications stayed with him for the rest of his life and proved particularly valuable during the Second World War. (Long after retirement and approaching 90 years old, he whiled away long, sleepless nights by deciphering the Morse Code messages of ships passing through the Channel whose lights he could sometimes see from his flat overlooking the sea at Hove.)

After the First World War the Navy had a surplus of men and although, by now, Delve had settled into the life, he was not overduly concerned at taking early retirement from the sea. Back home in Brighton he wanted to find work in which his skill at communications might be useful – the Post Office perhaps, the fire brigade or the police? He applied to all three and the letter from Brighton Fire Brigade arrived first. He joined, trained, and served them with courage and flair, being commended for bravery on several occasions. In 1927 he had passed the examinations of the Institution of Fire Engineers with distinction, making up for his lack of formal education by attending evening classes in science, engineering and building and was promoted rapidly until in 1929, after only eight years in the Brighton Service and at the age of 27, he was appointed Deputy Chief Officer – one of the youngest in the country.

Throughout his career he was always determined and, during those early years in Brighton, he had returned to his old recreation of swimming and had noticed a particularly attractive girl diving from a raft moored off the beach by the pier. Discreetly waylaying her, he invited her to tea in a local restaurant. Many years after she had become his wife, he admitted that he had set his heart on her from the moment he saw her diving. To his surprise, she in turn admitted that she had spotted him first and the diving was a deliberate move to attract his attention. His beloved 'Delvi' was to stay by his side throughout the rest of his distinguished career, including the wartime bombing when they lived at Lambeth headquarters, and well into his retirement, after he had received a knighthood. Her death, many years later, brought him great grief and loneliness.

To the regret of Brighton Corporation, Delve took up the appointment of Chief Officer of Croydon Fire Brigade in 1934. Croydon had a proud history of local firefighting long before it became part of the Greater London Brigade; it was larger than Brighton and Hove and offered more opportunities for his obvious talents. He completely reorganised their service, led part of it to the Crystal Palace fire and, soon afterwards, was one of the few senior fire officers in the country chosen by the Home Office to serve on its 1936 Committee planning the preparations for the AFS and what was to become the Second World War. By then he had equipped his Croydon Brigade with the first radio-communicating system in the country – the appliances able to keep in touch with headquarters wherever they were in the borough.

His service throughout the war, first in command of the Croydon service and later as deputy to Firebrace, adviser to the Home Office, Chief Officer of No 5 London Region of the NFS, official adviser to the Colonial Office on the war-time fire defences of the Colonies and, from 1941–1947, a member of the Fire Brigades Advisory Council, all provided a wealth of experience to qualify him to lead what was still the most prestigious fire brigade in the world.

The new Act had laid down certain standards including a system of ranks, uniforms and badges into which the local authorities could insert their own insignia and this now took place in London. Added to this, he was involved with the new Central Fire Brigades Advisory Council as well as a National Joint Council for Local Authorities' Fire Brigades, charged with helping to negotiate wages and conditions for the men. Women too, for included in the Act was the right of women to be employed in the fire service – albeit in typing, secretarial, telephone and control duties. There was never any question, at that time, of women carrying out the tough, physical work of fighting fires and rescuing victims.

As was expected, Delve knew exactly what he wanted in his new post and set to work, meticulously, to achieve his aims through the 2,500 men at his command. He enumerated them:

1   To restore as soon as possible the high standards of efficiency in fighting peace-time fires for which the LFB was famous.

2   Introduce radio transmitters and receivers on all fire appliances and reduce the existing Controls to one, at LFB HQ at Lambeth. This would speed up messages and enable central direction and control to be instituted.

3   Abolish the existing street fire alarm system.

4   Prepare a replacement programme for new fire appliances which should be diesel-driven instead of petrol. *'I had been impressed by the performance of diesel-driven military engines during the war and was convinced that they were more reliable and would last longer'* he explained, adding: *'no vehicles suitable for*

peace-time use had been provided during the war and it had been necessary to use government vehicles.'

5 Prepare a programme for building new fire stations.

There were, he agreed, other matters to look to, but these were of primary importance and these he put in hand immediately. He also changed some of the old recruiting shibboleths, doing away with the rigid pre-war requirements for height and chest measurements of potential recruits and their ability to lift certain weights.

Because there had been a 14% shortage of recruits in the immediate post-war period the Brigade had to retain in service many men who had served during the war but who could not now meet recruiting requirements. 'I felt it was not necessary for a man to reach 5 ft 9 ins in height to be a good fireman, or for his chest measurement to reach a certain figure', he explained. 'Provided he was medically fit and his chest expansion satisfied the medical examiners and, most important, that he was able to carry out the task that men were called upon to carry out at fires, he should be accepted.' As a result, many men on temporary employment were taken in to the permanent Service.

He was not, however, prepared to have a *'soft'* Brigade and for some time, called crews to headquarters for spur-of-the-moment drills to check whether they were, indeed, fit for the work. In the case of men who clearly were not fit, he advised their officers to deal with them gently, allow them time to come up to standard but, if they were still not capable of doing the work or lacked the necessary stamina, they must leave the Service. It was essential, he said, to ensure that the Brigade reached its pre-war standard as the best in the country.

Drills included carrying down a ladder a man of his own weight; using a hook ladder, operating a pump, wearing breathing apparatus in smoke, tying a chair knot and rescuing by 'lowering down', inserting and replacing lengths of charged hose on the ground, on an escape, on a ladder or on a staircase – in fact – the basic training for any recruit.

He was particularly concerned with fitness training – not necessarily arduous and punishing exercises but games in the drill yard, work-outs with a medicine ball on a regular basis which he regarded as all-important. Drills, he maintained, should be practice for the real thing. If a fireman was not confident enough to tie a chair knot in which he himself was prepared to be rescued it was not right that he should be trusted to experiment on members of the public. Crews were encouraged to compete with each other for speed and efficiency.

The strength of trade union power in peace-time was now beginning to be felt. The FBU objected to the drills, saying that the men were being subjected to greater danger

in carrying them out than they would be at fires. Massive press publicity followed and Delve took the unprecedented step of calling a press conference at Lambeth for journalists to see the *'dangerous drills'* for themselves. He himself went to the fifth floor of the drill tower (normally such a drill would be carried out from the third floor) and the crew went into action, lowering him safely to the ground without difficulty. The Union then applied for a High Court injunction to prohibit the drills but this was refused and they continued until Delve retired in 1962.

At this time too, the Unions reopened their demands for parity with the police which was also refused although a rent allowance of eleven shillings (55p) a week was awarded and consolidated into the basic wage. Soon after this the police received an award which put their basic wage to thirty five shillings (£1.75p) above the fire brigade and again, a Union protest was rejected by the LCC who ruled that the basis for wage increases should be a rate for the job.

Now came the start of real trouble in the LFB. The Union, in protest, organised a demonstration in which the men, for two days in November 1951, refused any duties except attending fires and other emergency calls. This was the first ever withdrawal of labour in the history of firefighting in London and although a minor one, it raised the whole principle of strikes by an emergency service. Under the Discipline Code it was an offence for a man to refuse to obey a lawful order. In London, 1,400 men were charged under the Code.

While the charges were being heard a serious fire broke out in December 1951 at a railway goods depot by Broad Street in the city, close to Liverpool Street Railway Station. The walls of the warehouse had been reinforced by steel girders which expanded during the blaze steadily pushing out the brickwork. Delve, who attended the fire himself, suddenly noticed the wall bulging and called to the men to run. Some escaped, but not all. The wall collapsed, killing three firemen and injuring many others including the Deputy Chief Officer, Mr C P McDuell OBE, whose right leg had to be amputated.

Praise was poured by the press and the public on the courage and devotion to duty shown by the firemen in fighting the fire and Delve immediately sought permission from the LCC for all the disciplinary charges to be withdrawn. This was agreed and as he commented, *'an unhappy episode was ended'*. The immediate pay dispute was referred for arbitration and it was decided not to relate firemen's pay invariably to that of the police but to consider it on the merits of each different claim. It was, however, to be the beginning of a long and unhappy period of industrial relations.

The situation was complicated by the fact that the

international situation was deteriorating also. The uneasy friendship with the Soviet Union, which had continued throughout the war, became increasingly strained as they began to threaten their neighbours with invasion. In 1948, the Auxiliary Fire Service was resuscitated and London, already 400 men under strength in its full-time Brigade, had to add recruitment and training of auxiliaries to its already difficult task of attracting men from the better paid industrial jobs. Nevertheless, many auxiliaries, men and women, rejoined and the new AFS formed a strong, loyal, independent adjunct to the full-time service joining in massive firefighting exercises with nostalgic enthusiasm.

Soon after this, there was general uproar when the Chief Officer decided to do away with the street fire alarm system. The red-painted pillars with fire alarm mechanisms fitted into their heads had been a familiar sight, dotted around the streets of London for more than half a century. When fire broke out, a member of the public needed only to break the glass in a small window and pull a brass handle to make instant contact with the nearest fire station where the site of that particular alarm was indicated by the ringing of an electric bell and a message on a printed tape. All the alarms had to be tested weekly by firemen. They were also a perpetual temptation for children or drunks to make false alarm calls. The alarms had been deliberately put out of action during the war lest they were set off by the bombing and no maintenance had been carried out. The system worked on a closed circuit needing an expensive continuous flow of electric current day and night at a time when power shortages were so acute that many shops were forbidden to light their windows and general power cuts, in homes as well as industry, were distressingly frequent.

After a long period of research, Delve decided that although the alarms had been useful when they were introduced, the fact that so many people now had telephones made them virtually redundant, particularly since 95% of the calls had, by 1939, been false alarms. The system was rented for tens of thousands of pounds a year and the cost of servicing and repairing the alarms after the war would have been phenomenal. The Post Office was organising a '999' service and Delve asked them whether, if the alarm pillars were removed from the streets, they would replace them with telephone boxes. The Post Office agreed and offered to include a free calling system for Fire, Police and Ambulance services in all the boxes. Once more the Trade Unions objected, but although they canvassed politicians and councils and organised demonstrations, statistics proved that the new scheme was justified and preferable to the old.

In due course all the pillars were removed – the last on 13th January 1958.

The '999' system which replaced them meant that some centre had to be established to monitor the calls. At the same time, and largely due to Delve's influence and pressure, two-way radio control had been increasingly introduced and this also needed to be linked with the emergency calling system. As a result, a new control room was opened at HQ which could receive all '999' calls from the public and quickly contact all fire stations within the service.

If he was anti-street fire alarms, Delve was certainly in favour of efficient fire appliances. Determined to convert to diesel engines, he decided to press the LCC to invest in them, knowing that although they cost more to buy, the increase would be offset by economies in maintenance costs. He also felt that pump outlets should be dual and fitted on both sides of the appliance so that the operator could work in safety from the pavement. At that time, the only suitable diesel engines available were the expensive Rolls Royce range. In his first report to the LCC after his appointment, Delve specified Rolls Royce engines for new diesel appliances and, somewhat to his surprise, the Council agreed – one member announcing that *'nothing was too good for the London Fire Brigade after all they had done during the war'*. Rolls Royce engines were supplied.

Delve had also been impressed by the high-pressure fog nozzles used by the US Navy on aircraft carriers and oil tankers. These were operated by powerful pumps which, in effect, emulsified the water and discharged it in the form of a fine spray. The method had three advantages – it protected the operator from the intense heat of an oil fire; its spray was so fine that it effectively excluded oxygen from the fire and so extinguished it and, being water, it cooled the area around the fire and prevented the risk of a flash-back. Another great advantage in its civilian use was that it reduced the amount of water needed when it was known that water often caused more damage than the fire it was meant to put out. He had hoped that the post-war pumps would have been of a capacity to produce high pressure fog, but larger and more powerful engines were not available then and he would be faced with the added problem of justifying the expense. Eventually he had fog nozzles fitted to hose reel equipment to save water and help to prevent excessive damage.

Although the LCC had been generous in its provision of new appliances, money had been short in London for so long that apart from the new Lambeth Headquarters, very little new building of fire stations had taken place in the 1920s and '30s or during the war and immediate post-war period. It was not until the mid-1950s that any major building work started although a great deal of clearing up and patching had gone on before this. Appliances were a different matter and by 1964 the Brigade was almost totally equipped with new, up-to-the-minute vehicles.

Now too, a Fire Prevention Branch was flourishing with particular emphasis on the new high-rise buildings which were going up rapidly all over the capital. Improved legislation meant that once the plans had been passed by the Brigade for fire safety, and the buildings erected, they had to be inspected regularly to see that the statutory fire precautions were being maintained efficiently. Among the Brigade's duties was to offer an advisory service to any organisation seeking expert opinions on fire hazards and through this, a whole new range of 'customers' was helped including historic buildings – Westminster Abbey, St Paul's and the national museums plus the underground railway system, hospitals, hotels, offices and private households. This was, however, essentially advisory and in many areas, particularly the underground railway system, the Brigade had no statutory power to insist on the safety measures they felt were needed.

A fire prevention officer went out to every serious incident to advise on checking the spread of fire and, when it was over, to examine and record its cause and effect. This later included a system of photographing such scenes in detail and maintaining the records in a special library for future reference if necessary – work carried out by the Photographic Section, started in 1935.

Yet again, the rapid developments in science and industry meant that radioactive materials, chemicals and in some cases, live bacteria were being stored and transported haphazardly around London. *(One crew, called to a road traffic accident involving a taxi in the heart of the West End, were shattered to discover that the passenger was travelling from one hospital research unit to another with a consignment of smallpox viruses.)* Special records had to be started to try to pin down the exact details of all hazardous loads which might be in transit and how best to deal with them. Added to all this extra work was the regular fire safety inspection of theatres, cinemas, concert halls, exhibitions and all the County's schools plus the normal regular inspection of hydrants.

Until now, the major part of the work of the Brigade had been firefighting, although statutory *'special services'* including rescues, were included among its regular duties and while the type was ever-changing (fewer small boys being stuck in milk churns, more in the drums of their mothers' washing machines – plus the now ever-present menace of children playing with lifts in high-rise flats and either getting trapped themselves or jamming the lift so that others were incarcerated until the firemen arrived) they were now beginning to form an increasing part of the Brigade's work. London's traffic was building up and more people

were being trapped in the wreckage of more accidents. Improved equipment for releasing them was needed and the Chief Officer's visits abroad, not least to America and Canada, produced ideas for adding to the items already carried for emergencies in tenders which had been steadily improving since the first world war. Normally, no charge was made for these special services, particularly if they came under the heading of 'humanitarian', but in some cases – householders calling out the Brigade because they had forgotten their door keys or where taps left running had caused floods – a small charge was imposed.

Neil Wallington, a former London fireman, (later Chief Officer of Devon and Cornwall Fire & Rescue Service) led one crew to an address in Maida Vale where the occupant was complaining of water pouring through from the flat above. There was no reply to the firemen's knock and they were about to break in when another neighbour emerged with the warning *'she keeps snakes in there…'* Wallington, who held the Queen's Award for Bravery, could face any fire, but not this. The police and the zoo were notified and the firemen – at arms' length – broke down the door and tiptoed in, finally reaching the bathroom where they discovered, in a cloud of steam, a collection of pythons clearly having a party. The flat belonged to a night-club dancer who used the snakes in her stage act. On her evening off she had washed her 'smalls', hung them on a line over the bath, left the hot tap dribbling to keep up the steamy atmosphere and let the pythons loose. Writhing round in their enjoyment they had knocked down the 'smalls', blocked the plug hole and started the flood. There was no question of police parity as the two services competed to evacuate the flat at speed, leaving the party-going snakes in the care of the zoo experts.

Basement fires were always a nightmare. Some of the larger stores in London, have what amounts to small villages beneath them, with winding 'roads' between massive storage areas and one of the duties of firemen with such stores on their ground was to acquaint themselves with the lay-out of these areas – a custom which paid off when, occasionally, small fires broke out. It was more difficult for the men when the fire was in an unknown house basement, filled with choking smoke and with the building liable to collapse at any time. Neil Wallington again recalls one such incident when a fireman was called over by an excited, gesticulating foreigner who appeared to be indicating that his mother was trapped in the basement. In plunged the fireman, groping his way through the dense smoke until he came upon the old lady huddled in the corner of a room. Although he could not see her through the smoke, she was obviously ready to leave, wearing her fur coat. With one arm round her shoulders he made his way slowly and with difficulty as she stumbled up the stairs, clutching his arm with her sharp, bony fingers. Only when they reached daylight did he discover that the 'lady' was a large, brown circus bear.

These were some of the lighter moments, but smoke was never a joke and research into improved breathing apparatus (BA) for firefighting has continued for more than 150 years. Not only do firemen face the dense smoke in these conditions but also a build-up of lethal carbon monoxide as well as the physical strain of heat and high humidity which mean that even an experienced fireman can collapse without warning. This was particularly evident at three major fires, in Covent Garden in 1949, Goodge Street Underground Station in 1956 and Smithfield Meat Market in 1958.

As a result of these incidents particularly, new BA equipment was introduced incorporating an automatic warning signal, 15 minutes before the oxygen supply ran out. Men going in to a fire wearing BA had to check in and

out using a special board which indicated the time of entry and the maximum time which they should spend inside – a system which was later adopted by many other brigades throughout the country and successively improved.

Transport accidents were not restricted to roads. In 1957 two trains collided at Lewisham killing 85 people and injuring a further 138. More than this, the accident had brought down a bridge carrying another train which was now balanced so precariously that it might fall at any moment. This headache was also dealt with by the Brigade, cutting, supporting, rescuing the casualties until the area was clear and safe.

In the thick of all this Chief Officer Delve continued his annual displays at headquarters, not quite so frequently as Shaw, but bringing in the Royal Family, famous war leaders and influential politicians, not just to view the skills of the men but because it gave him an opportunity for what was later to be known as good 'public relations'. He found the

The Duke of Edinburgh enjoyed visiting Lambeth. (LFCDA.)

Duke of Edinburgh particularly interested in the work of the Fire Service and welcomed his frequent visits to Lambeth headquarters as continuing the traditional concern of the Royal Family through the centuries over the hazards of fire. However, he had, reluctantly and diplomatically, to refuse the Duke's request to be called (as Edward VII had) if a particularly important fire broke out, so that he might attend in person. The responsibility of looking after so prominent a figure as well as fighting a major fire would be have been too onerous.

There was plenty to show the VIPs at Lambeth – and still more going on behind the scenes which few Londoners realised. The 1959 Factories Act and the 1963 Offices, Shops and Railway Premises Act had added enormously to the work of the Brigade's Fire Prevention department and now it was expected that every station should get to know its area in detail, visiting all the industrial premises and recording all potential problems or hazards as well as their lay-outs. An increasing number of 'back-up' departments providing expert background information were needed for the Service.

In 1962 Frederick Delve, now approaching his 60th birthday, became the first Chief Officer of the LFB to be knighted while still in office and in November that year, having reached 60, he retired after a lifetime of firefighting.

His brigade file shows not only details of his distinguished professional career within the service, but his appointments:

Joined Brighton Fire Brigade and appointed fireman, June 1923 (aged 19).

Station Officer, 1926.

3rd Officer, September 1929.

Deputy Chief Officer, November 1929 (aged 26).

Chief Officer, Croydon Fire Brigade, 1934.

Member of the Home Office Advisory Committee, 1936.

Special Instructor, ARP Civilian Anti-Gas Precautions, 1937–39.

Assistant Regional Fire Officer, London 'L' District, Sep 1939–June 1941.

Deputy Chief Inspector NFS, 1941.

President of the Institution of Fire Engineers, 1941

Chief Regional Officer, No 5 (London) Region, January 1943.

Chief Officer, London Fire Brigade, 1948–1962.

During that time, he was also:

Awarded CBE, 1942.

Founder Member of the Chief Officers' Association.

Member of the National Fire Protection Association of America.

Not surprisingly, the members of the London County Council recorded their high appreciation of all he had done for the Brigade and increased his annual salary on retirement from £4,200 to £4,400.

Never one to sit idly by, he moved back to Sussex, joined the Board of Securicor Ltd and served the Company for 20 years. On retiring from this – at 80 – he was elected Honorary President for Life, and still kept a positive interest in the work of the firm, maintaining his reputation for efficiency, firm discipline and the highest standards.

He was to be succeeded by the man who had been his Deputy Chief Officer since 1953, Leslie William Thomas Leete.

27

The Quiet Man

LESLIE LEETE WAS THE FIRST CHIEF OFFICER IN THE history of the Brigade to have risen through all the ranks in London. He had been educated at Bedford School and was one of the many 'white collar' workers who had volunteered for the AFS in May 1939.

Four months later when the war started, he became a full-time AFS fireman, trained and posted to the River

Leslie Leete, Chief Officer, LFB, 1962–1970. (LFCDA.)

Service, based at Blackfriars. There was a tradition of firefighting in the Leete family which owned the established hat-making business of W Leete Ltd in Luton. His grandfather had been Chief Officer of the Luton Volunteer Fire Brigade, and had even supplied his own horses to pull the 'steamer', but he could scarcely have predicted that his grandson would reach such heights in London.

There seems little doubt that Leete's knowledge of theory was excellent, but he was not a born fireman; his early practical work had sometimes left a lot to be desired and the officer in charge of training in 1942 had written 'Leete, although of intelligent type... does not appear to have the ability to take charge of men...' Others thought differently, reporting that he was 'upright, reliable and sober'; 'commands respect and obedience without effort' and 'has high intelligence... the type of officer who has great interest in his personnel... above average for his rank...' His Regional Interviewing Board noted: 'an exceptional Staff Officer with flair for Staff work. Type we need to retain for Staff duties in the post war Service...' When the NFS was formed in 1941 he was one of the first ten Company Officers to be selected in the London Fire Region, posted as officer-in-charge of Battersea River Station and taking command of a fireboat there (although like so many others, he had little experience on the water).

By 1943, after attending a course at the London Officers' Training School he was transferred to LFB headquarters at Lambeth and stayed there for the rest of his career in the Service, attached at first to the newly formed Regional Inspectorate and later made a Column Officer and put in charge of the Inspectorate.

Peace was on the horizon. By now a Divisional Officer he was appointed Senior Staff Officer in the department which was planning for the return of the fire service from the national body to the London County Council in 1948 and when the London Fire Brigade was restored he remained a

Senior Staff Officer until 1952. After the accident at the Broad Street fire which had led to the retirement of Mr McDuell, he was promoted, this time as Deputy Chief Officer to Frederick Delve and in the same year, awarded the MBE for 'distinguished services' – (he was later to receive the CBE). After 23 years of active firefighting and intensive staff work, few men were more qualified to take over the job of Chief Officer, particularly as it was already clear that big administrative changes were once more on the horizon.

London was adapting rapidly to keep up with the rest of the world. Centuries had passed since it had outgrown the walls of the old City, now only remembered in the names of small areas of the inner metropolis – 'Ludgate', Moorgate', 'Cripplegate', 'Aldgate'. From the earliest days of the Industrial Revolution it had been swallowing up the market gardens, the orchards and lavender fields on its outskirts and pushing on, further and further into the surrounding countryside until now it went far beyond the boundaries of the old London County Council. Politically, a new authority was deemed necessary to take in the sprawling area which now considered itself part of the capital.

The major upheaval came in 1965 when the London County Council joined its predecessor, the Metropolitan Board of Works as part of history. With it went Middlesex County Council, the county boroughs of Croydon, East Ham and West Ham and 83 other boroughs and county districts in the surrounding areas of Kent, Surrey, Essex and Hertfordshire. Taking their places came 32 new London boroughs, each with its own elected council under a new overall authority, the Greater London Council.

To say that this caused problems is to minimise its effect. The new, enormously powerful body brought with it a mass of difficulties in many areas but not least, the fire service. Under the new legislation, the London Fire Brigade was to remain 'in situ', but it would absorb eight proud local Brigades which had once been its neighbours – the 'crack' Middlesex, Croydon, East Ham and West Ham and others which had served in smaller areas. The expanded service would become one of the largest firefighting forces in the world with 6,500 men and women in uniform and a further 1,000 Auxiliaries and clerical staff.

Admittedly it had not all happened at once. Work on the new Service had started in 1963 with the creation of four Working Parties to gather facts about the constituent brigades and to work out the problems of differing procedures and equipment which would need to be ironed out before the 'D-Day' of amalgamation. Behind it all was the administrator *par excellence* who had already master-minded the rebirth of the LFB from the NFS – Leslie Leete. He had been responsible for the structure and organisation and was now to take over as Chief Officer of the new London Fire Brigade. (His shrewd administrative mind noted the financial consequences of moving to the Chief Officer's quarters at Lambeth and he suggested that since this was an official move, he should have a grant towards the cost of curtaining the windows 'of great size' – £32 – plus 40 yards of carpet for the passages and hall!)

Had it been a true amalgamation with all badges abandoned in favour of a new logo for the united service, it might have been easier. Instead, London changed its badge slightly to acknowledge the change from LCC to GLC and the rest had to adopt the London insignia. Senior officers could not all be accommodated at the same level as they had achieved in their own brigades and men who had held top ranks locally now found themselves demoted in an organisation where they were not always in agreement with the administration. There is no doubt that the men at the top had chosen Leete not just for his enormous administrative skill, but his quiet, non-abrasive manner, his tact and diplomacy. Even so, he was hard put to keep control in the years which immediately followed the change.

It had, among other things, brought in a massive assortment of new equipment including 360 first-line appliances and specialist vehicles – emergency tenders and such – 165 vans and cars, 285 pumping appliances, most of them able to carry a 50ft escape and some diesel driven and with two-way radio. There were 29 turntable ladders, all with an operational range of 100 feet, six foam tenders for oil or petrol fires or where water would be unsuitable, some carrying a 400 gallon foam-compound tank as well as extra foam compound in polythene containers. A fleet of hose-laying lorries were taken over, capable of laying 4,000–6,000 feet of 3½ inch rubber-lined hose at speeds of up to 20 mph.

With its own excellent stock of equipment, London now had a comprehensive range of 'gear', including emergency tenders carrying BA, special tools, lighting and cutting equipment, a breakdown lorry with a five-ton capacity crane and a two-ton hydraulic winch, mobile control units to provide headquarters for use at big incidents and a large new canteen van. The LFB also had its own two big fireboats, the famed 'Massey Shaw' and the newer 'Firebrace'.

From the earliest days, there had been workshops – Braidwood had absorbed the assorted smithies of the insurance brigades into his workshop at Watling Street and they had later expanded to a site near the Thames at Blackfriars where Shaw had inherited and improved them before making the transfer to Southwark. To the workshops at Lambeth HQ were now added new premises at Ruislip, Barking and Croydon along with six mobile repair vans equipped with benches, vices and small tools which could operate from fire stations close to a major incident and speed up any necessary repairs.

Hose repair shops were maintained at Lambeth and Willesden to provide new lengths or repair any which had been badly damaged. (Minor hose repairs were still carried out at fire stations.) The workshops at Lambeth and Ruislip not only repaired equipment but their civilian staff made all the hook ladders, extension ladders and first floor ladders. A turnery made the nozzles and other metal parts; wheelwrights mended the big wheels on the escapes; an engine shop dealt with general overhauls, and a central radio workshop was responsible for installing and maintaining all the radio equipment.

Training for recruits was now centred at Southwark and at Finchley where they were taught discipline and drill, how to use all the equipment, to carry out rescues of all kinds, to have basic knowledge of a range of technical subjects including hydraulics, building construction, chemistry, physics and the maintenance and testing of different items of equipment as well as a general education course. Specially designed smoke galleries were installed at Lambeth for training in BA work and every Command had its own driving schools. Before qualifying, new firemen had to pass examinations in all the subjects.

With the still constant shortage of recruits, a new training college was opened in a magnificent country house, surrounded by playing fields at Swanley, Kent, in February 1966. It was aimed at attracting boys between the ages of 16 and 17 to be Junior Firemen, taking on special educational, technical and practical training with the added temptation of being taught to drive and to swim as well as going on the adventurous 'Outward Bound' training courses. Apart from their firefighting training, they were encouraged to help with local handicapped children and others in need – preparing them for the mass of voluntary charity work for which London's firefighters are still famous.

The Brigade was still 1,500 men short of its authorised strength and, with 100 Junior Firemen in residence on the two-year course at Swanley, it hoped steadily to fill at least some of the vacancies. The Principal was Major William Anderson, an expert in guerilla warfare and an explorer who had led expeditions to the Arctic. Assisting him were DACO Packer from the Southwark Training School, ADO Fred Hurcombe, a senior officer and nine other instructors. The course included scientific and technical subjects with tutors from a local technical college brought in to help with theoretical training and practical work in the laboratories. Sports included table tennis, cricket, football, rugby, canoeing, sailing and riding. Although it ran well for a time, Swanley was never fully used and was eventually closed down and the scheme abandoned.

Promotion now depended on ability and ambition, with

in-service instruction available through all the ranks up to Chief Officer. When the Ocean Hotel Fire College at Brighton closed down, a new Fire Service Staff College was opened at Wotton House, near Dorking (an appropriate location as the 16th century manor had been the home of John Evelyn, the diarist who recorded much of the Great Fire of London in 1666 and became known as 'The Prophet of Fire Prevention'). The College was financed through the Home Office and was aimed at providing top management for the fire service nationally.

Under the control of the Joint Training Committee of the Central Fire Brigades Advisory Council, three basic courses were run: a new 12-month Accelerated Promotion Course for specially selected Firemen, Leading Firemen and Sub-Officers who had passed the Sub-Officers' examination or the equivalent exam of the Institution of Fire Engineers; a Command Course for selected officers from Assistant Divisional Officer to Assistant Chief Officer Rank, and a Junior Command Course for selected Station Officers, both of these covering a period of twelve weeks. All three courses involved management studies.

The Command Course students were selected by Home Office interviews. A place on the coveted Accelerated Promotion Course, which provided rapid advancement for the 'cream' – young men with enthusiasm, skill and obviously high ability – involved an extensive interview system similar to the old Army Officers Selection Board, and the course included some time spent at the fledgling Technical College, based at a huge former RAF bomber station at Moreton-in-Marsh in Gloucestershire. Later, the Dorking College was to be closed down and the whole system concentrated at what had become, by January 1970, the Fire Service College which has steadily expanded since that time.

By now radio control existed between all appliances and the Command Control Units at Wembley (Northern), Stratford (Eastern) and Croydon (Southern). For the first time, remote control 'walkie-talkie' apparatus was being used at fires in London.

By 1966 too, some of the sting was being taken out of the GLC changeover with preparations for the centenary celebrations commemorating the founding of the Metropolitan Fire Brigade – and – at the same time, the 300th anniversary of the Great Fire of London. The Brigade took a major role in the Lord Mayor's Show that year and a special commemorative display which included a great River Pageant at Lambeth and a spectacular firework display, was attended by the Queen and the Duke of Edinburgh. In a special message to mark the occasion, the Queen said:

'In the 100 years of its existence, the Brigade has established, in peace and war, a reputation for skill and gallantry and a tradition of service to the public which are second to none. I and my family share with the country as a whole, a deep pride in your history and achievements. Like many others, I have a personal reason for gratitude to the London Fire Brigade, for last year, I saw it in action at my own home at Buckingham Palace. But for its speed and skill the fire, which was quickly put out, would certainly have spread and become more serious. I am confident from what I hear and know of your work… that the high standard of efficiency which the Brigade has always displayed, is being not only maintained but improved……'

Lambeth now was looking ahead to the future, and discussion turned on the possibility of using a hovercraft on the Thames instead of the traditional fireboats. Serious thought was being given to basement fire extinguishing by an inert gas, from a completely new, jet-powered engine or by the use of bulk quantities of carbon dioxide. New paints and floor-coverings for fire stations were planned to reduce maintenance work; and terms such as alkaline batteries, synthetic material for hosepipes, automatic transmission, automatic power take-offs, and automatic lubrication systems as well as a hydraulic platform which could bridge parked cars for rescue purposes were all being bandied about. There was talk too of improved foam and new foam extinguishers.

Overtrousers were to replace the old black waterproof leggings; helmets made from cork and plastic were being tested as were new compressed air cylinders which would double the duration of BA. Even more revolutionary, the possible use of closed-circuit television to speed the transmission of vital information to the control room was on the horizon.

At the same time, the Fire Prevention Branch was pushing for better means of escape from clubs and cafés which were outside the range of existing legislation; some control on the sale to the public of flammable materials without any warning of their danger, and there was call for urgent action over the uncontrolled transport of highly dangerous materials. All this, and yet in 1966 annual fire losses in Britain were still exceeding £75,000,000.

Although money was never plentiful, plans were being made for simplified fire stations to replace the old buildings which often had elaborate, magnificent – and expensive Victorian decoration. The new stations were built for simplicity and efficiency with no frills and, wherever possible if two old stations were fairly close together and tactics allowed, only one would replace them.

An annual Sports Day was held regularly at the White City Stadium (the site of which was later absorbed into the BBC's Television Centre) and money raised by this helped support the Benevolent Fund, caring for sick and injured firemen and the dependents of those killed in the Service.

Post WW2 prizewinning architecture at Chelsea F.S.

The Brigade still had its own brass band, but this was soon to disappear as fewer recruits could play an instrument – or wanted to learn.

Added to all this, there was now a Welfare Section at headquarters with clubs catering for anyone interested in athletics, ski-ing, soccer, sub-aqua, ten-pin bowling, photography (run by the famed LFB photographer, Don Pye), horticulture, French, table tennis and even the cultivation of fuchsias. Money spent from London's own Welfare Fund included the provision of a *'Comfort Box'*, sent to any member of the Brigade who was in hospital and containing – at that time – 20 cigarettes, a box of sweets, a book of crossword puzzles and notepaper – *'a reminder that someone in the vast organisation knows of their misfortune'*.

To record and publicise all this, a new Press and Public Relations Department was established and a new magazine, *'The London Fireman'* was launched in 1966. (Later, as sex equality swept through the Brigade, the title was changed to *'The London Firefighter'*.)

The wealth of outside activities all gave a break from the job in hand which, in 1967 involved another train disaster. Soon after 9 o'clock on Guy Fawkes night, November 5th – several carriages of a twelve coach passenger train were derailed at Hither Green, close to Lewisham. Some overturned and many passengers were injured and trapped. More than 120 firemen from 'E' and 'B' Divisions worked to release the victims and the newly developed *Major Accident Procedure* was put into action.

For some time, representatives of the Police, Fire and ambulance services had been discussing the problem of rapid and efficient co-operation with hospital and other support groups in the event of a major accident (or incident), the definition of which was clearly laid down: *'A Major Accident is any incident which is determined as such by the Senior Police, Ambulance or Fire Officer first on the scene, or any incident in which the number of live casualties to be handled is estimated to exceed fifty. Or any incident at which, in the opinion of the Senior Officer of any of the essential services, the resources of all the essential services may be required or involved.'*

Hither Green railway crash was certainly a Major Accident. The call went out and instantly the emergency services dashed to the scene, each knowing what their own job was and also that the *'named'* hospitals in the area would not only be sending out a 'flying squad' of doctors and nurses but would be on stand-by to receive and treat casualties. At one stage 21 ambulances were lined up to take the passengers to hospital as they were cut free. With mobile lighting and heavy cutting equipment, all the trapped passengers were released within two hours and 66 people taken to hospital with maximum speed and efficiency.

Negotiations involving the Brigade, the Union and the LCC had resulted in a new wage agreement offering higher earnings for increased productivity and in 1967, a pensionable bonus. London was the first brigade in the country to bring in such an agreement. At the same time, the Brigade reported that experiments with automatic drive on their fire appliances had so far 'not fulfilled all our hopes' although the experiments were continuing. However, smaller bore hose with light alloy couplings and branches was being widely used and had been generally welcomed for its increased speed of handling which compensated for the greater delivery of the larger and heavier hose. *'There must be no halt in the search for technical improvements'* came the call from the top.

Without doubt, Leete had done a good job in moulding together a new firefighting force for London but it was not without constant problems in a society in which industrial unrest was endemic and into which a whole new breed of young people were emerging with very different ideas on life and work from their predecessors.

The scheme introduced during the war, of sending units of firefighters to help areas in particular need, was re-introduced and London's firemen helped local brigades at the Aberfan disaster in 1966 and during the East Coast floods of 1953 they travelled to the badly affected areas to help with pumping out of inundated houses. In June 1967 a team of 150 volunteers was sent to Land's End to join one of the earliest oil-pollution battles after the tanker *'Torrey Canyon'* broke its back off Land's End and released its cargo on to the Cornish beaches. Before long, similar teams would be flying off on overseas mercy missions.

Men were still very much the active part of the service, although the war-time break-through of employing women, mostly in office and telephone switchboard work and, to some extent, in Control, had been maintained. By now, they were a vital part of the administration. One woman took the opportunity to answer the question *'What is a Firewoman?'* in the *'London Fireman'* of Spring 1967. Her summing-up would have been furiously challenged twenty years later:

> Firewomen come in all shapes and sizes.
>
> Firewomen are blonde, brunette, redhead, or just plain mousy.
>
> Firewomen like dancing, ten-pin bowling, engagement rings,
>
> Sardine sandwiches and gooey cream cakes at three in the morning,
>
> Nattering, leave days, 20-pump fires and firemen.
> Firewomen dislike tidy lockers, canteen sausages,
> Service caps, working on Saturday nights

And being looked on as idiots by their male counterparts.

Firewomen are instantly alert at a sound from a bell or
buzzer;

Lie in bed trying to sleep when civilized people are out at
work

And wear a collar and tie and black stockings

When all the other females are clad in skinny sweaters
and mini-skirts.

Firewomen are hard-working, efficient, loyal, tolerant,

And full of love for their fellow MEN.'

Unisex and firefighters were still a long way off.

Joint exercises with the other emergency services –
police, ambulance and hospitals were still being held in
preparation for any possible disaster which might result,
particularly, from the increasing number of passenger
aircraft flying over the capital. Any Chief Officer's biggest
nightmare was said to be a jumbo-jet airliner crashing on
Oxford Street with its concentration of big stores, fashionable boutiques and huge crowds of shoppers.

In 1968 a combined practice took place assuming that a
plane had crashed into the 33rd floor of the 395ft high
Britannic House, headquarters of the BP oil company, in the
heart of the City, close to Moorgate Underground Station
and the Barbican fire station. Fire was reckoned to have
enveloped two floors and there were further outbreaks on
the roof and in the underground car park after a wing of the
plane had fallen into the yard of Barbican fire station and
burning fuel had escaped into the adjoining basement. All
lifts were out of action, including the firemen's lifts, and to
make the event really difficult, the wet rising main and hose
reels were 'out'. The Major Accident Procedure was initiated
with the Brigade, the London Ambulance Service, the City
Police and the Salvage Corps taking part. 2,000 staff were
evacuated from the building and 'casualties' were removed
to nearby St Bartholomew's Hospital which was involved in
the exercise.

It was a highly successful event and ironically, was to be
repeated 'for real' seven years later for a totally different
disaster when a rush-hour train hit the buffers 40 feet below
the surface at Moorgate Underground Station.

1968 saw the 'stand-down' again of the AFS, axed now
as an economy measure but with its members leaving
Lambeth in a glow of special parties and sincere tributes to
their sterling work. The autumn of the same year brought an
unprecedented number of calls from Londoners flooded out
in the storms. Between 11 am and 6 pm on 14th September
there were 114 calls for help and on the following day, 1,773
of which 1,660 came from south London. By the end of that
wet week, more than 3,000 calls for pumping out had been
received as well as more than 170 fire calls to the areas
involved.

Disaster struck again in 1969. Late in the morning of the
17th July the Brigade was called to a fire at Dudgeon's Wharf
in Manchester Road on the Isle of Dogs. A derelict area, with
enormous, empty 20,000-gallon tanks for storing oil and
spirits was being demolished ready for redevelopment.
Several small fires caused by workmen's hot cutting
equipment had already been put out in the past by the local
brigades but this time they were called to tank 97. The
workmen appeared to have put out the flames, although a
few wisps of smoke could still be seen. One group of firemen
climbed to the top to flush out the inside with water and
another was removing an inspection hatch at the bottom
when there was a massive explosion. Five firemen: *Sub
Officer Michael Gamble*, *Firemen John Appleby*, *Terry Breen*,
Trevor Carvosso and *Alfred Smee*, along with a site worker,
Mr Reginald Adams, were killed instantly. Two of the crew,
Station Officer Harold Snelling and *Fireman Ian Richards*
were awarded the BEM for gallantry when they took the
considerable risk of rescuing one of their mates from the
damaged tank. For years, efforts were made by the Brigade
to have some memorial to the men, but it was not until 1989
that the Chief Officer, Gerry Clarkson, was able to unveil two
memorial plaques, one on the site of the old wharf and the
other in Millwall Fire Station to the memory of the men
who died.

Despite so much activity and improving conditions there
was still a niggling feeling of lowered morale in the Service,
put into words in a letter to the *'London Fireman'* by a
Leading Fireman in the autumn of 1969. The reasons, he felt,
were:

1   Shortage of men.

2   Standing-by at another station too frequently.

3   Boredom (ie same thing every night, billiards, snooker,
    darts.)

4   Not enough practical drill.

5   Need for a workshop at every station.

6   Hobbies (more).

7   More inter-station activities.

8   More sporting activities.

For Leslie Leete it was sad, but immaterial. At the end of
1969 he retired. He had served the Brigade throughout the
war and had attended almost every major incident in
London since then, taking command personally at serious
fires at Goodge Street Underground in 1956, Buckingham
Palace and Grocers' Hall in 1965, a Tottenham timber yard
with all its attendant problems in 1966, the Silvertown sugar

refinery in 1968 and the Leinster Towers Hotel fire in 1969. He was a Member of the Institution of Fire Engineers, a member of the Central Fire Brigades Advisory Council, the Board of the Fire Service College and Chairman of the London Fire Liaison Panel co-ordinating the fire prevention activities of both fire service and insurance interests. He had paid official visits to Canada, Denmark, France, Hong Kong, Honolulu, India, Italy, Japan, Norway, Singapore, Sweden, West Germany and the USA and was an officer of the Order of St John.

Paying tribute to him, the Chairman of the GLC Fire Brigade Committee commended his outstanding personal qualities and his work in welding together the new brigade from so many different groups, adding *'despite the troubled times through which the Brigade has passed in the last year or so, Mr Leete has sought at all times to maintain a high level of Brigade operational efficiency within the limits of the manpower available and has followed worthily the best traditions of the Brigade'*.

The appointment of his successor was to cause an even bigger upheaval.

28

Out of the East – Joseph Milner

We're out and the Pump Escape's flying,
It's a 'shout' to a fire in a house
In a district where 'Persons Reported'
Is more common these days than a mouse.

Tom Arnold, our driver, is swearing –
'Curse the traffic, it's always at peaks'
Some eight tons of hope he is weaving,
Any hole we can get through, he seeks.

Two-tone horns are blasting – we're coming!
The Gov'nor is bashing the bell,
Lord God, though we know well our duty,
Give your aid and we'll save them from hell.

Policemen are running before us,
They're determined to break up a jam,
Return our salute as we pass them,
For they know we do well when we can.

The people are stopping to watch us
As emotion disturbs the most staid;
A feeling of pride grows inside us
Ev'ry Londoner loves the Brigade.

('Turn-out'. 1970–75. By DACO Charles Clisby).

OF ALL THE CHIEF OFFICERS OF THE LONDON FIRE Brigade, Joseph Milner was one of the most remarkable and although his leadership ended in early retirement and newspaper headlines, it was a vitally important stage in the history of the Service. The whole social situation in Britain was changing dramatically. With full employment and a shortage of personnel in the public sector, the boot of power was on the foot of the trades unions who were all too ready to use it. Now it was the turn of the 'bosses' to take the punishment. Sadly, Joe Milner was on the receiving end.

It is particularly important to understand his background and experience before taking on London. He seems always to have been known as 'Joe', (although not necessarily to his face). Nobody could have been nearer to the ordinary fireman than this extraordinary Mancunian who, like so many other Chief Officers, had come into firefighting almost by accident. He was born in Chorlton on Medlock, Manchester, in 1922 – it sounds like a cosy thatched hamlet

but was, in fact, one of the worst slums in the city. His father, an ex-regular soldier, was by then a labourer in an electric-cable makers and Joe went to the local elementary school. When his two brothers dreamed of being firemen when they grew up, Joe dreamed of joining the army. He left school just before his 14th birthday, worked briefly as an office boy, then as a parcel messenger and in 1938, at the age of 16, joined the Royal Corps of Signals as a boy soldier.

When the war started he was transferred to the King's (Liverpool) Regiment and spent two years on airfield defence around the coast of Britain. He was still only 20 years old when he was shipped to the Far East to serve with General Orde Wingate's elite jungle fighters, the *'Chindits'*, in Japanese occupied Burma. 'I was very lucky' he recalled. 'I suffered no wounds to speak of although, like so many other Chindits, I contracted typhus, had several bouts of malaria and had two toes amputated as a result of foot rot.'

The Chindits operated behind Japanese lines, relying on parachute drops for their supplies. Dead comrades were left

Joseph Milner, Chief Officer, LFB, 1970–1976. (LFCDA.)

where they fell as the men moved swiftly through the jungle carrying out their attacks and disappearing fast. In January 1945, Joe volunteered to join a small detachment to go back into the jungle and the mountains to recover the bodies of their comrades for interment in a military cemetery. 'It was six months of grisly, exhausting but rewarding work as they would, at last, have a decent burial' he recalled.

Back home in 1946 he was determined to stay in the Army, but a military muddle prevented this. As he waited for the matter to be sorted out, it was his wife who suggested the he might join the National Fire Service. 'It seemed a good idea. I went to Woolworths, bought a sixpenny arithmetic book and taught myself basic arithmetic, went along for the tests and passed. I was still not absolutely certain that this was what I wanted to do when I was sent to No 1 Regional Training School in Northumbria. The small group of recruits stood shivering on Riding Mill railway station on a bitterly cold night in October.

'A leading fireman met us and called out our names: "Milner"... "Sir!" Then, to my astonishment he said "It's your birthday isn't it? Many Happy Returns!" I couldn't believe it. Nothing like that would have happened in the

army. From that moment, from that small incident, I was a fireman.'

His training brought him the Home Office Prize for the best recruit. He went on to Middlesbrough, then Scarborough followed by two years in the North Riding. In 1950, hankering for more experience he transferred to Manchester. It was a big Brigade and he was still only a Fireman, albeit with the Graduate IFE examination behind him, when he replied to an advertisement for Station Officers for the Hong Kong Fire Brigade and was accepted. 'In Kipling's words' he said, years later, ' "The East it was a-calling and I couldn't 'eed naught else".' In March 1951 he flew to Hong Kong. His wife, son and daughter followed by boat.

It was a tough life. Officers were on virtually continuous duty and 'lived over the shop' – in an insalubrious, purely Chinese district. 'We lived and breathed Chinese customs, picked up colloquial Chinese and made staunch, lifelong friends.' It was a full colonial brigade, still suffering from war shortages, numbering about 490 men in half a dozen urban stations, the same number of rural stations and a couple of fire-boats, dominated by an intransigent Chief Officer who was opposed to any modernisation.

By this time thousands of refugees were pouring into Hong Kong from China and gradually the whole situation was changing from an entrepôt economy with traditional 'go downs' – primitive warehouses – and buildings of fir-pole rafters and clay-tiled roofs, to an industrial infrastructure with towering skyscrapers, bringing a major challenge to the fire service.

Clearly changes had to be made and with a new Chief Officer, Milner, by now a Divisional Officer, was in the team which, in 1958, drew up a ten-year development plan for the Hong Kong Fire Service. It included a dynamic Fire Prevention Bureau which came to be accepted as one of the best in the world. Changes were made to the Colony's Dangerous Goods legislation and a modern, residential training school was planned with a student capacity of 400, and courses for all levels, from recruits to senior command.

The Fire Service worked closely with the Hong Kong Government who, in turn, co-operated to the limits of its budget capability. Between them, they also worked fast. New appliances and equipment were bought. The future resources for firegrounds, marine fires, fire prevention and ambulance duties were constantly reviewed and the appropriate resources budgeted for, ordered and put into service at lightning speed. With increased respect among the community the Service began to work closely with the University. Milner put to the scientists the fact that infra-red rifle sights were being used by the US troops in Vietnam and questioned whether they might be of use to the fire service, for locating the sources of fires or possible unconscious victims beneath the rubble. He also asked if infra-red units might be used instead of photo-electric cells in the numerous lifts being installed in the new high-rise buildings. Ultimately, he felt, a remote-controlled robot might be produced which could be sent into a building to locate the seat of the fire and target a jet directly on to it. Building collapses were not uncommon in Hong Kong and they needed some way of locating trapped victims quickly. Unfortunately, the times were against him and the ideas had to be dropped on economy grounds.

In 1965, less than 20 years after he had shivered on the Northumbrian railway station as a 'rookie' fireman, Joe Milner took over as Director of the young, well established and equipped, efficient and respected Hong Kong Fire Service. He was also a Justice of the Peace, an active member of the Hong Kong Council of the Order of St John and was involved with several youth organisations.

'I had grown up with the Hong Kong Fire Service. I had seen it expand and had played my part in that expansion. I was proud of its reputation, its technical disciplines and its happy atmosphere' he said. 'By 1969 I was approaching 50. The pioneering challenge had gone out of the job and there were good officers, some of them older than I was, who deserved a chance of promotion.'

He was crossing the harbour on one of his larger fire-boats when he noticed the advertisement for the post of Chief Officer of the London Fire Brigade. His wife was ailing, and the enervating, humid summers were aggravating her illness. His children had grown up and left school. He had just drawn up the plan for the next ten years of the Service and once it was approved he would not want to move. Years later he looked back: 'I already commanded a happy, efficient brigade, the second largest fire service in the Commonwealth. I was particularly proud of our purpose-built residential training school which as well as educating our own officers and men, regularly undertook the training of officers from other Oriental and Middle East countries. What really decided me to apply for the London post was, I suppose, purely vain ambition.

'Leaving Hong Kong was one of the worst decisions of my life.'

Like a lamb to the slaughter, Joe Milner walked into Lambeth Headquarters.

'When I took on the post, I understood I would be responsible directly to the Fire Brigade Committee of the Greater London Council and that my immediate administrative superior would be the Director General' he wrote, many years later. 'In the event, I found another tier of GLC officials had been inserted into the hierarchy who were responsible, inter-alia, for the global co-ordination of departmental managements and resources.' No longer was he to have the rapid response, the face to face arguments and reasoning with the men who could trigger off the quick action to which he had been accustomed. 'My submissions and reports to the Fire Brigade Committee and all the other committees had first to be vetted by this tier and especially the Controller of Operational Services, a layman as far as Fire Service matters were concerned. They were good, competent administrators but were frustrating, time-consuming and in my opinion a superfluous link in the chain.'

He had assumed that as Chief Officer of the London Fire Brigade he would have personal control.

'In Hong Kong I was in command of a fire service and operationally responsible to the Governor. The Service had a very rigid but paternalistic discipline. When I got to London I was not in command in the same sense. I was part of a triumvirate – I as Chief Officer, plus the local politicians and trade unions whose influence really dictated the pace of developments.'

(In speaking of the trade unions, he was using a shorthand for all the representative bodies involved in the industrial relations including the Fire Brigades' Union, the National Association of Fire Officers and the non-uniformed staff associations. In this connection, he made the point that his officers often found themselves in the invidious position of being members of either the FBU or the NAFO but some had dual membership, so that on the one hand they had to represent the views of the Brigade while on the other they owed a loyalty to their union's dictates.)

Another major problem was not restricted to London but was nationwide. Unrest and discontent in all branches of industry had reached massive proportions. 'Winters of discontent' were followed by summers of strikes and controversies. The problem of police parity was ever present, particularly after the Ross Award of 1952 had firmly rejected it as a basis for pay determination, laying down that firemens' pay should be determined on its own merits. In 1967, the Home Office had commissioned a review of the Fire Service under the Chairmanship of Sir Ronald Holroyd. This Report was published in June 1970 – at about the time that Milner was taking over. In the intervening years, the development of the service had, it was generally felt, been retarded by a 'wait for Holroyd' mentality and now, Chief Fire Officers were asked to submit their views on the Report's 100 recommendations before any decision could be taken on their implementation or rejection.

Soon after this, another Government Inquiry was being held into Pay and Conditions in the Fire Service under the Chairmanship of Sir Charles Cunningham so to the Holroyd delay was added a 'wait for Cunningham' mentality.

The Holroyd Inquiry, had followed an examination of fire service pay in 1967 *(National Board for Prices and Incomes, Report No 32, May 1967)* and also an attitude survey carried out by the Government Social Survey Unit *('The Fire Service and its personnel' by Margaret Thomas, SS 417/B)*. At about the same time the GLC, the FBU and NAFO had jointly set up an inquiry into industrial relations in the London Fire Brigade so there was no shortage of interest in the pay and conditions of the Service at this period.

The purpose of the Holroyd Committee had been clear and concise:

'to inquire into and make recommendations on:

a the principles which should govern the organisation of the fire service in Great Britain.

b the relationship between the Central Government and local fire authorities; the functions of the fire service; measures for maintaining its efficiency; the arrangements for recruiting and training its members and ensuring that the best use is made of the manpower available and the machinery for determining pay and conditions of service.

c the need for further fire prevention measures.

d fire research and the application of its results.'

The findings included the remarkable fact that between 1957 and 1967 the number of building fires had increased by 88% – still due mostly to the same old causes of children playing with matches, rubbish burning, smoking and 'malicious actions'. At least 70% of these had been in private dwellings and other private 'occupancies' which were not directly subject to fire prevention legislation. Also, that there had been a 300% increase in the number of malicious false alarms. In addition, 'special services' were a growing burden on all brigades and the Committee recommended that these should be limited to 'those of a humanitarian nature requiring the special skills and equipment of the brigades which are not available elsewhere.' There had been an upward trend in fire casualties, with nearly 80% of these in private dwellings and more than 50% of the victims children or old people. Holroyd forecast that

'if the present trends continue, by 1977 the fire service may have to cope annually with some 500,000 to 600,000 calls of all kinds.' (Holroyd was right – and by 1990 the national figure for calls of all kinds had risen to 949,500. In London, the increase went from 84,538 in 1970 to 192,087 in 1990.)

The annual cost of the fire service nationally had increased nearly two and a half times between 1958 and 1968, reaching £61,000,000 by 1970 'and will inevitably continue to rise if firemen in sufficient number and of the right calibre are to be recruited and retained.'

The Committee's examination of the causes of the high-loss fires suggested that these were less likely to be affected by any extension of the fire brigade's cover than by the greater use of automatic detectors, particularly those which gave direct warning to the Brigades; more use of automatic sprinklers; stricter control of the use of old buildings for high fire risk activities and improvements in fire prevention measures. Indeed the Report constantly stressed the need for louder preaching of the gospel of fire prevention, including the widespread introduction, possibly by law, of sprinkler systems in hospitals and old people's homes, hotels and residential schools and perhaps, at some time in the future, the legal requirement that such protection should be installed in all new homes as they were built – with a rebate on fire insurance for homes in which they were included.

As for the cause of fires, they felt that the existing Fire Research Station at Borehamwood should be combined with the work of the Home Offices Scientific Advisory Branch and taken over by the Home Office Fire Department, with the Borehamwood premises used exclusively for research and testing on fire matters.

Although the Committee made a number of recommendations concerning other fire brigades, they agreed that London should be left, for the time being, to absorb the readjustments consequent on the so-recent reorganisation.

Nationally again, they pointed out that there was still no organisation with specific responsibility for the collation of information, the study of basic fire problems and the provision of managerial services and guidance to the fire service. This should, they recommended, be carried out by an enlarged and strengthened Fire Department of the Home Office with administrative and functional responsibility for the training colleges, for operational research on firefighting and fire prevention matters and other forms of research, with high calibre, trained and experienced staff. They did not feel that the fire service should provide a national emergency organisation to deal with peace-time disasters but should co-operate with their local authorities' contingency plans for these. Education had worried the Committee and they emphasised the need for entrants with a higher academic potential, and better facilities for improving the overall training of fireman, recommending an accelerated promotion course for those with outstanding potential. They were not in favour of a fire degree nor a post-graduate diploma in fire engineering although those who had the necessary qualifications, had given satisfactory service and who wished to take any advanced course, regardless of the subject, should be encouraged by having their fees, books, travelling expenses and normal pay borne centrally. The selection process could be organised by the Home Office and each Brigade would have a Training Officer. Future requirements of the Fire Service needed to be kept under constant review.

Pay had been one of the most anxiously awaited results of the Report and here, the Committee recommended that the National Joint Council should continue. Was a fireman skilled, semi-skilled or non-skilled? Holroyd declared that

'the earnings of a fully trained fireman with all-round operational experience should be comparable with the national average earnings of skilled craftsmen – with due regard to the fact that an operative in industry was paid for his actual working time, while a proportion of a fireman's weekly hours of duty is spent on standby. Meanwhile, all firemen should be trained in elementary fire-prevention duties and used for routine fire-prevention inspections and for giving advice on fire-prevention.

There should be a new grade of senior fireman with no supervisory duties and open to firemen of at least three years operational duties. Senior officers should be given more supervisory and management training, with particular emphasis on the skills of effective communication and the handling of human relations.

One of the minor recommendations at least relieved the men of a chore which had occupied firefighters for centuries – that of cleaning their station and 'domestic fittings'. It was some recognition of their new status that Holroyd suggested that civilian cleaners should be provided for the universally-hated station cleaning duties.

Although it had put forward a whole new range of recommendations, the Report was not accepted with open arms by the firemen themselves. A national delegate conference of the FBU had already been arranged to discuss Holroyd and this not only passed a resolution expressing lack of confidence in the machinery of the National Joint Council for dealing fairly with firemen's pay but called for a national demonstration, by answering emergency calls only, which took place for one week at the end of September, 1970.

Now followed a period of massive unrest within the Service with discussions between the Union and the Home Secretary culminating in the Union's request for an independent inquiry being accepted.

Early in 1971, Sir Charles Cunningham KBE KCB CVO, took the chair of an Inquiry into the work of the Fire Service, aimed at evaluating the fireman's job. *'What we have tried to do is to indicate the point at which, in the hierarchy of skilled and semi-skilled workers, the fireman can, having regard to the nature of his job, appropriately be put'* was the way in which this brilliant and experienced, leading Civil Servant explained their findings. They had visited a variety of fire brigades, examined a whole range of statistics and reports from the Office of Manpower Economics and taken evidence from a range of interested parties including the trades unions.

The FBU had stressed the increasing number of fires and other emergencies which the fire service was now having to deal with, emphasising that these were becoming increasingly complex with the rapid scientific and technological changes which were taking place, and underlining the amount of fire prevention work firemen had to carry out. They insisted that a fair and acceptable valuation of the fireman's job was essential to the morale and efficiency of the service. Skilled craftsmen in industry, firemen at some airports and the police were all getting a better deal than local authority firemen. They were particularly concerned that *'stand by'* time should not be taken into account when assessing a fireman's job, since the men could not leave the station at any time during their period of duty. Other unions added their views.

Cunningham's committee pondered on it and reached their conclusions. Their findings *that the job of the basic grade of fireman was broadly comparable with industrial jobs in the top semi-skilled categories or the lower ranges of the skilled trades – more specifically the equivalent of some of the crafts in the construction and heavy engineering industries* – did little to help industrial relations.

Their conclusions in the short term were:

i they could find no evidence that a fireman's pay was seriously out of line with that of most comparable workers but the danger and unpleasantness associated with it should be taken into account.

ii fireman's pay should be assessed and calculated in relation to a basic working week of 40 hours.

iii The rate of pay for a fully trained fireman with four year's service should be £1,850 pa (58p per hour) with rates of pay based on successful completion of 'modules' of training.

iv The rank of Leading Fireman should be withdrawn and replaced by the classification 'qualified fireman.'

v There should be one rate of pay nationally for the Service apart from the London weighting which should be increased to £160 pa for all ranks, but all other local allowances including the £54 London under-manning payment were to be removed.

Other recommendations dealt with pay and rank structure for officers.

Milner, who had arrived as all this was coming to a head, thought Cunningham had underestimated the job of firemen – and said so publicly. At the same time, the Unions were not happy with all the findings, but when it was suggested that the matter should be put to a further committee for consideration, threats of worse industrial action followed instantly.

In the thick of it all, Milner was still concerned with the actual problem of fighting fires efficiently in London. When he took over, he had inherited a generally well-equipped, highly trained and resourceful force, but, as he later admitted, he underestimated the militant influence of the unions and overestimated the durability of agreements with their delegates. As an example, he recalled one of the first big fires in his period of office:

'It was at Tooley Street – I remember I kept thinking of my illustrious predecessor, James Braidwood who had been killed there…This too, was a tremendous fire and I was fearful that we would not be able to bring it under control before it engulfed the whole waterfront area. Yet the men worked magnificently, keeping at the job until they were totally exhausted and then fighting not to be relieved.

To my amazement, I saw firemen servicing breathing apparatus on a tarpaulin laid on a pavement in all the dust and dirt. It alarmed me because the slightest grease or dirt in contact with oxygen is a potential hazard. Here, there was dirt, grease and it was pitch dark. You cannot service BA sets efficiently under these conditions.

'After the fire I had specifications drawn up for two new BA tenders, each on a single decker bus chassis. Sets used on the fireground would be handed into the tender, be recharged, serviced and tested in "sterile" surroundings and then put back in commission. There would also be provision for BA wearers to clean themselves up.'

The plans, together with two mobile control units on similar chassis were approved by the politicians and by the current Union representatives. When eventually, they were ready for service, the Union representatives had been replaced.

'Those I had reached agreement with were men who had been through the war and had moderate policies. Their successors were an entirely different breed' recalled Milner. 'The original agreement was that these vehicles would only be manned when they were specifically required on a fireground. The new representatives renounced the agreement and demanded that the vehicle be fully manned around the clock. This was financially impossible. The tenders would only be turned out at really major incidents – a few times a year perhaps – but for those occasions they were vital. Between those incidents the crews would have no role. When we pressed our case, the Union representatives threatened to put the entire Brigade on an 'Emergencies Only' footing, meaning their members would only turn out to emergency incidents and would not undertake other duties, including training and servicing appliances and equipment. Despite repeated negotiations, these vehicles were still not in commission when I retired some years later.'

The moderate ex-service and ex-NFS men who had joined the old LFB men to form the major part of London's firefighting force after the war were beginning to retire. Some of the younger men who were taking their place had less experience of discipline and service at a time when the word 'tradition' had become a national joke among many of their age group. The older men and the younger ones began to get across each other and to provide a fruitful ground for trouble. Adding to it was the feeling among some of the officers from outer London Brigades that they had been 'taken over' by London. Men who had, until now, tended to sort out money and administrative problems directly with clerks and executives whom they knew, were dealing with generally faceless officials who were totally unknown to them.

Without doubt, when Milner arrived, the new LFB under the Greater London Council was still a divided service with three operational commands, Northern, Southern and Eastern, each headed by an Assistant Chief Officer supported by a Deputy Assistant Chief Officer and their office staff. Milner thought that this was an unnecessary elongation of the chain of command which deprived Divisional Commanders of responsibility and initiative commensurate with their rank – apart from encouraging the 'split Brigade' mentality.

Among his priorities was the need to unify the Brigade. He made a point of visiting every fire station and attending as many incidents as possible. It was the way he had always worked in the past. Some of his officers felt that his 'chummy' methods were undermining their authority and affecting their discipline. At the same time he was setting his senior officers to work on a detailed review of Brigade procedure. Among its recommendations was the dissolving of the Commands and having their responsibilities devolved to the Divisions – a course which was eventually put into operation. He also strengthened his HQ staff by creating three new posts with the rank of Chief Staff Officer (a rank not included in the national rank code but "we overcame

Home Office opposition"). These officers were charged with the strategic development of fire prevention, research and logistics and operational resources.

Now too, a new operations Room, the first of its kind, was set up at Lambeth. This was to become the intelligence centre for the Brigade and although it was housed in somewhat cramped quarters, it accumulated an encyclopaedic mass of information, particularly on hazardous materials, and was often drawn on by other services including, on one occasion, the master of a ship on fire in the Caribbean, who radioed Lambeth for advice.

During his visits to fire stations, Milner had listened (often informally, over a cup of tea and a 'wad' of bread and cheese in the mess room – another source of attack from his critics) to many complaints over conditions and equipment. In Hong Kong negotiations to put right such matters meant dealing with one person. Milner soon learned that compromises had to be reached in long negotiations with the Unions, the Home Office-based Central Fire Brigades Advisory Council with its standards and doctrines to conform to and, in respect of pay and conditions, the National Joint Council's agreements to be adhered to as well as the financial controllers and the politicians. Provision of new fire stations, above all, was a nightmare – planning permission had to be obtained, objections from the public who did not want to lose their fire station and from the public who did not want a fire station on their doorstep had to be countered, as well as the phenomenal cost of building a station, particularly if the ground was not already owned by the Brigade. A fire station which before the war would have cost thousands was now reckoned in millions of pounds.

Milner quoted one example of his difficulties. He wanted to provide the men with an improved hand lamp. Once the decision to replace it was accepted, the search for, trials of and decision-making between all factions involved absorbed a whole year before the replacement could be issued.

This having been said, he was quick to emphasise that it did not mean he had met opposition at every turn. He knew that one or two of his senior officers were disdainful of his background as a 'colonial' who knew nothing about the traditional problems of London, and who were not averse to the odd remark about 'junk escapes', but these were rare exceptions – and he admitted that there was more than a grain of truth in some of their remarks. 'I was very vague about British regulations and practices and I leant heavily on my immediate subordinates to guide me through these minefields. Luckily, I was blessed with a supportive corps of loyal, dedicated and progressive-minded senior commanders and non-uniformed staff and I instilled the philosophy that there were no such things as problems, only challenges. I

was also fortunate in having a succession of amenable Committee chairmen and County Hall administrators. Operational matters, then, were always treated as "apolitical".'

With hindsight, there were times when the problems facing him must have seemed ludicrous, yet they all demanded time, nervous energy and public money to solve them. Beards were a perfect example. For almost half a century, men in the Brigade had been clean-shaven (before that, few firemen had worn BA). Now the 'hippy' fashions of the 'Swinging Age' demanded that beards should be worn and some of the younger firemen began appearing on duty with wild and bushy growths – fine for fashion but useless with breathing apparatus when the 'fuzz' broke the air-tight seal with the skin.

Milner tried to insist that all firemen should be clean-shaven but the Union argued that men had the right to grow beards if they wanted. Hours were spent in industrial negotiations over beards, always under the 'Emergencies Only' threat. Meanwhile, the already hard-pressed HQ staff were diligently trawling manufacturers for positive pressure masks. This, the ultimate solution, took months of research to perfect at pressure which would be efficient with even the most luxurious growth.

It was against these confrontations, which were eventually becoming almost a daily event, that he continued to assess the future needs of the Brigade and ways of meeting them with optimum efficiency. Industrial technology was advancing even faster now, bringing in its train a bewildering increase in the variety, quantity and use of hazardous substances in the home, in factories and on the roads.

'I could foresee the time when every domestic fire would present us with a highly toxic situation' *he recalled*. 'Polystyrene ceiling tiles, furniture upholstered with foam rubber or polyurethane, could produce dense volumes of lethal smoke and fumes, including cyanides. I therefore determined to implement a programme to provide a breathing set for every man on every appliance and hoped, ultimately, to extend it to providing each man with a personal set.'

The old 'tried and true' breathing apparatus of the LFB had always been the one-hour 'Proto' oxygen set which demanded a great deal of training time, technical competence and meticulous maintenance. Milner wanted compressed air sets which, although they lasted for a shorter period, needed less training, were quicker to put on and simpler to use and maintain. The minor outcry which this produced was placated when 'Proto' was retained for special incidents, but there was still the problem of the 'Old Sweat Smoke Eaters' who felt it was effete for the wearing of

BA to be the norm rather than the exception. Eventually even they were converted.

Although Milner, before he retired, failed to achieve his target of a personal BA set for every man, he at least increased their number to such an extent that their use at fires became almost routine.

This was the period in which many parts of the world were developing their motorway systems and Britain was among them. The first section of the first motorway, the M1, had been opened in 1958 and others were progressing rapidly, bringing to the fire services of the country another enormous headache. The fast, three-lane highways were perfect for transporting goods including an immense range of hazardous substances, usually carried in large, anonymous tankers.

Crisis point was reached when a fire brigade attended a motorway accident involving a tanker and a small car. The bewildered woman driver of the car, staggering through the spillage from the tanker towards the firemen, screamed as first her shoes and then her feet began to dissolve in the chemical. The tanker driver was unconscious. There was no immediate means of discovering what the liquid was or how to deal with it. The woman was rushed to hospital, but it was some considerable time later before the firemen discovered that the material was one of the most lethal chemicals in commercial use.

It was only the beginning. Some chemicals which were spilled became dangerous if sprayed with water. Some reacted to foam. Some were swilled down the drains only to explode in the sewers. Clearly, urgent action had to be taken at all levels to control their movements. The LFB had long provided a book of hazardous substances and firemen were issued with smaller editions, but thumbing through these, perhaps on a dark, wet night, trying to work out the nature of the spilled material and whether to use water, foam or some other means of control, was time-consuming and haphazard in itself as well as potentially increasing the risks of the accident. Clear, simple information was desperately needed. Something which would tell any fireman instantly what kind of substance was being carried; whether it would release poisonous fumes if he put water or foam on it; whether it would explode if he swilled it down the drains – in a nutshell, what it was and what to do about it. Milner, who had already refined an old-established system for instantly identifying and dealing with hazardous substances in Hong Kong, put the problem to his senior officers and one of them, Charles Clisby, offered a solution.

Clisby, Divisional Officer in the old Middlesex Brigade, had been working on just such a system but it had fallen into limbo when their Brigade had been absorbed into the new GLC Service. The Middlesex scheme involved a coded sign showing by only three or four numbers, letters and symbols the characteristics of a substance and the methods of dealing with it in an emergency. 'It was so beautifully simple, as near perfection as one could devise' said Milner. 'We called it 'HAZCHEM' and I set Charles Clisby to the task of getting it recognised world wide. He needed no urging and through him and the Brigade's senior officers, the code was soon being used by countries all over the world. On the European continent, there was another system, 'KEMLER' but this relied on a catalogue of United Nations – approved identification numbers – a slower business altogether. However, many European authorities were adamant that they wanted to retain their own invention and eventually a compromise was reached embracing HAZCHEM and the UN numbers. Soon after this, all vehicles carrying hazardous substances throughout the EEC area were required to display the HAZCHEM device – a regulation which also applied to any premises in which such substances were stored or used.

Milner and his Brigade were justifiably proud. Years later, he still maintained: 'I have no doubt that HAZCHEM was one of the finest pieces of fire defence intelligence ever developed and one of the most important contributions London has made to international fire service.'

The propagation of HAZCHEM was far from the only project the Brigade was pioneering at that time. Like Shaw, the Chief Officer was once more being besieged with new ideas from all quarters, particularly from within the Brigade. His hard-pressed staff were planning and subsequently supervising the installation of integrated Video Display Unit facilities – then in their infancy but of inestimable value in the Brigade's Control Rooms. Parallel with this, they were comprehensively modernising the radio network and progressively implementing a Brigade-wide 'paging' system – again in its infancy.

When Milner had arrived in London, plans were afoot to close several suburban stations as well as reducing the number of appliances at others. To the politician – as to the layman – the demands on stations did not seem to justify their retention but the Unions were bitterly opposed to the closures and in this, Milner supported them, arguing that with traffic increasingly dense in London he could not guarantee that adjacent stations could meet the statutory attendance times and, equally important, the stations housed crews and 'garaged' appliances that were valuable 'take pumps' and reinforcing resources for other areas. At the last minute, the closures were 'indefinitely postponed' and eventually forgotten.

The London docks, so much a part of London for centuries before World War Two, were now being run down as road and air transport and 'container' packaging took over. Pressure began to mount for all the fire boats to be replaced by 'franchising' a Thames tug company. Milner himself was unhappy about the river service with one fireboat moored at Lambeth, another at Greenwich and both moving away only for operational calls and exercises. They were slow vessels – particularly against the tide – and he felt that their value was being undermined by the time it took them to reach incidents.

With the full backing of the then Fire Brigade Committee, the Brigade bought two *'Sea Trucks'* for trials. These cost little more than a good saloon car and were shallow-draught vessels, their decks resembling the 'trays' of motor lorries. They were fitted with trailer pumps and needed a two or three man crew, a sore point with the Union. River traffic at this time consisted predominately of pleasure craft and the trucks seemed ideal for dealing with fires on such vessels. The intention was that they would patrol up and down the river throughout their period of duty but although the *'floaties'*, as they were very quickly nicknamed, were enjoyable new toys and were nippy enough, they lacked protection against bad weather; they were uncomfortable for long spells of patrolling and for fires, the crews needed augmenting to get the optimum effectiveness from their equipment. Eventually one ran aground (there were rumours of sabotage) and was stranded. The trials were abandoned and the trucks sold off.

Undoubtedly though, the existing fireboats needed replacing by more powerful vessels to deal with major ship fires and to support land appliances at waterfront fires. Funds for two new boats were approved and after a long-drawn-out period of ordering, building and commissioning the *'Fire Swift'* and *'Fire Hawk'* came into service. At the same time, the Brigade tried out an experiment in driving motor pumps aboard the Woolwich ferry and using them while she was under way. This proved successful and an agreement was signed to use the ferry in the event of a major dockland fire.

Another disappointment to Milner was the failure of trials of the small, *Haflinger*, narrow-tracked, four wheel drive trucks which were capable of travelling up and down staircases of subways and high-rise buildings. One of these was tried out in London, but the density of traffic and its modest operational payload – it could only carry a two man crew – more than offset its other advantages.

It was about this time too, that the Brigade chartered a helicopter and perfected drills for using them for rescue and firefighting. Financially it was impossible for the LFB to have its own helicopter but the hope existed that the GLC would buy a machine which could be shared by all its departments. Unfortunately, the Council at that time had set its face against planning consent for a heliport in Central London

and mainly for this reason, refused to buy a helicopter for any purpose. There had been other problems, including that of finding suitable landing pads close to incidents, of transporting enough equipment and of landing it at reasonable speed. It underlined Brigade policy however, of meeting minimum attendance times by sending appliances from stations in two different directions to any incident in an attempt to dodge the traffic.

Two other schemes were more successful: Milner's embryonic ideas on what became known as *'thermal imaging'* and a new system of radio communications. The GLC's Scientific Branch (lost to the capital when the GLC was dissolved but employed on a contract basis by the LFB after that date) took on the task of producing a prototype thermal imaging camera, while the Home Office scientists were researching a radio communication – dubbed 'Figaro' – which, among other things, would work efficiently in sub-surface situations including deep tunnels and underground railways. Communications between BA wearers and Entry Control officers to eliminate tele-line systems by providing some form of throat-microphone radio system was another challenge for the 'boffins' of the fire service.

Throughout this time, the Brigade was busy operationally with its customary quota of large and small fires, but fortuitously, no big disasters until one quiet spring morning in the heart of the City. In retirement, Milner remembered it:

'If the most Machiavellian Course Director at a Staff College had set a scenario for an emergency exercise, in timing and tragedy he could not have set one more complex and horrific than the Moorgate Disaster.'

On February 28th 1975, at 8.45 am, the peak of the rush hour, a mild, reliable London Underground motorman drove his crowded six coach train at 40 mph into a short dead-end tunnel, 51 feet underground at Moorgate Underground Station in the heart of the old City of London. The first fire officer on the scene faced the sight of the three leading coaches crushed into little more than the length of a London bus – 156 feet of metal, compressed and contorted round 42 dead and injured passengers in a 60-foot tunnel. It was the City Police Officer who summed up the immediate reaction of the emergency services: *'never, in our wildest imagination, had we dreamt of anything like this!'*

No time was wasted in astonishment. Major Accident Procedure was called for and the services acted instantly, combining to couple experience with common sense and instinct in dealing with the horror. The preparation was all there. For some time there had been regular meetings of the London Emergency Services Joint Planning Committee to decide on the action to be taken in the event of a disaster in the capital, particularly in the City with its high buildings and narrow streets, lanes and courtyards. Indeed, it was not long since a full exercise had been held at nearby Britannic House. Now BP's medical team from Britannic House was among the first to answer the call from the emergency services.

Because the incident was so deep underground, normal radio communications were virtually useless. Doctors working with the rescuers in the tunnel had no way of passing back messages other than by word of mouth – which all too often developed into a game of 'Chinese Whispers' against the roar of the Cengar saws and other cold cutting equipment. Sentences like 'the doctor needs Entonox' (a pain killing drug) became 'the doctor needs an empty box'. It was nobody's fault. These were exactly the conditions for which *'Figaro'* was being developed and now the Brigade appealed to Plessey, the company which had produced the experimental communication unit, to bring it out from under wraps for urgent use. It was released instantly and rushed to the scene where it proved a godsend. If the firemen were short of any item of equipment, police motor cyclists toured the City building sites to beg or borrow tools which were readily provided to be rushed back to the tunnel.

Firemen from every station in London arrived in shifts and worked for five days, in heat which which at times reached 120F. With foul air and an oxygen level down to 16% and at one time, such was the high risk of epidemic and infection, that every man was inoculated before he could descend to the tunnel and the slightest cut meant immediate withdrawal. The Brigade appealed to the Army who brought in decontamination and mobile ablution units, after which all firemen were put through full decontamination procedure on entering and leaving the scene, complete with a total change of clothing every time. (One of the better outcomes of "Moorgate" was the provision of such vans for the Brigade itself.)

Although the last of the live passengers, a young policewoman whose foot had to be amputated, was released by ten o'clock on the night of the accident, it was four days before the final victim – the driver – was released, under close scrutiny of independent advisers. There was no doubt that the cause of the accident was the failure of the driver to stop the train, but why he failed was never discovered and, indeed, became a perpetual source of discussion and speculation among pathologists world-wide. The inquest verdict was 'Accidental Death'.

Moorgate was one of the worst peace-time disasters ever to face the LFB and proved to be a triumph of organisation and co-operation between the Brigade, the City of London Police, the Metropolitan Police and the London Transport Police, the London Ambulance Service, the St John Ambulance Brigade and the WRVS. As always the Salvation Army,

who had an arrangement with the LFB, had set up a canteen on an adjoining platform where they fed and 'watered' exhausted firemen and offered a welcome counselling service, above all to the younger men for whom this was a particularly fearsome 'blooding.'

Moorgate was controlled by senior officers but the Chief Officer visited the scene throughout the five days of clearance work – so discreetly that many men failed to realise who he was. One said later 'I was trying to release a trapped passenger when my hacksaw blade snapped. I swore and shouted to a bloke standing nearby 'get me another one mate!' He went off immediately and returned with a new blade. It was only then that one of my mates told me that the 'bloke' was the Chief Officer.'

A Station Officer, collapsed with exhaustion, stripped in the heat and slouched with his men by the tunnel wall, did recognise him. 'I was sure I was in for a rollicking when I suddenly saw the Chief Officer approaching – no tunics, no belts, no helmets – you couldn't wear them in the heat and the cramped area of the crushed coaches. He just stopped and asked us how it had been, chatted for a bit then said "well done all of you" and went away. It was marvellous – just the boost we needed, he understood and said all the right things.' Moorgate was a triumph for the Brigade, but it brought more work for the 'Chief' and his HQ staff. Inquests, Inquiries, special meetings at the Home Office to respond to the public outcry which follows so many headline-making accidents. Improvements were demanded, recommendations made – but were they implemented?

Looking back, fifteen years later, Milner said 'in all honesty, I don't think so. *"We'll have to see to it"* was a well-worn delaying tactic of some authorities. While a disaster was "hot" publicity the intentions were good but when the outcry died down, the urgency seemed to give way to complacency. I suspect that many of the recommendations may have gathered dust on some planning officer's desk for a very long time.'

There is no doubt that the Moorgate disaster worsened the tense situation which already existed between the LFB and the London Transport authorities. Milner remembered an earlier top level meeting between him and his officers and the Underground 'hierarchy' which, he said, *'left me with the indelible impression that they were far too complacent about their safety record and precautions and somewhat cavalier in their dealings with other professionals.'*

London Transport had been seeking planning permission for a major hotel complex over one of their stations and not only the Brigade but the GLC Architects' Department objected to the scheme on safety grounds.

'At the meeting when they pressed for acceptance of the

plans, their officials were adamant to the point of arrogance that there was nothing that would burn in their Underground system, or that would pose a threat to the proposed hotel. They insisted that they would not have allowed people to travel on the system if there were any chance of this. Although the Brigade produced evidence from all over the world of underground railway fires, LT brushed it aside and persisted in their assertion that there was no real risk of fire from their coaches or stations. We were concerned, not just because we knew there was a risk from flammable and combustible material but also at their professional arrogance when confronted with clear evidence of this. The objections of the GLC and the LFB were upheld and planning consent was refused, but the last, tragic word came years later at Kings Cross.'

By the middle of the 1970s there was no doubt that the Brigade was beginning to change course, spurred on by nationwide industrial unrest in pursuit of higher pay and shorter hours. 'Emergencies Only' action at brigades all over the country was widespread. Glasgow Fire Brigade went on full strike. London and other brigades were threatening to follow suit.

Milner felt to some extent, there was justice in the men's claims and although tradition demanded that the Chief Officer remain silent, he felt he must declare his hand. In December 1974, a horrific fire at the Worsley Hotel in Paddington had trapped and nearly roasted alive several of his officers and one promising young fireman, *Hamish Pettit*, had been killed. (Four Queen's Gallantry Medals and three Queen's Commendations for Brave Conduct had been awarded after this incident alone, plus a Posthumous Queen's Commendation for Bravery to Hamish Pettit. The fire is described in Gordon Honeycombe's book 'Red Watch'.)

With, this and other recent fires in mind, no doubt, Milner, during an after-lunch speech to an influential group of Rotarians, gave one of the finest descriptions ever, of a modern firefighter's work. He quoted first, the conclusion of the Cunningham Report:

'the job of the basic grade of fireman is broadly comparable with industrial jobs in the top semi-skilled categories of the lower ranges of the skilled trades....' *Following that, came Shaw's words:* 'A fireman, to be successful, must enter buildings. He must get in below, above, on every side; from opposite houses, over back walls, over skylights, through holes cut by himself in gates, walls and the roof. He must know how to reach the attic from the basement by ladders placed on half-burned stairs, and the basement from the attic by a rope

made fast on a chimney. His whole success depends on his getting in and remaining there, and he must always carry his appliances with him as, without them, he is of no use.'

'Let me tell you', *said Milner,* 'what it is like to be a fireman in London to-day....

'The fireman begins each tour of duty by parading in full fire-fighting gear, when he is given precise directions about which appliance he is to ride during his shift. After an inspection, he places his gear on the appliance to which he has been assigned and always in the same place, so that when the calls come there can be no confusion, no hesitation. His routine continues with the checking of the appliance and the equipment. He makes sure his breathing apparatus fits and is properly adjusted and that his life-support gas-cylinder is functioning.

The appliance lockers are opened, their contents are checked .... so that they can be picked up in an emergency – whatever the time of day or night and whatever the weather. After this there will be continuation training drills, repeatedly practised, until each man instinctively knows his part and the roles of others on his team and can act speedily, efficiently, and virtually without any directive – as he will have to do, under great stress, when the chips are down.

'The bells go down. The firemen on duty, whether at drills, lectures, meals or at rest, race to their appliances. The drivers rev up impatiently, while the teleprinter chatters out the address of the emergency. Brief directions are given to the driver; the appliance-room doors swing open, and the appliances turn out. Now comes the often hair-raising drive through dense traffic. Speed is vital, but so is safety. Two-tone horns and flashing blue lights help to clear the road and serve also to reassure those in trouble that help is on the way. While the driver concentrates on the route, the others in the crew are struggling into their fire-gear and checking the location of the hydrants. The officer-in-charge is mentally running through his topographical knowledge of the area, wondering what kind of property will face them .... the adrenalin is pumping through each man, keying him up for action, making him ready for some as yet – unknown demand on his system .... often the arrival is an anti-climax, a false alarm .... the men feel washed-out and lethargic. Many times, the adrenalin is needed. Some superhuman effort is demanded of them and is always, thank God, forthcoming.'

It might be a fire in a supermarket – four floors and a basement, all smoke clogged. 'The officer-in-charge will radio for reinforcing appliances and to organise firemen wearing breathing apparatus in the search for any casualties and for the seat of the fire. The teams will grope their way forward, keeping close together, so that they may aid each other if trouble comes. They must remember each door they pass through, each turn they make, so that there can be no confusion about the way out. Each foot must be placed carefully, lest floors, weakened by fire, or rot, give way and plunge them into an inferno. Always they are aware of the heat. Its growing intensity tells them when they are approaching the source. And they must always be alert for a sudden build-up of superheated gases which may detonate a flash-over – a ball of flame scorching all in its path.

'Outside the building, other firemen are pumping water on the flames. Inside, as the search progresses, it may be found that the fire is in the basement. Tugging with them their heavy, charged hose, the firemen must find or force a way down. On their rumps or bellies now, they will be hot and sweaty, their clothing will be covered in filth and saturated with water. They stumble on to a stairway, and as they go down it the heat-band, a band of high temperature gases which builds up at ceiling level, toasts their exposed skin. Totally blinded by thick smoke, they feel their way down each step ..... spraying water to cool the atmosphere as they reach the foot of the stairs. They may be confronted with a confusion of passageways. These they must penetrate and explore..... Suddenly, the fire flares up somewhere in front. Jets of water are directed at the flames and a dense cloud of hissing scalding steam envelops them. Isolated from the outside, knowing only their own little part of the whole affair, they hang on, trusting that others are also playing their part and that their means of retreat are being securely held..... Soon they know they are winning. The scalding heat begins to lose its sting. The air at the lowest level begins to cool. By wiping their goggles and tucking their heads down they begin to see ..... they move on, searching for small pockets of fire ..... but now they are tired. That remarkable something that drove them on has evaporated. They are wet, chilled and will be glad to see the outside again....'

There were other risks. 'Stone staircases which heat and then cool suddenly, are prone to collapse without warning. There are gas-cylinders, heated up to explosive potential; chemicals which produce deadly gases; radiation risks – all adding their complications to a fireman's problems. Above all, there is the human tragedy..... Homes destroyed, burns, injuries, the suffering of children. Sometimes, sadly, we are too late........ Then there is the task of picking up the charred body of some unfortunate and wrapping it in a sheet, before taking it to a waiting ambulance outside. There are also the moments of sheer satisfaction – to snatch a child from peril and breathe back life into a seemingly lifeless body – to take a whimpering child the pet she prematurely

mourns – to be able to tell a distraught wife; *"he's alright dear. We've got him. He's alright."'*

And the special service call, with heavy rescue equipment and men finding themselves waist-deep in floodwaters, rescuing people or pumping out flooded premises. The rescues at train crashes, where the casualties suffer terrible injuries.

'Firemen risk injury to themselves releasing animals that have been sucked into sewage pits or bogged down in muddy river-beds; they climb trees and houses to rescue cats ..... they cut, pull, push at metal to get people from their crushed cars. They venture into clouds of ammonia fumes, seeking the valve that will close off the leak. They climb great heights and ... cajole, try to persuade some temporarily deranged person from jumping to his death. They release a child whose head is stuck in railings; they rescue people trapped in lifts and when, in the factory, people get their limbs caught in machinery, again, it's Mr Emergency who comes along to get them out.....'

With his audience by now transfixed, Milner finally described the fate of two firemen, caught in an explosion during a fire in the basement of a London restaurant: *'Both men were burned – severely burned. Taken to hospital, they were suspended above their beds, for there was no unburned part of their bodies on which they could lie. For three days they suffered; and then, one shortly after another, they died. They paid the full price and, some might say, much more.....'*

He apologised for the drama of his talk, but he explained *'I felt you would like to know something of what you get, as ratepayers, from your firemen, from every uniformed and non-uniformed man and woman in fire-stations, control rooms and workshops of the Brigade. Together, they help to make the London Fire Brigade second to none – and better than most.'*

Seldom can an after-lunch speech have made a greater impression. Two days later, Union leaders met Milner, his senior officers and the GLC Industrial Relations staff and hammered out a draft formula for new pay and conditions. Within the week Glasgow's strike was called off and industrial action throughout the country ended. Three weeks later, the National Joint Council for Fire Authorities had completed an agreement which, among other things, provided for what, in those days, was a substantial pay increase and a substantial reduction of a working week.

The Unions, recalling with some justice the historical procrastinations on fire brigade business, now demanded swift action and managed to secure an NJC undertaking that the 40-hour week would be implemented in nine months – an appallingly brief deadline. In London, several thousand men had to be recruited to allow for the shorter working hours. Uniforms and equipment needed to be found for them and they had to go through three months of essential training. It was a mammoth challenge which involved almost daily meetings, massive co-operation to cut through the 'red tape' of customary formal procedures, and a series of ad-hoc measures which finally resulted in the 40-hour week being implemented in London before any other brigade in the country.

At one stage, London had 40 recruit squads at emergency 'training schools', mostly prefabricated cabins based at fire stations throughout the GLC area. Even the suppliers of uniform had difficulty in keeping pace with the demands and at times Milner was sending his officers out to shop in the Old Kent Road for extra equipment. "Until then, men had been issued with two fire helmets, but at one stage we were so short that we had to ask them to return one for re-issue to recruits' he said.

The enormous and rapid influx naturally changed the nature of the Brigade and there were complaints from the 'old hands' that the LFB was *'lowering its standards'*. On the other hand, the slightest slowing down brought furious Union accusations that the Brigade was *'dragging its heels'*.

Officers who once dealt with a few men at a time, and understood them all well, were now overwhelmed with men they had no time to get to know. With more men and shorter shifts, more officers were needed and providing these took longer than taking in recruits. Milner realised with chagrin that men were becoming estranged from their officers – and the established customs of the LFB. *Esprit de corps* was suffering too; with so many men, individuals attended fewer fires and it was reaching the stage when retained firemen on 'round the clock' call in the 'shires' were getting more experience of real fires than the London professionals.

Milner recalled, 'the militant Union elements had become so *"all seeing"* that an officer could barely open a door, a fireman polish a piece of brass, without Union representatives presenting themselves at Lambeth HQ demanding negotiations on the subject, armed with the threat of imposing an *"Emergencies only"* action. Many of these actions were headed off by compromises, but when they were imposed they 'conned' the public who did not realise that the action placed an embargo on such jobs as servicing BA sets, repairs to appliances and generally keeping hose and equipment up to scratch. So, for example, equipment used at a fire often would not be replaced. That put those items out of commission for the duration of the action and the crew merely sat out the time in their stations, refusing to turn out. If we sent out a mechanic to repair a minor fault like a traffic indicator, the appliance would be

"blacked" and we would have to negotiate to get it *"un-blacked"*. Of the 114 fire stations in London there were occasions when 60%–80% were "off the run". The brigade eventually reached the stage where *"Emergencies only"* was sardonically referred to as *"Normal working"*.

'This was a period when laughter began to die in my soul' Milner admitted. 'At one period we had to arrange for the Metropolitan Police to respond to calls. It was humiliating and when, after the action was called off, I wrote to thank the Commissioner of Police, and he replied "it's all part of our service", I felt very inferior. Men were kept on full pay during these actions and, to be fair, most were very shamefaced and even opposed to *"Emergencies only"*. For the most part, they were in the thrall of their Union. If they ignored the Union edicts they feared they could be *"blacked"* for life, abused and ostracised in the Mess rooms. Whenever I pressed the ruling politicians to stop the pay of men who failed to respond to fires, I was castigated for being *"born with a gun in my mouth."'*

During one such dispute when he felt that the men were not fully au fait with what was on offer, he took the unprecedented step of broadcasting the full details over the Brigade's radio network – despite dire warnings that it was strictly illegal. 'All stations were instructed to stand by appliances at the morning change over of Watches and I spelled out details of what was on the table with a warning that there just wasn't any more left in the kitty.' It produced, he knew some ribald comments but there was no prosecution and the opposition seemed to moderate

Until this period, Joe Milner had taken the rough with the smooth and thrived on what he called the 'hurly burly' of his work in London. 'I can't recall a morning when I was reluctant to get to my office or wasn't at my desk by 8 am. I had a good supporting team to share the burden – top line officers like Chisnall, Burrell, Miller, Sennet, Watkins, Roundell; Albert Trewick, Chief Executive, and Tom Richardson, the Industrial Relations Officer. We worked hard and played hard in the social sense – the Annual Ball, the fêtes, the sports calendar and all the entertainments run by the Divisions – usually in aid of charity.' Even his relations with the Union representatives were not wholly hostile – 'daggers drawn across the negotiating table but I appreciated they had a job to do and outside negotiations, relations with most of them were amicable' he said.

By now, however, the meetings, the negotiations, the arguments and the delays were beginning to affect him. His official day was often split between the GLC at County Hall, discussions at the Home Office, the National Joint Council and half a dozen other official bodies and, above all, the Trades Unions who insisted on dealing with him alone or, in his absence, with his deputy, DCO Burrell.

Union officials had the advantage of being able to work in shifts and during protracted sessions of negotiating, they would change their staff while the Chief Officer and his team had to stay on, often late into the night, rather than allow the Brigade to be put on to 'Emergencies only' yet again. Ironically, the GLC actually paid Union representatives, or awarded them time off in lieu, for the time they spent in negotiations. At one time, the men had accumulated so much 'negotiating time' that it cost several thousand pounds to 'buy off' their time owing. While 'Emergencies only' could be imposed at a moment's notice, it often took several days for the union to put the Brigade back on to full duties when an agreement had been concluded.

Towards the end of 1975, Milner became depressed that the vital work of developing the Brigade to keep pace with the demands of London, was being held up by the welter of paperwork and negotiations. 'At meetings with the Home Office I got the impression that politicians were apathetic about the needs of the fire service generally. Unions were again demanding substantial increases in salaries and further changes in conditions of service, but I could not impress the authorities with the urgent need to take action on these claims. Meanwhile, the Unions were adept at leaving agreements with one more item to discuss and discovering this in the process of implementation to provide a loophole for re-opening negotiations.'

Complaints and demands ranged from the slow progress of the 'over-40s' medical examinations, differential qualification tests for long-serving and shorter service men; the abandonment of hook ladders; the abolition of 'live' carrying-down drills; new style uniforms; the restrictions on home-to-duty travelling allowances (Milner had agreed to the payment of travelling allowances to the new recruits and London firemen now included a sheep farmer from Northumberland and at least one man who travelled 200 miles from Devon for his spell of duty), down to the provision of sun-glasses for drivers. The repercussions were taking their toll of the long-suffering and hard-pressed clerical staff and engineering personnel.

In an effort to promote greater progress and to foster trust in the Brigade's integrity, Milner instituted a Joint Staff Relations Unit, chaired by a senior commander and composed of delegates of the various representative bodies. They were charged with speeding up the implementation of agreements, with investigating delays and promoting measures to eradicate them. 'It was akin to a Works Council' he explained 'but I'm afraid it was too far ahead of its time for a uniformed and disciplined service. It did achieve a great deal, but it became something of a "Star Chamber", rudely interrogating many personnel whom it called to its "presence" about some alleged tardiness or omission.' Some

officers refused, point blank, to submit to its interrogations.

'The enigma, the paradox of it all was that the London firemen were, with few exceptions, marvellous' said Milner. 'They were indefatigable on firegrounds, worked like stink in promoting charity projects especially for the Fire Services National Benevolent Fund. They would push a heavy, wheeled escape ladder from London to Brighton, organise and participate in top class AAA (Amateur Athletic Association) meetings and fêtes at their stations. I had always found that the successive Chairmen of the Fire Brigade Committee of the GLC, particularly my last one, John Henry, a former London fireman, treated me and my submissions with the greatest respect and the Committee was undoubtedly the best to be involved with. On the whole it was not so politically partisan as other committees. But they did not always have the last word. Their proposals had to be passed on through other committees for full Council assent. There had never been an occasion when I was finally denied anything for the Brigade, although I'd had to fight hard for some things. Now, it was all becoming too much.

'I was beginning to suffer from neurasthenia. I have to admit that there was another woman in my life whom I loved deeply. My wife and I had separated, but after 30 years together I still cared for her very much. Her deteriorating health worried me. Milner hoped that he might be allowed to take 'sabbatical' leave – as senior officers had in the Colonial Service, but this was not to be.

Early in 1976, after several searching examinations it was agreed that he should be retired on medical grounds. His retirement became effective on 30th June 1976, twelve days before his wife died.

The first major firemen's strike began at the end of the year. By then he had married again and begun a course in Business Management before moving to Norfolk.

Since the wintry day on which he had absorbed his sixpenny arithmetic book and decided to commit his future to the fire service, he had been awarded the CBE and the Queen's Fire Service Medal, had been Director of the Hong Kong Fire Services, Chief Officer of the London Fire Brigade, a member of the Board of the Fire Service College, the Central Fire Brigades Advisory Council, the National Joint Council for Local Authority Fire Brigades, Chairman of the London Fire Liaison Panel and London Local Radio Advisory Panel, Fire Adviser to the Association of Metropolitan Authorities, Chairman of the Fire Services National Benevolent Fund as well as a Fellow of the Institution of Fire Engineers, an Associate Member of the Institute of British Engineers and a Council Member of the Order of St John.

The post of Chief Officer now moved to another Northerner.

29

A Leader from the North

FIREMEN

Reporter asked me: 'What's it like?!
I shrugged him off: 'I couldn't say.
You see, I'm not a one for that,
Not one for bragging, anyway.'

He pressed me hard – and so I tried;
I hoped my tale he understood.
Could it be that telling him
Might do this job a bit of good?

'If you put on six overcoats –
And though you suffered hell from corns
You crammed your feet in army boots –
Wore on your head a crown of thorns –
Lay in a bath, first hot, then cold –
Got out and ran a mile or so –
Into an oven squeezed yourself

And turned to nine the Regulo;
If, with a bandage round your eyes,
A wooden peg clipped on your nose,
You then crawled through a concrete maze,
Your feet wrapped round with yards of hose –
You'd get a notion what it's like.'

Reporter laughed; 'It can't be true.'

I looked him in the eyes and said:
'You're right. Five overcoats will do'.

DACO Charles Clisby

PETER HOWARD DARBY CBE CStJ QFSM, TOOK OVER FROM Joe Milner on January 1st 1977 at a time of crisis for industry in the country generally and the fire service in particular. His unsurpassed experience and record, not just as a working fireman but as an organiser and administrator both in the north west of England and at government level had undoubtedly influenced the GLC members who appointed him. Here, above all, was a man who knew the full background of fire service legislation in Britain, who had commanded the prestigious Greater Manchester Fire Brigade and had worked at top level with the Home Office and with all the major firefighting organisations – and the trades unions.

It had not always been so. Once more, the new Chief

Officer had not nurtured a lifelong ambition to fight fires. His father had been an engineer and for generations their family had lived in the 'Black Country' where he was born. His mother had died when he was still a small boy and, along with his brothers, he had been moved round the family until he was finally sent to school at a Jesuit college in Oxford. When the Second World War started he was continuing his education on a part-time basis at the Birmingham College of Advanced Technology, very athletic, a swimmer, ABA boxer, cyclist, soccer player – 'one didn't want to be out of things…' He was 18 years old when he joined the Royal Navy and within three months saw action, helping to defend a convoy of merchant ships against attack from a 'wolf pack' of German U-boats in the North Atlantic. His work was defence and anti-sabotage, sailing as armed crew with the merchant fleet to protect them against air and submarine attacks and possible sabotage in foreign ports.

The job became even more hazardous when he was transferred to defending ammunition ships, crossing the Mediterranean in support of the Allied troops fighting in North Africa. On D-Day he had sailed from Cardiff, helping to protect the American Forces and was on one of the first ammunition ships to move up the River Seine, supplying the invasion troops advancing to liberate Paris. He recalled it calmly: 'Looking back, it was hair-raising at times. Had the ammunition exploded we would have all disappeared but at that age we weren't much troubled.' When the war in Europe ended, he was posted to a troopship, the 'Mooltan', armed to the teeth and sailing to help regain Singapore. They were still on the way when the atom bomb was dropped, the war ended and they put in to Colombo to help bring home the British troops who had been prisoners-of-war of the Japanese.

During the long periods at sea, Darby prevailed upon various ship's officers to help him improve his education. They appreciated the difficulties of a young man, missing out in this area and enjoyed the unusual challenge as something different from the routine.

When the war ended, he found himself in naval barracks in Liverpool, anticipating demobilisation and, again, anxious to improve his education – to such an extent that the Navy agreed to him attending their educational centre in the Liver Building until his demob papers eventually arrived.

Back home in Birmingham, the prospects of work looked poor. Industry was run down and he decided to join the police. On the way to enrol he and a mate passed the great Central Fire Station and remembered they had a friend serving there. 'He showed us round, mentioned that they were short of recruits and within a week we had sat the entrance examinations, were accepted and joined the NFS.' He trained at Sutton Coldfield but experienced his first big fire during his initial posting at Wednesbury – 'a timber yard – an enormous blaze and most exhilarating.' But Wednesbury was a rural brigade and he missed the discipline and dedication of the professional firefighters in the city so much that, at one point, he wondered whether he had chosen the right job. Soon after this he went back to Birmingham where the fire and ambulance service were being combined under the City Authority. He was already beginning to gain experience of organising and administration.

This increased when he became involved in the new national examinations for the Fire Service which had emerged with the growing realisation of the need to improve firemens' technical knowledge in the post-war build up of industry. Soon after this he was promoted to Staff Officer,

already facing the challenges of high-rise housing developments, motorway planning and the accident risks of road and rail tunnel incidents – at much the same time as Leete was struggling with them in London.

Eventually, he returned to the Central Fire Station in Birmingham, not as a wondering recruit but as Officer-in-Charge. 'By now I was married and we were living in the Fire Station. My two children were reared over the appliance room and every time the great doors flew open the whole of our flat shook, but we were a real family and we were a part of it all, living the Fire Brigade.'

Problems in Birmingham, like London and other big cities, included a massive influx of immigrants, mostly Asian, as the British Empire gradually dissolved. In Birmingham they were concentrated in the Handsworth area, bringing nightmares of overcrowding, rooms divided into two sections by a curtain and housing two families; of people who had been accustomed to a hot climate, struggling to keep warm with unsteady portable heaters and storing their paraffin in baths below the staircase. For the firefighters there were the added complications of language and of never knowing how many people were in a house or roof space when it caught fire.

Coupled with this, as industry recovered and began to expand, was the build-up of the car industry in Birmingham. The old, small factories were rapidly being replaced by open production lines in huge works where whole car bodies were dipped into great tanks of paint. Containers of an assortment of highly inflammable materials were scattered through open areas where there was nothing to stop a fire racing from end to end once it had got a hold. 'At one stage we had fires in almost every big car plant – Jaguar, Humber, Morris, General Motors – and there was very great concern for improved safety measures' Darby recalled. Teams of fire officers set to work to draw up fire prevention and protection procedure but meanwhile, the firemen themselves were facing a new danger.

Peter Darby had breathed smoke for long enough to recognise the problem – like many firemen of his era, he never lost the tell-tale sound in his voice and breathing.

'In those days you took some smoke, you sweated, had a glass of beer and a cough and cleared it all away. Now this was not so. The glass of beer didn't work and the men began to feel ill. Gradually we realised that the new products in the car industry, the vinyls and plastics, were producing dangerous fumes when they caught fire. It was something we hadn't experienced before and brought the urgent need for more effective breathing apparatus which would offer adequate protection to the firemen. We started a call for improved BA and this, slowly and steadily, has been provided, although it took some time to destroy the outdated "macho" image of the old "smoke-eaters".'

By the late 1950's, Darby had been promoted to Divisional Officer and had become one of the twelve Regional Staff Officers specifically concerned with Civil Defence. As the international situation worsened, he found himself involved not only in local firefighting but also in plans for setting up a seat of government for his Region in the event of nuclear attack or invasion when, as in the Second World War, the country would have been divided into twelve independent areas.

'We had thousands of fire engines stockpiled, mostly "Green Goddesses" – (green painted pumps produced primarily for the armed services) and thousands of plastic containers to make artificial lakes for water storage, with a variety of rural areas of land earmarked for siting them. There were plans for distributing supplies and for mobile columns of 100 vehicles if necessary, to move from one place to another.

As the crises in Berlin and in Cuba intensified, our preparations increased until we reached a day when the whole of Britain, unknown to most of the population, was poised on the brink of war. Aircraft were on stand-by to evacuate the government to Canada and I, along with my fellow senior officers, said goodbye to our families and headed for a specially prepared bunker, ready for the confrontation. Mercifully, nothing happened, the international situation quietened down and we all went home.' *It had been valuable experience.*

Darby's sights now were set on the post of Chief Officer of Birmingham and to this end he became Deputy Chief Officer of the joint Suffolk and Ipswich Brigade, followed by a Home Office Command Course to train as a Chief Officer. In 1966 he was appointed Chief Officer of Nottinghamshire and from there, went on to take over the largest County Brigade in the country – Lancashire. He stayed with them until 1974, by which time the Heath Government had decided to reorganise local government in Britain, which was traumatic for the north west. Great areas containing such cities as Manchester and Liverpool were split up and 25 local fire brigades reduced to three large units. As the re-appointment of officers began, Darby was offered two sought-after positions – Chief Officer of Lancashire and of the new Greater Manchester Fire Service. He opted for Greater Manchester and, in addition, became Fire Commander for the huge No. 10 North West Region. The new Local Government Act was coming into force and his work involved supporting 21 fire authorities in his area.

Once again, he was facing the problem which London had experienced when the outer boroughs struggled to make sure that the old London Fire Brigade would not dominate their own proud brigades. Equally, the surrounding towns fought to avoid being swallowed up by Greater Manchester and considerable tact and diplomacy was needed to mould the new fire service into one united force.

It was solved, to some extent, when Darby appointed a younger but experienced officer from the Midlands, Ronald Bullers, as his deputy. Between them they altered the Divisions, splitting the powerful old Manchester City Brigade and building a new, modern headquarters on a totally different site from the old one, partly to gain more space and partly to underline the determination to make this a totally new, united Force.

Life in the north was changing fast. Vast imports of cheap cotton goods meant that the home industry was in decline and Darby's men faced a succession of fires in the old, multi-storeyed 'dark, satanic' cotton mills. For generations, the solid wooden floors had absorbed the dust, the fluff and the spillage of oil from the spinning and weaving machinery. Now, as the mills were divided up into 'mini' production areas for smaller industries, there was a spate of fires.

'The mills burned quickly and collapsed rapidly as the supporting iron girders expanded in the heat and pushed out the walls' *explained Darby*, 'but there was also another hazard. The intense heat distilled the oil and grease which had gathered under the old machinery and the distillation released an explosive gas which gathered in any confined space. When fire eventually reached it, the concentration of gas exploded with enormous force. This was exactly the pattern at Kings Cross, and when I was called in as an independent assessor to examine the cause of that disaster, I came away convinced that the build up of dust, fluff and oil in the escalator machinery had been the fundamental cause of the disastrous fire and explosion there.'

Darby's had been a spectacular career in the north. Few men in the country could have had such wide experience of the whole range of firefighting, on both the practical and administrative sides, and at the period when 25% of the operational work of a fireman involved rescue work, particularly on the new network of motorways in the north of England. Crashes were almost daily events and fog brought the infamous multi-vehicle pile-ups.

But he also knew of the problems in the capital.

'By now, firemen in the rest of the country felt that London was behind in its technology and its attitudes, but was unaware of it. There was also a problem of industrial relations – the "Star Chamber" saga included. At one stage the officers' Trade Union was at odds with the firemens' trade Union and the administrative Unions. Eventually the matter went to arbitration and the ACAS (Advisory, Conciliation and Arbitration Service) Report was very critical of the whole situation.'

Partly because he was happy to continue in the north until his retirement, he did not apply for the London vacancy until it was suggested by the Home Office. 'I was very comfortable in Greater Manchester, I didn't really want to go to London but it was a challenge I couldn't resist. I applied and got the job. There was much trauma there because London, in its still-insular way, did not want anyone from outside. A lot of the elected members didn't and of course, the officers didn't. The GLC knew that there was trouble over the matter of fare allowances for firemen, trouble with the manning of appliances and in many other areas.' At his first meeting with one of the ACAS team, he had been somewhat taken aback when the Chairman shook him by the hand and said 'Well, Mr Darby, I wish you all the best in your new appointment, but I have never met such an intransigent crowd of people in all my life.....'

Darby felt that what the LFB needed was a strong lead. 'In the period between the retirement of Joe Milner and my appointment, the Brigade had been run with great efficiency by the Deputy Chief Officer, Don Burrell. When I arrived, he could have been very difficult, but he was not. He proved to be a wonderful man and I had a constant feed of background information from him. Because of the ACAS ruling and the recognition by the officers' and the mens' Unions that something had to be done, I had fantastic co-operation from them all and we used the ACAS Report as a basis for re-organising the whole management structure. We introduced a corporate management system, booked a hotel in Croydon with an independent management expert from a university as our Chairman and we argued, as a Board, the way we would run the London Fire Brigade. A new team, some of the old London officers, some new men, some longstanding and loyal officers like Mike Doherty (who was later to become Deputy Chief Officer and an expert on fire prevention, particularly in tunnels) – we debated the future and our corporate management system. From that, we introduced new procedures for industrial relations. It was so successful that within two years, in competition with industry, the London Fire Brigade won a national award for progress in industrial relations management.

In the midst of all this had come the Firemens' strike. 1977 had brought the beginning of the Great Winter of Discontent. Government promises of pay rises on all sides had failed to materialise and workers everywhere –

including the police – were threatening strike action. It was the, by now, hard-line Fire Brigades Union which took the plunge.

On November 14th 1977, some 43,000 members of the FBU in Britain began an official strike in support of their demand for higher pay and shorter hours which was far in excess of the government's 10% guideline. Apart from the brief 'dust-up' with work-to-rule just after the War, this was the first time in the history of the London Fire Brigade that its men had withdrawn their labour. Londoners on their way to work found fire stations closed and the firemen keeping warm beside braziers on the station forecourts, waving banners and seeking support with notices which included exhortations to passing drivers to '*hoot if you support the firemen*'. Many did.

Peter Darby faced a dilemma. On one side, he was sitting as an adviser on the National Council for determining pay and conditions for firemen. On the other, as Chief Officer of the LFB, he had, at a week's notice, to prepare independent fire cover for the whole of Greater London. So far as the stations were concerned, every one in London was likely to be closed, although the majority of the more senior fire officers stayed on duty while the younger ones went on strike with the men.

The over-riding fact remained. Londoners must not be left undefended against fire or accident.

Overnight, Darby provided a completely new fire service for the capital, using Army, Navy and RAF personnel. 'In the week before the strike, and once it seemed inevitable, I had instructions to approach the General Commanding the Household Division and we discussed the number of men he could make available. He also allocated a large detachment of Guards' officers from the Household Cavalry – the men more usually seen in glittering armour and plumed helmets on State occasions.

Their officers joined the talks and we explained that basically we needed a grid system of fire protection with good communications. They were fantastic, full of enthusiasm and quickly produced such an impressive and comprehensive control system for a skeleton fire brigade that – for this brief period – the people of London barely noticed the loss of the regulars.

'On the night the strike started, we moved, as arranged into an emergency control room in the old tram tunnel in Kingsway which had, for some time, been prepared as the Emergency Control for the London Flood Defence System, with all the essential communications. It was just our luck that, for the first time in years, the Thames chose that very night to rise to within an inch of flooding. The more immediately important Flood Protection Group moved in and we had to leave and re-organise ourselves in Scotland Yard.'

With the immediate flood crisis over, they moved back. 'We had decided not to antagonise the professional firemen by using fire stations and the normal equipment and relied entirely on emergency stations and the army's 'Green Goddess' fire engines. It worked very well on the whole, with the police guiding the Service drivers through areas which they didn't know as well as the firemen, who were more knowledgeable about their own 'patch'. Despite this, a number of major incidents occurred with considerable loss of valuable property, causing some concern in the insurance business.

In fact – and in secret – many firemen left the picket lines when they heard of a fire on their 'patch' and went along to help the servicemen. London had not voted to join the strike but had gone along with the will of the majority of firemen in the country. They were – and are – deeply conscientious professionals and could not bear the thought of Londoners suffering through the absence of their skills during the strike. Knowing the hazards of smoke and fumes they helped the troops with breathing apparatus and, in one bad hotel fire, quietly rescued 80 people before slipping back to the picketing. There was strictly no publicity. They did not want to be labelled "scabs" as had happened in some fire brigades outside London.'

It was impossible to use Lambeth as a headquarters and the Brigade's senior officers set up a new unit with a control point, communications and television facilities in a 'dug-out' at County Hall, on the south side of Westminster Bridge, where they stayed until the strike ended. Peter Darby continued in charge of the emergency service and, at the same time attended daily meetings with the Advisory Body trying to settle the strike in consultation with the local authorities' representatives including the Association of Metropolitan Boroughs, the County Councils' Association and the Secretariat of the National Joint Council for Local Authority Workers. The Home Secretary, then Mr Merlyn Rees, played an important part because of the nature of the problem and its relation to the defence of the country.

The strike went on for two months, ending early in 1978 when the discussions resulted in a mutually acceptable formula which recognised the value of the firemens' work and awarded them an index-linked pay system which was also adopted for the police and the armed services. London's firemen, the largest Brigade in the country representing one fifth of the British fire service, were among the quickest to resume normal operations, nor were there

any of the lasting problems of ostracism and 'scabbing' which bedevilled some other brigades. As Darby commentated: *'it said a lot for our corporate management system and our new relationship with the firemens' representative bodies.'* Nevertheless, many London firemen felt that the strike had damaged their image with the people of London and that it would be a long time before that could be restored.

Settled again, the Brigade started a planned programme of investment in the more heavy equipment which it badly needed. It had only one *'Simon Snorkel'*, an extending ladder with a small, enclosed platform on top, and that was on trial. Now, 50% of turntable ladders (TLs) were replaced by Snorkels with a programme for buying between three and four a year at £250,000 each – with top quality an essential specification.

The whole range of Brigade equipment was examined and replaced when necessary by more modern items. At this stage, it was found that the old-type wheeled wooden escape ladders were being bought second-hand from other Brigades and renovated for London by a team of carpenters. London was undoubtedly in love with these traditional escapes and the men fiercely resisted any change in them. Darby overcame the problem by getting rid of the carpenters. The consequent shortage of operational ladders resulted in the introduction of the new, up-to-date metal units.

The Brigade was looking now to its long-term future and officers travelled across the world, discussing the general problems of their work with other firefighters and with leading industrialists.

Plans were developed to reduce the existing system of eleven divisions to five, each of which would match the larger brigades in other parts of the country. Each would have a management structure and pay structure which would be the equivalent of a Chief Officer with his senior staff and administrative set-up, comparable with other large brigades in the country and fitting in with the general scheme of pay and conditions which applied nationally.

One of the major problems which Darby recognised throughout the Brigade was still the lack of general education among the men. Often, like himself, they had come from the Services or from other work, and lacked some of the basic elements of schooling. Darby, during his earlier years, had benefited from adult education in a variety of forms and, as an officer, from specialist courses at Birmingham University studying Local Government and Management Structure in depth, including the future of local government. At York University he had added Advanced Technology, Mathematics, Chemistry and Electricity. At Bristol it was a Youth Management course, *'Outward*

Bound' training and the progress of young people in industry.

'The Fire Service is an attractive job, but with its old "brass helmet" image, it tends not to bring in many candidates with "A" levels or degrees' he explained. 'Nevertheless, many of those who do come are intelligent and educable. We started a course of training to educate as many as we could. The Fire Service College was expanded steadily at Moreton-in-Marsh and made it easier for us to set up courses to match the requirements of the statutory national examinations for fire officers.'

London dropped much of its old insularity and responded with enthusiasm and vigour, working with new BA systems, new machines and new equipment. *'If there is one thing that London has above all, it is a vast amount of experience'* Darby admitted. *'The Brigade is continually active and has expertise on a massive scale. It was quick and easy to fit in the technology and as soon as we introduced something new it was tried, tested and operated with great enthusiasm.'*

The number of officers sent to Moreton was increased, as were the Brigade's own courses at Southwark and a new centre was set up in the Lake District, concentrating on management skills. The old system of *'dead man's shoes'* promotion was abandoned by stopping any man over 50 being promoted to senior level. 'We needed to give younger, more talented men who had no hope of promotion for years, a chance to prove their worth. It caused a lot of trouble among the older officers and I know that some of them disliked me intensely for it, but unpalatable things had to be done. This changed the whole face of the London Fire Brigade and men like Gerry Clarkson, who would not have had promotion for another ten years or more but who had immense potential, now had their chance. Clarkson was barely 40 when I made him an Assistant Chief Officer.' (The ebullient, ambitious and sparkling young Clarkson was to be Chief Officer before he was 50.)

Fitness was still important to Darby – by now a golf enthusiast – and as Chairman and Principal Adviser to the Central Fire Brigades Advisory Council he was responsible for the commissioning of a university study into the physical fitness of firemen generally. As a result of its findings, a whole new programme of Brigade health consciousness and care was launched, accompanied by a leaflet *'Physical Fitness for Firemen'*. London was among the first to install special physical training equipment in all its fire stations and in addition, Darby prevailed on the GLC to provide a sports ground for the Brigade at Ewell, on the southern edge of London.

Soon after this, a further study was carried out to assess whether the wearing of heavy protective clothing and breathing apparatus along with the normal, heavy physical strain on firemen, might affect their hearts. It found that although the men tended to have more accidents (partly by the nature of their work) than was normal in other industries, they were generally much healthier than the average worker.

Apart from the administrative work which Peter Darby coped with, two major events brought the LFB into the headlines during his term of office and one put it on the television screens of the world.

Millions of viewers, hypnotised by live TV coverage of the Iranian Embassy siege, were transfixed by their screens on the Bank Holiday evening of 5th May 1980. For some days the tall, stone-built Victorian building at 16, Princes Gate, close to the Albert Hall and facing Kensington Gardens, had been occupied by a group of Iranian terrorists holding a number of hostages. The LFB had been asked to reserve two appliances which could move in immediately if necessary, but otherwise to keep clear of the immediate neighbourhood. This presented problems, (already experienced at previous sieges including Balcombe Street and the 'Spaghetti House' in Knightsbridge) not least of fire protection for other residents in the sizeable restricted area surrounding the building which had been isolated. The Brigade had been warned particularly not to raise any ladders in case the terrorists thought they were there to attack, in which case they might shoot at the firemen.

Now, without public warning, troops of the SAS moved in. The Brigade had no idea it was to happen. What had been a patient, if tense period of watching and waiting was instantly transformed into a full-scale battle as the black-masked troops scaled the front and back of the building to 'take-out' the terrorists and rescue the hostages. Shots rang out from all directions, glass shattered, flames and smoke poured from the windows of the building as the SAS men smashed their way in.

Divisional Officer Roy Baldwin (known always as *'Bodies'* Baldwin for his long and vast experience, often of grim events) was in charge of the area that evening. He had been told that on no account was a fire engine to enter the danger zone until it was ordered, but now the crews had seen the television pictures and one, from Knightsbridge Fire Station, was already on its way to the burning Embassy. Leaping into his car, he gave chase and managed to stop it before it reached the firing area. Ordering it to wait, he approached the police with the intention of putting out the fire. At first he was warned to withdraw, but other police officers gave conflicting orders until eventually he demanded to see the commanding officer. It was like Sidney Street all over again. This time, however, it was the SAS Commander who came, still black-masked, and told him to stand by and await orders. Days of watching and listening with the latest anti-terrorist devices had given the authorities exact knowledge of what was happening inside the Embassy. Within minutes now, the SAS officer asked Baldwin if he could direct a jet through a particular window of the building. Baldwin agreed, knowing that the attending pump was one of the Brigade's older vehicles and praying that it would not let him down at this time of crisis.

With the fascinated eyes of television viewers all over the world fixed on him, he led three of his men, bent double and dragging the hose as they dashed for the protection of a low wall outside the Embassy, dropped to the ground and, as the water surged through from the obliging pump, directed their jet at the window. It hit the target 'bang-on' and the smoke began to subside.

It was an incident which brought other problems to the Brigade. Could the Embassy which, strictly speaking, was 'foreign territory' be entered without official permission from the Iranian Ambassador? Who would pay compensation if they did enter and a fireman was injured? They had peered through the front door and seen bodies in the hall – and boxes. Might these be booby-trapped? In the event, the SAS warned the firemen not to enter and the fires were extinguished from outside. Next day, Roy Baldwin returned to enter the building with the police and the SAS. The hazards were indeed there, including a dead terrorist with a string of hand grenades fastened to his belt – each one with the pin drawn out, two thirds of the way. Any attempt to move the man, jog the floor or direct a jet of water could have dislodged the pins to cause explosion and death all round.

Meetings and discussions with the Brigade, the Home Office and the Foreign Office followed the siege and as a result the whole procedure concerning Fire Brigade rights in relation to Diplomatic Status was made clear.

Not long after this, on 16th August 1980, came an incident which holds a macabre record for the greatest number of victims in a London fire since the war. For years, the Brigade had been warning that disaster would eventually result from the increasing number of illegal drinking clubs and gambling dens which proliferated, particularly in the Soho area, and were outside the legislation relating to other places of entertainment.

On this humid Saturday night, the bells went down in Soho Fire station for a fire in Denmark Place, in Soho. Fire had broken out in a tiny Victorian brick building where pimps, prostitutes and an assortment of young revellers of a variety of nationalities had gathered. On the previous night, police in plain clothes had visited the illegal Club and were planning to go to court on the Monday to have it closed again. The place was packed when a disgruntled reveller who had been 'bounced' out earlier in the evening, returned with a can of petrol. Passers by who saw him leaning against the door assumed that he was urinating. Instead, he was pouring petrol through the letter box. In the heat, the spirit began to evaporate and the fumes spread up the stairs. When he finally struck a match, the flames shot straight up the wooden staircase. Within seconds, the fire had spread through the two bars and across the fire exit doors. A few terrified club members managed to get down the crumbling iron fire-escape but the rest were trapped.

Soho fire station was a few hundred yards away and responded instantly to the call, but had problems penetrating the locked steel front door. The firefighters rushed to the back but by the time they managed to force an entry 37 people – mostly quite young – were dead. The intensity of the fire, which meant that some could only be identified by a fingerprint or a set of teeth, alerted the fire officers to the possibility of arson. The CID were called and, along with the Brigade's Fire Investigation Unit, (another LFB 'first') –trained specialists in working out the cause of suspect fires – discovered the reasons for the disaster. The arsonist, who admitted several similar fire-raising attacks, was later found guilty and jailed. Soon after this, the Brigade's warnings were finally heeded and new fire prevention legislation was introduced to cover such clubs and 'joints'. Like so many other rulings of its kind, it was *stable door legislation*', imposed only after the warnings had proved true.

London's firemen were regaining their image as a proud, leading Brigade and the news needed to be spread around. There was very little at that time in the way of public relations, but now, Darby deliberately opened the doors to the media. Press and Public Relations facilities were improved and a studio was installed at Lambeth. Now, all officers taking Advanced Training Courses at the Fire Service College were taught how to cope with the Press and TV at incidents. The lectures included special sessions – again in a custom-built studio – to which many TV personalities were invited to explain their work, their needs and the most efficient ways by which the Fire Service could respond to the 'media', to its own best advantage.

In less than four years, Peter Darby had turned the LFB round, dealt with its first strike, reorganised it, re-equipped it, provided it with a new form of management, expanded its horizons and planned for its future. By 1980 he was 57 years old, retirement was in view and the post of Chief Inspector of Fire Services at the Home Office had become vacant. He applied for and, not surprisingly, was offered the prestigious position and, on his retirement, a knighthood. London was bereft, but not for long. Darby knew whom he wanted to follow him and once more, he was successful.

30

From Firemen to Firefighters – Ronald Bullers

ALTHOUGH SUCCEEDING LONDON COUNCILS HAD CO-operated freely with the LFB, supporting them with the necessary by-laws, party politics had not, for the most part, affected the brigade, either at national or local level. Almost the contrary, in fact. For centuries, politicians had virtually ignored the problem until the exigencies of aerial bombardment forced it on them. By the 1980s, however, this was beginning to change and with it, the whole pattern of a Chief Officer's working day. Practical control of the fireground was being taken over, increasingly, by senior officers, with a visit by 'The Chief' if the fire was sufficiently important to merit his presence. It was a fact of life which restrained many Station Officers from seeking further promotion beyond the sound of the alarm bell and the surge of adrenalin as they leapt to the appliances and dashed off for the smoke and strife of another 'Shout'. Firemen still talked of 'a good fire', slightly embarrassed at their own enthusiasm over what, after all, was the disaster of a lifetime to the victim and might, by the end of the day, cost their own life. For the top-ranking officers, no matter how deeply their hearts were committed to the smoke and smell of the fireground, bureaucracy was advancing with all the rapidity of a burning circle of flame.

To constant contact with a far greater Home Office Fire Department and all its ramifications, were now added negotiations with a variety of trades unions, executive bodies, representative bodies and the Greater London Council. Clearly, the Chief Officer had to be not only a proven firefighter but one with the widest experience of the whole administrative cocoon which had developed at all levels of the Service.

Above all, at this stage, the 'grapevine' was already vibrating with rumours that the strongly established Conservative government, headed by Britain's first woman Prime Minister, Margaret Thatcher, was reaching the end of its tether over the extremist tactics of the Labour Party's Left

Wing which seemed to be gaining power, particularly in London.

Peter Darby had done well by the capital city. Who better to replace him than his former deputy, the man who had been at his side as they drew up the blueprints for the new Greater Manchester Fire Brigade and put them into action? His firefighting experience in the North-West of England was legendary. He was diplomatic, tough, and an ex-union representative who understood the problems of all sides, the Home Office, the employers, the unions and the men, His name was Ronald Alfred Bullers.

Ron Bullers was born in Aldridge, on the outskirts of Birmingham and won a place at Queen Mary's Grammar School in Walsall, leaving at 16 for a job with the Co-op. As a National Service entrant to the RAF he trained as a wireless operator, but with his period of service ended and no other immediate threat of war on the horizon, there was little to keep him in the peace-time air force and little in the way of jobs in 'civvy street'. He had enjoyed being in uniform, the discipline and the friendships. He had no wish to return to the Co-op. He considered the police force but, in his words – and with a smile – 'I was a lazy character and in the end I decided that the fire station was closer to home than the police station so I joined the local fire brigade.' He signed on in December 1954, 'determined to be the best fireman in the whole Brigade, which had all of two fire stations.'

The force was so small that within a week he was riding to fires.

'The local authorities couldn't afford to waste money on men who were going to change their minds and leave the service so they didn't start any sort of formal training for six months and then I was sent on a course in Birmingham.' He was shrewd enough to know that if he did too well he would get more work put on him, so he did just well enough to pass and after that, kept his head down. 'I didn't want promotion, I was very happy as an ordinary fireman with all the excitement of fighting fires and no particular responsibilities, although I always made sure that I was a good fireman. It was only when a colleague, whom I knew was totally incompetent on the fireground, passed his exams and was promoted to Leading Fireman that I decided I had better start thinking again about this exam business.'

Coincidentally at this time, fire broke out at a local aluminium works, a big factory using a lot of magnesium, and finding the road blocked by traffic as they answered the 'shout', Bullers mounted the kerb and drove his appliance along the empty pavement for some 60 yards. His old-time Chief was incensed and ordered the police to charge him with dangerous driving, driving without due care and attention and a variety of other offences. He was found guilty of driving 'without due care and attention' and fined £10 – a week's wages.

'By then I had read the fire service legalities and knew that I could claim back the money from the local authority but I was also very stubborn and obstinate. I decided to get the money back by earning promotion. After that, I volunteered for everything and I became the FBU representative, which didn't help me with the Chief. He vowed that I would never get promotion while he was in charge. I passed the IFE examinations and for six years I stayed a fireman. The Chief had kept his word.'

No Chiefs stay for ever and as soon as this one retired, Bullers became a sub-officer – 'almost overnight' – but in the Fire Protection Department. Disappointed, but determined still to succeed he read everything that came in to the office including Advisory Notes, Official Circulars and 'Dear Chief Officer' letters. (When the Home Office circulates advice on fire to local authorities and brigades it uses three main methods: *Advisory Notes* contain detailed specifications for dealing with certain situations such as motorway accidents, which are then included in training courses for firefighters; *Fire Service Circulars* inform local authorities and Chief Officers in a formal way of matters which require mandatory action; *'Dear Chief Officer' letters* are less formal and contain semi-mandatory advice and background notes on matters of current interest.)

From these, he discovered in advance that the Home Office was planning to launch its new system of training through 12 month Accelerated Promotion courses. He wasted no time, began studying at the local library, took a series of examinations and initiative tests and became one of 18 men who were sent on the first course. To the lad from the Co-op and the two-fire-station Brigade, it was an eye-opener. 'Until then, almost all my fire education had been

self-taught. Now we had physical and mental tests, lectures, practical and theoretical experience, we were seconded to major fire brigades to discover from top to bottom how they worked. Suddenly I realised there was a great big fire world outside Walsall!'

His experience was to lead him rapidly up the scale of promotion – Station Officer – then to Chorley ('it was the beginning of the package holiday era – I was called to Manchester Airport more than 50 times when they were using the old military aircraft to transport holidaymakers'.) On to North Nottingham, where, as an Assistant Divisional Officer he met Peter Darby, and on again until in 1969 he was a Divisional Officer in Lancashire County – heavily industrial and with a fine tradition. 'It was a busy area for fires and accidents and I never had one undisturbed night the whole time we were there'. From there to Commander of the Training School in Cheshire, then to the heavy cotton mill area of North Manchester.

Promotion continued until, in 1974, he was appointed Deputy Chief Officer to Peter Darby in the newly formed Greater Manchester Brigade. Here, as he tackled the administrative work of finding a suitable building to accommodate the new headquarters and then establishing the new Brigade, he was already learning the ropes for repeating the procedure in London when the life of the GLC ended.

'I had to deal with a whole range of councillors, a lot of them very angry, as well as the firefighters. With my senior officers, we were working from seven in the morning until midnight for weeks on end, but it was all useful experience. It was during this time that the Prince of Wales opened our new Control Centre, the first in the UK to have computer control – and it worked.'

Not surprisingly, when Darby took over in London in 1977, Bullers became Chief Officer of Greater Manchester. He had already spent 25 years in the fire service, had immense experience of everything from motorway accidents to ship, factory and tunnel fires and all aspects of fire prevention. After moving home 20 times, he and his wife had settled down in Bolton, close to a golf course, and were preparing for retirement. His work took him to London frequently, for Home Office talks, dispute panels between the unions and employers and multifarious meetings of the various fire-orientated bodies. He admitted quite honestly in later years that he had not liked London then.

'I thought it was a scruffy place and the London officers seemed a law unto themselves, insular, isolated from the provincial services. I was interested to hear that Peter Darby had been appointed to the Inspectorate and wondered who would take his place in charge of the LFB. I had not applied, but a late 'phone call one night suggested that perhaps I should. I thought about it long and hard. It was not what I had planned at all but, at the same time, London was the Ultimate Job. I went down for interview and was appointed. Within minutes of taking over, soon after midnight on 1st January, 1980, there was a bomb alert at Ruislip.'

Bomb alerts were nothing new in London, which had been under intermittent attack from the IRA – the terrorist Irish Republican Army – for many years. Men of the LFB had been in the forefront after devastating incidents at the Old Bailey and the Tower of London during Joe Milner's time in office. Usually the attacks involved death or serious injury to many innocent people, particularly the explosions at the Tower, when visiting children were among those badly hurt.

It was, however, the political bombshells which were to explode all round Bullers now. Years later, in retirement he spoke frankly of what he had found. 'London was still a divided Brigade, full of pig-headed, old-type fire officers, resentful of suggestions or questions. The uniformed staff resented the power held by the non-uniformed staff and the non-uniformed resented the pay of the uniformed.'

The GLC had a Conservative majority and within ten days of Bullers' arrival, a telephone call came through from the Chairman of the Fire Brigade Committee wanting to know why he had not been sent his daily report. He was, he said, accustomed to being in daily contact with the Chief Officer. Bullers was not happy at the amount of time a daily report of all that was happening would take up in his already busy timetable, but the matter was soon solved. Following the May 1981 elections, Labour gained control and within weeks, power had swung to the extreme Left Wing, led by Ken Livingstone. 'The new "Chair" of the Fire Brigade Committee was Simon Turney, a man I'd met and got on with quite well' Bullers recalled. *Two days after they took over, I had a letter from him with twenty orders to be carried out in the London Fire Brigade.'*

Bullers was astonished. 'I sat on it overnight. There were three items in it which I felt needed doing, but I disagreed with the rest. In the morning I sent him a letter explaining that I did not think that they had the power to order me directly to do something and I sent him a copy of the Council's Standing Orders, which made clear that any request from a Sub-Committee had to be agreed by the full Committee and then the whole Council before it could be put into action.

I was called in to see him and the Vice-Chairman of his Committee and they had to agree that they had not the power to give me direct orders. They then asked where I

stood politically and I declined to answer as I felt that this was not something which should affect my professional life.

The meeting ended but soon after this, I received another letter demanding that I increase the number of black firemen by 500 and also put into action all the matters dealing with the London Fire Brigade which had gone out in the Labour Party Manifesto. I was incensed and replied reiterating that they could not give me direct orders in this way, at the same time warning my officers that they were not to take orders from politicians of any party. I had found that many of the Brigade officers knew very little about the GLC and the political work of administration and because of this, I launched a scheme to try to give my men more knowledge and experience in this area.

It was an uneasy truce and we continued with the elected members sometimes accepting our advice rather than maintaining their political position. I tried to work towards the way they wanted to go, even if I disagreed with them, and I have to admit that they were always generous with their budgeting for the Brigade.'

One of the big bones of contention among the men and the Union was still the use of the hook ladder. 'For years the FBU had been urging that these should no longer be used, but like many officers – and men – I had always found them useful in certain situations when we couldn't get the big ladders close in to enclosed courtyards or other tight corners. I realised though, that the men needed to have confidence in them and to be using them frequently to maintain that confidence and skill. There had undoubtedly, been accidents and firemen had been killed using the ladders in training. In the end I decided to phase them out. We did it gradually, with 'A' Division in Westminster and West London the last to go – they were always a very traditional area. Half the Brigade were delighted to see the back of them, the other half were furious.' (The whole question of hook ladders was, indeed, an emotive one and as late as 1991, enthusiasts were calling for a 'demo' team to be formed to keep the skill alive within the Brigade.)

Meanwhile Bullers was faced with the question of possible prejudice against coloured recruits and women. The GLC was avidly committed to a positive policy of equal opportunity which meant not just that women should be allowed into the Brigade – which set no problem as they had been on the staff since before the Second World War, working as typists, secretaries, Control Room and Switch-board Staff. Equal Opportunity meant that women were to be encouraged to join, not only in the traditional roles but also as firefighters.

The media had a heyday over 'women firemen'. The Brigade was astounded. Nevertheless, the wave of immig-rants of the 50's had produced children who were now

London-born and concerned for their rights and 'Womens' Lib' was already established in many areas where, even twenty years before, it was unheard of.

'I suspected that there was racism against coloured applicants to the Brigade and against women, and examining the enrolment procedures more closely, I felt that this was indeed the case' Bullers said. 'I interviewed all the officers concerned with recruitment and, if I felt that they were so prejudiced that they could not change, I took them off the job and replaced them with officers who were impartial.

The problem was that while we only had ten black firemen out of a total strength now of 7,000, it was mostly because we had so few applications from them. We tried advertising. We took professional advice. We spent an enormous amount of money but very few came forward.'

It was a time when he was not particularly comfortable about his own position in London. He felt that many of the senior officers were taking over the full task of organising the Brigade, and the feeling was confirmed when, on a week-end off-duty, he heard of the Brixton riots on the radio. Nobody at headquarters had thought of reporting it to him. He drove straight to Lambeth, then on to Brixton. 'It was horrific. We were chased by a mob, the firemen were being attacked with bricks and bottles and 17 of our men were injured. I did feel that if we had more black firefighters in the Brigade it might have been better, and next day I went back to talk to the leaders of the black community there. They were angry because we had so few black firemen and I responded by asking them to encourage more youngsters to apply to join.'

Back at Lambeth, he also made it clear, throughout the Brigade, that he was Chief Officer in more than name and never again was he to be 'included out' of any incident.

Discussions on the problem of minority recruitment was, at this time, being organised at the highest level and as a result, a small study group, including the Chairman of the Authority, the Head of Recruiting, several trades union officials and the Chief Officer left London to discover for themselves how the problem of black and women firefighters had been dealt with in the USA.

'Newspaper headlines howled abuse at our so-called "junketings", but there were none', said Bullers. 'We worked hard and lived frugally, staying in hostels rather than hotels when we could, to cut expenses. We met many fire officers, both black and white. In Atlanta, Georgia, where they had a 54% black fire brigade they had been ordered by the Mayor to take in a set quota of black recruits, apparently regardless of their fitness for the job. I wanted no racism in the London Fire Brigade but at the same time, I wanted no ordering of artificial quotas.'

There was, too, the problem of women firefighters.

'Again, I had no strong feelings over this and if women wanted to join the Brigade and were capable of doing the job, I was prepared to accept them. We had, however, been advised in America, by a Californian university professor who had researched the difficulties experienced by women in firefighting, that women had a considerable physiological problem insofar as their main body strength was concentrated naturally below the waist. For men, the most power was above the waist.'

Although the American experience had suggested that few women were likely to be interested in the work, (research there had shown that the figure was 0.01%) it was, nevertheless, decided to open recruitment to women and in October 1982 the first female to be employed by the London Fire Brigade to carry out the same duties as a male, 30 year old Susan Batten, finished her training and took her place among the crew of Lewisham Fire Station in South London.

Her arrival did not pass un-noticed, nor without comment in the Brigade or the world outside. There is no doubt that many firemen who were not 'sexist' genuinely felt that this was no job for a woman. The very nature of a firefighter's work tended to attract men who were physically and mentally tough and who, at that time, still regarded women as a race apart. Even those who welcomed women found it difficult not to shield them from the harsher aspects of the duties. Those who were openly 'anti' maintained simply that this was mens' work, concentrated on male comradeship, and dependent on the knowledge that when they were 'up against it' in the teeth of the smoke and flames, there could be no risk of possible weak links in the chain of survival. There were times when all their lives might depend on their individual strength and stamina. It was a strong, traditional, almost mystical power which none could or would put into words, but which they felt was a comforting buffer against the danger they faced.

Susan Batten could not have been a better ambassador to counter this, although at first, many senior officers were among those who felt that she was a 'plant', put in by the feminists of the Left to check on any possible continuing 'sexism' in the Brigade. Certainly her qualifications were not only impeccable but educationally a great deal better than most of the men. Her family kept a smallholding in Somerset. She had left school with 11 good 'O' levels (including Maths, Sciences, three foreign languages, Latin and English) and three 'A' levels in French, German and Spanish. Several years at Polytechnic had added a diploma in Business Studies after which she worked for a year with the British Institute of Management before setting up a soft furnishing business with her sister and running it, seven days a week with virtually no spare time. She was looking for something completely different when the GLC began to

Elizabeth Nuttall's advertisement for fire engines. (Merryweather.)

ELIZABETH, Widow of ADAM NUTTALL, of *Long-acre, London,*
Engine Maker to all his MAJESTY's Public Offices, Dock-Yards, Forts and Garrisons, &c. belonging to his MAJESTY's Royal Navy.

CONTINUES to make and sell Engines of all sorts for extinguishing of Fires and watering Gardens, which play with a constant stream and prodigious force a large bore of water closely collected together, and thereby sooner extinguish the flames in Buildings, than any Engines hitherto contrived. The Engines I make, have a suction-pipe seven feet long, or longer if required, to feed themselves with water from any pond, river, well, channel, or main where it may stand, and has twice the room to pour in water, where the suction-pipe cannot be applied, than any other Engines, whose levers work at the sides of the cistern.

I make five different sizes of these Engines, and three smaller for watering of Gardens, two of which are in cisterns to be carried like a chair, or run upon wheels if required, and by having a fan fixed on the branch, will sprinkle the water like rain; and these small Engines are likewise exceeding useful at fires, being handy to be carried where a fire begins, and thereby speedily extinguish it; and by having a convenient length of leather pipe, the screws whereof fit each other, they will be rendered much more beneficial, inasmuch as the water may be thereby conveyed through any narrow passage, or up the stair-case, or in at the window of any house, and by that means prevent the fire's spreading any farther.

All that is possible to be required of an Engine is performed by mine, the parts being made of the best and most substantial materials; the cisterns are made of good large *English* Oak quartered and well seasoned, the joints of the cisterns are lined with copper and nailed with brass nails, and the wheels are compleatly shod with iron.

The largest of these Engines may not only be drawn through a passage three feet and half wide, but may be worked in the same either by suction or out of the cistern, there being room to pour in water by four buckets at a time, through large copper strainers, which those Engines work'd by treddles cannot. The smaller sort are proportionably narrower, may be turned about at either end, and will stand firm on uneven ground.

The preference given to these Engines for many years by the Hon. the Commissioners of his Majesty's Navy, and several other ingenious mathematicians, well skill'd in the principles of mechanical powers, sufficiently testifies their allowing them to be the best; and that it is, and always has been the constant and chief study of a good mechanick to reduce friction as much as possible in all machines, and particularly in Engines, but more especially those designed to work in salt water, cannot be controverted; and the fatal consequence of the contrary system hath lately been sufficiently demonstrated by Engines, whose moving parts have been many, and friction great, they having been in a short time rendered incapable of working, and consequently entirely useless. The many improvements lately made in Engines for working in salt water, and otherwise, are worthy of notice and encouragement, as I will maintain they will work many years without wanting the least repair, whereas Engines that have racks and chains become useless in a short time, and liable so to be when most wanted.

The following are the Sizes, Prices, and Performances of the Engines, Leather Pipes, &c.

How many men may be applied to each Engine.	How many gallons discharged per Minute.	At what number of yards Distance.	Prices with seven feet of Suction pipe.	Prices of leather pipe, forty feet each, with brass screws.
Men	Gallons	Yards	l. s. d.	l. s. d.
First size Fire Engine — 8	First size Fire Engine — 70	First size Fire Engine — 37	First size Fire Eng. 24 0 0	First size Fire Eng. 3 4 0
Second ditto — 12	Second ditto — 100	Second ditto — 40	Second ditto — 34 0 0	Second ditto — 3 6 0
Third ditto — 16	Third ditto — 120	Third ditto — 45	Third ditto — 40 0 0	Third ditto — 3 10 0
Fourth ditto — 18	Fourth ditto — 150	Fourth ditto — 48	Fourth ditto — 48 0 0	Fourth ditto — 3 14 0
Fifth ditto — 22	Fifth ditto — 170	Fifth ditto — 50	Fifth ditto — 55 0 0	Fifth ditto — 4 0 0
First size Garden Engine 2	First size Garden Engine 30	First size Garden Engine 25	First size Gar. Eng. 12 0 0	First size Gar. Eng. 2 10 0
Second ditto — 4	Second ditto — 50	Second ditto — 35	Second ditto — 18 0 0	Second ditto — 2 18 0
Hand Engine — 2	Hand Engine — 16	Hand Engine — 12	Hand Engine — 7 7 0	Hand Engine — 2 0 0

N. B. I make all sorts of Engines for supplying of towns, Noblemen's and Gentlemen's houses, fish-ponds, reservoirs, &c. to be wrought by water, wind, horses, or men, and for bringing the water from any depth, and forcing it to any height or distance that is possible to be done by the power of hydrostaticks.

I likewise make all sorts of leather buckets and leather pipes for brewhouses, engines, &c. in the best manner, and all sorts of old Engines, leather pipes and buckets, repaired at the most reasonable rates.

In order to make the above Engines and leather pipes easy to be understood and kept in order by any person, I have fixed printed directions within-side the doors of each Engine.

advertise for women firefighters. She applied in October 1981, was tested in January, 1982 and began training in May. Although her father had served briefly in the NFS after his 'demob' at the end of the war, she had only learned the 'fireman's lift' from him and had played it as a game with the rest of the children. Carrying the necessary 12 stone man for 100 yards in less than a minute was a different matter, but she passed all her entrance tests successfully and her arrival in the Brigade as a full-time firefighters coincided with her 30th birthday at the end of September 1982.

Her passing-out parade became a stampede as she was photographed and filmed by the Press and TV. The first weeks of her service were not made easier by a succession of magazine articles assuring readers that she slept in the same room as the men and took them morning tea in bed. 'It embarrassed me and other members of the Watch' she commented. 'I just wanted to settle in and get on with the job. They had accepted me as a firefighter and that was how I wanted it to be. I know that some thought I was in it for sensationalism; that I wanted to do the training, spend a few weeks in the Brigade and then leave and write a book, or that I was a feminist trying to make a gesture. None of it was true.'

Time proved her right. Sue Batten became an accepted and respected member of the Brigade and their only disappointment was that she never sought promotion. She enjoyed being a firefighter and stayed in that rank in the stations to which she was posted in south east London for many ensuing years.

Although she was the first woman in the LFB as a full firefighter, she was by no means the first woman member of the Brigade, nor the first to fight fires in the capital. From as far back as the Romans – or earlier – women had stood alongside men in bucket chains. After Queen Anne's 'parish pump' legislation was passed, women were often in charge of the engines belonging to the parishes and, in some cases, the insurance company fire engine houses were in the charge of women.

In the late 1700's a woman engineer, Elizabeth Nuttall, had taken over her late husband's business in Long Acre and was advertising, on the customary handbills of the period with an illustrated heading showing her products at work, and assuring customers that she 'continued to make and sell engines of all sorts for extinguishing of Fires and watering Gardens which play with constant stream and prodigious force…' She described herself as 'Engine Maker to all His Majesty's Public Offices, Dockyards, Forts and Garrisons &c belonging to His Majesty's Royal Navy.'

In 1843 Braidwood had received a letter from a Mrs Smith, widow of the parish sexton of a City church, which read:

'E A Smith respect to Mr. Braidwood, and will feel obliged if he will permit one of his men to look at the engines belonging to St Michael Royal and St Martin Vintry for her. The church having undergone a thorough repair and they are very dirty.

I remain, your humble Servant,

E A Smith.'

At least Widow Smith was concerned for the efficiency of her pumps and the 'Quarterly Review' for 1854 reported that 'she might be seen at conflagrations, hurrying about in her pattens (clogs), directing the firemen at the engines'.

Shaw himself, after some initial refusals, had eventually given in and helped to train the lady students at Girton College, Cambridge, in firefighting skills. In 1880 a year after the College was built there, the women had been so alarmed at the length of time it took the local fire brigade to attend a nearby fire, that they organised themselves into a brigade which became highly efficient with its ladders, stirrup-pumps and fashionable glass grenade extinguishers. Two of these firefighters were later to become Mistresses of the College.

The fashion set up at Girton spread rapidly until, by the mid-1880's many other womens' colleges and schools as well as a number of stores in the West End of London were training their 'ladies' in the skills of firefighting. When fire broke out at a hospital in Woking, the hospital Ladies' Brigade worked alone for two hours and extinguished the flames before the local fire brigade reached the scene. Some of the women wore special uniforms, usually navy blue and faintly nautical. At Holloway College, between 40 and 50 members drilled in a uniform of blue serge suits, blouses and sailor hats which was the recommended outfit for lady firefighters at the time. All this sparked off a lively if sexist correspondence in 'The Fireman' on the pros and cons for women wearing or not wearing stays when manning the pumps.

Americans, equally flippantly, spread tales of a women's brigade which carried out 'hands-on' drill with a jumping sheet, using a fiancé of one of the women as the 'fall guy'. The shock of seeing him jump so terrified the 'lady firemen', it was said, that, to a woman, they screamed and covered their faces with their hands. The fiancé recovered in hospital.

There was nothing flippant about the work of the women who served with the AFS and the NFS during World War II. Their toughness, courage and perpetual sense of humour shines through all the stories of the horror and devastation of the Blitz in London. They manned the Control Rooms, the telephone switchboards, 'chauffeured' officers, wove their way through the devastated streets on motor bikes, dodging

Lady firefighters of the 1880s. (LFCDA.)

the falling bombs and shrapnel to deliver messages when all else had been blown apart – and still found time to joke.

Lady Cuthbert conceded that the men might have been physically stronger, but insisted that the women had more stamina. Her women were often mothers who had brought up their families without any help and they were used to working long days with broken nights caring for their children. She was quite sure that this was why they had far greater stamina than the men and could, if necessary, keep going for far longer periods at a stretch.

Later, when the Berlin Wall was built and the Cuba crisis was reaching a peak, many of them returned to give up time and enthusiasm to the resurgent AFS, and when, eventually, this too came to an end, there were loud protests and a succession of nostalgic farewell parties.

So it was, that Sue Batten led a new era of female firefighters, brought into the Brigade through the massive publicity campaign by the GLC, with thousands of advertisements and leaflets pointing out that firefighting was '*an active way of life that is attracting women as well as men from all sections of London's racial community. One that gets you out and about and offers a more varied range of involvement, broader career prospects and greater earnings potential than you might have imagined .... if you are a woman in search of an active career that's really different, this could be it.*' Specifications included living in the Greater London area, physical fitness, age between 18 and 30, at least 5ft 6 ins tall, with a minimum 36 inch chest and two inch expansion as well as good, unaided eyesight. '*The GLC is an equal opportunities employer*' asserted the advertisements. '*We invite applications from women and men from all sections of the community, irrespective of their ethnic origin, colour, sexual orientation or*' (strangely, perhaps, for a firefighter) '*disability, who have the necessary attributes to do the job*'.

Thousands of pounds were spent in the effort to attract women to firefighting but the predictions of the American researchers proved correct and very few applied, (although an advertisement in *'Woman's Own'* magazine brought in a wave of male recruits, spurred on by their wives.) Some senior officers reckoned that every woman recruit had cost Londoners nearly £1,000,000 per head in research, recruitment campaigns, the provision of a special toughening-up course and changes in fire station accommodation.

Those who did come tended to stay. Out of some 60 females who were trained in the first ten years of the campaign, only half a dozen left, and by 1991 London still had 50 female firefighters, settled in and, for the most part, accepted by their male colleagues. It had not been without problems and one of Ron Bullers' less pleasant duties had been to deal with a complaint from a female based at Soho fire station. It was known that for some time, and in some stations, part of the *'macho'* scene had been the *'initiation'* of recruits by hosing them down or playing other practical jokes. This time, the jokes appeared to have gone too far and although the woman gritted her teeth and tolerated them, assuming that they were part of accepted tradition, she rebelled when the crew attended an incident in Regent Street and a fellow firefighter made a remark about her morals to a policeman. Because she felt that the insults had now been taken outside the confines of the Brigade, she made a formal complaint, outlining also some of the indignities which she had been put through.

An immediate Brigade Inquiry was instituted and after all the evidence had been heard, one man was dismissed from the Service, others were reprimanded and the Station Officer of Soho, a man with a fine record of dedicated and courageous service who had made the mistake of not taking firm action over the offences, was reduced in rank to Firefighter. This caused uproar in the Brigade, only equalled by the fury when the verdicts were inexplicably overturned on Appeal to the Fire Brigade Committee of the GLC, which included a woman among its members.

The whole sad affair ended when the Chief Officer sent an official letter to all stations on standards of behaviour.

He wrote:

'I am determined to make it absolutely clear, in terms which cannot be misunderstood, that any action by an on-duty member of the Brigade which is abusive or oppressive towards another member of the Brigade will not be tolerated. I shall continue to deal with any cases of such behaviour with the utmost severity. My total commitment to rooting out all forms of offensive behaviour is fully supported by the Fire Brigades Union and the National Association of Fire Officers of the London Fire Brigade.' *All had agreed to a joint statement in which they made it clear that* 'initiation rites' *were not part of the Brigade tradition and that these* 'or any other form of behaviour, verbal, physical or by intent which is abusive, offensive or intimidating towards a member of the Brigade, should not and will not be tolerated and will be dealt with as a discipline matter of extreme seriousness.

'The job of a firefighter is a prized and respected occupation which calls for mature behaviour and judgement by caring individuals who take a pride in the service to the community. Any firefighter who is not prepared to accept this responsibility should not be a member of the London Fire Brigade.'

(It was a message which had clearly been ignored or forgotten when, in 1991, a television series depicting life in the Brigade showed a recruit in wooden stocks having the contents of a dustbin emptied over his head as part of his 'initiation' rites. Eleven firemen were suspended as a result but some were later reinstated. Although many members of the public telephoned to complain against the suspensions, pointing out that the men had probably been 'playing up' to the cameras, the fact remained that this was flouting of a clearly laid down ruling which constituted part of the Brigade's disciplinary code.)

The Soho case was followed by what is believed to have been the first libel action by a Chief Officer of the LFB against a newspaper. Ronald Bullers and his Deputy, Gerald Clarkson, successfully sued the Daily Telegraph after it had suggested, in a series of articles in October 1984, that the two officers had conducted the Soho Tribunal in an injudicial, unfair and improper manner. It had also alleged that, during the course of the hearing, they had ordered one of the men to plead guilty 'if he wanted to keep his job.'

Counsel for the officers, Mr Richard Walker, told the High Court that there was no foundation whatsoever for these allegations and that the two officers had conducted the proceedings in 'an impartial and lawful manner.' At no time did either of them order or advise the accused as to how they should plead to the charges.

On behalf of the Daily Telegraph, Mr Desmond Browne acknowledged that their reports of this matter had been 'ill-founded' and he expressed the apologies of the newspaper to both men, confirming that it had agreed to pay them a suitable amount in compensation.

There were calmer times in May, 1985, when the old fire boat *'Massey Shaw'* took to the water again on a sentimental journey. For twelve years after the War she had lain forgotten until she was discovered by a group of LFB enthusiasts. Slowly, raising money as they went along, they set to work to restore her in time to cross the Channel for the 45th anniversary of the famous Dunkirk evacuation, when she had played so valiant a part. The deadline was achieved and the 'Massey' sailed again, carrying among her crew Dick Helyer, who had swum ashore with the line along which so many stranded soldiers had clung to reach her deck and eventual safety. The crew, all members of the 'Massey Shaw' Preservation Group, included the Skipper, Tom Bell (later to retire and join the famous clipper, 'Cutty Sark' at Greenwich) and the rest, all firefighters, included Ernie Fenlon (First Engineer, Workshops); Alan Gosling (Second Engineer, Workshops); Paul Head (Cook and General Hand); Len Hinkley (Bo'sun); Mike Green, Derek Marney, Terry Howes, David Rogers and by now Assistant Chief Officer of the Brigade, Gerry Clarkson, who navigated the boat back from Dunkirk to Ramsgate with skill and panache. She returned again for the 50th anniversary in 1990, taking with her one of the soldiers who had been rescued by her in 1940 and laying a wreath to the memory of the men who had died there.

Some of the money for the restoration had been contributed by the Prudential Assurance Company and by the GLC, with a tremendous amount of practical back-up from the Brigade Workshops and the Operational Branch of the Service, but fund-raising remained a constant concern for her devoted carers. By now, the work of the River Service had dwindled as bulk carriers and container ships needing deep-water docks took over from the older freight ships and air cargo became cheaper and easier. Gradually, the great area of London's docks became derelict and, with more reliable water supplies ashore, there was, until the development of Dockland during the 1980s, less need for a full force of fireboats. What was needed now, was a fast, well-equipped boat, capable of navigating the river in any weather and at considerable speed. The answer came in the form of a catamaran, the 'London Phoenix'.

She followed a long line of craft used for firefighting on the Thames. It seems likely that the earliest of these carried manual pumps on their decks and were powered by oarsmen or towed along the shore by horses. Two were certainly owned by the Sun Assurance Company in the 1760s and are shown in action in illustrations of the great fire at the Albion Mill, Blackfriars, in 1782. Another royal concern with fire came when the Duke of Clarence (later to become King William IV) was reportedly 'seen very active on board the extraordinary floating engine of The London Assurance' in 1791. Pumpers would be paid at the going rate of one shilling (5p) for the first hour and sixpence (2½p) from then, plus beer. Like the 'landlubbers', they would refuse to continue pumping if the beer supply ran out – and did so at a fire at Humphrey's Warehouse in 1852.

It was this early strike action which drove Braidwood to introduce two steam floats, pulled by tugs, and in 1853, to commission a steam driven fireboat. There were no embankments on the Thames at this time and the river had wide areas of shallow water along its banks. The heavier 'steamer' proved useless as its draught prevented it from approaching sufficiently close to the riverside fires and it was abandoned.

Although the Albert Embankment had been built in 1868, and the Victoria Embankment followed soon after this, Shaw reverted to steam pumps mounted on barges drawn by tugs, but still had problems of reaching warehouse fires along the riverside. By the time of Wells's command, land water supplies had improved and the embankment extended. Because of this, and his naval experience, he replaced the barges with a new, steam-driven fireboat which he had designed himself with a two-foot draught, enabling it to sail close in to the river banks. The first of these, 'Alpha II', came into service in 1900. It cost £6,300, was built in a Thames-side boatyard and was considered a wild extravagance by some members of the LCC.

Alpha II was stationed at Blackfriars and was followed in 1913 by three similar boats: Beta II, Gamma II and Delta II, stationed at Blackfriars, Battersea and Rotherhithe. These formed the backbone of the River Service until 1935 when the 'Massey Shaw' was commissioned. After extensive research at the National Physical Laboratory to ensure that her design would produce the least possible wave formation and wash when she was travelling at her full speed of 12 knots, she was built by J Samuel White at Cowes. In 1939, the 'Gamma II' was replaced by a smaller, faster boat, the 'James Braidwood' (also built in White's yard at Cowes), which could run at 20 knots and discharge water at 750 gpm from its single monitor.

As war started, the 'Gamma II' came out of retirement and was joined by a new vessel, the 'Atash Kush', which had been awaiting delivery to a customer in the Middle East, but was now commandeered for London's fire defence. Added to these was a fleet of small, wooden-hulled vessels, built in the yard of Frank Curtis of Looe, in Cornwall, plus several barges with pumps mounted on their decks. In 1940, the River Service became a separate Command, not only used for fighting fires but pumping water ashore from the Thames when mains had been smashed by the bombing of the Blitz.

1943 saw the advent of the 'Jewel' class of fireboats, 'Amethyst', 'Sapphire' and 'Diamond', each fitted with four heavy pumps discharging 3,600 gpm, but by 1957, their maintenance costs made them uneconomic and they were sold, along with the 'James Braidwood'. Replacing them came the 'Firebrace' and the 'Fireflair', each 65 ft long, steel-hulled vessels with a pumping capacity of 2,000 gallons.

'The Massey Shaw', which had served so gallantly at Dunkirk, was pensioned off in 1971 and by 1975 and 1976 the 'Firebrace' and the 'Fireflair' were replaced by the 'Fireswift' and 'Firehawk', costing £46,000 and £60,000 respectively.

Eventually, the river craft were reduced to the £500,000 'London Phoenix', built of steel and aluminium, able to navigate the shallowest reaches of the river and whose sophisticated steering equipment and radar allowed it to travel safely at speed in any weather conditions. The twin-hulled, catamaran design provided stability for the long, hydraulic platform which could be extended for ten metres above water level to allow greater access to riverside buildings or other river craft and the fireboat had the capacity to pump water at 8,000 litres (approx 2,000 galls) per minute (and could, if her engines failed, propel herself along by means of her monitors). She also carried 4,500 litres (more than 1,000 gallons) of foam compound for oil fires. For a brief period, the Brigade had a contract with a company operating firefighting tugs in the lower reaches of the Thames, but this was abandoned soon after the 'London Phoenix' came into operation. Added to the force, were a number of inflatable dinghies, based strategically at land fire stations close to the Thames or to London's big reservoirs.

Whether on land or water, the Brigade continued to answer calls for help from all over the capital. Gas had still caused problems, not least when gas meters were burgled and the feedpipes broken. One major incident involving gas took place at Ronan Point, an East London tower block of flats where an explosion tore a hole half way up the side of the building and the Brigade was called in to rescue the terrified families from below and above the dangerously shattered floors which had been closest to the source. Another incident, in Putney in 1985, again called for a massive Brigade attendance and it was here that several new items of equipment were used including, for the first time 'in action', the thermal imaging units – several stages on from those which Joe Milner had pioneered in Hong Kong, developed for tracing victims who might be buried and unconscious beneath the rubble.

In the block of flats on Putney Hill, leaking gas had caused an explosion which blew down most of a building, several storeys high. Not only thermal imaging was used, but another recent development, the Vibraphone, to track down victims buried in the rubble. Gerry Clarkson, one of the most senior officers in charge at the incident, described the scene:

'We feared that there were almost certainly people still trapped below the piles of bricks and concrete, but there was no way of telling where they were. The only course

open to us was to call for silence and then, using the Vibraphones to listen and, if we heard anyone, to seek them out. There was the usual tremendous noise of saws, diggers, people shouting and a huge crowd of media people, all talking. We went out with loud hailers and called for absolute silence and they responded. Gradually, all noise stopped and the area became totally silent.

We had stationed officers at intervals the length and breadth of the site and now one could hear, very faintly, what we later discovered to be the sound of something hitting the side of a bath. It was an amazing moment. A crew went in immediately, quickly but carefully dragging away the rubble and tunnelling until a hospital worker managed to get through the hole. He discovered a woman who had been in her bathroom when the explosion came. Her sister was alongside her, dead, but although she had serious spinal injuries, the rescued woman survived and was taken to hospital. She eventually recovered, to some extent, from her injuries.'

It was the year which brought another remarkable and unpleasant event in the history of the LFB – and of London. Calls for help from the Brigade went out late on the evening of 6th October 1985 when rioters swept through the Broadwater Farm Estate of council houses and flats in Tottenham, north London, setting fire to a supermarket as they went. Firemen from nearby stations rushed to the scene, and, to their amazement, had to be given police protection from the attacking crowds. As they attempted to run out their hoses, nearly 200 youths brandishing knives, machetes and home-made spears, advanced on them, slashing at equipment and subjecting the firemen to a hailstorm of bricks and bottles.

At the height of the attack, when both firemen and police had to retreat from the onslaught, Divisional Officer Trevor Stratford and Assistant Divisional Officer Graham Holloway, along with two police officers, were waiting to make sure that all their personnel had escaped when they noticed that two policemen had fallen and were being attacked by the mob. They turned, confronted the rioters and still facing a hail of missiles, managed to pick up one of the constables and carry him to a fire appliance with orders that he be taken to the nearest hospital. Trevor Stratford, along with a police officer, returned to the second police victim, manhandling aside the armed rioters and eventually managing to grab the man by the overalls and drag him several hundred yards to a place of relative safety. By now, his pulse had ceased, but ADO Stratford started cardiac resuscitation which brought back both a pulse and respiratory response. Eventually, an ambulance was escorted through the still fighting mobs, but although Stratford maintained the emergency treatment throughout the ambulance journey to hospital, the police constable died from his injuries. For their bravery, courage and determination, both officers were awarded Certificates of Commendation from the Chief Officer and Leading Fireman James Ryan received the Chief Officer's Letter of Congratulations for his work in helping to rescue one of the policemen. Later, DO Stratford was awarded the Queen's Gallantry Medal at a ceremony in Buckingham Palace.

Paying tribute after the event, the Chief Officer said: *'the tragic sequence of events on that night in October 1985, will never be forgotten and this award, honouring the bravery and courage displayed by DO Stratford, is a tribute not only to him but to his colleagues at the incident, whose actions epitomised the spirit, bravery and determination required of London's firefighters in carrying out their duties.'*

Support and rescue had always been part of the ethos of the Brigade and during the following year, 1986, the first Emergency Rescue Team of three London firefighters, *Divisional Officer Joe Bishop (36), Assistant Divisional Officer Paul Quick (45) and Station Officer John Elliott (43)*, accompanied by a former LFB officer, *Norman Roundell*, (who was, by now, an Inspector of Fire Services based at the Home Office) set off for Mexico to help with the aftermath of the earthquake, where they were to use both thermal imaging and the Vibraphone to trace victims. Bishop was not only an experienced firefighter but spoke fluent Spanish.

For everyone who could afford the increasing amount of cheap air travel the world had, for many years, been opening up and, now, with diminishing national and international insularity, the LFB was building up new links with firefighters throughout the world, not least through the Chief Officers' own international organisation.

Although the AFS team which had set off for Finland in 1940 had probably been the first to go abroad from London to assist firemen in other lands, the Mexico expedition began a new wave of help from the London Fire Brigade at disasters in other countries. Soon after they had returned, the Mexico City Government asked London to send out a team to train their own firemen in operational and rescue techniques and two senior Brigade officers spent three months there, supported by the words of the Leader of the LFCDA, Cllr Robert Neill: *'Londoners should be proud that the standard of excellence shown by their own fire brigade is a model for those in other parts of the world'*. Soon after, the Brigade made a series of educational video tapes to help overseas brigades with specific problems.

In the years to come, similar teams were to go out from London to disasters in El Salvador, Armenia, Afghanistan and to help the Kurdish refugees in Northern Iraq.

Eventually, a specialist LFB Emergency Rescue Team was organised, to be ready, with full equipment, to leave at a moment's notice for any part of the world which might need their help.

After the nuclear disaster at Chernobyl, in the Soviet Union, the Brigade's experience and resources were again used to formulate CIRUS, the Chemical Information Retrieval and Update System, which could, in any emergency, supply detailed information on 27,000 chemicals which might cause problems to firefighters as well as more than 1,000 companies which might be producing them. The information, stored on microfiche, is, again, available to any country throughout the world which might need it and many have taken up the opportunity to use this and the Brigade's informative technical video service.

There were celebrations too, and in 1986, the 50th anniversary of the opening of the Brigade headquarters at Lambeth was commemorated with displays of drill and with meetings of many old members of the Service. Dramatically, on the night before the event, the *'Massey Shaw'*, which had been moored off Lambeth pontoon, mysteriously blew up and sank. Fortunately, none of her crew was on board and she was later raised with the help of the Port of London Authority and re-built by her devoted volunteers.

For Ron Bullers there was even more happening on the home front. The strong majority power of the Conservative Government had finally managed to break the Greater London Council and although its demise would mean that for the first time since the foundation of the Board of Works, the capital would no longer have its own overall ruling body, the *Local Government Act of 1985* was passed and on 31st March 1986, the GLC was abolished. Clearly, provision had to be made for the protection of the capital and for this purpose, on *1st April 1986*, the *London Fire and Civil Defence Authority* was set up under the aegis of the same Act. The Authority was composed of one councillor nominated by the majority party of each of the 32 London boroughs and the City of London. The London Fire Brigade became by far its biggest element.

Simultaneously, Bullers and his senior officers had reorganised the Brigade into a five area Command Structure. This time, each area was to be aligned with groups of London boroughs; each incorporating a broad mix of city centre, commercial, industrial, residential and semi-urban development and each under the command of an Assistant Chief Officer. From now, North West Area HQ would be at Harrow Road, Wembley; North Area HQ: Harrow Road, Paddington; North East Area HQ: Stratford; South East Area HQ: Lewisham and South West Area HQ: Croydon.

For twenty years, demands on the Brigade's resources had been increasing steadily and, by the time of the change-over to the LFCDA, had reached a record total of 148,737 emergency calls compared with 55,516 in 1966. The Brigade had 114 fire stations, staffed round-the-clock, seven days a week by firefighters working a four-shift duty system to provide a non-stop service throughout the 620 square miles of Greater London. Calls now covered far more than fires alone. When the bells went down for a 'shout', it might be for a road, rail or air crash, people trapped in sewers, tunnels, lifts, as well as to chemical spillage or nuclear leak. The Salvage Corps, always run by the insurance companies since its inception in 1866, had been phased out in 1984 and its work of minimising the effects of fire and water on property and protecting it when the firefighters' work had ended, was an added responsibility for the LFB.

Finance was essential. The Authority's capital allocation for 1986/87 (prescribed by the Secretary of State for the Environment under Section 72 of the *Local Government Planning and Land Act, 1980*) was £4 million. Already, new fire stations were being planned at Barnet and at Islington, which were reckoned to increase the contractual commitments of the new Authority to £6 million by 1987/88. The magic figure of a penny rate for the fire service, which Shaw had sought for so long, was at last being realised.

Once more, the Brigade re-shuffled and settled down into the new mould. Bullers had promised the LFCDA that he would see them through the change-over period before he retired. A year after they took control, he handed over to his successor. This time it was a Glasgow-born Londoner. For the first time, the LFB was under the command of a man who had entered it as a full-time professional fireman, literally at the bottom of the ladder.

Map showing fire stations of LFB, 1992.

31

The Live Wire – Gerald Clarkson

GERALD DAWSON CLARKSON CBE QFSM BA (HONS), WAS ready for action from the moment he took command on 1st August 1987 and the Brigade had a shrewd idea what to expect from the first man to have joined the LFB as a 'regular' fireman and to have reached the top rank. (Leete had started as a fireman, but in the AFS). This former electrician was indeed a live wire.

Clarkson was a sturdy figure, strong and athletic and there were many who remembered him as a young instructor at the Training School, enthusiastically working a hook ladder to the top of the tower and finishing with a flourish by performing a hand-stand on its 'horns' – at roof level. Eventually he was summoned to appear before the Officer-in-Charge of the School. 'You are a young man', said the officer; 'I am an older man and my heart won't take the strain of you doing hand-stands on top of the tower. I also keep visualising the paper work involved if you fall off. Kindly don't do it any more!'

Tracing his career through the Service gives some idea of the extensive experience and the powerful personality which had led up to his appointment.

Clarkson himself was to become a strict disciplinarian at the time when discipline was beginning to be a dirty word on the London fire scene, but he always had three great loves in his life – his wife, Rose, his family and the London Fire Brigade. One of his men summed him up frankly: 'He was tough, he always spoke his mind in no uncertain terms but he was always fair and, you have to admit, whatever he did, it was for sheer love of the Brigade and for the traditions of firefighting in London.'

There was no firefighting tradition in the Clarkson family. Gerry, as he was always known, had been born in Glasgow where his father was a bus driver. The family moved south when he was still a toddler and set up their home in Battersea. As one of five children, he went to the local state school and then on to the Westminster Technical College for engineering, lathe and forge work before starting his first job, apprenticed to an electrical engineering firm in nearby Balham. Later he moved and finished his apprenticeship with the Central Electricity Board at Battersea Power Station. At about this time he had met and fallen head over heels in love with Rose, a local girl who worked in a bank. Against the advice of their families, they were married when they were still only 19 years old.

Thirty one years later he was able to say 'the parents were right to be worried. Everyone said it wouldn't last but we're beginning to get used to each other now.' Within days of the wedding he was called up for National Service – one of the last to be conscripted before the system was abolished.

He served for two years in the Royal Engineers – 'quite an experience but I enjoyed it' – and emerged older and much wiser, questioning what he wanted to do with the rest of his life. 'I couldn't bring myself to go back to Battersea Power Station where we worked in tremendous heat and noise. You couldn't hear yourself speak for the uproar of the crushers, pulverising the coal. We were always in boiler suits with scrims round our necks to mop up the sweat that poured down. I was absolutely convinced that I should not stay there any longer. After army life, I wanted the comradeship of a disciplined service and it was then that I thought of the Fire Brigade.'

In the army he had been very keen on gymnastics and was, at one time, the corps champion. He felt that the Brigade would be physically active – and challenging – as a career. 'By then I was 22 years old. I entered the training squad at Southwark and thoroughly enjoyed it. I used to walk over Clapham Common with Rose testing me on the questions and answers for the weekly quiz which was held then, and I was always top. I felt devastated if I got less than 85% and was in fierce competition with a friend I'd made on the course.'

From training school, he went to Whitefriars fire station,

then to Clerkenwell and on to Shoreditch where, on Blue Watch, he was so high-spirited and 'cocky' that, like Bullers, he was warned that he would never be promoted while his present senior officer was in command. Nevertheless, his enthusiasm was unquenchable and he took a succession of examinations which eventually qualified him as a sub-officer, but on this Watch he remained a fireman – not even 'acted up' for a day.

The period of stagnation ended when he was moved to a different Watch and immediately promoted to Leading Fireman.

Within nine months he was a Sub-Officer and posted to Lewisham. Here, he considered that the discipline was lax and tried to do something about it, but found himself thwarted at every move. Returning from a course at the Fire Service College he was, to his surprise, accused of exceeding his public holiday leave, but with the suggestion that if he were prepared to be more lenient with the men and relax the discipline, the matter might be overlooked. He refused and, at the height of the furore which followed, he was called in to see the Chief Officer, Leslie Leete.

'He was a man with great presence and his office was the holy of holies – hallowed ground. I went in full of apprehension and was asked to explain the situation. I did this, not knowing what would happen next. The Chief listened, then said "go back to your station, take tomorrow off, find a good tailor and have your Station Officer's uniform made. Then report to the Head of the Training Centre to start work as a temporary Station Officer/Instructor pending you passing your examinations, when you will be made substantive.'

The Training School was one of the happiest periods of his career. He was working with a group of instructors who, although they were mostly older than him, were friendly and had a great deal more experience which they passed on willingly.

'Even so, I felt that I had to compete by making the most of my physical fitness.' Hence, the ladder handstands. 'We worked at the School from Monday to Friday and would stay on in the evenings to study. I wanted to get my Station Officer's examination and my Institution of Fire Engineers qualifications, and we would sit round asking each other questions which demanded specific answers. We all worked and studied hard and when the time came, we all sat down to take the examinations utterly confident that we could take anything they threw at us. We all passed.'

It was during a visit from one particular senior officer that his hackles rose. The man suggested that a specific recruit should be treated differently from the rest because he had three 'A' levels. In the somewhat acrimonious conversation which ensued, Clarkson had to admit that he had not even passed one 'O' level. It didn't alter the fact that he was a good firefighter but it stuck in his throat. 'It so happened that I had a free afternoon and after a lot of questioning of colleagues I found out that London University was involved with 'O' levels. I looked up the address in the telephone book and presented myself at the Reception Desk of the Senate House. I think they were a bit surprised when they asked what I wanted and I said 'eight "O" levels.' With the help of the Reception clerks, he selected eight suitable subjects which he could study in his spare time and, concurrent with taking his Fire Service examinations, he managed to pass them. He followed them eventually with a Bachelor of Arts Honours Degree in Social Sciences, after a five-year study course in Economics and Politics at the Polytechnic of Central London, still working in tandem with his professional courses and examinations and his full-time job as an LFB officer.

His first Command was Cannon Street, in the heart of the City (later to become Dowgate), and soon after arriving, he was asked to become a Staff Officer at Shoreditch, but he demurred, saying that he felt he needed a full two years of experience as a Station Officer before being promoted further. At the end of the two years, he moved to Shoreditch as Station Officer in Charge and it was during this time that he earned a reputation for his impeccable knowledge of Brigade Orders. He had his own set and Rose, with her meticulous banking background, kept them up to date, entering every amendment with the date on which the change was made. 'I was always able, instantly, to produce the exact, up-to-the-minute answer on Brigade Orders, but it was Rose's hard work which was responsible for the accuracy of the file' he admitted.

At about this time he bought a 31-foot sailing boat, learned navigation and seamanship (in addition to everything else he was studying), and started sailing from Faversham, often crossing the Channel to France and Belgium as a relaxation from the job. He was all of 30 years old by now, with a growing young family.

Within two years he was asked to move to Headquarters, but again, hesitated as he enjoyed his work at Shoreditch. This time, however, there were to be no delaying tactics. A senior officer from Lambeth arrived at the fire station, called on the Commander and then ordered the recalcitrant firefighter to his office. Many years later, Clarkson smiled as he recalled the moment. 'It was one of the shortest conversations of my life. I think I said "Sir!" twice. He told me "I've had enough of you Clarkson! Be at Brigade Headquarters on Monday morning otherwise your career is finished!" On Monday morning I was at HQ. It was 1972. Joe Milner was Chief Officer. I looked like staying there for the rest of my career.'

Initially he was a Station Officer, working with the famed and respected Charles Clisby on Policy, evaluating and implementing the HAZCHEM system, sorting out the problems of the new intake for the 42-hour week and learning all the time as he sat in on the committees and negotiations with the Council, the Home Office and the Unions, absorbing not just the advanced practical work but the delicate art of tact and diplomacy in industrial relations.

Despite this, he was not cut off from the practical work of a firefighter and he remembered walking across the yard at Lambeth on a fine Spring morning when the light on the balcony (switched on when a Major Incident was reported) began to flash and his bleeper started up. It called him to the Moorgate Underground disaster

'I was there for the duration and it's a memory which will stick, a horrific incident. I arrived soon after it started and we were crouched double in the heat and din, supporting some of the victims physically, young men and women, as we tried to release them from the wreckage; holding their hands, trying to joke with them and bring them some comfort as they literally died in our arms. As time went by the heat, the stench and the lack of ventilation were appalling.'

It was at Moorgate that he learned for the first time, the importance of silence during a rescue and was to use it again at the Putney gas disaster.

'More than 12 hours after the crash, when we had released the young man and policewoman who were the last known survivors, we had to be sure that nobody else was trapped, alive. A senior officer, Norman Roundell, called for silence. It was an unforgettable moment. In the heat and the glow of the emergency lighting, the roar of the cutting equipment and the shouts of the men gradually died away and deep down in that terrible scene there was total quiet and tremendous tension. We walked the length of the wreckage, calling and listening, knowing that there were still many people unaccounted for. There was no sound. We knew then that there was no further hope of bringing out anyone alive. It was the reason why, years later, at the Putney gas explosion, I remembered Moorgate and we carried out the same exercise. That time, it worked and we found a survivor.'

During the 1977 firemens' strike he was given a co-ordinating role with the Brigade officers, the police and the military.

'Fascinating. We stayed on duty day and night, only going home for a bath and to get a change of clothes. On the night of the flood warning the troops moved in and ate all our food – to our fury. It was all taken in good part though, particularly when they moved out again, leaving so much of their food for us that we could hardly get through it all.'

By now, he was a Divisional Officer in charge of Fire Prevention at New Cross where half his officers were on strike and half were working.

'I knew that when the strike was over we would all have to work together again and I asked that, in spite of the industrial situation, our traditional Christmas Party for the men and their families should go ahead normally, and this was achieved via the good offices of my Staff Officer, Graham Collins. There was only one condition – that there was to be no mention of the strike. At the peak of the industrial action, the party took place in the Bromley Court Hotel and everyone – strikers, the men who had stayed at work and their families all joined in and made it a very happy occasion. Next morning some went back to work and some went back on strike. There were no recriminations when it was all over and the men started to work together again.'

The after-effects of the strike, made worse by the general spread of indiscipline in the social world outside the Brigade, was causing problems, and his reputation as a disciplinarian was strengthened when he took part in the removal of the drinking bars in the 'B' Division, having by now been made the Divisional Commander. Some fire stations in the 1970s had set up bars and clubs on LFB premises and even named them after their Brigade code: 'L's a Poppin' – 'J's Nest'.... They were rooted out, lock, stock and, in more cases than one, barrels.

'We felt strongly that there was no place for alcohol in a fire station, called the men together, told them that this was LFB property and turned the bars into lecture halls. It was all part of Peter Darby's tightening up of discipline and very necessary. Some of the bars were hidden away, but we found them all in the end and after that we had so many exercises and drills that there was no time for drinking on duty.'

Clarkson was a stickler for instant action. 'I have always felt that we are all on this earth for such a short time, however long we live, and we need to make the most of every moment.' On taking up his appointment as Deputy Assistant Chief Officer in Command of 'B' Division, he was appalled at the state of decoration at his headquarters –

particularly his office. Attempts to have the work done prior to taking up his appointment had failed. He recalled vividly, arriving one Saturday morning with Rose, both of them donning overalls and painting the office completely before laying a new carpet, to the astonishment of the officers on duty. Subsequently, after prolonged discussions with the architects and appearing to meet with much bureaucratic red tape in trying to have some minor partition walls removed to improve the headquarters accommodation, he sent for a large sledge hammer from one of the appliances below, and proceeded to demolish the offending partition walls. The process left the wiring hanging from the ceiling. He called the architects back and suggested that it might be wise to make good and re-site the electrical wiring. The work was immediately put in hand by the architects – who added a stiff letter to the Chief Officer complaining bitterly about Clarkson's action.

Added to his drive, now, was knowledge and experience and so it was that Clarkson found himself an Assistant Chief Officer, still only 38 years old, with many good friends around him and some who were less happy with his tough approach and his lightning rise to power. This time he was in command of the Training School at Southwark, where someone was foolish enough to tell him that everything was running smoothly and there was nothing for him to do but sit back and enjoy himself.

'I asked to be shown round the building, not mentioning that I had worked there previously. At the end of the tour I showed my guide places in Winchester House that he never knew existed, had a couple of store rooms full of rubbish turned out and made into my new office, then I turned to the School itself. We had no gymnasium, the garage was hopeless, we had 20 old appliances, some with parts missing, some that wouldn't start and all with no locker doors. This was no way to train our recruits. I called in 20 drivers and had the whole lot removed – including some which had to be towed away. It was costing more to try to maintain them than to instal new ones. Through the good offices of CSO Norman Roundell, who was Head of Technical Services, a new fleet arrived, drawn from our spare fleet. The garages were cleared and turned into a gymnasium and the whole building re-organised and brought up to date before it knew what had hit it.'

By this time, the GLC had launched its 'Equal Opportunities' policy, aimed at full integration of ethnic minorities and women into the life of the Capital.

Under the Command of Ron Bullers, Clarkson had joined the Working Party which went to the US to study the equal opportunities situation as it affected the fire service there. 'I had prepared a questionnaire with 100 questions for every Brigade we visited and based my report on these when we returned. It was an interesting visit. I came back much more aware of the equal opportunity issues and delighted that it was I, at the training school, who recruited our first woman firefighter.'

It was only a matter of months before Gerry Clarkson was promoted to Chief Staff Officer dealing with the budget, the capital programme, and the expansion of the press and public relations department. From that, it was one, small step to the post of Deputy Chief Officer.

These were the uneasy years preceding the demise of the GLC and Clarkson recalled the astonishment of the senior Brigade officers when the Council and the Government reached a state of open conflict.

'The officers of the Brigade were issued with written instructions from the majority party on the GLC forbidding them to communicate with the Home Office, the Inspectorate or any other government department. It was quite amazing. Nevertheless, we carried on steadily planning for the scheduled end of the Council and because many of us had good friends, often former colleagues, in the government departments, the consultations continued quietly and sensibly.'

It was a time when the more extreme members of the GLC Left Wing were demanding that the Brigade put stickers on their fire appliances with slogans such as *'Hands off the GLC'* and *'Keep London Nuclear Free'*. Bullers had replied that if this were done under a Labour majority, there would be nothing to prevent stickers promoting private enterprise being stuck all over London's fire appliances if political power changed hands. Appliances remained sticker-free.

'We had made it quite clear that the LFB serves all the public in the community, whatever their colour, race or gender, their political leanings or religious beliefs' Clarkson said later. *'I think that some people, particularly in the government failed to realise how difficult it was to maintain the dignity of the Brigade at that time.'*

At about the same time, access to the classified 'Secret' information dealing particularly with war planning, was demanded by some Council members. *'To my understanding, it was an offence for them even to ask for such information'* Clarkson said. *'Of course, we had to refuse, but it was a very strange period in the history of the Brigade. Indeed, Mr Bullers and I were asked to see Leading Counsel employed by the GLC to assure us both that we could advise Elected Members regarding certain information secured in the course of our duties under war planning.'*

The LFCDA came into power, Ronald Bullers retired and, not without the customary turbulence which seemed to surge round Gerry Clarkson as he forged his way through life, he took command of his beloved LFB.

It was now reasonably well-off for equipment, but the Home Office was expecting a Review of Fire Cover in London and because of the problems surrounding the demise of the GLC and of re-organising the Brigade into the five new areas, it had been delayed. This was now put in hand as a matter of urgency.

Clarkson felt that his recent predecessors had, perhaps, been justified in describing London as being 'insular', aloof from the rest of the country, and he set to work to examine and structure not only the future of of its work in London but in relation to the rest of the country and, as international communications improved, the rest of the world.

He had appointed loyal and efficient senior officers, all experts in every aspect of running the Brigade, and saw his own task now as concentrating primarily on extending the outside links. He talked to Command Courses at the Fire Service College, began giving papers on firefighting in London and beyond, at national and international conferences. Within a few months of taking over, he was invited by the government to join an official overseas mission to help forge new links with China. The group included the Assistant Under Secretary of State at the Home Office, Alan Turney; the Chief of the Fire Inspectorate, Sir Reginald Doyle, the Commandant of the College, George Clarke and the Chief Officer of the West Midlands Fire Service.

'It was a successful and enjoyable visit' he said, 'and on 18th November 1987, I was about to sit down at an official luncheon in a magnificent garden in Beijing when the Naval Attaché from the British Embassy brought me news of the Kings Cross Underground Station disaster. Thirty members of the public and one of my Station Officers, Colin Townsley, had been killed when fire broke out under an escalator, swept through the whole booking hall area and exploded in a sheet of flame. Many more, including firefighters and police officers were injured.

'Back in Beijing, my mind was racing. I knew that my senior officers would be coping efficiently, but I felt that I should be there myself to advise elected members of the Authority. There would be much to do, including the possibility of a full public inquiry with all that it entailed. The Embassy managed to get me on to a flight and I arrived back for a meeting with my own senior officers and Home Office officials. We had tried to summon the three elected leaders of the LFCDA together, but one politician said he was not prepared to sit down with the other two. I had just finished a long, tiring flight. There were many problems to discuss. I told him 'if you don't come, we'll carry on with the business without you and then I'm going home to bed.' He came. We all sat down and had a valuable talk. I visited the scene at Kings Cross, talked to Mrs Townsley and we then embarked on the first stages of the major public inquiry which was to last for six months. The legal fees alone cost us more than £500,000, which had to come from our Fire Brigade budget, paid for by the people of London, and that was before one reckoned the cost of staff time and all the other expenses.'

The Kings Cross disaster was a particularly bitter event. For years the Brigade – and others – had been warning the transport authorities for London of the high risk of fire in their system, but still it had no statutory powers to enforce its constant requests for the clearance of rubbish, removal of inflammable hoardings and facings in and around the stations and platforms, and for better training of staff in what to do in the event of an incident. It was not the first time there had been problems with the Underground. There had been a succession of small fires, some more serious than others, including one at Goodge Street in 1981, caused by rubbish and scrap material catching fire.

In November 1984, a snack-bar owner had noticed smoke coming from a ventilator in the nearby Oxford Circus Underground station, and called the Brigade. This was reckoned to be the second busiest Underground station in London, built on four levels with three platform levels for the Victoria, Bakerloo and Central lines, plus booking halls, and with an estimated 2,000 trains and 200,000 passengers passing through it daily. 'A' Division firefighters, answering the '999' call, found thick smoke issuing from one exit and, as the electric current was turned off, passengers in at least five trains were reported trapped in the tunnels. By now, smoke was emerging from Piccadilly, the next station down the line and from Green Park, nearly a mile further on. Lack of communication between stations meant that while the smoke was pouring into the Piccadilly platforms, its booking office staff were still issuing tickets to passengers and allowing them to descend the escalators.

Before the 'Stop' message was sent by the LFB, one train and a system of cross-tunnels between the Victoria and Bakerloo lines had been 100% damaged by fire, 10% of a Bakerloo line platform, tunnel and train was damaged by fire, three miles of tunnel damaged by heat and smoke and nearly 400 people rescued from the five trains involved, 15 of whom needed hospital treatment. London Transport staff had not initially alerted the brigade and it was only later that asbestos was discovered in the area and special procedures had to be implemented for the safety of the firefighters. Further examination by the Brigade's expert Fire Investigation Unit discovered that the incident had been started by a carelessly tossed aside cigarette end which had landed in a temporary wire 'cage', set up to hold workmens' materials but which had been generally misused as a litter bin.

Following this incident, Gerry Clarkson, as the then

Deputy Chief Officer, took the quite unprecedented step of calling a high level meeting with London Underground Limited and the Brigade's principal officers to discuss the incident which had been so near a catastrophic disaster, and to impress on LUL the need for a better approach to fire safety matters. The LFB increased still further its pressure on the Government to grant statutory powers to force London Regional Transport to improve its safety standards, but, despite all this, no action was taken and LRT made scant effort to act on the Brigade's exhortations. Nor did they show any enthusiastic response to a report from the London Passenger Transport Research Group, following the Oxford Street incident, which recommended a number of changes in the Underground system. Almost all would have helped prevent the Kings Cross disaster.

They included alarm bells at all stations to speed up the evacuation of passengers in the event of an incident; improved alternative 'emergency exit' signs; smoke detectors at all stations (which might activate the emergency exit signs); closed emergency exit staircases to be re-opened; sprinkler systems extended to booking halls and passageways; an urgent review of all plastics and treated woods used in deep-level underground tunnels and all remotely inflammable or smoke-producing materials to be stored in closed steel bins. A review of internal communication systems was urgently needed, and of those between London Regional Transport and the emergency services, 'with considerable improvements in mind'. Plans of stations needed to be provided for the use of the emergency services; consideration given to installing smoke-proof doors in passages, kept open by electromagnetic locks and closed by the activation of the fire alarm and, finally, staff needed better training in what to do on the outbreak of fire.

Somehow, the old 'stable door' mentality persisted, very little was done and if ever a catastrophe were waiting to happen, it was Kings Cross. One could see, more than a century on, the blind refusal of the authorities to recognise the danger signs which had persisted through Braidwood's warnings on the Thames-side warehouses, and had culminated in the Tooley Street disaster. It seems remarkable that such vital arguments on passenger safety had been almost totally ignored in the three years which followed the Oxford Circus incident, and that ACO Mike Doherty, and LFB international expert on tunnel disasters, could still be observing in October 1987: 'ever since Oxford Circus, the Brigade has been terrified that another fire will come and that next time it will bring fatalities.'

A few weeks later, Kings Cross had proved him right. Remarkable too, that twelve years after the Moorgate disaster, there were still problems of communication between the subterranean levels and the surface, so that fire

officers had to call for a field telephone system to be installed as a matter of urgency.

Although smoking on underground trains had been banned following the Oxford Circus fire, it was not banned on platforms until after Kings Cross, when an instant and total ban on smoking was introduced throughout the Underground system, to the ghostly echo of yet another clanging stable door.

The Kings Cross inquiry brought allegations that the brigade had been slow in attending. In fact, there had, once more, been delay in calling the Fire Service. Euston – the nearest station, had its appliances out, answering a false alarm call, and the first attendance came from Soho, nearly a mile away. Soho had three minutes – Clarkson emphasised the phrase as he gave evidence to the Inquiry – 'three unforgiving minutes' – between their arrival and the fatal flashover which caused the major damage. Station Officer Colin Townsley had been leading his men in a race to save the trapped passengers when he was suddenly faced with a searing inferno which swept the booking hall. He died in his attempt to rescue the victims he could see through the flames. The initial outbreak had been small, but Sir Peter Darby, called in as an expert to advise, pointed out that inflammable fumes had been building up from the oil-soaked dust round the escalator machinery and it was this, he believed, gathering above the false ceiling of the booking hall, which finally exploded and caused the sheet of flame. Not all the experts agreed but there was no doubt that there had been a flashover.

The Chairman of the Kings Cross Inquiry, Desmond Fennell QC, was rigorous and searching in his questioning and, with eight counsel representing the bereaved, the railway trades unions, London Underground, British Rail, the London Fire Brigade and other interested parties, it was something of an ordeal for the firefighters who had to give evidence.

Despite some minor criticisms of the fire service in the final Report, many lessons had been learned, on all sides. Protective equipment for firefighters, Command Control procedures, first aid generally and the mens' skill in advanced medical first-aid in such a hostile environment – all these needed to be improved. 'At Kings Cross it was impossible to get the Ambulance crews through the fire in the initial stages. We had people burning, choking, dying, and firefighters had to have the first aid skills to help them' Clarkson maintained.

At least, Fennell praised the Brigade too, and the courage of its personnel. Clarkson set to work to activate at top speed the necessary changes which would prevent any further criticisms, giving ACO Knight, who had recently joined the Brigade from the Home Office, the task of spearheading a vigorous Research and Development Section, charged with implementing improved equipment and procedures. London became the first Brigade in the country to introduce new breathing apparatus using compressed air (instead of the re-circulatory oxygen) to provide protection for a longer period of time – 82 minutes – with positive pressure to prevent gases from entering the face mask. An added advantage was its lightness compared with the existing sets. Tunics were improved with higher specifications – said to be more comfortable and more fire-resistant (although crews were not so sure) – and there were better leggings. There were no buttons which could be snagged, greater resistance to water and to flash-over and all the new outfits had high-luminous reflective markings. Improved gloves were issued and, in 1991, new boots came into service. Boots, ever a source of active concern since the days of the insurance firemen, had been made of leather for centuries, but in comparatively recent years, had been replaced by rubber 'wellington' style footwear, with steel – reinforced toes and insteps. These had never been totally successful and now, leather boots were back, calf-length, but still with reinforced toe-caps and insteps but with leather soles and heels and treated to give additional chemical resistant protection to the wearers.

Above all, every breathing apparatus set carried automatic distress warning equipment. There was no need for manual pressure to activate it. The 'tally' which firefighters handed in at the Breathing Apparatus check-point when they entered a burning building was pulled out of the *ADSU* – the *Automatic Distress Signal Unit*, activating it instantly so that there was not even a chance of forgetting to switch it on. If the operator collapsed in a fire and could not move or remained motionless for 20 seconds, it automatically entered '*alert*' mode and then went into '*full alarm*'. '*Dosimeters*' – instruments for measuring radiation – were also provided for use at any incident where radioactive leakage might be suspected.

First-aid instruction for firefighters was improved, and objections from the Ambulance Service answered by pointing out that they were not trained or equipped, as firefighters are, to work in such hostile environments as chemical clouds, radiation, irrespirable atmospheres or under collapsed buildings or trains.

Another change made Londoners considerably more aware of their firefighters. Ever since the early days of the 20th century when the bells took over from the '*Hi! Hi!*' men to clear the way, there had been gradual changes. The hand-rung brass bells with their leather thongs were slowly replaced after the war by bells rung by rapidly turning a brass handle on the dashboard of the appliance, but this system, in turn, gradually gave way to electric bells.

Although Firebrace had seen – and heard – sirens on fire engines in New York in 1936, it was not until the late 1960s that the new sound alerted London's traffic as the Brigade installed its first sirens with a two-tone 'nee-naw' warning. These were gradually improved with electronic devices until, in 1990, an even more sophisticated system appeared, giving firefighters a choice of sounds: a '*two-tone*', a '*wail*' and a '*yelp*'. Firm instructions were issued as to their use: the '*two-tone*' was a normal warning, the '*wail*' indicated a more urgent need to penetrate the traffic and only in cases when drivers adamantly refused to give way should the frenetic '*yelp*' be put into operation.

As all the changes were in the process of being carried out and with the ink hardly dry on the Kings Cross Report, the Major Accident Procedure was initiated again, on 12th December 1988, and the howl of sirens reverberated through the suburban streets as the emergency services raced to a railway cutting off Wandsworth Common in south west London, a few hundred years from Clapham Junction Station. Faulty signals had caused a British Rail train disaster with 37 passengers killed and many critically injured. Once more there were scenes of carriages burst open, distorted metal trapping seriously injured victims and of rescuers struggling to carry the injured on stretchers away from the scene, in this case, up the grassy slopes of a deep cutting.

Gerry Clarkson, who had himself, surveyed the site from a police helicopter, took the then Minister of Transport, Paul Channon, over the wreckage to show him the task facing his firefighters, the carnage, the injuries sustained by so many passengers. It was all followed by the customary public inquiry, and by the Brigade's own formal inquiry. For many years there had been demands for a helicopter for the use of the LFB, but although tests had been held and assessed, the matter was not pursued, partly through financial stringencies and partly through operational difficulties of carrying enough essential equipment and of finding suitable landing places close to an incident.

These were busy times, and it was not until several weeks after the Clapham disaster that Clarkson had the opportunity of taking a rare Saturday afternoon off duty to sample a new experience. By now it was March 1989 and for the first time in his life he was to watch an international rugby union game at Twickenham. 'Amazing' he recalled. 'I loved it all, the crowds, the atmosphere, the game. Then the loudspeakers started up and I heard my name. My car and driver were waiting outside with the blue light flashing on top and my uniform ready to put on. Alongside was an escort of police motor cyclists. They accompanied us at top speed to Purley, near Croydon where there had been yet another train accident, this time with five dead and more than 80 injured. It didn't seem possible that it could happen yet again.'

It seemed inevitable that when he attended a major international firefighting conference in America soon after this, the San Francisco earthquake erupted. By now, he was used to disasters – and to travelling. He had already made official visits to China, Hong Kong, Singapore, Finland, Sweden, Switzerland, Spain and France.

At home, the Fire Cover Review, delayed yet again by the essential work on the Kings Cross Inquiry, had been completed. It included among its reports, the fact that the Port of London had been gradually diminishing and mentioned Clarkson's concern that the 'London Phoenix' had too big an area to cover – 44 miles from Teddington Lock, to the Thames Estuary. History had shown that there had, for more than a century, been the occasional accident with Thames shipping. Now it seemed more of a hazard. With the development of the Isle of Dogs and the obvious increase in pleasure boats and water buses on the River, as well as the normal traffic of large and small vessels, barges and the added dimension of the recently opened Thames Barrage, there was all the potential for another accident. It was ironic that on 20th August 1989, only a few weeks after the Report's publication, a large dredger, the 'Bow Belle' was in collision with a small passenger cruiser, the 'Marchioness' within sight of London Bridge in the heart of the City. Despite the efforts of the 'London Phoenix' and a small fleet of police and other vessels, 51 people were drowned.

Next day – a Sunday – firefighters were posted on every bridge across the Thames in an effort to recover the bodies of missing victims as they drifted on the tides. There was an immediate public outcry over lack of safety on the Thames.

Gerry Clarkson had been fully aware of the safety problem of the river and full publicity was given to his statement concerning this in the Fire Cover Review. His flights over London from time to time had made it obvious to him that there was not only the hazard of the River itself. Whole areas of lakes and reservoirs existed in and around the capital which might be the future site of another disaster – not necessarily with boats but possibly an air crash. Heathrow and Northolt were in the Greater London area; there was a Helipad at Battersea; the City Airport had been opened in the new Dockland Development. Gatwick and Stanstead were both within flying miutes of the LFCDA.

Add to that the enormous overflying of London and there was certainly a risk of a future air disaster which might involve an aircraft falling into water. Looking ahead for future needs, (and bearing in mind the Air Florida plane which had crashed into the Potomac River in the USA) Clarkson had called for special equipment to be made available for such a possibility. Firefighters trained in diving techniques were needed as well as light and heavy rescue boats with winches, a rapid intervention unit and several dozen small vehicles with medical first-aid and lifesaving rescue equipment. The recommendations were made but although the Marchioness incident stayed in the headlines as prosecutions and court actions followed, there was little headway in providing the LFB with the equipment it might need for a similar event in the future.

By now, the streets of central London particularly, were beginning to grind to a halt through sheer weight of traffic. It became commonplace in the rush hour to sit for half an hour without moving and a nightmare to get a fire appliance to a fire within the designated time – or at all – regardless of two-tones, wails or yelps. Clarkson felt that there was a need for smaller, more compact vehicles, both for firefighting and for rescue work, which might be able to weave their way through more quickly than the bigger, traditional equipment for first attendance. Above all, though, he wanted the public to be made more aware of the danger of fire and the part they could all play in preventing it.

However much fire prevention was stressed, there would still be a need for fire appliances and in the summer of 1990, a fleet of 34 new fire tenders was on order, each with a Volvo chassis carrying equipment and bodywork by Saxon Sandbec and bringing to 52 the number of Volvo-based vehicles in the LFB's 500-strong fleet, (although there was still a sizeable force of Dennis appliances which had produced 'fire engines' for the LFB throughout the century, and others, plus six hydraulic platforms and 12 designed to operate as heavy emergency tenders or for a wide range of demountable systems).

These were joined, at about the same time, by new FRUs – Fire and Rescue Units, to replace the ageing ERTs – Emergency Rescue Tenders. The vehicles had been produced after close consultation between the Area Commanders, the ERT crews themselves and the representative bodies of all the staff involved. The outcome of the discussion, which had been sifted by the Brigade's Research and Development Section, showed that if all the equipment needed was to be provided, a total of 1.5 vehicles would be required as there was too much to fit into a manageable truck. As a result, two vehicles were produced: the HRU or Heavy Rescue Unit, was built on a standard FL6 Volvo chassis, carrying most of the latest equipment needed for heavy rescue work, and designed to attend large fires, rail, underground, shipping and aircraft incidents, or collapsed buildings. It would carry the latest equipment for heavy lifting, pulling, cutting and forced entry, as well as extended duration breathing apparatus and an inflatable boat.

The LRU, the Light Rescue Unit, was built on a four-wheel

drive Mercedes 917, and its main objective would be saving lives, in fires, transport accidents, shafts or sewers and its equipment would include cutting and spreading tools, special line rescue 'gear' and an advanced first-aid capability as well as extended duration BA. All the units had been built to LFB specification, carefully monitored by its Engineering Section.

The problems of improved breathing apparatus, which had emerged after the Kings Cross disaster particularly, faced the Research and Development Section with the task of meeting the British Standard specification restricting the maximum weight of a BA set to 18 kg, but still giving a 60 minute nominal working duration time, using compressed air. To solve this, the Brigade's teams looked to *NASA* – the American space research programme, which had recently developed a suitable lightweight cylinder and once more the LFB scored a 'first' by putting the latest space technology into service, with the full co-operation and approval of the Health and Safety Executive and the Home Office.

At the same time, the research section had been evaluating new developments in hot cutting equipment. The need was for a neat, compact, portable and safe item of equipment, capable of cutting rapidly and efficiently through a variety of modern materials ranging from reinforced concrete to hardened steel. It was soon clear that thermic cutting cable and similar thermic lances available at that time were not suitable for the Brigade's work, due chiefly to their lack of safety features. Instead, it opted for a *'slice pak'* using the exothermic process from a torch feeding oxygen and power to a carbon steel cutting rod. Once the exothermic reaction started, the cutting rod would continue to burn only if an oxygen flow were delivered via a pistol grip and trigger mechanism, giving the operator instant control of the oxygen and cutting processes. Were the torch to be dropped, the cutting power would cease instantly.

Both items took their place among equipment on the new Rescue Units.

Now, too, the helmet shape which had been a tradition in London since Shaw's time, was changed. After months of evaluation by firefighters at Old Kent Road, Plumstead, Manchester Square and Finchley fire stations, a new-style, more compact and lighter helmet came into general use, developed by a New Zealand based company, *Pacific Helmets*. Gone were the high 'comb' and the long back and front peaks which Shaw had designed for the men's safety under the prevailing conditions of his period. The new helmet used the latest materials – kevlar and fibreglass, and gave London yet another 'first' in the UK by providing the added protection of a tough, transparent visor.

In addition to all this, Clarkson was still concerned particularly with hammering home to the public the need for fire prevention. Television, newspaper and magazine advertising and editorial and radio programmes were all used to publicise the need for Fire Safety. *'Don't Let a Fire Be Your Fault'* became the great slogan. For years, firefighters had hoped for a television serial based on their work. London Weekend Television's *'London's Burning'*, produced by Paul Knight, was at times controversial in depicting firefighting men and women in their fictionally steamy private lives, as well as at work, but it had the full support and co-operation of the LFB and certainly made the public more aware of the Brigade's existence. Its cast, who had all been through a special training course, organised by the Brigade, before they began recording the series, were generous in giving their time to publicising fire safety, particularly with children, as well as helping to raise money for charity with the firefighters.

As part of the London safety campaign, smoke alarms, not only for public buidlings and industry, but for use in the home, were promoted on a massive scale. Fire Stations, now organised into Watches to accommodate the duty rosters of two full days and nights on duty or stand-by and four days off, had a Station Commander in overall charge of the various Watches, each of which, Blue, Red, White and Green, had their own Station Officers. On them, to a great extent, was placed the responsibility for improving the standard of what was now becoming a major Brigade policy of fire prevention.

This had become the age of the computer and in 1990 the Brigade Installed a new, up-to-the-minute Command and Mobilising Centre, aimed at speeding up communications and providing quicker attendance times after a '999' call from the public. It was believed to be the most advanced fire service mobilising and command system in the world, handling over 250,000 emergency calls in its first year of operation. Its primary aim was to shorten the time taken between receiving a '999' call to an incident and getting a fire appliance on its way – possibly only a matter of seconds, but time which could, even so, be vital in saving life.

The high-technology *'CMC'* complex, built on the site of the former band-stand at Lambeth headquarters, replaced the previous Control Rooms at Stratford, Wembley and Croydon, which had relied on manual systems and basic technology to mobilise the Brigade's resources. The new Control had 12 operator consoles dominated by a huge electronic wall map of London, displaying clearly the positions of the entire available fleet of fire engines and specialist equipment. The system, based around two identical computers, was designed by Marconi experts who had been in close touch with the Brigade for a long period in order to work out exactly what would be needed in this sophisticated piece of technology, to cope with all the demands to be made on it. The complex also housed a *Major Incident Command* area for use in the event of any disaster in the capital, which could provide instant information on chemical or radioactive problems and, all too necessary, a comprehensive plan of the entire London Underground system.

'Improvements are beginning to be made' Clarkson said, shortly before his retirement. 'Nevertheless, we still have disasters and a sad loss of life in fire, and much more remains to be done in the way of fire prevention. I want our firefighters to be sorry to be in the busiest areas for fires which might have been prevented. I want them to be proud of being in the most safety conscious areas where there are the fewest incidents. If we can succeed with domestic smoke alarms, we must move on into the field of domestic sprinkler systems. Officers in London can no longer be promoted unless they have experience of fire prevention. The 450 hours of training for recruits has been extended by 60 hours to provide for fire prevention. I want them to do this before they train in fighting fires. Future plans must concentrate on smaller, more streamlined, more effective fire brigades with the accent on speed of response and weight of attack. We need small, compact vehicles with good output and equipment.'

The old days of building without any thought given to fire protection were long past. Every new building development in London was now taking place within strictly enforced statutory building regulations, be it suburban 'semi' or City skyscraper. Many, like the National Westminster Bank's high-rise headquarters, were divided into fireproof sections, each with its own rising main water supply and with special lifts for firefighters from roof to basement. Developers of the even-taller Canary Wharf building on the Isle of Dogs, consulted closely with the Brigade and employed a retired senior officer of the LFB to advise on fire prevention. As a result of the Brigade's foresight and co-operation with the developers, this building is 'state of the art' in terms of fire safety. The whole subject of fire safety and protection formed an important part of the sales drive in promoting the great Canary Wharf Development.

In looking to the future, Clarkson had not forgotten the past. The history of firefighting in London was a subject which fascinated him and it was a memory which, again, he was determined to preserve. When two volumes of Sir Eyre Massey Shaw's Order Books appeared in a London auction room, he managed to buy them, and the Brigade not only had the chance to see the Introduction, written by Shaw himself, but to read, through the entries, some vivid highlights of the earliest days of the Metropolitan Fire Brigade, including details of the tragic incident in which the

Victorian fireman Joseph Ford had been trapped on his escape and killed.

Many fire brigades throughout the country had adopted mess dress for certain social and ceremonial occasions. London's was based on a military pattern. Clarkson went to Samuel Brothers of Clerkenwell, who had been making uniforms since 1830, and asked, firstly, if it was appropriate for the London Fire Brigade to have its own, historically-based mess dress and secondly, if it was, what would be the appropriate design. The Company researched the background and advised that it was most fitting because the London Fire Brigade and its history was older than many regiments of the Army. They produced a design based on that history – in dark grey, faced on the lapels with smoke grey, with flame red piping set into the grey on the trousers. A full gauntlet cuff represented the naval traditions of the Fire Service and the button configuration symbolised 1666. The design produced a dignified, formal outfit which was remarkably like that of Braidwood's men in their grey with silver buttons. As in Braidwood's time, no pattern was produced for women although it was agreed that, as soon as a woman was appointed as a senior officer in the Brigade, a suitable mess kit would be forthcoming.

Throughout his time in the Service, Clarkson had been surprised that of all the Guilds in the old City of London, (and they ranged from Mercers and Goldsmiths to the newer Guild of Air Pilots and Navigators), none had represented the firefighters who had contributed so much to its survival through the centuries. Added to all his other responsibilities, he set to work to rectify the omission, and with the help of many good friends and sympathetic industries, the Guild of Firefighters was established in 1988 and through the generosity of the Chartered Institute of Insurance, it shared their premises and their Hall. Its telephone number, significantly, was 1666.

At the same time, he was determined that the courage of the firefighters in the Blitz on London and many provincial towns and cities, the professionals, the AFS and NFS, should have some tangible recognition. One of his first projects as Founder Master of the Guild was to raise enough money for a statue in memory of these men and women. Years before, fire officer Cyril Demarne OBE, had presented the London Fire Brigade with a small bronze model of three wartime firemen which stood in the entrance hall of the Lambeth headquarters. The sculptor John Mills was his son-in-law and for years the two men had wanted a similar statue to be erected in some part of the docks or the City to commemorate the courage of the wartime firemen and women. Now, Gerry Clarkson asked him if he could produce a similar group of anonymous firefighters, larger than life size, for a permanent monument. He did so. The City of London Corporation granted permission for it to be sited in Old Change Court – a perfect position, close to St Paul's Cathedral, London's great symbol of survival throughout World War II, which the firefighters had struggled so hard to save. It was paid for by public subscription.

Cyril Demarne, who had published several books on the heroism of the wartime fire force, was one of many veterans at the Service in St Paul's Cathedral for the dedication of the memorial and was in the front ranks of the crowd which watched as the Queen Mother unveiled it on 4th May 1991. As the wraps fell away, there were those among Demarne's friends who looked at the standing bronze figure, arms outstretched and dominating the group, with surprised recognition on their faces. This was no unknown firefighter – this was Cyril. As one of them commented *'I'd know him a mile off. He was always waving his arms round like that when he was telling us what to do!'* As if to confirm it, the sharper-eyed noticed, half-hidden among the moulded debris at the firemens' feet, a single letter *'D'*. The bronze plinth of the statue is engraved with the name of every firefighter, man and woman, not only of London but all the cities in Britain which suffered aerial bombardment during World War II.

The Blitz itself was remembered during a special service held in St Paul's on 25th October 1990. The Cathedral was packed to the doors with London's firefighters and was attended by HRH the Princess of Wales, bringing with her for the first time on a public engagement, Prince William and Prince Harry. After the service, the two young Princes inspected a display of vintage fire engines outside the Cathedral and – instinctively following in the footsteps of so many Royal ancestors – climbed aboard the largest fire escape and while Prince Harry took the wheel, Prince William rang the bell. The Princess met many VIPs, including former wartime fireman Harry Errington, who had won the George Cross for his rescue at a Soho sub-station, and Dick Helyer from the Dunkirk crew of the *'Massey Shaw'*.

Between the happy events and the sad, disaster was to strike yet again before Clarkson retired. In July 1991, what appeared to be not a large fire, but a particularly difficult one, broke out in an old bonded warehouse, now used as a secure document store belonging to the Hay's Business Services Company at Bow, in east London. During the operation, two firefighters lost their lives after some confusion over their safety lines in the dense smoke and labyrinthine passages. Unusually, after hearing evidence that the fire had been started by arson, the jury at the inquest on the two men returned a verdict of 'unlawful killing'. Once more the Brigade held its own inquiry to discover what had gone wrong and how it could be avoided in future.

Satisfied that this had been carried out correctly, and after 30 years service, Gerry Clarkson was now looking ahead to retirement – still in his early 50's and still with much to offer in expertise. He stepped down as Chief Officer in October, 1991. His place was taken by another man who had come up through the Brigade from its own Training School. Clarkson's Deputy Chief Officer, at 44, was also the youngest London Chief Officer since Shaw.

32

Into 2,000 AD – Brian Robinson

BRIAN GORDON ROBINSON WAS GOING TO BE A printer. There was no doubt in his parents' mind, and very little doubt in his as he left school to take his place at the North East Essex Technical College to follow the course which would continue the long family printing tradition in the ancient Roman town of Colchester, famous for its fine printing companies. He had been born there in 1947 and looked like staying there for the rest of his life. It was only during his five-year apprenticeship that he began to wonder whether this was, in fact, his life's ambition. Printing technology was changing fast and family tradition or not, he had his doubts.

At about this time his closest friend had joined the AFS and suggested that he might try it too. In the course of his training as an auxiliary fireman, he visited the Lambeth HQ of the London Fire Brigade. The experience impressed him sufficiently to make him apply to the Essex Fire Brigade, but rather than be posted to Grays, he changed his mind, wrote to the LFB and was accepted as a recruit. It was the period in which the AFS was being stood down. On a Friday afternoon in 1968 he finished his training and became a qualified journeyman compositor. On the following Monday, he joined the London Fire Brigade training school at Southwark.

The first stages accomplished, he was posted to Islington ('every firefighter has a soft spot for their first station') then on to Shoreditch, Silvertown, and as a Leading Fireman; Ilford and Cannon Street as a Sub-Officer. Within six years he was taking the Home Office Accelerated Promotion Course at the Fire Service College, returning to Lambeth as a Station Officer in the Operations Section. From there, the promotion continued rapidly – SO Fire Prevention; Assistant Divisional Officer, General Staff; another course, at the Dorking Fire College; then Divisional Officer to 'F' Division. This led to a Brigade Command Course at the new Fire Service College at Moreton-in-Marsh, which was followed by a two-year spell as a Senior Course Director at Moreton. Back in London in

1983, he became Deputy Assistant Chief Officer in 'K' Division (south west London), Assistant Chief Officer in Personnel at Lambeth HQ, then, as the LFCDA took over, he was appointed Brigade Senior Staff Officer followed by Assistant Chief Officer and Area Commander for the North West Area of London.

He had been in the Brigade for just 20 years when he was appointed Deputy Chief Officer. Although he had not experienced a war, or even a spell in an armed service, he had attended many of the major incidents in London during those two decades.

Robinson was vehement in answering the question 'had you always set your sights on the Chief Officer's post?' 'Never' he asserted. 'It had never occurred to me. When I joined, a Station Officer was the highest command I ever aspired to. Then, when I'd reached that, I thought I might go a little higher and so it went on. It was not until I became a senior officer that I began to think of one of the top positions but even then I had not considered reaching the post of Chief Officer.'

He was appointed to lead the LFB on 23rd October 1991, determined to take the Service into the 21st Century. Significantly now, his qualifications included not only the Membership of the Institution of Fire Engineers but also a Fellowship of the British Institute of Management.

It was a very different Brigade from that which Shaw had found when he took command of the new Metropolitan Fire Brigade in 1866. Shaw had his headquarters in a room 'over the shop' at the Watling Street Headquarters of the old LFEE. As far as we know, there was little secretarial or administrative help, other than from his wife and daughters and his senior officers.

Many of Braidwood's officers and men had left, disgusted with the conditions offered by the Board of Works, which compared so badly with their old insurance company employers. Shaw had been faced not only with planning to

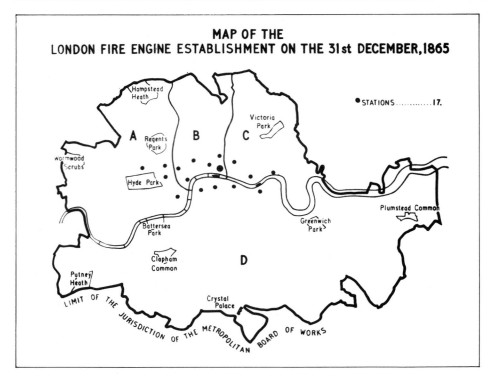

Map showing fire
stations of the LFEE.
(LFCDA.)

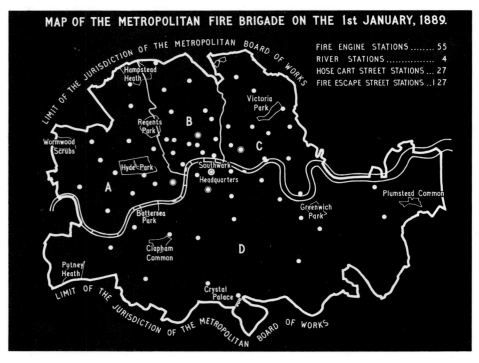

Map showing fire
stations of MFB in
1889. (LFCDA.)

cope with fires but with training new officers and men to do the job, dealing with a stream of suppliers offering engines and equipment, assessing the increasing hazards which surrounded his Service, paying the bills – and the men – and dealing with all the paper work. Added to which, he put in a regular appearance at every major and many minor fires.

Life was very different in the 1990s. Only stubborn pressure from the Brigade in 1985 had kept its name from being changed to the LFCDA, but it was interesting to note that Gerry Clarkson's official title was not Chief Officer of the London Fire Brigade, but Chief Fire Officer and Chief Executive of the London Fire and Civil Defence Authority. Responsibility for London's fire protection now lay not with a solitary Chief Officer but more than 40 different committees, sub-committees, departments and sections with a back-up of 1,000 administrative staff.

In 1990, the London Fire and Civil Defence Authority Review and Statement of Accounts, 'People Protecting People', showed a Committee structure of ten, including Disciplinary Appeals, Personnel, Urgency, Policy and Resources, Fire Brigade and Civil Defence, plus sub-committees dealing with Senior Staff Appointments, Disputes, Scrutiny and Fire Prevention. Politically, by 1991, the Authority was controlled by 15 Conservative, 14 Labour, 3 Liberal Democrats and one Independent representative.

The five centrally-based departments – Personnel and Training, Treasurer's, Clerk's, Information and Fire Safety and Technical Services were sub-divided into a variety of further sections. The Brigade was divided into five Area Commands and by 1989/90 the accounts showed that fire staff were costing £113.2 million a year; running expenses cost £28.5 million; pensions, £37.9 million, with 'other staff' £23.6 million, from a total expenditure of £212.6 million. (The previous year's expenditure had been £191.2 million.)

The projected cost of fire and civil defence for London in 1992–93 was £242,000,000 – compared with Shaw's £50,000. After allowing for the Central Government contribution, the Community Charge payers of the capital would be paying £9 a year – 17p a week – for 115 fire stations, 8,000 fire staff and full cover for both fire and civil defence.

Pay, even taking inflation into account, would have delighted a Massey Shaw fireman. The lowest rate – for an 18 year old firefighter with less than 6 months' service – was £239.15 per week (£14,907 per annum) and for a senior divisional officer after 15 years' service: £36,270. A Station Officer with 15 years' service would be paid £22,407 per annum.

The number of calls to the Brigade had risen from 159,482 in 1989/90 to 184,862 in 1990. Of these, 31% in each year had been calls to fires. Casualties had fallen from 130 deaths and 1,643 injured in 1988/89 to 129 deaths and 1,519 injuries in 1989/90. On average there were 400 false alarms per week, 15% of calls were to people locked in or out of their homes or cars; 10% to people stuck in lifts; 4% to flooding and to accidents. Over two years, one per cent of 'shouts' were calls to deal with dangerous substances. Other assorted calls amounted to 4%

The LFB fleet comprised 282 pumping appliances, 15 hydraulic platforms, 9 emergency rescue tenders, 7 foam tenders, 12 hose-laying lorries, 6 damage control tenders, 11 turntable ladders, 5 area control units, 6 area forward control units, 5 fire investigation units and 2 fireboats.

Of the fires during the period 1989–1990, statistics showed that 882 needed 4–6 pumps; 32 needed 7–12 pumps; 3 needed 13–19 pumps and 1 needed more than 20 pumps.

For Brian Robinson, the new Command meant comfortable quarters in the Chief Officer's suite on the top floor of the Headquarters building at Lambeth surrounded by a back-up secretarial force with all the latest equipment – word processors, computers and telephones which were not only on his desk but in his car and at his belt on the fireground – and included a 'bleep' which would keep him in permanent contact with the Brigade.

The LFB had survived the problems of the post-war years and was concerned now with a whole new scene. Young Londoners entering the Brigade had grown up in a city of comprehensive schools and a society of sex and ethnic equality. For many of them, their strongest influences came from videos, films and radio-cassette players which could be carried on the person and played day and night. They were inured to a massive range of television programmes, cheap and easy travel to all parts of the world and a 'pop' music scene which had no time for discipline or tradition. Nevertheless, they were not basically so different from those who had entered in the past. They may not have done particularly well at school. They certainly lacked the discipline of the ex-servicemen, but many of them had the very special qualities needed in firefighters – natural intelligence, a quickness in assessing a situation and responding to it, the ability to learn about a job if they were interested in it, compassion and above all, courage in generous quantities.

The Single European Market seemed only a few months away and the LFCDA procedures included the harmonisation of technical standards both on fire fighting and fire safety; problems of fire-safe furniture and the transportation of hazardous materials. A major stumbling block was the Brigade's anxiety to preserve the highly efficient HAZCHEM system in the face of opposition from other European countries which preferred the less stringent provisions of their own schemes.

As he took over command, the new Chief Officer explained his attitude towards the fire protection of London in the 1990s:

'I think we have to realise that the old, military service-style Brigade with its marching and saluting is difficult for a lot of young people to accept, but, at the same time, they are being firmly taught, and are realising that while this may be less a part of the Brigade generally than it was in the past, the need for discipline, particularly on the fireground, is still essential. There is no time for questioning an order at the height of a fire. Instant obedience to a command becomes an absolutely vital part of the job. This is the message we are emphasising.'

Like Gerry Clarkson, he too, was anxious that their education, particularly their technical knowledge, should be constantly upgraded, planning that evening shifts, when the firefighters were not called out, should be used for lectures and videos on a whole range of relevant issues. In 1991, any firefighters who genuinely wished to take a degree course in a subject which would be of use to them in their work, including such topics as Economics, Management or a foreign language, would have their expenses paid by the LFCDA. He was determined to follow the same path as his predecessor helped by the agreement of two London polytechnics to offer among their subjects, degree courses in Fire Engineering and in Social Sciences.

London itself was still building up as well as out, with new developments including great shopping centres and the vast Canary Wharf area with its 50-storey main tower, reckoned to be the highest in Europe. All these, along with modern building materials and commercial changes brought, yet again, a new challenge to the firefighters, but now, thanks largely to the persistence of London's fire officers, one which was being dealt with in advance. The Canary Wharf Project fire protection equipment included electronically supervised automatic sprinkler systems in conjunction with mechanical smoke exhaust systems, increased fire resistance of protected stairways, phased and planned evacuation, a two-stage fire-alarm system combined with a voice communication system, backed up by floor-wardens to oversee any safety problems.

Response was very different from the old days. The mediaeval housewife whose roast sucking pig caught fire would have screamed for the scullion to run for a bucket chain. The City Puritans would have called for the 'squrt' or for one of London's new-fangled fire 'enjins' from Germany; the ladies and gentlemen of the 18th century would have paid their insurance money and sent a boy running to the fire-house of their company for a manual pump with one of the latest 'sucking worm' hoses – (their poorer neighbours

would have called out the perspiring beadle with the parish pump and a team of beer-swilling pumpers). Braidwood and Shaw had risen to the heights of a speaking-tube in contact with a duty fireman in the fire station below, but still most of the communication was by runners on foot or horseback. The late 19th century brought a telegraph system between fire stations and street fire alarms which demanded no knowledge of English to bring a steamer galloping to the scene. World War Two saw the introduction of radio-communications and in the post-war years the '999' system, connected to manually operated control centres. By the 1990's all that had changed.

A Londoner who had heeded the massive publicity concerning fire safety in the home might have installed a domestic smoke alarm, so could hear its shrill whistled warning that the chip pan or the electric blanket was alight. Dashing to the telephone, a '999' call would be answered by a telephone operator asking which emergency service was needed. The cry of 'Fire!' would bring an instant contact with the new fully-computerised Brigade Control in the Command Mobilising Centre at Lambeth and a voice would ask for the exact address of the fire. If by this time, the caller was in hysterics, the operator, trained to cope in such a common situation, would calm them before gently and steadily eliciting the essential information needed. As soon as the address was known, the details would appear on the operator's display unit and at a touch of a button, the bells would go down in the nearest fire station to the site of the fire.

Back in the station, the navy-style six rings of the bell would alert the firefighters as the address of the fire was tapped out on the teleprinter. The 'Duty Person' would look for the code on the message, open a drawer by the machine and pull out a Route Card with the same code number. On it would be exact directions for reaching the fire. Waterproof trousers would be tucked into the fireboots, in line alongside the appliances, as the crews slid down the brass pole, leapt into them and grabbed their helmets and coats before leaping aboard. Every firefighter had a set of breathing apparatus and could be expected to use it.

As the station doors opened automatically, the blue strobe lights would flash on the appliance roofs and the sirens howl with a 'two-tone', 'wail' or 'yelp' as the drivers edged out into the traffic. From the cabin, the Station Officer would call Control on his VHF radio to receive the computerised notes from the CRR – the Central Risks Register – on what sort of incident he could expect at their destination. (By 1992, much of this contact was by a 'button box' with fingertip pressure to make instant contact with Control.) All London fire stations would, as a matter of routine, have checked every thoroughfare on their 'patch', and provided the central computer with notes on each building, its potential hazards and where they would be situated – in or outside – although even a suburban 'semi' which looked innocent enough, would be treated with caution.

'It's surprising what you can find in a quiet house in the suburbs' said one firefighter. 'We take particular care over garages and garden sheds. It's usually there that the keen hobby fans or DIY fanatics keep their supplies. A shopkeeper has to inform us if he keeps hazardous materials, cans of camping gas, paraffin or paint on his premises. A householder has no such restrictions and quite often we find all these – and more in the out-buildings.' (Legislation covering hazardous goods on private premises was soon to be sought.) 'It's not unusual to discover oxy-acetylene cylinders under the sofa and in one house where the firefighters could detect a peculiar smell, they discovered a bath full of acid. Nothing sinister – the occupier supplied skeletons for medical purposes and used the acid to strip the bones clean....'

Fire risk categories in the London of the 1990's fall into four sections – A,B,C and D. Minimum attendance of appliances and the time in which they must arrive, is officially laid down.

'A' category, usually in a high risk area in the centre of the capital, automatically receives three pumping appliances, two carrying 13.5 m 'Lacon' (tripod) pump ladders complete with handling poles; the third a pump with a 9 m 'Dewhurst' ladder capable of reaching the second floor of a building. If necessary, there is a back-up of an 'aerial' ladder, which might be a 'Simon Snorkel' hydraulic platform, a turntable ladder or, from 1991, a 'CAMIVA' ladder which could reach 180 feet when fully extended or be bent in the middle to reach over parked cars or low buildings in a similar way to the Simon Snorkel. Attendance times would be five minutes for the first two appliances and eight for the third.

'B' category, the most common in London, would involve incidents in built-up areas, perhaps with small factories or shopping centres. These would have a first attendance of two pumps with ladders, the first to arrive within five minutes, the second within eight minutes. Other equipment could be called in as needed.

'C' category, the less built-up areas, would normally merit one pumping appliance with ladder, to arrive within 8–10 minutes but London always sends two appliances to both 'C' and 'D' risk areas.

'D', which would affect only the semi-rural areas on the extreme edge of the Greater London region would, again, officially merit only one appliance initially, to arrive within 20 minutes.

Every Watch in London would have a Station Officer or Sub-Officer on duty and the 'Rider SO' would be expected to attend every 'Shout'. (The exact origin of the widely used word 'Shout' for a call-out, is obscure, but one senior officer explained its source as the Brigade's new Lambeth headquarters in the 1930s. The building had a small box containing a telephone, fixed to its front wall, so that any member of the public could open the door, pick up the 'phone and call out the Brigade immediately. Usually they were so excited that they bellowed down the receiver at such a pitch that the firemen referred to it as another 'shout.' The name stuck and spread rapidly after it was used in the 1941 film of the Blitz, 'The Bells Go Down'.)

A serious or major fire, road or rail crash, or a fire involving trapped people would merit an attendance of anything from four to 30 appliances. Any incident which appeared to be serious could call on the Brigade's resources and support vehicles, including foam tenders for oil fires, road or aircraft accidents; emergency tenders, giving way by now to the 'HRUs' – (Heavy Rescue Units), heavy or light vans stocked with a full supply of spare BA equipment and the means of servicing it.

An Area Control Unit, a mobile control van, attends all fires of more than four pumps, to provide plans of the area and a full co-ordinating system with links to the headquarters Control. The Fire Investigation Unit carries the specialists trained to discover the cause of every fire, with a staff of two, trained in forensic science. The old Salvage Corps has been replaced by the Damage Control Unit with its tender and its supply of rakes, shovels, black bags, sponges, mops and waterproof sheeting to restrict fire damage to a minimum. Fast hose-laying lorries carry the modern version of the 'sucking worm' – hosepipes – mass-produced now in plastic-coated man-made fibres, and a supply of hose bandages to carry out instant 'on-the-spot' repairs. These lorries are still needed in parts of London where the water pressure might still be unreliable or at a distance from the fire. The 'London Phoenix' and the old 'Firehawk' are still available for river fires or for pumping, where necessary. Senior officers move in a fleet of Brigade cars in constant telephone contact.

Every firefighter needs refreshment and at fire stations, the crews are still responsible for providing their own food – as they always have been. On the fireground, the wartime refreshment vans had worn out and with their replacements reaching the end of their working lives, the Brigade phased them out and resorted to the Salvation Army for physical and spiritual succour. For many years it was the famous SA Major Joe Burlison who brought his team of bonnetted 'lassies' to the scenes of fire and disaster to dispense tea, sandwiches, sympathy and treatment for minor cuts and

Ranks and Markings

Chief Officer
White helmet with
38mm black band

Cap
Two rows of silver oak
leaves on peak

Epaulet

On lapel of jacket a
gorget patch of black
with a centre cord of
red embroidered oak
leaves

**Deputy
Chief Officer
and Assistant
Chief Officer**
White helmet with two
19mm black bands with
12.5mm separation

Cap
One row of silver oak
leaves on peak

Epaulet

Deputy
Chief Officer

Assistant
Chief Officer
On lapel of jacket a
gorget patch of black
with a centre cord of red

**Deputy Assistant
Chief Officer,
Senior Divisional
Officer and
Divisional Officer**
White helmet with
19mm and 12.5mm
black bands with
12.5mm separation

Cap
12.5mm raised silver
embroidery on peak

Epaulet

Deputy Assistant
Chief Officer

Senior Divisional
Officer

Divisional Officer

**Assistant Divisional
Officer**
White helmet with
19mm black band

Cap
Plain cloth peak

Epaulet

Control Officers play a vital role within
the Brigade; taking emergency calls —
often from stressed members of the
public — ascertaining details of
incidents in as short a time as possible
and then mobilising appliances and
deploying Brigade resources.

Principal
Controller

Senior
Controller

Area
Controller

Control
Officer I

Control
Officer II

Control
Officer III

Station Officer
White helmet with
12.5mm black band

Cap
Plain cloth peak

Epaulet

Sub Officer
Yellow helmet with two
12.5mm black bands
12.5mm separation

Cap
Standard pattern
Firefighter

Epaulet

Leading Firefighter
Yellow helmet with
one 12.5mm black
band

Cap
Standard pattern
Firefighter

Epaulet

Firefighter
Yellow helmet

Cap
Standard pattern
Firefighter

Epaulet

Ranks and markings, London Fire Brigade, 1992.

bruises or 'foreign bodies' in the eye. At incidents like the
Moorgate disaster, 'Major Joe' and his team were on hand,
ready if necessary to offer respite, refreshment and the often
welcome on-the-spot word of quiet counselling. As a matter of
policy, the S.A. team attends all fires of eight pumps or more.

Religion appears never to have played a major part in the
lives of many firefighters, but nevertheless, the LFB has, for
many years, had its own Chaplains. One simple appeal came
in 'A Fireman's Prayer', its author identified only by the
initials 'EJH':

'When I am called to duty
Whenever flames may rage
Give me some strength to save some life
Whatever be its age.

Help me embrace a little child
Before it is too late;
Or save an older person from
The horror of that fate.

Enable me to be alert
And hear the weakest shout;
And quickly and efficiently
To put the fire out.

And if, according to your will,
I have to lose my life,
Please, bless with your protecting hands
My children and my wife.'

The official LFB Prayer reads:

'O Almighty God, Who cares for all your people, we thank you for those who are willing to face great dangers on behalf of others. Especially now, we pray for all who serve in the London Fire Brigade; grant to each one courage, an alert mind and sound judgement so that they may be kept safe in the midst of danger. This we ask through Him who gave His life for our salvation, even Jesus Christ our Lord. Amen.'

The Brigade also has an annual Service of Carols, often attended by a member of the Royal Family, where there is always a large and enthusiastic turn-out of firefighters and their families.

By the beginning of the 1990s, the Brigade also had six trained counsellors available to provide a professional service for personnel suffering from stress as a result of their work and several firefighters received financial payments after claiming compensation for stress brought on by their experiences at the Kings Cross fire. It was an industrial award which brought divided opinions in the Brigade between those who felt it was justified and others who believed that facing situations of stress was part of a firefighter's normal duties.

For many victims, fire is a devastating event which numbs their senses and leaves them unable physically, mentally and often, financially to cope with the problem after the Brigade has withdrawn. In some cases, particularly with elderly people or those who can hardly speak English, the firefighters have often stayed on briefly to help and advise. Now such help forms part of normal Brigade policy, with some firefighters remaining after a fire to offer help and advice on insurance claims, social security, clearing up and restoring the damaged homes, and there is a specially prepared Brigade booklet to help victims.

Robinson's aim was to bring the whole of the LFB closer to the people in their area, not only to be there in the event of fire but, more important, to impress on the people living and working around them, the importance of treating fire seriously and taking every possible precaution to prevent it.

This included a scheme: 'Learn Not to Burn', aimed at London's schoolchildren, in which a fire safety package, tailored to the needs of the National Curriculum for 9–11 year olds, was pioneered by the Brigade, which spent £60,000 and months of research on its development. In the preceding two years, 36 children had died in fires in the capital and nearly 500 more had been injured. The idea was developed from a similar project, brought back from America by Gerry Clarkson when he was Chief Officer, and the National Fire Protection Association of the USA granted London permission to adapt it for its own schools. Some of the material was designed specifically for children with special needs and those with sight, hearing or physical impairment. With the success of the first venture a second scheme, aimed at younger children was being planned.

From the single unit of Shaw's Brigade, the LFB had expanded until now, even Lambeth headquarters was too small to accommodate the specialist and administrative support staff which had expanded into two adjoining buildings. These also housed the library and the Brigade's extensive reference collection of photographs. The Museum had been moved to the 'Massey Shaw' wing of the old Southwark Headquarters and was completely overhauled in 1991 under the surveillance of its two former firefighter curators, John Rodwell and Roy Still, who not only welcomed the many visitors from all over the world to the Museum, but for the 50th anniversary of the 1940 Blitz, had organised comprehensive exhibitions showing the work of London's firefighters in World War Two.

The major departments of the LFB in the 1990's include:

TECHNICAL & SERVICES dealing with the evaluation of new equipment, from uniforms to the largest appliances. This also covers repair and maintenance of equipment, through workshops at Lambeth HQ, Ruislip, Eltham and Barking.

INFORMATION, COMMUNICATIONS, SUPPLIES, ENGINEERING AND FIRE SAFETY, dealing with Fire Precautions legislation, Fire Safety Education, the issuing of Certificates of Fire Safety and the Press and Public Relations Section of the Brigade. Duties include arranging links with schools throughout London and with the many visits from overseas firefighters and by London's staff to other countries.

PERSONNEL AND TRAINING, covering all aspects of a London firefighter's training within the Brigade, including encouragement to improve their education and to take the Degree Course in Fire Engineering. The Personnel Section deals with pay policy, medical claims, retirement pensions, or problems and conditions of service. Post-Incident and Stress Counselling comes under this umbrella.

CENTRAL OPERATIONS includes all operational procedures and practices with COPE – Command Operational Planning Emergencies, which is concerned at government level with preparations for any possible major national emergency, including nuclear accidents similar to Chernobyl. COPE is in touch with the Home Office and the Emergency Planning Officers of every county throughout the country, its officers are trained and kept up to date with the changing situations by attending special courses at the Home Office controlled Civil Defence College at Easingwold.

Valuable legislative support in dealing with serious incidents came with the Control of Industrial Major Accident Hazards (CIMAH) Regulations of the mid 1980s and those of 1990–91 – the Control of Substances Hazardous to Health (COSHH).

London's Fire Brigade still rests on the firm foundation of

its history. Even its naval traditions survive in the fire station bell codes with the 9 am six bells for 'Roll-Call'; 11 am, six bells for 'Stand-Down' when, in almost every fire station, the Capital's firefighters sit down to inch-thick wads of bread and butter with slices of strong cheese and a dish of raw onion to add savour to the snack. (One man, asked what would happen if he had to give the kiss-of-life to an unconscious victim after eating raw onions replied instantly – 'they wouldn't be in any position to object would they!') Tea remains the favoured on-duty drink – it is provided free, but coffee has to be paid for, unlike the practice in Braidwood's time when coffee was the cheaper and more common beverage. 11.15 am brings 'Muster all Hands' and so it continues until the 6 pm 'Off Duty' bells. Shifts are still called 'Watches' and firefighters are still referred to as 'hands'.

Raising money for charity or other good causes is still a major spare-time occupation, with whole stations producing elaborate fund-raising equipment. Hauling a 6-ton fire engine from Westminster to Brighton is a 'regular', but climbing Ben Nevis wearing breathing apparatus was one of

Fund-raising for charity – climbing Ben Nevis in breathing apparatus. (Stn Officer Amos, LFB.)

the more inspired pieces of profitable lunacy, raising thousands of pounds for a children's hospital. Another favourite cause is the National Fire Services Benevolent Fund, which not only supports firefighters and their families throughout the country in time of need, but maintains two convalescent homes, in Sussex and Devon. Under the Brigade Welfare Department, a London Fire Brigade Sports Ground was maintained at Ewell, in south west London, but this was a long journey for personnel from the north and east. The need for a second field became so pressing that the firefighters themselves not only raised enough money to buy the site at Aveley, in Essex but set to work and built the new club house. Brigade sports, apart from the usual athletics, cricket and football now include parachuting, cycle-racing, rock-climbing, field archery, sea-angling, squash, skiing and bowls.

Courage can never be sufficiently rewarded. In Braidwood's time and the early days of the MFB, medals were presented by the RSPLF but in 1888 Shaw persuaded the Metropolitan Board of Works to introduce a silver medal for gallantry. It was designed by a 'Mr Waldeck of the Engineer's Drawing Office' and depicted Britannia presenting a laurel wreath to a kneeling fireman, flanked by two colleagues and with a burning building in the background. The reverse was inscribed 'For Bravery'.

Later a similar medal in bronze, was introduced for long service and good conduct, and in the early 1900s the design was changed to a horsed manual with Grecian-style firemen aboard. Both medals had been withdrawn by 1936 when rewards for bravery were introduced on a national basis, including the George Cross, the George Medal, the CBE, OBE and BEM. Award ceremonies are still held within the Service, when the Chief Officer's Certificate of Commendation or Letter of Congratulation are presented, as well as the Royal Humane Society's awards for resuscitation.

Within seven months of taking over, Brian Robinson had produced a new Authority Plan, laying down as the principal aims of the LFCDA 'to protect and serve the people of London in the most competent and effective manner' and outlining his aims for the next five years as well as the key issues to be faced in the decade which would take the Brigade into the 20th century.

The 35-page document explained how, initially, a more structured approach to strategic planning, linked to financial planning and performance, would be developed 'so that Budget options are considered in the context of agreed priorities rather than policy options assessed in the light of externally applied financial constraints.' Objectives already achieved included decisions on the number, type and location of fire appliances in the light of the Fire Cover Review, implementation of revised top management structure and of revised procedures for fire safety, including the continued devolvement of fire safety work to fire stations. New sets of output measures and performance indications would improve monitoring information and participation in the parallel Home Office study to develop a national set of such indicators for the fire service. There would be continued implementation of the Equality Action Plan and agreement of a Building Maintenance Strategy, arrangements for fleet management, efficiency targets for Brigade workshops and safe working practices.

Co-operation with the Home Office on plans for any major emergency in London would be constantly reviewed.

Also on the horizon was the problem of providing new headquarters accommodation in 1998.

By the 1990s, with the challenge of Britain's entry into Europe, of high-rise building, high-speed trains and high-risk materials in transit, the Brigade looks ahead with a background of full Home Office, Government and LFCDA support and with every scientific method available to them, for all possible ways of dealing effectively with the hazards which no amount of fire protection nor fire prevention, nor cajoling or legislation will ever completely prevent in any part of the world – the hazards of accident and fire. With their expertise – and public support – the day may yet come when we no longer hear the centuries-old cry: 'London's burning!'

Bibliography

ANON. *London's Hour as seen through the eyes of the firefighters.* Staples Books, 1942.

ANON. *Jim Braidy. The Story of Britain's Firemen.* Lindsay Drummond, 1943.

'AUNT LILY' *Jack the Fire Dog.* H R Allenson Ltd.

BAILIE REYNOLDS P W. *Vigiles of Imperial Rome.* Soc of Antiquaries.

BALLANTYNE R M. *Fighting the Flames.* Nelson, 1867.

BAUMER E. *Early Days of the Sun Fire Office.*

BERESFORD ELLIS Peter. *The Great Fire of London.* New English Library, 1976.

BELL Walter G. *The Story of London's Great Fire.* Bodley Head, 1920.

BETTS Ben. *Heroes with Grimy Faces (cartoons).* Pearson, 1941.

BEVIR Harold. *The Fire Brigades Act, 1938 Explained.* NFBA 1942

BLACKSTONE G V. *A History of the British Fire Service.* Routledge & Kegan Paul, 1957.

BRAIDWOOD James. *The Construction of Fire Engines & Apparatus, the Training of Firemen and Proceeding in Cases of Fire. Fire Prevention & Fire Extinction.*

BUTCHER T K. *The Firefighters.* Batsford 1977.

CHARTERED INSURANCE INSTITUTE. *British Fire Marks and Plates Catalogue.*

COI HOME OFFICE. *Home Fire Safety Guide, 1987.*

CEREMONIAL PAMPHLETS. *Details of Parades etc.* GLC Records Office.

CHIEF OFFICERS' REPORTS. GLC Records Office.

COX Ronald. *Oh! Captain Shaw.* Victor Geen Publications, 1984.

CUNNINGHAM Sir Charles. *Report of Cunningham Enquiry into the Work of the Fire Service.* HMSO, 1971.

DAVIES E A. *Early Days of the Westminster Fire Office.*

DE CAUS Saloman. *Les Raisons des Forces Mouvantes.*

DEMARNE Cyril. *The London Blitz – A Fireman's Tale.* After the Battle, 1992.

DIAPER James Charles. *Fire Brigade History – 70 years in Uniform – Braidwood to Firebrace.* Private publication.

DICKSON P G M. *The Sun Insurance Office, 1710–1960.* Oxford, 1960.

DREW Bernard. *The London Assurance.*

DYER, Arthur. *Questions & Answers on Fire Brigade Work.* 1921.

EVERTON Ann R. *Fire and the Law.* Butterworth. 1972.

FIRE ALARMS *positions of fire alarms and stations to which they and some buildings are connected.* 1939 GLC Records Office.

FIREBRACE Sir Aylmer. *London Fire Brigade Drill Book, 1936; Fire Service Memories,* Andrew Melrose, 1949. *Questions & Answers on Fire Brigade Work.*

FIRE DRILLS. Manuals of. GLC Records Office.

FIRE SERVICE TO-DAY. Oxford University Press. 1953.

FITZGIBBON Constantine. *London's Burning; The Blitz.* 1941.

GAMBLE S G. *A Practical Treatise on Outbreaks of Fire.* Bell & Bain, Glasgow. 1926.

GILBERT K R. *Fire Engines and other Fire-fighting appliances.* Science Museum/HMSO. 1966.

GLAWARDS COMMISSION REPORT. *Nuclear War, London Under Attack.* 1986.

GOODENOUGH Simon. *Fire! The Story of the Fire Engine.* Orbis 1978.

GOUDSBLOM Prof Johan. *Fire and Civilisation.* Allen Lane/The Penguin Press. 1992.

GREAT FIRE OF LONDON. *Report of Parliamentary Inquiry, 1667.*

GREATER LONDON COUNCIL. *Future of LFB – statement of policies 1981.* GLC Archives.

GREEN, Henry. Extracts from *'Surviving',* Chatto & Windus, 1992, and from *'Fire & Water.'*

HAMILTON Alice B. *An Outline of Firefighting in England until the 20th Century.*

HARDWICKE Arthur. *Memorable Fires in London.* 1926.

HAZARDOUS SUBSTANCES. *Fireman's Handbook of –* LCC, 1958.

HENHAM & SHARP *Badges of Extinction.* Quiller Press. 1989.

HMSO. *Front Line – 1940–41.* 1942.

HMSO. *Auxiliary Fire Service uniforms and equipment.* 1938.

HMSO. *Manual of Basic Training for Atomic Warfare.* 1950.

HMSO. *Annual Reports of HM's Chief Inspectors of Fire Services for England, Wales & Scotland.*

HMSO. *Report of the Joint Committee on Standards of Fire Cover, 1985.*

HMSO. *Report of Inquiry into the Kings Cross disaster.*

HIRST Rev. Joseph. *On a Roman Fire Brigade in Britain.* Soc. of Antiquaries.

HOLLIS Barry R. *37 Fire Force (Fire & Rescue) SE London,*

1941–45. Enthusiasts Publications. 1988.

HOLLOWAY Sally. *London's Noble Fire Brigades*. Cassell. 1973.

HOLLOWAY Sally. *Moorgate: Anatomy of a Railway Disaster*. David & Charles. 1987.

HOLMES F M. *Firemen and their Exploits*. S W Partridge & Co. 1902.

HOME OFFICE. *Report on firefighting in underground buildings*. 1968.

HOME OFFICE. *Fire Precautions Act*. 1971.

HOME OFFICE. *Health Monitoring Schemes for Firemen*.

HONEYCOMBE Gordon. *Red Watch*. Hutchinson. 1976.

HOWGEGO George L. *The Guildhall Fire Judges*.

INGHAM H S. *'Fire & Water'* – a NFS Anthology.

INGRAM Arthur. *A History of Fire-Fighting and Equipment*. New English Library. 1978.

INSURANCE INSTITUTE OF LONDON. *Work of the insurance companies in combating fire*. 1966.

JACKSON W. Eric. *London's Fire Brigades*. Longman. 1966.

JONES David. *Early Works of the LCC Architects Department*. GLC Records Office.

LESLIE Anita. *Edwardians in Love*.

LLOYD-ELLIOTT Martin. *City Ablaze*. Bloomsbury, 1992.

LONDON COUNTY COUNCIL: *Firemen's Handbook of Hazardous Substances*, 1958.

LONDON FIRE BRIGADE. *Fire Over London. 1940–41*.

LONDON FIRE BRIGADE. *Centenary History of LFB*. GLC. 1966.

LONDON FIRE BRIGADE. *Extra Hands. 1944*.

LONDON FIRE BRIGADE. *The London Fireman & The London Firefighter* (magazine).

LONDON FIRE BRIGADE. *Assorted Reports on major fires*.

LONDON FIRE BRIGADE. *Report on USA Study Tour, 1982*.

LONDON FIRE BRIGADE. *London Salvage Corps, History, Organisation & Work*. 1980.

LFCDA *The Blitz Remembered 1940*. 1991.

LFCDA *A Study and Review of Fire Safety in Underground Systems*. 1988.

LFCDA *Kings Cross: How London's Firefighters answered the call*. (Ed. Helen Atha). 1990.

LFCDA *Kings Cross: Learning the Lessons*.

LFCDA *'Out of the Ashes': 50 years of HQ*.

'LM OF LONDON' *Seasonable Advice, 1643*. Harleian Misc. Vol V. p 346–349.

MARTIN Nancy. *The Fire Service To-day*. J M Dent. 1972.

MILNE Gustav. *The Great Fire of London*. Historical Publications. 1986.

MORRIS Maj. C C B. *'Fire'*.

MERRYWEATHER J C. *The Fire Brigade Handbook*.

FIRE! *Magazine*.

FIRE & WATER. *Magazine*.

METROPOLITAN BOARD OF WORKS. *Divisional boundaries and fire stations, 1866–1966*. GLC Archives.

MORRIS, Maj C C B. *Handbook on Hydraulics*.

NEWSON Sir Frank. The Home Office.

NICHOLLS Arthur. *Going to Blazes*. Hale. 1978.

NOAKES Aubrey. *The County Fire Office, 1807–1957*. Witherby 1957.

PAIN Peter. *The Struggle of the AFS*. FBU. 1941.   *Manual of Fire Service Law*. Thames Bank, 1951.

McELLIGOTT John J. *Wartime Defense in London*, Carey Press Corporation, New York. 1941.

MUNDELL Frank. *Stories of the Fire Brigade*. Sunday School Union. 1895.

NFS Members. *Fire and Water, anthology*. Lindsay Drummond 1942.

'PHOENIX'. *The Decay of London's Fire Brigade*. 1902.

RADFORD Frederick H. *The Official History of the Fire Brigades Union*. FBU 1951.

READ & MORRIS. *Aspects of fire precautions in buildings. Building Research Establishment*. Pub Dept of the Environment. 1983, 1988.

RICHARDSON L. *London's Burning*. Robert Hale. 1941.

ROYAL SOCIETY FOR THE PROTECTION OF LIFE FROM FIRE. *Plain directions for helping people to escape from buildings on fire*.

SAINT Andrew. *London's Architects and the LFB, 1866–1938 Exhibition of RIBA drawings*.

SANSOM William. *Fire Over London – London Fire Force's official account of its work during World War Two*. Also, contributions to 'Fire & Water' (see under 'Ingham'.)

SCOTT Donald. *Fire and Fire Raisers*. Duckworth, 1974.

SENCERA Rege. *Observations on the Fire of London*. Harleiian Miscellanies, iii 295–350.

SHAW Sir Eyre Massey. *A Complete Manual of Fire Protection.   A Complete Manual on the Working of the Fire Brigade of London.   Fires in Theatres.   Report on LFEE.   The State of the Fire Brigade*.

SMITH James & Horace. *Rejected Addresses*. John Murray. 1855.

SPENDER Sir Stephen. *Citizens in War and After. 1945*.

SPENDER Sir Stephen. *World Within World*. Faber. 1951.

STONESTREET George. *Reflections on the Frequency of fires. 1740*.

UNDERGROUND CAR PARKS. *Precautions against explosions*. 1978.

WALDO F S. *City of London Fire Inquests*.

WALLINGTON Nehemia. *Personal Diary, 1632*.

WALLINGTON Neil. *Fireman! A Personal Account*.

WALLINGTON Neil. *Firemen at War*. David & Charles. 1981.

WALLINGTON Neil. *Images of Fire – 150 years of Fire-Fighting*. David & Charles. 1989.

WALLINGTON Neil. *'999' – The Accident and Crash Rescue Work of the London Fire Brigade*.

WASSEY Michael. *Ordeal by Fire*. Secker & Warburg, 1941.

WELLS Lionel de Latour. *Manual of Fire Drill, 1898*.

WHILE Jack. *Fifty Years of Firefighting in London.   'Fire! Fire!'*

WHITEHALL PALACE *Fire at, 1698*. Harlelan Misc. 1698.

WASSEY Michael. *Ordeal by Fire*. Secker and Warburg. 1941.

WATKIN W. Thompson. *Roman Forces in Britain*. Soc of Antiquaries.

WILMOTH V J. *The Auxiliary Fireman*. Lomax Erskine. 1939.

WILMOTH V J. *The Advanced Auxiliary Fireman*. Lomax Erskine. 1941.

WRIGHT Brian. *The British Fire Mark*. Woodhead Faulkner, 1982.

WRIGHT Brian & BAIN Fergus. *Fire Insurance Company Buttons.* Fire Mark Circle. 1985.

WRIGHT Brian. *A Fire in the House.* Woodhead Faulkner. 1962.

WYNTER Andrew. *Curiosities of Civilisation* – (chapter on Fires and Fire Insurance). Hardwicke. 1845.

YARRANTON Andrew. *England's Improvement by Sea & Land.*

YOUNG C F T. *Fires, Fire Engines and Fire Brigades.*

PERIODICALS INCLUDING: *'Fire'*; *'The Fireman'* (vols 1–80); *Protection Review*; FPA Journals; *The London Fireman/Firefighter*; IFE Quarterlies.

OFFICIAL REPORTS Including Select Committee for Protection against Fire in the Metropolis, 1862. Select Committee for Protection Against Fire in the UK. 1867. Select Committee to Enquire into the MFB in 1876. Select Committee to Enquire into Arrangements for Fire Brigades in England & Wales, 1899. Report of the Royal Commission on Fire Brigades & Fire Prevention, 1925. Report of the Departmental Committee on Fire Brigade Services. (Riverdale) 1938. Report of the Departmental Committee on the Fire Service. (Holroyd) 1970. Report of the Cunningham Inquiry into the Work of the Fire Service. 1971. Home Office Review of Fire Policy. 1980. Central Fire Brigades Advisory Councils' Report of the Joint Committee on Standards of Fire Cover. Chief Officers' Reports,

FILMS:

Fires Were Started. Crown Film Unit. WW2 National Film Archive, Central Film Library.

The Bells Go Down. 1941.

Who Started It? Fire Prevention Film. 1948–1952.

THE GREAT FIRE OF LONDON:

BELL Walter G. *The Great Fire of London.* Bodley Head.

BROADSIDE (1666). *A True and Exact Relation of the Most Dreadful Fire of 1666.*

PHILANTHROPUS PHILAGATHUS. *An Humble Remonstrance to the King and Parliament in behalf of Many Decayed and Decaying Citizens and Families of London occasioned solely by the late Dreadful Fire in that City.* 1675.

AN ACT OF COMMON COUNCIL FOR THE SUPPRESSION OF FIRES. 1668.

De LAUNE Thomas. *The Present State of London.* 1681.

EVELYN John. *Diaries of.*

FORD Simon. *Poemata Londinensia, Iam tandem Consumata. 1667. Conflagration of London poetically delineated 1667.*

LONDON GAZETTE *No 85, 3–10 September, 1666.*

MILNE Gustav. *The Great Fire of London. Historical Publications* 1986.

Index

(note: *'passim'* indicates subject is mentioned throughout)

Printed in the United Kingdom for HMSO
Dd 295757   C50   11/92   5673